Rudi Matthee holds a Ph.D. in Islamic Studies from the University of California in Los Angeles. He taught at the University of Delaware from 1993 to 2011, the last four years as Unidel Distinguished Professor of History. He is currently the Roshan Professor of Persian Studies at the University of Maryland, College Park.

"This is an extensive and authoritative study of the history of Iran from the second quarter of the seventeenth century until the fateful year of 1722, which ended the rule of one the country's most successful dynasties—the Safavids. It fills a gap in our understanding of the Safavid period by emphasizing the political, administrative and economic structure of the time. A rich palette of personalities and events are critically assessed, and the study is intelligently but also thoughtfully composed and well documented. The author displays an admirable knowledge of the sources in Persian, a rich vein of contemporary archival material and the studies written in all major European languages, clearly a feat that will not be easy to follow. The result is a rich mine of information which will undoubtedly allow the reader to come to new insights into the character and structure of the Iranian polity during the second half of the seventeenth century."

J. P. Luft, Centre for Iranian Cultural Studies,
University of Durham, UK

Persia in Crisis

Safavid Decline and the Fall of Isfahan

Rudi Matthee

I.B.TAURIS
LONDON • NEW YORK • OXFORD • NEW DELHI • SYDNEY

I.B. TAURIS
Bloomsbury Publishing Plc
50 Bedford Square, London, WC1B 3DP, UK
1385 Broadway, New York, NY 10018, USA

BLOOMSBURY, I.B. TAURIS and the I.B. Tauris logo
are trademarks of Bloomsbury Publishing Plc

First published in Great Britain 2012
This paperback edition published 2020

Copyright © Rudi Matthee, 2012

Rudi Matthee has asserted their right under the Copyright,
Designs and Patents Act, 1988, to be identified as Author of this work.

All rights reserved. No part of this publication may be reproduced or
transmitted in any form or by any means, electronic or mechanical,
including photocopying, recording, or any information storage or retrieval
system, without prior permission in writing from the publishers.

Bloomsbury Publishing Plc does not have any control over, or responsibility for,
any third-party websites referred to or in this book. All internet addresses given
in this book were correct at the time of going to press. The author and publisher
regret any inconvenience caused if addresses have changed or sites have
ceased to exist, but can accept no responsibility for any such changes.

A catalogue record for this book is available from the British Library.

A catalog record for this book is available from the Library of Congress.

ISBN: HB: 978-1-8451-1745-0
PB: 978-1-8386-0707-4
ePDF: 978-0-8577-2094-8
eBook: 978-0-8577-3181-4

International Library of Iranian Studies, 17

To find out more about our authors and books visit
www.bloomsbury.com and sign up for our newsletters.

For Fariba

Contents

List of Maps and Illustrations	ix
Note on Transliteration	xi
Abbreviations	xiii
Acknowledgments	xv
Preface	xvii
Introduction	xxi

1.	Patterns: Iran in the Late Safavid Period	1
2.	Politics at the Safavid Court, I: Shahs and Grand Viziers, 1629–1666	27
3.	Safavid Politics, II: Shahs, Grand Viziers, and Eunuchs, 1666–1699	55
4.	Monetary Policy and the Disappearing Mints, 1600–1700	75
5.	From Perpetual War to Lasting Peace: Safavid Military Politics in the Seventeenth Century	109
6.	Weakening Links: The Center and the Provinces, 1600–1700	139
7.	Religion in Late Safavid Iran: Shi`i Clerics and Minorities	173
8.	From Stability to Turmoil: The Final Decades, 1700–1722	197

Conclusion	243
Glossary	257
Notes	259
Bibliography	329
Index	359

Maps and Illustrations

Maps

1. Safavid Iran and the surrounding world   xxxvi
2. Locations of Safavid mints 907–995/1501–1587   82
3. Locations of Safavid mints 995–1052/1587–1642   84
4. Locations of Safavid mints 1052–1105/1642–1694   95
5. Late Safavid Iran: tribal pressure on the periphery   224

Illustrations

Plate section located between pages 166 and 167

1. View of Isfahan, 1703, from Cornelis de Bruyn, *Reizen over Moskovie, door Persie en Indie*, 2nd ed., 1714.
2. Royal Square of Isfahan, 1703, from Cornelis de Bruyn, *Reizen over Moskovie, door Persie en Indie*, 2nd ed., 1714.
3. Mint of Isfahan, from Ambrosio Bembo, "Viaggio e giornale per parte dell'Asia di quattro anni incirc fatto da me Ambrosio Bembo Nob. Veneto" (courtesy of the James Ford Bell Library at the University of Minnesota).
4. View of Sa'adabad, 1703, from Cornelis de Bruyn, *Reizen over Moskovie, door Persie en Indie*, 2nd ed., 1714.
5. View of Shamakhi, 1702, from Cornelis de Bruyn, *Reizen over Moskovie, door Persie en Indie*, 2nd ed., 1714.
6. View of Lar, 1704, from Cornelis de Bruyn, *Reizen over Moskovie, door Persie en Indie*, 2nd ed., 1714.
7. Grand Vizier Khalifah Sultan, by Mu'in Musavvir, *c*.1650, opaque watercolor, ink and gold on paper. (Lent by the Art and History Collection, Courtesy of the Arthur M. Sackler Gallery, Smithsonian Institution, Washington, D.C.: LTS1995.2.88)
8. Safavid surrender at Qandahar, *c*.1640. (Courtesy of the Musée Guimet, Paris; Réunion des Musées Nationaux / Art Resource, NY)

9. Shah Sulayman, *c.*1680, opaque watercolor on paper. (Lent by the Art and History Collection, Courtesy of the Arthur M. Sackler Gallery, Smithsonian Institution, Washington, D.C.: LTS2003.1.6)
10. Grand Vizier Shah Quli Khan, by Hajii Muhammad, 1696, opaque watercolor, ink and gold on paper. (Lent by the Art and History Collection, Courtesy of the Arthur M. Sackler Gallery, Smithsonian Institution, Washington, D.C.: LTS1995.2.182)
11. Shah Sultan Husayn, 1703, from Cornelis de Bruyn, *Reizen over Moskovie, door Persie en Indie*, 2nd ed., 1714.

Note on Transliteration

The Arabic, Persian, and Russian transliteration used in this book follows the Library of Congress system without the diacritic marks. Exceptions are non-Roman place names such as Herat, Tehran, and Yerevan, terms such as *jiz'ya* and shari`a, which are spelled without the final *h*, and some originally Turkish words, such as *bey, beglerbeg,* and *Shah-seven*. Dates in the text are given according to the Common Era calendar, except when there is a compelling reason to give the Islamic lunar or the Iranian solar *hijri* date as well.

Abbreviations

AAE	Archives des Affaires Etrangères, Paris
AME	Archives des Missions Etrangères, Paris
ARSI	Archivum Romanum Societatis Iesu, Rome
BA	Biblioteca da Ajuda, Lisbon
BN	Bibliothèque Nationale, Paris
BSOAS	*Bulletin of the School of Oriental and African Studies*
CA	Carmelite Archives, Rome
CHI	*The Cambridge History of Iran*
EI²	*The Encyclopedia of Islam*, 2nd edition
EIr.	*Encyclopaedia Iranica*
HHSt	Haus-, Hof- und Staatsarchiv, Vienna
IJMES	*International Journal of Middle East Studies*
IOR	India Office Records, British Library, London
IS	*Iranian Studies*
JESHO	*Journal of the Economic and Social History of the Orient*
NA	Nationaal Archief (Dutch National Archives), The Hague
PF	Propaganda Fide Archives, Rome
St.Ir.	*Studia Iranica*
ZDMG	*Zeitschrift der Deutschen Morgenländischen Gesellschaft*

Acknowledgments

This book is the result of a long process of research and thinking, going back to the moment that I chose the reign of the much neglected Shah Sulayman as the topic of my dissertation some twenty-five years ago. It grapples with some of the same questions that I encountered working on my thesis, and I can only hope that the analysis and answers offered here show my intellectual progress over a quarter of a century.

It gives me great pleasure to acknowledge my debt to a number of friends and colleagues who have guided me in my intellectual development and helped me improve this study by prodding me to sharpen its argument. As always, my first expression of gratitude goes to Nikki Keddie for being the great mentor that she is, quietly supportive by way of the intellectual community she maintains, while reminding us all of the importance of comparative history and of the imperative to present ideas clearly and intelligibly.

I am grateful to the various colleagues who went over the manuscript in full or in part. Needless to say, none is responsible for any remaining gaps and errors; those remain mine alone. Michael Axworthy read the entire penultimate draft with great care and greatly improved it with his pertinent comments and suggestions. I am grateful to those who read multiple parts of the book or commented on individual chapters, including Saïd Amir Arjomand, Jeremy Black, Stephen Dale, Willem Floor, Vazken Ghougassian, Hirotake Maeda, Vera Moreen, Monica Ringer, Giorgio Rota, and Devin Stewart. I also would like to thank Giorgio Rota and Hasan Zandieh for providing me with source material, Massumeh Farhad and Farhad Hakimzadeh for assisting me in procuring images, Anandaroop Roy for drafting the general map, and Stephen Album and Angie Hoseth for helping me to create the mint maps. I owe a special debt of gratitude to the professional staff and my colleagues at the University of Delaware, my academic home for the last eighteen years, for their support and encouragement and, in general, for helping create a congenial and intellectually stimulating environment. I thank Joanna Godfrey at I.B.Tauris and Elizabeth Stone for overseeing the editing and the production of the book with diligence and efficacy.

I also would like to express my gratitude to the helpful and efficient staff of the various archives and libraries that I have visited over the years. These include the Dutch National Archives in The Hague, the India Office Library in London, the Bibliothèque Nationale and the Archives des Missions Etrangères in Paris, the Biblioteca da Ajuda in Lisbon, and the Archivum Romanum Societatis Iesu in Rome.

My sons Max and Theo still think their dad does boring work. They are voracious readers yet for now their X-Box and the games they play on it are a greater source of excitement than the library. Given their age, I can hardly take issue with them, although I do hope that they will one day read this book and change their mind—if only a bit. In the meantime, their lust for life and their ironic wit inspires me more than they can imagine.

My greatest thanks go to Fariba Amini, the most caring person I have ever known. She, too, reminds me from time to time that the past may be fascinating but that it is also important to live in the present. To which I always respond that there's no present without the past, as the history of Iran demonstrates in particular. But then, living in the present with Fariba is pure joy, so I dedicate this book to her.

Preface

This book addresses the problematic question of decline for Iran in a period which most Iranians and a good many scholars consider to be not just a crucially formative phase in the country's history but one of its more glorious epochs. As the nationalist narrative goes, the Safavids were the first dynasty since the Mongols to knit Iran together as an integrated territorial unit. They did so by giving their realm a distinct identity marked by overlapping territorial and religious boundaries, which endures until today. In time Safavid Iran became an urban-centered society of great cultural achievement, a nation imbued with an outward-looking elan connecting it to a globalizing world by way of long-distance commerce and diplomacy. The lead actor in this script is Shah `Abbas the "Great," who plays the role of Renaissance prince, equal in fortitude and sophistication to the greatest contemporary European monarchs. After "reconquering" Iran, this most formidable of Safavid rulers put his realm on a sound military and administrative footing, sidelining its unruly tribal elements by replacing them with a new military-bureaucratic elite, endowing his new capital, the centrally located city of Isfahan, with a dazzlingly new commercial and administrative center. The outcome of his efforts was a centrally controlled country under visionary leadership, a nexus of long-distance trade and diplomacy, from which the Armenian merchants of New Julfa, the suburb of Isfahan that `Abbas had created for them, plied their trade under royal patronage from England to the Philippines, and which dispatched envoys to far-flung courts in Europe and Asia.[1] Such is the image, one that has only grown in radiance with time, evoking a blend of royal grandeur and justice and, ultimately, the promise of transformative change.

The transformation, of course, never materialized. Indeed, Iran—as much of Asia—and Western Europe embarked on rather different trajectories precisely in this period, the sixteenth to the early eighteenth century, spanning the high Renaissance and the onset of the Enlightenment and the early Industrial Revolution. European thinkers in this period gradually moved away from an epistemological framework based exclusively on the Bible and its truth toward a more experimental and open-ended approach to the fundamental questions of human life and society. English and French political philosophers, operating in an atmosphere of widening intellectual and geographical horizons, formulated fresh ideas that summoned accountable government and popular sovereignty and that proclaimed the commensurability of self-interest and the common good; scientists began to put science at the service of trades and crafts, allowing entrepreneurs to tap into vast reservoirs of newly available "useful" knowledge, prefiguring the synergetic interplay between government and private initiative that soon was to harness nature's resources beyond anyone's imagination. All this—in addition to great advances in military technology—enabled the nations of northwestern Europe to expand tremendously, militarily, economically, but above all in terms of applied knowledge. While European visitors were dazzled by the splendor of the mid-seventeenth-century Safavid court, gazed admiringly at the wondrous architecture of Isfahan, and marveled at the safety of the country's road system, Europe's objective economic power, organizational capacity, and cognitive grasp of the world already far surpassed that of Iran (and most other non-Western nations).[2]

Any lingering indeterminacy with regard to Iran's direction ended abruptly with the fall of Isfahan in 1722 and the country's subsequent disintegration at the hand of tribal warlords, the extortionate Nadir Shah in first place. The resulting anarchy would persist for almost a century, with consequences that reverberated into the modern age, leaving Iran far behind metropolitan Russia, India, and the core area of the Ottoman Empire in developmental terms. After 1722 Europeans no longer visited what was now seen as a dark and dangerous land. When they returned to Iran in the early nineteenth century they looked in vain for the splendor of the realm of the legendary Sophi; what they encountered instead was a bedraggled, backward country of ruined towns inhabited by impoverished, ignorant people who seemed in dire need of Western tutelage.

Iranians have been baffled at this devolution ever since. They have found it hard to come to terms with the yawning gap between their self-perception as the proud inheritors of a great civilization and the inhabitants of a country endowed with abundant material resources and a magnificent culture, and the reality of a land rapidly turning into a backwater ripe for the imperialist picking in these two centuries. In their search for answers, they have generally looked to outside forces. Externalizing the "blame," they have tended to ascribe the slide to second-rate power status to the machinations of greedy and power-hungry foreigners—not the lowly Afghans so much as the foreigners they take seriously, the ones who evoke a mixture of envy, admiration, and resentment—first the Portuguese, prone to bullying Iran from the isle of Hurmuz, their stronghold in the Persian Gulf, then the Dutch, determined to despoil their country of its vast natural riches, and finally the crafty English, who are thought to have completed the job of stifling Iran's autonomy while robbing it of its wealth.

I draw attention to this radical divergence between perception and reality, not to indict Iranians for indulging in a myopic collective memory but to enable the reader to understand some of this book's premises. One is that, if the Safavid state had not disintegrated, Iran's future might not have been drastically different from what it became. There are no interruptions here. To recognize the Safavids as an important phase in Iranian history is not the same as presenting their reign as a teleologically predetermined chapter in a heroic national narrative. The pages that follow are offered as an interpretive study that grapples with the complex range of reasons—environmental, economic, and, above all, political—explaining why the interaction between the state and society and the outside world evolved the way it did, causing the Safavids to falter and fail. It is an attempt to explain the fate of the Safavids, not Iran's "failure" to follow a European-like path to modernity. That would be a different project. In his recent study on the rise of Britain as an industrial power, Joel Mokyr observes that for much of recorded history "the arch-enemy of economic growth was [...] predators, pirates, and parasites, often known euphemistically by economists as 'rent-seekers,' who found it easier to pillage and plunder the work of others than to engage in economically productive activities themselves."[3] There is precious little evidence to suggest that, absent the Afghans (or any other "outsiders"), rent-seeking would have ceased to be the dominant mode of making money in Iran.[4]

This leads to the second premise, which is that, whereas from the early nineteenth century onward outside pressure and meddling inarguably had a significant impact on Iran's political and economic conditions, to connect Safavid decline directly to the (deliberate) design of external forces is as misleading as it is anachronistic.[5] Iran, then as now, was embedded in a larger regional and international context that helped shape its fortunes, yet its destiny was not *determined* by "foreigners." Foreigners and foreign lands naturally are not excluded from the discussion in this book; long-distance trade and transcontinental money flows are an integral part of the analysis; it will be seen how wars, natural disasters and government policies in Europe, the Ottoman Empire, India, and even Japan influenced the commercial and monetary conditions of the Safavid realm. Yet this study identifies the causes of Iran's malaise at the turn of the eighteenth century primarily in terms of internal dynamics, having to do with political and economic weaknesses which were domestic in origin even if they played themselves out as part of and in interaction with larger global currents. The Afghans finally—hardly "foreigners"—emerge from this book not as a cause but as a symptom, for being the most successful peripheral tribesmen who, alienated by the center, broke out of their frontier zone and ended up overwhelming a severely weakened heartland.

Introduction

Since the publication, more than half a century ago, of Laurence Lockhart's massive study *The Fall of the Safavi Dynasty and the Afghan Occupation of Persia*, little that is new and noteworthy has been written about events and developments during the reigns of the last two Safavid rulers, Shah Sulayman (1666–94), and Sultan Husayn (1694–1722), or in general about the decades leading up to the collapse of the Safavid dynasty in 1722.[1] The presumed reasons for this reticence range from the apparent comprehensiveness of Lockhart's book, which may have daunted scholars from revisiting the period, to the relative dearth of Persian-language sources for the last half century of Safavid rule. Studying the decline of Muslim states and the demise of the dynasties that ruled them also seems less exciting than examining the rise of new and promising political configurations—especially at a time when "decline" has become a loaded term. New sources have since come to light and our ideas about the motivating forces of history have changed, yet Lockhart's work continues to stand as a formidable challenge to a full reassessment of the Safavid dynasty's dying days.[2]

This does not mean that Lockhart's approach and interpretation have gone unchallenged. Martin Dickson's famously trenchant—and somewhat unfair—review drew attention to the peculiarly (British) Orientalist and Whiggish biases that inform the book. Dickson chided Lockhart for paying insufficient attention to social and economic conditions and developments, for according undue importance to the role European envoys, merchants and missionaries played in Safavid society, and for singling out royal debauchery and the "oppression" of minorities as the primary reasons for its downward slide.[3] Ironically, already at the time of its publication, this aspect of Lockhart's book was somewhat dated. A full fifteen years earlier, the Russian scholar Vladimir Minorsky, paying scant attention to foreign missionaries and merchants, had suggested a series of proximate political, military, and economic causes for the many problems that plagued late Safavid Iran.[4] In 1966, K. M. Röhrborn's *Provinzen und Zentralgewalt Persiens* added a new dimension to Safavid studies by laying the groundwork for a thorough mapping of the makeup and evolution of the Safavid bureaucracy.

Minorsky's and Röhrborn's studies were sturdy building blocks for further exploration along the lines of the critical approach meanwhile taken by Ottomanists and Mughalists, who in the past thirty years have sought to avoid the "Orientalist" biases found in Lockhart's book in analyzing the forces that weakened their empires. Yet even with a plethora of newly available source material, few scholars of early modern Iran have risen to the occasion. They have either stayed away from the topic or chosen to focus on politics and religion in discussing late Safavid Iran.[5] The result is that, the odd article aside, little effort has been made to re-examine the period in a comprehensive manner.[6]

This study seeks to do just that. It revisits the second century of Safavid rule, the period between the death of Shah 'Abbas I in 1629 and the fall of Isfahan to Afghan invaders in 1722, and takes a fresh look at the interplay between the forces that continued to animate the Safavid dynasty and the ones that helped bring it down. Although for reasons to be pointed out below, I do not embrace Lockhart's vision of "decline," I do use the term, and I naturally do so in a self-conscious manner. Long embedded in the Christian as well as the Islamic historiographical tradition, the "decline" paradigm has fallen out of favor in modern Western scholarship about the non-West, and in the case of early modern Muslim states it has almost become a taboo. Scholars still legitimately talk about the decline of sixteenth-century Venice, Spain after the reign of Philip II or the Dutch Republic following its Golden Age, but in addressing states such as the Ottoman Empire or Mughal India they are suspicious of it, reject it by arguing that the term is vague and imprecise or that a slide spanning a century or more lacks any meaning as an organizing principle. They circumvent it if they can, and talk it out of existence if they have to address it. In the context of the early modern Middle East, decline, in Cemal Kafadar's words, has become the "d-word, shunned simply because it seems the incorrect thing to say...."[7]

One way of evading the problematic decline scenario in the case of late Safavid Iran is to highlight political stability and cultural efflorescence. More than a little justification exists for this approach. For decades after the death of Shah 'Abbas I in 1629, foreign visitors continued to find Iran a safe and agreeable place, and especially the reign of his great-grandson, Shah 'Abbas II (1642–66) earned a reputation for relative peace and prosperity—an "Indian Summer,"

Lockhart called it.⁸ The shah continued to make efforts to stay on top of competing bureaucratic interests. The turnover rate of high-ranking officials remained comparatively low.⁹ Politically, matters were far less chaotic than in the Ottoman Empire or Mughal India— and much more stable than in the sixteenth century. The transition between 'Abbas II and Safi II in 1666 was as peaceful as the accession of Shah Sultan Husayn in 1694. No seventeenth-century Safavid ruler met a violent end or was even deposed.¹⁰ Whether this reflects an unassailable legitimacy on the part of Safavid shahs or says something about the weakness of their enemies, the record stands in sharp contrast to conditions in Istanbul, where between 1622 and 1703 several sultans were either murdered or cast aside, or to developments in India, where the internecine strife that preceded the accession of Shah Jahan in 1628 was as intense as the turmoil that led to the same ruler's deposition thirty years later. Iran's record is equally as impressive if the length of incumbency of grand viziers is any measure of stability. Between 1624 and 1720 Safavid shahs were served by ten grand viziers, one of whom, Shaykh 'Ali Khan Zanganah, was in office for a full twenty years. Several were dismissed but only Mirza Abu Talib Khan Urdubadi (1634) and Mirza Muhammad "Saru" Taqi (1645) met a violent death at the shah's orders. Istanbul in the same period saw a succession of eighteen grand viziers. Four of these were executed, eleven were deposed, two resigned; only one died a natural death in office.¹¹

Safavid society in this period looks vigorous in other respects as well. Isfahan was at the peak of its economic energy and cultural vitality, its population growing until after the middle of the century.¹² Merchants from all over Eurasia frequented its well-stocked bazaars; coffeehouses were as ubiquitous as (officially sanctioned) brothels; and everyone marveled at the splendor of the architectural wonders flanking the grand royal square that Shah 'Abbas I had built. The flowering of philosophy and architecture concentrated in the city was such that it prompted Marshall Hodgson to speak of a renaissance.¹³ Operating from the suburb that Shah 'Abbas I had created for them, the Armenians of New Julfa oversaw a trading empire that spanned the breadth of Eurasia.¹⁴ Conditions beyond Isfahan were not necessarily depressed either. Tabriz, the center of Azerbaijan and Iran's second city, expanded until the mid-seventeenth century.¹⁵ Europeans at that time described Shiraz as pleasant and sophisticated. The country at large remained at peace and saw few insurrections until the 1690s. Agriculture and trade still flourished, new caravanserais continued to be built, and road security remained relatively good throughout the country, certainly compared with conditions in the eastern half of the Ottoman Empire, not to mention Russia.[16] Jean Chardin, who wrote the best informed outside account of Safavid Iran, made a famous claim that Iran's peasants were better off than their French counterparts; and his equally telling observation that, at least until the end of Shah 'Abbas II's reign, its roads remained relatively safe, epitomizes this tranquility.[17] No one, in sum, foresaw that the entire edifice would crumble within a few decades.

Yet the notion of Safavid decline is not so easily exorcized, and any scholar dealing with the period will have to find an explanation for the sudden demise of the dynasty that goes beyond (small numbers of) predatory nomads swooping in from the east. Neither of the two neighboring empires descended from glory to ruin in quite the same abrupt fashion. Rather than dissolving, the Ottomans, in traditional historiographical terms, went on to "decline" for another 350 years after their "halcyon days" under Süleyman the Lawgiver. The Mughal collapse, too, was a more gradual and inchoate process, involving the mutation of the central state into a series of regional power centers and, ultimately, a creeping incorporation into a new, colonial dispensation.[18]

The Safavid decline trope is firmly embedded in the literature, going back to first-hand sources written by participants and outside observers alike. Even more than in the case of the Ottoman Empire and Mughal India, in Safavid Iran one ruler represents the gold standard, the ideal from which his successors are thought to have fallen away. Sultan Süleyman (r. 1520–66) remains the most celebrated Ottoman ruler; and the consensus that Mughal India reached its apogee under Sultan Akbar (r. 1556–1605) remains in place. Yet neither ruler rises to the stature of Shah 'Abbas the "Great" in embodying the acme of the dynasty as well as the empire he helped create.[19] This is not merely a question of retroactively applied gloss. Shortly after his death in 1629, European observers already hailed Shah 'Abbas I as a wise and just monarch, and within a few decades his reign was fondly remembered as a golden age of good governance.[20] These same observers were quick to blame what they saw as a dysfunctional state apparatus on the harem education of 'Abbas's successors. They spoke of rulers determined to keep the heir to the throne ignorant by restricting his formal education to religious matters and weak by plying him with drink and drugs instead of encouraging him to engage in physical exercise.[21] In the 1670s Chardin set the tone for this assessment with his remark that, after Shah 'Abbas I, Iran had ceased to prosper. 'Abbas's successors, he argued, did not live long enough to rise above the factional fray at the court, hence failed to put their imprint on the system as `Abbas had done during four decades of firm rule. Shah `Abbas II, the last strong ruler of the dynasty, had died young, and after him Iran had gone to waste. The reign of his immediate successor, Shah Sulayman, was so short on noteworthy events that it did not even prompt the writing of any court chronicles.[22] As the shah succumbed to the pleasures of the harem, women and eunuchs came to dominate the inner palace.

Following the fall of Isfahan, the Polish Jesuit Thaddeus Krusinski endorsed this verdict and gave it authoritative treatment as well as a distinctly moralizing coloring. An eyewitness to the Afghan takeover, he described how a meek, pleasure-seeking Shah Sultan Husayn had hastened Iran's irreversible decline.[23] A century later, John Malcolm's seminal *A History of Persia*, the first comprehensive history of Iran in a Western language, raised the moral decline scenario to historiographical respectability. Malcolm's treatment also put a distinctly British stamp on it. Published in 1815, *A History of Persia* is deeply informed by Persian sources available to the author (some of which are no longer extant) but it also represents a way of thinking steeped in admiration for Roman virtue and virility entwined with an age-old biological theory of decline, going back to the ancient Greeks and revived by Enlightenment thinkers wont to link Oriental despotism to an "air of softness and effeminacy" exemplified by royal debauchery and the baleful influence of harem women.[24] Both interpretations heavily depended on the moral character of the ruler and the elite. Molded in a stern Georgian-era intellectual environment that hailed Republican Rome as a civic model, Malcolm thought in strictly dichotomous terms, contrasting the "virtues of reason" with the "vices of passion." Shah `Abbas I, he wrote, although reportedly cruel and severe, was also courageous. He had "punished and rewarded his nobles ... without fear and without suspicion," and he had "acted more from the dictates of policy than of passion." With the exception of Shah `Abbas II, all of his successors had been "unworthy" rulers, avaricious, indolent, or bigoted.[25]

Malcolm's views, feeding on age-old notions of (Oriental) degeneracy in which lubricity equaled fateful effeminacy rather than virility, have been repeated in one way or another by Westerners writing on Iran until Lockhart put a Victorian-inspired scholarly imprimatur on them. Modern scholars have added a cultural dimension to this verdict. E. G. Browne at the turn of the twentieth century lamented the "extraordinary dearth of notable poets" in the Safavid period and dismissed its entire literature as overwrought and derivative.[26] More recently, Alessandro Bausani has drawn attention to the stagnating effect of the definitive turn to gnosis as opposed to science supposedly taken by Iran's literati in the Safavid period.[27] Art historians echoed all this by insisting that, a few highlights aside, the seventeenth-century Safavid pictorial arts stand out for "overrefinement and effete sophistication," and that even the period's hallowed religious architecture lacks the originality and purity of that of earlier times.[28] The overall verdict is epitomized in Roger Savory's assessment of the period after Shah `Abbas I as one of "gradual but continuous decline."[29]

From the last days of Safavid rule, an indigenous Iranian perspective of related provenance and similar tenor has powerfully reinforced this assessment. Focusing on "prophets and princes," *rusul-u-muluk*, Iranian-Islamic historiography pairs a strong idealist foundation to a firm belief in the trajectory of civilization along biological lines, and combines all this with the assumption that "it is kings and the character of kings which constitute polities, for men are by nature evil and fractious and can be curbed only by overweening, omnipotent authority."[30] A tendency to view the state as an "abstract activity personified in the detailed actions of the king and to describe its history as that of a particular royal line" has compounded the image.[31] Muhammad Baqir Sabzavari, the mid-seventeenth-century *shaykh al-islam* of Isfahan, in his *Rawzat al-anvar-i `Abbasi* presents a list of what he sees as causes of decline. These include kingly pride and selfishness (*ghurur va khud-bini*), injustice (*zulm*) vis-à-vis the peasantry, a lack of royal attention to the greed and abuse among subordinate officials, wanton sexuality, extreme parsimony or the opposite, excessively spendthrift, and military neglect.[32] By this time a mood of nostalgia had already set in among Safavid literati. The 1670s and 1680s saw the earliest example of so-called "anonymous histories" of Shah Isma`il, pseudo-historical works that, harking back to the inspiring days of the early Safavids, presented that ruler's exploits as a series of entertaining and gripping stories.[33] By then Shah `Abbas I, too, had come to be celebrated as an ideal monarch, a legendary ruler whose valiant deeds provided public story tellers in Iranian coffeehouses with rich material.[34]

Like their European peers, Iran's post-Safavid literati, presenting the king as the personification of the body politic, typically ascribed the weakening of the Safavid state and its tragic demise to a loss of moral fiber at the top, to the insouciance of the elite and the hedonism of a court led by a spineless shah only interested in religious matters.³⁵ Shushtari praises the Safavids for their building efforts, for granting *suyurghal*s (fiefs) and endowing *vaqf*, for their concern for religious education and their efforts to bring prosperity to the common people. But, Shushtari insists, matters deteriorated with the feeble-minded Shah Sultan Husayn, whose incompetence made the country fall into disarray.³⁶ `Ali Muhammad Hazin Lahiji, who lived through the last days of the Safavid regime, attributed the easy Afghan victory to a careless elite and an army that had not seen war for close to a century.³⁷ Writing shortly after the fall of Isfahan, Muhammad Shafi` recounts the well-known, "over-determined" story of how on his deathbed Shah Sulayman suggested to his courtiers that they had a choice between Sultan Husayn and his brother `Abbas Mirza. If they chose the pious, pusillanimous Sultan Husayn, they would be able to sit beside their wives without having to worry about war; if, by contrast, they preferred to spend their lives in the saddle amid the sound of whizzing arrows and thunderous guns, they should go for `Abbas Mirza.³⁸ The late eighteenth-century man of letters Rustam al-Hukama suggested how royal indulgence did not preclude legitimacy. Echoing an old adage of Middle Eastern kingship, he insisted on the right of rulers to indulge in pleasure and entertainment provided they also take care of their subjects' well-being. Late Safavid rulers, and especially Shah Sultan Husayn, clearly did not live up to the latter mandate.³⁹ In the twentieth century Iranian historiography, now coming under the influence of European models, began to coat the story with thickening layers of secular-nationalist paint, contrasting the slothful, superstitious late Safavid rulers and the ruin they brought upon society to the energetic, strong-willed Nadir Shah, Iran's Napoleon, who restored the country's national honor by rebuilding its military might.⁴⁰

In today's academic climate, skeptical about (non-Western) decline and especially averse to decline as a moral category, one is almost forced to reject this type of interpretation out of hand and to focus on manifestations of continued vitality in the form of artistic expression, religious disputation, or overlooked provincial initiative. But to do so would be to ignore the many unmistakable signs of trouble. One would have to disregard the sober words of the Isfahan-based agents of the Dutch East India Company (VOC). They, too, pointed to the ineptitude and insouciance of the last few shahs, calling them "slaves of Bacchus and Venus" who rarely left their harems to apprise themselves of the true state of affairs of the realm beyond the palace walls. VOC officials drew attention to the excessive flattery of sycophantic courtiers who kept the shah in the dark about events outside the capital, and lamented the result, irresponsible rule and rampant corruption.[41] They arguably did so less from an "Orientalist" perspective than as clear-eyed observers interested in keeping abreast of the shifting matrix of power and influence at the court, the better to be able to do business with its decision-makers. They experienced first-hand the damaging effect a retreating shah had on effective policy-making; the absence of a clearly defined center of power confronted them with a highly factionalized court filled with officials unwilling to assume any responsibility for fear that doing so might help their competitors bring them down through slander and intrigue.

There were yet other warning signs, some of them proffered by sympathetic foreigners. Tavernier and Chardin generally wrote positively about Iran, but they also discerned a decrease in economic vitality as well as in the quality of political leadership. True, they followed a Western trope by associating the opulence they witnessed at the Safavid court with an inherent Oriental penchant for wastefulness, but their assessment does not just hinge on a court sinking into lascivious lethargy.[42] They spoke of agricultural mismanagement. They pointed to a series of disasters that struck Iran around the accession of Shah Sulayman in the form of poor harvests, famine, and outside attack. They also offered some telling diachronic comparisons. When Chardin says he saw a marked difference in prosperity between the first time he was in Iran in 1665 and when he last left in 1677, with riches diminished by half and the money debased, we have to take him seriously—not just because he was a keen observer of Iran, but also because his remarks are corroborated by a wealth of other, more specific documentation. Five years into the reign of Shah Safi, the Dutch claimed that under his predecessor Iranian officials had been much less demanding in their quest for bribes in the form of "gifts."[43] In the 1680s, their agents spoke of a general impoverishment of the country as reflected in lower sales of spices and decreased sugar consumption among the elite, who had taken to using cheaper sources of fructose than imported sugar.[44] And in 1692 Russian merchants protested to the shah's envoy in Moscow about the worsening quality of Iranian manufactured goods exported to Russia. The hardest possible evidence for economic trouble, finally, is found in a stagnating influx of silver, which led to a precipitous closing of Iran's mints and was accompanied by a worsening of its currency through debasement and loss of value in this same period.

The term decline seems appropriate for this period and these conditions—even before road security deteriorated and tributary arrangements with the nomadic fringe broke down, leading to a series of tribal revolts followed by outside invasions—with the following caveats. As John Elliot, writing on early modern Spain, suggests, we need to study how reality interacts with the perception of decline.[45] Decline is a normative term as well as a relative one, and is thus always used comparatively. The "decline" of one society looks all the more ominous in the face of the simultaneous ascent of another, more energetic or innovative one.[46] Late Safavid Iran juxtaposed with early Enlightenment Europe with its scientific breakthroughs, its radical new political ideas, and its global commercial reach, is the obvious case in point. Similarly, a period of "decline" often derives half its drama from being contrasted with a preceding, more "brilliant" era full of vigor and discipline. The Safavids arguably reached their apogee of power and control in the early seventeenth century, yet the idea that Shah `Abbas *monopolized* power, that he achieved a panoptic kind of control over society, and that all this was lost under his successors, is as simplistic as it is misleading. For all his centralizing measures, `Abbas never controlled Iranian society. State control arguably weakened under his successors. But even as they whiled away much of their time engaged in pleasurable activities, later Safavid shahs typically chose their grand viziers on the basis of past experience and proven competence. Once in office, the latter showed themselves well aware of the problems at hand and worked hard to address them.

This leads to the second caveat, which is that we should be careful not to use decline as an all-embracing category implying that the entire system was drained of vitality and dynamism. Countervailing forces—the administrators who were not corrupt, the soldiers who still fought, the thriving exports—continued to abound in late Safavid times. The Qizilbash lost their dominant position in the military, but the Georgians who partly replaced them proved to be no less courageous fighters. Money in circulation became ever scarcer, yet the volume of Iran's silk and wool exports continued to grow. It is, in other words, important to "define what it is that is declining."[47] Economic vitality and military resilience are relatively easy categories in this regard—especially if concrete measures and events are on record and if quantitative data are available. Following Minorsky's analysis, it is clear that the upsetting of the balance between crown and state lands, a byproduct of the attempt to curtail the Qizilbash, contributed to a serious drop in fiscal revenue after the reign of Shah `Abbas I. There is also no doubt that military alertness diminished in the course of the seventeenth century, and especially after the

Safavids concluded the Peace of Zuhab with the Ottomans in 1639. The question of leadership is far more elusive for being a qualitative one. Yet here, too, we are not without some compelling evidence. The harem upbringing of Safavid rulers after Shah ʿAbbas I demonstrably produced rulers of lesser quality who even after ascending the throne spent more time within the confines of the palace than on the battlefield. It is important to note that court carousing per se is not the issue here. Royal debauchery is of all time; emperors and kings in East and West have always whiled away much time in their private quarters and dissipated treasure on lavish banquets and costly hunting parties. Safavid commentators saw such behavior as integral to kingship for reflecting the realm's prosperity and the king's prestige; they accepted, even expected it—as long as it was balanced by royal vigilance, forcefulness, and generosity.[48]

Finally, we should beware of teleology, and not just because as late as 1700 no one knew that the Safavid state would collapse a mere two decades later. If various practices initiated or intensified by Shah ʿAbbas were detrimental to the effective execution of central power, we should never assume that cause and effect are automatic or simple; nor should we automatically attribute all apparent weakness to elite incompetence and sloth. The Peace of Zuhab may be emblematic of Safavid apathy and the signal moment of Iran's military retrenchment. But we might also call the Safavid decision to end the state of war with the Ottomans a judicious move on the part of the ruling elite, based on a realistic assessment of relative military strength. And Zuhab certainly did not mark the *beginning* of the erosion of Safavid military might and vigilance. The same is true for economic issues. There were various structural reasons of Iran's weaknesses, including a harsh natural environment, a fragmented economy, and a dearth of exportable commodities, all of which transcend the reign of any single shah, indeed the lifespan of the dynasty. There is little question that, over time, productive forces faltered and scarce money became scarcer still. But did the economy just deteriorate because of nonchalant rulers who allowed provincial underlings to abuse the populace and raise taxes to unbearable levels? Or did international conditions leading to a diminished influx of bullion play a role in the malaise? Did environmental factors in the form of a prolonged period of drought contribute to the growing incidence of incursions by nomads driven to despair into Iran's eastern marches? And if religious minorities were prime targets of growing fiscal pressure, did this just reflect clerical bigotry or was it rather a function of their presumed wealth and vulnerability?

ORGANIZATION

The book blends a thematic organization with a chronological narrative. Chapter 1, called "Patterns," offers a schematic introduction to the working of the Safavid state and society, seeking to find a middle ground between the notion that the state was a Leviathan capable of bending society to its will, and the idea that state power was just nominal and abstract, that the shah's writ hardly ran outside of the capital, leaving the outlying regions largely autonomous. It presents Safavid society as a series of tensions between strong centrifugal and equally strong centripetal forces. The former, which ranged from physical barriers to easy communication to Iran's tribal makeup and its economic fragmentation, bred disunity and helped subordinate groups achieve much leeway. The latter, composed of elements like the centrality of the Persian language and culture, shared assumptions about divine kingship, and a strongly integrative religious vision, contributed to social and societal cohesion, facilitating central control beyond purely logistical means and, at the best of times, a measure of stability.

Leaving the static, functionalist analysis in the introductory chapter behind, the remainder of the book pursues a dynamic and evolving model, in which political structures turn into "units in action" performed by political actors.[49] Chapters 2 and 3 explore the politics of the central administration between 1629 and 1694, tracing the evolution of the court from an ambulant royal entourage engaged in perpetual campaigning to a stationary, palace-bound administration dominated by eunuchs and women. Chapter 2 discusses this process for the period from the accession of Shah Safi in 1629 until 1666, the year of Shah ʿAbbas II's death. Chapter 3 considers the reign of Shah Sulayman, the period from 1666 to 1694. It will be seen that, though it was strictly hierarchical in theory, the Safavid political order in practice was flexible and fluid. Individual players and the ethnic or status groups they belonged to or formed sought to maximize and solidify their interests in temporary alliances with others, leading to the creation and maintenance of formal and informal networks of power and influence. Yet all danced around the shah—the apex of a pyramid, seen as divinely appointed and acting as the one party above all other parties, as well as the center of a vortex, one faction among a multitude of feuding factions, albeit the most powerful one. The focus of the discussion about the shifting constellation of power will thus be on his relationship with his main courtiers, with special attention to the grand vizier.

Chapter 4 shifts the focus from the struggle over privilege and wealth to economic policy-making, a topic on which Persian-language sources and foreign travel narratives shed little light and which therefore often gets short shrift in discussions of the period. Based largely on the documentation left by the agents of the European maritime companies, this chapter looks at official monetary policy in an environment of scarce resources and relatively open borders. It analyzes how the state handled its finances; it focuses on fiscal policies and the management of the mints in an effort to explain the deterioration in the quality and volume of the Safavid coinage. It also examines the constant outflow of specie and bullion to India via the Persian Gulf ports, its causes, its effects, and the measures taken by Isfahan to prevent or tax this bullion drain.

The military naturally was a pivotal institution, the chief instrument for the Safavid state to maintain its supremacy and guarantee its survival against domestic rebels and external enemies. Its role in seventeenth-century Iran is peculiar. Historians agree that one of the factors contributing to the decline of the Roman Empire was the perpetual urge to expand, which depleted the treasury by expending too many resources on war-making. The Safavids, by contrast, not only gave up in their attempts to enlarge their territory; they deliberately retrenched in 1639, willingly ceding Mesopotamia to the Ottomans as part of the Treaty of Zuhab. Chapter 5 centers on this accord—how it came about and in what circumstances it was concluded—as part of a discussion about the army, its makeup and its evolution, with a particular focus on the causes and circumstances of the weakening of its command structure and of its diminishing battle-readiness in the course of the seventeenth century.

Moving away from the capital, Chapter 6 explores the interaction between the central government and the provinces. Claiming that the chain of command was not unilinear, flowing from the center to the outlying areas, nor simply based on coercion, it presents the practice of power as a blend of intimidation and violence, and negotiation involving compromise and accommodation. It discusses the various administrative arrangements made between the two, showing varying degrees of central control and different forms of fiscal income and how these changed as the state sought simultaneously to increase its authority and extract more revenue from outlying areas. This chapter examines economic activities beyond trade, most notably agriculture, yet in surveying Iran's economic conditions it inevitably gives unequal coverage to the country. Mostly written from the perspective of the center, the Persian-language material reflects a distinct bias towards the capital and the court. Its authors portray the shah as the protector of the common people, the ri`ayat, but pay virtually no attention to the latter except in cases of insubordination and rebellion, which they unhelpfully tend to dismiss as acts of ingratitude and disloyalty.[50] The reports of the various East India Companies do inform us about commoners, but they focus on the south, where their operations were concentrated. The chapter of needs follows this focus; it pays attention to conditions in Iran's northern regions, but is most detailed about events in the town of Kirman and the eponymous region, and the port of Bandar `Abbas on the Persian Gulf coast, in their interaction with the center.[51]

Chapter 7 addresses the interplay between religion and politics in the late Safavid state. It charts how the clerical establishment rose to prominence and became an integral part of the bureaucratic elite; it examines the tensions that existed, worsened, or erupted between various religious interest groups and professional elites—immigrant "Arab" ulama, Sufi-minded scholars, and literal-minded jurists—and how especially the latter came to play an increasingly activist role in the upper echelons of power. The chapter pays particular attention to clerical attitudes toward Iran's non-Shi`i population. This includes the treatment of Iran's domestic Armenian Christians, Jews, and Zoroastrians in connection with the presence of a small cohort of European missionaries and the resentment their activities created within the ranks of the ulama and Isfahan's badly divided Armenian community. The more important issue, the increasingly precarious position of Iran's far larger Sunni population, will be discussed with an eye to the paradoxical fact that these mostly peripheral inhabitants of the Safavid state suffered growing discrimination under the auspices of a grand vizier who was an avowed Sunni. The chapter finally weighs growing fiscal demands, a decreasing willingness to enlist marginal groups by way of tributary arrangements, and an ever sharper focus on the Shi`i character of the state as factors in the deteriorating conditions of Iran's "minorities."

Chapter 8 brings together the various events and processes discussed in the preceding chapters—weakening political authority, growing court factionalism, the increasing difficulty of mustering and equipping troops to face military challenges, mounting financial troubles, and the alienation of the Sunni fringe—in a grand finale covering the last twenty years of Safavid rule. It charts how court eunuchs, women, and literal-minded clerical forces came to dominate the court of the feeble Shah Sultan Husayn, and how rampant corruption, growing abuse of power, and fierce intra-elite competition in the form of factionalism scuttled any chance for a coherent response to the mounting domestic and external challenges. It finally examines how a diminishing willingness to accommodate and coopt marginal groups as part of a growing emphasis on the Shi`i character of the state alienated the Sunni tribesmen of the borderlands. The result was a series of rebellions and depredations that metastasized into a full-scale invasion—the first installment of what C. A. Bayly calls a series of eighteenth-century "tribal breakouts."[52] In the last years before the fall of Isfahan, Lezghi marauders wreaked havoc in the Caucasus, the Kurds in the Ottoman borderlands rose in revolt, and Baluchi and Afghan tribesmen, possibly driven to despair by recurrent periods of drought, began to pose a serious threat to Iran's vulnerable eastern flank. The Afghans faced fierce resistance in their attempts to take Kirman, but otherwise met with few obstacles as they advanced into Iran's heartland before laying siege to Isfahan, by then the panicked capital of a severely weakened state.

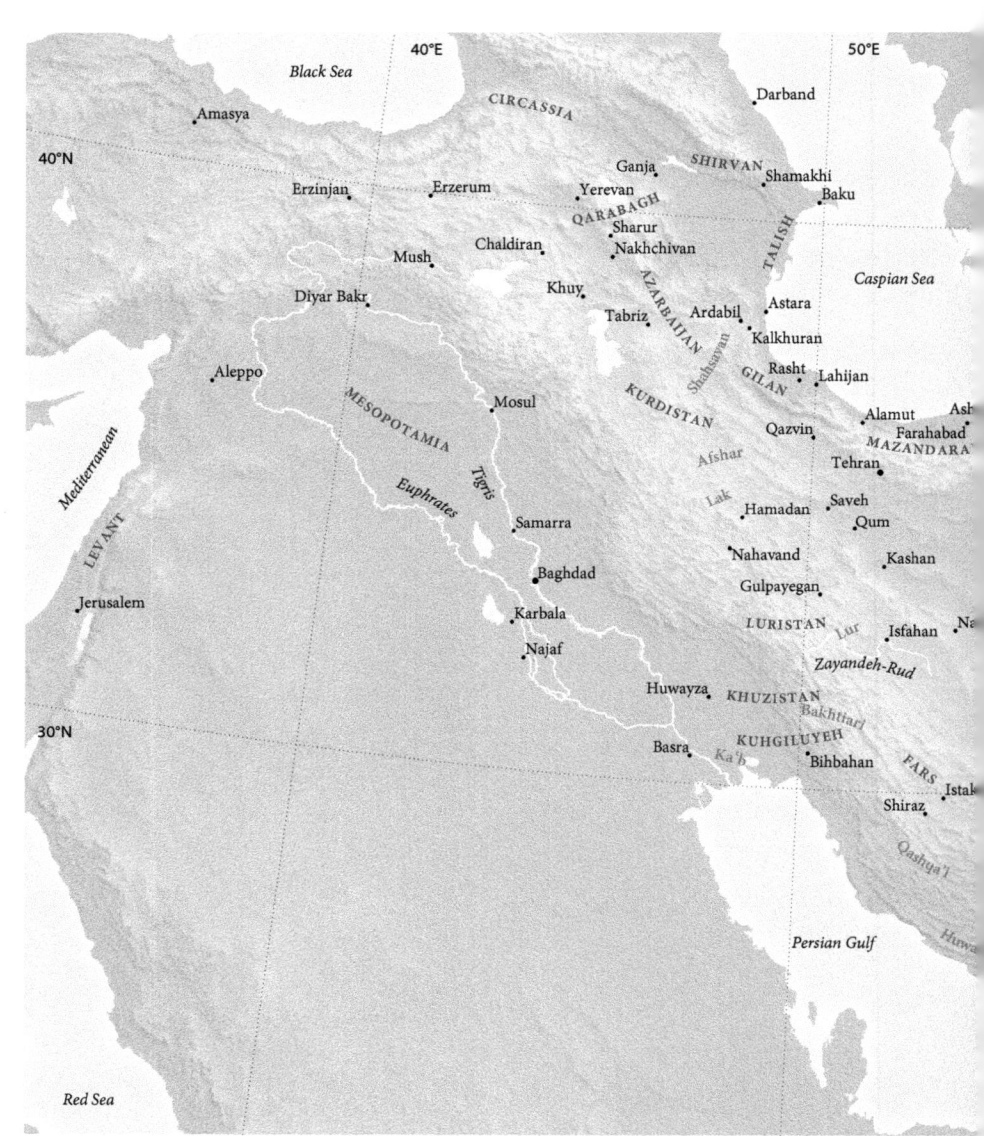

Map 1. Safavid Iran and the surrounding world

Map

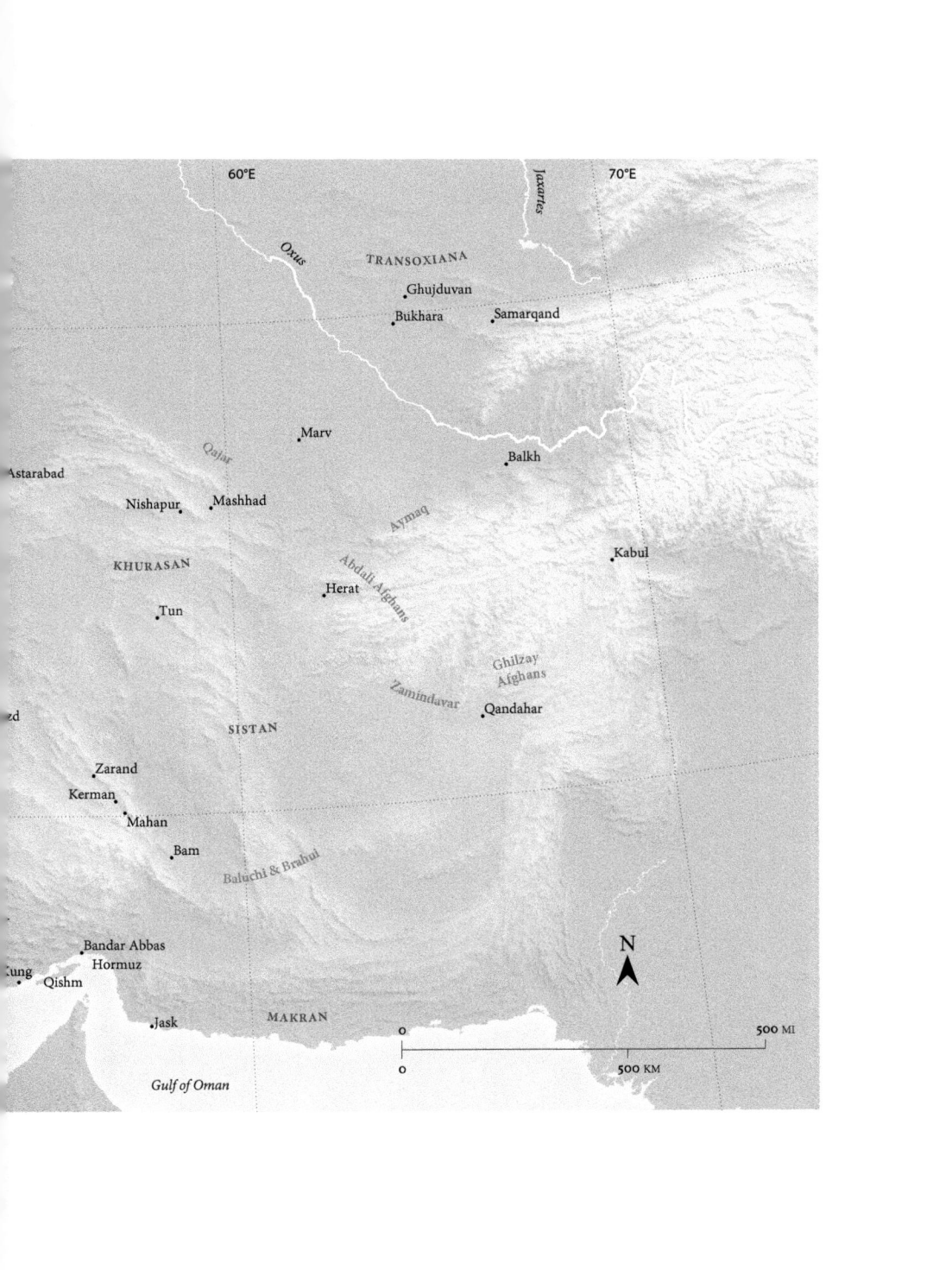

- 60°E, 70°E
- Jaxartes
- Oxus
- TRANSOXIANA
  - Ghujduvan
  - Bukhara
  - Samarqand
- Marv
- Balkh
- Astarabad
- Qajar
- Nishapur
- Mashhad
- KHURASAN
- Aymaq
- Abdali Afghans
- Herat
- Kabul
- Tun
- Zamindavar
- Ghilzay Afghans
- Qandahar
- SISTAN
- Zarand
- Kerman
- Mahan
- Bam
- Baluchi & Brahui
- Bandar Abbas
- Hormuz
- Kung
- Qishm
- Jask
- MAKRAN
- Gulf of Oman

N

0 — 500 MI
0 — 500 KM

Chapter 1

Patterns: Iran in the Late Safavid Period

پس معلوم شد که عدالت پادشاهی با صلاح و کم آزاری دخلی ندارد ، چه بسیاری از سیاست پادشاهان باشد که باعث امنیت شود ، و بسیاری از خونریزی های ایشان باشد که باعث این شود که کسی به نا حق خون کسی را نریزد ، و از بیم بازخواست و سیاست بر قتل کسی اقدام ننماید .

It is thus clear that royal justice has nothing to do with rectitude and the absence of causing harm. Some harsh policies of rulers generate security; and much of the blood-letting they engage in prevents people from unjustly shedding other people's blood and, for fear of retribution, keeps them from killing others.

Findiriski, *Tuhfat al-`alam*, 128

در عفو لذتی است که د ر انتقام نیست

In forgiveness there's a pleasure which doesn't exist in revenge.

Nawzad, *Namah'ha-yi Khan Ahmad Khan*, 94

INTRODUCTION

Several features of the late Safavid state make it appear as a west Asian example of the early modern state. Its rise in the early sixteenth century was fueled by tribal military power, charismatic leadership, and religious messianism. Over time, these forces grew weaker, to be replaced or supplanted by new sources of support and legitimacy. As the ruler's divine aura faded and the chiliastic enthusiasm of his followers abated, a more scriptural form of religion espoused by a newly formed clerical class came to replace it; as the Qizilbash, the Turkoman warriors (descendants of the Ghuzz Turks who had invaded the eastern Islamic world in the tenth/eleventh century) who had brought the Safavids to power, proved to be an unruly and destructive force, a new military and administrative elite was brought in and groomed to neutralize them. Over time these changes generated an urban-based system of governance blending traditional patterns of Iranian-Islamic kingship and institutionalized religion.[1]

These changes notwithstanding, the Safavid state remained a premodern formation along Weberian, patrimonial-bureaucratic lines, and not just because Iran did not undergo the social disciplining that set some contemporary European societies on the road to (bureaucratic) modernity.[2] The state endured as an extension of the royal household, its administrative offices knew little functional division, and private and public spheres overlapped. Coercive power, in sum, continued to be the ruler's personal property.[3]

This represents reality only up to a point, though. A common criticism of Weber's theory is that it presupposes static, even immutable structures. Weber was explicit about the fragility of patrimonial rule, yet he formulated state and society as a unitary system and, in his nineteenth-century (German) tendency to overrate the ability of the state to control, manage, and arbitrate, he paid insufficient attention to societal challenges to its power. Michael Mann's reformulation of Weber's ideas, taking this into account, rejects a simple antithesis between the all-powerful state, and society, the populace, the objects of its coercion. Mann sees a dialectic relationship between the two, a relationship in which a "range of infrastructural techniques are pioneered by despotic states, then appropriated by civil societies (or vice versa); then further opportunities for centralized coordination present themselves, and the process begins anew."[4] He also views society less as a structure than as a series of "multiple overlapping and intersecting sociopolitical networks of power."[5] This study follows these propositions, including Mann's distinction between "despotic" (immediate) and "infrastructural" (logistical) power.

It is useful to broaden Weber's conception of the patrimonial state even further by emphasizing the tributary dimension of relationships.[6] Power relations in Safavid Iran were fueled by *zar-u-zur*, gold and force, monetary inducement coupled with coercion including violence. The latter—military force—was the more important of the two. The shah was first and foremost a warrior-in-chief, the head of a band of fighters, and violence, or the threat of violence, was what made his opponents retreat or submit, and it was always the means of last resort for the state. Following Walther Hinz's focus on idealist—ideological and religious—pursuits in his analysis of the rise of the Safavids, we have perhaps paid too much attention to ideology and not enough to the more mundane motives of the warrior band that carried the Safavids to success—booty, a lust for power and glory, and the manly urge to conquer and subdue.[7] Effective and lasting power, however, could only be secured by way of tributary relationships involving the exchange of money. This, in turn, presupposed negotiation, resulting in a dynamic interaction between state and societal groups. Not just political domination but all forms of surplus extraction in Safavid Iran, from regular taxation to rent and confiscation, from state monopolies on commodities to forced partnership, were the outcome of bargaining processes pitting central power and its quest for domination against local resistance and subterfuge. Tributary relations were primarily extractive, applied to state centralization. But, following ancient patterns, they also knew a reciprocal, redistributive element.[8] Extraction could only be legitimate if balanced by the spread of resources and power among the members of the ruling clans. Only thus could (temporary and instrumental) loyalty and cooperation be expected.[9]

The Safavid state became centrally organized, but it was never able to overcome the political, social, and economic fragmentation of society. Its leaders naturally pursued maximal administrative and fiscal control. Shah ʿAbbas I's policies, most notably his efforts to replace tribal power with a new military and bureaucratic elite and his choice of Isfahan as the realm's administrative and economic center, represented a major step on the road from a tribal nomadic to an urban sedentary order. Despite all efforts, however, the Qizilbash warrior, the mainstay of the Safavid army, never became fully subordinated to the urban scribe, the pillar of bureaucratic management and order. The ancient tribal tradition, decentralized, exploitative, redistributive, and built on corporate legitimacy, continued to challenge its urban-based, agrarian Iranian counterpart, with its tendency toward accumulating revenue and concentrating power in the hands of a single supreme ruler.[10]

ANALYZING SAFAVID SOCIETY

This opening chapter presents Safavid Iran as a set of tensions. Some characteristics of its state and society enhanced order, cohesion, and stability, while others fostered fission and fragmentation. The purpose of this approach is to move away from a simple dichotomy between state and society as well as to dispel the idea that the state controlled society. We may blame long-standing Western notions of Oriental despotism for this as much as the Persian-language sources with their tendency to portray a state fully in charge of society—with a divinely ordained ruler at the head of a bureaucratic apparatus administering appointments and collecting large surpluses, and armies patrolling a well-defined territory. Once we collate these highly stylized sources with other, more realistic documentation and view the country in its proper environmental and political-historical context, a different picture emerges—one of a minimalist state masquerading as an absolutist court, highly factionalized, limited in its ability to collect information, dependent on fickle tribal forces for military support, and forced to negotiate with myriad societal groups over power and control.[11] The shah's power was awe-inspiring and Safavid ideology was a commanding force, but state absolutism was a relative concept and centralization was at best uneven. Like Mughal India, Safavid Iran was a "strange mix of despotism, traditional rights and equally traditional freedoms."[12]

CENTRIFUGAL FORCES

Physical and economic aspects

It took Iran much longer than most other parts of the Middle East to form a strong central state. Well into the twentieth century concentrated power faced formidable obstacles, with a harsh natural environment, causing communication to be slow and difficult, in first place. Iran's heartland, the plateau, is made up of vast stretches of semi-desert and piedmont terrain flanked by formidable mountain ranges—a saucer, Chahriyar Adle calls it. Human habitation, irrigated agriculture, and the traffic of people and goods have always clustered on its rims, the triangle that connects Mashhad with Tabriz via Tehran and that swerves south to the cities of Kashan, Isfahan, Shiraz, Yazd, and Kirman.[13] The western Zagros range constituted a natural barrier against attack from the Mesopotamian alluvial lowlands, but the same mountains also impeded access from the country's heartland to Kurdistan and Luristan, in addition to weakening the hold of the central state over ultramontane 'Arabistan (modern Khuzistan), and making lasting control over Iraq nearly impossible. The northern Alburz range, separating the central deserts from the lush Caspian forests, in turn hampered communication between Isfahan and the silk-producing areas of Gilan and Mazandaran. All this was made worse by the fact that, unlike Europe, Russia, and India with their profuse waterways, Iran barely has any navigable rivers. This resulted in scattered villages, economic isolation, and affinities and loyalties that were intensely local and regional.

Perhaps the most important geographical distinction in Safavid times, dictated by climate, cultural particularism, economic orientation, and military concern, was the "inner frontier" that separated the north and the south, especially the Persian Gulf littoral, the "hot lands," *Garmsir(at)*.[14] Ethnic, linguistic, and economic ties bound the north and the northwest to Anatolia and the Caucasus, and northeastern Khurasan to inner Asia. Of Kurdish origin, the Safavids hailed from the Turkish-speaking highlands of Anatolia; Tabriz and Qazvin had been their early capitals. Their military supporters, the Qizilbash tribes, had their origins and grazing grounds mostly in the same region. Georgians and Armenians, two groups that came to play a crucial military, administrative, and commercial role in Safavid society, had northern roots as well. Military challenges, too, tended to come from the northeast, the frontier with the Uzbeks, and the northwest, where the Safavids faced unruly mountaineers such as Kurds and Lezghis as well as the formidable Ottoman armies.[15] Much of the country's agricultural resource base was located in fertile Azerbaijan and the silk-producing Caspian provinces. All these factors made northern Iran a natural focus of Safavid attention and concern.

The southern littoral, by contrast, was alien territory for the Safavids. Its weather, swelteringly hot and humid for most of the year, must have been repellent to warriors used to the bracing climate of the high plateau. Most of its land was barren and unproductive. Ethnically and linguistically, too, the Garmsir was cut off from Iran's interior; many of its inhabitants were Arabs, with a sprinkling of Hindus from Gujarat and Sind; the region interacted with semi-autonomous Basra and the Arab shaykhdoms across the water as much as with Iran's heartland; its economy was oriented toward Oman—which received most of its food from Iran—and, most importantly, toward the Indian subcontinent.[16] Emblematic of this orientation is the distinct currency, the *larin*, a coin that was current throughout the Persian Gulf basin and in the Indian Ocean as far as Ceylon and the Maldive islands.[17] Aside from Fars, no part of the south ever elicited any special interest from the royal court other than for the revenue it produced. For all his concerns about trade, and despite the fact that he incorporated Bahrain and parts of the Gulf coast into his realm, even Shah ʿAbbas I himself is hardly an exception to this rule. He traveled a good deal during his long years in office, yet none of his campaigns ever took him beyond Shiraz.[18] Instead, he spent much time in Mazandaran, the region from which his mother hailed, which he loved, and where he built the two resort towns Ashraf and Farahabad. His successors were no different, except that they paid even less attention to the south. They, too, often spent their winters in the lush Caspian region, hunting and relaxing. Otherwise they might go on pilgrimage to Mashhad or Qum. Armed expeditions to the south were rare, and the Safavids never really developed a solid military connection with the Gulf. Even the growing seaborne threat by the Omani Arabs at the turn of the eighteenth century did not inspire them to build a navy. The minor role the Garmsir played in the Safavid imagination is well illustrated in the way the region is represented in the seventeenth-century geographical compendium *Mukhtasar-i mufid*, which has the Persian Gulf littoral in last place.[19]

Economic realities arising from geopolitical conditions were a major cause of weak infrastructural state control. As a productive and consumer market, Safavid Iran was of modest size. Overwhelmingly arid, the country was poorly endowed with arable land and low in population density. Jean Chardin reckoned that barely one-twelfth of Iran was cultivated.[20] According to the most plausible estimate, its population in the early to mid-seventeenth century did not exceed 8 million.[21] About a third of those, moreover, were pastoralists, people who, living at the near-subsistence level, made only a modest contribution to the country's economy. Safavid state income in the seventeenth century tells the story. Combined state and crown revenue is generally given as somewhere around 700,000 *tumans*, or no more than one-tenth of a tuman per inhabitant. Less than 200,000 tumans of this was crown revenue.[22]

The absence of significant gold and silver deposits was especially significant in this regard, since it made Iran dependent on the outside world for bullion and coinage. Other sources of wealth did exist, but few could be relied on for a sustained productive yield. Agriculture, heavily dependent on irrigation in most parts of the country, required intensive initial investment as well as high maintenance expenditure. Some of the empire's richest agricultural regions eluded central control. Fertile plains around major cities such as Tabriz, Qazvin, and Isfahan ordinarily produced enough to feed the urban areas and their surroundings. Wheat and barley were grown throughout the country, even on the Persian Gulf coast.[23] But some of the most productive areas, among them Shirvan, Azerbaijan, and the Caspian provinces, were situated on the periphery of the country and thus dangerously exposed to unrest and attack. The entire northwest faced Ottoman and, ultimately, Russian aggression. The inaccessible interior of heavily forested Gilan and Mazandaran had repelled land-based invaders since the seventh-century Arab conquest, but the Caspian littoral, where most of Iran's silk was grown, was open to seaborne Cossack raids.

Iran's low production of goods for which foreign demand existed combined with its scarce precious metal deposits gave it a perennial trade deficit, especially with the Indian subcontinent, from which it received many consumer goods and to which it exported substantial sums of bullion in return. Safavid authorities naturally did all they could to regulate precious metal exports through bans and taxation, but a policing system riddled with corruption doomed most of these efforts. The problems Shah 'Abbas I faced in enforcing his silk export monopoly epitomize the limitations of the state's ability to harness economic resources.[24]

Commerce played an important role in Iran's economy, and caravan trade was its most conspicuous manifestation. But the volume of long-distance trade as a proportion of all exchange was much smaller than the eye-catching caravan trade suggests. By highlighting the caravan network, making it look like the backbone of a national economy, the writings of contemporary travelers and maritime company agents obscure the fragmentation of commercial life. Caravan travel did connect urban centers and create links between Iran and the outside world. But it was slow and it was relatively costly. On average, it took forty days for a camel caravan to travel from Isfahan to Mashhad, as long to Qandahar, and nearly one month to cover the distance between the capital and Bandar 'Abbas via Shiraz.[25] At times of heavy snow or rainfall much more time was needed, or roads might be blocked altogether. Horses or mules were about twice as fast as camels, but their carrying capacity was smaller and they were not very useful in hot desert conditions. Long distances between major cities, a lack of navigable rivers, and the absence of wheeled traffic made long-distance traffic in most bulk commodities barely cost-effective.[26] Transportation costs, including overhead expenses, commonly made up 50 percent of the price of goods.[27] Not surprisingly, long-distance trade was largely confined to items of a high volume-to-weight ratio, silk, luxury goods such as spices, furs, and fine wool, and finished products such as manufactured textiles. This, in addition to a low level of specialization, poor investment, and a tendency among the elite to hoard, created limited market exchange. Agricultural production and manufacturing mostly served local consumption, and the bulk of transactions took place locally or within regional circuits, typically between towns and their immediate hinterland. The result, the absence of a national market, exemplifies the premodern character of the Safavid economy.

This fragmentation caused—and was exacerbated by—a low velocity of money and limited monetization. Parts of the country and some aspects of the economy were fully monetized. Examples are the sericulture in the Caspian provinces and the goat wool trade of Kirman. Yet various observers noted a pressing scarcity of current coin.[28] In 1618 English merchants called ready money the "principall want of this Countrey," attributing its scarcity to the state of war with the Ottomans. The same observers called Iran "a most miserable poore countrey of money [with] little Commerce and trade within itselfe."[29] Eight years later, money was so scarce that merchants had difficulty buying goods in bulk with a single purchase, forcing the VOC (the Dutch East India Company) to distribute its wares in small quantities over various cities.[30]

The limits of monetary circulation are reflected in the use of copper for most small and local transactions. Since such transactions comprised the bulk of commercial traffic, copper coin was tremendously important for economic life as a whole.[31] The validity of these coins, a different kind of which was struck in each city, was purely local and was determined by the governor who had issued them. Coins from one place could not be used elsewhere, or at least were worth much less, and a governor's dismissal was often followed by an abatement of the coins minted under his auspices.[32]

In some remote parts of Safavid territory, tribal areas and regions far from producer access to markets, cash money hardly played a role at all. Barter trade was ubiquitous, extending to the royal court. Chardin even claimed that most of the shah's revenue was in kind. Indeed, many regions paid a substantial part of their tribute to Isfahan in this manner. Gilan usually remitted its taxes in silk; Georgia often paid in the form of slaves; Kirman sent fine goat's wool to Isfahan; Kurdistan was made to provide soldiers to the state; the governor of Shiraz was supposed to furnish an annual supply of limes to the court; and the Armenians of Yerevan supplied all the wax that was burned in the royal palace.[33] Conversely, royal expenditure, especially under the last two Safavid rulers, often took the form of drafts on future provincial production, and salaries were frequently paid in the form of precious wares.[34]

SOCIAL AND POLITICAL ASPECTS

Iran's ethnic, religious, and linguistic diversity formed a major impediment to central control. A large percentage of the population was engaged in nomadic pastoralism. None of the myriad tribes in the country's central parts posed a direct threat to Safavid authority in the seventeenth century but, armed and mobile, they all defied fiscal and administrative control. Until 1639 the court itself was largely peripatetic, exemplifying tribal mobility and its centrifugal effects, one of which is that, with the exception of the late Safavid period, Iran never had a fixed capital until the Qajars opted for Tehran at the turn of the nineteenth century.[35]

More important was the connection between tribal power and military power, which the Safavids inherited from previous regimes. No Iranian state from the Mongols to the Qajars managed to shake itself entirely free from tribal domination (with Nadir Shah as a brief exception).[36] The Ottomans and Mughals, with far greater resources at their disposal, in time broke the military monopoly of the refractory tribes that had brought them to power. Iranian dynasties never achieved the same autonomy despite periodic attempts at introducing sources of non-tribal military power.[37]

Naturally, the most autonomous tribes lived on the margins of Safavid jurisdiction, in the Ottoman, Mughal, and Uzbek borderlands, on the frontiers of the Caucasus and Central Asia, and the barren deserts of Sistan and Makran, all of which were exposed to tribal incursions. The fertile Georgian lowlands invited attack by Lezghi mountaineers; Uzbeks and Turkmen often raided deep into the interior of Khurasan, and Baluchis and Afghans constantly threatened the vast regions of Kirman and Yazd. At times these depredations inflicted heavy damage on local economies. In an effort to neutralize them and even make them safeguard the frontier zones, the Safavids made various arrangements with the tribal peoples living on their frontiers. All of these involved tribute. A tribe formally subordinated to Isfahan ordinarily paid an annual sum as a token of submission, and Isfahan often held an important relative of the chief, typically a son, hostage as a guarantee for good behavior. But tribute might work the other way as well. In cases where the central government lacked military deterrence or needed their services to gather intelligence or facilitate the passing of troops, the Safavids might *pay* tribal chiefs for peace and cooperation.[38] Obedience and collaboration were never assured, though. The Kurds and Arabs in the borderlands between Iran and the Ottoman Empire, especially, could always defect to the other side, and often did. A few examples should suffice to illustrate this. As long as Shah Isma'il was alive, the Kurdish leader Taymur Khan was content to be his protégé. Upon the shah's death, fearing instability in Iran, the khan threw in his lot with the Ottomans—in exchange for an annual stipend of 100,000 *akçe*s.[39] An envoy from the Arab Musha`sha` expressed it best in his admonishing remarks to Shah Isma`il I: "Each year we send taxes and tolls to the shah's court. Do not make claims on our territory, for if you apply force, we will flee and retreat. You will not stay in these borderlands forever. When you put the region under someone else's control, we will return once you are gone to overthrow your appointee. If, on the other hand, you treat us with kindness and justice, we will remain your tributaries."[40]

The Safavids managed to convert most but not all inhabitants of the territory to Twelver Shi`ism. Of the remaining minorities the non-Muslim ones, Jews, Zoroastrians, and Armenians, were numerically far less significant in Iran than in the Ottoman Empire, even though they were economically important beyond their numbers. Of far greater political consequence were the many Sunnis who refused to bow to Safavid pressure to convert. Even in the early eighteenth century, an estimated one-third of Safavid subjects still adhered to the Sunni creed.[41] Most of these happened to live in the peripheral areas, in the frontier zone bordering on the Sunni Ottoman, Uzbek, and Mughal states, so that their loyalty could not be taken for granted either. The growing harassment they suffered in the religiously sensitive atmosphere of the late Safavid period tested their identification with the polity and demonstrably counts as one of the reasons why the Sunni Baluchis and Afghans met with so little resistance when they invaded Iran.

Language had a divisive component as well, albeit a minor one. With its three grammatically unrelated main languages, Safavid Iran was more fragmented than most European countries. Persian was the language of culture and diplomacy as well as that of most urbanites on the plateau. Court chronicles and royal edicts had long been written in Persian. Yet the shah and his courtiers conversed in Azeri Turkish. This created few obstacles between rulers and subjects, though, for Turkic languages and dialects were the mother tongue of many of Iran's inhabitants, especially those living in tribal environments.[42] Arabic served as the religious language and was spoken by the people of `Arabistan and parts of the Gulf coast. Kurdish and a host of minor languages and dialects further complicated the picture.

More destabilizing was the inherent antagonism of ruler–subject relations. Few linkages existed between various societal groups, making it impossible for dissenting forces to create a unified front.[43] As in most Middle Eastern, tribally organized societies, the social order in the Safavid Iran was based on vertically based, segmented social structures rooted in patronage networks. This segmentation, unlike horizontal distinctions based on class, made personal relationships and alliances play a larger role in shaping social identity than wealth, regional background, or even religious faith. A strongly developed conception of a private realm revolving around the extended family as a refuge against the outside world worked as a buffer against governmental intrusion. Iran also had a long tradition of what today we call "freedom of conscience," the liberty to question the truth, including the divinely revealed truth. Foreign visitors frequently noted how Iranians freely criticized the authorities and their actions in public.[44] This, too, created a safety valve.

In practice, people, especially in rural society, seeing little more than the extractive aspects of the state, sought to keep interaction with its representatives to a minimum. Not surprisingly, they did all they could to avoid tax collectors. Peasants naturally lived in terror of marauding bandits but they also dreaded the depredations of passing armies and the costly obligation of provisioning soldiers and providing for the upkeep of diplomats traveling through their region.[45] A visit by the shah might be especially ruinous for a region, so much so that local officials would often offer large bribes to avoid having to play host to the royal retinue.[46] The result was that, as in contemporary Europe, in Safavid Iran the most prosperous villages were situated at some distance from the main roads.[47]

Power in Safavid Iran combined Turko-Mongol nomadic political notions, in which legitimacy was vested in the entire ruling clan, and the "Iranian" agrarian-based tradition, with its concept of power revolving around individual, divinely legitimized rule. In the absence of primogeniture, each succession in the Turko-Mongol tradition tended to generate a round of internecine warfare. From this bloody struggle one survivor would ultimately emerge to take power, after eliminating surviving family members who might still challenge him, killing or blinding them. In the Iranian tradition, by contrast, succession was a matter of heredity, and the shah ruled as God's shadow on earth.[48] Under the Safavids the "Iranian" tradition prevailed. The shah's legitimacy was unquestioned—at least until the late Safavid period when it occasionally came to be questioned by some—and with the exception of the succession of Shah Tahmasb, no power struggle preceded a shah's ascent to power. At the same time, especially in the sixteenth century, a transfer of power often entailed a conflict between the powerful Qizilbash tribes over control of the state. After his enthronement, the shah would also engage in a bloody purge of any and all potential rivals, including those who had helped him secure the throne. After Shah ʿAbbas I, succession based on sovereignty vested in the entire clan was supplanted by a more formalized form of succession of which male primogeniture formed the basis even if it was not strictly applied.[49] Under Shah Safi and ʿAbbas II, as the polity further evolved to a palace-bound monarchy, the battle over succession moved to the ranks of the court, with eunuchs and women competing to advance their favorites. Once selected, the new monarch was instantaneously revered as divinely ordained and typically had little to fear from his immediate surroundings, although he still had to maneuver for effective control.

The elaborate bureaucracy reflected in administrative manuals such as the *Tadhkirat al-muluk* and the *Dastur al-muluk* appears well organized and structured but in reality was fluid, highly personalized, and, above all, riddled with perennial conflict in the form of factionalism.[50] V. V. Barthold called the division between the palace (*dargah*), and more specifically the inner court (*haram*) composed of eunuchs and women, on the one hand, and the chancery (the *divan*), on the other, the most enduring feature of Iranian politics.[51] Personal animosity permeated all echelons of the bureaucracy, and any two high officials might become engaged in a personal feud filled with mutual slander and intrigue. Each would form a faction with the strongest possible links to the shah.

A palace connection was essential for holding on to a position in this fiercely competitive environment. Any high-ranking official automatically faced envious rivals determined to bring him down. There were several ways of keeping one's rivals at bay beyond trying to undermine them through calumny. One was to reward them with rich gifts. Another one was to have a presence in Isfahan—the center of political action and intrigue. A prolonged absence from the capital weakened an official's ability to act and react, and the farther away he was sent and the longer he stayed away, the greater the chances that his enemies might succeed in bringing him down. Rivals would typically try to hasten the downfall of a provincial official by making sure that the court was flooded with complaints about his oppression, greed, and disloyalty.[52] Especially if they already served in top positions, appointees to provincial posts often sent a relative, who could be minor, to take up the actual post.[53] The incumbent who did go himself was well advised to keep a representative (*vakil*) in the capital, preferably one with a line to the court's inner circle.[54] Direct access to the shah or at least to his intimates was essential. The "power of proximity," as James Bill has called it in reference to Iran under the Pahlavi dynasty, helped an official build a power base at the expense of his rivals, spreading rumors about their lack of loyalty and their treacherous scheming. Having a female relative in the inner palace offered the best chances for intercession with the shah himself. Every official thus aspired to having at least one of his daughters in the royal harem.[55]

The shah was both a separate faction and a privileged arbiter in the welter of feuding factions. In some ways, his relationship with state officials was a zero-sum game. Either the shah was strong and the members of his direct entourage were weak, or he was weak and they were strong. The shah accumulated wealth and power at their expense; they, in turn, enriched themselves on the backs of the populace and thus indirectly at the expense of royal income. In any direct conflict the shah naturally had the upper hand; he could always dismiss an official or have him executed, at which point the latter's property automatically fell to the crown—a custom that often created an incentive for the ruler to do away with underlings. In practice, officials had myriad ways of enriching themselves and enhancing their power base without directly confronting the shah. More fundamentally, the monarch depended as much on the loyalty and cooperation of his courtiers and his political appointees as they were beholden to him for their positions and prestige. The ruler thus had to court his top officials, but also needed to keep a watchful eye on them lest their ambitions become a threat to royal power. This the shah did by dividing them, sowing discord among them, preventing them from forming alliances or at least preventing alliances from congealing into a challenge to the prevailing order. The shah had various techniques at his disposal to achieve this. One was to tour their realm on a regular basis. Like their Mughal peers, most Safavid shahs heavily relied on travel to stay in touch with their territory, to put down rebellions, but also to check on outlying parts of the country.[56] Another was not to appoint officials to the region of their origin; a third one was to keep tenure short; a fourth one was to appoint counter officials with shared responsibilities, shadow officials, whose task it was to inform the ruler of any signs of the appointee's ingratitude, disloyalty, or rebellious tendencies.[57]

CENTRIPETAL TENDENCIES

Political, cultural, and religious aspects

An enumeration of unifying elements in late Safavid Iran begins with the intertwined notion of territory and faith. It would be anachronistic to label early modern Iran a nation-state in the modern sense of the term. Affinity and loyalty lay with kin, clan, and faith rather than with abstract political concepts; political affiliation followed lineage and rarely went beyond one's region of origin or residence. Late Safavid Iran nevertheless was a contiguous territorial entity or at least comprised a clearly defined core territory. In the thirteenth century, after an absence of six centuries, the Il-Khanids reintroduced the term "Iran." The land thus named had long remained fragmented, until the Safavids united its eastern and western halves. As the *Mukhtasar-i mufid* with its notion of a "greater Iran" suggests, the political elite used the term self-consciously to refer to a bounded political entity.[58] The term *mulk-i vasi` al-faza-yi Iran*, the expansive realm of Iran, found in the *Khuld-i barin*, conveys a similar self-consciousness and pride.[59]

Persian culture, its legacy, and its continued production, played a vital part in the overarching Iranian sense of self, to the point where Safavid Iran may be called an incarnation of the age-old Iranian "empire of the mind," in Michael Axworthy's apt phrase.[60] As noted, Iran was multilingual; as they do today, the country's inhabitants spoke a number of different languages, from Persian and Kurdish to Turkish and Arabic. While Safavid shahs usually conversed in Azeri Turkish, Persian was the mother tongue of the country's urban elite and the core political and administrative language of the entire realm. Persian was also the language of high culture, above all of poetry, the supreme expression of the Persian language, which linked the past, including the pre-Islamic past, to the present and served as a shared cultural repertoire, not just for the elite but for the common people, at least in urban areas.[61]

The other (inherited) term employed in Safavid chronicles, *mamalik-i mahrusah*, the "protected realm," adds a religious dimension to the notion of territory. In what was to be their greatest political accomplishment, the Safavids connected faith with land by imposing Twelver Shi`ism on their realm. Under their auspices, territory and religion came to overlap in ways that have characterized the country ever since. A minority faith within Islam, Shi`ism imbued the Iranian state with a sense of unity by way of particularism. Even if this unity remained far from complete, the Safavids used Shi`ism as an effective propaganda tool to set themselves apart from their Sunni neighbors, the Ottoman, the Mughal, and the Uzbek states. They cultivated Twelver Shi`ism as a mark of distinction in a variety of ways, ranging from the ritual cursing of the first three caliphs to the propagation of festivals commemorating the faith's foundational events.[62] They patronized Iran's Shi`i shrines, including the mausoleum of the dynasty's founder, Shaykh Safi, in Ardabil, and at times when they controlled Iraq, took special care of the `atabat, the tombs of the imams. After Iraq was lost to the Ottomans in 1638, the Safavids spent large amounts of money on the restoration and embellishment of Iran's own shrine cities, Mashhad and Qum, which evolved into devotional centers of pilgrimage in competition with the Iraqi `atabat.[63] A shift in the language used for religious writing reflects a growing congruence between territory and religion as well. In contemporary Protestant Europe, vernacular languages began to supplant Church Latin. Late Safavid religious scholars similarly began to make their writings more accessible to ordinary literate people by composing their treatises in Persian rather than in Arabic. In the process, the status of Persian as a unifying idiom increased, further enhancing the role of the ulama as spokesmen for a nascent national-religious identity.

Twelver Shi`ism was well suited to weld the nation and the dynasty together. Its symbols and doctrines—and especially its focus on authority as a hierarchical series of emanations—were easily adapted to the traditional notion of the Iranian ruler as the divinely appointed protector of people, territory, and faith. God was the lord of the universe and the Imam his vicegerent; in the latter's absence, the shah was God's "shadow on earth," charged with the task of upholding the cosmic order until his return. The Safavids' claim of descent from `Ali, the first Imam, and their deference to the Hidden Imam—whose servant the shah called himself—combined with the ancient Iranian divine right of kingship to produce a strong basis for dynastic legitimacy.[64]

All this made the shah a crucial unifying force. He was the sole link between the divine and the terrestrial spheres, the only force to cut across societal ranks and divisions, and thus the foremost centripetal element in the realm. Initially, the Safavid ruler was revered as the *murshid-i kamil*, the divinely guided perfect Sufi shaykh. The terrible defeat the Safavids suffered against the Ottomans at Chaldiran in 1514 damaged their divine charisma and cost them in tribal allegiance. Yet Isma`il's successor, Shah Tahmasb (r. 1524–76) continued to be venerated as a god-like figure to the point where people would reverentially kiss the doors of his palace and consider any water the shah had touched a cure against fever.[65] Shah `Abbas I similarly was credited with supernatural powers. One chronicler recounts how in 1598–9 the construction of a fortress near Astarabad (modern Gurgan) was held up by persistent rains until the shah successfully begged the heavens for a dry spell.[66] For the remainder of the dynasty's lifespan the shah retained supreme power and legitimacy as an Iranian king, demanding his subjects' continuing loyalty. Safavid chroniclers proclaimed unqualified obedience to him a self-evident obligation.[67] What Iran's rulers meanwhile lost in messianic luster they regained in part through the *shah-seven*, "love for the shah" phenomenon—whereby his subjects declared their loyalty to him and contributed funds or labor to public works undertaken by the crown. Shah 'Abbas, in particular, would cultivate the shah-seven bond as an alternative to tribal loyalty.[68]

Their growing connection with a clerical establishment whose rise to prominence they facilitated further solidified the status of Iran's rulers. The new bond between politics and religion thus forged manifested itself in crowning ceremonies filled with religious symbolism and presided over by the *sadr-i mamalik* and the *sadr-i khassah*, the highest religious officials in the state, respectively the palace, administration, in the continued practice of granting religious officials generous allowances and landed property in the form of *vazifah*s (pensions) and *suyurghal*s (fiefs), and in the intensification of intermarriage between court and clergy from the time of Shah 'Abbas I onward.[69] Dependent on the crown for positions, landed property, and emoluments, the Safavid religious establishment never challenged the idea of divine kingship. Under Shah 'Abbas I the ulama grumbled as large numbers of Christians, Armenians, and Georgians were transferred to Isfahan and given positions of privilege in the administration, the military, and state-directed commerce.[70] And under Shah 'Abbas II some clerics began to criticize the shah for behavior unbecoming for a Shi'i ruler, including excessive drinking. Yet, overall, the literati, including the ulama, continued to uphold the traditional legitimacy, arguing that society needed a monarch with a heavenly mandate, a just ruler counteracting the forces of evil and decline through a policy equal parts benevolence and coercion.[71]

Iran's rulers, in sum, enjoyed tremendous legitimacy—exceeding even that of their Ottoman and Mughal counterparts—which perhaps explains why no Safavid ruler was ever deposed and why only one, Shah Isma'il II, r. 1576–7, may have been assassinated.[72] Over time, cracks appeared in this edifice: At least one treatise from the early eighteenth century raises doubts about the divine nature of the shah, suggesting a crisis in royal legitimacy that was likely related to a faltering martial performance and the insularity of the shah since the days of Sulayman.[73] Meanwhile, de facto power shifted from the monarch to the grand vizier, to the point where, after Shah 'Abbas I, this official often acted as the ruler's stand-in. Yet, unlike the Ottoman vizier, the Safavid chief minister remained beholden to the shah as the ultimate source of power and thus never operated as a quasi monarch.[74]

The shah enjoyed unfettered arbitrary power. Yet he was also supposed to protect his subjects and he had a mandate to treat them equitably. Royal justice, pivotal to the age-old theory of Iranian statecraft, figured prominently in Safavid ideology.[75] Justice was enshrined in a cultural heritage that invoked ancient rulers, real and mythical ones, as exemplars. It was also an integral part of manuals of good governance and reiterated in every single royal decree (*farman*). Conceived as a cycle, justice mandated royal kindness and benevolence with the aim of fostering the welfare of the people and thus securing the dynasty's longevity.[76] Royal justice found concrete expression in tax rebates following the enthronement of a new shah or at times of economic hardship, as well as in the habit of distributing money to the poor as part of coronation celebrations, during the New Year's ceremony, and whenever the shah fell ill.[77]

Royal justice mandated accessibility as well, giving those who had suffered injustice a chance to seek recourse with the ruler himself. Its purpose was twofold: It showed royal concern for commoners and it allowed rulers to gather first-hand, unmediated intelligence. Several shahs are known to have mingled with the people in an informal public setting. Known for his "melancholy disposition," Shah Tahmasb in the last years of this reign lived within the confines of his palace, out of reach for the people, leaving his subjects without a symbol of justice and at the mercy of greedy subordinate officers, including the judiciary powers.[78] Shah Isma'il II, otherwise known for the bloody havoc he wreaked on the elite, would go around Qazvin to apprize himself of the state of his realm.[79] Shah 'Abbas's famously casual governing style included his habit of strolling through the streets of Isfahan during festivals, accompanied by his female retinue, joking with people of various walks of life, and visiting their homes.[80] It was also customary for petitioners to try to attract the shah's attention when he went out riding by grabbing the bridle of his horse and handing him petitions. Popular discontent often manifested itself in bread riots, but more formal outlets existed as well.[81] In the period of Shah 'Abbas I, the vizier of Isfahan would collect petitions from people.[82] Under the same ruler a grievance council existed.[83] 'Abbas II instituted a semi-weekly tribunal (*majlis*) for the same purpose.[84] Rendering justice also was among the explicit responsibilities of various offices. A good example is the city prefect (*kalantar*). The shah appointed him but in accordance with the wishes of the populace—and for good reason, for he acted as a middleman. It was his task to defend people against the vexations of other local officials as well as to protect them from unscrupulous vendors.[85]

Naturally, none of this was quick or easy; serious obstacles, from poor communications to obstructionist bureaucrats, made it difficult for ordinary people, especially in the outlying areas, to stand up to fiscal oppression by local officials, let alone make their case in Isfahan. Yet a community with enough resolve was not without legal recourse. Numerous examples underscore the power of the "popular vote" and show even the late Safavid monarch in his role as a brake on extortion and abuse by intermediate forces.[86] In 1662 the viziers of Gaskar, Kashan, Daylaman, and Shirvan all lost their jobs following complaints by the local population, *ra`iyat*; in 1680, popular protest about the tyrannical rule of Khusraw Khan, the governor of Kurdistan, caused this official to be recalled to Isfahan and executed; and in 1695 the kalantar of Rasht in Gilan was dismissed after his subjects voiced their displeasure with his conduct.[87] Several farmans from the 1650s and 1660s document successful village resistance in Armenia against the usurpation of their land by provincial officials.[88]

In Iran's fractious political environment, nothing was more important than balancing competing interests. At the upper administrative level, only the shah was capable of doing so. The more skilled he was at this task, the greater his actual influence. Factionalism was the gravest threat to the system whenever a shah was new, under-age, or otherwise weak. Shah Tahmasb, engulfed by Qizilbash infighting for the first ten years of his reign, almost lost his throne in this manner. Throughout the sixteenth century, the Safavids sought to maintain a careful balance between Turks and Tajiks, as well as among the various Qizilbash clans, coopting the latter by appealing to their loyalty to the shah and by creating new, artificial "tribes." Examples of the latter are the Shaykhavand, whose origins go back to the reign of Shah Tahmasb, and the Shah-seven and Muqaddam, who were both created by Shah `Abbas I. The age-old practice of resettling entire tribes from one part of the country to another served the same purpose—in addition to strengthening border areas.[89]

From the reign of Shah Tahmasb onward, the Safavids increasingly used newly imported Armenian, Georgian, and Circassian elements from the Caucasus, the *ghulaman-i sarkar-i sharifah*, the ghulams of the noble court, to offset Qizilbash power. Designed to create a new military and administrative elite without tribal ties, the Safavid ghulam system was a variant on the age-old Middle Eastern *mamluk* device. The term ghulams is often translated as slaves (of the shah), but, since not all of them were originally Caucasian slaves, they might more appropriately be called servants of the shah.[90] These were given a new identity, which included their conversion to Islam. But, the better to manipulate them for his centralizing purposes, the ruler also allowed them to maintain ties with the power elite in their homeland. The ghulams attained the highest bureaucratic positions, including control over the most important provinces and supreme military command, often replacing the local notables who previously had been in charge. Yet they never managed to monopolize power. At least until Shah Sulayman, the Safavids maintained a balance between the old and the new elements, making sure that the ghulams continued to face competition, most notably from the Qizilbash who, though weakened, remained a formidable force.[91]

Creating alliances was vital for any authority figure who wished to remain in power and see it transferred to his offspring after his death. Heredity remained the norm, even after ʿAbbas I abolished it as an automatic principle as part of his administrative reforms in order to curtail the autonomous tendencies inherent in it.[92] But heredity presupposed a solid power base in the form of an alliance network. And it was above all contingent upon the shah's favor. Only a royal confirmation would guarantee the transmission of a suyurghal, a hereditary land grant, from a father to a son, and only with the ruler's approval did an official succeed his parent in an administrative post.

The shah, meanwhile, was no exception to the need to create and maintain ties through alliances. Such alliances could take the form of concrete quid pro quo arrangements, such as making access to water rights for Kurdish vassals contingent on political fealty and military support for the crown.[93] Alliances manifested themselves in the form of hereditary positions vested in one group, such as the mayor (*darughah*) of Isfahan who from the late sixteenth century onward was always a Georgian. Or they might involve affinitive ties resulting from elite intermarriage (*musahirat*). In some ways Iranian politics operated as a vast network of intermarriage among the ruling class, with the shah at the center. From their early days, the Safavids had followed an intricate policy of solidifying ties through marriages between royal daughters and amirs of leading Qizilbash families or the semi-autonomous ruling houses of Gilan, Mazandaran, and Shirvan. Such alliances worked both ways; they enhanced the shah's power over provincial affairs, and they enabled tribal elders and local rulers to increase their wealth and the standing of their clan.[94] In the late sixteenth century, sexual politics began to involve the Georgian elite as well. Two of the wives of Shah ʿAbbas's half-brother Hamzah Mirza were Georgian princesses.[95] Shah 'Abbas I married the daughter of King Giorgi X of Kartli, the central part of Georgia, and a daughter of Prince David of Kakheti, its eastern half. Other daughters of Georgian noble families entered his harem as well.[96] In due time, musahirat with members of the religious classes became common.[97]

If the royal household collected massive amounts of tribute, it also dispensed a great deal of patronage. A direct relationship existed between the ruler's munificence and his prestige. Most of this munificence was redistributive, taking the form of monetary rewards, allowances, and pensions. The shah also had to be generous with land assignments. He also expected to be especially lavish with his "robes of honor," *khal`ats*, tokens of good standing handed to officials at the beginning of their tenure and during the Iranian New Year, *Nawruz*, and to visiting foreign envoys upon their departure. In exchange, subjects, dependents, and visiting foreigners were expected to express fealty to the monarch. A high-ranking official who wished to retain royal favor was obliged to offer gifts to the shah when he was appointed, on the occasion of the New Year, and on religious holidays. If the shah honored him by accepting an invitation to his residence, the host had to arrange for an elaborate "sugar banquet," cover the streets leading to his house with expensive cloth, and scatter gold and silver coins around upon the ruler's entry.[98] Similarly, foreign embassies were not received or merely granted a perfunctory welcome if they did not bring rich and exotic presents.

Gift-giving was all pervasive, combining the symbolic and the pragmatic. *Pishkash* (gifts) functioned as social and political glue. It solidified ties and confirmed loyalties, defined and reaffirmed the hierarchical order, and served to placate and mollify rivals and superiors. All political relationships involved the exchange of presents. Reciprocity demanded that the recipient reward the donor with a counter gift. Subordinates presented gifts to their superiors to propitiate them and to offset complaints about their behavior; the latter reciprocated to secure continued loyalty from their underlings. Gifts also served as the material acknowledgment of past and anticipated favors. On religious holidays a so-called `*aydi* was expected; whenever a new high-ranking public official took up his post, a welcoming present (*salamat*) was required from his subordinates.[99] Gift-giving was even integral to court-sponsored commerce, albeit in ambiguous ways that occasionally were cause for misunderstandings abroad, as happened when Shah 'Abbas sent a supply of silk to the King of Spain in 1609 and had it presented as a gift whereas in reality it was meant as a vendible commodity.[100] Gift-giving was also highly institutionalized. All gifts to the shah had to be appraised for their value and the donor had to pay a 25 percent surcharge above the value.[101] Some 10 percent of this went to the major-domo of the palace, the *ishik-aqasi-bashi*, and 5 percent was pocketed by the scribe who recorded the gifts, the *pishkash-nivis*.[102]

Perhaps the system's most centripetal force was its capacity for accommodation and inclusiveness. Both were crucial ingredients of Safavid political culture—as they were, to varying degrees, among the Ottomans and the Mughals. This tendency is exemplified by the assimilation of the ghulams as administrators and soldiers as well as by the practice of intermarriage between the Safavid dynasty and members of the tribal and clerical elite. Chardin called the openness of the ruling order one of the remarkable features of the Safavid polity, citing the habit of appointing former rulers to conquered lands, of rehabilitating and even reappointing disgraced officials, and of offering refuge to fugitive foreign princes. Circular patterns of dismissal and reappointment confirm the validity of his observations. The practice varied with the character of the ruler, but at all times it was quite common for disgraced officials to be allowed back into the fold, even to recapture their former rank and prestige after a period of dismissal and imprisonment.[103] Perhaps the most spectacular case is that of Mirza Muhammad "Saru" Taqi, who was castrated at Shah 'Abbas I's orders for engaging in pederasty with a minor child that he had kidnapped, yet subsequently managed to stage a come-back culminating in his appointment as grand vizier under Shah Safi. Rehabilitation might even include the return of possessions confiscated at the time of discomfiture.[104] An extreme example is 'Ali Khan, the ruler of Bih Pas in Gilan, who under Shah 'Abbas I rebelled no less than three times but was forgiven in each instance.[105] Or if the culprit was not allowed to return to the fold himself, his territory and position might be given to relatives. A case in point is Sulayman Khan, *beglerbeg* (governor) of Kurdistan, who in 1657 was punished for treason by being sent into exile to Mashhad, while Kurdistan was divided between his sons and brothers.[106] Naturally, such forms of clemency and indulgence were not just a matter of royal kindness but rather a strategy based on the realization that coming down too hard on provincial rulers would invite great resentment to the point of provoking outright rebellion. So striking was royal leniency in the face of rebellious and untoward conduct by officials under Shah Sultan Husayn that Europeans saw it as one of the causes of the country's ills.[107]

Accommodation was linked to social mobility. Top officials tended to be recruited from a limited pool and most high-ranking officials came from families that were closely connected to the center of power. Yet, as had been true under the Il-Khans, loyalty and competence counted for more than ethnic or religious affiliation, allowing smart, ambitious men from relatively humble backgrounds to attain high rank.[108] There was a degree of self-consciousness about this. Abu Talib Musavi Findiriski asserts that Shah Safi was explicit about his insistence on talent rather than heritage as a qualification for high office, resulting in the elevation of such officials of (relatively) humble background as Mirza Muhammad "Saru" Taqi and Mirza Habib Allah to the most exalted positions in the realm.[109] The premium put on merit was an outgrowth of a harsh Turko-Mongol environment in which weakness equaled defeat and death, but it also allowed for greater royal control, since the more humble the background of an official, the greater his dependence on the monarch. The rise from marginality to high rank of the ghulams exemplifies this aspect. Needless to say, officials might fall as fast and hard as they had risen. The careers of grand viziers such as Mirza Taqi, Shaykh ʿAli Khan, and Fath ʿAli Khan Daghistani—discussed in later chapters—illustrate this point.

The second epigraph at the top of this chapter might seem incongruous in light of the harsh retribution generally meted out to opponents and enemies. Punishment, *siyasat*, and revenge, *intiqam*, were integral to statecraft. The shah was expected to mete out justice, and for it to be compelling it had to be swift and severe. Like all rulers, the Safavids engaged in negotiation, but violent reprisal was the method of last—and often first—resort. A weak ruler or, rather, a ruler who was perceived as weak, invited sedition.[110] Not only did Iranians expect their rulers to be violent, as Chardin said, but, in the words of Findiriski mentioned above, violence was considered an integral ingredient of royal justice for creating stability and prosperity. Royal justice, he submitted, involved neither rectitude nor the absence of inflicting harm. Instead, the bloodshed perpetrated by rulers served to strike fear in people, preventing them from unjustly oppressing or killing others.[111] But royal severity was balanced and mitigated by clemency (*mudara*), the other ingredient of royal policy, which had been enshrined in political doctrine at least since Nasir al-Din Tusi, who lists its absence as a factor in the decline of states.[112] The ideal ruler was one who knew when to punish and when to forgive, who held "fire with one hand, water with the other," *bih yik dast atish, bih yik dast ab*, in the immortal words of Firdawsi.

The official who had incurred the shah's wrath was often deposed and killed together with other members of his clan. When Shah

'Abbas I had his former tutor (*lalah*), Murshid Quli Khan, executed in 1588, the relatives and clients of this powerful vakil lost their positions as well.¹¹³ Shah Safi brutally exterminated the Imam Quli Khan clan four years after coming to power in 1629. His successor, Shah 'Abbas II, engaged in a major purge early on in his reign. In 1645 Jani Khan, the *qurchibashi* (head of the praetorian guard), was given the green light to execute grand vizier Muhammad Taqi, only to perish with his fellow conspirators and a large number of his fellow clan members shortly thereafter. Yet the more inclusionary elements of the Safavid polity gained in prominence as well under 'Abbas II. Jani Khan's son, 'Abd al-Qasim Khan, far from having to pay for his father's sins, received the double function of *divanbegi* (Chief Justice), and darughah of Qazvin, and was later appointed governor of Hamadan.¹¹⁴ In 1644 Khalil Khan, the governor of the Bakhtiyaris, provoked a revolt among the Bakhtiyari clans with his harsh and violent rule. A Safavid expedition was sent to quell the uprising, but Khalil Khan, though found guilty of the charges, was only deposed, to regain his former post twelve years later.¹¹⁵ The later Safavid period shows many such cases of relatives left unaffected by the demotion of high officials.

ECONOMIC ASPECTS

The period of Shah Tahmasb's reign gave Iran a unified monetary system.¹¹⁶ This unity, reflected in the issuance and circulation of locally minted coins of striking uniformity in style, legend, and standard, naturally benefited trade, even if much (long-distance) commerce was conducted with non-Iranian coinage.

Trade enjoyed various other forms of government support. Shah 'Abbas chose Isfahan as his new capital, redesigning its center with a royal palace, major mosques, and a commercial district surrounding a huge central square, and thus gave Iran a territorial nexus, located in the center of the country, halfway between Azerbaijan and the Persian Gulf.¹¹⁷ Iran's largest and most important city, Isfahan in the mid-seventeenth century had a few hundred thousand inhabitants, and the entire oasis may well have been home to the 600,000 people several travelers attribute to the city proper.¹¹⁸ As Shah 'Abbas's successors turned more sedentary, Isfahan further expanded in size and importance. The shah's buying power and the size of his entourage—estimates in mid-century range from 3,000 to 4,000, excluding women—had a direct impact on market conditions in the capital.¹¹⁹

The size of the *urdu bazar*, the ambulant market that accompanied the royal suite en route, reflects the court's importance as a commercial magnet.[120] Du Mans insisted that an army of 50,000 required a total train of 400,000 people.[121] Chardin in 1667 claimed that the shah's return to Isfahan would increase the city's population by one half.[122] The Dutch in 1706 echoed this by noting how Shah Sultan Husayn's departure for Mashhad emptied the capital of people.[123] It is therefore little surprising that the market slumped as soon as the shah left Isfahan, and that a prolonged absence of the royal suite from Isfahan tended to cut into VOC profits for draining thousands of people from the city. Dutch commerce also suffered because the upkeep of the royal retinue—in the form of travel costs and expenses of servants, horses, and tents—imposed an enormous burden on provincial governors, leaving them with few means to purchase luxury goods.[124] Just as prices fell once the court left the capital, so they rose again upon its return.[125]

The Safavids solicited industry and commerce in other ways as well. They oversaw an extensive system of factories (*karkhanah'ha*), manufacturing goods for the state.[126] Following Central Asian practice, Iran's rulers concluded commercial agreements with foreign merchants, most notably the East India Companies.[127] They also harnessed the entrepreneurial energy of their domestic merchants. The most famous case is that of Shah 'Abbas I who pressed Iran's Armenian merchant community into royal service by resetting the community of Julfa on the Aras River to a newly built suburb of Isfahan, called New Julfa, where they received commercial rights and privileges. Armenian merchants were frequently dispatched on foreign missions combining trade and diplomacy; the authorities consulted leading (Armenian) merchants on commercial matters, and a council composed of these same merchants often represented the state in dealing with foreign envoys and merchants.

Nothing facilitated long-distance trade more than its actual infrastructure. Caravanserais, with storage and animal-parking facilities on the first level and sleeping quarters above, were essential to communication throughout the Middle East until the advent of the motor car. Foreigners generally praised the Safavid caravanserais, comparing them favorably to their Ottoman counterparts.[128] Many were built during the reign of Shah 'Abbas I, even if the number of 999 traditionally attributed to him is clearly exaggerated. Under his successors, construction continued, albeit on a lesser scale, until the reign of Shah Sultan Husayn, who preferred building pleasure gardens and embellishing religious structures.[129]

The judicial system benefited commerce, too. In the Iranian tradition the state was to provide safe communications and security of trade.[130] Armed soldiers, who might number up to 1,000, often accompanied caravans.[131] Far into the seventeenth century, foreign observers found the effectiveness of laws regulating commercial security in Iran superior to those of the Ottoman Empire.[132] Some saw a link with the harshness of the penal system: Highway robbery as well as merchant fraud met with swift and severe retribution. Merchants found guilty of using counterfeit weights or of price gouging were subjected to the *tahtah-kulah*, or pillory.[133]

The system was as simple as it was pragmatic in its approach to robbery. Anyone who had goods stolen from him was to be reimbursed for their value, and the responsibility lay with the officials under whose jurisdiction the theft had occurred. This practice, too, goes back to Mongol times, when collective responsibility for commercial safety served to protect merchants in a nomadic environment.[134] In Safavid times, the policy was enforced regardless of the victim's identity. During the 1629 rebellion in Gilan it was Russian merchants who were compensated for the loss of some 500 bales of silk.[135] For goods stolen from a caravanserai, its supervisor, the *karavansaray-bashi*, was held accountable. This official also kept a record of transactions between merchants and was held liable if these involved bad credit and led to bankruptcy. Officials had four months and ten days to find a robber and retrieve stolen goods. They had an incentive to act, for they received a fee of 20 percent of the value of recovered ware. They often paid promptly to prevent complaints from reaching the shah's ears.[136] If the crime remained unsolved, the nearest village might be forced to collect two to three times the amount stolen. Chardin described the procedure as quick and efficient; an Armenian merchant he knew had lost goods worth nearly 300 tumans and had been reimbursed within six days by the governor of Jahrum in Fars. Tavernier personally experienced the working of the system when the same khan reimbursed him for two bales of merchandise that he had lost to thieves.[137]

CONCLUSION

Like all societies, Safavid Iran may be viewed as a series of evolving tensions. Amin Banani identified tensions between the center and the periphery, between settled and unsettled forces, Persian and non-Persian elements and, finally, between forces of social stratification and mobility.[138] Following this approach, the state becomes less a unified entity in opposition to "civil" society than a blend of competing factions deeply embedded in society and rarely effectively controlled by the ruler. The state amassed power and extracted revenue but also redistributed income and conferred prestige and influence; it used coercive force but ultimately it had to coax its subjects into participation and collaboration by heeding local voices and peripheral interests. The Safavid state was a patrimonial state headed by a ruler endowed with tremendous "despotic" power; it had all the trappings of early modern absolutism, but a limited resource base and significant environmental and logistical obstacles severely circumscribed its effective coercive power, forcing perpetual negotiation with subaltern groups upon policy-makers.

A proper understanding of the working of late Safavid Iran requires identifying a series of additional, environmental, economic, political, and cultural features, distinguishing the ones conducive to tension and fission from those that lent a degree of cohesion and balance to society.

An unforgiving natural environment, slow communications, the regional character of most exchange and limited monetization made commercial life precarious and fragmented, resulting in a series of regional economies each of which clustered around a regional center.[139] Iran's ethnic diversity, its tribal makeup, and its endemic political factionalism created further disunity. These centrifugal tendencies were offset by a series of centripetal elements that attenuated conflict and allowed the ruling elite a modicum of control over key resources. These included shared cultural notions centering on the Persian language and its literary tradition, a conception of entwined territory, faith and of divinely sanctioned kingship fashioning a proto-national collective identity, state policies facilitating commercial exchange, and forms of inclusiveness and accommodation that mitigated the competitiveness and factionalism of political life.

Chapter 2

Politics at the Safavid Court, I: Shahs and Grand Viziers, 1629–1666

It is impossible to give an exact description of the duties which the prime minister of a King of Persia has to perform. These depend upon the degree of favour and confidence he enjoys, and upon the activity and energy, or indolence and incompetency, of his sovereign.

John Malcolm, *A History of Persia*, 2:435

INTRODUCTION

From its inception the Safavid state had relied on the military power of the Qizilbash, the Turkoman tribesmen who controlled territory in exchange for providing military service to the crown. These unruly warriors soon came to pose a grave threat to stability, however, to the point of almost bringing down the shah and his regime in the sixteenth century. Over time, Safavid rulers devised ways to marginalize the Qizilbash by breaking the tribal land for service arrangement. Most significantly, they created a new elite class of so-called *ghulam*s (Arabic pl. *ghilman*), servants of the shah, who derived their standing solely from their affiliation with the crown. Most ghulams were imported Armenian, Georgian, and Circassian "slaves" from the Caucasus region, although examples of "Turk" and Tajik (ethnic Persian) ghulams are known as well. Initiated by Shah Tahmasb, the process of integrating them into the ranks of the bureaucracy and military was intensified by Shah ʿAbbas I. He transformed the ghulam corps into a major fighting force and appointed the first ghulams as provincial governors, beginning with the Georgian Allah Virdi Khan, who in 1595 was given control over the important province of Fars.[1]

The tensions between the Qizilbash and these new forces in combination with the growing power of the inner palace following the reign of Shah ʿAbbas I, with eunuchs and harem women gaining influence at the expense of the members of the chancery, have long been considered among the main causes of growing Safavid weakness.[2] Historians used to view this process in linear terms, as part of a larger story focusing on decline, positing a simple Qizilbash-ghulam/eunuch conflict reified as a struggle between tribal virility and courtly effeminacy. They also tended to identify the period following the reign of Shah ʿAbbas I as the beginning of this struggle. The result, a rather undifferentiated treatment of the fractured political order of late Safavid Iran, yielded little insight into either the stages of the conflict or the precise nature of the players and their interests.

In recent decades, a more sophisticated analysis has gained currency, one that recognizes that attempts to break Qizilbash dominance go back to early Safavid times and that the resulting power struggle was not simply a matter of ghulams trumping the Qizilbash. As early as 1508, a mere seven years into the Safavid period, the important function of *vakil* or deputy of the shah was taken away from the Qizilbash and offered to an ethnic Iranian.[3] Ghulams were involved in Iran's affairs from the beginning as well. Georgians thus had a role in the army as early as the reign of Shah Ismaʿil I. Ghulam influence and power accelerated under Shah ʿAbbas, to be sure, and his death did nothing to halt their ascendance. Between 1629 and 1666, the number of ghulams serving as provincial governors rose from eight out of fourteen major provinces to twenty-three to twenty-five out of thirty-seven newly appointed governor generals.[4] They intermarried with members of the royal household, as the Qizilbash had done and as leading members of the religious estate would soon be doing.[5] But, unlike the Ottoman slave regiments, the ghulams were able to pass on their domains to their offspring.[6] By forming hereditary households, they came to represent a landed nobility of sorts. Good examples are the Georgian Allah Virdi Khan and his son, Imam Quli Khan, who ruled Fars from 1595 until 1632; and the Armenian Qarchaqay Khan (d. 1624), his son Manuchihr (d. 1636), and grandson Qarchaqay Khan II (d. 1668?), who collectively held sway over Mashhad from 1595 until 1664.[7] Ghulams not only played a preeminent role in politics, but also gained prestige and influence by patronizing the arts and by leaving a substantial architectural legacy.[8]

While the ghulams brought a new dynamic to the state and became major players in its politics, they did not fully supplant the tribal element. Rather than breaking the power of the Qizilbash completely, their ascent complicated the political arena by adding more players—as did the growing power of the court eunuchs, who over time would emerge as the single most important force in court politics. Consequently, historians of late have begun to view the tensions between the "tribal" forces of the old-guard Qizilbash and the newly introduced ghulams as a complex phenomenon involving a multiplicity of competing interests—between Turks and Tajiks, between the representatives of the old religious order and the newcomers from Arab lands, as well as between various households within individual groups, and, ultimately, between individuals.[9]

This raises the issue of identity and the terms in which it is cast. Put simply, does the terminology applied by modern historians correspond to that used in the contemporary sources, and does it do justice to the way the people in question identified themselves? There are no easy answers to the question of identity and how it shaped conflict. Then, as now, Iran's political system was in some ways individualistic to the point of being amoebic. Joseph-Arthur de Gobineau, writing in the mid-nineteenth century, exaggerated only slightly when he declared that there was no Iranian state, just individuals.[10] Yet this does not mean that its many conflicts can be reduced to individual quarrels over wealth and power. To do so would render any discussion beyond individual players meaningless. It is true that terms such as "tribal" and "ghulam" remain unclear and are used only with great infrequency in the Persian sources, certainly not to denote any type of group solidarity—in terms of either ethnicity or class. A Qizilbash tribe was less an ascriptive group than a war band consisting of a chieftain and his retainers, men who shared a common experience as warriors but whose loyalty to one another—and to the shah—was nevertheless instrumental rather than inherent and automatic. The same is true of the ghulams. Tahmasb Quli Khan, the official who oversaw the brutal deportation of the Armenians from Old Julfa to Isfahan in 1603–4, was himself an Armenian.[11] It is also little more than romantic make-believe to view ghulams as loyal servants of the shah, tied to him in a blood-brotherhood based on trust. Safavid history is littered with cases of betrayal by all and sundry officials, including ghulams.[12]

There are, in sum, good reasons to be cautious of treating the ghulams as status groups with a high degree of self-identification. The distinction between Qizilbash and ghulams is real, albeit vague, for we have examples of ghulams classified as Qizilbash, and even of ghulams leading tribal Qurchi regiments.[13] All Georgian and Armenian officials were ghulams but not all ghulams were of

Georgian, Armenian, or Circassian background. Indeed, the term "ghulam" seems to have been a generic one used for anyone who served the shah.[14] Muzaffar Beg, a Turk of Tajik background originally active in the retinue of Allah Virdi Khan, appears to us as a ghulam.[15] Ghulams, we might conclude, were simply servants of the shah who were mostly recruited from the Caucasus.

Willem Floor's suggestion that it is most productive to identify key political figures and to look for and analyze their political networks is therefore well taken.[16] This is valid for the Qizilbash as much as for ghulams, who, in contrast to slave soldiers in most of Islamic history, continued to be embedded in family networks originating in their ancestral lands. But it is also important to keep an eye on wider associative links. Individual interests are always pursued as part of larger group interests, and the network of individuals tended to coincide or overlap with kin and extended family. Rivalries followed the same lines, even if they were fluid, perpetually shifting, and, at bottom, always personal. Rivalry between and among Georgian families and factions was fierce, with momentous repercussions for the composition of the court. Beyond that, there was an ascriptive element to group status. Individuals may not necessarily have identified themselves as members of such groups, but others often saw and judged them as such. Sanson observed in the early 1690s that, while the grand vizier, Muhammad Mirza Tahir, was generally popular because he was a Tajik, the Qizilbash disliked him for the same reason.[17] Individuals also had to forge at least temporary alliances based on self-interest beyond their direct family, with members of the same profession or the same social category.[18] The animosities and conflicts generated by these alliances often followed tribal and ethnic in-group divisions, or were religious in nature. Rula Abisaab has identified the Shi`i clerics from Arab lands who migrated to Iran and gained prominence as a distinct social group with specific interests.[19] In the period of Shah `Abbas I we hear of a religious court faction opposing the arrival of Roman Catholic missionaries and thousands of Armenian Christians from the Caucasus.[20] The reign of Shah Safi saw the rise of a xenophobic faction among the ruling elite. Under Shah `Abbas II there appears to have been an anti-ghulam cabal composed of Qizilbash forces and religious officials whose main grievance was the admission of formerly Christian ghulams to high office.[21] In the later Safavid period many resented the eunuchs as a group for the tremendous power they had accumulated and the arbitrariness with which they wielded it. As will be seen in Chapter 8, an anti-Georgian court faction made up of eunuchs in the last days of the dynasty thwarted military initiatives, thus hastening the demise of the regime.[22] The Georgians were deeply divided amongst themselves, yet others clearly perceived them as a group with distinct traits, most notably fierceness and bellicosity, which made them feared and unpopular. A missionary who traveled from Tabriz to Isfahan in 1692–3 noted that the Georgians in his company did not pay dues at any of the toll stations on the way because the toll masters (*rahdars*) were afraid of them.[23] The decision by the French cleric Avril and his companions to travel disguised as Georgians on account of the awe they inspired among people conveys the same image.[24] A mutual dislike between Georgians and Armenians is also documented, at the royal court as well as in society at large.[25] Jean Chardin claimed that the two groups hated each other to the point of being unable to live together in the same village.[26] The Georgians, he insisted, despised the pusillanimity of the Armenians. The Armenians, in turn, lived in fear of their quarrelsome Caucasian neighbors. The ease with which Georgians reputedly converted to Islam only fueled the contempt others felt for them.[27]

Officials, moreover, operated as members of institutions. Without any type of institutional arrangement guided by a professional ethos, no administrative structure can function and endure. Suraiya Faroqhi's observation about the Ottoman Empire is pertinent here: "it is an Orientalist assumption of the most outmoded variety to postulate an atomized Ottoman elite unable to formulate even a loose consensual framework, within which its individual members might pursue interests of the state, that alone could guarantee their positions and—as was true also of other polities—their personal financial concerns as well."[28] The same applies to Safavid Iran, even if it is often hard to discern any overarching public interest beyond the person of the shah, his well-being and his glory. Ultimately individuals acted as individuals, serving their own interests and, beyond that, favoring next of kin above anyone else, yet they also formed groups, identified with these groups, built networks of patronage around them, and competed with each other in part in alliances based on them.

THE COURT AND ITS PLAYERS: INDIVIDUALS, FACTIONS, AND ETHNO-RELIGIOUS GROUPS

The Safavid court was a contentious universe. It was made up of a multitude of officials who in theory held rank and wielded power and influence according to their formal functions. Yet, following Weber's categorization of premodern states, this structure, if we can call it that, was far more fluid than one would assume to have been the case on the basis of administrative manuals such as the *Tadhkirat al-muluk* and the *Dastur al-muluk*. In practice if not in theory, it operated on hereditary principles. Most bureaucratic positions were attached to a particular family or clan, and officials typically were succeeded by their sons or other male family members.[29] Kinship ties were ordinarily instrumental in a bureaucrat's initial appointment. Once installed, an official worked tirelessly to reward members of his extended kin by helping them too to gain high positions. In turn, being surrounded by high-ranking members of one's extended family served as a cushion against intrigue and possible dismissal.

Royal favor was the sine qua non of an official's standing. The ruler was the pivot of the system, as he tended to be in Western Europe until the nineteenth century.[30] The "personal and unequal relation of each subordinate to the ruler" animated the court and gave it coherence.[31] Access and, during official functions, literal proximity to the shah reflected the actual power and influence of a functionary, in a ranking that often deviated from the official hierarchy and that might be reshuffled depending on changing circumstances.[32] To be in the shah's favor was indispensable for any ambitious official. The attendant status and privilege facilitated the building of a durable power base, which in turn helped ward off the competition and prevent quick demotion or dismissal.

Factionalism was not just the inevitable result of a perpetual power struggle among greedy, power-hungry officials, but an institutionalized aspect of governance, the outcome of deliberate policy, encouraged by the ruler as part of a divide-and-rule strategy. Ideally, the shah would assert control by making sure that his courtiers, including the grand vizier, remained dependent on him.[33] One way of achieving this was by having officials screened by shadow officials—a long-standing practice in Iranian statecraft with roots in the Achaemenid period. An official was typically seconded by a *janishin*, a substitute who had the task of checking and reporting on his superior. High-ranking functionaries were kept in check by counterparts. The grand vizier was shadowed by the *nazir* (the steward of the royal household). Although the former handled monetary matters, he had no insight into the workings of the royal treasury and thus depended on the nazir in this regard.[34]

Another strategy used by shahs was to foster discord between their subordinates. Shah ʿAbbas I favored the Georgians in an effort to weaken the political and economic power of the Qizilbash, but in turn made sure to keep the former as divided as they already were.[35]

He also used Iran's domestic Armenians and resident Christian missionaries as a counterweight to the ulama, but simultaneously he maintained good relations with the Shi`i clerics, allowing them to vilify non-Shi`i minorities whenever it suited him, and he exploited the divisions in Isfahan's Armenian community for his own benefit.[36] The success of such a policy depended on the ruler's personality and skills, and especially on his ability to stay above the factional fray. A new shah would be beholden to the grandees of his predecessors, especially if he was under age. Rivalries at this stage would often spin out of control and have a deleterious, even paralyzing, effect on the decision-making process. Typically the shah would grow out of this as he reached maturity, at which point he often asserted his authority by liquidating the players who hitherto had dominated the court. A strong shah typically meant weak and subordinate courtiers, whereas a weak shah would give great leeway to his administrators. But since even the most ambitious officials could not aspire to the ruler's full sovereign power, this combination ultimately weakened the system.[37]

This chapter and the next concentrate on some of the most pivotal players in the political arena, with an eye toward exploring the multiple rivalries between and inside the *dargah* (the palace), and the *divan* (the state administration). The particular focus will be the grand vizier and his relationship with the shah in the period following the reign of Shah `Abbas I. The grand vizier was the shah's personal servant. Since he was responsible for both the *mamalik* (state) and *khassah* (crown, administration), he straddled the two branches of government.[38] In addition to approving the appointment of all civil servants in both, he also oversaw monetary matters and issues of royal income, even if he did not control the royal treasury. In the late Safavid period all treaties had to be confirmed by him.[39]

The grand vizier was the ruler's main counselor, in the case of an absent or weak shah often his stand-in, and in some ways his counterweight and even antithesis. In the Safavid shah we see elements of the Turko-Mongol tradition of mobile steppe warfare coupled with conspicuous consumption. He was expected to project his power through conquest as much as through outsized generosity, which included organizing sumptuous banquets for his warriors and visiting dignitaries, lavishly rewarding officials for loyalty and good service, and granting tax remissions to his subjects. The vizier stood for the Iranian urban, sedentary order of concentrated wealth precariously produced through agrarian surplus. It was his task to increase royal revenue as well as to husband the resources of the realm judiciously.[40] This made him the most important of all courtiers. At representative functions, he was always seated closest to the shah, even if occasionally other officials overshadowed him in actual influence and power.[41] Engelbert Kaempfer, who saw the grand vizier as crucial to the system, claimed that any official's ascent to office, prestige, influence, and riches required his blessing and favor.[42] The Safavid cleric Muhammad Baqir Sabzavari concurred by calling him the indispensable official.[43] The eighteenth-century man of letters Rustam al-Hukama used a cosmological metaphor to drive the same point home, arguing that rulers needed viziers like planets circling in their orbit.[44]

Yet, for all his power and influence, the grand vizier was vulnerable. No one else was so exposed to the jealousy of other high-placed courtiers. Sabzavari called the grand vizierate the most precarious post in the realm for being the target of merciless intrigue by envious rivals. As the Dutch traveler Cornelis de Bruyn put it, the grand vizier could never be at ease, for he could never trust anyone. His closest colleagues were often the first to attack him at the slightest sign of weakness shown by him.[45] The vizier also lacked an independent power base. He did not represent any obvious tribal interests; nor did the vizierate come with the governorate of an important province, as some other high positions did. The grand vizier was solely beholden to the shah, unable to accomplish anything without the latter's consent.[46] The relationship between the two was fraught with problems. A strong and vigilant shah would give his vizier free rein in fiscal and administrative affairs, but was well advised never to let him out of sight or to rely on his advice alone. Shah `Abbas I is said to have remarked once that a judicious ruler should not listen only to his grand vizier, for to do so would undermine royal control.[47] A weak, indecisive shah might fall under the spell of his grand vizier, who would start building his own power base while keeping his master occupied with various forms of carousing. A vizier faced with a whimsical, erratic shah would often become passive, trying to avoid bouts of royal anger. The result would be administrative paralysis.[48] The grand vizier, finally, served as a lightning rod; he was always at hand to defuse criticism of the ruler for bad management or calamities. As Heinrich Brugsch observed in early Qajar times, a shah needed a grand vizier to deflect the wrath of his populace or he might himself become the object of popular criticism.[49] This explains in part the frequency with which grand viziers have fallen from favor, often leading to their execution, in Iranian history. Studying the Safavid grand vizier is thus bound to yield valuable insight into the working of the financial and administrative system, the balance of power between the ruler and his entourage, the evolving nature of the chain of command emanating from the palace, and thus into the transformation of the Safavid state from a tribal polity into a patrimonial-bureaucratic empire.

From the early days of Safavid rule, when the grand vizierate had a short-lived independent, albeit subordinate, status, the function had mostly been combined with the position of viceroy (*vakil*), an official who often simultaneously held the highest military post of *amir al-umara*. In 1509–10, the grand vizier received the right to put his seal on *farmans* (royal edicts).[50] It was only under Shah 'Abbas I, when no more vakils were appointed, that the vizier came into his own as a separate functionary.[51] Shah 'Abbas enhanced the post of *majlis-nivis* (secretary of the royal council), in part to curb the power of the grand vizier, and made sure that none of the incumbents established an independent power base. Under his successors, the vizier rose to unprecedented prominence—a process that went hand in hand with the growing importance of the crown domain as well as the gradual retreat of the shah from the center of politics.[52] The seventeenth-century grand vizier played a role of great complexity and ambiguity in the evolving constellation of power. He was neither a figure-head in an increasingly decadent court,[53] nor a mere extension of the shadow government formed by the inner palace.[54] More and more he turned into the official through whose eyes the ruler "saw the world." Yet even the most forceful grand vizier, a strong-willed one serving an insouciant master, never turned into the shah's "alter ego."[55] The common perception of later Safavid rulers as having retreated into a state of oblivion ignores the fact that even an indolent shah remained not just the apex of the system, the sole source of legitimacy, but its pivot as well, the figure for whose "heart and mind" all courtiers continued to compete. However high a grand vizier's star might rise, he never acquired the ruler's aura and he therefore continued to be a full-blown competitor in the perpetual struggle for his master's favor.

SHAH SAFI: THE QUEST FOR ABSOLUTE ROYAL CONTROL

Shah 'Abbas I died in January 1629, to be succeeded by his grandson, Safi. Safi was not the only or even the most obvious heir to the throne. Only in the last months of his life did Shah 'Abbas consult with his court astronomers and single him—the son of his own son, Safi Mirza—out as his successor. Safi managed to ascend to power with the assistance of various officials, among them Khusraw Mirza, the Georgian *darughah* (city prefect) of Isfahan, who, following an outbreak of unrest in the capital, ensured an orderly transition by stationing his troops in the town and proclaiming him `Abbas's rightful successor. Following the coronation, Safi honored Khusraw Mirza by calling him not his "son"—the customary epithet for royal favorites—but his "brother." Renaming him Rustam Khan, he also rewarded him with the important position of *qullar-aqasi* (head of the ghulams) and, beyond that, with the governorship of eastern Georgia, Kartli.[56]

Shah Safi initially found it difficult to establish personal control over the court. The young lad—barely eighteen years old and a product of the harem system—mounted the throne with little life experience of any kind.[57] The heavy drinking and opium abuse that he soon engaged in with his courtiers—a habit carried over from his harem years—naturally did little to improve matters. As a result, the shah seems at first to have enjoyed but minimal respect. Aside from unrest in the capital, he immediately faced several rebellious provincial subalterns who, clearly viewing the death of his formidable grandfather as an opportunity to reassert local autonomy, initially refused to recognize the authority of the new ruler. Gilan was the scene of a millenarian uprising led by the charismatic Gharib Shah. Uzbeks stepped up their raids into Khurasan, and the Portuguese attacked the Persian Gulf island of Qishm. Disrespect even extended to the palace itself, where drunken courtiers are said to have quarreled in front of the new shah.[58]

It took Shah Safi five years to establish full control. This entailed a series of brutal purges which left all of his real and potential rivals incapacitated—dead, blind, or imprisoned. The casualties included all male offspring of Shah `Abbas's daughters, some of the courtiers who had been most prominent under the same ruler, and those who had been instrumental in bringing Shah Safi himself to power. Among the latter, the sources mention an assortment of Qizilbash, ghulams, and ethnic Iranians, such as Zaynal Khan Shamlu, `Isa Khan Shaykhavand, and Yusuf Agha. Khalifah Sultan, grand vizier since 1624, was also among the victims.[59] The shah's principal advisers and executioners in the purge were Chiragh Khan Zahidi (or Pirzadah), Rustam Beg, a Georgian ghulam who served as *divanbegi* (Chief Justice) and, most prominently, the aforementioned qullar-aqasi Rustam Khan, who had become the shah's main confidant.[60]

One of the first to be eliminated was the *ishik-aqasi-bashi* (master of ceremonies), Zaynal Khan. This official had been the first to approach the shah upon the latter's coronation in 1629. Appointed *vakil-i divan*, the shah's tutor, some days later on account of his favored status with the new king, he soon managed to accumulate even more power and prestige by becoming *sipahsalar* (army commander). Yet after barely a year the shah had him executed for failing to halt the Ottomans at a narrow mountain pass prior to the battle of Marivan in early May 1630. His head, put on a stick, was paraded around the army camp as a deterrent against treason and military weakness.[61] Abu'l Qasim Beg Iv Ughli, the eighty-year-old *ishik-aqasi-bashi-yi haram* (chamberlain of the inner palace), who took care of all of Safi's affairs, paid the ultimate price as well; his more agile sons managed to escape from Isfahan and find refuge elsewhere.[62] Yusuf Agha, a castrated ghulam of Circassian background who enjoyed great prestige in the shah's harem and who, as *amir-mirshikar-bashi* (master of the hunt), represented the interests of the Armenian community of Isfahan, was next in line. After his execution, the staggering—although surely exaggerated—sum of 450,000 *tumans* was found in his estate.[63]

The main targets of Shah Safi's wrath were all males with potential claims to the throne, most notably the various sons of Shah 'Abbas's daughters.[64] The first to be decapitated by Rustam Beg and Chiragh Khan Pirzadah were the three sons of *qurchibashi* (head of the praetorian guard), 'Isa Khan Shaykhavand and Zubaydah Bigum, one of Shah 'Abbas's daughters. 'Isa Khan himself was also killed, as were two of his retainers, Takhtah Khan Ustajlu, a *qurchi-yi Turkaman*, and Mir Muhammad Tahir Simnani, the qurchibashi's vizier. 'Isa Khan's successor, Chirag Khan Pirzadah, perished a year later, in 1632.[65] So as to "eradicate matrilinear and collateral lines," women were targeted as well.[66] Zubaydah Bigum, who had conspired to have her own son, Sayyid Muhammad Khan, put on the throne, was killed, and some forty other harem women died with her. Zaynab Bigum, Shah 'Abbas's aunt and confidant, was expelled from the harem. Next, in February 1632, came the dismissal of Khalifah Sultan and the blinding of the four sons he had with one of Shah 'Abbas's daughters.[67] The same fate befell the two sons of Mir Rafi' al-Din Muhammad Shahristani, the *sadr*, who was probably married to another daughter of the former shah. The four sons of Hasan Khan Ustajlu, whose mother was a granddaughter of Shah Tahmasb, were cut down as well.

The killings and blindings went well beyond Safavid offspring to include Muhammad Khan, the governor of Mashhad; 'Asab Khan, the governor of Baghdad; Ughurlu Beg Shamlu, the ishik-aqasi-bashi; and grand vizier Mirza Abu Talib Khan Urdubadi, with his vizier, Muhammad Tahir, and his son-in-law, Hasan Beg, the *yasavul-bashi*.

Head of the aides-de-camp, Mirza Abu Talib Khan's three sons were deprived of their eyesight.[68] Yusuf Khan, *yuzbashi* (centurion) of the ghulams and head of the secret royal council, another high official from the reign of Shah 'Abbas, was also executed, with at least one of his relatives. 'Ali Quli Beg took control of his considerable assets.[69]

In late 1632 the string of executions culminated with the brutal murder of Imam Quli Khan, the country's most powerful and wealthiest man after the shah. This scion of the Georgian Undiladze family, whose father, Allah Virdi Khan, had been brought to Iran under Shah Tahmasb, ruled virtually autonomously over the entire southwestern half of the country. He was governor of Fars as well as of the regions of Kuh-i Giluyah, Gulpaygan, Lar, Jirun/Hurmuz, and Bahrain. He also had the country's best military forces at his disposal, regiments whose assistance Shah 'Abbas frequently called up to engage in campaigns on his behalf. Imam Quli Khan's demise, with two of his sons, ordered during one of the drinking sessions to which the young shah was increasingly given, formed the prelude to the killing of all of his offspring, variously given as sixteen or even fifty-two. The carnage may have been triggered by the shah's decision to eliminate one of his sons, born of a wife impregnated by Shah 'Abbas, who thus was a potential pretender to the throne.

The underlying reasons for the purge remain a matter of speculation. The Dutch, watching developments from Isfahan, suggested two possibilities: Either a palace conspiracy had come to light, or the shah had decided that, rather than continuing to be at the mercy of his courtiers, it was time to begin administering his realm himself.[70] The two scenarios are not mutually exclusive and, indeed, elements of both are visible in the unfolding of events. We see a young ruler, untrained in feeling compassion, acting out his whims by targeting older courtiers who may have treated him, a mere adolescent, with unforgivable condescension. The victims were all potential rivals, either as blood relatives or because they wielded considerable power in the administration. The events contained an element of conspiracy as well. Jean-Baptiste Tavernier later ascribed the demise of Imam Quli Khan and his clan to jealousy on the part of the queen-mother and her protégé, Mirza Muhammad "Saru" Taqi.[71]

Bitter rivalry between various Georgian families is also likely to have played a role in the bloody purge. Imam Quli Khan, the main representative of the house of Undiladze, was flanked by his younger brother Da'ud Khan, who had been governor of Ganja-Qarabagh since 1627–8. Shah 'Abbas had designated Imam Quli Khan as his successor's main adviser, but it was Rustam Khan who had in fact assumed the role of royal confidant. And it was Rustam Khan, now qullar-aqasi, who was instrumental in bringing down the members of the Undiladze clan. His first target had been Da'ud Khan, who at his behest was expelled from the royal council in 1631. In this he was clearly encouraged by the Qizilbash, who had suffered terribly at Da'ud Khan's hands, both in Fars and in the Caucasus. Da'ud Khan thereupon conspired with King Taymuraz I of Georgia, with whom he maintained close ties, having married one of his sisters, with the aim of invading Azerbaijan. He evaded the shah's wrath by taking refuge in Georgia, and it was his elder brother who would pay the price for his perfidy.[72]

Kathryn Babayan sees in this massacre a turning point in Safavid history, the definitive triumph of the ghulams. This is an overstatement, even if their numbers grew tremendously under Shah Safi, as the *Tarikh-i Shah Safi* avers they did.[73] First of all, the episode exemplifies a recurrent process of rulers acting out a coming-of-age ritual by eliminating actual and potential rivals. The removal of Imam Quli Khan is reminiscent of the various purges undertaken by Shah 'Abbas I, beginning with the elimination of the person who had brought him to power, his vakil and erstwhile tutor Murshid Quli Khan Ustajlu, in 1589, and extending to the execution of his powerful general Farhad Khan Qaramanlu in 1598.[74] Those acts, too, had removed formidable army commanders and governors of important provinces whose power far exceeded that of ordinary *beglerbegs* (governors of large provinces), and whose wealth rivaled that of the shah himself.[75]

Secondly, as many ghulams as members of the Qizilbash perished in the purges. As stated, the undermining of the Qizilbash goes back all the way to the reign of Shah Isma'il I, and Caucasian elements had had a significant place in the administrative system since the time of Shah Tahmasb I. There is no question but that the ghulams acquired greater power, including military power, in this period, and that much of this came at the expense of the Qizilbash. Thus the highest military post, that of sipahsalar, was successively held by two prominent ghulams, Rustam Khan and his brother 'Ali Quli Khan, almost uninterruptedly for some twenty-five years between 1631 and 1655. When Rustam Khan departed for Georgia as *vali*, viceroy, of Kartli in 1632, Georgian substitutes, *na'ibs*, appointed by him, continued to hold the position of darughah of Isfahan.[76] Yet the Qizilbash continued to play a prominent role in all administrative sectors.

The events of 1630–3 were important, not because they marked the definitive rise of the ghulams but because they were a phase in a gradual process of curtailing the power of the Qizilbash, a process that was never completed—intentionally so. Rather than seeking to destroy the Qizilbash and replace them with ghulams, the Safavids sought to balance old forces with new ones, all with the aim of enhancing central control. Powerful as he was as sipahsalar, and governor of Azerbaijan, Rustam Khan too was eventually killed. The ghulams were allowed to assume many key positions in this period, but this did not necessarily come at the expense of the Qizilbash. Masashi Haneda has argued that quite a few provincial governors in the reign of Shah 'Abbas I were originally Qurchis, examples being Husayn Khan Shamlu of Herat, Ganj 'Ali Khan of Kirman, and Hasan Khan Ustajlu of Hamadan.[77] This pattern continued beyond 1629. In Kirman, for instance, the monopoly of the Afshar—which had its roots in the reign of Shah Isma'il I—was broken only to be replaced by Kurdish rule. Later on, control over the province alternated between the Jala'ir, the Shamlu, and the Qajar. Only in the final two decades of Safavid rule were Georgian ghulams appointed to Kirman as governors, at which point the Afshar were called back in to help defend the province against tribal attack.[78]

MIRZA MUHAMMAD "SARU" TAQI KHAN

One official who played an important role in the elimination of both Abu Talib Khan and Imam Quli Khan was Mirza Muhammad "Saru" (blond) Taqi Khan. A scion of a middle-ranking, rather poor family, and castrated after being accused of sodomy, he was neither a member of the Qizilbash nor a representative of the ghulams. He exemplifies what Babayan calls the "broader conception of so called *ghulam*hood," which "not only encompassed the converted Christian slaves or the lovers of the Shah, the shahsevan, but also allowed a castrated commoner such as Mirza Taqi to enter the arena of politics."[79]

Exemplifying the meritocratic tendencies of Safavid administrative practice, Mirza Taqi does not seem to have relied on family connections when he first made a name for himself as financial supervisor (*mushrif*) of the ruler of Ardabil, Zu'l Fiqar Qaramanlu. He next held the same post in Ganja, Shirvan, and later became vizier to the ruler of Qarabagh. He was subsequently appointed vizier to revenue-rich Mazandaran, to become governor-general (*vazir-i kull*) of the equally lucrative region of Gilan in 1617–18—whether through bribery, as his enemies alleged, or as a reward for having overseen the completion of the famous paved causeway that ran along the southern shore of the Caspian Sea.⁸⁰ Upon taking up his post in Gilan, he set out to investigate the financial dealings of Mirza Isma'il, his predecessor in Biya Pas, the region's western half. He also drew up a balance sheet of the losses suffered by the royal treasury as a result of the Gharib Shah rebellion.⁸¹ Mirza Taqi continued to enjoy the shah's favor during the transition of power from 'Abbas to Safi, surviving the massacres. As Floor points out, this probably reflects his good standing with grand vizier Khalifah Sultan.⁸² Two years into the reign of Shah Safi, Mirza Taqi was sent to Baghdad to supervise the renovation of the *'atabat*, Iraq's Shi'i shrines.⁸³

In August 1633, Mirza Taqi succeeded Mirza Abu Talib Khan as grand vizier.⁸⁴ According to Tavernier, Shah 'Abbas I was responsible for this appointment, for he left a note to his successor urging him to elevate Mirza Taqi to the highest bureaucratic post.⁸⁵ We are otherwise poorly informed about the circumstances of Mirza Taqi's promotion. Mirza Abu Talib had been his enemy for a while, and Mirza Taqi may have had a hand in his predecessor's downfall, but proof for this is lacking. The *Khuld-i barin* states that Mirza Taqi acquired a position of influence because of his friendship with Ughulru Beg, a ghulam, but the sources do not provide any details about the consequences of that connection either.⁸⁶ Political connections no doubt played a role in the choice of Mirza Taqi, but his close relationship with the shah may have been decisive. According to Adam Olearius, he gained the post because he had made the shah his sole inheritor while promising to regale him regularly with rich presents.⁸⁷ Equally significant may have been his organizational and financial talent. Previous grand viziers such as Hatim Beg Urdubadi and 'Ali Kirmani, too, had served as *mustawfi* (comptroller) before acceding to the highest bureaucratic post.⁸⁸ The Dutch called Mirza Taqi the best administrator in the entire country.⁸⁹

Mirza Taqi proved to be a competent grand vizier. He also was the first in a long time to take an active, hands-on approach to his job.⁹⁰ He immediately set out to increase royal revenue, reduce spending, and combat corruption. He arranged for a number of provinces to be converted from mamalik to khassah land. (See Chapter 6 for details.) He also cut back on military expenditure, in a policy that clearly targeted the Qizilbash. He further continued the policy that he had initiated while serving as governor of Mazandaran, curbing the power of that province's traditional elite, the Sayyids of Mar'ashi, by making sure that his own relatives were put in charge of the territory. His brother, Muhammad Salih Beg, was appointed in 1634, and when he died his son, Qasim Beg, took control of Mazandaran, ruling the province until the end of Shah Safi's reign.⁹¹

Mirza Taqi ruffled many feathers with these policies. He had a run-in with Husayn Khan Beg, the nazir, who supervised the shah's household. He also confronted Khajah Mahabbat, a eunuch, the *sahib-i jam`*, *rish-sifid* (department head of the royal treasury) as well as the supervisor of the royal harem, who was replaced by Khajah Mushfiq after being investigated for corruption. Another official he took to task for financial irregularities was Mirza Ma`sum, the *mustawfi baqaya* (comptroller of arrears) who had been instrumental in bringing down Mirza Taqi's predecessor, Mirza Abu Talib Khan. Mirza Taqi also investigated the malversations of `Ali Quli Beg, the *shahbandar* (harbor master) of Bandar `Abbas, who fled to India in an attempt to escape the consequences of the inquiry.[92] The grand vizier, finally, proved to be an able negotiator in dealing with agents of the VOC and EIC, conceding but little to these foreign merchants while keeping a keen eye on the financial interests of the Safavid crown.[93] As chair of the royal council, Mirza Taqi continued to wield extraordinary power at the court until the end of his life. After the accession of Shah `Abbas II in 1642, he headed a ruling troika which operated at the command of Anna Khanum, the shah's grandmother, until the monarch reached maturity. Some even argued that the country was run by him and the queen-mother.[94]

SHAH `ABBAS II

In 1642, after a thirteen-year reign, Shah Safi died, exhausted from excessive drinking. During the reign of his successor, Shah `Abbas II, various forces continued to vie with one another over the legacy of the tribal dominance that had marked the Safavid state until the days of Shah `Abbas I. It is not easy to identify the role Shah `Abbas II played in this rivalry and the changing power constellation it generated. Some have praised him as a strong and open-minded ruler, a worthy heir to his great-grandfather. Others have condemned him as an intolerant despot oppressing religious minorities. Neither view does justice to the complex and varying characteristics of the different phases into which his reign can be divided. Mounting the throne at the tender age of nine, `Abbas II was at first supervised and overshadowed by a few high-ranking courtiers. Once he reached maturity, he emerged as a forceful leader determined to take control. This phase ended when the shah fell victim to chronic drinking and began to indulge in his other favorite pastime, hunting. The resulting period of relative weakness coincided with the rise of Muhammad Beg as his grand vizier, and in no small measure accounts for the autonomy this official enjoyed.

A triumvirate consisting of Mirza Taqi, Muhammad ʿAli Beg, and Jani Khan Shamlu, who worked in alliance with the queen-mother, Anna Khanum, effectively wielded power at the court for the first three years of Shah ʿAbbas II's reign.[95] The second of these served as *nazir-i buyutat* (steward of the royal household). Jani Khan, an originally rather humble member of the Shamlu tribe, had earned his stripes in the military, until in 1637 he was appointed qurchibashi in addition to receiving the governorship of Kirman. In 1643 Jani Khan became related to Mirza Taqi through his daughter, who was given in marriage to Mirza Qasim, a nephew of the grand vizier.[96] This liaison solidified a family alliance that also included Anna Khanum and that was designed to do away with a mutual rival, the formidable Rustam Khan, a ghulam who wielded tremendous power as sipahsalar and beglerbeg of Azerbaijan.[97] When ʿAbbas II had this popular official killed, he apparently did so at the instigation of his mother, Jani Khan and Mirza Taqi.[98]

Mirza Taqi himself soon came to grief as well, his fate entwined with that of Jani Khan. The outline of their fall is as follows: The marriage alliance between the two clearly did not outlive its immediate objective, for Jani Khan would soon emerge as the main conspirator in the assassination of Mirza Taqi. The resentment fueling the plot involved disagreement over fiscal and military policy, with Jani Khan favoring a strong military and Mirza Taqi, taking the side of the cash-strapped court, determined to cut the salaries of the Qizilbash-dominated army.[99] Various sources suggest that Jani Khan sought to poison Shah ʿAbbas II's mind against the grand vizier, insinuating that he was driving the country to ruin and posed a threat to the shah himself.[100] Acting on the shah's authority, Jani Khan on 11 October 1645 went to Mirza Taqi's house and cut the octogenarian grand vizier down.[101] The subsequent investigation into the vizier's assets brought fabulous riches to light. According to the Dutch, a notebook kept by Mirza Taqi was found that revealed that the grand vizier had amassed the jaw-dropping sum of 340,000 tumans in gifts in the previous four years—compared with 40,000 for the shah, who ordered a comparative assessment. In late October seven camels transported jewels and treasure, cash, gold, and silver totaling 250,000 tumans from the vizier's mansion to the royal treasury.[102]

Following the murder, Jani Khan himself was betrayed by the royal *shirahchi-bashi* (sommelier), Safi Quli Beg, who feared that the ultimate objective of the conspiracy was the overthrow of the shah himself (especially since Jani Khan had reportedly called up 30,000 troops). But the real inspiration behind the terrible revenge that followed was Anna Khanum, the shah's mother, whose protégé Mirza Taqi had been. Jani Khan was assassinated four days after executing Mirza Taqi, and with him perished a large number of his fellow conspirators and clan members. Among the victims were Naqdi Khan, 'Arab Khan Shamlu, and Da'ud Khan Shamlu, the governor of Gilan, who had been a bitter enemy of Mirza Taqi since the latter had indicted him for embezzlement. Jani Khan's possessions in Kirman and Hamadan were confiscated, and the post of qurchibashi devolved on Murtaza Quli Khan, who also became governor of Kirman.[103]

The Taqi Khan–Jani Khan affair is analogous to the massacres of 1630–2 in more than one way. Most importantly, the execution marked the moment when a young and inexperienced shah emerged from the shadows to take control of state affairs. It also involved fierce factionalism among and between courtiers. If we can speak of collective interests at all, both the ghulams and the Qizilbash suffered, though neither group was dealt a mortal blow. The purge was bloody, though not as bloody as the one that had accompanied the ascent of Shah Safi. Most importantly, it was the last time a Safavid shah engaged in large-scale bloodletting with the aim of establishing his own supremacy.

THE TENURE OF KHALIFAH SULTAN, 1645–54

Mirza Taqi's successor, Sultan al-'Ulama, better known as Khalifah Sultan, a cleric known for his erudition and accounting skills, initially declined to assume the post of grand vizier, but accepted the shah's call on 14 October 1645.[104] A scion of a well-known family of Mar'ashi sayyids from Mazandaran, this son-in-law of Shah 'Abbas I had served the same ruler as grand vizier between 1623–4 and 1632, when for reasons unknown he had been dismissed and sent into early retirement.[105]

Not much is known about Khalifah Sultan's role and activities during his first term as grand vizier. This low profile, which emerges from both the Persian and the European sources, probably reflects his minor stature vis-à-vis a shah who, just coming into his own, must have been determined to wield real power rather than be overshadowed by his entourage.[106] We lack explicit information about the reasons why Khalifah Sultan was invited to serve again. His track record as a skillful administrator was no doubt the determining factor, although it is quite possible that the shah called this "spokesman for the propertied and pedigreed Persian clerical elite" back into service in part with the aim of tamping down clerical disgruntlement about the lack of high positions offered to the turbaned class under his predecessor.[107]

We are better informed about Khalifah Sultan's activities following his reappointment as grand vizier in 1645. These reveal a complex personality—a cleric who liked to drink. Living up to his reputation for piety, he launched his second term with an anti-vice campaign that targeted gambling, prostitution, and wine drinking, all of which were common activities in Isfahan's ubiquitous coffeehouses, taverns, and brothels.[108] He also took measures against Armenian Christians, forbidding them from selling their wares in the center of Isfahan and urging the shah to force them to wear distinctive clothing—thus confirming the impression among foreigners that he was an inveterate enemy of Christians.[109] These issues will be discussed more fully in Chapter 7.

His second term found Khalifah Sultan more actively involved in the administration of the country in other ways as well. He took a keen interest in the 1648 Qandahar campaign against the Mughals, accompanying Shah ʿAbbas II on his march to this eastern frontier city. He is also said to have held frequent public audiences for people with requests and grievances, a practice that was discontinued under his successors.[110] Finally, like Mirza Taqi, he proved to be an astute negotiator with the agents of the maritime companies.[111]

Naturally Khalifah Sultan faced serious competition. His main rival was Allah Virdi Khan, an Armenian ghulam and a boyhood friend of the shah who in 1644 was appointed mirshikar-bashi (master of the hunt), succeeding his father Khusraw Khan. ʿAbbas II appears to have favored Allah Virdi Khan so much that in 1649 he honored him with an appointment as qullar-aqasi. A year later, he briefly served as governor of Astarabad as well as mirshikar-bashi, a position that included representing the interests of the Julfan Armenians at the royal court.[112] The early 1650s saw Allah Virdi Khan as the shah's absolute favorite, exceeding the grand vizier himself in standing.[113]

Following a forty-day illness, Khalifah Sultan died on 5 March 1654 in his ancestral Mazandaran, to be buried in Najaf.[114] His relatives continued to occupy prominent positions in the Safavid administration long after his death. His brother, Mirza Qavam al-Din Muhammad, thus became *sadr-i mamalik* (the realm's spiritual chief), in 1661. The post of sadr remained in his family under his descendants and, indeed, until the end of the Safavid dynasty. The grand vizierate went to Muhammad Beg.[115]

THE VIZIERATE OF MUHAMMAD BEG, 1654–61

Hailing from Tabriz, Muhammad Beg was born at an unspecified date into an Armenian family of tailors who had risen at the Safavid court as ghulams. His father, Husayn Beg Tabrizi, had served Shah Safi in the capacity of head tailor in the royal workshops (*qaychachi-bashi*).[116]

Unfortunately, little is known about Muhammad Beg's early youth and career. Tavernier called him a person with a keen mind determined to get ahead in the world despite his humble background.[117] His father's position at the court, which belies an overly humble lineage, must have helped Muhammad Beg stake his own claim in the state administration. In 1643 we find him first mentioned as the darughah or city prefect of the Armenian community of New Julfa, an administrative function which included the prosecution of criminal cases. In his further rise through the ranks he enjoyed the support of another Armenian ghulam, Allah Virdi Khan. In 1646 he was appointed shahbandar of Bandar 'Abbas.[118] Shortly thereafter, perhaps as early as 1648, he acceded to the important post of controller of assay, *mu'ayyir al-mamalik*. Muhammad Beg distinguished himself in this latter function to the point where, on Allah Virdi Khan's recommendation, in late 1651 he was appointed *nazir-i buyutat*, steward of the royal household, succeeding Muhammad 'Ali Beg. In 1652 the shah showed his continued affection for Muhammad Beg by appointing him beglerbeg of the southern province of Kuh-i Giluyah.[119]

In the same year Muhammad Beg's relationship with Allah Virdi Khan seems to have soured and the two men became bitter rivals. Rumor had it that Allah Virdi Khan had fallen out of favor with the shah, although some claimed that this was a ploy designed to find out who were the mirshikar-bashi's real enemies.[120] At any rate, he was reinstated soon thereafter, and from then on sought to gain influence with the shah at Muhammad Beg's expense.[121] Yet by that time the latter had gained the upper hand. Shortly before Muhammad Beg's appointment as grand vizier, the Dutch commented that the nazir's influence exceeded that of the mirshikar-bashi and even of Khalifah Sultan.[122]

With Muhammad Beg's appointment another strong personality assumed the highest bureaucratic post. The choice must be seen above all in light of Iran's continuing economic problems. The loss of Iraq in 1638 and the costly campaign waged to regain Qandahar a decade later had helped intensify the drain on the country's meager resources. Whereas to foreign visitors the Safavid realm still seemed in good shape, its apparent prosperity represented reality only up to a point. The harsh winter of 1653–4, which was marked by inflationary prices and famine, underscored the urgency of the financial crisis, which may well have been why the shah selected Muhammad Beg as his grand vizier.[123] With his monetary expertise, gained during his tenure as controller of assay, Muhammad Beg might have been expected substantially to enhance the flow of revenue toward the royal treasury. He had also played a skillful role in the court's negotiations with the Dutch embassy of Joan Cunaeus in 1652, the outcome of which, an annual obligation for the Dutch to purchase a fixed number of 600 bales of raw silk at a price that was almost always above market rates, was a windfall for the court.[124]

As grand vizier, Muhammad Beg lost no time in enacting various measures designed to increase royal revenue. Cutting back on expenditure was the main objective. As had been the case with Mirza Taqi, one of his targets was the army. In 1654 he made sure that the post of sipahsalar was left unfilled.[125] The following year the function of the artillery commander (*tupchibashi*) met the same fate, and with his dismissal the entire artillery department was eliminated.[126] To enhance revenue, he suggested selling the numerous palaces—reportedly numbering 137—belonging to members of the elite who over time had lost the shah's favor and whose property had thereby fallen to the crown.[127] The export of gold was prohibited as well. Supervised by the assayer of the mint, Muhammad Amin Beg, a son of his, this ban was enforced quite strictly between 1658 and 1661.[128] Vulnerable religious minorities felt the burden of tax increases, although they were not the only ones, judging from a Dutch remark in 1660 that people all over the country were complaining about onerous new imposts.[129] The policy of converting state land to crown land reached its apogee during Muhammad Beg's tenure as grand vizier. Initially, central regions, located beyond the reach of external aggression, had been freed from tribal overlordship. In the 1650s provinces such as Kirman, Ardabil, Simnan, and Hamadan were added to the shah's domains.[130]

Among the most disastrous of Muhammad Beg's measures was his plan to unlock some of the country's natural resources. This included an effort to mine deposits of precious metal in the vicinity of Isfahan. The circulation of growing amounts of adulterated coin in this period must have made Muhammad Beg lend an attentive ear to the persistent rumors that a short distance east of the capital gold, silver, and copper deposits were to be found. He engaged a self-styled French mineralogist by the name of Chapelle de Han in an effort to exploit these riches.[131] However, the assistance of this gentleman, who proved little more than a fraud, failed to produce results. Another of his projects involved an attempt to reopen old coal mines. Nothing came of this either, since the coal extracted from these quarries proved largely unusable. Continued exploration resulted in the discovery of lead mines, but as the metal found did not yield the hoped-for percentage of silver, this ended in failure as well. Muhammad Beg also forced the country's artisans to use lapis lazuli found in local copper mines, but had to give up these efforts when its quality proved much lower than that of the variety imported from Central Asia.[132] The vizier also failed in his plan to secure the water supply for Isfahan's royal gardens by digging a canal between the waters of the Karun River and those of the Zayandah Rud, a project which had been contemplated before and would be explored again by grand vizier Shaykh 'Ali Khan in the 1680s.[133] A final project initiated by Muhammad Beg was the search for methods to improve on the traditional *badzan* air-conditioning system.[134]

SECURING A POSITION

Muhammad Beg's career might be considered typical of the relative openness of the Safavid bureaucratic system, yet moving up the ranks was impossible without the right connections. He thus began to cultivate his own power base as soon as he attained high rank. Like all top officials intent on keeping their posts, Muhammad took great pains to appoint the widest possible variety of family members to high-level positions. Muhammad Beg's kinsmen acquired something of a monopoly over two important posts. One was that of shahbandar of Bandar 'Abbas, which held the key to the rich income from harbor tolls and which was customarily assigned for a one-year period. In 1651–2, while Muhammad Beg was still nazir, one of his brothers, Ughan Beg, was sent to Bandar 'Abbas.[135] The latter's successor, Tahir Mirza, who took over in 1652, does not seem to have been a family member, but it was no doubt Muhammad Beg himself who in 1653 made sure that another of his brothers, Husayn Beg, received the assignment.[136] In the same year we meet Husayn Beg's son, Muhammad Amin Beg, as the new incumbent.[137] It is unclear if his successor, Muhammad Quli Beg, who held the post from 1655 to 1656, was a member of the Muhammad Beg clan, but we do know that the man who took over from him, Shamshir Beg, was an uncle of the grand vizier.[138] Shamshir Beg, in turn, was succeeded in 1658 by his nephew 'Isa Khan Beg, who was at the same time a cousin of Muhammad Beg.[139]

The other function, mu'ayyir al-mamalik, had also been held by Muhammad Beg himself. In 1651, when he was appointed nazir, this post was awarded to a brother named Hasan Beg.[140] Upon Muhammad Beg's appointment as grand vizier, Hasan Beg became the court master tailor, qaychachi-bashi. On that same occasion, Husayn Beg, the harbor master of 1653, took over as assayer of the mint.[141] Finally, Muhammad Amin Beg, the son who was shahbandar in 1654, held the same post in 1658 and may have kept it for as long as his father served as grand vizier.[142] We have little information about other high positions going to members of the Muhammad Beg clan. Father de Rhodes refers to a nephew of the grand vizier, a "young man of excellent intelligence ... who already holds an important position in the country," adding that he had been appointed to an important embassy sent to the Mughal Empire.[143]

FALL FROM GRACE AND REHABILITATION

The exalted rank of grand vizier gave Muhammad Beg extensive power at the court but failed to endear him to his colleagues. Grand viziers always had more enemies than friends, but certain unsympathetic character traits made Muhammad Beg even less liked than he otherwise might have been. The Dutch commented in 1657 on the vizier's aloofness from administrative affairs, noting that he had suspended Khalifah Sultan's custom of holding frequent public audiences where people could air grievances and submit requests.[144] The height of power also seems to have brought out what Tavernier called the man's vindictiveness. This caused the downfall of a number of high officials, beginning with the darughah of Isfahan, Mir Qasim Beg.[145] Their enmity went back to the days when Muhammad Beg was controller of assay and had its origin in the theft of some gold vessels from the royal kitchen. For this, Mir Qasim Beg had imprisoned some of Isfahan's goldsmiths, who had had no part in the act. The goldsmiths had turned to Muhammad Beg, who succeeded in getting them released but in the process was humiliated by Mir Qasim Beg. His chance for revenge came when he became grand vizier. Counting on Mir Qasim Beg's greediness, Muhammad Beg persuaded the shah to charge the darughah with the recruitment of soldiers from Isfahan and environs to meet Mughal aggression on the southeastern border. He next accused Mir Qasim Beg of taking bribes from peasants in return for draft exemptions, thus causing him to be hanged in the royal square.¹⁴⁶

Mir Qasim Beg's demise apparently did not sate Muhammad Beg's thirst for revenge. Angry that the shah had not ordered the confiscation of his goods, he plotted further conflict, involving both Mir Qasim Beg's successor, the ghulam Farsadan (Gorgijanidze), and the country's divanbegi or Chief Justice, Ughurlu Beg.¹⁴⁷ The grand vizier apparently encouraged the newly appointed Farsadan to enrich himself through bribery and extortion, in hopes of showing that, if a venal official like him could amass substantial wealth in such a short period, Mir Qasim Beg must have pocketed fantastic amounts of money during his thirty years in office. Farsadan duly followed Muhammad Beg's advice. Before long, however, his harsh regime got him embroiled with his superior, the divanbegi, following complaints about Farsadan's oppression of the people of Isfahan and in particular the city's craftsmen. The divanbegi, an enemy of the darughah, took the side of the people and even had a hand in the rioting that ensued. Muhammad Beg, seeing his plans thwarted by the divanbegi, thereupon arranged to make the unrest look like a threat to security. He implicated the divanbegi in fomenting the riots and convinced the shah to have Ughurlu Beg blinded.¹⁴⁸

Muhammad Beg eventually managed to rid himself of all his adversaries.¹⁴⁹ At least four provincial governors, Mirza Hadi of Fars, Nazir 'Ali Khan Süglün of Ardabil, Qurkhmas Khan of Marv, and, probably, Muhammad Quli Khan of Yerevan, lost their jobs as a result of his scheming.¹⁵⁰ At the top of his game, Muhammad Beg now went out of his way to bamboozle the shah into granting him a virtual monopoly over state affairs, even allowing the ruler access to his own harem. The shah took to spending most of his time either in the inner palace or on hunting outings and drinking parties, while his grand vizier managed the affairs of state without consulting the other members of the state council.¹⁵¹ Muhammad Beg also kept his master in good spirits by hiding unpleasant news from him. He thus failed to inform 'Abbas about the defeat of his forces in the north, including the loss of 12,000 men, concealing the letters with the news to that effect sent by the commander-in-chief, Allah Virdi Khan. Instead, he reported great military successes and ordered preparations for a "sumptuous show," to be paid for by the inhabitants of Isfahan. He kept the cost of the spectacle, a reported 20,000 tumans, hidden from the shah, telling his master that the expense would be no more than 300 tumans, a sum which he claimed the city's inhabitants were only too happy to raise.¹⁵²

In the process, Muhammad Beg seems to have lost sight of the fact that not even the grand vizier could afford to neglect the cultivation of political alliances. Naturally, none were more upset by his behavior than those who had assisted him in his rise to power. And among the disgruntled no one was more prominent than Allah Virdi Khan, now his most bitter enemy and the only serious competitor for the shah's favor. Allah Virdi Khan believed Muhammad Beg owed him deference on account of the past; Muhammad Beg demanded respect from Allah Virdi Khan as a subordinate.[153]

Muhammad Beg's dismissal in 1661 is the story of a failed attempt to marginalize his main rival.[154] He apparently persuaded the shah to expedite Allah Virdi Khan in the latter's new capacity as qullar-aqasi to Yerevan, where a rumored uprising had broken out. Finding no evidence of unrest upon his arrival in Armenia, Allah Virdi Khan asked the shah for permission to return to Isfahan with his soldiers. Muhammad Beg, presumably intercepting the messages coming from Armenia, convinced Shah 'Abbas that circumstances required him to keep the qullar-aqasi and his troops at the borders for a while longer. When Allah Virdi Khan finally managed to bypass the grand vizier in his communication with the shah, the latter found out how his chief minister had deceived him. Only his genuine affection for Muhammad Beg is said to have kept 'Abbas from having him executed; instead, he sent him and his family to Qum "to pray for the eternal well-being of the shah."[155] The post of grand vizier was given to Sayyid Mirza Muhammad Mahdi, like Khalifah Sultan a member of the ulama, who continued in his function until his death in 1669.

Muhammad Beg's dismissal and exile did not relegate him to oblivion, or even spell the end of his career. Many, the VOC agent insisted, missed this competent administrator. The Dutch, who claimed that Muhammad Beg's dismissal was widely seen as a loss, had good reason to be unhappy with the transfer of power. His fiscal vigilance notwithstanding, Muhammad Beg had usually abetted them in their clandestine export of gold—in return for a handsome reward, to be sure. They also appreciated him for his energy and can-do attitude. The shah himself, the VOC director maintained, at times complained that none of his courtiers measured up to Muhammad Beg, whose administrative and military skills had no equal in the entire country. Meanwhile, Shah 'Abbas must have been unhappy with Allah Virdi Khan, the instigator of the grand vizier's dismissal, for in 1662 he is said to have treated him to a flogging.[156] Everyone expected that, sooner or later, Muhammad Beg would be called back to serve again.[157]

Muhammad Beg was indeed asked once more to serve the shah, albeit by Shah Sulayman, 'Abbas II's successor. A partial rehabilitation took the form of an appointment as governor of Astarabad, in 1666 or 1667. Some five years later, Muhammad Beg had a second chance to rise to the top. In 1672 grand vizier Shaykh 'Ali Khan fell out of grace. Shah Sulayman dismissed him and summoned Muhammad Beg to Isfahan. He was never able to prove his administrative skill again, however, for he died en route. Commenting on his sudden death, Chardin noted that everyone believed that Muhammad Beg had been poisoned by the current grand vizier, Shaykh 'Ali Khan. The grieving shah did not leave his palace for five days after he received the news.[158]

MIRZA MUHAMMAD MAHDI, 1661–9

Muhammad Beg's successor, Mirza Muhammad Mahdi, was appointed grand vizier on 11 March 1661.[159] A descendant of the famous Shaykh 'Ali al-Karaki, the highest ranking *alim* (cleric) under Shah Tahmasb, he was a member of the so-called 'Amili clerics who in the sixteenth century had migrated in large numbers to Iran from Lebanon. Before his appointment as grand vizier, he had been *mutavalli* (supervisor) of the shrine of Qum, as well as sadr-i mamalik.[160]

It remains unclear why Shah 'Abbas II chose Mirza Muhammad Mahdi as his new grand vizier, other than on account of a satisfactory performance as sadr and perhaps because he was well integrated into the ruling elite, being a brother of Isfahan's shaykh al-islam, with one of his sons having married a daughter of Khalifah Sultan in 1651.[161] Abu Talib Musavi Findiriski, who insists that Shah 'Abbas was not in the habit of consulting with any of his courtiers about appointments, also claims that Mirza Muhammad Mahdi was a surprise choice, since he was not on anyone's list of candidates for the position.[162] Regardless of the shah's motives, once appointed, the new grand vizier proved to be sluggish and impractical, at least according to the Dutch, who called him a man of inaction.[163] Floor makes a valiant effort to rehabilitate Mirza Muhammad Mahdi, but almost all the examples he adduces suggest that he was rather weak, certainly compared with his immediate predecessor and, as will be seen in the next chapter, his direct successor as well. In their sparing references to him, both the Persian sources and foreign reports suggest that Mirza Mahdi had a minor role in the executive affairs of the administration. He seems to have played second fiddle to Zaman

Beg and especially to Maqsud Beg, who was appointed nazir in 1664. In later years, his power also trailed that of the *tufangchi-aqasi* (head of the musketeers), the formidable Budaq Sultan, as well as that of the qullar-aqasi, Jamshid Khan.[164] He seems to have been marginal to some of the turmoil that marked the last years of Shah ʿAbbas II's rule, when first qurchibashi Murtaza Quli Khan Qajar was decapitated in 1663 and next his candidate-successor, Haydar Beg, also lost his life on the orders of the shah.[165] Even the cautiousness with which he interacted with the monarch can be interpreted as the pusillanimity of an official reluctant to carve out a profile for himself. This is all the more striking since precisely in this period Shah ʿAbbas II, already given to various forms of carousing, freely delegated power, creating a wide berth of agency for major courtiers.[166] How much of an outsider Mirza Mahdi really was was revealed upon Shah ʿAbbas II's death in 1666, at which point he expressed ignorance about the existence of the eldest son of the deceased ruler, Sam Mirza—the one who ended up succeeding ʿAbbas as Safi II, to be renamed Sulayman. "What do I know?" he famously is said to have responded to a query about the succession process. "I have no knowledge of what goes on in the interior of the palace."[167]

Chapter 3

Safavid Politics, II: Shahs, Grand Viziers, and Eunuchs, 1666–1699

هر کمالی را زوالی مودر است
و هربهاری را خریف مقرر

All perfection is surrounded by decline
And autumn is sure to follow every spring.
Mustawfi Bafqi, Jami`-i Mufidi, 3:226

DEVELOPMENTS AT THE COURT OF SHAH SULAYMAN, 1666–99

Mirza Muhammad Mahdi's self-professed ignorance about conditions in the inner palace suggests that there was nothing inevitable about the trend toward the greater visibility and influence of the *i`timad al-dawlah* (grand vizier). A chief minister's actual power naturally depended in part on the incumbent's personality and the strength of his rivals. The trend meanwhile was undermined by a decrease in communication between the *divan* administration and the *dargah*, the inner palace. That development, in turn, was intimately linked to the rise to prominence of the court eunuchs. Jean Chardin, reporting on the accession of Shah Safi II, `Abbas II's son and successor, in 1666, emphasized their pivotal role in the process. The eunuchs were the ones who arranged the transfer of power, delegating two from their ranks, Agha Mubarak, the *mihtar* (chamberlain), and Agha Kafur, the *khazanah-dar* (royal treasurer), to inform the court about the death of the shah and the name of his successor. Chardin, who received his information from a court eunuch and whose rendering of events is corroborated by the Persian-language sources, also recounts how the eunuchs were instrumental in the choice of the elder of the deceased shah's two sons, Safi, who had been born in 1647 to the Circassian concubine Nikahat Khanum. His father supposedly had favored the younger son, the seven-year-old Hamzah Mirza, whose mother was Georgian and who, in Chardin's words, displayed a certain nobility and generosity of character. As the Frenchman tells the story, the eunuchs, eager to have a pliable child on the throne and ready to believe the rumor that the deceased shah had blinded or even killed the older candidate, initially agreed on Hamzah Mirza. At this point, Agha Mubarak, Hamzah Mirza's *lalah* (tutor), stepped in. Going against his own interests and those of his fellow eunuchs, he made an eloquent plea in support of the elder son, accusing his colleagues of opting for the younger one for selfish reasons, so that they could rule unchecked. Safi, he argued, was alive *and* the worthier heir. Agha Mubarak's view prevailed. *Tufangchi-aqasi* Khusraw Khan, by reputation the least untrustworthy among the eunuchs, was chosen to go to Isfahan to notify the shah-elect before word of the death of Shah 'Abbas II would spread. Safi, who had been surrounded by women and eunuchs all his life, was next brought into the light, dazzled and unsure what to do with the awesome responsibility thrust upon him.[1]

Shah Safi II, as he was initially known, mounted the Safavid throne in the fall of 1666. Following a period of royal illness and natural disaster, which the astrologers attributed to an inauspicious date chosen for the initial enthronement, the shah went through a second inauguration a year and a half later. Taking the name Sulayman on that occasion, he would rule until his death in 1694. His reputation is that of a weak and erratically cruel ruler whose drug-addled insouciance and predilection for the pleasures of the harem caused a great deal of harm to the country. Jonas Hanway, visiting Iran a few decades after the fall of Isfahan, called Sulayman's reign "remarkable for nothing but a slavish indolence, a savage and inhuman cruelty."[2] Laurence Lockhart intones that "with such a king—one cannot say 'ruler'—on the throne, it was inevitable that the process of decay should become more manifest."[3] Shah Sulayman's reign became known in particular for its lack of events worth recording, which mostly means a lack of military exploits, to the point of not generating any known court chronicles.

Shah Sulayman may have been cruel and disengaged, but he should not be dismissed because he did not initiate any wars. He may, at times, have been more active than he is given credit for. Of the eleven *farmans* collected in Heribert Busse's compendium, seven were directly ordered by him; only four suggest the hand of the grand vizier.[4] Still, Sulayman clearly failed to project the kind of power expected from a Safavid ruler, and under him the link between the monarch and his subjects grew weaker. Most of his predecessors had been roving warriors, vigilant in patrolling their realm to quell internal uprisings and keep external enemies at bay. Even Shah ʿAbbas II lived up to this image in the first half of his reign. In keeping with nomadic traditions, early shahs had also been highly visible and approachable and, in the case of Shah ʿAbbas I, even informal in their governing style. Iranian rulers never completely lost the mobility involved in moving between winter and summer pastures; far into the nineteenth century they still preferred the open space of the steppe to the confinement of the city, frequently camping in tents outside its walls, in the extramural garden, *bagh*. But, as Iran made peace with the Ottomans, the court gradually ceased to be peripatetic. Shah ʿAbbas II still led an expedition to recover Qandahar from the Mughals; Sulayman and Sultan Husayn, by contrast, reigned as stationary monarchs. Aside from occasional hunting parties or pilgrimages, both preferred to live—invisible to all but the most intimate of their courtiers—ensconced in the palace in the heart of the capital, or in Hazar Jarib, the retreat that Shah ʿAbbas I had built in the suburb across the Zayandah Rud, or, in the case of Shah Sultan, in Farahabad, the pleasure garden that he designed toward the end of his reign. Hardly interested in administrative affairs, they relied on their grand viziers for the daily management of state business, while allowing the inner palace to obstruct these same viziers by granting its members ultimate decision-making power.[5]

THE RETREAT OF THE SHAH

The retreat of the shah from the public eye was a gradual process. Emblematic of diminishing royal accessibility was the growing incidence of *quruq*, the ban on adult male presence during royal outings, in the later Safavid period. Quruq was declared whenever the shah went out riding with his female retinue. No males aged over six were to be in the vicinity of the route taken by the shah. Not only were the streets cleared but all men had to vacate their homes and move to a different part of town for the duration of the shah's outing. A day prior to his event, so-called *quruqchi*s would ride through the streets announcing the outing. On the day itself, they would clear the streets hours before the visit. Any male person caught during the event risked execution on the spot.[6] With the exception of Shah ʿAbbas I, who occasionally mingled freely with his subjects, Safavid rulers generally appeared in public under quruq. Sulayman and Sultan Husayn practiced it with great frequency. Shah Sulayman especially was fond of going out riding with his female entourage. He is said to have engaged in sixty-two such excursions in the first five months of his reign, taking advantage of the freedom denied to him during long years of secluded harem life.[7]

Royal alienation took other forms as well. The retreat of the shah from public view limited the opportunity for people to make themselves heard in an orderly fashion. Known for his "melancholy disposition," Shah Tahmasb in the last years of his reign had lived within the confines of his palace, out of reach, leaving his subjects, now at the mercy of greedy subordinate officers, clamoring for royal justice.[8] Something similar happened under Shah Sulayman. In keeping with long-standing Irano-Islamic custom, the Safavids knew a system of public petitioning. This operated on different levels. Under Shah ʿAbbas I the vizier of Isfahan would ride around town a few times each week, ready to accept petitions from common people approaching him.[9] During Khalifah Sultan's tenure, the grand vizier himself was available for people to air their grievances. In 1655 Shah ʿAbbas II instituted a complaint system over which he presided himself. Three days a week were set aside for this: two days to collect complaints and to render justice, one of which was reserved for soldiers and ghulams and one for commoners, and one day to receive envoys and accept presents. In 1657 Muhammad Beg ended this petition system. At the outset of Sulayman's reign, the three days set aside for petitions were reduced to two.[10] The shah also developed the habit of not emerging from his palace for periods of up to twelve days, during which time he could not be approached with complaints.[11] Yet during the first fifteen years of his tenure it was still possible for people to accost Sulayman during his morning ride. In 1683 this access was formally abolished altogether. People seeking to approach the monarch as he left the palace were now shunted aside by cudgel-wielding officials.[12]

Equally deleterious was the increasingly meager stream of reliable information that reached the ruler's ears. To be surrounded by sycophants is, of course, the fate of rulers and especially despots of all times. Courtiers, naturally inclined to bamboozle the shah about the state of the country, were eager to proffer only positive news. We saw how Muhammad Beg failed to apprize Shah ʿAbbas II of a military defeat, opting instead to report success on the battlefield.[13] Sulayman, reared in the harem and endowed with scant natural curiosity, was particularly susceptible to this type of misinformation, and only reinforced it with his habit of punishing the bearers of unpleasant news. He would also switch topics whenever something came up that exceeded his intellectual abilities. The result was that courtiers only raised important issues with him when he was in good spirits, leaving him mostly unaware of existing problems in his realm, so that Sulayman ended up being entertained—by acrobats, ropewalkers, magicians, and wrestlers—rather than informed.[14]

Especially detrimental to bureaucratic efficiency was the decline in operational funds under Shah Sulayman. This manifested itself, among other things, in a reduction in the daily allowance granted to official representatives from abroad, the much celebrated *mihmandari*. Raphaël du Mans claims that, previously, mihmandari worth four times an envoy's actual expenses was allocated but that under Shah Sulayman foreigners received only a quarter of what they spent.[15] Another example of cost reduction was the shah's habit of leaving offices vacant on the death of their incumbents. Shah `Abbas II had already chosen not to appoint a *sadr-i khassah* at the end of his reign.[16] Sulayman assumed that function himself in 1680, and over time left several other posts open as well.[17] The post of *ishik-aqasi-yi divan* (royal chamberlain), for instance, remained unfilled for some time, during which the *divanbegi* (Chief Justice) took on his responsibilities. Notoriously avaricious, the shah pocketed the savings.[18]

Royal stinginess affected more than the treasury; it eroded loyalty among state officials. This diminished the ruler's standing, even if the grand vizier was often the one to bear the brunt. Ancient tradition mandated conspicuous royal consumption and generosity with gifts, titles, and tax breaks. Yet a country like Iran, low on reliable income, ultimately needed frugality. This necessity was built into the ancient formula as well, for it was one of the grand vizier's tasks to caution the ruler against profligacy. The blame for tightness at the top was thus often laid at his door. Just as the early eighteenth-century Mughal grand vizier Zu'l Fiqar Khan came to grief because of royal stinginess, so Shaykh `Ali Khan and, later, Fath `Ali Khan Daghistani owed their downfall in part to the opposition they encountered from frustrated officials who blamed the grand vizier for encouraging frugality in the shah's entourage.[19]

THE RISE OF THE PALACE EUNUCHS

Relatively little is known about the eunuchs in court circles. In charge of the harem, a realm by definition out of sight to all (male) observers, they remained invisible to the outside world. This is true of the white eunuchs, who guarded the entrance to the harem, and even more so of the black ones, who oversaw the palace interior. Eunuchs did not even have the right to sit in the presence of the shah during public ceremonies, at least not until the late seventeenth century.[20] The Persian-language sources barely mention their names, and we get mere glimpses of their activities from foreign observers who may have relied on inside informants but had no direct access to the inner palace. These report that the eunuchs were little liked, even despised.[21] Much antagonism seems to have existed between them and the tribal qurchis.[22] We also know that the number of eunuchs had steadily increased between early Safavid times and the mid-seventeenth century. Judasz Tadeusz Krusinski later claimed that the percentage of Iranians among them, small in the beginning, had also grown over time.[23] Under Shah ʿAbbas I, whose reign saw an influx of 100 Georgian eunuchs, their collective influence was apparently still relatively small.[24] Chardin relates how in the 1620s ʿAbbas had relegated a large number of "useless" eunuchs to a palace in Isfahan. Thirty years later, ʿAbbas II, learning that many were still alive, one night had the youngest ones killed, so that by 1667 only fifteen or sixteen survived.[25] It is clear, though, that some already wielded considerable influence in the late reign of Shah ʿAbbas I, among them Agha Hajji, the *ishik-aqasi-bashi-yi haram*, and *mirshikar-bashi* (master of the hunt), Yusuf Agha, the official of most consequence in the shah's inner palace.[26] Eunuchs also occupied sensitive positions under Shah Safi I. Prominent examples are Khajah Mahabbat, who served as *khazanah-dar* (treasurer), as well as the *rish-sifid-i haram*, the official in charge of all black eunuchs.[27] As shown by Mirza Muhammad "Saru" Taqi's success in having Khajah Mahabbat dismissed for financial impropriety, the eunuchs at this point did not yet have absolute power. This changed during the (later) reign of Shah ʿAbbas II when, growing in numbers, they turned into a major counterweight to the grand vizier.[28] By the 1670s the royal entourage is said to have included some 3,000 eunuchs, including 500 black ones.[29]

François Sanson insisted that the eunuchs held the most lucrative posts in the Safavid administration, explaining that since they had no heirs the fortunes accumulated by them would revert to the shah upon their death.[30] Two posts were particularly powerful. One was that of khazanah-dar. Nothing of financial import was done without his knowledge and participation. The grand vizier and the shah's secretary each month presented him with an account of state revenue and expenditure; the *nazir* did the same with regard to the outlays of the royal household.[31] The other was the mihtar, or royal chamberlain. Invariably a Georgian by birth, the mihtar served as the chief of the white eunuchs.[32] Referring to a prevailing stereotype about eunuchs, Du Mans claimed that mihtars tended to be exceedingly greedy and often amassed fantastic amounts of wealth during their time in office.[33] The mihtar's function as the shah's personal attendant gave him the royal ear, enabling him to wield great influence over the monarch himself, especially when the latter was a minor.[34] Never straying from the shah's side, he acted as the royal second food taster (the first one being the *tushmal-bashi*); he helped the shah dress and undress, handled his jewelry and ornaments, and carried the *hizar-pishah*, the huge wine receptacle used during royal drinking parties. His signature accoutrement was a small gold casket attached to his belt that contained several very fine kerchiefs in addition to a watch, seals, perfume, opium, and other cordials, as well as some of the shah's personal items, such as scissors, nail clippers, files, and needles.[35] The size of his annual salary, 4,890 *tumans* in late Safavid times, suggests the position's importance.[36]

At the time of Shah 'Abbas II, Mihtar Da'ud was among the most prominent court eunuchs. His brother 'Ivaz Beg long occupied the post of governor of Lar and later was appointed divanbegi and governor of Rasht. For most of the reign of Shah Sulayman the most influential eunuchs were Agha Mubarak, who served as mihtar, and Agha Kafur, who held the post of khazanah-dar. Both had served under Shah Safi and Shah 'Abbas II, and both were renowned for their cleverness and outstanding counsel. Agha Kafur especially became the shah's confidant, trusted for his discretion and appreciated for his common sense.[37] According to Engelbert Kaempfer, the influence of these two men reached such heights that Shah Sulayman would not decide on any issue of importance before consulting with them. Both died in old age in 1683 or 1684.[38] Subsequently Agha Kamal became the most powerful palace eunuch. Writing in 1691, Sanson claimed that at that time—when Sulayman was often ill and withdrawn—Agha Kamal was given total authority in matters of state.[39] He continued to be the most influential state official under Shah Sultan Husayn, maintaining this position until at least 1716.[40]

Already under Shah 'Abbas II, the eunuchs often worked at cross purposes with other government agents. As Jean Baptiste Tavernier put it, any of the decisions taken by the i'timad al-dawlah and the royal council during the day might be repealed at night by the eunuchs.[41] The situation worsened under Shah Sulayman, who, prompted by his mother, would consult the eunuchs about each and every issue. The queen-mother and the black eunuchs thus came to dominate the court, jealously guarding their influence and keen to prevent the shah from communicating with anyone but themselves. Shaykh `Ali Khan, for instance, dealt mostly with the eunuchs, turning now to Agha Kafur, now to Agha Mubarak. Toward the end of Sulayman's reign, when the shah was severely ill, the court eunuchs acted as the sole intermediaries between the ruler and the outside world.[42]

The institution of a privy council alongside the royal advisory council further increased their power. Composed of the queen-mother, the principal eunuchs, and the shah's favored female consorts, this assembly became the ultimate decision-making body. The grand vizier continued to head an advisory council composed of the state comptroller, *mustawfi al-mamalik*, the royal comptroller, *mustawfi khassah*, the *darughah-i daftar* (the keeper of the general register of revenues), the *vazir al-muli* (an official with unclear responsibilities), or the *darughah* (mayor of Isfahan), the *vazir-i khassah* (the keeper of the accounts of the king's household), and the *kalantar*.[43] But he and his colleagues were left in the dark about the operations of the privy council, even as it intervened in the affairs of state and at times overturned the decisions of the regular advisory council.[44] Each morning they were left to congregate in the *kishik-khanah*, a residence at the entrance of the seraglio, waiting for the shah to come out of the palace in hopes of being able to address him before he left on his morning ride.[45]

THE GRAND VIZIERATE OF SHAYKH `ALI KHAN ZANGANAH, 1669–89

Given Shah Sulayman's insularity and the inherent secrecy surrounding the inner court, the sources offer scant insight into its working. The way of circumventing this problem is to focus on the grand vizier, the official who straddled the dargah and the outer, more visible divan part of the court. For the reign of Shah Sulayman, this means examining the career of Shaykh `Ali Khan, who was appointed i`timad al-dawlah three years into the shah's reign, served him for a full twenty years, and in this period became one of the most remarkable administrators of Safavid times.[46]

Shaykh `Ali Khan Zanganah was born in 1611 or 1613 as a member of the prominent Kurdish Zanganah tribe.[47] His father, `Ali Beg Zanganah, was a "holder of the rein" (*jilawdar*) under Shah `Abbas I who in 1618 had moved up to the position of master of the king's stables (*amir-akhur-bashi*) and, under Shah Safi, had become a qurchi (a member of the tribal cavalry). Rising from the position of stable boy, Shaykh ʿAli Khan in 1639 succeeded his brother Shahrukh Sultan as amir-akhur-bashi, at which point the latter became amir of the Zanganah. On Shahrukh Sultan's death less than a year later, Shaykh ʿAli Khan took on his post again.[48] From 1653 onward, Shaykh ʿAli Khan served as khan and landholder (*tuyuldar*) of Kalhur, Sunqur, and Kirmanshah, the homeland of the Zanganah.[49] In this period he demonstrated his negotiating skills by successfully mediating a conflict between the Lurs and their newly appointed leader, Manuchihr Khan. Over the years he must have acquired a reputation as a competent military commander as well, for in 1666 Shah ʿAbbas II called him with a contingent of the Zanganah to Isfahan and sent him as a military commander (*sardar*) to Khurasan with the task of putting a halt to Uzbek border raids.[50]

ʿAbbas II's death later that year and the enthronement of Sulayman did nothing to interrupt Shaykh ʿAli Khan's political career. On the contrary, the new shah in 1668 called him back to Isfahan, and, clearly impressed with his military competence, appointed him *tufangchi-aqasi* (head of the musketeers). In June 1669, finally, Shaykh ʿAli Khan succeeded the deposed Muhammad Mirza Mahdi as grand vizier.[51]

THE HEIGHT OF POWER

Shaykh ʿAli Khan's appointment as grand vizier must be placed in the context of the severe crisis that plagued the Safavid state in the mid- to late 1660s, when parts of the country suffered multiple bad harvests followed by outbreaks of famine and plague. A poor harvest in 1666, caused by widespread drought and locust swarms, followed by another meager yield in 1667, made provisions in Isfahan grow extremely scarce. Hoarding by bakers and grain merchants caused prices to go up nearly threefold, driving the urban population to penury. Conditions in the capital further worsened when, following the shah's enthronement, the court returned to the city before adequate measures had been taken for provisioning the huge numbers of people involved.[52]

The insolvency of the government, compounded by the effects of natural disaster, was brought into stark relief during Sulayman's enthronement. Setting the tone for his future legitimacy, the accession of a new shah entailed a hugely expensive display of panoply—including the actual ceremony as well as tax remissions designed to buy popular support. Involving two coronations, the inauguration of Shah Sulayman put a particularly onerous burden on the taxpaying population. This flux of famine and royal extravagance coincided with a series of military threats to Iran's borders. Uzbeks from Central Asia as well as Kalmyks and Cossacks from the steppes of South Russia—the latter led by the notorious rebel Sten'ka Razin—took advantage of the power vacuum caused by 'Abbas II's death to put pressure on the northern flank.[53] The Cossacks in particular did great damage in the lands around the Caspian Sea, ravaging the southern littoral, Iran's most productive silk-growing area, where they destroyed Shah 'Abbas's winter capital, Farahabad.[54]

The heightened military alertness this unrest necessitated depressed the income derived from landed property known as *tuyuls*. Tuyuls, assignments of land or its revenue to individuals in return for service to the crown, usually in the form of providing troops, were officially granted for limited periods but in practice tended to become hereditary. Since the late sixteenth century a great deal of land thus alienated had been reappropriated as crown land (*khassah*). This process culminated under Shah 'Abbas II but saw a partial reversal at the end of the same ruler's reign, when the need for troops to counter the tribal threat in the north forced the state to reassign some territory as tuyuls. This renewed alienation of land, which continued into Shah Sulayman's reign, naturally depressed royal income. Faced with a depleted treasury shortly after her son's accession, the queen-mother is said to have persuaded him to transform his spendthrift habits into a policy of parsimony.[55]

Shaykh 'Ali Khan immediately embarked on a financial policy that combined cutting expenses with increasing revenue. Among the first problems he tackled was that of the tuyuls, which he set out to reappropriate for the crown. He also sought to rationalize the bureaucracy that oversaw the supply of silk from the Caspian provinces to the capital.[56] He thus decreed a stricter observation of the annual silk supply to the VOC, demanding that the northern governors supply the full quota of 600 bales to the Dutch and forcing the latter to take whatever amount was actually delivered in Isfahan.[57] Other trade-related measures taken by Shaykh 'Ali Khan included attempts to extend state control over sugar, an important commodity used in great quantity by the populace, and the institution of a 5 percent tax on all bullion that merchants carried to the Persian Gulf coast with the aim of shipping it to India. New taxes were imposed on the churches in New Julfa and the Armenian villages surrounding Isfahan. Tolls went up, too. Traditionally, merchants, aside from having to pay minor fees to *rahdars* (road toll takers), were charged road tolls only at the country's entrance and exit points. In 1671, a 5 percent toll was instituted on merchandise leaving Isfahan.[58]

In all this Shaykh ʿAli Khan displayed a remarkable degree of diligence. Categorically refusing to indulge in the common practice of accepting bribes, he soon became known for his incorruptibility.[59] Kaempfer insists that the vizier never relented in his uncompromising stand vis-à-vis bribery.[60] It is true that few of his fiscal projects were wholly successful. Most foundered on the strength of vested landed and commercial interests or the ingenuity of private subterfuge. Shaykh ʿAli Khan nevertheless appears to have been highly effective in collecting revenue for the royal treasury. He also garnered tremendous power in the process; less than a year after his installation, he was said to be in sole charge of the affairs of state.[61] Nothing illustrated this better than the departure for Mecca of his main rival, Maqsud Beg, the nazir, who had been a major power broker in the last years of Shah ʿAbbas II's reign. Maqsud Beg was temporarily replaced by his nephew, Najaf Quli Beg, but everyone saw the shah's authorization of the nazir's journey for what it was—a sign of Shaykh ʿAli Khan's ascendancy.[62]

OPPOSITION AND FALL FROM GRACE

Shaykh ʿAli Khan did not enjoy his unchallenged power for long. In the spring of 1672, less than three years after his appointment, the news broke that the grand vizier had fallen out of grace with the shah, who had ordered him to stay in his palace.[63] The story of the dismissal is told in more than one version, but centers on one of Shah Sulayman's periodic outbursts of anger involving the vizier's refusal to drink wine in his presence.[64]

Shaykh ʿAli Khan's formal removal from office was relatively brief; he was reinstated in June 1673. Yet it had immediate and long-lasting repercussions for the conduct of government. One observer spoke of a country in turmoil following the events at the court culminating in Shaykh ʿAli Khan's dismissal. In 1672, one of his sons took refuge with the Ottomans, suggesting the precariousness of the former vizier's position.[65] The immediate effect was a severe interruption in the execution of daily government under the officials who took over from him: commander of the musketeers Khusraw Khan and state treasurer Mirza Sadiq. Some of his policies were also reversed. The 5 percent fee on money transported from Isfahan fell into disuse, as did the tax on drawing bills of exchange. The tuyul reform may have been aborted in this period as well. However, Isfahan's Armenians continued to pay their additional taxes.

Shaykh ʿAli Khan's removal resonated beyond his rehabilitation in other ways as well. He resumed his duties as soon as he was back in the shah's favor, though in a manner that was a far cry from his earlier performance. He now shunned responsibilities, and procrastinated in managing the state affairs that he had formerly expedited so promptly. Most disastrously, his former self-assuredness had given way to insecurity. He never again seems to have performed the grand vizier's quintessential task of informing the shah about the true state of the country. Shaykh ʿAli Khan's diffidence and restraint, best reflected in his new habit of handing over requests to Sulayman without unsealing and reading them himself first, naturally hampered the speed and efficiency of day-to-day politics. Many who came to the court for business were subjected to long periods of idle waiting before receiving attention, ran out of means in the process, and had to return home unsuccessful.[66]

There were good reasons for the prudence Shaykh ʿAli Khan henceforth displayed, for the dignified minister continued to be exposed to the shah's whimsical behavior. In particular, his persistent refusal to drink alcohol periodically provoked the monarch's wrath and mockery, leading to humiliating scenes of forced drinking. Most unsettling was the inconsistency in Sulayman's behavior, with instances of cruelty alternating with demonstrations of remorse: after a night of gross insult, the shah would frequently offer his minister a robe of honor as a token of appreciation for his services.[67]

Shaykh ʿAli Khan's aversion to ostentation and his lack of venality were uncommon traits in Safavid government circles. He disliked astrology and fortune-telling—a rare attitude at a court whose ruler led his life according to the forecasts of his astrologers. Known for his simple ways of dressing and eating, the vizier, who was married to only one wife, also led a strictly ordered life.[68] All of this may have filled the shah with admiration mixed with jealousy, offering a partial explanation for his erratic treatment of the chief minister. Sulayman certainly did not skimp on expenses when it came to his own entertainment. In 1683 the shah organized a hunting trip that lasted from May until late July. Rumor had it that it cost the staggering (and no doubt exaggerated) amount of 200,000 tumans and the lives of some 800 people who perished from exposure and lack of food during the drive.[69] But psychology alone does not explain Shaykh ʿAli Khan's dismissal and the precariousness of his position after his rehabilitation. We also need to consider issues of social status, of factionalism based on tribe and kin, vested interests among courtiers, and the changing political order in the late Safavid state. The first issue concerns Shaykh ʿAli Khan's Kurdish background and presumed religious affiliation, which reflect a Safavid tendency to recruit officials from a wide pool of talent—for reasons that combine considerations of merit and intended vulnerability. The Kurds suffered a reputation in metropolitan circles that went well beyond a general urban bias against rustics and mountain dwellers.⁷⁰ Kaempfer claimed that the "Iranians" made a clear racial distinction between themselves and the Kurds, whom they considered stubborn, morose, and treacherous.⁷¹ Shaykh ʿAli Khan's rise from the ranks of a group with a pejorative reputation is aptly captured in the mocking verse:

رفته رفته قشو قلمدان شد
شیخ علی خان وزیر ایران شد

Gradually the horse comb became a pen box
Shaykh ʿAli Khan became Iran's chief minister⁷²

Kurdistan was not only marginal but also mostly Sunni, and Shaykh ʿAli Khan was widely suspected of being a crypto-Sunni. If true, this is likely to have played a role in his strict observance of Islamic law, including his refusal to drink alcohol. His zeal in this expressed itself in measures such as a prohibition on the Armenian fur cap makers of Isfahan working in the city's royal square, as well as the imposition of a new church tax on the Armenian community of New Julfa, earning him the reputation of being a "grimme and seveare man espetially to Christians whom he greatly hates."⁷³ Yet he also put pressure on Zoroastrians in villages around Isfahan to convert to Islam, suggesting that he was less anti-Christian than favorably disposed to Islam.⁷⁴ Indeed, the extraordinary piety Shaykh ʿAli Khan displayed may be interpreted as the concern of an official from a non-Shiʿi region suspected of harboring Sunnite sentiments to emphasize his religious conformism by strictly abiding by the letter of the religious law.⁷⁵ His enemies, in turn, are likely to have used every possible opportunity for innuendo on this sensitive point.

Shaykh ʿAli himself meanwhile made his own enemies. Sanson called attention to his tendency to engage in divide-and-rule tactics.⁷⁶ This strategy was common, and increasingly involved Georgians and other people from the Caucasus, Daghistanis and Circassians, whose number in Isfahan alone reached an estimated 20,000 by the time of Sulayman's reign.⁷⁷ It often took the form of appointments of Georgian officials to provinces inhabited by non-Georgians. An example of the resulting tensions occurred in 1674, when the people of Luristan revolted against Shah Virdi Khan, a Georgian governor who had been imposed on them.[78] Suggesting that animosity existed between the vizier and the Georgians, Chardin recounts how Shah Sulayman humiliated Shaykh `Ali Khan by forcing him to shave his beard, which he was said to wear distinctly different from the short "Georgian" fashion popular with most courtiers.

Problems also arose over Georgia, where the proconsul of Kartli, Shahnavaz I (Vakhtang V), sought to balance Safavid control with Russian protection. Shaykh `Ali Khan, who allegedly harbored a grudge against Shahnavaz for having refused the shah his daughter Anusa in marriage, reacted by calling his loyalty to the Safavid crown into question. He next plotted to incite civil war in Georgia, inviting Prince Erekle of Kakhet'i, a rival claimant to the throne of Georgia who had fled to Moscow, to return from exile. Capitalizing on the power vacuum following Shahnavaz's death in 1676, the vizier fostered renewed unrest in Georgia with the aim of bringing it under full Safavid control.[79]

Shaykh `Ali Khan's animus toward Georgians comes out in other ways as well. Giovanni Gemelli Careri tells the story of a conflict between the grand vizier and the Georgian governor of Azerbaijan, Bizhan Beg, who was the son of the former *sipahsalar*, Rustam Khan, and an uncle of the divanbegi and the current sipahsalar, also called Rustam Khan. The family, Gemelli Careri noted, had always been among the shah's favorites, but Bizhan Beg had fallen into disgrace during the tenure of Shaykh `Ali Khan, who had made him suspect with Sulayman by claiming he was a madman and a drunkard. It was, the Italian concluded, only through the intercession of Bizhan Beg's powerful nephew that the shah could finally be convinced of the governor's sanity.[80]

Distrust and discord in Isfahan expressed themselves along the lines of tribe and kinship, but were underpinned by divergent individual political and economic interests. High-ranking officials, among them ghulams, had good reasons to resent Shaykh `Ali Khan, for the frugality he imposed on the court hurt all those whose income depended on royal largesse. As Chardin put it, courtiers were poor as long as the shah was not liberal in his personal spending habits.[81] In their capacity as landholders, moreover, they must also have felt threatened by the vizier's attempts to reconvert the tuyuls whose revenues they enjoyed. Their disgruntlement most likely played a major role in Shaykh `Ali Khan's disgrace and might explain why, on his dismissal, some of his policy initiatives were rescinded.

Resentment in court circles would have posed a serious threat to Shaykh `Ali Khan's position under any circumstances. Yet it might not have led to his disgrace and marginalization without the profound change in government that occurred in this period, with power increasingly shifting from the chancery to the royal domain and, within the latter, to the inner palace. One manifestation of this trend—and one that involved Shaykh ʿAli Khan—was the shift of control over the treasury away from the chancery. This was seen in the conflict between the vizier and Mirza Razi, comptroller of the royal domain (mustawfi khassah), in the 1680s. Whereas European travel accounts present an ambiguous picture of the precise function and authority of the mustawfi khassah, the *Tadhkirat al-muluk* indicates that he remained formally subordinate to the grand vizier, who appointed him. The case of Mirza Razi, however, suggests that the formal status of a bureaucratic position cannot automatically be taken as an index of its real power and prestige. Mirza Razi became one of the shah's favorites, and his authority in financial affairs, which overlapped with that of the grand vizier, began to exceed that of the latter.[82] He was the official who handled the Dutch silk payments to the court in 1682.[83] Their rivalry inevitably led to mutual slander. Shaykh ʿAli Khan thus accused the treasurer of having accepted money from the European maritime companies and having conspired with them against him.[84] When Mirza Razi, in good health, suddenly died in 1684, rumor had it that he had been poisoned by Shaykh ʿAli Khan.[85]

THE MAINTENANCE OF POWER

Communication between the shah and members of the divan did not improve during the second decade of Shaykh ʿAli Khan's tenure as grand vizier. On the contrary, in late 1679 and early 1680 Sulayman struck new fears into the hearts of his state officials by treating Shaykh ʿAli Khan and the nazir, Najaf Quli Beg, to the bastinado and by blinding the divanbegi, Zaynal Khan. Najaf Quli Beg was so intimidated by these latest events that he no longer attended to state affairs and requested permission to undertake the pilgrimage to Mecca.[86] In early 1681 Shaykh ʿAli Khan himself reportedly joined the nazir in asking the shah for permission to perform the hajj.[87] He never left Isfahan. The reason why his request had been rejected—if he indeed made such a request—remains unknown.

Despite this continued insecurity and his limited contact with the shah, now mostly confined to joint evening horseback rides, Shaykh ʿAli Khan managed to maintain himself in his high post until his death in 1689.[88] Not only that, but in the early 1680s, a period when many high posts fallen vacant in earlier years were left unfilled, the vizier's stock seems to have risen again. The nazir was all but dismissed in 1682–3[89] and, aside from Mirza Razi, the only significant rival in the divan administration he was to face in his last years was qurchibashi Saru Khan Sahandlu. Appointed mint master as well in 1682, this official temporarily eclipsed Shaykh `Ali Khan and survived the vizier in his position as qurchibashi, only to come to an ignominious end himself in 1691.[90]

Shaykh `Ali Khan's remarkable staying power in the face of formidable opposition raises a number of questions. The first, Shah Sulayman's personal motives for sparing his life, may be attributed to the shah's alleged promise not to kill a vizier who had performed the hajj. What prompted the shah to reinstate his vizier may have been his own lack of ambition. Unlike his predecessors, Shah Sulayman never usurped direct executive power by getting rid of the most ambitious of his courtiers. Following his reinstatement, Shaykh `Ali Khan, in turn, was careful never again to antagonize his master. In 1684, for instance, he chose to present the news of a bloody Uzbek raid in Khurasan to the shah as an Iranian victory.[91] Sheer common sense may have been another reason for Sulayman to reinstate his competent minister. The Dutch were not alone in believing that Shaykh `Ali's authority guaranteed peace and stability in the country.[92] When in 1675 the shah mistreated Shaykh `Ali Khan, qurchibashi Kalb `Ali Khan, who was known as one of his enemies, pleaded for his life, arguing that the entire country would be thrown into turmoil if the grand vizier were to die.[93] Shaykh `Ali Khan's track record in fiscal matters must have been especially compelling. Clearly, no inner council could match his efficiency and effectiveness in raising revenue. Barely three weeks after his reinstatement, the vizier confirmed the validity of the church tax that he had imposed on the Armenians of New Julfa shortly after his initial appointment.[94] Shaykh `Ali Khan also kept sending tax collectors to outlying regions. Time and again his officials visited Kirman with demands for revenue, imposing fines for sums in arrears. In 1683, one of his men was sent with the task of conducting a census of the Zoroastrians living in the city so that the poll tax to be paid by them could be accurately assessed.[95] Shaykh `Ali Khan's continued efforts to fill the shah's coffers appear to have been very successful. The Dutch in 1682 claimed an increase of the royal treasury by 150,000 tumans under Shaykh `Ali Khan's vizierate, attributing most of it to the absence of war and the resulting lack of high military expenditure.[96] Writing shortly before Sulayman's death, Sanson echoed this opinion by insisting that 50,000 *livres* (more than 1,100 tumans) accrued to the treasury each day.[97]

Shaykh ʿAli Khan's political survival did not hinge solely upon his service to the crown. Equally important was his shrewdness in catering to his private interests, his integrity in public financial matters notwithstanding. These centered on his ancestral homeland, more specifically Kirmanshah and Hamadan, where he managed *vaqf* (religiously endowed) property.[98] He is said to have sabotaged a plan to irrigate the plain of Isfahan by connecting the waters of the Zayandah Rud with those of the Karun River for fear that the fertility of the Isfahan region would come at the detriment of the produce from the many villages he himself possessed around Kirmanshah and Hamadan.[99] Most significantly, Shaykh ʿAli Khan followed the strategy by means of which every official of high rank solidified his post: he filled key functions with his own clients, relatives, and tribesmen. Unsurprisingly, Kirmanshah remained under his family's control. In 1666, as Shaykh ʿAli Khan was appointed sardar, army commander, Husayn ʿAli Khan succeeded his father as the area's *beglerbeg*. In 1667–8 Sulayman Khan, another of Shaykh ʿAli Khan's sons, acceded to this position again. In the 1680s the region was ruled by Shaykh ʿAli Khan's third son, Shah Quli Khan, who was to become qurchibashi in 1692 and grand vizier under Shah Sultan Husayn.[100]

We are well informed about the numerous other relatives Shaykh ʿAli Khan managed to appoint to prominent political positions. When he became grand vizier in 1669, his function as tufangchi-aqasi was taken over by one of his sons.[101] This was only the first of a series of strategic appointments based on kinship. By 1679 the vizier had been in power long enough to have built a solid network of family members in high-ranking positions across the country. VOC director Casembroot gives a figure of twenty-five to thirty.[102] Kaempfer claimed that a large segment of the country's administration was in the hands of the Shaykh ʿAli Khan clan.[103] Some of its members held rank from earlier dates or changed posts over time. His brother Najaf Quli Beg, for example, had been beglerbeg of Qandahar under ʿAbbas II, later fell into disgrace and was imprisoned, but rose again to become *vali* (governor) of Marv shortly after Sulayman's accession and coinciding with his brother's appointment to the rank of grand vizier.[104] Some held sensitive posts in the hierarchy. An unnamed relative was assayer of the mint (*muʿayyir al-mamalik*) in the late 1680s. There is also the unspecified relative Dust ʿAli Khan, possibly his second son, who in 1645 had received Khʷaf and Bakharz in Khurasan as a tuyul and in 1648 was reportedly made ruler (*hakim*) of the Garmsir.[105] The Dutch director, possibly referring to Ibrahim Beg, mentions a nephew of the vizier as occupying the post of "murason bassa" (*amir-akhur-bashi?*).[106] Kaempfer refers to Hajji `Ali Khan, another nephew, as beglerbeg of Azerbaijan, and as sardar at the head of 20,000 troops who provided security at the borders of Turkey and Georgia.[107] The same person also served as tufangchi-aqasi.[108] The vizier's eldest son, `Abbas Beg, appears as the amir-shikar-bashi.[109] Several later sources, on the other hand, mention Husayn `Ali Khan, another of the vizier's sons and possibly the second eldest, as becoming beglerbeg of Bihbahan and Kuh-i Giluyah in 1675–6. Khatunabadi, in addition, mentions Isma`il Beg as a son of Shaykh `Ali Khan who attained the military rank of centurion (*yuzbashi*). His youngest son, `Abbas Quli Beg, was said to be the police chief (darughah) and governor of the city of Qazvin.[110]

Lastly, there is a clear connection between Shaykh `Ali Khan and the prominence of Kurds in high administrative posts in the 1670s. Kalb `Ali Khan, the ruler of Kurdistan under Shah `Abbas II, may have owed his appointment as qurchibashi in 1672 to Shaykh `Ali Khan, even if the two became enemies at a later date. Two of Kalb `Ali Khan's sons, Shah Virdi Khan and Khan Ahmad Beg, became the governor and darughah, respectively, of Kirman. That city in particular saw a great influx of Kurdish officials, appointed to high positions or sent as tax collectors.[111] This network helped Shaykh `Ali Khan to retain far more influence than his low public profile and apparent lack of preoccupation with state affairs would suggest. Relying on his ties and contacts in the provinces, he remained the official "on whom the entire administration of the realm rests."[112]

In 1689 Shaykh `Ali Khan fell ill. Sanson expressed how much, in spite of everything, the vizier had managed to stay in command until his last days when he said that "the entire country languished with the vizier, for no one is able to take over the management of affairs during his illness."[113] In the autumn of the same year he died a natural death.[114] Terribly upset at the passing of the grand vizier he had mistreated so badly, Shah Sulayman did not leave his palace or even mount a horse for a full year.[115] Nor did he immediately appoint a successor, most likely in an attempt to save money.[116]

POWER AT THE COURT, 1689–99

It took Shah Sulayman one and a half years to decide on a successor to Shaykh `Ali Khan. In March 1691 the position of grand vizier was given to Mirza Muhammad Tahir Vahid Qazvini, a renowned bureaucrat with an illustrious career as court registrar, *vaqa'i`-nivis*, a position that had long been in his family.[117]

Following Tahir Vahid's appointment, the shah presented him with a full hizar pishah, and subsequently made him explain what he considered to be the most urgent needs of the country. Tahir Vahid responded by listing four pressing issues: 1) the pay of Iran's soldiers, 2) monetary reform, 3) the filling of vacant positions, and 4) the regeneration of trade. In response, the shah granted his new grand vizier full and unprecedented executive powers.[118]

In spite of his excellent credentials and his perspicacious analysis of the country's major problems, Tahir Vahid proved to be of lesser standing than his predecessor. His advanced age—he was about seventy when he was appointed—and attendant lack of energy account in part for this. He also proved to be extraordinarily venal, even by the standards of the time. Several eyewitnesses commented on this trait, among them the Dutch, who, faced with this magistrate during negotiations, were forced to hand him and his vizier, his son-in-law Mirza Yahya, the substantial present of 1,250 ducats before he would make any concessions to them.[119] Under Tahir Vahid, and really until the tenure of Fath `Ali Khan Daghistani (1715–20), the position of the i`timad al-dawlah was temporarily eclipsed by other high-ranking officials, suggesting once again that there was nothing inherent about the rise of the grand vizier in the face of a weakening shah: the field was open to any high official who could build enough of a power base by currying favor with the ruler while keeping his rivals at bay. Tahir Vahid had many rivals, among them the sipahsalar and the ishik-aqasi-bashi.[120] Yet none was as formidable as the qurchibashi, Saru Khan Sahandlu (in office 1682–91), who was close in age to Tahir Vahid and whose father, Murtaza Quli Khan Sa`dlu, had been qurchibashi himself in the early 1670s.[121] Aside from controlling the Qurchis, Saru Khan served as governor of Hamadan, Simnan, and Khurasan, held Kazirun as a tuyul, and in 1682 had been appointed mu`ayyir al-mamalik as well.[122] In the latter capacity he was in charge of the mint reform discussed in the next chapter. Already a formidable player—and a major adversary of the grand vizier—during Shaykh `Ali Khan's last years in office, Saru Khan rose to become the dominant courtier after the latter's death in 1689.

When Sanson claimed that the qurchibashi used to be of higher standing than the grand vizier, in reference to the relationship between Tahir Vahid and Saru Khan, he implicitly explained why, as grand vizier, Tahir Vahid figures so sparingly in the surviving sources.[123] The office of qurchibashi officially trailed that of the grand vizier, though not by much. In the *Tadhkirat al-muluk* he is called one of the most important pillars of the state, the senior officer of all the tribes, responsible for appointing valis, governors, yuzbashis, and sultans, and assigning tuyuls and the salaries of the qurchis.[124] He was one of the four officers who were always present at the shah's side.[125] The qurchibashi had long been an important official. If anything, he only became more important in the course of the seventeenth century, belying the notion that the Qizilbash had become a spent force.[126] `Isa Khan and Jani Khan are good examples of this, as is Murtaza Quli Khan Bigdili Shamlu (in office 1645/6–8), whom the Dutch called the "third person of the realm," and Saru Khan's father, who also served as sipahsalar.

The diary of Dutch ambassador Van Leene, written in 1691, makes clear that Saru Khan effectively ranked not third but first in the administration. Shah Sulayman's favor was of crucial importance in this. In 1690 Shah Quli Khan, the governor of Kirmanshah, complained that Saru Khan had disgraced the name of his late father, Shaykh `Ali Khan, by killing up to forty members of his family.[127] This is no doubt what Sanson meant when he said that Shah Sulayman loved Saru Khan so much that he overlooked crimes that would have spelled death in anyone else's case. Yet Saru Khan's turn would come soon enough. Forgiven for murder and, as the next chapter will show, for enriching himself at the expense of the treasury, he incurred Sulayman's wrath for having an affair with Maryam Bigum, the shah's aunt, following the death of her husband, the *sadr*. During an assembly in late 1691, Shah Sulayman offered the royal wine cup to all the courtiers in attendance with the exception of Saru Khan Sahandlu. The qurchibashi was beheaded following the meeting.[128]

Following the execution of Saru Khan, the shah appointed another member of the Zanganah tribe, Shah Quli Khan Zanganah, as the new qurchibashi. Shah Quli Khan became Tahir Vahid's new main rival. Yet with the demise of Saru Khan the position of qurchibashi once again lost some of its importance, as is suggested by the fact that the official apparently no longer automatically served as army commander.[129] Tahir Vahid was to become Shah Sultan Husayn's ultimate favorite. Envious rivals soon initiated a whispering campaign with the ruler, insinuating that the grand vizier did not take care of the royal treasury.[130] This damaging innuendo notwithstanding, Tahir Vahid managed to remain in office until 1699, five years into Sultan Husayn's reign.

Chapter 4

Monetary Policy and the Disappearing Mints, 1600–1700

[Money is] the principall want of this countrey.
                  EIC agents Edward Pettus and Thomas Barker, 1618

INTRODUCTION

In Chapters 2 and 3 we saw how, following the reign of Shah 'Abbas I, the Safavid political system showed myriad signs of weakening central control, manifesting itself in growing court factionalism and infighting over diminishing resources. These same chapters also suggested that, even though 'Abbas's successors did not stand out for vigor and vision, what came out of Isfahan at this time was more than unmitigated torpor. Safavid authorities continued to pay attention to the economy or at least to the income it generated, showed an acute awareness of the growing shortfall in royal revenue, and sought to find ways to reverse the trend.

That Iran's elite remained concerned about income and kept up a policy of economic vigilance which included monetary matters is no more than a truism—all states are necessarily preoccupied with the question of revenue. This chapter addresses the more important issue of the methods employed by the Safavids to generate income and the effectiveness of these methods within the parameters of intentions and constraints set by the time and the place. The first part offers a brief overview of the Safavid monetary system. This is followed by a discussion of the origins and effects of the scarcity of coin in seventeenth-century Iran, focusing on the drastic long-term reduction in the number of operational mints between the reign of Shah Tahmasb and that of Shah 'Abbas II. Also to be examined are the strategies employed by the state to garner revenue beyond the regular profits it made on the striking of coins—either by preventing bullion and specie from leaving the country or by manipulating the coinage through weight reductions. The more controversial question to be addressed in this regard is whether and under what circumstances Safavid rulers tampered with the coinage by reducing its precious metal content.

THE SAFAVID CURRENCY: ANTECEDENTS AND STRUCTURE

Cash played a limited role in the Safavid economy. In many parts of the country and for most of the population, current coin occupied a place of minor importance. The maritime sources show that economic activity involving major commodities such as silk and goat's wool, and exchange in general by way of long-distance trade, was fully monetized. Long-distance trade was also conducted by way of a sophisticated credit system that allowed deferred payment for goods using bills of exchange. Much of the trade between Isfahan and the Persian Gulf ports took place in this manner.[1] Yet a substantial part of the economy, especially in remote rural areas of low productivity and without cash crops, operated on the basis of barter. All of our direct evidence for this comes from the north, most notably Georgia, but there is little doubt that the situation was no different in other parts of the country. Michele Membré in 1540 claimed that, in western Georgia, people would come to the market "with silks, which they exchange for cloth, without other money being used."[2] The Ottoman traveler Evliya Chelebi, writing a century later, observed that in Daghistan trade took place "not for money, but by exchange."[3] An eyewitness reporting from Georgia from 1687 affirms that cash only played a limited role in the region's economy.[4] Jean Pitton de Tournefort, who visited Georgia in 1701, agreed, insisting that in many of its regions people preferred to be paid in bracelets, rings, glass necklaces, and other items.[5]

Major commercial transactions involved the exchange of cash. Yet, even in the case of tax remittances to the state, payment was not necessarily effected in current coin. The tax obligation was expressed in monetary units, but actual payment was often settled in kind. According to Jean Chardin, most royal taxes were in kind and consequently many of its payment orders were in kind as well.[6] Gilan, for instance, submitted its taxes in raw silk. Officials received their salaries in the same manner: they were paid with assignments of the produce of land, not in coin. The conversion of the wares into cash took place via a system called *tas`ir*, which facilitated transfers by fixing actual payment according to the demand–supply situation of the commodity in question.[7]

The Safavid monetary system was heir to the unified coinage introduced by the Il-Khans. Ghazan Khan at the turn of the fourteenth century introduced a uniform monetary system in Iran as part of his overall administrative reforms, suppressing local coinages throughout his realm. Coins of three metals, gold, silver, and copper, circulated simultaneously. We might call this a trimetallic system, except that the government did not set the ratio between the three metals, leaving this to market forces. Silver *dirhams* comprised the bulk of the coins struck in this period,[8] and silver was the only real currency in that only coins of that metal were minted according to a fixed weight standard. The Il-Khans struck gold coins primarily for commemorative and donative purposes and sometimes for economic reasons, not to any standard but at random weight, presumably in response to an erratic supply of gold owing to the fact that only one gold mine was found in all of Iran.[9] Copper coins were in wide circulation too, used for local purposes and in low-volume transactions.

A feature that the Safavids inherited from the Mongols by way of the Tumurids and the Aq-Quyunlu is the money of account they used. The value of a unit of a given name could vary substantially from place to place, as well as from time to time. The Iranians adapted to this situation by keeping records in a money of account, a standard of value used in everyday transactions. Whereas the dinar had been the unit of account from the early Islamic period, the Mongols had introduced the *tuman*, a word meaning 10,000, and a unit originally denoting 10,000 gold dinars. The Safavids used the tuman as well, even though the term never referred to an actual coin. During the first century of the dynasty's reign, one tuman equaled 200 *shahis* or 10,000 *dinars*.

The trimetallic system established under the Mongols persisted in the Safavid period. Silver was used for commercial transactions beyond small-scale exchange. From the reign of Shah `Abbas I until the end of the Safavid period, the following main monetary face values existed for silver coins: the `*abbasi*, equal to 200 dinars; the *mahmudi*, worth half an `abbasi; the shahi, valued at one-quarter of an `abbasi; and the *bisti*, equal to one-tenth of an `abbasi. In addition, the Safavid market accommodated a host of foreign silver currencies, from Dutch lion dollars to Spanish *reals of eight*. Traded at market rates and mostly exported to India, these coins too were mainly used as commodity money. Yet, unlike the situation in the Ottoman Empire, where such currencies began to replace the domestic coinage as the latter lost its value and credibility, Safavid Iran retained its domestic silver coinage, and only coins struck in Iran were generally accepted in the market place.[10]

As before, copper money was used for local and low-value transactions. Instead of showing a face value, copper coins featured pictures of animals to facilitate handling by illiterate users. Copper coins were represented by the *qazbaki*, which was worth one-fortieth of an `abbasi.[11] Provincial governors issued their own copper coins. These were cried down each year before Nawruz, forcing people to return them to the mint. Those that were not handed in lost 50 percent of their value. Come Nawruz, new coins were minted from the available stock of copper and issued with a new mark. The profits from the operation fell to the mint farmer and the governor.[12] The value of copper coins was also tied to the place of issuance: a coin lost half of its value outside the governor's jurisdiction and following the replacement of one governor by another.[13]

Gold coins were struck only infrequently, typically for donative purposes. They were produced in the period between Isma`il I and Shah `Abbas I, and again in the late reign of Sultan Husayn. This does not mean that no gold circulated in the Safavid realm; it did, in great quantities in fact, mostly in the form of gold ducats, both Venetian ones and imitations—so-called Moorish ones—struck in Ottoman territory. These, however, were used for export purposes. High-ranking officials going on pilgrimage in Iraq and Arabia had to pay for their expenses abroad in gold and thus carried large quantities, causing the price of gold in Iran to spike each year shortly before the departure of the hajj caravan. Most importantly, gold served as commodity money exported by merchants forced to take out money for lack of viable Iranian export products.

The separation in the use of each of the three metals created a workable, relatively stable monetary system in which arbitrage remained limited as long as the discrepancy between the official value and the market value of the currency did not become excessive.

THE STATE AND MONEY: BETWEEN POLITICAL SOVEREIGNTY AND THE MARKET

The working of the Safavid economy, or at least the role money played in it, can only be understood in light of Iran's persistent bullion shortage. Much of the state's monetary policy, from its minting practices to its preoccupation with bullion exports and its urge to maximize silk exports, was driven by a constant need to replenish the country's silver stock. The state used the system of mints to direct the inflow of specie, it collected revenue by levying a 2 percent seigniorage fee on minted coins, and it imposed an export fee on specie.[14]

This preoccupation with revenue begins with the mints, the operation of which combined royal sovereignty with private enterprise. The state exercised a monopoly in striking coins, and it periodically took old coins out of circulation, exchanging them for newly minted ones through a system of discounting. But, while the mints were state regulated, they were also farmed out to the highest bidder. Before 1879, when mechanized minting was introduced in Iran, the activities of provincial mints were not of great concern to the central authorities. As long as a mint remained profitable, "it was up to each farmer to recover what he had paid in advance for the right to operate the mint. The central government was only concerned, in a general way, that the mints remained lucrative enough to attract reasonable bids from prospective farmers."[15]

To ensure profitability, the Safavid border mints were to receive all specie imported from outside the Safavid realm. Anyone bringing silver into the country was supposed to submit it to the mint upon crossing the border, where it was to be restruck into Safavid coins of standard types bearing uniform legends. Iranian rulers used the issuing of money as a significant means to project their power and legitimacy. Yet monetary sovereignty did not extend much beyond symbolism with regard to the enforcement of the extrinsic value of the coinage or the convertibility of currencies.[16] Given porous borders and a decentralized minting system—coins were struck at many provincial mints—the state was not in a position to fix currency rates. The circulation of a host of foreign currencies, from Venetian gold ducats to Dutch lion dollars and Spanish reals of eight, traded at market rates, was symptomatic of this lack of control.[17]

THE LONG-TERM CONTRACTION OF THE MINTS

Currency shortages were a common problem in the early modern world at large, but they were particularly acute in a country such as Iran, with its severe constraints on the supply of precious metal. A lack of indigenous precious metal deposits coupled with low economic output created a precarious balance between state income and expenditure.[18] Since time immemorial, the important immediate source of Iran's bullion supply had been the Ottoman state and, to a lesser extent, Russia. In the early 1500s, the influx of New World treasure further intensified this movement, flooding the entire Mediterranean basin with precious metal. Most of this precious metal left for India, Iran's principal trading partner, where market prices for silver especially tended to be higher than in Iran; it was either siphoned off via the southern ports or carried via the overland caravan route.[19] All of this is summed up by Raphaël du Mans, who in an eloquent metaphor likened Iran to a caravanserai from which as much money exited as entered.[20]

The main reason why gold and silver disappeared to India in such large quantities was Iran's much noted trade deficit with the subcontinent—as opposed to its position vis-à-vis the Ottoman Empire and Russia. Safavid long-distance commerce was essentially a transit trade, having to do with Iran's strategic location between India, at the time the workshop of the world, and Western Europe, with its rapidly growing demand for a variety of consumer goods.[21] India offered spices and textiles, and, being largely self-sufficient, demanded bullion in return. Europe craved spices, textiles, and raw silk, and had as yet little to offer but silver and gold, which were abundantly available through the influx from the New World. Iran itself simply did not produce enough exportable wares to compensate for the huge quantities of spices and manufactured goods, mainly cloth in myriad varieties, brought in from India. Iran's dependence on bullion imports naturally made the country vulnerable to political events and economic conditions beyond its borders. Political turmoil in Europe or war in the Mediterranean might cause the flow of gold and silver coming from the West via the Ottoman Empire to dry up. Conversely, the persistent trade imbalance with India made attempts to prevent the incoming bullion from leaving the country largely futile.[22]

Low economic output combined with a perennial money shortage prevented country-wide long-term inflation—as opposed to short-term and typically local price hikes in the wake of natural disaster and as a function of the hoarding of foodstuffs, especially cereals.[23] Even at times of substantial inflows, almost as much money left the country as came in, mitigating the inflationary effect of the occasional debasements undertaken by the state.[24] This was exacerbated by a tendency among the elite and especially by the shah to hoard. As a result, monetary problems often stemmed less from a lack of available money than from a shortage of circulating coin. The chronic arrears in Safavid military pay, for instance, did not necessarily reflect empty royal coffers. Whereas Shah Isma`il's treasury may truly have been poorly stocked,[25] the case of his successor is different. Shah Tahmasb did not pay his troops during the last fourteen years of his reign, prompting thousands of Iranian soldiers to take refuge in India and Central Asia.[26] Part of the problem may have been the Ottoman–Venetian war of 1570–3 and rebellions in Anatolia in the same period, which surely had a negative effect on the inflow of money into the shah's vaults.[27] Yet the same ruler, avaricious to the extent of putting his own clothes up for sale at the bazaar, also engaged in massive hoarding, to the point where, upon his death in 1576, the royal treasury is said to have contained more than 80 million ducats.[28] As will be seen below, similar conditions—a well-stocked royal treasury coinciding with official penury—existed under Shah Sulayman and Shah Sultan Husayn.

For all his celebrated economic acumen, Shah `Abbas I proved unable fundamentally to improve Iran's financial health. Iskandar Beg Munshi reports how, before putting `Abbas on the throne, king-maker Murshid Quli Khan in 1581–2 "announced that his troops would receive a handout of gold, intending to raise the money from the rich citizens of Mashhad." Having exhausted this source, he proceeded to "lay hands on the shrine treasury; he seized possessions of the shrine ornaments, including all the gold and silver chandeliers and candlesticks ... and used the money to provide his men with pay and allowances."[29] In 1618, EIC agents Pettus and Barker remarked that money was "the principall want of this countrey." Attributing the scarcity to the wars between the Ottomans and the Safavids and their negative effect on trade, they pointed to Iran's dependence on outside sources for its precious metal supply.[30] In 1626, current coin was in such short supply in Iran that the Dutch had to distribute their merchandise over various cities to make any money.[31]

Persian-language sources tell the same story, focusing on the effects of war, both for the ruin it brought to trade and because of its cost. Shah `Abbas I, hampered by a severe lack of money in his campaign to drive the Uzbeks from Mashhad in 1590, ordered that all his gold and silver ware be melted down, overruling his officials, who cautioned him that it would be a waste to lose vessels that had cost 900,000 ducats to manufacture.[32] Such problems continued to plague the state throughout his reign. The cash-strapped ruler habitually paid his soldiers with cloth that had been supplied by foreign merchants and that they were forced to resell for far less than its face value.[33] During the siege of Baghdad in 1622 `Abbas remunerated his soldiers with promissory notes in the form of round pieces of leather stamped with his name and that of Baghdad.[34]

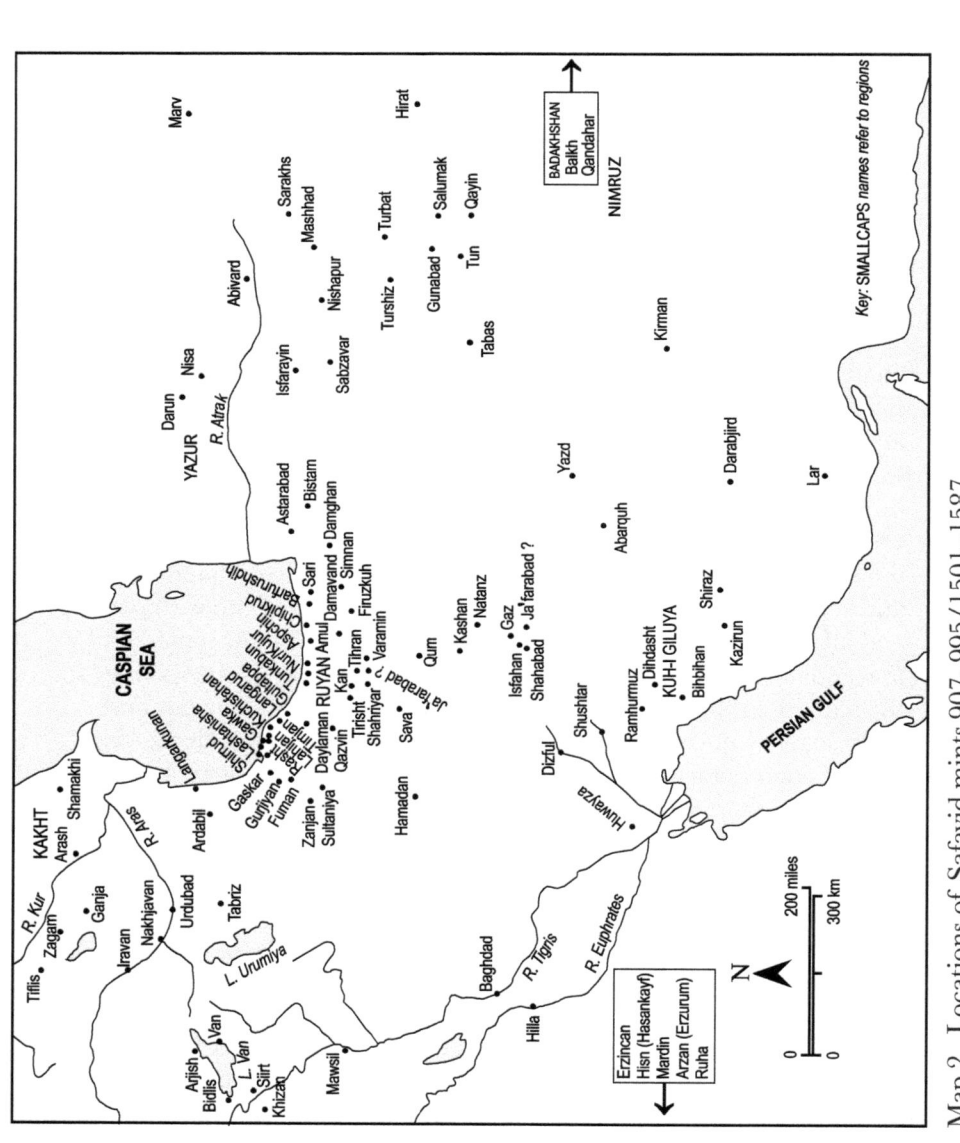

Map 2. Locations of Safavid mints 907–995/1501–1587

The most tangible effect of this protracted monetary crisis was a steady contraction in the number of mints operating on Iranian soil. Between the early reign of Shah Isma`il I and the end of that of Shah Muhammad Khudabandah (1501–87), Iran's mints numbered approximately seventy. Of these, no more than forty were operational at any given time, and many were ephemeral. In some cases no more than one or two coins have survived. Map 2 shows the location of these mints. Not surprisingly, the heaviest concentration is found in the northwest, in the border area with the Ottoman Empire and Russia, the entry points of most precious metal, and throughout the north as far as Khurasan. The large number of mints in Gilan and Mazandaran is striking. It probably reflects the lingering local nature of monetary politics due to the existence of the semi-autonomous kingdoms in the region, in addition to the intensity of economic life, which centered on the lucrative and fully monetized silk cultivation and trade.[35] Few mints existed in the south and the southeast, a vast area of relatively low agricultural yield.

Map 3 shows the Safavid mints during the reign of Shah `Abbas I, when their number had decreased to forty, and that of Shah Safi I, by which time the number had gradually dropped to twenty-six. The main reason for the initial closing of so many mints was a diminished inflow of silver, which in turn was related to instability in the Mediterranean as well as the outbreak of a new round of Ottoman–Safavid warfare in 1576. All of this had a profound impact on Ottoman monetary policy. In 1584–5 Istanbul engaged in the first of what would be a series of currency debasements. All mints except those of Istanbul and Cairo were closed, and attempts were made to limit the outflow of silver to Iran.[36] A long-term contraction of the mints was the result. Whereas the silver *akçe* was struck at almost forty mints under Sultan Mehmet III (1595–1603), the number dropped to about thirty during the reign of Sultan Murad IV (1623–40).[37] India, too, felt the effect of a dwindling influx of precious metal in the late sixteenth century. Across the Mughal realm, coin production came to a virtual halt in 1580–1 and, with the exception of the mint of Ahmadabad and Sultan Akbar's camp mint, all mints striking silver ceased operation for years.

Shah `Abbas I's reign saw a continuation of these developments. The frequent Safavid–Ottoman wars fought in the borderlands between the two states exacerbated existing money shortages and caused the mints to contract further.[38] This process was also a function of the centralization undertaken at the time.[39] This is especially true of the mints in the Caspian provinces, which were brought

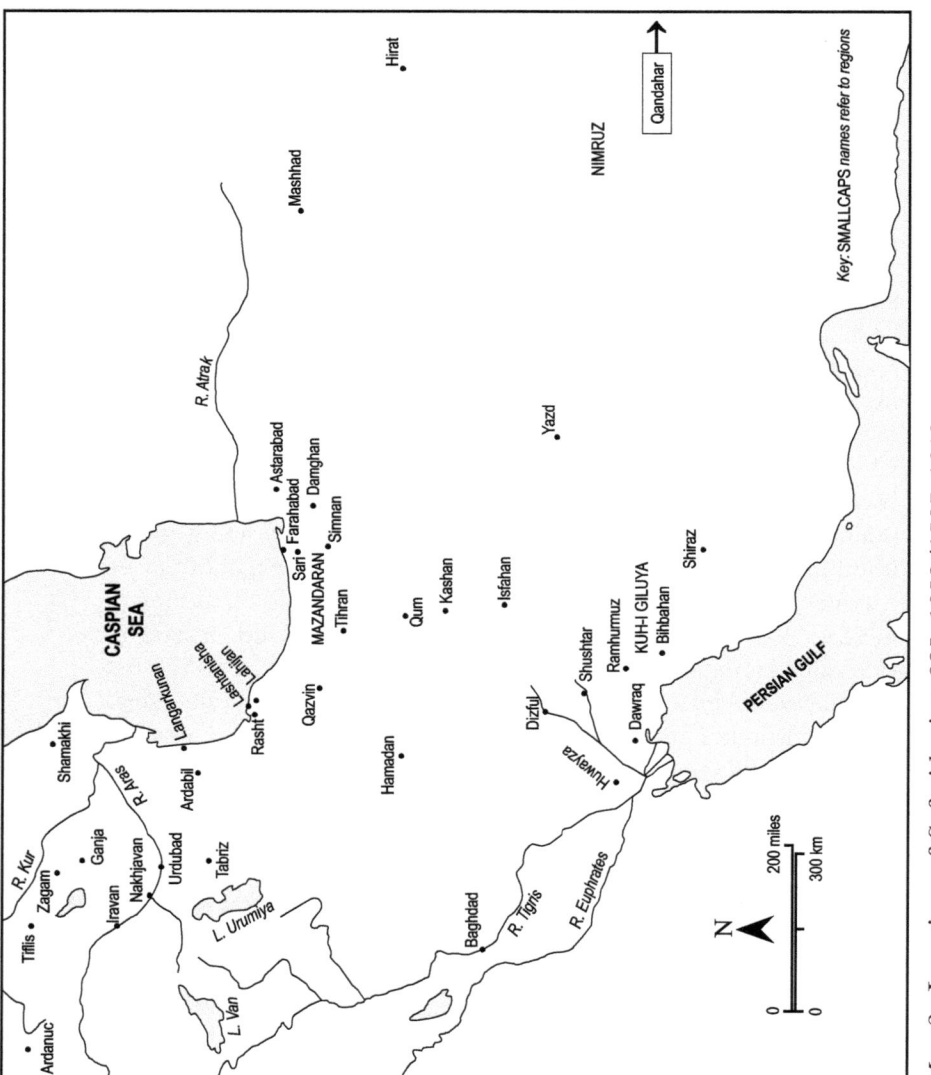

Map 3. Locations of Safavid mints 995–1052/1587–1642

under definitive Safavid control by ʿAbbas I. The shah's conquest of Azerbaijan in 1613 and his subjugation of eastern Georgia three years later similarly obviated the need for the continued operation of the many mints in that region. Meanwhile, in the provinces of Azerbaijan and Armenia a large number remained open, kept busy by the precious metal that still flowed into the country from the Ottoman Empire and Russia.

MONETARY ISSUES AFTER SHAH ʿABBAS I

Following Shah ʿAbbas's death in 1629, Iran's monetary problems only grew worse. The causes varied. A terrible outbreak of plague resulting in famine that struck all of West and South Asia in the 1630s wreaked havoc in Iran's silk-producing regions. In 1638 the Iranians lost Baghdad and Qandahar to the Ottomans and the Mughals, respectively, and thus gave up two important commercial transit centers.[40] The so-called War of Candia that broke out between the Ottomans and the Venetians in 1645 soon impeded the flow of money carried from Aleppo and Baghdad to Isfahan.[41] All of this caused the mints, which could only be maintained on imported reals, to shrink further in number and output, severely constraining the state's ability to pay for vital functions.

Given these persistent problems, the Safavid authorities found themselves in a perpetual dilemma. To do nothing was to see great amounts of bullion being siphoned off abroad. As the official mint value of silver coin in Iran tended to be lower than the price the market was willing to pay, huge amounts of specie disappeared to India via the mechanism of arbitrage.[42] To prevent this from happening, rulers had several options. One was to prohibit the export of specie. This was logistically difficult to enforce, however, and it did not deter imaginative profit-seeking exporters from finding ways around such bans through bribery and concealment. The only real solution might have been for the government to follow a Dutch suggestion: to offer prices for imported silver bullion and coins commensurate with the market price of silver. However, without a change in the underlying economic structure—that is, without increased production and improvement in the ratio between imports and exports—this measure only accelerated the bullion exports.

The alternative lay in the handling of the currency itself. The strategy of compromising the weight or quality of the currency was attractive, for it carried a double advantage: it enhanced immediate revenue and, theoretically at least, prevented the capital flight of most current money.[43] However, the fixation of currency was, as Minorsky observed, a "delicate task, for on the one hand it was desirable to squeeze out as much profit as possible, and on the other a debasement of coin might upset the market and even provoke trouble."[44] In practice, state policy was a blend of the three approaches, with results that typically raised immediate revenue while harming the long-term soundness of the coins without diminishing the urge of merchants to ferry out specie.

In keeping with contemporary notions about the best way to react to the working of Gresham's Law—which caused money whose metallic value exceeded its face value to disappear from circulation—the Safavids frequently issued bans on bullion exports. Rather than representing an aggressive hunt for treasure, this was mostly a defensive policy.[45] Since the Ottomans, faced with their own monetary problems, banned the export of bullion in the 1570s, it is likely that Iran's rulers took similar measures at the time. Yet no bans on bullion or specie exports are on record prior to Shah 'Abbas I's reign.[46] 'Abbas is known to have prohibited the export of precious metal in 1618. The agents of the EIC in that year wrote of the "Bannians in returne of their Linens carryinge of the Silver, and gould out of the country." Merchants, they noted, "at their comming into Persia ... are used with great favour.... But at their going into India they use all extremitie, searching them to the skinne for gold, which to transport, or any coyne of silver out of Persia, but the King's, is death."[47] They also reported the execution at Qazvin of several Banyans, Indian merchants, accused of exporting bullion.[48] The ban seems to have remained in place for the duration of the shah's reign, forcing the Dutch to pay for part of their silk purchases in cash rather than with commodities.

After 'Abbas I's death, the ban was allowed to lapse. Money could now be borrowed in the market and exported. This was a temporary situation, however, no doubt a function of Shah Safi's initially weak leadership. 'Abbas's successors persisted in their attempts to keep as much bullion as possible inside the country. The recurrent conflicts with the Dutch in the subsequent period were due in part to a Safavid demand that one-third of their imports into Iran be in precious metal.[49] Instead, the Dutch not only paid for most of their silk exports in spices, but as silk deliveries decreased they began to export more and more bullion from Iran. In 1644, Isfahan issued another decree, making it illegal to export reals of eight, gold ducats—the Hungarian and Venetian ones as well as the "Moorish" (Ottoman) ones—or "new money," that is, new 'abbasis, to India.[50] These severe restrictions increased the risk of transporting money but did not stop the practice. In 1652, a year of great financial strain, the Safavid government tried to curb the Dutch export of bullion through a separate arrangement. The new commercial treaty concluded with the VOC in that year contained a clause that prohibited the Dutch from exporting Spanish money or "Moorish" ducats (*sultanis* struck in the Ottoman Empire in imitation of European ducats).[51]

These restrictive measures had a noticeable effect on the money trade, causing the Dutch to complain about a diminished supply of specie from the interior.[52] Yet they did not prevent the continued drain of treasure. Like everyone else, the VOC agents, while impeded in their activities, continued to export cash in defiance of the various bans, circumventing regulations by bribing conniving officials and hiding coins among their regular merchandise. In fact, forced to remit money for lack of viable Iranian export products, they managed to increase their remittances relative to the previous period, with annual exports that averaged half a million guilders after 1644.[53] Batavia headquarters in 1658 expressed their great satisfaction with the more than fl. 100,000 in gold shipped to Coromandel, calling Iran one of their most profitable factories.[54] Between 1642 and 1660 the VOC exported an estimated equivalent of more than 9 million guilders from Iran.[55]

The appointment of Muhammad Beg as grand vizier in 1656 suggests the political dynamic behind the export bans. A former assayer of the mint, Muhammad Beg launched a campaign to increase revenue soon after becoming grand vizier. Several of his family members had held the post of *shahbandar* (toll master) in Bandar ʿAbbas, giving him an intimate knowledge of how money was "processed" onward toward India. It is therefore not surprising that the measures taken by Muhammad Beg included a reinstatement of the export ban on bullion, specifically prohibiting the export of gold. As with other such proclamations, restrictions on clandestine transports seem to have been rather strictly enforced for some time, with the new assayer of the mint, Amin Beg, sending out spies to ferret out violators. The money changers of Isfahan responded to this and other forms of intimidation by closing their shops and by refusing to assay coins any longer. Everyone else involved in the gold business kept a low profile, too, so that little gold could be obtained.[56] Due to rising demand, by May 1660 prices reached 14.5 mahmudis per European ducat.[57]

Fortunately for all precious metal exporters, Muhammad Beg fell from power in 1661. Under his successor, Mirza Muhammad Mahdi, control over trade and in particular the export of specie loosened.

In 1662 the government, realizing that gold still leeched out of the country and that merchants coming from Ottoman lands now chose to take their money to Basra instead of Isfahan or Shiraz, replaced the ban on gold exports with a tax, imposing a fee of three-fifths of a mahmudi on every ducat that left Isfahan. The *sarraf-bashi* (head of the moneychangers) received the right to inspect all caravans for clandestine transports.[58] The Dutch, who had refrained from exporting any ducats between June 1660 and late 1662 so as not to endanger their profitable trade with Iran, now reconsidered their policy. Lured by growing profits on gold and excited to learn that merchants were returning to Isfahan, they decided to pay the export duty and resume their gold exports.

TAMPERING WITH THE COINAGE

At the same time as the Safavid authorities sought to keep bullion from leaving the country, they reduced the value of the main silver coin, the `abbasi, by lowering its weight. The new `abbasi that was introduced in 1645 was valued at 2 mahmudis, as opposed to 2.5 mahmudis for the previous ones.[59] Various sources confirm this reduction, even if they differ in their assessment of its extent. An EIC agent claimed that, whereas the old `abbasis had weighed "10 grains," the reduction amounted to 10 percent, so that the new ones weighed only 9 grains.[60] According to the Dutch, the new `abbasi were 5 percent lighter than the old ones.[61] This reform aimed to increase government revenue but, like all such measures, it was palliative; it may have alleviated the most urgent shortages but it offered no solution to the underlying scarcity of current coin. In spite of the ban on silver exports that was issued simultaneously, the old coins, most of which had already been exported to various parts of India, now disappeared altogether.[62] Within three years most of the "old" `abbasis had been spirited out of the country, leaving the market with only the new ones.[63] What remained of the old `abbasis flowed into the royal treasury, there to be reminted into the new lighter ones.[64] Interest rates on the Persian Gulf coast in this period remained relatively high, at an annual rate of between 12 and 20 percent.[65] Money, in other words, continued to be scarce.

Muhammad Beg's dismissal in 1661 did not end the experimentation with the currency. A year later, Shah `Abbas II ordered all mints to strike `abbasis weighing 2 *misqal* (9.2 grams) and to issue them at a value of 250 dinars, or 5 shahis, as opposed to the previous 200 dinars, or 4 shahis. These new large `abbasis were also called *panj shahi* (5-shahi) coins. The old coins became known as small `abbasis.[66] The new ones continued to be struck until the accession of Shah Sulayman; the mint of Tiflis appears to have produced nothing else until 1667.[67] Zakariya Aguletsi reports how in that year Agha Vali, the new mint master of Yerevan, received an order from the shah to "strike `abbasis worth four shahis," as a result of which the panj shahis gradually went out of circulation.[68]

Did the Safavids, in addition to lowering the value of the coinage by decreasing its weight, debase their coinage, that is, lower its fineness, as a way of increasing state revenue? J. Simmons, one of the few scholars who have dealt with the issue, argues that Safavid shahs did not engage in debasement as a matter of principle. He bases this on the notion that in Islamic treatises the prestige of the king was judged by the quality of his money, so that tampering with the alloy could never be official policy. If any depreciation occurred at all, it would have been the work of individual mint masters rather than official policy.[69] Such mint masters, Simmons argues, were punished whenever their abuse was detected. As an example he cites Engelbert Kaempfer's story of the *mu`ayyir al-mamalik* (assayer of the mint) who in 1685 was blinded for tampering with the silver content of the coinage while a recoinage was under way.

Simmons's claim about the continued purity of Safavid coins is problematic. His moral argument can be dismissed for reflecting an idealist perspective that ignores the profit-driven aspect of the state's monetary concerns. Heeding religious and moral strictures against tampering with the purity of the coinage would have made Safavid Iran unique among contemporary states, including European ones. Rising military expenditure in the late 1500s prompted the Ottomans to undertake the first of a protracted series of debasements and weight reductions of the akçe.[70] Europe's sixteenth-century wars of religion were largely financed through currency debasement. The French seventeenth-century ministers of state Colbert and Pontchartrain continually sought to raise government revenue in this manner, and England went through a major recoinage in the same period.[71]

More importantly, Simmons implies a distinction between public good and private gain that did not exist anywhere at the time, and certainly not in Iran. It was no doubt risky for mint masters to tamper with the mint for private gain or to cause money to deteriorate by neglect. Hajji Muhammad Baqir Beg was demoted. The fraudulent mint master of 1685 was indeed deposed and blinded. Saru Khan

Sahandlu, too, was to suffer his demise shortly after his fraud was detected, albeit more directly for treason than for malfeasance. But to suggest that individual mint masters pursued their own interests whereas the "state" stood for the common good is to ignore the fact that "raisons d'état" largely coincided with the interests of the shah. If individual mint masters were punished for misbehavior, it was—despite public claims to the contrary—most likely not because they had contravened some symbolic law or harmed the public interest but because their behavior had impaired the flow of resources to the center. The shah was seen as the guarantor of monetary soundness, to be sure, but punishing fraudulent mint masters for having violated the god-given order might well be a matter of "plausible deniability," a way to mask official tampering with the coinage.

The fact that most of the coins that survive from the period exhibit a continued purity and suggest hardly any compromised alloy does not support Simmons's thesis either. Hoards, the source of most of the extant coins, tend to yield flawed or at least incomplete data in that the specimens they contain are unlikely to be representative of the actual money that circulated at the time and in fact may be expected to contain the better pieces. Most importantly, the claim does not quite stand up to the evidence found in the sources, the Persian-language ones as much as the European ones. As will be seen below, Shah Tahmasb was not the last Safavid shah to have money restruck each year, putting out coins with the same face value but of lower metal content and pocketing the difference.[72] Powerful textual evidence of compromised money is found in the *Tazkirah-i Nasrabadi*, a rare contemporary Persian source of economic importance. Speaking of the harsh winter of 1064/1653–4 in Isfahan, its author cites the following poem by the Isfahani draper-poet Mulla Qudrati.[73]

ز خواب گران فتنه بیدار شد
چو ماهی به مردم درم بار شد

فلوس صفاهان چنان ناروا ست
که گویی به هرکیسه پول اژدهاست

نگیرد گدا پول از بس پراست
تو گویی مگر شیرش آدم خوراست

زمسان چنان دهر درهم شده
که ماهی به زیر زمین خم شده

زر از دست مردم نگردد سفید
که از دور کف میزند هرکه دید

Monetary Policy and the Disappearing Mints, 1600–1700

چنان گشته خوار از خلایق درم
که شخص غنی گشته صاحب کرم

چو شیرست نقش فلوس این زمان
ز بیمش گریزند پیر و جوان

گریزد طلبکار از قرض دار
ندیدست رسم چنین روزگار

مگر شاه عالم ز روی کرم
کند خلق را شیر گیر درم

دو آن فلس ناجنس را یک کند
رواجش در آفاق بی شک کند

شود دست قلابیان ستم
به تیغ عدالت قلم یک قلم

به تاریخ این انقلاب درم
دلم داشت اندیشه از بیش و کم

خرد گفت با من بگو راست زود
"درم چون دوگروید زرو نمود"

Unrest rose from a deep sleep. People were weighed down with dirhams, like the fish[74]

Isfahan's money is so unworthy, as if there were a dragon in each money bag

The beggar doesn't take money, which is so abundant that one would say its lion is a man-eater

The world has become so topsy-turvy because of copper that the fish has become bent under the earth

Gold does not turn white by people's touch. Everyone who sees it claps his hands from afar

The dirham has become so despised by people that even the rich person has become generous

The money's face is like a lion these days old and young flee for fear of it

The creditor flees from the borrower never did the world see such ways

One wishes that the lord of the world in his bounty would make the dirham a lion catcher

Let him make two of those unworthy coins one so that they become of unquestioned currency

The hand of counterfeiters would be cut by the sword of justice from limb to limb

> At the time of this upheaval of the dirham I was worried about abundance and scarcity
>
> Reason said: tell me the truth, quickly
> When the dirham doubled, gold showed its true value

Sa'ib of Tabriz, Shah 'Abbas II's court poet, similarly captured the deplorable state of the currency when he said:

سکه سان رویی از آهن به کف آور صائب
کاین متاعی است که امروز به زر نزدیک است

> Sa'ib, get yourself some iron object looking like a coin
> because it's merchandise today that's close to gold[75]

Both poems bear eloquent testimony to debasement in a period marked by severe shortages of cash, prompting anyone who could afford it to shun silver and deal in gold. There is of course no reason to assume that the debased coins the poems refer to had been struck and disseminated by the central mint. The reference to counterfeiters in Mulla Qudrati's poem suggests other culprits than the shah, and not just because the author implores him to remedy the situation, for that may just be a poetic trope. As Simmons surmises, in various cases private agents or provincial governors might have been responsible. The misrule of Hajji Muhammad Baqir Beg, the vizier of Yazd in the 1660s, apparently resulted in a severe devaluation of the silver 'abbasi in his province.[76] And, as will be seen below, the deterioration of Iran's coinage in the 1670s first showed up in the mahmudi of Huwayza, a regional currency. Regardless of the culprits, the entire population suffered under the bad state of the money, although ordinary people, especially those on small and fixed incomes, must have been particularly hard hit by the debased currency and the attendant price hikes. They did not have the same option as merchants, who increasingly avoided Iran's silver currency, preferring gold ducats of foreign provenance. It is, in other words, very difficult to argue, on the basis of the perceived purity of extant coins, that Safavid coins remained of sound alloy.

FURTHER CONSOLIDATION OF THE MINTS

Unlike conditions in Mughal India, where by the end of Sultan Akbar's reign many mints had resumed operation and new ones came into production as well, the number of Safavid mints continued to fall under Shah ʿAbbas's successors.[77] Whereas under Shah Safi some twenty-six mints were still operational, their number had dropped to nineteen by the time Shah ʿAbbas II assumed power in 1642. In the last decade of his reign, no more than ten of those were still putting out coins.[78] This was clearly a function of a new, more severe round in the silver scarcity. The flow of silver into the Ottoman Empire all but dried up in the 1640s, forcing most Ottoman mints to close down. As the production of the akçe came to a virtual halt, the country was flooded with a multitude of counterfeit European coins.[79] In the next few decades, as hostilities between the Ottomans and the European nations resumed and rumors spoke of an imminent Ottoman–Safavid war, the volume of silver imports from the West fell even further.

Bullionist measures taken by Russia and Japan in this period also affected Iran, as did monetary changes in India. In 1667 the Russians, keen to prevent specie from leaving their territory, imposed restrictions on the export of ducats and rix-dollars (rijksdaalders, a Dutch coin) by Iranian and other "Eastern" merchants.[80] Japan pursued a similar policy. The Tokugawa shogunate, dismayed at the continued efflux of silver and the prospective depletion of Japan's silver mines, had begun to restrict silver exports in the 1640s, and banned these outright in 1668.[81] India meanwhile became more silver-hungry than ever. With the incorporation of the Deccan into the Mughal realm, traditionally gold-based Golconda was integrated into a monetary system operating on silver. Revenue and tribute thenceforth were mostly collected in coins of that metal.[82] As a result, the value of silver underwent a sharp increase in the subcontinent: in 1675–6 the price of gold suddenly fell in the Mughal state, making silver highly profitable.[83] So strong did the pull of silver from India become that for the VOC it more than compensated for the falling profitability of silk.[84]

Some silver still reached Iran, to be sure, but it did not necessarily end up in Isfahan. Much of it now began to be diverted to the southwest. As many northwestern mints closed, new ones opened up, or at least became newly productive, in ʿArabistan. Given a fragmented economy and the fact that, as Carlo Cipolla reminds us, scarcity of precious metals in one area might well coincide with abundance elsewhere, there is nothing surprising about this.[85] The intensified minting activity in ʿArabistan most likely followed the working of Gresham's Law. Since export bans focused on the Bandar ʿAbbas trade route, merchants now began to take good coins to Basra. Adjacent ʿArabistan, remote and difficult to control from Isfahan, may have reaped the benefits. Authorities there, anxious to share in the profits, probably decided to "tax" the exports through striking coins, thus legalizing the export trade. The mints of Dawraq Shushtar, Dizful, Ramhurmuz, and Huwayza fell under Safavid suzerainty but preserved a considerable amount of autonomy. Of these, Huwayza became by far the most productive, striking mahmudis in accelerating quantities, especially under Shah Sulayman. In time, the Huwayza mahmudi would become the main trade currency of southern Iran and the Persian Gulf basin.[86]

The acute silver famine continued for the next decade and a half, causing the habitual Dutch complaints about the scarcity of silver money to turn into a chronic jeremiad.[87] It is most tangibly reflected in the small number of surviving Safavid coins from the mid-1660s onward. Between 1076/1666 and 1092/1682 most centrally located mints ceased operation. Only Qazvin and Isfahan are known to have struck coins in this period. Of the border mints, only those in Azerbaijan and Armenia continued to operate, albeit on a reduced scale.[88] In the next few years, between 1092/1682 and 1096/1685, almost no Safavid coins were issued, with the exception of some activity at the mints of Tabriz and Tiflis, a rare representation piece struck at Isfahan, and, presumably, continued production at Huwayza.[89] Map 4 shows the distribution of Iran's mints from the early reign of Shah ʿAbbas II to the end of that of Shah Sulayman, when the shortage reached its peak and the total number of mints had decreased to fifteen. This development was not confined to Iran. Quite a few Ottoman mints also ceased operation in this period.[90] In India, a shortage of mintable silver caused a precipitous drop in mint output between 1075 and 1096/1665 and 1685.[91]

MONETARY POLICY BETWEEN 1669 AND 1684

The acuteness of many problems plaguing Iran at the time when Shah Safi II came to power in 1666 quickly prompted the clerical elite to suggest that the shah had been enthroned at an inauspicious moment and that a new accession ceremony was in order. A dire currency situation reached crisis proportions during an unusual dry spell that resulted in a series of bad harvests which were followed by official grain hoarding. The result, a famine followed by an outbreak of plague in 1668, affected Isfahan as well as large parts of the Persian Gulf coast and possibly other regions of the country too.[92] Subsequent years brought little relief. The winter of 1672 saw bitter cold and heavy snowfall in central Iran. Prices in Isfahan rose steeply.

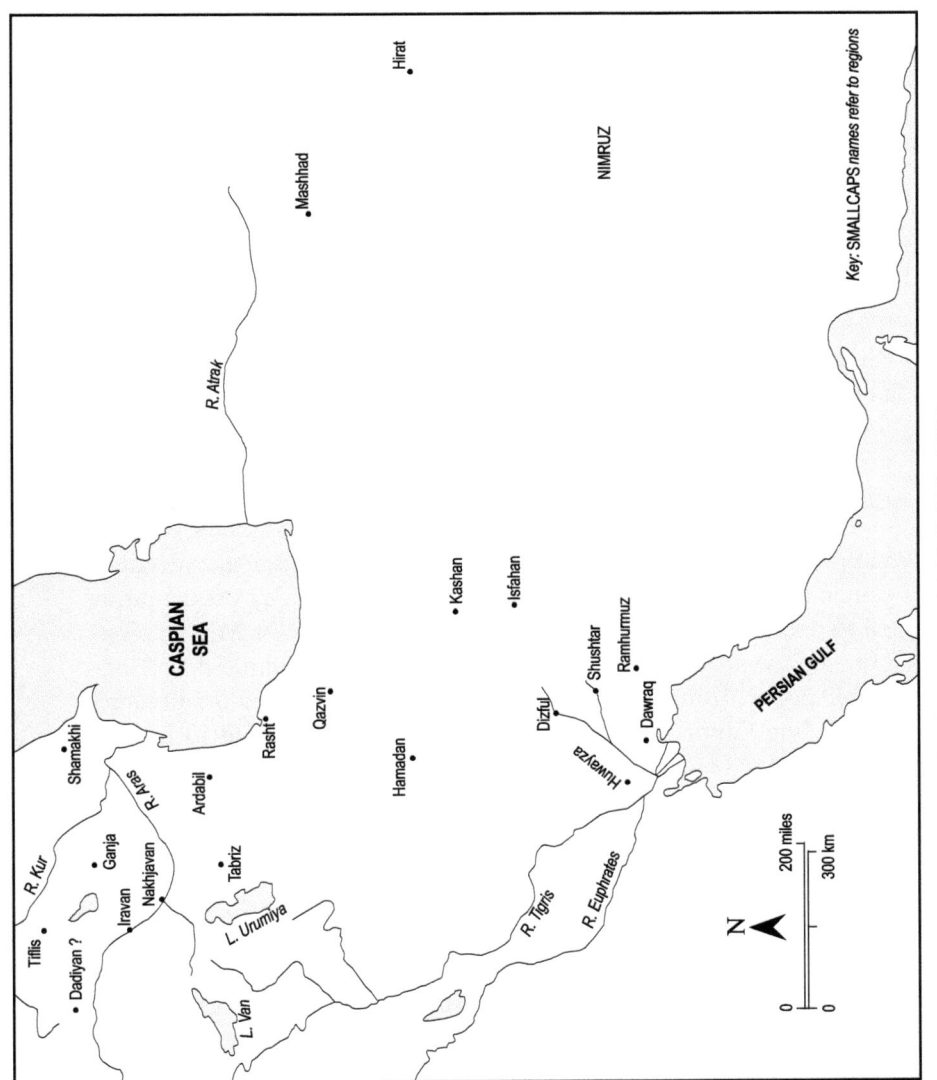

Map 4. Locations of Safavid mints 1052–1105/1642–1694

Bread, which in 1667 had been fixed at 1 `abbasi per *mann-i shah* (5.8 kilos), went up by 50 percent.⁹³

Iran's currency, buffeted by dwindling silver imports, suffered terribly as a result. Chardin noted the change for the worse between his first visit in the 1660s and his second a decade later. In 1677, the year he left Iran for good, he reckoned that the country's wealth had diminished by half in the intervening period, adding that one no longer saw any good coins.⁹⁴ The Dutch in 1682 called the `abbasi a coin that "used to be of pure specie."⁹⁵ They may have had the mid-1660s in mind, when Jean de Thevenot and Jean Baptiste Tavernier could still praise the soundness of Iran's money (although they may inadvertently have referred to the coins struck in the border areas with the Ottoman Empire, which remained sound long after many of the coins in other parts of the country had been tampered with).⁹⁶ Two decades later, Kaempfer testified to the bad quality of the currency in Isfahan. He recounts how in February 1684 Shah Sulayman inspected the funds kept for the maintenance of foreign envoys and found that out of 30,000 tumans only 300, a mere 1 percent, were in good order.⁹⁷ His remarks, joined by those of others and supported by the material evidence, provide more evidence for debasement.

The seventeenth-century "crisis theory," which postulates that the interruption of especially silver imports precipitated a sharp reduction in the circulation of money, necessitating escalating tax demands on the part of the state, has been called in question for Ming China, but does seem to apply to Safavid Iran. With its limited productive capacity, Iran was much more vulnerable to silver fluctuations than Ming China (and Mughal India), which continued to receive large amounts of silver even after the global flow of silver slowed in the second half of the seventeenth century. Since taxes were often extracted arbitrarily and largely hoarded, the silver famine combined with the measures taken to combat it significantly contributed to the country's economic weakening.⁹⁸

The process can be charted in some detail through the official monetary policy, beginning with the measures to enhance royal income taken by Shaykh `Ali Khan, some of which were discussed in Chapter 3. Kaempfer implicated Shaykh `Ali Khan in the decision to defray a visiting Uzbek envoy with bad money. The vizier, he claimed, questioned why the delegate should be paid in good money from the state treasury. Following consultation with the shah, it was secretly decided to pay him his 3,000 tumans in coins especially struck for the occasion, containing only one-quarter as much silver as regular coins. The money offered to the Uzbek envoy eventually found its way to merchants and thus entered the system, where it contributed to the deterioration of the currency.[99]

The effect of this one case may have been exaggerated by Kaempfer, and as an isolated example of deliberate policy it says more about the craftiness of the Safavid authorities in dealing with hapless foreign envoys from lands that the Iranians held in little esteem than about the overall worsening of the coinage. Nevertheless, in the late 1670s it was becoming abundantly clear that the deterioration of the Safavid currency was not an isolated or passing phenomenon. Fewer and fewer `abbasis were available, and those minted in Tabriz, by far everyone's favorite, were especially hard to come by. In the late 1670s `abbasis became nearly impossible to obtain.

As stated, the main cause of the silver shortage was the scant supply from Ottoman lands and Russia. Rumors about an impending Safavid-Ottoman war, a series of spectacular caravan robberies, and deteriorating political and economic conditions, made merchants reluctant to come to Iran via Anatolia.[100] Hoarding by the elite made matters worse (and by siphoning off good coins may have created the false impression that nothing but compromised money was available in the country).[101] A notoriously parsimonious shah took the lead in this. Chardin, referring to Sulayman's habit of hoarding much of the revenue that flowed into his treasury, claimed that the ruler spent no more than one-twentieth of what he received in income.[102]

Official government policies only exacerbated the crisis. Shaykh `Ali Khan, seeking to make it less profitable for merchants to take their money abroad via the Gulf ports, in 1670 instituted a 5 percent tax on all silver exports. A replay of the measures taken eight years earlier, this was a pragmatic measure, informed by the realization that money was going to be exported regardless of restrictions and that it would be more profitable to tax this traffic than to outlaw it. Initially, the fee appears to have been payable in Bandar `Abbas. A year later the government, keen to assert direct control over the traffic, opted to have goods inspected near Isfahan, on the routes leading out of the city. This did not just affect the route to the Persian Gulf coast. Whereas formerly it had been routine to open bales for scrutiny at the country's borders, now all merchandise was subjected to checking and taxation in the interior.[103]

All of this had a counterproductive effect. Gold, the export of which remained banned but which merchants found easier to conceal from the tax and toll inspectors because of its smaller volume, turned more expensive. Faced with a dwindling silver supply from Anatolia, the Dutch worried that, eventually, they might have to accept expensive gold ducats for their wares—ducats that would yield a loss in India. As they put it in 1673:

> The strict control that has been exercised on the export of silver for several years now is the cause that gold, of which a great capital is being carried down and transported, has become very expensive. The European ducats are now valued at 16⅔ and 16½ mahmudis, for which reason little silver and many ducats now arrive from the northern quarters of the country, and silver is very scarce, not only here but even in Isfahan, which is to the great disadvantage of the trade.[104]

Many Armenian merchants arriving from Ottoman lands with silver now began to take their specie to freewheeling Basra. This shows up in the increased minting activity in `Arabistan mentioned before. As `abbasis grew scarce, the alternative, mahmudis struck in Huwayza, gradually became more abundant. Yet this came at the expense of quality. The two phenomena are linked, involving opportunities for speculation and profit offered by the decentralized monetary system of Safavid Iran to those engaged in striking coins. Officials in `Arabistan purchased `abbasis at prices above their intrinsic value. In 1679 and 1680 the `abbasi commanded premiums of between 10 and 19 percent. The minters recouped the rising costs by restriking the `abbasis into adulterated mahmudis. The mahmudis they struck also had to cover the growing fees they paid to the *basha* (governor) and the shahbandar for the privilege of minting and the right of export, and still leave room for the handsome seigniorage profit that the Dutch claimed they made on their operation. The decline of the coins they put out did not manifest itself in any consistent loss of weight. The minters made sure the weight was acceptable—even if there was a slight deviation from the Safavid norm. Instead, it shows up in reduced precious metal content.[105] Huwayza mahmudis struck under Shah `Abbas I and Shah Safi have a silver content consistently above 90 percent. Under Shah `Abbas II we see a drop to the 80–90 percent range. A further decrease occurs in the reign of Shah Sulayman, when for the dated coins, spanning the period 1084–92/1673–81, the highest reading is 85 percent, while examples of 70–75 are common. The lowest are off-scale, representing a silver content of less than 50 percent and thus a severe debasement. The undated coins from the same period yield similar results. A specific gravity test shows many to be off-scale, suggesting billon coins, or coins whose alloy is less than 50 percent silver.[106]

Almost all Huwayza mahmudis from the 1660s onward, moreover, give the impression of having been struck in great haste in an apparent effort to maximize output. Most are of an irregular shape and vary in size; a great many are oval; some are extremely worn, and the edges of many are cracked. Many of what appear to be later Huwayza mahmudis do not even bear dates and some are almost illegible. Local mint masters, successful in attracting silver and now perhaps without firm supervision, may have been tempted to continue to strike coins in great haste and volume without paying much attention to appearance and aesthetics. With the accession of Sayyid Faraj Allah b. `Ali Khan to the post of *vali* in 1687, regular minting of the Huwayza mahmudi appears to have ceased altogether.

The adulteration of coins, until the mid-1670s largely confined to the mahmudi from Huwayza, in subsequent years spread to the `abbasi as well. For years, merchants chased `abbasis as the alternative to the debased mahmudis. `Abbasis struck in Tabriz were especially sought after. They may not have met the standard of the old "large" ones minted under Shah `Abbas II, few of which were still available at that time, but they were certainly of much better quality than the regular small `abbasis that made up the majority of the coins produced under Sulayman.[107] All the other `abbasis were swept up in the decline. Writing in early 1677, the Dutch called the `abbasis from most mints deficient in quality.[108]

No relief was found in the issuance of a series of new `abbasis in 1680. Far from improving on the overall quality of currency, these new coins were found to be deficient in weight as well as in silver content. According to initial VOC findings, they differed by 15 to 20 percent in value from the old `abbasis.[109] In 1682 the Dutch could be even more specific. When they melted down a number of the new `abbasis, they found these to differ by between 20 and 24 percent in purity from the `abbasis struck under Shah `Abbas II. The new `abbasis were also 2 to 3 percent worse in alloy than the ones that had been produced during Sulayman's early reign.[110] It is not altogether clear what triggered the issuance of 1680, though the Dutch suspected that the adulteration of the coin was part of a deliberate policy designed to prevent capital flight.[111]

The worsening of the currency in the late 1670s and early 1680s put a severe strain on commerce. Numerous merchant bankruptcies between 1665 and 1675 underscore the severity of a crisis that only worsened with time.[112] All parties involved in trade became reluctant to accept mahmudis. Some, such as the Dutch, were in a position categorically to reject payment in these coins. Safavid officials, too, began to demand money with a minimal guarantee of soundness. In 1677, for instance, the royal treasurer refused to accept anything but `abbasis minted in Tabriz and weighing "*nuh dang nim*" (9½ *dang* or

7.30 grams) by way of Dutch silk payments.[113] The reason given was that "it had been found that the 'abbasis minted in other cities were not of such good alloy."[114] The Dutch responded by arguing that they could only pay with coins current among the local merchants, the kind they received in exchange for their own goods. They therefore continued to pay for their silk in mahmudis of bad alloy, wondering how long they would be able to continue their refusal to accept these coins as payment for their merchandise.

When the 5 percent fee was introduced, the Dutch factors in Bandar 'Abbas wishfully predicted that opposition by domestic merchants would render the new policy a dead letter, yet nonetheless voiced concern about the consequences for trade, particularly their own.[115] Such worries proved justified, for the new fee quickly proved to have a negative effect on commerce in the southern ports, including on that conducted with fiduciary money. The first season after its introduction, VOC agents complained that few merchants had come down to the coast and that those who did make the journey had brought little money with them in hopes that the fee would soon be abolished.[116] Many tried to make purchases on condition that they would be allowed to pay later in Isfahan. The Dutch factors in Bandar 'Abbas, fearful of bankruptcies and unpaid loans, refused such credit arrangements—which were anyhow prohibited by their superiors in Batavia.[117] In late 1671 the 5 percent fee on money transports was, according to English merchants, "strictly looked after, and paid at Spahan before permitted to come thence."[118] Two years later, the Dutch complained about renewed checks on their shipments.[119] The tax farmers in Isfahan levied the fee on bills of exchange as well. Since this took away one of the attractive features of this way of making payments—the option of transferring money to Bandar 'Abbas anonymously and without having to pay dues—money lenders no longer issued such bills. Yet the new impost did not prevent large quantities of silver from being taken to the coast. Bad money, in other words, continued to drive out good money regardless of government regulations. Just as the earlier lifting of the ban on gold export had done nothing to keep gold in the country, so too the new policy did not stop the best-quality money from leaving.

THE MONETARY CRISIS OF 1684–5

The merchants' call for redress in the monetary situation went unheeded in much the same way as Mulla Qudrati's plea had gone ignored during the reign of Shah 'Abbas II. In 1678 poets and merchants clamoring for change were joined by the common people of Isfahan, who rose in revolt against penury and famine. Ordinary folk on small and fixed incomes did not have the same option as merchants, who did not ordinarily handle copper coins and who increasingly sought to avoid Iran's silver currency. Yet it was not until 1684 that the authorities were willing to concede what everyone else had known for years: that drastic action was needed.

Exactly what triggered the monetary "reform" of that year remains unclear. Official awareness of the problem had existed long before 1684, and plans to bring about change seem to have preceded this date as well. Developments immediately preceding the "reform" illustrate the fragility of a monetary system in crisis. In 1683 news circulated that the shah had decided to bring new money into circulation. The mere rumor of this made it much more difficult to obtain credit; in anticipation of things to come, Iranian merchants refused to enter into transactions involving bills of exchange. The Dutch, who conducted much of their trade with fiduciary money, also began to demand cash payment for their wares, only to find that fewer than a quarter of the `abbasis they received were of acceptable standard. The remaining coins were found so debased that the VOC factors decided to send them back to their trading partners with the warning that they would have to stop distributing goods if no better money was forthcoming.[120]

In the subsequent period of commercial standstill the Dutch managed to garner only a small portion of the money they were owed from local merchants in good `abbasis. They soon realized that little more was to be expected, for their local debtors insisted that they had been forced to change the mahmudis in their possession at 2¼ to 2¾ mahmudis per good `abbasi (as opposed to the official ratio of 2 mahmudis per `abbasi) and that they would have to give up on the contracted goods if the VOC insisted on further cash payment in good `abbasis on the spot. Just as dependent on the merchants as the latter were on them, the Dutch realized that their merchandise was too large in volume to seek a different market if the domestic merchants were to turn their backs on them. They therefore decided to consent to the usual procedure of letting the merchants pay part of what they owed via bills of exchange drawn on Isfahan.[121] Later reports suggest that the Iranian merchants in this period had great difficulty in meeting their commitment to pay their bills in Isfahan on the due date and in proper coin.[122]

On the eve of the 1684 trading season it looked as if the problems with bills of exchange from the previous year were about to be repeated. By then, many current ʿabbasis contained little more than half of their supposed silver content and were accordingly valued at about 1¼ to 1½ mahmudis at most. The English captured the seriousness of the problem by saying that owing to the "bad money" Isfahan saw "neither buying nor selling, all the Bazars being shut up, and if you melt down one Tomand you will hardly find 5 abassis Silver in it, soe that Spahaune is now all in uproare...."[123] In the summer the rumor spread that a beginning had been made with the anticipated recoinage.[124] The news was not substantiated until the early autumn, when the English insisted that the shah had ordered new money to be struck, cautioning that the actual recoinage would not happen until Nawruz—March of the following year—at the earliest.[125] On 13 October 1684 Du Mans wrote in a letter to Kaempfer that new coins were being produced while the old ones were left in place.[126] The Dutch claimed around the same time that a total of 90,000 tumans in new coins had been struck. According to them, royal *sarrafs* (moneychangers) in the bazaar offered these coins for exchange against old ʿabbasis.[127] Everyone was frantically trying to convert old ʿabbasis into the new currency.[128]

Hopes for continued reform were soon dashed. The Persian New Year came and went, yet the first limited run did not have a follow-up. The Dutch put it this way: "It is true that, according to rumor, the shah intends to mint large quantities of new ʿabbasis, and new ones have indeed been coined, but this has been of so little significance that it is considered a curiosity if someone manages to lay his hands on one...."[129] The ʿabbasis that had been struck, they asserted, were equal in their fine silver content and weight to the ones issued under Shah ʿAbbas II. Director Casembroot, writing from Bandar ʿAbbas, claimed that the new ʿabbasis had suffered a weight reduction of 20 percent or 2 dang.[130] A later report from Isfahan, written in the autumn of 1685, contradicts that assessment, however, affirming that the weight was the same as that of the old ʿabbasis, that is, 9½ dang. Their silver content, on the other hand, was ¼ dang less than that of the ones struck under ʿAbbas II. The silver content of the latter had been valued at 5¾ dang, only ¼ less than the full alloy of pure silver.[131] Despite the slight debasement in alloy, however, the VOC agents saw neither the weight nor the silver content of the new ʿabbasis as the problem. The real problem, they asserted, was that after the initial issue production had stopped altogether. The official to blame for this suspension, Director Casembroot asserted, was the grand vizier, Shaykh ʿAli Khan. He had dissuaded the shah from bringing more money into circulation with the argument that all the unminted silver that used to be brought into the country from outside was now being taken to Basra and that putting out new coins in large volume would only deplete the treasury. This had apparently persuaded the shah to discontinue striking new `abbasis.[132]

The Dutch agreed to some extent, calling the dearth of silver and the fact that merchants had been taking most of it to Basra highly relevant to the crisis of 1684. Reals of eight, they said, were valued 1 to 1¼ mahmudis higher in Basra than in Iran. Nor was there much chance that conditions would change any time soon. Improvement would only come if Spanish reals, which were officially valued at 6¾ mahmudis, were raised to a price of 7 mahmudis.[133] The Iranian merchants, they insisted, had pledged that such a revaluation would prompt them to resume their silver transports to Isfahan. However, the desired increase had not met with approval in court circles, mainly, the VOC agent surmised, because many state officials, including the shah himself, were in possession of huge amounts in old `abbasis. They would sustain a significant loss if more mahmudis were offered for the rival silver real.[134] Instead of agreeing to an increase in the price of the real as a solution to the silver shortage, the shah at the behest of Shaykh `Ali Khan had issued an order to procure a few camel loads of silver from the mountains around Kirmanshah. From this batch a number of `abbasis had been struck at minimal cost, all of which had disappeared into the shah's treasury. While this seemed logical from the court's (short-sighted) perspective, its next step left observers puzzled. After striking a number of new `abbasis, the royal treasury proceeded to accept only mahmudis struck in Huwayza and `abbasis minted in Yerevan, notwithstanding the fact, as the Dutch noted with surprise, that these coins were scarce and had to be bought at a premium. Moreover, they were of lesser alloy than mahmudis and `abbasis struck elsewhere. In an even more bizarre turn, the court next outlawed all coins but the mahmudis and `abbasis that it was now soliciting, after making sure to drain the central treasury of all other money.[135]

In the context of the prevailing monetary crisis, this seemingly irrational measure suggests a desperate move after other salvaging efforts had been exhausted. Shaykh `Ali Khan, if he was indeed the driving force behind the decision to suspend the recoinage, was of course correct in suspecting that, regardless of output and the nominal price attached to the new coins, putting out more money would only lead to an immediate increase in export of whatever coin was released in the market.[136] That was precisely the dilemma the state faced. The aim of the government's policy may have been to safeguard the holdings of the royal treasury by giving preference to a coin that was little exported, after first securing a large quantity for the royal coffers. This scenario tallies with a principal objective of the attempted reform: to curb the currency flight that had plagued the system for so long. As the first new `abbasis were issued, new restrictions on cross-border money traffic were announced. In Dhu'l hijjah 1095/Nov.–Dec. 1684, the shah issued farmans prohibiting (the striking of) adulterated coins and banning his subjects from visiting Ottoman territory in an attempt to prevent (the importation of) adulterated money. He also sent orders to the province of `Arabistan for merchants not to export gold from the country. In addition, restrictions were imposed on the local vali's right to strike coins, although it is not clear whether this represented a total ban on minting activity or simply a tightening of existing rules.[137] These decrees seem to have been issued for all of the country's exit points. In December the English reported from Bandar `Abbas that an order had arrived from the shah for the shahbandar "not to let any Money Gold or Silver be carried out of his Countrey...."[138] The experience of William Hedges, passing through Kirmanshah on his way to Baghdad in January of 1686, suggests enforcement by way of increased scrutiny of cross-border traffic. Shah Quli Khan, the city's governor and a son of Shaykh `Ali Khan, suspecting hidden gold and silver, forced the caravan Hedges traveled with to open various bales. The price the Englishman was forced to pay to avoid further probing was 15 tumans in cash and goods.[139]

The mint "reform" of 1684–5 made a great impression on everyone. It is the only monetary issue referred to in Khatunabadi's chronicle.[140] This may be because the actual consequences of the measure were counterproductive, causing great consternation and driving many to destitution. The confusion it created is voiced by a resident European missionary who noted that "for now, as new money has been coined, and the old coinage retouched, in part allowed to remain, there are three kinds of currency—of higher, medium, and lowest value...."[141] For their part, the VOC agents predictably complained that the half-finished reform was highly detrimental to commerce, since it made it much harder to obtain credit. It also fueled inflation. Everything had become very expensive, the Dutch insisted in 1686, and little could be obtained for anything but the Huwayza mahmudi. This would be tolerable, they added, if only these coins circulated in sufficient quantities. In reality, however, they were so scarce that people bought them at rates that exceeded their face value by 10 to 15 percent. Gold was no alternative either, at least not for ordinary people, for how could they afford the 17½ to 18 mahmudis for which each ducat was sold by speculators who took advantage of the confused circumstances?[142]

The lack of confidence in the soundness of money that had developed did not stop there. Even those who could afford to buy ducats as an alternative, the Dutch reported, found that the shopkeepers would not accept them. The owner was then forced to take these coins to the official mint, only to be paid in new money worth a mere 14 to 14½ mahmudis. After all, it was court policy to have those who brought their specie to the mint and those who received their newly struck money from the mint bear the loss that accrued from melting specie and turning it into new coinage. This, among other things, was the reason, the same Dutch report noted, why in the circumstances no Armenian merchants were willing to come to Isfahan from Anatolia with ducats, or reals for that matter, the latter still being valued at no more than 6¾ to 6⅕ mahmudis. The upshot of these conditions was that the collective merchants—including the foreign ones—no longer knew what kind of currency they should demand for their goods. By now, good old 'abbasis had ceased to circulate, either because they had been siphoned off to India or because of hoarding. New money, by contrast, continued to be so scarce that, for the few commercial transactions that were still conducted, merchants would reserve it eight to nine months in advance, anticipating that by that time the new coin might be more widely available.[143]

DEVELOPMENTS AFTER 1684

The decade after the events of 1684–5 saw no improvement in Iran's monetary situation. Badly adulterated coins continued to be a problem for the Safavid government as much as for merchants bent on exporting treasure. The persistent impecuniousness of the Iranian state is reflected in the modest value of the gifts accompanying the embassy of Husayn Khan Beg to Moscow in 1691.[144] The Dutch, the biggest exporters, were temporarily reduced to idleness when a conflict over their silk contract with the Safavid crown escalated to the point where they occupied the island of Qishm, off the coast of Bandar 'Abbas, in 1684. The conflict came to an end when they surrendered the island a year later, yet only in 1687 was the VOC able to fully resume its commercial activities in Iran, including its bullion transports to India. Never mind that much of the specie the company had procured in the interim, current `abbasis and mahmudis, proved to be deficient in weight.[145] The only good `abbasis, the ones struck under `Abbas II, could be had only at rates that exceeded their face value by up to 11½ percent. Newer `abbasis received by the VOC yielded a 40 percent loss upon melting.[146] So many adulterated Safavid coins were carried to Ceylon by private traders in this period that the VOC agents on the island began to differentiate between the `abbasis and mahmudis they themselves brought from Iran and the privately imported, compromised ones by overstriking the former with a VOC stamp.[147]

The Dutch at this point adopted several measures to minimize their losses in the subcontinent. They limited the quantity of mahmudis they received for their wares to the equivalent of the cash needed to buy goods, insisting on ducats for payment of the rest.[148] They also sought to convert as much of their profits as possible into commodities. This did not include Iranian silk, which at this point commanded low prices. Instead, the VOC found a partial alternative in the export of goat's wool from Kirman.[149] The Company also cast an eye on pearls from Bahrain as a way to process income earned from the sale of spices.[150] The Dutch were not alone in this predicament; Banyan merchants, too, in the early 1690s unloaded profits by buying up commodities such as pearls, madder, fruit, and tobacco.[151] Yet none of these was capable of absorbing the substantial profits they and the maritime companies began to earn in the closing decade of the century with the importation of ever larger quantities of Indian cloth. As a result, foreign as well as domestic merchants continued to remit most of their revenue in specie.

Contrary to appearances, the monetary crisis continued to preoccupy the Safavid authorities following the aborted recoinage of 1685. Control of the ban on bullion exports momentarily slackened after Shaykh `Ali Khan's death in 1689. The following year, large amounts of smuggled specie belonging to Turks, Arabs, and Indians and destined for India went undetected, even as 400,000 Armenian-owned rix-dollars transported on Dutch ships were discovered and confiscated.[152] In the spring of 1691 Mirza Tahir Vahid was appointed grand vizier. Asked by the shah to name the most pressing problems facing the state, he mentioned the need for currency reform.[153] One casualty of the new attention to monetary issues that seems to have resulted was Saru Khan Sahandlu, qurchibashi as well as mu`ayyir al-mamalik, who in the summer of 1691 was put to death, accused, among other crimes, of putting out substandard money.[154] Tahir Vahid showed a special interest in the large sums of money that bypassed Iran by being taken to India via Basra. When he asked Johan van Leene, special Dutch envoy to the Safavid court, about the reason why so many Spanish reals were taken to Basra, to be ferried from there to India, the latter listed low mint prices for silver and the debased character of the Safavid silver currency. The remedy, Van Leene suggested, would be to raise the mint price of reals, that is, to pay for them according to their market value, to improve the quality of silver coin, and to leave merchants alone.[155]

Van Leene's first recommendation was heeded soon enough, for in 1692 it was announced that the royal treasury would henceforth accept reals at 7 mahmudis as opposed to the former rate of 6½, causing the Dutch to anticipate a great increase of silver imports into Iran.[156] Isfahan's official appreciation of silver, combined with lower gold prices in Europe, indeed led to a (temporary) influx of silver into the country, causing a fall in the value of gold. By 1691 the "Moorish" ducat sold at 12½ and the European ducat at 13½ mahmudis in Isfahan, making export to India once again profitable. Even when the price went up to 14 mahmudis in 1692 and 1693, they still made a profit in the subcontinent. Taking advantage of these conditions, the Dutch decided further to minimize their dependence on the persistently unreliable `abbasi and mahmudi by buying up large quantities of these ducats.[157]

Not surprisingly, the Safavid authorities chose to ignore Van Leene's last piece of advice, his suggestion that merchants be left free and undisturbed. They instead followed a time-honored impulse by reaffirming the ban on the export of reals from the southern ports.[158] Still, with the ducat down in price and the appointment of Hajji Piri, a renegade Armenian and a merchant himself, as the new mint master in 1692, expectations in Isfahan ran high for genuine mint improvement and a revival of commerce. Hajji Piri, however, resigned his post in March of the following year, to die a month later. The succession of Isfahan's *kalantar*-cum-vizier to the position dashed any hope of improvement.[159] Neither the court nor merchants seem to have benefited much from the increase in the denominative value of silver coin. Beyond a momentary spike in imports, there is no record that substantially more silver was brought to the mints as a result of the 1692 measure. Nor did the capital flight diminish, despite stepped-up vigilance by inspectors. In 1694, Banyan money changers purchased newly struck `abbasis and mahmudis at a premium of 1 to 3 percent before dispatching them to Surat. Huwayza mahmudis were still the only current coin, even though half were compromised in their silver alloy.[160] Clandestine money exports continued unabated. The EIC in 1695 sent 23,000 ducats packed in a consignment of galbanum; and in 1697 they hid some 17,000 ducats in a load of ammoniacum, remitting a total of 83,000 to Bombay that year.[161] The VOC factors, too, continued to take specie out of the country at a fast clip. In response, the Safavid authorities in 1699 issued another export ban. In an obvious sign of limited success, such bans kept being issued until 1720.[162]

Chapter 5

From Perpetual War to Lasting Peace: Safavid Military Politics in the Seventeenth Century

> Les armées persanes luttent contre la faim, la soif, les aspérités des montagnes, les solitudes des déserts, les distances entre les différents lieux, la disette, etc.
>
> The Persian armies fight against hunger, thirst, the harshness of the mountains, the loneliness of the deserts, the distances between the various places, deprivation, etc.
>   Raphaël du Mans, "De Persia 1684," in Richard, ed.,
>   *Raphaël du Mans*, 2:287

QIZILBASH VERSUS GHULAMS

A long-standing assumption, reiterated in numerous accounts, holds that after the reign of Shah `Abbas I the Safavid army declined from a position of superior strength to a state of lamentable weakness. Following Minorsky's analysis of the root causes of Iran's overall "decline" in the seventeenth century, the reasons have generally been associated with `Abbas's military and administrative reforms, which he enacted precisely to strengthen his realm by tightening his personal grip on it. Pointing to the demise of the Qizilbash as the realm's stalwart warriors and their replacement by officers and soldiers recruited from the ranks of the *ghulams*, scholars have identified a shift from military strength based on tribal prowess to military weakness related to bureaucratic inertia and urban softness.

We now know that the deliberate undermining of Qizilbash influence did not start with Shah `Abbas I but goes all the way back to the beginning of Safavid rule. It was Shah Isma`il I who first appointed Iranian *vakils* (counselors) in order to balance Qizilbash power. Following his victory in the civil war that marked the first decade of his rule, Shah Tahmasb continued this policy in judicious ways, seeking to weaken the Qizilbash without humiliating them. He thus promoted Ma`sum Beg, neither a Qizilbash warrior nor a bureaucrat but a member of the extended Safavid clan, to the post of vakil in 1553, and through him created the Shaykhavand "tribe" as an artificial entity on par with the Turkoman tribes. Tahmasb tampered with Iran's tribal makeup in other ways as well, most notably by making sure that tribes were no longer ruled by individual chieftains. This divide-and-rule policy, which also manifested itself in appointments of *mirzas*, men of Iranian stock, to high administrative office, paved the way for the subsequent bureaucratic and military measures undertaken by Shah `Abbas I.[1]

If the long-term weakening of the Safavid military is an inarguable fact, it was also a complex process. A good understanding of its causes, its evolution, and its outcome requires paying attention to the nature of the Safavid military, including its fighting traditions and the weaponry and logistics it employed in relation to Iran's physical environment, as well as to the financial means made available to the military, and the politics this involved.

The first observation to be made is that Iran's military might was inherently limited, in absolute as well as in relative terms. The Qizilbash were a formidable fighting force with a well-deserved reputation for courage and ferocity. Utterly devoted to a leader whom they venerated as an incarnation of the divine, and convinced of their own invincibility, they are said to have thrown themselves into battle without armor. Yet, even if their surprise attacks were often effectively lethal, as a war machine the Qizilbash army was far from perfect. Consisting of tribal irregulars, the Qizilbash were notorious for their lack of discipline and organization, which manifested itself in a great diversity of arms as well as in the habit of camping out in a disorganized fashion in multi-colored tents, with little concern for surprise enemy attacks.[2] Divided by tribal affiliation, they also rarely fought as a united front.

From their early days as a political dynasty, the Safavid army had to bow to the Ottomans both in numerical terms and with regard to discipline, logistical strength, and strategic effectiveness. Safavid chroniclers occasionally acknowledge this weakness and evince a grudging admiration for Ottoman military power.[3] In the aftermath of the Iranian defeat at Chaldiran in 1514, the Ottomans estimated that the Safavid army numbered no more than 18,000 men, 10,000 of whom were equipped with firearms.[4] This seems a suspiciously low number. Perhaps more realistically, some fifty years later an Italian source comparing the strength of the Iranian and the Turkish armies insisted that the Safavids could field at most 50,000 to 60,000 men.[5] The number of 50,000, given by the Dutch one century later, suggests long-term continuity.[6] Unfortunately, the sixteenth-century Italian report does not give figures for the Ottoman army, but other sources indicate that Istanbul was able to mobilize at least 100,000 men at any time. One report from 1548 even speaks of 200,000 Ottoman soldiers confronting 120,000 Iranian ones.[7]

The Safavid rout at Chaldiran might not have been as disastrous as it was if Shah Isma'il and his troops had not engaged in a raucous drinking party on the eve of the battle, yet the Safavids owed their defeat above all to structural weaknesses, including inferior fire power. A deficiency in firearms remained a problem in the Safavid army even after Isma'il introduced a (small) body of firearm infantry in the aftermath of Chaldiran.[8] And Ottoman superiority did not rest solely on a larger arsenal; it also involved greater familiarity with the use of fire power. The papal envoy Giovanni Battista Vecchietti, an eyewitness to the battles around Tabriz in 1585–6, noted the bravery and skill of Iran's soldiers, calling them better than the Ottomans in their use of sword, lance, and bow. He was much less sanguine about their adeptness at handling firearms, though, claiming that they cared but little for harquebus and that they had less expertise with artillery than the Ottomans, relying on foreign experts for its operation.[9] Firearms had been known in Safavid Iran from the outset; the people of Kirman employed fire power against Uzbek marauders in 1509, and Safavid troops defeated the Uzbeks at Jam in 1528 with mass firearms.[10] Isma'il in his later reign even sought to intimidate the Ottomans by spreading rumors about the Qizilbash having adopted cannons and firearms in great numbers.[11] Still, separated by the Ottoman Empire from the main source of innovative technology, Western Europe, and effectively landlocked owing to the great distance between the Persian Gulf ports and the capital, Iran was at a disadvantage with regard to outside military expertise. The Safavids did benefit from the assistance of mostly European military experts, foundrymen, gunners, and artillerymen, who sold their skills to anyone willing to pay, though not as much as the neighboring Mughals, who in the sixteenth century employed numerous Ottoman military advisors, widely reputed as expert gunners and musketeers.[12]

Similar problems attended the use of artillery. The Ottomans were surefooted in their ability to mount a coordinated and sustained ground attack and, using field artillery, often managed to prevail in prolonged combat. The Safavid army primarily remained a cavalry formation, employing the swift dash, attacking with volleys of arrows and retreating just as quickly in rather disorganized fashion. This might take the enemy by surprise and inflict heavy casualties, but it was not very helpful in open combat on a fixed battlefield, which the Iranians tried, not always successfully, to avoid.[13] Field artillery especially remained underdeveloped, and siege artillery, if not unknown, remained heavily underused in Iran. Cannons, known in Iran at the time of the Aq-Quyunlu in the late fifteenth century, were cast in Azerbaijan during Safavid campaigns in the sixteenth century, and later continued to be employed in wars that involved strongholds, such as Yerevan in the 1630s and Qandahar in 1648. Yet the country's physical environment posed insurmountable obstacles to the full use of cannon. Muscovy held sway wherever navigable rivers allowed for the transportation of artillery. The Ottoman army used the Tigris and Euphrates for the movement of big guns to cities such as Mosul and Baghdad. Iran, by contrast, lacked waterways that would have facilitated the transportation of this kind of heavy equipment.[14] Several observers comment on the relative paucity of cannon in the Safavid arsenal, the low skills the Iranians displayed in handling cannon, and their tendency to neglect the pieces that were available. Vecchietti attributed the difficulty the Qizilbash had in driving the Turks out of the fortress of Tabriz to their "inexperience in this kind of combat."[15]

Iran's backwardness in firearms was also linked to the fighting tradition of the steppes. The Qizilbash idea of manliness, *javanmardi*, was ill at ease with firearms, which forced the rider to dismount and get down to the level of the lowly infantry soldier.[16] A serious adoption of firearms by the Qizilbash would have come at the expense of their mobility and speed, just as it would have undermined their warrior pride in riding and archery skills that were intimately bound up with a millennia-old warrior ethos. This, in addition to a desire to break the connection between land and service, was precisely why the ghulams were introduced as an alternative military corps. Yet, as Geoffrey Parker puts it with regard to armies of slave soldiers, the ghulams were "not a system that favored strategic or tactical innovation."[17] Even the ghulams mostly continued to adhere to traditional weaponry. Firearm troops, recruited from the peasantry and the laboring classes, were generally held in low esteem by the cavalry troops, who despised them as "cannon fodder."[18]

All of this means that the distinction between the Qizilbash and the mostly Georgian ghulam fighting force on which the Safavids increasingly came to depend is not as stark as it is often made out to be. The ghulams neither supplanted the Qizilbash entirely, nor were they necessarily of lesser military stature. The *qurchis*, members of the tribal cavalry, came to represent the Qizilbash, but as officers loyal to the shah rather than as representatives of their tribes. It is true that in Shah `Abbas I's later reign the ghulams began to fill some high-ranking officer posts in the army. A conspicuous example of this development is the *sipahsalar kull-i lashklar-i Iran*, the commander-in-chief of all of Iran's troops, a function that appears to have been called into being by Shah `Abbas I in a desire to "strike a balance between Qizilbash and ghulams" by creating a post "superior in status to both the qurchibashi and the qullar-aqasi."[19] The first official to hold this position de facto was Allah Virdi Khan. Several ghulams carried the title in subsequent decades, among them Qarchaqay Khan (1616/17–1624/5) and Rustam Khan (1630–43).[20] Georgians also came to make up a large part of the actual fighting forces, reaching a contested number of 40,000 in the 1670s.[21] Yet, though challenged by the ghulams, the Qizilbash—a term that gradually lost its tribal connotations and more and more came to refer to Persian troops in general[22]—continued to represent the majority in the military throughout the seventeenth century, both as officers and as warriors. The sipahsalar, for one, hardly reflects the new power and influence of the ghulams. After all, the position lapsed under Shah `Abbas II (to be revived in the 1690s, most likely in response to the new military threats looming on Iran's eastern border).

Meanwhile, the head of the qurchis, the *qurchibashi*, who was always a Qizilbash, continued to be the most important military commander. If anything, his stature and standing only grew in later Safavid times. Saru Khan Sahandlu, discussed in Chapter 3, is not the only example of a qurchibashi who vied with the grand vizier for supremacy. From the mid-seventeenth century onward, the qurchibashi was seated in second place next to the shah, just behind the grand vizier, and in front of the sipahsalar.[23] The continued high standing of the Qizilbash also comes through in the *Tarikh-i jahan-ara-yi `Abbasi*. Writing in the 1650s, Vahid Qazvini praises their loyalty and their willingness to fight and die in battle.[24] They had indeed been in the frontline fighting at Qandahar a few years earlier.[25] Five Qizilbash officers were among the top court *amirs* in this period: the qurchibashi, the *amir-akhur-bashi*, the *tupchibashi* (cannon master), the *tufangchi-bashi* (head of the musketeers), and the *ishik-aqasi-bashi*.[26]

Aside from the ishik-aqasi-bashi, these all represent the highest military offices. In sum, much of the army command at this point was still in the hands of the Qizilbash. Even in the 1690s, when Georgians formed the mainstay of the Safavid military, the Qizilbash played a significant role in the army.[27] The Georgians earned the respect of contemporary observers for their fighting skills and morale. Yet, common perceptions notwithstanding, they were not the only ones to fight for the survival of the Safavid state in the early 1720s.[28] For instance, as Iran's eastern borderlands came under intense pressure at the turn of the eighteenth century, the Afshar of Kirman, who had long been marginalized by Kurds, were once again pressed into service and joined the Georgians in the struggle against the Baluchis and Afghans on the Sistan frontier.[29]

MONEY PROBLEMS AND GROWING MILITARY WEAKNESS

All the available evidence suggests a diminished fighting capacity for the Safavid military in the course of the seventeenth century. Inherent weaknesses as well as changes in the makeup of the army played a role in this process, but financial problems were by far of most consequence to the outcome. The nexus between war and economy is inherently complex, involving the financial outlays required to mobilize and equip an army, the damage to land and property caused by hostilities, and the fiscal revenue accruing from conquered lands. In the case of the wars that the Safavids and Ottomans intermittently fought until the 1630s, it is doubtful if any long-term financial benefit derived from, say, Iraq, made up for the initial war-related costs. The Iranian army's scorched-earth tactics, designed to prevent the enemy from being able to feed off the land, only made matters worse. The fertile provinces of Azerbaijan, Armenia, and Shirvan bore the brunt of this policy, resulting in scarred, desolate landscapes filled with destroyed villages, ruined bridges, poisoned wells, and burned crops. Add to that the habit of depopulating areas, resettling the inhabitants to far-off places with the aim of weakening loyalties and strengthening borders, which the Safavids inherited from previous dynasties, and one gets an idea of the destructiveness involved—as well as of the dread the Ottomans apparently felt when going on campaign against the Iranians.[30]

Uruch Beg, better known as Don Juan, the Iranian diplomat who converted to Christianity while on a mission in Spain, observed that "gold is the motive and the true motive power of war; he who has money will always find soldiers."[31] Gold, indeed ready money of any kind, is precisely what Iran was chronically short of, for reasons that were discussed in Chapter 4. Safavid impecuniousness showed up as early as the days of Shah Isma'il in the form of a state treasury that was frequently empty.[32] Matters hardly improved under his successors. Toward the end of Shah Tahmasb's reign, a period of severe money shortages in Iran as well as the Ottoman Empire, soldiers had not been paid for fourteen years. Any wages they received were in kind.[33] A Venetian report from 1580 claimed that 15,000 destitute Iranian soldiers had taken refuge in India and Central Asia, blaming this state of affairs on the shah's avarice.[34] Almost a century later, little had changed. Soldiers' pay was constantly in arrears, and their predicament was worsened by Iran's sparsely populated and inhospitable environment. Their pay, one observer insisted, was inadequate, so that they suffered while on campaign, where victuals were very expensive because of the barrenness of the soil and the great distances between towns and villages. As long as no opportunity for plunder presented itself, they quickly exhausted their financial means.[35] The words of Raphaël du Mans quoted at the head of the chapter convey the same image of famished and dehydrated soldiers straggling through arid, empty territory.

A burst of royal munificence often accompanied the accession of a new shah, enabling soldiers to recover some of their back pay. With the enthronement of Shah Muhammad Khudabandah in 1578, for instance, the qurchis recouped decade-old arrears.[36] Four years later, soldiers received three years of back pay before going on campaign to Khurasan, suggesting that the previous disbursement had been a one-time operation—as it tended to be—and that regular payments had not been kept up since.[37] Hamzah Mirza, Khudabandah's son, in 1586 out of necessity broke up "all the gold and silver vessels belonging to his establishment and distributed them among the Qizilbash."[38] Shah 'Abbas I was a paragon of military strategy and strength; if we are to believe Jean Chardin, he raised the number of his armed forces to 120,000.[39] With these, this most capable of all Safavid military strategists successfully resisted the mighty Ottomans, retook all the lands that had been lost since the days of Shah Tahmasb, including Iraq and the province of Qandahar, and added the Caucasus to the Safavid realm. Yet, like his predecessors—and quite a few of his European contemporaries—, he waged war under a financial cloud. Pietro della Valle reported in 1619 how a number of Iranian recruits had defected to the Portuguese for lack of pay.[40] Safavid soldiers, he observed, received their wages partly in cloth, which they had to purchase from the court at above-market rates, losing considerable money upon selling it.⁴¹ During his expedition against Baghdad in 1623 'Abbas was forced to remunerate his soldiers with money printed on leather.⁴² A Venetian consul in Aleppo claimed that the Ottoman–Safavid wars fought between 1623 and 1638 left the region in a state of utter poverty.⁴³

DEVELOPMENTS UNDER SHAH SAFI, 1629–42

The reign of Shah Safi was to be a crucial phase in the interplay between financial distress and a weakening army. As the Safavids faced renewed Ottoman aggression following his accession in 1629, Isfahan decided to meet the country's structural monetary problems with budget cuts, including a reduction in military spending. The results soon showed. In 1631 Iranian soldiers were paid in broadcloth of very poor quality, English imports that had lain in storage for long periods for lack of buyers.⁴⁴ The Safavids in 1630 lost the battle of Marivan against the Ottomans and in 1635 were forced to cede Yerevan to their main enemies. The latter city was recovered a year later, but this hardly made up for the definitive loss of Baghdad to the Ottomans in 1638. In the latter year, the Iranians also lost Qandahar to the Mughals, so that a decade after the accession of Shah Safi most of 'Abbas's conquests had been lost.

Instrumental in the decision to reduce military expenditure was Mirza Muhammad "Saru" Taqi. His tenure as grand vizier from 1634 to 1645, in particular, proved to be a mixed blessing with regard to state finances. In many ways he was an excellent administrator. Relatively uncorrupt and relying on broad experience gained in the course of a long career in financial administration, he found numerous ways to increase royal revenue. As vizier of Mazandaran under Shah 'Abbas I, he successfully investigated various cases of corruption. Later on, he looked into the fiscal practices of the *mustawfi-yi baqaya* (comptroller of the arrears), Mirza Ma'sum, and the *shahbandar* of Bandar 'Abbas, 'Ali Quli Khan.⁴⁵ This diligence, in addition to his tough negotiating style with agents of the European maritime companies, made him a royal favorite.⁴⁶

Yet not everyone benefited from Mirza Taqi's projects and policies, and the army suffered greatly. The grand vizier alienated a number of important officials with his heavy-handedness, some of them strong characters and competent military commanders. One was

'Ali Mardan Khan, the able governor of Qandahar, who, faced with a grand vizier demanding large payments and intent on having him dismissed, rebelled and proceeded to offer the strategically important stronghold of Qandahar to the Mughals, thus necessitating a costly Safavid campaign.[47] Another was Imam Quli Khan. This powerful governor of a large swath of the country's southern regions was brought down in a conspiracy led by Mirza Taqi and the queen-mother.[48] For decades, Imam Quli Khan and, before him, his father Allah Virdi Khan had been among Shah 'Abbas's most reliable commanders, assisting him in conquering the entire southern half of the country. Allah Virdi Khan is said to have commanded 50,000 troops, who "ranked with the best in the world."[49] The son was as competent a general as the father. He, too, led some of the best troops in the country, a reported 10,000 foot soldiers and cavalrymen. His elimination in 1632 thus dealt a severe blow to Iran's military strength—as did the conversion of state land to crown land in general.[50] A generation after Imam Quli Khan's death the Dutch declared southern Iran vulnerable to attack from the Arab shores of the Persian Gulf, insisting that the soldiers recruited from areas south of Isfahan were "all peasants with little military experience."[51]

Modern historians have hailed Mirza Taqi as a paragon of ghulam ascendance, singling out his various building activities.[52] But these same activities also siphoned off resources that might, and arguably should, have gone to the defense of the country.[53] Politics beyond architectural patronage probably played the determining role in his stinginess vis-à-vis the army. The grand vizier is known deliberately to have withheld funds from the military in an effort to undermine the Qizilbash. He thus decided to curtail the salaries of the qurchis.[54] In this he worked closely together with the women and eunuchs of the inner palace, both groups that were fervently anti-Qizilbash. In 1635, forced to prop up the army in the face of Ottoman attempts to regain Mesopotamia, he asked the Dutch for an 8,000-*tuman* loan so as to be able to pay the troops.[55] The sum he received, 4,200 tumans, clearly fell short of the need, for a year later reports spoke of scenes of mass desertion by unpaid Safavid soldiers fighting before Baghdad.[56]

The conspiracy that in 1645 ended the life of both Mirza Taqi and his nemesis, qurchibashi Jani Khan, provides yet more evidence for the struggle between two court factions over expenditure.[57] One of the grievances Jani Khan and his fellow conspirators harbored against Mirza Taqi was precisely that the latter had undermined the Qizilbash-dominated army by cutting the wages of soldiers. As detailed in Chapter 2, the animus that existed between the two officials was linked to differences over fiscal and military policy. A military officer and a member of the Qizilbash, Jani Khan naturally favored strong armed forces. As the official responsible for well-padded royal coffers, Mirza Taqi, in turn, took the side of the cash-strapped court by advocating military cutbacks. Nothing illustrates this dispute better than their respective suggestions about the policy to be pursued with regard to Qandahar. Mirza Taqi insisted that its governor, `Ali Mardan Khan, pay his dues to Isfahan or be summoned to court to be replaced. Jani Khan, concerned about the simultaneous Ottoman threat to Baghdad, counseled the shah against replacing `Ali Mardan Khan so as not to create turmoil on the eastern border.

THE PEACE OF ZUHAB AND ITS AFTERMATH

The Accord of Zuhab (or Qasr-i Shirin) of 1639 and its result, a durable peace between the Safavids and the Ottomans, exemplified a new approach to war and peace among Iran's decision-makers.[58] In the acknowledgment of military inferiority implied by the accord we see the culmination of a process with origins in Shah Isma`il's rout at Chaldiran and his subsequent decision not to resume hostilities with the Ottomans. Following Isma`il's death in 1524 the Safavids once again became embroiled in conflict with their archenemies, yet until Shah `Abbas I took the offensive the Iranians were rarely the aggressors. It was the Ottomans who invaded Iran three times during the reign of Shah Tahmasb. The main reason why they managed to retake Baghdad in 1638 lies in a glaring imbalance in troop strength. An eyewitness claimed that the Ottoman army consisted of almost 110,000 men, whereas the Safavids, having sent "away all unprofitable and unserviceable persons (as old men, women and children), unto other retired cities and strong holds in Persia," were left with only 40,000 soldiers to defend the garrison.[59] No doubt partly inspired by strategic considerations, the accord was also a function of domestic politics, most notably the (selective) pacifism pursued by the same elements at court that schemed against the Qizilbash. Already under Shah `Abbas I some courtiers had advocated making peace with the Ottomans, even at the price of far-reaching territorial concessions, possibly in response to Ottoman suggestions for peaceful relations in the face of Europe's ability to benefit from the existing enmity between the two states.[60] The faction they represented continued to make itself heard under his successors. In 1629, shortly after Shah Safi's accession, the ruler's great-grandmother appeared in the royal council to plead against renewed anti-Ottoman campaigning.[61] And following the conclusion of the Accord of Zuhab, Mirza Taqi counseled the shah that doing away with the costly necessity of maintaining provincial governors and troops was an excellent way of saving money, especially at a time of peace and in the absence of any war plans.[62]

Regardless of the impetus behind it, Zuhab must be considered a watershed in Safavid military, commercial, and diplomatic history. Terminating almost a century and a half of hostilities between two bitter enemies, it obviated the need for either state to be prepared for imminent war over Azerbaijan and Mesopotamia. This was a remarkable step for a state built upon perpetual warfare—even if it was arguably a sensible solution to an intractable problem for both states, in keeping with a historical pattern set by previous adversaries over the same territory, the Romans and the Byzantines on the one hand, and the Parthians and Sasanians on the other. Even more remarkably, unlike the Peace of Amasya, which was only observed for a few decades following its conclusion in 1555, the Accord of Zuhab proved to be durable. It was to last until the 1720s, when the eclipse of Safavid power prompted the Ottomans to join the Russians in occupying parts of northern and western Iran. Its legacy endures until today, for its boundaries were, with minor adjustments, reaffirmed in all subsequent border arrangements between Iran and the Ottoman Empire and, indeed, continue to mark the borders between modern Iran, Iraq, and Turkey.[63]

The agreement did not preclude all tension and conflict, to be sure. Dutch reports written in Basra in 1645 mention Iranian incursions into the region.[64] Five years later, Shah 'Abbas II organized an expedition to take Basra shortly after its governorship had devolved on Husayn Basha, son of 'Ali Basha Afrasiyab. But the shah's attention was soon diverted by developments around Qandahar, which became his next target. A more serious provocation was the assistance the Iranians lent to Husayn Basha to regain control of Basra after being ousted from the city in 1654. He managed to do so with a band of hastily recruited Arab warriors and an undefined contingent of Iranians numbering in the thousands, who are likely to have been supported and perhaps even supplied by the Safavid government.[65]

It is nevertheless clear that neither the Iranians nor the Ottomans had any desire to resume a full-scale war. The peace accord signed, both parties repeatedly confirmed its status and verified future peaceful intentions through diplomatic exchange. In the period from 1640 to 1662, Isfahan received four Ottoman missions, and as many Safavid delegations headed for Istanbul.[66] In the aftermath of the

1654 conflict, the two states exchanged ambassadors to confirm that no damage had been done to their good relations. Kalb ʿAli Khan went to Istanbul in 1655 and returned with an Ottoman envoy by the name of Ismaʿil Aqa Mutafarriqeh Aqasi, who, the Safavid chroniclers insist, was received with the highest honors and respect in Isfahan.[67] In the following three decades the exchange continued, albeit on a reduced level. Aside from the congratulatory Ottoman and Safavid missions of 1667 and 1692, respectively, the Ottomans seem to have dispatched envoys to Isfahan only in 1673 and 1684–5, years in which new crises once again threatened to disrupt the peace. The Iranians, for their part, do not seem to have reciprocated with a substantive embassy in this period.[68]

A paucity of published sources makes it difficult to draw definitive conclusions about the motivations of both states in their mutual pacifism. The Ottoman diplomatic record beyond 1612 is limited to a few scattered letters.[69] As for Iran, the available court chronicles do not provide us with any information between 1072/1662, the last year covered in the *Tarikh-i jahan-ara-yi ʿAbbasi*, and 1105/1694, the first year narrated in the *Dastur-i shahriyaran*.[70] The information contained in the Persian-language sources generally concerns the factual exchange of embassies and missions and fails to throw much light on their mandates and objectives. In the absence of archival repositories of Ottoman–Safavid diplomatic correspondence, we are therefore unable to probe Iranian objectives and intentions from within.

Even without explicit documentation, it is easy to see what motivated the Ottomans to abstain from aggression in the east beyond eastern Anatolia and Mesopotamia. Baghdad, the city that had frequently changed hands between the Ottomans and the Safavids, had definitively fallen under Ottoman control in 1638. Afterwards, Sultan Ibrahim I (r. 1640–8) seems to have been content with the extent of the Ottoman eastward expansion. The Janissaries are said to have lost interest in Iran after fighting a series of inglorious and unrewarding wars in Armenia. Istanbul meanwhile found it difficult to establish even a modicum of control over tribal and remote Mesopotamia. Following the execution of grand vizier Kemankesh Kara Mustafa Pasha in 1644, the Ottoman state went through a long period of disarray, involving the rapid succession of no fewer than eighteen grand viziers in a period of twelve years, four of whom were executed and eleven of whom were dismissed.[71] Military developments on their western borders played a role as well. In the 1640s their attention shifted toward the Mediterranean, where they became entangled with Venice in a prolonged conflict over Crete, known as the Candian Wars.[72]

It is, at first glance, more difficult to understand what made the Iranians refrain from provocations that might have led to a resumption of hostilities. Having lost Iraq, including the shrine cities of Shi'ism, the Safavids might reasonably be expected to have used every opportunity, and especially the Ottoman imbroglio over Crete, to regain these territories. There are several parts to the answer. One is the perennial shortage of liquid funds, as well as a long-standing, instinctive Safavid reluctance to get involved in a two-front war. There was also more to Iraq than its religious significance. By moving as far as Hamadan in 1630 and by briefly occupying and devastating Tabriz in 1635, the Ottomans once again had exposed Iran's vulnerability.[73] Mesopotamia, with its tribal, Arab population and its many Sunnis, was also alien territory for the Safavids. Iran's soldiers, used to the bracing climate of the plateau, no doubt felt uncomfortable in the humid and waterlogged lowlands of Iraq. The Qizilbash were out of their depth in an environment where the quick dash followed by a retreat into the mountains did not work and where the enemy—the local Arab population rather than the Ottomans—might disappear into impenetrable marshes. Finally, Iraq lay beyond Iran's natural boundaries, the mountains that surround the central plateau. Della Valle, writing two decades before Zuhab, noted the futility of trying to conquer Mesopotamia in light of the difficulty of defending the plains beyond the mountains.[74] The Safavids indeed barely controlled the mountains and their indomitable inhabitants. In Iraq proper, they had never held more than the main cities; in the countryside, they depended on the tribal population, Kurds in the north and Arabs in the south, and they could do little more than make ad hoc arrangements whereby they received military support in the form of supplies and intelligence, and in some cases tribute, in exchange for de facto autonomy. The Ottomans hardly fared any better, and it is probably safe to say that Iraq was a drain on the coffers of whichever state nominally ruled the territory. In sum, the urge to make peace was inspired by profound realism—with regard to the poor financial state of the Safavids, the superior strength of the Ottoman armies, and the difficulty of holding on to Iraq.

THE WAR OVER QANDAHAR, 1648–53

The Accord of Zuhab established a durable peace on Iran's western borders, but did nothing to pacify its northern and eastern frontiers. Shah 'Abbas II became involved in a confrontation in the restive

Caucasus, where the Safavid sphere of influence collided with those of the Russians and the Ottomans. The main issue involved the expansion of a Russian garrison on the Koy Su River and the construction of new fortresses, in particular the one they had built on the Terek River in support of Taymuraz, the deposed ruler of Georgia who had turned to them for aid. When the shah learned of this, he decided to act, even in the face of a new conflict over Qandahar. Orders went out to the governors of Ardabil, Chugur-i Sa`d, Qarabagh, and Astara and parts of Azerbaijan to send armed forces to assist Khusraw Khan, the governor of Shirvan. The assembled troops, reinforced by various tribal formations including contingents sent by the Daghistani ruler (the *shamkhal*), the *hakim* of Darband, and the ruler of the Kara Qaytaq, in 1653 attacked the fortress and drove out its occupants, the Russians and the Nogay, before destroying it.[75] `Abbas II followed up by sending Allah Virdi Khan, the *amir-shikar-bashi*, master of the hunt, with the order to build fortresses to secure the settlement of Qizilbash warriors. This led to unrest among the tribes of Daghistan. Safavid attempts to bring that region's various local amirs under the control of the governor of Shirvan, Hajji Manuchihr Khan, failed. In reaction, the Safavids sent an army numbering 30,000, which managed to defeat the tribal forces. Yet the result was the status quo ante: In keeping with tradition, Sorkhay Khan Shamkhal sent a son, Gul-Mihr Beg, as hostage to Isfahan and was allowed to regain his throne.

On the eastern border, meanwhile, the Safavids continued to tangle with the Mughals over the long-contested city of Qandahar, the key to control over the vast frontier zone between the two states, located at the outer limits of the radius of military action of either state.[76] Qandahar had been in Safavid hands since 1622, when Shah `Abbas I had wrested the city and its eponymous province from Mughal control, appointing one of his protégés, Ganj `Ali Khan, as its governor. When Ganj `Ali Khan died a year later, his son, `Ali-Mardan Khan succeeded him. `Ali Mardan Khan would rule the province for the next fifteen years, during which time he amassed a fortune, creating jealousy among the courtiers, who incited Shah Safi against him. Chief among those was grand vizier Muhammad Mirza "Saru" Taqi Khan, who demanded large payments from him and who was clearly intent on having him dismissed. Under financial pressure and the object of intrigue on the Safavid side, `Ali Mardan Khan was also approached by the Mughals, who invited him to defect with a promise of rich rewards. Thus lured, he rebelled against the shah, proceeded to offer the city and the province to Shah Jahan, and fled to India, where he subsequently attained high rank in the Mughal administration.[77]

Shah 'Abbas II acquiesced in the definitive takeover of Baghdad by the Ottomans, but did not give up on Qandahar. Both decisions—to forsake further adventurism in the west and to try and recover Qandahar—were no doubt a matter of deliberate choice, involving strategic calculations with regard to relative military strength and the chance of success, as well as royal prestige. With his eastward campaign Shah 'Abbas II continued his father's policy. In 1641 Shah Safi, apparently more galled by the loss of Qandahar than that of Baghdad, was about to mount an expedition against the Mughals, but until the late summer of that year it remained unclear whether the Ottomans would ratify the Accord of Zuhab, so that no action was undertaken until the arrival of the embassy that had been dispatched to Istanbul with the purpose of finding out.[78] When the news confirming Ottoman agreement arrived in September, Safi, having been apprized of the outbreak of a series of anti-Mughal rebellions in India, immediately proceeded to launch a campaign against Qandahar. In the spring of the following year, a huge army was ordered to assemble near Sabzavar, the gateway to Khurasan. The troops indeed left in early 1642, with the shah following a few months later. But Shah Safi died on 11 May.[79] By that time the Mughals had sent their own army to Qandahar, and Shah 'Abbas II, put on the throne on 15 May, dispatched troops as well, but the momentum for Iran's thrust was lost in the change of power.[80]

It was some time before the Safavids were able to resume their drive to retake Qandahar, with its fortress which was generally known as the strongest in all of West Asia and which under the Mughals had been further strengthened by European engineers.[81] It took 'Abbas II more than three years and the conspiracy that resulted in the execution of Mirza Taqi and the subsequent removal of Jani Khan to take effective control of state affairs. Soon after the dust of this coup had settled, the young shah turned his attention to military matters. In late 1645, following Mirza Taqi's death, a sum of 100,000 tumans was distributed among Iran's soldiers, whose pay had been in arrears for years.[82] The following spring Jamshid Khan, the *qullar-aqasi* (head of the slave soldiers) set out to mobilize an army from Isfahan.[83] Other parts of the country were pressed into action as well. The authorities of Kirman received orders to provide *suyursat* (provisions) in the amount of 300,000 *man* of wheat, in addition to lead and gunpowder.[84] The royal treasury made 5,000 tumans available for the purchase of wheat in Khurasan and Sistan.[85] The Mughals were not in a bellicose mood, however, and indeed sought to obtain Safavid neutrality with regard to Shah Jahan's venture to regain the ancestral lands of the Mughals in Central Asia. In early 1647 an Indian embassy dispatched for this purpose reached Isfahan. The Safavids agreed to remain neutral, yet in effect decided to proceed with their advance against Qandahar, taking advantage of the disastrous defeat Shah Jahan had just suffered in Badakhshan.[86]

Led by sipahsalar Hajji Manuchihr Khan, an army numbering 40,000—the bulk of Iran's armed forces if we are to believe a Dutch estimate of 50,000 as their aggregate number—set out from Isfahan in the summer of 1648.[87] Traveling via Mashhad and Farah, it reached Bust, near present-day Lashkargah, in January 1649. After taking Bust, the army marched on Qandahar itself and after a brief siege took the city on 11 February.[88] During the siege the Iranians, demoralized by oppressive commanders, lack of pay, and substandard accommodation, suffered great losses. The huge army of Qizilbash soldiers went "famisht for want of victuals," and the 30,000 tumans sent to them failed to provide sufficient relief.[89] During a parade in 1648 each horseman had received, for himself, his servant, and his two horses, the risible sum of one tuman for the entire year. At the same time soldiers in Mashhad were forced to pass review with horses and clothing borrowed from merchants. It is thus hardly surprising that 6,000 of the men fighting at Qandahar reportedly defected to the Mughals and that more than half of the horses in the Safavid forces died from hunger and exhaustion.[90]

There are various reasons why Qandahar nevertheless surrendered to the Safavids. Sanson (retrospectively) offered one by calling the Iranian troops better disciplined and much more robust than the troops the Mughals were able to field.[91] The Dutch noted the superiority of the Safavid artillery—enhanced by the assistance of European artillery experts.[92] But the Iranians may have owed their victory above all to factional fighting between Shah Jahan's sons, Dara Shikuh and Aurangzeb, leading to disarray in the Mughal command structure.[93] All Mughal attempts to retake Qandahar in the next few years failed. In early 1651 they marched against the city and spent four months before its walls, after which they had to give up their siege because of the onset of the cold season. Aurangzeb tried again the following year, but invading Uzbeks sidelined the effort, forcing him to lift another siege. Dara Shikuh made one last attempt in 1653, prompting Shah 'Abbas II to mobilize an army while seeking assistance from the governors of Kirman and Sistan in the form of cereals, lead, and gunpowder. Iran's deepening financial crisis severely hampered these efforts, however.[94] The same crisis cut deeply into Iran's military in other ways as well. In 1654 the post of sipahsalar was left vacant and a year later the *tupchibashi* (cannon master) was made to retire. In the same year, we hear of merchants being forced to take care of the upkeep of soldiers.[95]

None of this benefited the Mughals enough to recover Qandahar. Supplied with heavy artillery brought in from Lahore, Dara Shikuh managed to take Bust, but the low quality of the stone cannon balls used by the Mughal army and the limited range of their medium-sized guns made it impossible for them to sustain a siege.[96] This, as well as organizational problems, intrigue, and a lack of military resolve, caused the expedition to fail, forcing the Mughals to retreat.[97] Sanson, playing upon an age-old stereotype about Indian pusillanimity, argued that the Iranians held an inherent advantage over the Indians because their soldiers were superior, more disciplined fighters, which is why, in his words, Shah 'Abbas I had always sent fewer troops against the Mughals than they sent against the Iranians.[98] One observer even insisted that Shah Jahan's best soldiers were Iranians—presumably the ones who had defected from their own army—adding that the Mughal ruler could not "utilize them against their own king of Persia," and that his other crack troops, consisting of Rajputs, were no good against "men from cold countries."[99] According to Judasz Tadeusz Krusinski, Aurangzeb contemplated mounting a new campaign to retake the city but was dissuaded by his sister with the argument that the military odds were against him, that failure would be a terrible blemish on the sultan's reputation, and that success would bring but small gain.[100] In the end, the reason that the city remained in Iranian hands until the Afghan revolt of 1709 probably owed as much to Indian ineptitude caused by internal rivalries as to Iranian military prowess.

MILITARY DEVELOPMENTS UNDER SHAH SULAYMAN (1666–94)

From 1639 onward the Iranians enjoyed relative peace, even outward prosperity, a happy state that at least one Safavid chronicler ascribes to the Accord of Zuhab and that caused many a foreign observer to exult in the stability of Iran in mid-century.[101] The Safavid political elite henceforth counted on strategic territorial depth as a defense mechanism. Urban Iranians felt safe behind the mountains and deserts that surrounded the central plateau on three sides, viewing the same sparsely populated desert expanses that made life difficult for their own soldiers as a shield protecting the heartland against enemy attack.[102]

None of this is to say that no more money was spent on the army, that soldiers were no longer recruited, or that the Safavids completely gave up on military action. The power vacuum created by Shah ʿAbbas II's death in 1666, which Iran's enemies were quick to exploit, meant that they had no choice but to fight. In the case of Qandahar, new tensions actually preceded the shah's death. In early 1666, Indian sources spoke of Shah ʿAbbas II's plans to wage war against the Mughals. In Isfahan, by contrast, many were convinced that the Mughals, keen to avenge the poor treatment that Sultan Aurangzeb's lavish embassy had suffered in Iran in 1664, were about to invade Iran. This sentiment only grew stronger when news reached the capital that the Mughal ruler had ordered the shins of the 120 horses the shah had sent him cut, while publicly burning all the fine cloth and precious stones presented to him; he had also forbidden his subjects from engaging in trade with Iran over land and by sea. Jamshid Khan, Qandahar's newly appointed Safavid governor, spread his own rumors about an impending war, claiming that the Mughals were organizing an expedition against his city and had provided the Uzbeks with 50 *lak* (5 million) rupees as an incentive to open hostilities against Iran.[103]

The Safavids struck first. The governors of Kirman and Sistan having been instructed to assist Qandahar, the Iranian army crossed the border and engaged in raids.[104] Sultan Aurangzeb responded with preparations for a counteroffensive. Yet when in the fall the news broke that ʿAbbas II had died, Aurangzeb called off the planned campaign, reportedly with the excuse that, for the time being, "it would not be generous and heroic to send an army against the country of Iran," in an apparent reference to the tender age of the ruler who had just mounted the throne.[105] In reality, Mughal war preparations continued for another three months, as did the trade boycott that the Indians had instituted.[106] The Iranians, too, kept at it. In 1667, as Shah Safi II (Sulayman) was enjoying himself in his harem with Armenian women specially selected for him, his qullar-aqasi led an army toward Qandahar. The tufangchi-aqasi, too, made preparations for an eastern expedition, and the new sipahsalar, ʿAli Quli Khan, had set out for Afghanistan as well.[107]

As the Mughals retreated from the front around Qandahar in 1667, new Uzbek raids into Khurasan forced Isfahan to send troops to the northeast. This confrontation, too, had antecedents that long preceded Shah Sulayman's enthronement. As Chardin tells the story, Shah Safi had made arrangements with the Uzbeks after capturing the ruler of Urganj in Kharazm, Abu'l Ghazi Khan. Abu'l Ghazi Khan had been taken to Isfahan to be kept there for a decade as a gilded prisoner, enjoying many privileges in addition to an annual stipend of 1,500 tumans. In the early reign of Shah 'Abbas II, taking advantage of lax security, he had managed to escape, returning to Central Asia, where he had taken up power again. In a characteristically pragmatic gesture, the Iranians had continued to pay his allowance with the understanding that this would keep him from bothering Khurasan. On the death of Abu'l Ghazi Khan in 1663, 'Abbas II had terminated the annuity. This had prompted the ruler's son, Anusha Khan, who considered this stipend a form of tribute to be paid as insurance against aggression, to turn against Iran by forming a coalition with the khans of Balkh and Bukhara. Mashhad, Astarabad, and Farahabad were laid waste in the ensuing assault, prompting 'Abbas II to move to Mazandaran with an army of 50,000 in 1665. The Uzbeks thereupon sent an embassy to sue for peace. The shah's death a year later turned the tables, however. The Central Asian powers, aware that Iran's new ruler was more interested in wine and women than war, resumed their raiding on Khurasan, causing the death of some 8,000 Iranian soldiers.[108] Isfahan reacted by sending the governor of Kirman and Shaykh 'Ali Khan, at that point in charge of Kirmanshah, to the northeast with some 4,000 troops, joining those already stationed in the area. At the same time, Cossack incursions into the region of Astarabad prompted the central government to order local governors to recruit troops and dispatch those to Astarabad. The campaign foundered for lack of funding, however. Isfahan sent a caravan carrying money in the amount of 40,000 tumans to finance the operation, but it was intercepted and plundered by an army of 3,000 Uzbeks.[109]

The Ottomans also took advantage of Shah 'Abbas II's death. In 1667 they made another attempt to gain mastery over Basra, ordering the governors of Baghdad, Diarbakr, Aleppo, and Mardin to organize a campaign against the city. Istanbul also seems to have secured the assistance of the Muntafiq tribe, promising them control over Iraq's Jaza'ir region in exchange for switching sides.[110] Basra's governor, Husayn Basha, furious at the betrayal, sent his women to Iran and destroyed his palace while getting ready to depart the city.[111] He offered Basra to the Iranians but these declined.[112] On 18 November, despairing of his ability to defend his city, he gave orders for its evacuation. In keeping with the scorched-earth warfare typical of the times, all inhabitants were told to leave for Iran within three days and with all their possessions, after which the town would be torched. This is indeed what happened: Basra, now devoid of people, was first sacked by Husayn Basha's soldiers and subsequently laid in ashes.

All of these conflicts abated within a few years, either because Iran's enemies lacked the strength to mount an all-out assault on its territory, as in the case of the Uzbeks and the Mughals, or because they had settled on peaceful relations, as was true of the Ottomans. The Iranians were also lucky, for by the time Shah Sulayman took power the Safavid army was in shambles, hollowed out in terms of numbers, underpaid, and poorly served by incompetent leadership. In 1657 a visiting Ottoman ambassador had still been sufficiently impressed with the Safavid army to express the hope that its force would not be directed against the Ottoman military.[113] A decade later, matters had changed. A series of poor harvests and the enormous cost of Sulayman's two accession ceremonies had depleted the treasury. As the English put it in 1668, Iran "was never in a poorer condition to defende itself having neither men nor moneys."[114] Chardin, who was in the country at the time, estimated that the military still absorbed substantial sums of money amounting to 38.2 percent of total state spending.[115] Yet he also hinted at the qualitative and numerical deterioration of the standing army since the days of Shah `Abbas I. At that time, he insists, the Safavid army had numbered 120,000 men: 50,000 royal forces troops, 60,000 provincial forces, and a 10,000-strong special palace guard. By 1666, the preponderance of crown land had led to a decrease in military leadership and discipline, and the numbers had dwindled to the point where, during a military parade watched by Shah `Abbas II, the same troops with their armaments and horses kept up the fiction of sizeable numbers by passing the review stand ten to twelve times.[116] Engelbert Kaempfer, while offering a still respectable number of 90,000 for Iran's total armed forces, provides more detail by putting the army's weakening in the context of tensions and divergent interests between the center and the periphery. It was, he said, the responsibility of provincial governors to maintain the troops assigned to them. Their greed made them underreport the numbers, though, prompting the shah to hold frequent and unannounced reviews. Yet, Kaempfer adds, the officers in charge of mustering troops were either venal or unintelligent and thus easily fooled.[117]

Unsurprisingly, low and intermittently paid wages played an important role in the deterioration of the army. Chardin claimed that the pay of soldiers had been reduced by one-fourth since the days of Shah ʿAbbas II, prompting many soldiers to desert. According to him, the *barat* (promissory note) system that underlay the payment of soldiers' wages had led to arrears of seven to eight months and an attendant loss of one-fourth of their money through corruption and commissions. He had seen officers and artisans working for the shah who for two years had received their pay in the form of barats. As wages fell and prices went up, he insisted, many soldiers deserted to find different forms of employment, while refusing to bring up their sons as soldiers.[118] The French cleric De la Maze, very familiar with the northern regions, in these years referred to the utter poverty of the country's few military forces, assuring his superiors that they would concur with him if they saw conditions in Iran with their own eyes.[119] The south fared little better. In 1681, the soldiers stationed around Bandar ʿAbbas had not received any pay for a full five years.[120] Soldiers only received 25 to 30 *écus* (1.80 to 2 tumans) per annum from provincial governors, who handed them their wages in the form of barats for cereals or other goods to be recouped in villages.

Unlike their counterparts in Europe and the Ottoman Empire, who received a daily food allowance, Safavid soldiers had to take care of their own provisioning, which meant that they had to fend for themselves at the *urdu bazaar*, the traveling market that accompanied the army on campaign.[121] The local population bore the brunt. In Armenia the common people were made to pay for the salaries of the army that was assembled to resist the Cossacks in 1668, and several instances of theft and violence accompanying demands for irregular contributions by agents of the shah are on record from the same region.[122] Perhaps most tellingly, growing financial distress seems to have made soldiers increasingly dependent on the civilian population. Della Valle, writing in 1619, had observed that, unlike conditions in Europe, where villagers and peasants would flee in the face of approaching armies for fear of looting and extortion, Shah ʿAbbas's soldiers behaved well in their contact with people in the countryside. Not only did they abstain from plunder; they even paid in cash for every single item they acquired.[123] In the same vein, ʿAbbas's army, upon reaching Qazvin, had camped outside of the city so as not to impose hardship on its inhabitants.[124] Such concerns eroded over time. Later reports insist that the treatment of peasants by officials and especially passing army regiments was abominable to the point where villages were often located far from the thoroughfares.[125]

STRATEGIES OF WAR AND PEACE: THE EUROPEAN CONNECTION

With Qandahar back in Iranian hands and the Mughals too preoccupied with their domestic problems to mount a full counteroffensive, Sulayman's officials could (momentarily) relax about the eastern front. Vis-à-vis the Ottomans the shah continued his father's policy of peace as principle, albeit not as unconditionally as is often argued.

Meanwhile, the Peace of Zuhab and the Safavid weakness it reflected could not but diminish Europe's interest in bringing Iran into a projected anti-Ottoman alliance—a project with antecedents that go back to the reign of Shah Isma'il I. As the Venetian Bailo Francesco Gritti wrote in retrospect, the Iranians had "fallen into such idleness" after the Ottoman conquest of Baghdad in 1638 that it "extinguished all their previous bravery together with all their credit among Christian powers as possible allies."[126] That the Christian nations nevertheless showed renewed interest in Iran around the time of Shah Sulayman's accession relates to fresh developments in their anti-Ottoman struggle, which included a rare instance of intra-European cooperation. In 1667 Russia concluded the Peace of Andrusovo with Poland. This enabled these two countries to coordinate their anti-Ottoman policies by way of a joint diplomatic and economic initiative toward Iran. In early 1668 the Polish envoy Bogdan Gurdziecki left Warsaw for Isfahan, charged with the task of congratulating Shah Sulayman on his accession, of informing the Iranians of the recently concluded Russo-Polish treaty, and of securing continued missionary privileges in the Safavid realm. Informally, he was also to persuade Isfahan to join the anti-Ottoman league and to ratify a commercial treaty between Russia and the Armenians that had been concluded a year earlier, provided that part of Iran's exports would be directed to Poland.[127] The Franco-Spanish Peace of Aix-la-Chapelle of May 1668, meanwhile, prompted Pope Clement IX, anxious to forge a coalition to relieve the siege of Candia, to dispatch embassies to numerous courts, including those of Russia and Iran.[128]

Shah Sulayman sent an envoy named Muhammad Beg to Poland in response to the Gurdziecki mission. Yet he did not agree to the military and commercial proposals conveyed by the Polish emissary. Nor did he accede to similar requests in 1673–4, as Safavid–Ottoman tension threatened to erupt into yet another war and Russian, English, and French envoys all vied for attention at the Safavid court—prompting one visitor to comment about Iran that "no country in the world sends fewer and receives more ambassadors."[129] In the autumn of 1673 Sulayman left Isfahan and headed north in a move that some saw as preparation for a new war over Baghdad.[130] While in Qazvin he received the Spanish cleric Pedro Cubero Sebastian, who carried with him a letter from the Polish marshal and future king Jan III Sobieski (r. 1674–96). Written in June of 1673, it contained yet another proposal for joint military operations against the Porte.[131] Similar pressure came from the Arabs of southern Iraq, always eager to solicit outside assistance against the Ottomans, who in 1674 are said to have sought Iranian military support. In Baghdad rumors went around about the impending arrival of a Safavid army.[132] In the same year a potential *casus belli* presented itself with the arrival of envoys from the Kuchab, an autonomous part of Kurdistan that, feeling threatened by Ottoman designs to annex it, offered to become tributary to the Safavid state. Yet the shah stood his ground. After deliberations with his ministers, he declined the offer, telling the ruler of Kuchab to accommodate himself as best he could with the Porte.[133]

The Safavid decision to defuse the mounting tensions may have been inspired by the Ottoman reaction, which was to move artillery and other military equipment from Alexandretta (modern Iskenderun) to Baghdad.[134] The same reaction may have influenced the outcome of a meeting the shah held with his officers on 5 August 1674 to discuss a Russian request for the sending of 20,000 troops against the Ottomans. The request was conveyed by a mission led by A. Priklonskii and K. Khristoforov, who had come to Isfahan to urge the shah to try and retake Baghdad. The Safavid ruler once again rejected the suggestion. Since he had made peace with the Ottomans, Sulayman is reported to have said, he could not renege on his word; it would be better to dishonor a contract with the Russians than to break the peace with the Ottomans.[135] In reply to the argument that, having concluded their wars with the Christian powers, the Turks would not hesitate to resume hostilities against Iran, he let it be known that he would be content to be left with Isfahan.[136] This last statement may be apocryphal; at least, it is not found in any eyewitness account. In time it would, however, become a metaphor for the lax and irresolute image of Shah Sulayman that has persisted until today.[137]

In truth, Shah Sulayman's aversion to waging war was neither unconditional nor comprehensive, and the Iranian decision to maintain amicable relations with the Ottomans was motivated by more than royal lethargy. Lethargy, after all, does not explain why in 1671 troops were mobilized in Kirman, reinforced by contingents from the Persian Gulf coast, Lar, and Shiraz, to combat rebel Baluchis from Makran and Kitch.[138] Barthélemy Carré, passing though

Kirmanshah, in the same year observed a *yasaq*, army recruitment, with recruiters in town who summoned all those old enough to carry arms to keep themselves ready to march (against an undefined enemy).[139] In 1673, when a new war with the Ottomans seemed imminent, prompting the shah to move to Qazvin, Iranian army commanders were present in all the border provinces, reviewing troops and matériel, and assessing the governors' readiness to fight in case the Turks would declare war.[140] Villagers were recruited to strengthen the fortress of Yerevan.[141]

Some European observers attributed the Safavid reluctance to resume hostilities with the Ottomans to Shaykh ʿAli Khan and the fact that most of his landholdings were located at the frontiers of Mesopotamia, in the vicinity of Kirmanshah, in Kurdistan, his homeland.[142] Others pointed to the vizier's attempts to solve Iran's persistent monetary problems, emphasizing the energy with which he tried to reduce expenses as well as increase revenue.[143] Iran's penury, exacerbated by Shah Sulayman's notorious stinginess, certainly played a role in the pacific policies pursued by the state. Kaempfer noted how parade troops numbering 2,000 were originally paid from the royal treasury but that, upon assuming office, the parsimonious shah had taken over only 700, with an equal number being transferred to the payroll of the actual fighting force.[144]

Yet, with all that, the Safavid court arguably pursued a prudent policy inspired by strategic consideration. The story of the aforementioned Husayn Basha, the governor of Basra, suggests the nature of the debates in court circles with regard to the strategy to be pursued vis-à-vis the Porte. Having fled to Iran in early 1668, as the Turks laid siege to his city, Husayn Basha momentarily stayed in Shiraz at the shah's expense, in hopes that the Iranians might either restore him to the governorship of Basra or appoint him as governor somewhere in the Safavid realm. Sultan Mehmet IV next requested his extradition by way of a mission dispatched by the new basha of Basra.[145] This mission generated considerable controversy among Iranian authorities. Du Mans claims that there were two camps at the Safavid court, those who leaned toward extradition and those who favored standing up to the Ottomans. In the end, Shah Sulayman, loath to endanger his peace agreement with Istanbul yet concerned about his southwestern frontier, sent troops to ʿArabistan, just in case there might be trouble, but chose a third option by forcing his guest to leave Safavid territory.[146]

Giovanni Gemelli Careri alludes to another possible rationale for Sulayman's pacific sentiments. He points to Shaykh ʿAli Khan as the inspiration, referring to the vizier's alleged anti-Christian and secretly Sunni convictions. He also calls attention to various counselors who apparently saw the Ottomans as a buffer against the Christian countries. These courtiers, Gemelli Careri avers, were afraid that, once the Christian forces had overpowered the Ottoman state, they would take on Iran as well.[147] His observation about Shaykh 'Ali Khan's suspected Sunni leanings echoes the rumors that had surrounded this formidable magistrate from the time he was appointed grand vizier.[148] Yet religion was probably subordinate to clear-headed political calculations based on an awareness of historical patterns. The European powers had long seen the Ottoman–Safavid wars as a divine blessing for involving two adversarial Muslim powers engaged in mutual destruction, thus providing relief for the Christian West.[149] The Safavids, thinking along similar lines, saw an Ottoman state strong enough to keep the Europeans at bay as crucial to their security. When Shah Sulayman rejected the Russian suggestion of joint action against Istanbul in 1674, he promised to attack Baghdad once Russia and Poland were actually engaged in a war against the Turks and provided they were to assure him that they would not make peace without him.[150] The obvious long-term frustration with European power politics reflected in these caustic words is underscored by a remark made by Shaykh 'Ali Khan during the same talks. In response to a request for a more detailed answer to the proposal for an anti-Ottoman alliance, the grand vizier—who is said to have been in the forefront of an anti-Russian faction at the court—retorted that the "Christian powers had at various times engaged the kings of Iran to join them in making war against the Turks, after which they had [always] made peace without their participation."[151]

At no point did Shah Sulayman take any serious initiative to break the peace, even at times when the Ottomans were engaged in war in southeastern Europe. Occasionally he must have been tempted, though. The event that spoke to the imagination more than any other was the Ottoman defeat at Vienna in 1683. This Christian victory, the magnitude of which was greatly exaggerated by the informants who insisted that the Poles had not just defeated the Turks but taken Istanbul, was cause for great celebration in Iran. The news was apparently transmitted in such a sensational manner that the shah decided to dispatch special agents to Ottoman territory to foment a rebellion.[152] Emperor Leopold I of Austria sent letters to Isfahan, referring to his recent military success and the ignominious defeat of the Turks, and requesting the shah's assistance in the struggle against the Ottomans.[153] Shah Sulayman in response appears to have contemplated a move to recover Baghdad.[154] Sebastianus Knab, one of the envoys seeking a hearing in Isfahan at the time, added that the only sign of readiness for war among the Safavids was the presence in parts of Georgia of an army which, decimated by the plague of the year before, had been recalled. Knab claimed that the Porte had sent an envoy to Isfahan with the aim of bringing back under its authority several families subject to the sultan but living in Iran. According to Knab, the envoy had been told that no one wishing to live in Iran would be evicted by force.[155]

A more activist policy is also reflected in the Safavid reaction to the information coming out of Europe. In his letters, the Polish King Sobieski informed the Safavid ruler about his victories and, in general, about the progress of the anti-Ottoman struggle. Du Mans, who was in a position to know since he translated the court's foreign correspondence (and who, being French, may be trusted to have encouraged the shah not to resume war with the Ottomans), asserted that Sobieski exhorted Shah Sulayman to mount a campaign against Baghdad and other spots along the Tigris that had formerly belonged to Iran, swearing that peace with the Ottomans could never come to pass until the restitution to Iran of its former possessions.[156] Shah Sulayman, in turn, was apparently inspired to engage in irredentism by taking back Baghdad after reading the accounts of the liberation of Vienna. Spies sent to Turkey confirmed the Ottoman defeat.[157] At the same time, Sultan Mehmet IV is said to have responded to the disquieting news that the Polish king had sent an ambassador to Isfahan by dispatching his own mission to Iran (which may have been different from the one noted by Knab). The rich gifts the mission brought were designed to change the Safavid court's mind and apparently achieved their goal.[158] Rumor also had it that the Ottomans had mollified Iran and secured a continued peaceful relationship with the Safavids by paying them money and by easing restrictions on the pilgrim traffic to Mecca, the latter being a perennial source of conflict between the two states.[159] The Ottomans even seem to have pleaded for Safavid assistance against the Christian powers on the basis of a shared religion. To this request Shah Sulayman reportedly reacted by announcing that the Safavids were not going to take sides and meddle in the conflict.[160] The Safavid monarch similarly responded to Ottoman solicitations with a reference to long-lost Baghdad, declaring that "when Babylon had been restored to him, he might be induced to assist the Porte, but that otherwise, when the war with the Christians was over, his objective would be to get back that fortress which belonged to his domain of old."[161]

The patience of the various foreign delegates present in Isfahan in 1685 would be tested for another year, for it was only in the summer of 1686, more than two years after arriving in the Safavid capital, that one of them, the Swedish envoy Ludvig Fabritius, finally received permission to depart. To the Europeans, the court's procrastination in expediting the matter only seemed to amplify the widely accepted notion that the European powers courted an Iranian ruler who, in response, showed a glaring lack of interest in any proposals urging him to rise from his inertia. The nature of the shah's final message to the various envoys suggests otherwise, though. To be sure, the results were meager indeed: in the end, the Safavid court rejected all suggestions of joint action. Fabritius relates how the shah informed him that he would be happy to oblige the Swedish king in all his wishes except for any proposal to resume hostilities with the Ottomans. "My forebears," Fabritius had Shah Sulayman continue, "made peace, and I have confirmed and formalized this for eternity. Cursed be the one who will first draw the sword again.... We let ourselves be prompted by the Christian powers to greatly distract the Turks, but then the Christian powers made peace without so much as mentioning us once."[162]

Sulayman's message for the Russian envoy was equally trenchant and even more revealing. It should, the Russians argued, be easy for Iran to defeat the Ottomans given the predicament they were in. "May the Sultan be humiliated," the shah replied, "but may he not perish.... It is not in our interest to have a Grand Seigneur who is too weak. His territory functions as a barrier between our empire and the Christian powers." Shaykh `Ali Khan is said to have completed this homily with a graphic metaphor by declaring that it was dangerous to open up a plugged-up beehive since one might be stung by the bees. He also showed himself satisfied that Iran was tranquil whereas its most redoubtable enemy was engaged in war with the Christians. By joining an anti-Ottoman league, he concluded, Iran might provoke an attack by a Sunni coalition of Tatars, Uzbeks, and Mughals.[163]

Leaving the issue of the quality of Shah Sulayman's personal leadership aside, we might conclude that, rather than sheer inertia, astute strategic and geopolitical considerations informed the court in its inaction. By the 1680s Safavid officials must have been fully cognizant of the lamentable state of their armed forces. In 1680, as rumors spread in Isfahan that an Ottoman army of 50,000 was advancing on Yerevan, the shah had appointed a new commander-in-chief, charging him with the task of recruiting 50,000 to 60,000 soldiers. The

Dutch, voicing skepticism about the ability of the Iranians to muster an army of that size, insisted that the country was bereft of soldiers, that the old ones had died, and that poverty had forced new recruits to desert.[164] A careful calculation of the relative strength of potential allies and foes, moreover, must have convinced the Iranians that it would be unwise to upset the fragile peace with their neighbors. At this point, around 1690, the Safavids did not have enough troops to defend the Darband area against Cossack raids; all available soldiers were needed against the Uzbeks in Khurasan and the restive Afghans and Baluchis near Qandahar. Isfahan had also been forced to send troops led by the new khan of Hamadan to punish the Lurs and the Bakhtiyaris, who had risen in revolt after the shah had executed the last of their leaders, Shah Navaz Khan, and imposed a non-native successor.[165] In light of these challenges, it is probably best to follow the assessment of Kaempfer. The shah, he insisted, from time to time proclaimed that he would rather leave minor challenges [to the peace with the Ottomans] unanswered than undertake a revenge campaign the outcome of which would be uncertain.[166]

A story about Sulayman's treatment of Prince Akbar, son of Aurangzeb, who sought refuge in Iran against his father, suggests a similarly cautious approach vis-à-vis the Mughals. Having confronted the Imam of Masqat, who had taken Akbar hostage, he welcomed the latter warmly in Isfahan, but refused to support him against his father with the words that he would have assisted him if anyone other than his father was involved.[167] The continued strength of the Ottoman armies and a history of empty promises coming out of Europe combined to make the Iranians leery of tampering with the peace they had made with Istanbul and to maintain a neutral stance in the conflict between the Ottomans and the Christian powers. Toward the end of Shah Sulayman's reign, Sanson echoed a refrain asserting that the palace eunuchs were averse to the destruction of Ottoman power—presumably because they saw the Turks as a barrier against European aggression.[168] A final concern, little appreciated by Westerners, was the possibility that Iran's immediate neighbors might come together in an anti-Safavid coalition. The specter of a Sunni league directed against Shi`i Iran was hardly far-fetched; the Ottomans, Mughals, and Uzbeks had at various times suggested the formation of such a league, and only Mughal-Uzbek enmity had, at times, prevented the implementation of that idea.[169]

Until the end of Safavid rule it remained one of the principles of Iran's foreign policy to keep a cordon sanitaire in place around the Ottoman state by maintaining friendly relations with Christian powers inimical to the Ottomans. As the German traveler Franz Caspar Schillinger observed at the turn of the eighteenth century: "It is one of his [Shah Sultan Husayn's] maxims of state to maintain everlasting friendship with the Muscovites, the Poles and the Germans in order to keep the Turks in check."[170] Geopolitical considerations, however, dictated that friendship should never extend beyond the exchange of embassies.

Chapter 6

Weakening Links: The Center and the Provinces, 1600–1700

Les Persans [disent] que les intendants sont des sangsues insatiables, qui épuisent les sujets pour remplir le trésor royal, et qui, pour cet effet, négligent les plaintes des peuples sur l'oppression qui leur est faite, prétendant que l'intérêt du roi ne leur permet pas d'avoir égard, comme ils le voudroient, quoiqu'en effet ils ne pillent que pour s'enrichir eux-mêmes.

The Persians say that the intendants are insatiable bloodsuckers, who bleed the (shah's) subjects dry to fill the royal treasury, and who thus ignore the complaints of the people about the oppression they suffer, while pretending that the interest of the king does not allow them to pay attention to this the way they would like to, even though in reality they only plunder to enrich themselves.

Jean Chardin, Voyages, 5:252–3

INTRODUCTION

The discussion in the preceding five chapters mostly concerned the working of the seventeenth-century Safavid central government. Chapter 5, dealing with the army, took the discussion beyond Isfahan and the confines of the royal court. But even there the vantage point was the capital and, more specifically, the royal court in Isfahan. The present chapter moves away from a concentration on the center to explore relations between Isfahan and the outlying regions. Information about the degree of political cohesion and changes therein, as well as clues to related matters of economic performance and financial management, must be sought not just in the narrow circle of the political establishment in the capital but above all in the chain of command that tied the royal court via the central bureaucracy to the provincial administration—by way of bureaucratic representation, landholding patterns, and fiscal organization. The first part of the chapter offers an outline of these arrangements, their rationale, their way of operating, and the changes they underwent from the reign of Shah `Abbas I onward. The second, more specific part examines a number of outlying areas for which we have sufficient data to substantiate these changes and assess their import and impact, involving matters of productivity, tax revenue, and security, allowing us to evaluate the state of affairs in various urban centers and surrounding areas. This discussion will first survey the country in general terms, then look in greater detail at two relatively well-documented regions, Shirvan in the north and Fars in the south, and finally examine two locations for which we have much more detailed information with regard to events and agents, the province of Kirman and its eponymous capital in the southeast, and the port of Bandar `Abbas on the Persian Gulf coast.

CHARACTERISTICS OF CENTER–PERIPHERY RELATIONS

Guided by a presentist perspective and perforce relying on sources originating from the center—in many cases the only ones that have survived—one would be tempted to regard most premodern and early modern societies as marked by a strong, coherent, and articulate center in opposition to a weak, inexpressive periphery inhabited by people with a dim self-awareness and a poorly developed sense of overarching identity. Safavid Iran is no exception to this tendency, especially during the reign of Shah `Abbas I. The state and the "capital," consisting of the shah and his entourage, appear to have controlled the "country," if not in equal measure all the way to its formal borders, at least along a sliding scale, maintaining a grip that became less tight yet never fully dissolved with distance. Scholars of early modern Europe long ago learned to question the extent to which "absolute" monarchs managed to project power evenly across their territories. In the case of the Safavids, a forbidding physical geography, harsh climatic conditions, and a largely tribal and partly nomadic population provide even greater justification for a healthy skepticism about the state's ability to wield effective control. Severely limited infrastructural capabilities and fragile institutions gave the state weak effective control over all but the capital, the main provincial cities, and the arteries that connected them.

With distances as great as communications were poor, ties and affinities in Safavid Iran were mostly local, based on kinship and tribe. Regular caravan trade linked the main towns, most of which were located on the rims of the inner triangle framed by the Zagros Mountains in the west, the Alburz mountain range in the north, and the vast eastern salt and sand deserts, Dasht-i Kavir and Dasht-i Lut. Vast stretches of the country, about which we know next to nothing, remained unaffected by such communication. Yet, far from creating a supine periphery, this very isolation gave Iranian villages and towns a large measure of self-sufficiency and political autonomy, with officials chosen by the local population regulating most of their own affairs.[1] The central state might appoint the supervising officials, but it had to be cautious in its selection. John Malcolm's remark, written in the early 1800s, that the voice of the people "counted in the selection of officials and that if the king should appoint a magistrate disagreeable to the citizens, he could not perform his duties. ..." is as valid for Safavid Iran as it was for the early Qajar period.[2] The same isolation had long made Iran's major towns the fulcrum of civilized life, causing their inhabitants to develop a strong sense of local pride and historical memory. For this we need look no further than Mufid Mustawfi Yazdi, who, suffering in far-away Hyderabad in the mid-seventeenth century, nostalgically called his hometown Yazd the most beautiful of all cities. Half a century later, `Ali Muhammad Hazin, languishing in India as well, pined for his beloved homeland in similar ways.[3] In a more institutionalized manner, such self-awareness was habitually expressed through local history-writing—a genre that provides us with valuable information about some far-flung regions in the Safavid period.[4] The final part of this chapter will show examples of such local strength translated as resistance against the power of the central state.

Arrangements between the center and the provinces

Various landed and administrative arrangements tied the periphery to the capital, the royal court, and its administrative apparatus. These were *mamalik* or *divani*, state lands, *khassah*, royal domain lands, and *vilayats*, autonomously administered regions.

A variant of the Buyid *iqta`*, the mamalik arrangement—a form of prebendalism in which landed property was alienated as fiefs—reflected the government's dependence on tribal military troops for the defense of the realm. The granting of mamalik land was a way of rewarding the regime's supporters, the Qizilbash chieftains, for military vigilance and the payment of a limited fixed annual sum to the royal treasury.[5] In early Safavid times all of Iran was mamalik land. Over time, as the regime consolidated its authority and security increased, some centrally located regions were converted to crown land, khassah. The frontier provinces, where the need for military vigilance remained urgent, continued to be mamalik territory, which explains why outlying regions such as Khurasan, Azerbaijan, and Qarabagh remained tribally controlled state domain throughout the Safavid period. Such control was not fixed, though. Tribes tended to have a long-standing connection with a region; yet the influence and power of individual tribes fluctuated over time. In the early sixteenth century, for instance, the Takallu wielded disproportional power in Iran. They lost their dominance under Shah Tahmasb, to be overtaken by the Ustajlu, whose rise was so spectacular that in the 1570s they held two-thirds of all governorships.[6] The Shamlu, who had been associated with Khurasan from the time Shah Isma'il conquered the region in the early 1500s, fell into disgrace during Shah Tahmasb's reign, but rose again under Shah 'Abbas I, gaining a monopoly on Khurasan's governorship following the death of Farhad Khan Qaramanlu, after which they controlled the region until the end of Safavid rule. The Qajar and the Afshar were two other tribes with great power in later times. The former, who hailed from the north, ruled the area of Astarabad—a frontier region perennially exposed to Uzbek incursions—throughout the seventeenth century. They also came to control Yerevan and Tiflis in the northwest after Shah 'Abbas I seized those cities from the Ottomans.[7] The Ziyad Ughlu, one of their subgroups, commanded the borderlands of Qarabagh, Ganja, and Chughur-i Sa'd in the southern Caucasus from the days of Shah Tahmasb onward. The Afshar were not just concentrated in Khurasan, but held sway over parts of Khuzistan and Kuh-i Giluyah. In early Safavid times they also came to rule Kirman province. Kirman remained under their control until the early reign of Shah 'Abbas I, who appointed the Kurd Ganj 'Ali Khan, one of his most loyal servants, as its governor.[8] The Afshar were subsequently forced to cede power to the Kurds in the Kirman area, although in the late Safavid period intensifying Baluchi attacks prompted the central state to allow them to return to help defend the province.

Mamalik land was also routinely linked to specific administrative offices, by way of governance or income. From the time of Shah

Isma'il I onward, the governor of Azerbaijan, a rich province and a recruiting ground for some of Iran's best soldiers, regularly held the post of *amir al-umara* (an old term for commander-in-chief) and *sipahsalar*, commander of the armed forces.[9] The district of Abarquh was assigned to the *tufangchi-aqasi*, head of the musketeers, and as of 1645 the post of *qullar-aqasi*, head of the slave soldiers, was tied to the governorship of Kuh-i Giluyah. The *amir-shikar-bashi* (master of the hunt) derived (part of) his income from the revenue of Abhar, between Qazvin and Sultaniyah.[10] The position of *ishik-aqasi-bashi* (royal chamberlain) was vested in the Shamlu tribe.[11] Members of the Afshar had a lock on the position of *ishik-aqasi-yi khassah*.[12] And from the reign of Shah Safi I, the governorate of Kirman came with the post of *qurchibashi*.[13]

Mamalik land secured border regions with tribal military power but gave the central government little direct control and scant revenue. To increase both, the state over time transferred a great deal of land to crown domain. The long-term conversion to khassah land reflects a shift from a decentralized polity beholden to tribal military power to an agrarian-based system in which tribal chieftains came to be subordinated to the new, centrally appointed ghulam class of soldiers and bureaucrats.[14]

As stated, the centrally located, most secure parts of the country were the first to be turned into crown domain. Shah 'Abbas declared Kashan crown land in 1590 and, upon seizing Isfahan in the same year, gave that city and its surroundings similar status.[15] The conversion of Gilan and Mazandaran to crown land in 1599 spelled the end of local dynastic rule in the Caspian region. Contrary to conventional wisdom, crown land and *ghulam* rule were not inherently connected. Ghulams came to dominate Fars with the appointment of Allah Virdi Khan in 1595, but the province only became crown domain in 1633, after his son, Imam Quli Khan, was killed on Shah Safi's orders. Conversely, when Kirman was turned into khassah land in 1658–9, it was not brought under ghulam control but rather saw a growing influx of Kurds.

Vilayats were located in border regions beyond the mountain ranges that framed the central plateau. These were mostly mountainous areas, located on the edge of Safavid jurisdiction and inhabited by fiercely independent tribal people. The five vilayats in late Safavid times were 'Arabistan (modern Khuzistan), Luristan, Georgia, Kurdistan, and Bakhtiyari territory, in that order of ranking.[16] *Valis* were all but independent governors. Hailing from leading local families, they usually ruled in hereditary fashion even if they were officially appointed by the shah, who in a concession to regional autonomy almost always chose a candidate from the region. Appointing someone from outside the resident tribe might create more problems than it solved, as is shown by the example of Kurdistan, where in the 1680s a non-Kurdish governor dispatched by Shah Sulayman was run out of town by the local population.[17] Good behavior by chieftains was enforced by means of keeping a family member, typically a son, in Isfahan as a hostage. Valis formally expressed allegiance to Isfahan and had coins struck in the shah's name. Unlike regular governors, however, valis oversaw their regions' administrative apparatus, controlled their own budgets, maintained their own militia, and managed their own vassal relations, in all of which the shah rarely intervened.[18] The tributary strategy the Safavids employed vis-à-vis vilayats varied with circumstances. Ordinarily, the exactions were light. Thus Luristan in late Safavid times annually supplied only twenty Arabian horses in addition to 200 mules and a quantity of valuables. In time of war, however, the Lurs were held to provide up to 12,000 cavalrymen and the same number of foot soldiers.[19]

Other forms of control

To achieve a modicum of control around the country, the Safavid state resorted to various strategies beyond punitive expeditions to regions in revolt. One way of reducing subaltern power was to try and restrict the spread of firearms, a relatively new form of weaponry that was initially limited to the state. Like many contemporary states, the Safavids sought to halt their spread among the wider population. The people of Lar—a major manufacturing center of firearms—were prohibited from carrying guns at the time of Shah `Abbas I. In the late seventeenth century such orders were still in place in remote areas. Bénigne Vachet, traveling in western Iran in 1690, claimed that in all of Iran mountaineers were forbidden from carrying any other arms than batons.[20] Such bans naturally had little effect. Ambrosio Bembo, traveling in the Kurdish Ottoman–Safavid borderlands in the 1670s, observed how not even peasants in those regions were without "an arquebus or sword or bows and arrows."[21]

Much more effective was the forcible resettlement of populations, a long-standing practice pioneered by the ancient Assyrians. Resettling a recalcitrant border tribe into the interior was typically designed to break up vested tribal power. Shah `Abbas thus deported the Qazaqlu from Qarabagh to Fars.[22] Deportation was often a precautionary measure. We hear of tribes being moved away from the front lines in the face of imminent war, for fear that they might side with the enemy.[23] Depopulation was also a byproduct of the scorched-earth policy that the Safavids often engaged in. An example is Shah ʿAbbas's removal of the entire Armenian population from the Aras River region in the face of Ottoman aggression in 1603–4.[24] Most often the aim was the protection of borderlands. The northern frontiers, perennially exposed to raids by Uzbek, Turkmen, and Lezghi tribesmen, were a favored destination for deportations of this kind. Dividing the Qajar tribe into three groups, Shah ʿAbbas resettled many of its members to the north, making them guard Ganja in the Caucasus and Astarabad and Marv on the Central Asian frontier.[25] The same ruler sought to strengthen central control by relocating a large number of Qizilbash tribal folk to Georgia. ʿAbbas encouraged the Turkmen Göklen to settle around Astarabad so as to protect the Khurasan border against raids by the Yomut, a rival Turkmen tribe.[26] Frequent raids by Lezghi marauders as well as Russian pressure on Daghistan made Shah ʿAbbas II move large numbers of Turks to Georgia, prompting an uprising against Safavid rule in 1659.[27] Kurds, renowned for their martial qualities, were often deployed for defensive purposes. Many thus ended up in Khurasan.[28] A number of Kurds were also sent to Kitch and Makran in Baluchistan to help defend those remote marches.[29] Chardin gave the following numbers for troops defending the borders in the mid-seventeenth century: 6,000 for Kirmanshah; 50,000 each in Armenia and Georgia; and 8,000 each in Khurasan and Qandahar.[30]

State authority was not founded on military means alone. In fact, force was not the principal form of control, even if the threat of armed intervention was always the ultimate deterrent. Isfahan used "soft" power much more widely and, arguably, more effectively to keep the provinces in check. This came in different forms, ranging from the appointment of shadow officials to alliance building by way of marriage and various tributary arrangements. In all of this, the ultimate purpose was to secure loyalty, a commodity that was structurally in short supply. As Patricia Crone puts it, the premodern state did not inspire any loyalty.[31] Yet managing a state was predicated on at least some form of (temporary) loyalty. To achieve this was to engage in perpetual negotiation and bargaining.[32] And negotiation typically involved some form of mediation by brokers or middlemen, *vakil*s. The vakil, a person who could deal with both parties and a central figure in Iranian politics, operated on different levels. Provincial governors were well advised not to take up their position in provincial outposts without good representation in Isfahan, since leaving the court would unleash a wave of intrigue against them. They would often stay in the capital themselves, dispatching a relative in their stead; and if they took up their post, they would leave a vakil to represent their interest. Until they were recalled to Isfahan to account for their behavior, these officials usually remained at a safe distance from the capital, where agents and family members interceded on their behalf. Some hardly ever showed up in the region to which they had been appointed, although few would go to such extremes as the *muhrdar*, keeper of the royal seals, who waited twenty years before visiting Qum, the province assigned to him by Shah Tahmasb.[33]

One time-honored way of keeping individual power in check was to appoint mutually controlling officers. This began at the central court, where the *nazir* (steward of the royal household) checked on the grand vizier and in turn was controlled by a number of other officials. The vizier of a khassah province typically had a nazir and a *vaqa'i`-nivis* (registrar) as assistants, who acted as shadow officials charged with the task of monitoring him.[34] According to Chardin, in Mazandaran the vizier and his assistant were expected to report on each other. The fiscally important Caspian provinces, moreover, were headed by a *vazir-i kull*, whose task it was to control the vizier in financial and juridical matters. In Bandar `Abbas, the *shahbandar*, harbor master, and the local khan operated in similar fashion. Chardin attributed the relative lack of rebellion in Safavid Iran to the ubiquity of such institutionalized mutual control.[35]

Alliance building was the most commonly used control strategy. It came in various forms. One was to keep the sons of local rulers as hostages in the capital, conditioning them as loyal Safavid subjects. This age-old practice was especially common with regard to outlying regions such as Georgia, Daghistan, and `Arabistan. Shah `Abbas kept Constantin Mirza, son of the Georgian King Alexander, in Isfahan.[36] Alqas Mirza, a Lezghi prince, was sent at a young age as a hostage to Isfahan, renamed Safi Quli Khan, reared in the harem, and in 1666 appointed governor of Yerevan.[37]

A more benevolent form of cementing loyalty through alliances involved marriage arrangements between the Safavids and ruling families, officials in high military, administrative, and religious positions. This type of arrangement was particularly common in the case of Georgia. Shah `Abbas solidified the nexus with its royal house by giving Constantin Mirza's sister in marriage to Prince Hamzah Mirza. A century later, Gurgin Khan, the Georgian commander-in-chief of the Safavid army, married a daughter of Ja`far Quli Khan of Sistan in a union designed to strengthen ties between Isfahan and that remote area.³⁸ Sexual politics might even extend to the "barbarian" periphery. Shah Tahmasb gave a daughter in marriage to `Adil Giray, a Tartar chief whom he kept as a hostage, in hopes of preventing the Tatars from siding with the Ottomans.³⁹

In the borderlands, where power was by definition a matter of negotiation, operating with tact and sensitivity was especially important. Borders looked linear to foreigners entering and leaving Iran at clearly defined transit stations, yet they were above all permeable frontier zones, unpacified mountains and deserts inhabited by tribal peoples whose loyalty might be temporarily bought but could never be taken for granted.⁴⁰ The Arabs and Kurds along the Ottoman borders, the Lezghis in the Caucasus, the Turkmen in Khurasan, and the Baluchis and Afghans on the eastern marches were notorious for their unwillingness to submit to outside authority. In an approach that goes back to antiquity, the Safavids sought to bring security to such areas by making alliances with tribal chiefs, enlisting them through arrangements in which the latter pledged to defend the frontier in exchange for maintaining their local autonomy.⁴¹ This might take the form of a tribe submitting to the shah as "lovers of the shah," *shah-seven*, as Kurds from the Hakkari region did when they disavowed loyalty to the Ottomans and offered their service to the Safavids, thus facilitating the taking of Van by the latter.⁴²

The tribal support the state needed, for intelligence and actual assistance in case of war, gave great leverage to the chieftains. The shah picked the Lezghi ruler, the *shamkhal*, but always from one of the local princes and with the consent of local forces, thus ensuring the stability that was the ultimate rationale of any such arrangement.⁴³ In 1595 Shah `Abbas I agreed to a temporary subordination of the shamkhal to Russia, stressing that he was an Iranian vassal even if he was an underling of the czar.⁴⁴ In the Safavid–Ottoman borderlands, especially, too much pressure from Isfahan or Istanbul might drive a tribe into the arms of the other regime.⁴⁵ Iskandar Beg Munshi called the Kurds fickle, deploring their tendency to switch sides in the conflict with the Ottomans.⁴⁶ A policy of leniency and accommodation was vital in such conditions. This is probably why Khalil Khan, the governor of Bakhtiyari territory, was just deposed—as opposed to executed—after his people had risen in revolt against his violent oppression, and why he managed to regain his post twelve years later. Similarly, Shah `Abbas II received Mansur Khan, the ruler of Huwayza, with great pomp and circumstance in Isfahan in 1645, after he had led a rebellion against the Safavids.⁴⁷

Sulayman Khan, the Kurdish *beglerbeg* of Ardalan, in 1657 took the side of Istanbul and tried to escape to Ottoman territory. Caught, he was only exiled to Mashhad for this act of treason. Not only that, but Shah `Abbas II, who had little interest in conflict with either the Kurds or the Ottomans, allowed him to be succeeded by his oldest son, Kalb `Ali Khan.[48]

Loyalty was often literally bought, either with cash or by way of lucrative concessions.[49] When Imam Quli Khan, the governor of Fars, marched against Basra in 1628, he got the Arab tribes en route to render him a variety of services by handing out "cash grants, robes of honor, and other gifts in profusion."[50] The Afghan warlord Mir Ways in the early eighteenth century served as *qafilah-salar*, supervisor of the caravan trade between Iran and India.[51] The Safavids also made more institutionalized arrangements with various tribal peoples.[52] Shah `Abbas II coopted the Lezghis through a mutually beneficial tributary arrangement: They sent gifts to Isfahan as a token of fealty, and in turn received 1,700 tumans per annum from the shah to ensure stability and the protection of the border against other marauders. This arrangement included the resettling of large numbers of tribesmen from the mountains of Darband and Qubbah.[53] The same ruler paid the Kharazmian ruler Abu'l Ghazi Khan an annual allowance of 1,500 tumans during a decade of gilded captivity in Isfahan, and kept disbursing this sum even after Abu'l Ghazi had escaped and regained power in Central Asia, simply to keep him from turning against Iran.[54] After the shah had conducted several campaigns against the Uzbeks, he struck a deal whereby they received an annual stipend in exchange for a promise to desist from raiding—a promise they promptly broke following the shah's death in 1666.[55]

Long-term changes

Although extending crown land allowed the central state to increase its political control over outlying territories, revenue enhancement was the main purpose of such conversion. Collecting the one-third of khassah revenue that accrued to the crown was the main task of the viziers, the administrators appointed to head crown land, the equivalent of the contemporary French *intendants*.[56]

The practice of converting mamalik to khassah land goes all the way back to the reign of Shah Isma`il I. It gained momentum under Shah `Abbas, reflecting the growing need for immediate revenue to pay for the upkeep of the ever larger numbers of new ghulam troops and administrators. From early Safavid times it had been customary for princes to be appointed as provincial governors in order to gain experience. Muhammad Baqir Mirza, ʿAbbas's eldest son, was the last one to be groomed in this way—he was sent to Hamadan in 1591–2—yet the shah had him executed in 1614.[57]

The amount of khassah land expanded considerably after Shah ʿAbbas I, culminating under Shah ʿAbbas II with the incorporation of Bakhtiyari territory, which followed the suppression of a rebellion in the region in 1645.[58] This expansion reflected a growing sense of military security, which was reinforced when the Safavids made peace with the Ottomans in 1639. Grand vizier Mirza Taqi initiated the subsequent acceleration, suggesting that, with the risk of war reduced, reliance on semi-independent governors was no longer necessary, so that land should be appropriated by the crown.[59] Between 1645 and 1654, the years of Khalifah Sultan's tenure as grand vizier, the reappearance of external threats, and especially the need for support from the country's Turkish tribal elements in the war over Qandahar, temporarily stalled the conversion of state land. In the later 1650s, a period of relative peace coinciding with undiminished financial stringency, the practice was resumed under the auspices of the newly appointed grand vizier Muhammad Beg. Hamadan was added to the stock of khassah land in 1654; Ardabil, Simnan, and Khʿar followed suit in 1656–7, and Kirman in 1658–9.[60] The process was interrupted once again in the early reign of Shah Sulayman, a period when frequent Cossack irruptions into the Caspian littoral prompted the administration to restore Gilan and Mazandaran to mamalik status, with the latter going to a Qajar governor. As soon as the threat subsided, however, the region once again became khassah. (Chardin's claim that Azerbaijan and Khurasan were also turned into khassah land at this point remains unproven and unlikely.)[61]

The premodern practice of revenue farming was not necessarily detrimental to the land affected by it.[62] In some parts of Mughal India it apparently had a beneficial effect by stabilizing or even enhancing government income.[63] But this presupposes the preservation of a balance between productive forces and the need for income coupled with judicious expenditure. In the Safavid case, the advantages of mamalik land—a landholder interested in maintaining the long-term productivity and prosperity of his land, limited government interference, and the fact that most revenue remained within the territory—typically far outweighed the (short-term) benefits of the khassah system. The author of the *Tarikh-i jahan-ara-yi ʿAbbasi* insists that tax income tended to decrease once state land was converted to crown land.⁶⁴ Chardin concurred. He famously pointed out the drawbacks of the khassah system by calling the viziers of crown lands bloodsuckers, adding that, when he was in Iran, these converted territories no longer yielded good soldiers and that money which used to circulate in the country now disappeared and was hoarded in the shah's treasury. The peasants, who naturally bore the brunt of this, responded by engaging in fraud, passive resistance, and ultimately flight.⁶⁵ It is impossible to say how much the economy suffered from all this. We are faced with a severe lack of economic data, especially with regard to agricultural output. But since agriculture perhaps accounted for some 70 percent of GDP, the negative effect of this change in landholding patterns must have been substantial.⁶⁶

A particularly detrimental effect of the conversion was the rapid turnover of officials, who had to buy themselves into their rank and, once settled, work hard to recoup their investment at the expense of the populace. Their tenure was brief, for there were many bidders and the one who held out the highest tender would quickly oust the incumbent.⁶⁷ With a new khan came a large entourage consisting of a cadre of officials who were often unfamiliar with local conditions. Such rotation imposed a heavy burden on the populace, all the more so because locals also bore the cost of welcoming each new governor with a lavish display of fireworks and other celebratory outlays.⁶⁸ At times, more than one governor per year was appointed. It is instructive to compare the continuity in Azerbaijan, which remained mamalik land, with the rapid turnover in Fars after the province was turned into crown land. Under Shah 'Abbas II, the provincial vizier of Azerbaijan was Mirza Sadiq, who later became governor of Fars. With the accession of Shah Sulayman, his brother Mirza Ibrahim was appointed to Azerbaijan. Mirza Ibrahim, whom various travelers praised for his erudition and curiosity, stayed on as vizier until 1684, at which point he was succeeded by his son Mirza Tahir, who had previously substituted for his father and who was still in charge in 1694, when Gemelli Careri visited Iran.⁶⁹ As will be seen later, Fars meanwhile was split up into several districts and subsequently ruled by a series of mostly abusive governors.

Not only were the viziers appointed to rule over crown lands frequently recalled, dismissed, and replaced, but an increasingly rapid turnover occurred on all levels, especially during the reign of Shah Sulayman. This affected the post of *kalantar* of New Julfa and that of shahbandar in Bandar 'Abbas as much as the governorate of any khassah province.⁷⁰ The *rahdari* (road security system), too, was farmed out in this period, probably by Shaykh `Ali Khan. As Engelbert Kaempfer explained, the system as set up by Shah `Abbas I had functioned well, involving the payment of a small sum to the officers for each traveler and pack animal to help defray the cost of providing security. Over time, however, this contribution had become a real tax, and the rahdari business became so lucrative that it ended up being farmed out, so that the guardians turned into robbers, leading to diminishing security.[71]

THE GENERAL STATE OF IRAN, 1650–1700

Sources of significant economic information—mainly reports by foreign travelers, often our only informants on the subject—offer a mixed picture of the state of Iran in the mid- to late seventeenth century. Isfahan continued to dazzle foreign visitors and did not appear to any of them as a city in decline. On the contrary: Du Mans insisted that the capital had grown by a fifth or even a quarter in the two decades between 1645 and 1665.[72] The court lived lavishly and spent prodigiously. The first thing `Abbas II did upon acceding to the throne was to grant a tax amnesty to all officials whose salaries were in arrears. The sum thus forfeited was said to amount to (a no doubt exaggerated) 500,000 tumans.[73] And, judging by the fantastic sum spent on the wedding in 1673 of the son of Nazir Najaf Quli Khan to the daughter of the *divanbegi*, the shah was not the only one with large amounts of disposable income.[74] To the average outsider who entered Safavid territory at various points, traveled its main roads, and stayed in its numerous hostels, much of the country beyond the capital seemed stable and prosperous as well. Until the late seventeenth century, Europeans almost without exception praised the famous Iranian hospitality, marveled at the unique *mihmandari* system, which provided foreign visitors on official business with free food, lodging, and even a *per diem* allowance, and spoke highly of the security of the roads, which, as the travelers tell it, contrasted starkly with the lawlessness in the eastern marches of the Ottoman Empire.[75] These observations only gain in saliency in light of the fact that, as mentioned, Iran's most prosperous villages were not located along the main roads. The Italian Nicolao Manucci in the 1650s characterized Safavid Iran as "very well governed, having no rebellions or treasons, neither robbers nor highwaymen on the roads…."[76] The people seemed not to be in want of anything. Boullaye-le-Gouze, visiting the southern part of the country in the same period, commented on the absence of thieves. Crediting the khan of Lar and the governor of Bandar ʿAbbas for the prevailing security, he explained that he had traveled alone without having heard about or experienced any untoward encounter.[77] Barthélemy Carré in 1671 called Hamadan "a great and pleasant city."[78] Two years later, André Daulier Deslandes said about Tabriz that it had been much restored from the destructions caused by the Turkish wars and was now "thickly populated, rich and well supplied with every sort of trade."[79] Bembo in 1674 referred to what seemed to him like an abundant wheat harvest in Fars. Upon leaving Iran he fondly spoke of a country where he had felt safe from brigands and murderers and where good lodging was available and food was plentiful and reasonably priced. The very first inn where he stayed upon entering Ottoman territory had the owner watch the animals entrusted to him—a sign, to Bembo, that Iranian security had been left behind.[80] In a much-quoted statement, Chardin insisted that Iranian peasants were often better off than their European counterparts.[81] Even in 1690, a time when various regions saw a serious breakdown in security, Vachet could still breathe a sense of relief entering Iran from Iraq, optimistic that the road would be safe all the way to Isfahan.[82] The Carmelite Francesco Maria di S. Siro, who a few years later traveled in the opposite direction, shared in this optimism, describing the region around Hamadan as a fertile valley where cereals, fruit, and tobacco were cultivated in abundance, and the town itself as a commercial center inhabited by "Persians, Armenians, Turks and Jews," and ruled by a khan who had the trust of the shah.[83]

Appearances did not necessarily correspond to underlying realities, however. A more detailed examination of conditions as described by perceptive observers suggests that their generally positive assessment should not be taken at face value. Jean-Baptiste Tavernier, writing in the 1660s, claimed that Iran's agricultural output had markedly declined over time. Iran, he said, used to be one of the more fertile lands of the Middle East because of the prodigious number of irrigation canals, *qanats*. Yet over time their number had fallen considerably, the Frenchman insisted, in part because of the recurrent wars against the Ottomans, in part because of official neglect. Azerbaijan is said to have recovered from the devastating Ottoman–Safavid conflict only in the mid-seventeenth century, when its cities regained their former fame as centers of commerce and manufacture.[84] Yet Mirza Ibrahim, the provincial vizier, told Tavernier that around Tabriz alone 400 wells had dried up in the previous eighty years.[85] In 1663, a few years before Tavernier's visit, no snow or rain had fallen for six months from Nakhjavan to Tabriz. Wells had become depleted and crops had withered.⁸⁶ In the early 1670s Deslandes and Struys echoed each other, claiming that Sultaniyah had declined from previous times. The former called Zanjan "now half ruined."⁸⁷ Kaempfer spoke of the decline of various cities he traveled through in 1684, singling out Savah and Qum as examples.⁸⁸ Du Mans in the same period recalled the effectiveness of the traditional Safavid security system as established by Shah 'Abbas I, which held the governor of a region in which a robbery took place accountable for the stolen goods. Nowadays, Du Mans lamented, any money retrieved would end up in the shah's coffers, complaints fell on deaf ears in Isfahan, and governors often worked in cahoots with highway robbers, claiming the largest share of the loot in premeditated heists. Rahdars, he added, echoing Kaempfer, were now prone to shake down travelers, considering anyone who passed through their territory a gift of God, or *bad-avurdah*, "brought by the wind." Du Mans specifically mentioned the Bakhtiyari, who at the time of his writing were roaming around Isfahan, looking to plunder caravans.⁸⁹

A closer look at various individual regions reveals complex conditions in which enduring stability might exist side by side with deepening poverty and where an extortionate governor might be succeeded by a benevolent one, even if the general trend was toward greater oppression in the face of an increasingly ineffective central government.

The north: Shirvan

The north was important to the financial health of the Safavid realm; the Caspian provinces, especially, generated large amounts of money for the royal treasury. Taxes on the silk production in Gilan and Shirvan amounted to 100,000 tumans per year, contributing greatly to overall state revenue.⁹⁰ But Iran's northwestern provinces also bore the brunt of the Ottoman–Safavid wars, and Shamakhi, Shirvan's capital, suffered tremendously when in 1667 it was struck by a devastating earthquake.⁹¹ In the same period Gilan and Talish were dealt a heavy blow with the irruptions of Cossack marauders led by Sten'ka Razin. The Cossacks took Astrakhan, temporarily disrupting the trade link between Iran and Russia, and almost seized Darband. They devastated large tracts of Gilan and Mazandaran, including the royal winter resort of Farahabad and the town of Astarabad, and did great damage to the silk cultivation in those regions.⁹²

We get a fairly detailed overview of the misery in the northern countryside, as well as an idea about its causes, from a lengthy report written by the Jesuit Father Jean-Baptiste de la Maze (1624–1709), who for many years served as his order's representative in Shamakhi, and who thus was as familiar with the state of the country as any foreigner could be expected to be.[93] Traveling through Shirvan and Azerbaijan in 1684, he called the thirty-four villages in the Baku region all poor, adding that the city itself was no exception, having been terribly neglected for generations. Most of the houses were ruined or abandoned, and in the entire city one saw no more than ten or twelve shops that were open. He listed two reasons for these sorry conditions—one structural, the other contingent and manmade. The first was the poor quality of the soil, which was either rocky or sandy and, lacking water, best suited as grazing ground for nomads. Of the crops he saw he singled out cotton, which grew in great abundance, enabling large-scale local textile manufacturing, and saffron. De la Maze speculated that the production of saffron between Baku and Nizovoi could be for the region what silk was for Shirvan, but that the second reason of the depressed state of the land, the abuse and violence by local officials, prevented this from coming about. The tax farmers in particular were keen immediately to recoup the money they had invested to obtain a three-year lease on the land, including all the presents and bribes they had been forced to disburse in the process. The present tax farmer, De la Maze noted, was supposed to send an annual sum of 7,000 tumans to Isfahan. The region's petroleum—used as a medicine and as a lighting fuel, among other things—only yielded 600 tumans, so that the remainder had to come from salt and additional exactions, which were so onerous, De la Maze insisted, that they drove the region's inhabitants to ruin. By way of example he offered the case of one peasant he had spoken to, who owned no more than a small garden and yet had to pay 100 *livres*, or more than one tuman, per annum—a very large sum indeed given a 3-tuman average salary for a government servant at the time.[94] At the end of a tax farmer's term, a new one, even hungrier for revenue, would arrive, making the hapless peasants abandon their land out of sheer desperation. Everyone, the French Jesuit maintained, was anxiously anticipating the arrival of Mirza Tahir, who had been sent by Isfahan to take stock of the province and bring relief to the suffering inhabitants. In the meantime only four villages retained a semblance of prosperity, their inhabitants eking out a living on the basis of rotating weekly markets. Two of these were exceptions to the general misery. Shah

`Abbas I had given both as a hereditary fief (*suyurghal*) to a shaykh, and the latter and his descendants had governed their property with justice, only forcing the peasants to engage in light corvée labor, which meant that they worked for the owner no more than six days per year.⁹⁵

Not everything spoke of deprivation, to be sure. The region might be suffering economically, De la Maze observed, but it was also safe—so safe, in fact, that even a small child could carry a bag full of money from village to village without being bothered. The only threat to regional security was posed by the Cossacks, who from time to time engaged in piracy, landing on the southern shores of the Caspian Sea to raid the coastal towns and villages. Hence the defensive towers that had been built in almost all of them and that now were falling to ruin because of neglect.⁹⁶ Yet by the late seventeenth century cracks were appearing in Iran's much-vaunted road safety, and the north had its fair share of the growing turmoil. In the winter of 1680 a caravan coming from Izmir was robbed of 20,000 tumans near Yerevan. Aside from costing the lives of thirty men, this robbery ruined a number of merchants, Muslim as well as Armenian. The governor of Yerevan was suspected of having had a hand in the affair, one of several caravan robberies that remained unresolved.⁹⁷

The south: Fars

Our information about Fars is just as scattered, and the picture it yields is as variegated and complex as that projected by Shirvan, pairing signs of stability in the continued prosperity and safe roads with evidence of underlying problems. In terms of the revenue it produced, Fars was one of Iran's most important provinces. Its economic significance is suggested by Bembo, who estimated its income at 60,000 tumans per annum, on a par with Gilan.⁹⁸ Shiraz, the most important southern city, had attained a level of high cultural efflorescence in the mid-sixteenth century, and for quite some time afterward it remained a center of manuscript production.⁹⁹ Under Shah Isma`il it may have had a population of 75,000, a number that seems hardly to have changed until the city's decline in the second half of the seventeenth century.¹⁰⁰ Shah `Abbas brought Fars under central control in 1590 by executing Ya`qub Khan Zu'l Qadr, whose clan had ruled the area since the days of Shah Isma`il I. Five years later, the shah appointed Allah Virdi Khan, perhaps his most renowned general, as its beglerbeg. Allah Virdi Khan ruled as the province's virtually autonomous governor until his death, when control passed to his son, the equally famous Imam Quli Khan, who helped to make the region prosper.

Most travelers who visited the region offer positive descriptions, especially of Shiraz, suggesting that, on the surface, this prosperity lasted far into the century. Jean de Thevenot, visiting in 1665, found a pleasant city with rich bazaars and beautiful gardens, as well as a surrounding region abundant in fruit.[101] Speaking more specifically, Carré claimed in 1671 that Shiraz had formerly been a city of nobles and warriors but that it was now a commercial center. Its people, he explained, had grown rich from the maritime trade with India, the Red Sea, China, and Japan, where they took carpets, brocades, horses, Georgian slaves, porcelain, faience work, wine, dried fruits, and rose water, as well as from the caravan trade with Arabia, Mesopotamia, and the Levant, where each year they sent caravans consisting of 10,000 to 12,000 camels laden with spices, precious stones, pearls, and fine textiles coming from the Orient.[102] A few years later, Shiraz struck Petis de la Croix as a prosperous city, with its well-stocked bazaars offering an abundance of goods.[103] In 1677 John Fryer called the town a very agreeable place, with its many gardens and markets, "of which there are innumerable, large and splendid, abounding with rich merchandize...." The same observer drew attention to the stately palaces of the khan and the notables, the city's pleasant walks and gardens, the colleges and mosques, tombs and water-courses.[104] Bembo, visiting in the same period, similarly praised the "large, beautiful and majestic bazaars" of Shiraz. Coming from Jahrum, he had traveled through "beautiful and fully cultivated countryside," filled with numerous villages, where farmers were cutting wheat all around."[105] Hedges, finally, in 1685 spoke of the city's handsome bazaars and public buildings.[106]

Yet, here too, we are faced with a counter-narrative offered by outsiders with a deeper knowledge of the country, and one that is corroborated by Persian-language sources. Tavernier spoke of the diminished income of Fars.[107] The most insightful of the European observers, Chardin, said about Shiraz that the city had flourished until the death of Imam Quli Khan in 1632. Shah Safi, intent on weakening a potential regional rival to his own power, Chardin insisted, had divided the region into three parts, giving each to a vizier, and siphoned off all its revenue, causing the province to spiral into steep decline. Suggesting the paradoxical effect of the conversion, the Frenchman claimed that, with Fars converted to crown land, provincial income had gone up by some 175,000 tumans, while the population had diminished by half and Shiraz had lost more than 80,000 inhabitants.[108]

Although Chardin's assertions are surely exaggerated as far as the population loss of Shiraz is concerned, there is enough additional evidence to suggest that, even if life in the city seemed agreeable to outside visitors, all was not well in the wider region of Fars. Many people are said to have left Lar in the 1620s, weary of the growing tax burden and shrinking commercial opportunities.[109] In 1645 VOC official Winnincx observed that in former times nearby Jahrum had been a pleasant town full of trade activity but that it was now totally dilapidated.[110] Other reports corroborate Chardin's argument about economic decline resulting from poor governance. As early as 1652, Speelman, the secretary to the Dutch Cuneaus embassy, claimed that Shiraz had fared poorly since the death of Imam Quli Khan. He called Fars overtaxed on account of its fiscal obligations to the local and central governments. Several years later, another VOC agent invoked credible informants to confirm the decline of the productive base of Fars since the days of Imam Quli Khan.[111] The Persian-language sources, too, suggest that the problems in Fars went back to the days of Shah Safi and echo foreign views with information about local abuse. Shah `Abbas II had Mirza Mu`in al-Din Muhammad, Imam Quli Khan's successor as provincial vizier, dismissed for financial malfeasance.[112] Mirza Mu`in's son and successor, Mirza Hadi, too, was recalled in 1656 for fiscal impropriety. The Dutch accused him of fleecing the province.[113] Tavernier adds a political element, explaining that Mirza Hadi had been called to account for the revenue figures he submitted because of a feud that had developed with grand vizier Muhammad Beg. Calling Mirza Hadi rich and wise, Tavernier claimed that the governor had become an irritant to Muhammad Beg for pointing out the latter's flaws and bad conduct. In retaliation, the grand vizier had complaints about Mirza Hadi whipped up, prompting his dismissal.[114] Afterwards, Fars was split up into five districts, one of which went to Babunah Beg and one to the latter's brother, Muhammad Isma`il.[115]

The financial problems persisted, however. According to the *Tarikh-i jahan-ara-yi `Abbasi* Fars showed a huge deficit in the 1650s. Vahid Qazvini, lending credibility to Chardin's comment about the population loss, insists that the economic crisis had prompted many peasants and other inhabitants to move elsewhere. In 1663, the province was offered to Mirza Sadiq, formerly vizier of Azerbaijan and Mazandaran. This was clearly an attempt at reform on the part of Isfahan, for the region's revenue assessment was subsequently changed, making it more realistically conform to the actual yield.[116]

But by 1668 Mirza Sadiq, disgraced, was dismissed and imprisoned, ostensibly because he had allowed Hasan Basha of Basra to escape. Yet, as the English surmised, his removal was more likely related to his formidable wealth and the shah's acute need for money. Indeed, soon after his incarceration a sum of 20,000 tumans was found in the khan's possession and that of officials in his entourage.[117]

In the following years conditions hardly improved. Fars, for instance, was swept up in the series of natural disasters that afflicted large parts of southern Iran. In 1677 the entire south was plagued by drought and visited by swarms of locusts.[118] Two years later Shiraz suffered from "great penury," with food costing four and five times as much as before. The famine of 1679 extended to Isfahan as well, prompting the government to try and fix food prices.[119] The year 1688 brought new locust swarms.[120] In early 1689 a missionary described Shiraz as utterly desolate because of extraordinary rains followed by an outbreak of the plague which killed thousands.[121] These natural events clearly took their toll, yet fiscal pressure by a government desperate for revenue contributed to the deepening crisis as well. Governors, meanwhile, came and went in rapid succession. In early 1674, the ruler of Fars, possibly Safi Quli Khan, who in 1668 had succeeded Mirza Sadiq, was dismissed.[122] Fryer tells the story of the imprisonment of the next khan, Murtaza Quli Khan, in 1677, claiming that he was taken to Isfahan in shackles because of rumors that he possessed "unheard of treasuries." Some, Fryer added, alleged that the same official had incurred the shah's wrath for neglecting to send the annual tribute to the court. The shah confiscated whatever wealth he could lay his hands on, dismissed Murtaza Quli Khan from his position—with the assurance that there was hope for reinstatement if he disclosed the remainder of his wealth—and replaced him with the brother of the nazir, the chief favorite at court, as Fryer called him.[123]

Kirman

Kirman town and the surrounding province are among the few areas for which we have information beyond the occasional remarks and observations left by passing travelers or the formulaic capsule written from the perspective of the court—which typically refers to the appointment of an official or his dismissal for "disobedience." From the reign of Shah Safi until 1693, the region's vicissitudes are covered in a rare provincial chronicle, the *Tazkirah-i Safaviyah-i Kirman*. For the period after the 1660s, we have extensive documentation from the

Dutch sources, with Armenian VOC agents reporting on the city's trade and politics.

Kirman had been a stronghold of the Afshar since early Safavid times.[124] The Afshar retained their hold on the region until Shah ʿAbbas I brought down the formidable Biktash Khan, who had expanded his power beyond Kirman to Yazd, after which he set his sights on Fars as well. ʿAbbas, determined to bring down the Afshar, moved a large number of Kurds to the area, appointing one of them, Ganj ʿAli Khan, a trusted official, as its governor. In 1618 Qandahar was added to Ganj ʿAli Khan's domain. Upon his death in 1624, he was succeeded by his son, ʿAli Mardan Khan. Both oversaw a huge area, all the way from Qandahar to Nayriz and from Birjand as far as Minab, about one million square kilometers in all.[125]

The case of Kirman reminds us that it is hazardous to extrapolate from individual examples, however well documented, to conclude that the entire south went into decline following the death of Shah ʿAbbas I. Bastani-Parizi argues that from the reign of Shah ʿAbbas I no more good governors were sent to Kirman and that the appointees had far more limited financial and military jurisdiction than their predecessors. Other changes he sees as detrimental to conditions in Kirman include the extraction of local wealth by way of taxes, confiscation, and forced provisioning, an increase in clerical interference in local politics, growing intolerance vis-à-vis minorities, especially the Zoroastrians, and the religious tensions that came with an influx of large numbers of (Sunni) Kurds.[126] These trends are unmistakable in the long term, yet for decades after Shah ʿAbbas I's reign the province continued to prosper. Several caravanserais were constructed in Kirman in the mid-seventeenth century.[127] Responding to growing local demand, the city's pottery industry saw an increase in production as of the 1660s.[128] Kirman also drew outside commercial attention in the same period on account of its famous goat's wool. The VOC and EIC, looking to expand their business in Iran, in the 1650s entered the trade in Kirman goat's-hair (*kurk*) fleeces, which were produced in the region of Rayin and locally used for the manufacture of precious shawls. In 1656, a Dutch private merchant sought to invest the profit he had made selling cloth to buy kurk.[129] A year or two later, the VOC decided to try its hand at the trade and sent an assistant merchant to Kirman. Both the VOC and the EIC were usually represented locally by Armenian brokers. Purchasing and handling kurk presented the Europeans with many problems concerning price and quality; yet, with interruptions, they would stay on in Kirman doing business long after the end of Safavid rule.[130]

Several governors in this period are also said to have ruled benevolently and to good effect. These include Jani Khan Shamlu, who in the spring of 1637 became qurchibashi as well as governor of Kirman. He seems to have performed well in the latter function, even though he was mostly an absentee governor who let himself be represented by his brother, Ulugh Khan. Mashizi, for one, lauds Kirman's stability and prosperity in this period and the good care Jani Khan took of the peasants. Another governor who worked to enhance the city's well-being rather than to line his own pockets was `Abbas Quli Khan. Appointed in 1653, he built qanats and constructed caravanserais. Many people flocked to Kirman town and numerous houses were built while he was in power, so that his benevolent rule was remembered long after his death.[131]

Conditions in Kirman seem to have deteriorated only in the second half of the century, following the region's conversion to khassah land. Jani Khan's demise in 1645 and the death of his brothers, Ulugh Khan and Qara Khan, entailed the confiscation of all his assets, including his landholdings in Kirman and Hamadan.[132] As Kirman was turned into crown domain, Isfahan began to interfere in local affairs without being familiar with these, and especially with the life-giving qanat system. The absence of responsible landowners made the agricultural yield fall. Ultimately, this destroyed the inherently fragile equilibrium of an environment in which the effects of frequent drought and famine could only be countered through judicious management of resources.[133] Trade seems to have diminished in volume. Tavernier claimed that traffic on the caravan route through Qandahar had fallen off by the 1650s compared with previous times.[134]

The situation became particularly acute under Shaykh `Ali Khan, with his fervent attempts to increase central control and fiscal revenue. In 1671, the position of hakim was downgraded to that of vizier, presumably to curb autonomous tendencies. Shaykh `Ali Khan began to interfere not just in the choice of the city's vizier, but also in the appointment of its other high functionaries, from the kalantar to the *darughah* and the *mustawfi*. Worse, under his administration Kirman was flooded with Kurdish officials connected to him, men who were obviously unfamiliar with the city and its ways.[135] Shaykh `Ali Khan also sent to Kirman a stream of tax collectors and officials charged with the investigation of crimes.[136] The town's Zoroastrian inhabitants, in particular, suffered from increasingly onerous imposts, including the *jiz'ya*, poll tax, prompting them to file repeated complaints in Isfahan.[137]

All of this created conflict between the various constituent groups in the city: between ethnic "Iranians," who were mostly Shi`i, and

Kurds, who were predominantly Sunni; and between local Muslims and Zoroastrians. Conditions in the city worsened to the point where thieves and robbers roamed freely in the streets, forcing people to organize their own neighborhood watches. Tensions between the religious and civil authorities, involving the *shaykh al-islam*, the second most prominent official after the vizier and a local magistrate with landholdings in Bam, exacerbated the situation. Muzaffar Husayn, the incumbent of the hereditary post of shaykh al-islam, was a venal type who enriched himself at the expense of the common people. He also got on badly with the vizier, the kalantar, and other local officials. In 1676, Muzaffar Husayn became embroiled in a conflict with the vizier, Hatim Beg, causing the latter to try and oust him through slander. Muzaffar Husayn also schemed against the *sadr-i mamalik*, who was married to an aunt of the shah, associating this religious official with a portrait that depicted Sulayman as a donkey. He was found out and exiled to Shiraz, but managed to stage a comeback with the assistance of Shaykh `Ali Khan, as a result of which the vizier of Kirman was put under arrest and his goods were confiscated. The shaykh al-islam, meanwhile, was rehabilitated.[138]

In 1690, Mirza Tahir Vahid succeeded Shaykh `Ali Khan as grand vizier. With his appointment came an order to investigate Kirman's account books and the need to select a new governor. Yet several years went by before Shah Virdi Khan was appointed, chosen from a pool of five candidates. This delay corresponded to the time it had taken Tahir Vahid himself to succeed Shaykh `Ali Khan, and reflects administrative paralysis as much as efforts to cut costs. Unsurprisingly, the resulting power vacuum created a decline in administrative order and safety. Matters became so dire that the officials of the vizier no longer dared to go into the bazaar or the alleys. The shah thereupon consulted with Tahir Vahid so that finally, after four years of pleading and bribery, the appointment of Shah Virdi Khan as vizier of Kirman was approved in May of 1693.[139]

Kirman's proximity to the eastern border zone created additional problems. The city served as a jumping-off point for the repeated campaigns that the Safavid army undertook against the Mughals and, with increasing frequency, against the Baluchis of Kitch and Makran. Each time the region was called upon to fulfill its tax obligation by provisioning troops and supplying resources in the form of cereals, lead, and gunpowder. Regional alliances grew weaker, too. The tyrannical behavior of Kirman's darughah, Mansur Khan, alienated the rulers of Bam, who were vital to the defense of the hinterland of Baluchistan, stretching all the way to Qandahar.[140] Chardin tells the story of Jamshid Khan, the qullar-aqasi, a favorite of the shah and very cunning, who set out to recruit troops against the Mughals shortly after he had successfully schemed to be appointed governor of Qandahar and military commander (*sardar*) in the early reign of the shah, having fostered rumors about an impending Indian attack. After arriving in Qandahar he began to behave as a despot, causing alarming reports to reach Isfahan. He next made the mistake of demanding a girl in marriage from an unnamed local Baluchi ruler, who happened to be tributary to Isfahan. When the ruler refused, Jamshid invited him to a banquet and had him killed during the course of it. Chardin claims that 300 Iranians and 700–800 Baluchis perished in the ensuing battles.[141]

During the final years of Sulayman's reign, the long-term repercussions of these developments became fully apparent. Roads became unsafe. In 1673 the governor of Qandahar, Zal Khan, was put on trial for being an accomplice to the robbery of a caravan crossing his territory, an incident in which millions had been lost.[142] Not just moving caravans but villages and oases became the target of highway robbers and roaming bands of Baluchi tribesmen. Recurrent droughts may have driven the nomadic forces into settled territory. The first of these struck in 1652; the next occurred in 1666, to be followed by another in 1677. In 1689 the region experienced its first major Baluchi attack, directed against the town of Khabis. A year later the Afghans staged their first raids into the area, robbing a caravan coming from Isfahan. In October 1691 the Baluchis attacked Kubnan and Zarand. More than 200 people were killed in the various skirmishes. In late 1692 a Baluchi chieftain named Pur Dil Khan attacked Rudbar, plundering its inhabitants. When he realized that the central government lacked the resources to resist him, he threatened to move on and lay siege to Kirman itself, demanding 5,000 tumans, one for each of his warriors, as the price for desisting.[143]

In Isfahan, little serious attention seems to have been given to these threats. Local leaders, left to their own devices, therefore entered into their own negotiations with the Baluchis. The ruler of Rayin, Giyas al-Din Mansur, fearing that his town would become the next target and despairing of any assistance from Kirman, engaged in talks with Pur Dil Khan. He saved his own city from assault and persuaded the Baluchi chief not to attack Kirman either. Not only did the central government neglect to mobilize an adequate force to counter the Baluchis and the Afghans but, in a reflection of the lamentable state of the administration, officials did their best to hush up the various incidents. Local authorities falsely claimed that Pur Dil Khan and his son had written a letter stating that if Isfahan would recognize them as leaders of the Baluchis they would take responsibility for regional security.[144]

Bandar ʿAbbas and the Persian Gulf coast

The Persian Gulf littoral was not an integral part of Iran in the early days of the Safavid dynasty. Shah Ismaʿil I never established any form of control over the southern coast. Shah ʿAbbas I went much farther in achieving that goal by taking Bahrain, by establishing the port of Bandar ʿAbbas as an alternative to Portuguese-held Hurmuz, and by ousting the Portuguese from that stronghold in 1622. Still, until the end of the dynasty and really into modern times, the Persian Gulf littoral remained a series of "outward-looking maritime port cit[ies]" existing in a dichotomous relationship with an "inward-looking, agrarian-based inland empire."[145] The economic significance of the Persian Gulf trade to the Safavid treasury was nevertheless considerable. In the 1690s, Sanson estimated the revenue generated by the southern ports at some 65,000 tumans.[146]

The shahbandar was the functionary in charge of collecting tolls in Bandar ʿAbbas, the largest of the Persian Gulf ports. Unlike the situation in Ottoman ports, where shahbandars were chosen from among wealthy merchants,[147] the post in Bandar ʿAbbas was a purely political one, on a par with that of the local khan, his superior. If they worked in tandem, the khan and the shahbandar could be a formidable team. They rarely did, however, and the inherent tensions between the two functionaries—deriving from the fact that they were each other's shadow official, sent by Isfahan to engage in mutual supervision—frequently erupted into strife. Most conflicts seem to have revolved around jurisdiction over the management and receipt of tolls. The stakes were high, for whoever controlled the tolls held the key to private enrichment. Matters were further complicated by the presence of a substitute official to both the khan and the shahbandar, the so-called *janishin*. The janishins, who took charge during the long and frequent periods when their superiors were absent, duplicated the rivalry between the khan and the shahbandar.

Bandar ʿAbbas's officialdom reflected overall Safavid political culture in this and several other ways. One was the tendency for certain clans and families to have a hereditary claim on positions. This tendency is amply documented. Mirza Tahir, the shahbandar in 1653, was the brother-in-law of the governor of Shiraz.[148] The official who received the post in 1654, Muhammad Amin Beg, succeeded his father Husayn Beg. Husayn Beg, who a year later became master of the mint (*zarrabi-bashi*) in Isfahan, was a brother of the grand vizier Muhammad Beg.[149] Muhammad Quli Beg Lalah, who in 1655 succeeded Muhammad Amin Beg, had held the post of shahbandar before. Shamshir Beg, who acceded in late 1656 or early 1657, died in the latter year and was succeeded by his brother's son.[150] Both `Isa Beg, who received the post in 1658, and the shahbandar who succeeded him were again close relatives of Muhammad Beg. The town's new governor in 1678 was Muhammad `Ali Beg, the official who had been shahbandar between 1671 and 1675. Mirza Sharif Jahan, who in 1691 succeeded Mirza Masih, was a nephew of one Mirza Sadiq, who in turn was the brother of Mirza Masih.[151] Mirza Sharif Jahan succeeded his paternal uncle, Mirza Murtaza, and married the latter's wife in order to lay claim to all of his uncle's possessions.[152] Mirza Sadiq, who was mustawfi in Isfahan, became shahbandar in 1697 (after an interim tenure by one `Abdal-Qasim Beg following Mirza Sharif Jahan's disgrace in 1695) and held the position until 1704, when he was succeeded by his son Mirza Sayyid `Ali.

Diminishing returns in Bandar `Abbas
Michael Pearson cautions against automatically connecting the decline of states with the decline of maritime trade in and out of ports belonging to those states.[153] Yet in the case of late Safavid Bandar `Abbas it is impossible to ignore such a connection. Toward the end of Shah `Abbas II's reign, the once flourishing port witnessed a marked decrease in commercial activity and an even steeper decline in officially registered revenue. Fiscal oppression by state officials and customs fraud committed by local magistrates and merchants, sometimes in collusion with each other, appear to have been the principal causes of this decline. Growing fiscal abuse was largely a function of increased supervision on the part of a central state desperate to tap new sources of revenue. The conversion of Fars to crown land after the death of Imam Quli Khan in 1632 increased Isfahan's grip on the coast, and, especially during the tenure of Muhammad Beg as grand vizier, ghulams came to dominate as appointees in Lar and Bandar `Abbas. The old Qizilbash, the Dutch noted in an interesting comment on the perceived efficiency of the new bureaucratic class, had not been as "diligent in executing their functions as the new Sofis."[154] Greater oversight created as many problems as it solved, and certainly did nothing to end the prevailing corruption.

The problems first became visible on a grand scale in the 1650s. A good place to start an overview of the process is the tenure of `Isa

Khan, a paternal nephew of Muhammad Beg, as shahbandar. Soon after arriving in Bandar ʿAbbas, in late February 1658, he summoned the Banyan brokers of the EIC and the VOC to his office, alleging that the shah had foregone much income because of the toll-free import and export of third-party goods under the companies' names, a practice known as "coloring." He claimed to have a royal farman ordering the brokers to be sent to Isfahan, adding that the decree also gave him the right to call up all local Banyan women and girls for the purpose of selecting the prettiest for the shah's harem. He next had the brokers put into chains, without ever producing the said farman, and threatened his prisoners with the bastinado. He only released the men after they had paid him 2,400 tumans in cash. He also demanded 600 tumans from the Dutch and extorted a sum of between 1,500 and 1,800 tumans from the English. One Banyan paid 241 tumans to prevent his wife from being sent to Isfahan. The local kalantar, who until the shahbandar's arrival had temporarily managed the tollhouse, did not escape the latter's "strange humor" either. He was incarcerated for several days, accused of having embezzled money, and forced to pay 500 tumans for his release. The Dutch director would, in his own words, have confronted ʿIsa Khan about these acts, but the Banyan brokers implored him to refrain, arguing that they dreaded further sanctions and would rather pay the shahbandar than see their wives and daughters carted off to Isfahan.[155]

ʿIsa Khan's behavior did not fail to have repercussions for trade in Bandar ʿAbbas. The EIC agent reported in early 1659 that the merchants who had come to town were "so terrifyed with a powerfull and troublesome shawbunder that they dare not do yett adventure to buy...."[156] A year later the English put it this way:

> The merchants of this place are all in readiness to complain of the bad usage of late Shahbandar which have much preiudiced the port of Gombroone for merchants chuse rather to goe to Bunder Congo where they finde better usage and have likewise lately found ways to land their goods at Bundar Reebe and other pettie ports betwene Congo and Bussora...[157]

The problem of diminishing revenue continued in the following years. We lack good information about the shahbandars succeeding ʿIsa Khan—who was removed, probably at the time of his uncle's dismissal as grand vizier in 1661—but their abuse must have been quite brazen, since it led Isfahan in 1664 to conduct an investigation. The new shahbandar, Murtaza Quli Khan, the former royal coffee master (*qahvahchi-bashi*), who was said to have the ear of the shah, came down with the task of finding out why trade at Bandar 'Abbas had languished so badly that its toll revenue had declined from between 20,000 and 28,000 tumans in the early reign of Shah 'Abbas II to between 3,000 and 5,000 tumans at present.[158]

The reasons were not far to seek. Among them was the "coloring" of goods by the Dutch and, above all, the English, who had been involved in a long-standing dispute with previous shahbandars regarding the same issue and who had been instrumental in having the last one recalled to Isfahan.[159] The VOC, asked to draw up a list of the goods it handled, soon found itself in conflict with Murtaza Quli Khan.[160] The issue concerned the interpretation of the farman the Dutch had received in 1652 and in particular the question of whether the annual amount the VOC was entitled to trade toll-free was limited to 20,000 tumans, as the shahbandar alleged, or whether it exceeded that sum, as the Dutch maintained. Through their efforts, Murtaza Quli Khan returned to Isfahan within six months with the promise that he would intercede with the court on behalf of the VOC and the assurance that, if he were to succeed, the VOC would reward him with a handsome gift.[161]

"Coloring" and bribery were not the only reasons why toll revenue did not reflect the real volume of trade in Bandar 'Abbas. The shahbandars themselves were clearly part of the problem. An EIC agent in 1661 overheard a tollhouse official mention to his friends that the shah's customs income for that year totaled anywhere between 15,000 and 16,000 tumans. Since the shahbandar was cheating Isfahan on the real figure, the same agent estimated the actual sum to be in the 20,000-tuman range.[162] One scheme shahbandars employed to defraud the shah was to allow merchants to bring their goods ashore in return for the payment of a personal fee to them in lieu of the official custom charges. In 1682 the English claimed that, in the previous five years, Mirza Masih had struck deals with private merchants by letting them pass directly through him instead of through the tollhouse. These were willing to pay 6 percent above the customary toll rate for this privilege.[163] Chardin, too, speaks of merchant brokers bribing shahbandars to let the choicest merchandise go through.[164] Carré is more specific. Suggesting that such deals were routine practice, he reports that, upon landing in Bandar 'Abbas in 1664, the captain of his ship went ashore to ask the shahbandar for a "mafi" (*mu'afi*), an exemption from the fee the official usually demanded from the captain of a ship—which the captain, in turn, retrieved from the merchants—"in order to get him to pass their private merchandise without paying duty."[165]

Bandar 'Abbas in the reign of Shah Sulayman

In 1665 Firaydun Khan, who a year earlier had succeeded his father as city governor, became embroiled in a conflict with Mirza Yusuf, the shahbandar, over the payment of tolls. An investigation by Isfahan led to the dismissal of both.[166] After their departure, the posts of khan and shahbandar were temporarily combined in one person, beginning with Mahmud Mu'min, a ghulam and the former governor of Huwayza. Mahmud Mu'min never took up his new post, however, for he died on the way from Isfahan, in the vicinity of Shiraz. The double position was next left vacant for some time due to the death of Shah 'Abbas II. The habit of combining both functions in one person continued for a while under Shah Sulayman. While still ruling as Shah Safi II, Sulayman sent a new khan and offered the post of shahbandar of both Bandar 'Abbas and Kung, for two successive years, to the same person. This individual, whose name has not been preserved, managed Bandar 'Abbas while his son was in charge of Kung.[167] The next few years witnessed a renewed separation of the posts of khan and shahbandar and a rapid succession of men who seemed mostly concerned to fill their own pockets as quickly as they could. In late 1668 the shah recalled the shahbandar and Zaynal Khan, the local khan, to account for their behavior. The latter died in Shiraz en route to Isfahan, having poisoned himself. The reason, many claimed, was his realization that the shah was aware that he and his assistant had embezzled 2,000 tumans in toll revenue.[168] The next khan, Mihrab Khan, a former muhrdar, arrived in Bandar 'Abbas on 5 December 1668, but died after little more than a month from excessive drinking. He was succeeded by another ghulam, a Georgian by the name of Talib Khan. Said to be a decent person, he did not last long either. Later that year the same Murtaza Quli Khan who had been shahbandar in 1664 arrived in Bandar 'Abbas, no doubt appointed following persistent reports about fraud on the part of local officials and merchants, indigenous and foreign alike. This time, he took up the combined position of shahbandar and khan.[169] Murtaza Quli Khan remained governor for at least four years, spending much of his tenure fighting marauding Baluchi nomads with the assistance of the khans of Lar and Shiraz and their armies.[170]

With Murtaza Quli Khan the rapid succession of shahbandars and khans came to an end. The decision to make officials serve longer terms was no doubt a response to the continuing decrease in the profitability of commerce, with a particularly precipitous slide in the period immediately following Shah Sulayman's accession, when large parts of the country were afflicted by famine.[171] Chardin claimed that after 1666 customs revenues dwindled to the point where Bandar 'Abbas and Kung combined reported no more than annual proceeds of some 10,000 tumans, less than half the amount generated at the time of Shah 'Abbas II. The magnitude of the disaster can also be gauged from a report in 1668 claiming that the price of pack animals had gone up three- to sixfold and that the extra expense ruined the profits of many ordinary merchants.[172]

The decision to farm out the positions of shahbandar and khan for a longer period was put into effect in 1670, not in 1674, as Chardin alleged. The newly appointed Shaykh 'Ali Khan is likely to have been responsible for the measure.[173] The port was leased for a period of five years against an annual sum of 23,000 tumans. When Allah Virdi Beg died in 1669, his teenage son, Muhammad 'Ali Beg, succeeded him. He would serve until 1677.[174] This pattern of longer tenure was to continue well into the reign of Shah Sultan Husayn.[175] In 1684 Mirza Masih, who had been in post since 1678, received an extension of his tenure by another seven years and simultaneously became shahbandar of Kung. As for the khans, Murtaza Quli Khan served from 1670 to 1674, and Nasir 'Ali Khan, who was appointed in 1674, held the post until he was deposed in 1681.

While the practice of long tenure was clearly deliberate, an attempt by the central government to increase revenue through continuity, it may also have been a function of Isfahan's growing weakness, enabling officials to extend their tenure through bribery and malfeasance. Whereas earlier the shah had often recalled abusive officials, the central authorities in the 1670s appear to have become increasingly negligent in keeping track of matters in Bandar 'Abbas. In 1675 the annual due date for renewal of the customs farming passed without a new farmer being appointed or the incumbent being reconfirmed in his position. Meanwhile, tolls were managed by the assistants of the khan and the previous year's shahbandar. Contrary to Chardin's claim, longer tenure did not necessarily mean higher revenue or improved justice, either. In a vicious circle, the growing oppression attending efforts to extract more money made merchants increasingly reluctant to engage in business, resulting in falling trade and profit, which in turn prompted officials to use even more violence to extract revenue. The sums the shahbandars were to submit to the royal treasury went up from an annual 22,800 tumans in 1672 to 24,000 in 1675 and 25,200 in 1678, dropping to 23,000 in 1699.[176] The volume of merchandise going through Bandar 'Abbas, meanwhile, failed to keep pace with this increase. The shahbandars paid the difference partly by defrauding the shah of toll income and partly by extorting money from the local population and the merchants who frequented Bandar 'Abbas in ever smaller numbers.

The aforementioned Muhammad 'Ali Beg provides a good example of the dubious practices port officials engaged in. The Dutch claimed that, while in office, he managed to extort 60,000 tumans from local merchants.[177] In 1672 he deceived merchants as well as the state by persuading the shah to abolish the 5-percent duty on money brought from Isfahan. When the merchants responded by resuming the transport of large amounts of cash to the coast, he forced them to pay the same duty directly to him.[178] Another stratagem for self-enrichment was direct participation in trade. Political officials routinely took part in commercial ventures. The shah might make forced purchases through his own factors, and court eunuchs are known to have invested in trade.[179] As has been seen, officials in Bandar 'Abbas, too, engaged in business initiatives, often by way of intimidation and coercion. Muhammad 'Ali Beg in 1677 tried to appropriate the choicest sugar and pepper imports.[180] His successor, Mirza Masih, in 1681 scared away many of the merchants who usually came down to Bandar 'Abbas in the winter by declaring that he intended to take one-fourth of all goods imported by the Dutch.[181] In the 1690s the central court sequestered 7,000 kilos of tin, creating great disruption in the market.[182] In the face of such meddling, the local merchants frequently turned to the VOC for support. Using their financial clout, the Dutch often successfully intervened with Isfahan in defense of the aggrieved (and of their own interests). In the case of the shah's order to purchase tin, for instance, they were able to show that the shahbandar had used the royal command as a cover to enrich himself, as a result of which Mirza Sharif Jahan was sent up to Isfahan in shackles.[183]

Bandar 'Abbas's khans were hardly better than its shahbandars during this bleak period of drought and famine. Nasir 'Ali Khan, a former governor of Sarvistan in the province of Fars, was a particularly bad specimen in a series of shady officials. Appointed khan of Bandar 'Abbas in 1674, he cared more for his wine than for his duties, choosing to stay indoors for eight to ten days at a time soon after arriving in town. He also took advantage of his prerogatives by meddling in the handling of merchandise brought to the port. Artificially fixing prices and prohibiting anyone but his own appointees from buying or selling victuals, he caused food prices to go up beyond the means of ordinary people. This prompted villagers to stop bringing food to the port, leading to yet higher prices. The soldiers in town, meanwhile, whose provisioning was in the hands of the local administration, did not receive their wages. Frustrated, they sent representatives to Isfahan to seek redress. In 1679, three years after traveling to the capital, they were still waiting fruitlessly at the court.[184]

The foreign merchants had problems with the khan as well, ranging from a quarrel over the rent owed by the VOC for a house in town to the value of the annual present given to the khan: Nasir `Ali Khan claimed it was too low, whereas the Dutch refused to be pinned down to a specific amount, arguing that gifts were meant as a bonus, dependent on past behavior and promises of future civility. The khan tried to blackmail the Dutch, threatening to inform Isfahan that their trade was worth twice as much as reported and that they also exported many goods illegally for Armenian merchants. Nasir `Ali Khan also targeted the English, demanding 350 tumans from them and warning that, if they refused to pay, he would ask the shah to give half of the EIC's toll share to the Portuguese.[185] For the time being, it seemed that little could be done against Nasir `Ali Khan. Shaykh `Ali Khan harbored a personal grudge toward him, but his animosity was offset by the good relations between the khan and the grand vizier's secretary, Hajji Mu'min.[186] Nasir `Ali Khan had many other powerful friends in the capital, all of whom had received lavish bribes from him. Keeping friends in Isfahan, including the shah himself, was costly. Nasir `Ali Khan was in financial trouble indeed. To cover up his dirty business he had to send 5,000 tumans to Isfahan, a sum he procured with the help of a VOC broker. Fryer, visiting Bandar `Abbas in 1677, informs us that the "large sums of money" Nasir `Ali Khan had disbursed hardly made up for his misdeeds, but that the shah had nevertheless given him a robe of honor.[187]

As always, the local population bore the brunt of the violence Nasir `Ali Khan used in extracting money to make up for his debts. In Shamil, a village near Minab, the khan's tax collectors had the local kalantar bastinadoed so badly that the poor man died. The people of Minab thereupon closed the gates of their town and returned the tax collectors to Bandar `Abbas bound on the backs of donkeys.[188] In Bandar `Abbas itself, people were forced to pay fines for fictitious crimes. The Banyan broker of the EIC was fined, supposedly for monopolizing rice imported by the English and for speaking in contempt of Islam. Other Banyans were victimized too, and at least one was slain for his wealth. Offering money to persuade Isfahan to remove the khan, as the Dutch did, was pointless; as Fryer surmised, the shah remained unaware of the extent of the problem. Nasir `Ali

Khan himself had a hand in this: To prevent news of his outrageous behavior from reaching Isfahan, he asked his couriers to intercept all letters destined for the capital, thus forcing the Dutch to reroute their postal service.[189]

In 1678 Bandar ʿAbbas was a shambles, depleted by fiscal oppression and badly affected by the famine that had gripped large parts of the country. The port, the English commented, was "wholly ruinated, there being not a merchant in Towne, nor a penny of money, nor any trade stirring, nor any freight goods in Towne."[190] Unusual locust swarms had wrought havoc on the region in 1676 and 1677; and the latter year saw the onset of a terrible drought which was to last for at least two years, leading to a doubling of transport costs between Isfahan and the coast.[191] The English summed up the situation by commenting on "all sorts of provisions being now here very scarce and deare, by reason of the great want of raine the last season." The following spring, "not an orange nor a turnip nor anything of the like nature" was found in town, while the people around Lar cried "for rain, both to fill their water-stores, and to bedew the earth."[192]

The accumulated misery and suffering eventually worked against Nasir ʿAli Khan. The Dutch refused to take silk in Isfahan, arguing that they first wished to see the oppressive governor removed. Nasir ʿAli Khan, aware of his growing weakness, thereupon became conciliatory, offering to reimburse the representatives of the local military, who had spent years in futile complaining, for all their expenses provided they were willing to drop their charges.[193] He made similar gestures toward the English and the Dutch, the latter having spent 2,450 mahmudis in bribes at the court to get the governor dismissed.[194] But his efforts to mend relations bore no fruit. The petitioners from the army rejected his offer and, with his powerful friends in Isfahan deserting him, he decamped, first to his ancestral Sarvistan and next to Shiraz. In late 1679 he managed to return to Bandar ʿAbbas. This time, however, the local population did not stand idly by. They gathered some 900 men from surrounding villages to protest at his arrival. Nasir ʿAli Khan, realizing that his posse was no match for the angry crowd, asked the deputy of the shahbandar to mediate, pledging that he would henceforth rule in justice provided his former conduct would not be held against him. He was admitted on those terms and for a while ruled in deference to the people of Bandar ʿAbbas.[195] Before long his conduct drew new complaints, however. This time there were no lengthy negotiations: in 1681 he was deposed and imprisoned for life in a nearby fortress, while his assets were confiscated in the name of the shah.[196] His successor, Murtaza Quli Beg, proved to be a reasonable man whose rule came as a relief for the port's stricken population. He abolished a number of the onerous fees Nasir 'Ali Khan had levied, saw to it that no one was harassed, and, most importantly, made sure that the local soldiers, who by then had not been paid for five years, received their money.[197]

Despite such popular resistance and Isfahan's various attempts at redress, by the late 1670s oppressive officials and uncompetitive fees had caused Bandar 'Abbas's most prosperous inhabitants to leave the town and head for Kung. Fryer, writing in 1678, commented that no Banyans were left in town, all having left for Kung to escape "tyranny and inhumanity."[198] Kung had grown since the early 1630s, attracting merchants through better treatment and a reasonable toll tariff of 7 percent—as opposed to an ordinary impost of at least 10 percent in Bandar 'Abbas.[199] In addition, merchants increasingly chose to call at the smaller ports situated farther along the coast toward Basra, places such as Bandar Rig, which did not have a tollhouse, or even at Basra itself.[200] Thevenot, writing in 1665, insists that for some years Armenians had been avoiding the tolls at Kung by going directly from Shiraz to Bandar Rig. Isfahan did not stand idly by as revenue was siphoned off, to be sure. The Arab shaykhs presiding over the remote small ports only consented to Safavid tutelage on their own terms, which included the right to retain revenue and not to have to consent to a shahbandar sent from the capital. Yet the Safavid government did manage to establish a customs house in Bandar Rig—which functioned until the town was destroyed in 1678.[201]

The authorities in Isfahan were also keen to direct traffic back to Bandar 'Abbas, so as to cut into the income of the Portuguese, who by agreement enjoyed half of Kung's toll revenue. In 1669, following an outbreak of Portuguese–Omani hostilities, the shah issued an order prohibiting all non-European ships from calling on Kung.[202] In response, the Portuguese in 1675 began to hold up merchant vessels, threatening to redirect all ships to Basra. This provocation inspired a plan—most likely instigated by Shaykh 'Ali Khan, who was known for his aversion to the Portuguese—to destroy Kung altogether. Its inhabitants were told to leave and caravans received orders to avoid the town.[203] Yet nothing ever came of this project. Kung would continue to thrive until the Omanis raided and partly destroyed the port in 1695.

Chapter 7

Religion in Late Safavid Iran: Shi`i Clerics and Minorities

Schah `Abbâs II. zeichnete sich durch hochfliegendes und sehr unternehmungslustiges Wesen aus ; er war gerecht, klug und leutselig, dabei den Fremden oft mehr zugetan als seinen eigenen Untertanen.

Shah `Abbas II stood out for his high-spirited and very energetic character; he was just, judicious, and affable; and with all that often more devoted to foreigners than to his own subjects.
Engelbert Kaempfer, *Am Hofe des persischen Grosskönigs*, 46

SUNNI VERSUS SHI`I IRAN

The Safavid state came into being, and, until its demise, presented itself, as a religiously inspired polity. It derived its legitimacy from its founder's status as the incarnation of the divine, and Twelver Shi`ism played a defining role in its evolving identity. As Shah Isma`il I embarked on his territorial conquest, he sought to bring Shi`ism to a population that in majority adhered to the Sunni branch of Islam. Like the conquest itself, the process of conversion was anything but peaceful. Isma`il's efforts to make Iran's population turn to the Twelver Shi`i creed were marked by great brutality. The forcible conversion of large numbers of people accompanied the subjugation of eastern Anatolia, Shirvan, and Azerbaijan, where the Qizilbash sowed terror among the largely Sunni inhabitants, ordering people to publicly condemn the first three caliphs and desecrating the graves of the previous Aq-Quyunlu rulers.[1] Conquering Isfahan in 1503, the shah caused a bloodbath among Sunnis—ostensibly in retaliation for the killing of many of the city's Shi`i inhabitants under the Aq-Quyunlu regime. The Portuguese traveler António Tenreiro, visiting Isfahan in 1524, reports seeing bones sticking out of mounts of dirt, the remains of 5,000 people killed and burned by the Safavids.² Sunnis bore the brunt of these campaigns, but members of Sufi orders were targeted as well. In Fars Isma`il massacred 4,000 members of the order of Abu Ishaq Kaziruni, and destroyed the tombs of their shaykhs in the region.³ Shah `Abbas I deported the inhabitants of Andkhud in Khurasan to Iraq, where they were made to convert to Shi`ism.⁴

If the conversion progress was largely involuntary, it was also never completed. Despite ongoing attempts by the Safavids to put a Shi`i stamp on the territory, a significant segment of Iran's population never gave up its loyalty to the Sunni faith or continued to follow semi-pagan heterodox beliefs. Some cities, such as Isfahan, had long been Shi`i in character and thus were "ready" for the Safavid takeover, but many towns and regions remained heavily or even exclusively Sunni in orientation.⁵ The population of Qazvin, which was mainly Sunni in the early Safavid period, only turned Shi`i reluctantly.⁶ During the reign of Shah `Abbas I, Hamadan was part Sunni, part Shi`i.⁷ In the seventeenth century the people of Gilan still mostly adhered to the Hanafi school of Sunni Islam.⁸ The Afshar, who initially mostly inhabited Kuh-i Giluyah and Khuzistan in the southwest, gave up their Sunni beliefs long after they had been dispersed to regions such as western Azerbaijan, Kirman, and Khurasan.⁹ Sunnism continued to have a particularly tenacious hold over the periphery. The Lezghis and Afghans are a case in point. The nomadic Yomut Turkmen of Khurasan, too were—and are—Sunnis, causing friction with the heavily Shi`i frontier town of Astarabad, which they often threatened with their slave-raiding practices.¹⁰ The sixteenth-century *siyah-push* revolt in Astarabad was rooted in Sunni resistance to local Shi`i hegemony.¹¹ The surroundings of the southern town of Lar remained mostly Sunni as well, as did much of the Persian Gulf littoral at large.¹² Many Kurds in the western parts of Iran, too, stuck to their Sunni beliefs, although many tribes were and remain heterodox, adhering to a series of beliefs blending Islamic and pre-Islamic syncretistic, Mazdean, and Manichean notions. An early eighteenth-century Persian survey of tribes categorizes the Kurdish Garusi and Kalhuri clans as "Sunni."¹³ So many parts of Iran remained Sunni that in 1721 the Ottoman envoy Dürri Efendi famously claimed that one-third of Iran's population still adhered to the Sunni branch of Islam.¹⁴ As the state religion and the majority faith, Shi`ism over time lent a measure of cohesion to the country. Yet this cohesion remained fragile, for political and religious boundaries never fully overlapped, and it thus was incapable of instilling a state-directed unity of purpose. Indeed, the more the Safavids articulated their cause as a Shi`i one, the more those who inhabited the frontier regions and did not subscribe to the official belief system remained not just outsiders but potentially traitors to a perceived common cause.

The story of the rise and early evolution of the Safavids is a textbook example of the routinization of faith in the Weberian sense of the term. Their consolidation of power went hand in hand with the institutionalization of the faith that legitimized it. This was a protracted process, too. Twelver Shi`ism as practiced by the Qizilbash was as fluid and ill-defined as it was syncretistic. Theirs was a primordial semi-pagan universe in which heterodox beliefs and orgiastic ritual awkwardly mixed with an appeal to Islamic legitimation. An early catalyst in the process of institutionalization was Shah Isma`il's defeat at Chaldiran in 1514. Shattering the image of the Safavid ruler as an incarnation of the divine, this rout prompted a search for new, more scriptural forms of legitimacy, in which the shah represented the Hidden Imam rather than competed with him in stature. The onset of Shah Tahmasb's reign a decade later saw a greater emphasis on outward religious behavior, a rejection of the heterodox elements of the Qizilbash variety, and a process by which religion was transformed from an inchoate set of folk beliefs to an institutionalized urban-based faith underpinning the state.

Two additional motives inspired this search, and both became fully visible during the reign of Shah Tahmasb as well. One was the need for the state to rein in the unruly tribal element. Having survived a Qizilbash rebellion during the civil war that marked the first decade of his reign, Shah Tahmasb looked for ways to shift his power base away from tribal support. The other was the need for unity through loyalty, leading to a growing emphasis on the Safavid state as a Shi`i polity—in contradistinction to the Sunni states surrounding it. This orientation was directed against the Uzbeks and, to a lesser extent, the Mughals, but its principal target was the staunchly Sunni Ottomans, whose troops invaded Iran three times between 1534 and 1554 and whose vilification of the Safavids reached all the way to Mecca.[15] Twelver Shi`ism thus became the Safavid rallying cry in their propaganda wars with the Ottomans, even if, initially, they knew little about its formal beliefs.

To help make his elite familiar with the true tenets of Twelver Shi`ism, to shore up his legitimacy as the ruler of a Shi`i state, and to build a religious cadre without ties to any domestic tribal and ethnic factions, Shah Tahmasb intensified his father's habit of courting scholars from such Ithna`ashari strongholds as Bahrain and especially

Jabal ʿAmil in Lebanon, promising them landed property and high positions in return for loyalty. Many heeded the call and moved to Iran, where they became the nucleus of a new religious-bureaucratic class.[16] As a distinct status group, these clerics served the state and buttressed its legitimacy, encouraging popular anti-Sunni practices, such as the ritual cursing of the early caliphs, and suppressing narratives that did not fit the Safavid self-perception, most notably that of Abu Muslim (d. 755), a legendary figure whose life story animated warrior epics and hagiographies popular among the Qizilbash and the Sufis.[17] Their most illustrious representative was ʿAli al-Karaki, who, invited by Shah Ismaʿil, visited Iran as early as 1504. By the time he died in 1534 he was the supreme cleric of his age, and a close relationship had developed between him and Shah Tahmasb, who showered him with honors and conferred lofty titles on him, including that of *shaykh al-islam*.[18] The attendant increase in clerical influence at the heart of the state also manifested itself in the growing practice of intermarriage between royal ladies and members of the new clerical classes.

Yet, just as they failed fully to eradicate Sunnism, so the immigrant ulama did not succeed in monopolizing the political arena. For as long as the Safavids lasted, Iran's religio-political landscape presents a complicated picture rife with paradox and ambiguity. Shiʿism became the realm's official and legitimizing creed, but in its claim to exclusivity and in its inclination to reject other belief systems it had to compete with a long tradition of toleration on the Iranian plateau marked by an inherited tendency to indulge alternative viewpoints concerning questions of life's meaning and purpose. Over time, the ulama became a powerful pressure group, articulating its truth with growing insistence. Yet, for all their assertiveness, they proved unable to eliminate some of the deeply rooted countervailing tendencies of the Iranian cultural universe—its mystical and heretical inclinations, its irrepressible speculative propensities, its relative openness to "heresy" resulting from a long history of interaction with people of diverse creeds. Its apparent ideological single-mindedness notwithstanding, the Safavid polity retained a certain capacity to absorb and assimilate confessional elements of peripheral and foreign provenance.

The stubbornness of Sunni convictions in the Safavid period attests to this tendency. The Safavid state increasingly mobilized Shiʿi Islam as a propaganda tool, yet Sunni Islam did not just maintain a hold over peripheral peoples but even continued to stir at the very heart of the polity. The most telling example of this is, of course, Shah Ismaʿil II (r. 1576–7), a ruler of Sunni proclivities who, assisted by a Sunni grand vizier, Mirza Makhdum Khan, briefly reinstated Sunni

Islam. There are other cases; all through Safavid times one encounters prominent administrators who were avowed or suspected Sunnis. Qazi Jahan Qazvini, a high official in Herat who later would become Shah Tahmasb's grand vizier, was known as a crypto-Sunni.[19] The religious tendencies, real or suspected, of Shaykh `Ali Khan demonstrate that, even in later times, the Safavids continued to draw on a variety of groups in their recruitment of officials, suggesting that political loyalty remained more important than religious credentials. And as the following chapter will show, even the last decade of Safavid rule, when Shi`ism at its most self-righteous had taken center stage at the court, left room for a Sunni grand vizier.

The process of integration and assimilation reached a new level of intensity and consequence during the administration of Shah `Abbas I. `Abbas is known for savagely repressing heretical elements in his realm, most notably the Nuqtavis, an offshoot of the Hurufiya sect who espoused a cyclical conception of time and a belief in reincarnation and the transmigration of souls.[20] His treatment of Sunnis reveals a mixed picture. At times he showed clemency and treated them with his proverbial tolerance. When he took Marv and Nisa in Khurasan in 1600–1, he issued an order not to harass Sunnis or put pressure on them to convert, evincing an attitude that seems astonishing given the brutality with which the Uzbeks had treated the Shi`i inhabitants of Mashhad upon capturing that city in 1589. At other times the shah dealt with them in shockingly violent ways. When his army descended on rebellious Simnan in 1599–1600, he fed the noses and ears of the town's Sunni ulama to the people; and upon seizing Abivard four years later, he allowed the Qizilbash to put many of its Sunni inhabitants to the sword and to take the rest into slavery. Seven years later, `Abbas ordered a massacre among the mostly Sunni Mukri tribe of Kurdistan, whom he suspected of disloyalty.[21] Anthony Sherley's assessment of the shah's religious policies was that, "knowing how potent uniter of mens [*sic*] minds the self-same religion is for the tranquility of an estate ... he is exceedingly curious and vigilant to suppress through all his dominions that religion of Mahomet, which followeth the interpretation of Ussen (`Uthman) and Omar. ..."[22]

CHRISTIANS AND CLERICS

With the accelerated influx of large numbers of Armenians and Georgians and the greater interaction with representatives from Christian Europe, Christianity, rather than Sunnism, became a major issue in Shah ʿAbbas's new capital, Isfahan. ʿAbbas transplanted a good number of the Armenian community of Julfa on the Aras River to the newly built suburb of Isfahan, called New Julfa, in 1604, granting its members commercial and fiscal privileges as well as a measure of religious protection. The Armenian and Georgian ghulams, who were introduced in unprecedented numbers in this period, also infused a Christian element into Safavid society. Prior to receiving high administrative positions, they were made to convert to Shiʿi Islam. They retained many of their original beliefs and customs, though, which posed a challenge to the Safavid polity as a Twelver Shiʿi project. In Minorsky's words, the Georgians especially were known to wear their religion lightly; they apparently converted mostly for reasons of expediency, while holding on to their Christian beliefs and practices.[23] The hogs kept near Allah Verdi Khan's palace in Shiraz offer a graphic example of this.[24]

European Christianity played a role, too. Foreigners, especially visitors from Europe, were typically well received in Iran during Shah ʿAbbas's reign, contributing to his reputation as an open-minded, tolerant ruler. He welcomed Iberian missionaries, allowing them to open convents, build churches, and engage in (limited) proselytizing in his realm. Like Sultan Akbar in the neighboring Mughal state, ʿAbbas showed great interest in people of different faiths and liked to converse with Christians, both the ones living in his own realm and visitors from abroad. He also seemed curious about Christianity as a belief system, as well as about its symbols and rituals, its crosses and relics, its art and architecture. As hopeful missionaries report it, the shah professed not just great admiration for their faith but at times gave the distinct impression that he was but one step away from converting himself.[25]

It would be a mistake to view Shah ʿAbbas's receptiveness to Christians and their faith as a manifestation of a predilection for Christianity, just as it would be erroneous to see in his generally cordial treatment of Christians a form of tolerance as a philosophical principle. As said, the shah ruthlessly suppressed various mystical and heretical sects in his realm. Nor did he embrace Iran's Christian population as a whole. Shah ʿAbbas may have broken with the Shiʿi custom of considering non-believers to be *najis*, ritually impure, in his contact with Christians, freely mingling with his Armenian subjects and even allowing his European visitors to drink from his own wine cup.[26] But, in Edmund Herzig's words, he also was "responsible for more instances of anti-Christian persecution than any of his successors."[27] This was in part a function of deteriorating relations with the

Portuguese. Following the attack on Hurmuz, Shah `Abbas decreed that the Armenians and other Christians who had been settled on the border of Bakhtiyari and Lur territory would have to convert to Islam and that their churches were to be turned into mosques. Rather than a precautionary measure designed to safeguard them against Lur attack, as Iskandar Beg Munshi portrays the campaign, this conversion drive seems to have been part of a larger offensive.[28] In the same year a large number of Armenians and Assyrians who had been captured as part of the seizure of Tabriz, as well as the Armenian inhabitants of a village near Isfahan, were all made to convert to Islam.[29] Having taken Baghdad in late 1624, the shah forced the Armenians living in Mesopotamia to be circumcised.[30] Della Valle recounts instances of Christians refusing to convert being tortured and killed.[31] And just before his death, `Abbas resorted to a practice rooted in Islamic jurisprudence by issuing an edict giving any *dhimmi* apostate the right to inherit the "possession of the property of all his relatives, up to the seventh generation." [32]

The more sober ones among European missionaries wondered whether in his praise of Christianity the Safavid ruler was divinely inspired or just deceitful. In truth, Shah `Abbas was above all a shrewd and pragmatic politician. His curiosity about Christianity and its symbols was no doubt genuine, but his first concern was to enhance and maximize his own power, and to this everything else was subordinate—Christian missionaries, Iran's religious minorities as much as his own clerics and their agenda. His solicitation of Christians did nothing to protect Armenians and Georgians from his terrible wrath following rebellions in 1616–17 and 1619, when he had large tracts of the Caucasus ravaged. The shah's benevolent treatment of the Julfan Armenians was a function of political calculation involving their perceived usefulness as entrepreneurs, cultural brokers, and diplomats, and did not prevent him from putting pressure on their coreligionists in outlying areas to convert.[33] He treated Christian missionaries cordially, not because he was ready to embrace their faith, but because he saw them as useful intermediaries in his efforts to obtain European military assistance against his Ottoman enemies.[34] To that end, he was ready to go to extreme rhetorical lengths. He thus offered the famous Armenian cathedral of Echmiadzin near Yerevan to the pope and, in an even more grandiose gesture, played into an age-old dream of Western Christianity by pledging to hand over Jerusalem to the Christians as soon as he had taken the city from the Turks—with whom he was discussing peace at the same time.[35] As the Portuguese Augustinian diplomat António de Gouvea put it, the shah intended to isolate Istanbul by forging a strategic alliance with the Christian powers of Europe, and thought the surest way to obtain their cooperation would be by having missionaries in his country.[36] At times he appeared receptive to their suggestion to have his Armenian subjects obey the pope. Yet this, too, was politically motivated, involving a strategy designed to curry favor with the missionaries as well as to sow discord among the various groups within Iran's Armenian community.[37] When in 1607 the shah was informed that the Austrians had made a peace treaty with Istanbul a short while before, he flew into a rage and threatened to expel the Iberian missionaries.[38] Two decades later he did expel them, or at least the Augustinians, for a year, suspecting collusion between the fathers and the Portuguese, whom he fervently disliked.[39]

'Abbas's pragmatism extended to his approach to the various religious currents in his realm. To strengthen the legitimacy of his rule, he continued the policy of the predecessors by creating a symbiotic bond between the authority of the state and that of a (carefully monitored) high clergy, who in this period became fully integrated into the state structure, while also fostering selected forms of popular, devotional religiosity. As always, balance was a key component of his policies. Keen to employ religious forces as a counterweight against the Qizilbash and their ecstatic Sufi beliefs, the shah maintained a good relationship with his high-ranking ulama, showering them with gifts and positions. The most prominent cleric of the age, Shaykh Baha' al Din al-'Amili, who briefly served as Isfahan's shaykh al-islam, was a personal friend as well as one of the shah's main astrologers, and as such could often be found on his side.[40] Like most of his peers, Baha' al-Din endorsed the authority of the Safavids and showed himself quite willing to do their bidding. As long as it served his purposes, 'Abbas propitiated the clerics in their concerns and sensibilities.[41] The arrival of thousands of Christians from the Caucasus in Isfahan must have seemed like an alien invasion to the Safavid ulama, and naturally raised suspicion among them. They also voiced strong opposition to the entry of Christian missionaries in the capital. We know that clerical agitation contributed to the lack of warmth with which the shah treated members of the Augustinian delegation that visited Iran in 1607.[42] And it surely is no coincidence that in the early 1620s, a time of mounting tensions with the Portuguese, the ulama succeeded in persuading 'Abbas to institute a ban on drinking. Nor is it accidental that a prominent religious scholar like Ahmad b. Zayn al-'Abidin 'Alavi (d. 1644), penned two anti-Christian treatises in this period. Shaykh Baha' al-Din, finally, who is known to have advised the shah to persecute Iran's Zoroastrians (although not Jews), is likely to have played a role in instigating the 1623 conversion campaign targeting Armenians living in villages around Isfahan.[43]

Shah ʿAbbas I might mollify the ulama and benefit from cooperating with them, enhancing the legitimacy of both parties, but he only allowed them to interfere in politics on his terms. One missionary speculated that the monarch meant to engage the European powers in a military coalition against the Ottomans prior to granting their friars the right to build convents and churches in order to "shut up" his own mullahs, who were keen on the destruction of the Ottomans as well, albeit for reasons of religion rather than state.[44] Shaykh Baha' al-Din's writings suggest one of the shah's ways of steering Iran's clerics for the possible purpose of facilitating "social integration" for ghulams. A hardliner on most issues concerning worship and conduct, the same jurist also issued a series of (undated) rulings urging flexibility in matters of relations with Christians, possibly at the behest of a ruler concerned to create a congenial environment for the newcomers and to make it easier for pious Muslims to interact with them.[45]

The most astute of all Safavid rulers was a master at balancing competing elements in his orbit, Christian missionaries, domestic Armenians, and Shiʿi clerics. Shah ʿAbbas may have been broadminded but he was also a mercurial potentate, apt to cajole or intimidate, depending on mood and circumstances. He might impress his foreign guest with his magnanimity one moment, to cow his subordinates the next by engaging in an act of unspeakable cruelty. He forced his entourage, including the highest religious authorities of the land, to drink wine in the presence of Gouvea, exhorting his guest to report the incident to the pope as a sign of his absolute control.[46] He treated the missionaries well, expressing his affection for Christianity to them, but he did not allow the Iberian fathers to coopt the Julfan Armenians by bringing the latter under papal jurisdiction. In 1613, during one of his visits to Iran, Gouvea made cavalier remarks about this issue. In response the shah temporarily banned the New Julfans from visiting the Augustinian convent and forced them to repay the loan he had given them during their resettlement in 1604–5.[47] Reportedly averse to fasting, ʿAbbas embodies the notion that, as Chardin put it, temporal concerns trumped spiritual matters at the court, and that with some exceptions Safavid rulers were all but orthodox in their beliefs and in some cases not even particularly religious.[48] Occasionally they treated religious minorities with brutality, although rarely for religious reasons alone. Resolutely secular in his will for power and determined not to be bullied by the ulama, Shah 'Abbas was also pragmatic. He thus called off the aforementioned conversion campaign when, in response, an Armenian caravan traveling in Ottoman territory threatened not to return to Iran. In 1624, in a similar display of pragmatism fueled by financial concerns, the shah accepted 1,000 tumans in extra annual taxes in exchange for putting a halt to the forced conversion of Armenians.[49]

THE PERIOD OF SHAH SAFI I AND SHAH 'ABBAS II, 1629–66

Much remained the same under Shah 'Abbas I's successors with regard to the position of Iran's non-Shi'i population, but some things changed. For all his well-attested cruelty, Shah Safi I resembled his grandfather in his relative openness in religious matters. Despite their complaints about his many misdeeds, Safi on balance came to enjoy a good reputation among Western missionaries for permitting them to continue their activities in the Safavid realm. Iran's Armenians and Jews, too, fared well under his rule: he allowed many of the Armenians who had been transplanted to Mazandaran under 'Abbas I to return to their homeland in Armenia, and gave permission for the Jews of Isfahan to return to their faith.[50]

The formerly cordial relations between the court and the agents of European nations cooled off somewhat in this period, mostly, it seems, because Shah Safi lacked his grandfather's interest in maintaining comprehensive diplomatic relations with the West. This change in attitude became particularly pronounced after 1639, the year of the Accord of Zuhab, which restored Turkish rule to Iraq and definitively ended Safavid–Ottoman hostilities. As the Ottoman threat receded, the need to curry favor with agents and emissaries of potential European allies grew less urgent, and especially relations with the missionary orders diminished in intensity, if not in cordiality.[51]

A diminished need for European allies was not the only catalyst for this change in attitude. Growing suspicions about Christians—European missionaries as well as local Armenians—may have been a contributing factor as well. There is some evidence for the growing assertiveness in this period of a court faction with xenophobic tendencies. The European men of the cloth formed its main target, but the ghulams appear to have been the object of the group's scheming as well. Clerical pressure doubtless played a role in this. Shah Safi was the first Safavid ruler to be enthroned by an `alim, the famous Mir Damad (d. 1631–2), a descendant of `Ali al-Karaki.[52] The spate of clerical writings criticizing the ghulams and arguing for a greater role for the ulama in the affairs of state that marked the next few decades reflects the growing influence of these opinions.[53] Shah Safi may have acted in deference to this type of criticism when he curbed the proselytizing activities of the missionaries at the behest of the sadr.[54] Yet, like his grandfather, Safi was neither particularly religious nor willing to be cowed by the ulama and their agenda. He managed to keep hard-line clerics at bay, showed no particular animus vis-à-vis non-Shi`is, and was well disposed to Christian visitors from abroad, something that contributed in no small measure to the positive rating he received from resident missionaries.[55]

Matters turned more complicated under Shah `Abbas II, whose reign evinces great paradox with regard to the treatment of non-Shi`is. Chardin's famous claim that many upper-class Iranians were really deists certainly applies to this ruler. Sayyids and ulama prominently participated in `Abbas's accession ceremony.[56] Once in power, the shah emphatically propagated Shi`ism as a matter of official policy. Like Shah `Abbas I before him, he had Shi`i works on jurisprudence translated into Persian, and he reportedly consulted the ulama on taxes.[57] But, like his immediate predecessors, `Abbas II was not known for zealotry in his religious beliefs. He harbored a great fondness for Sufism and Sufis, whom he patronized to the point of becoming known as the "dervish-loving monarch," and he exhibited a remarkable openness in other ways as well. In Chardin's words, the shah considered himself put on the throne by God to rule as a king responsible for the welfare of all his subjects, not as a tyrant bent on the curtailment of freedom, including the freedom of conscience.[58] `Abbas II, enraged at a murder committed during Ramadan, at one point ordered the killing of all the Jews of his realm; yet Mulla Muhsin Fayz-i Kashani managed to persuade him to reverse this decision, and he is otherwise not personally associated with the persecution of Iran's Jews.[59] With visitors from Christian lands, he maintained cordial personal relations, inviting European envoys and agents to join him in his drinking sessions and even allowing them to quaff from his own goblet.[60] Like his great-grandfather, Shah `Abbas II was keenly interested in intellectual debate, and this passion, too, he indulged by way of long conversations with his European guests. In all this he may have been influenced by his preceptor, Rajab `Ali Beg (d. 1669–70), whose moral ways, Du Mans insisted, were close to those of Christians and who was often at the shah's side.[61] So great was the hope this congeniality generated among missionaries that even the canard about the Christian leanings of Safavid rulers surfaced in the form of a spurious claim, posthumously conveyed by Krusinski, that, on his deathbed, Shah ʿAbbas II had converted to Christianity and was baptized by Raphaël du Mans.[62]

Shah ʿAbbas II continued the policies of his predecessors in other respects as well, including the habit of receiving missionaries as diplomats and allowing them to operate in his realm. In the fall of 1653 French Jesuits led by Fathers Aimé Chézaud and François Rigordi managed to obtain a royal decree for the establishment of a Jesuit mission in Isfahan-New Julfa, Tabriz, and Shiraz. They owed part of their success to letters of recommendation from Louis XIII they brought with them, which contained grandiose promises of French assistance against the Ottomans and other enemies of Iran, including the prospect of a French assault on Istanbul, a siege of Surat in India, and French help with the ouster of the Dutch from Bandar ʿAbbas.[63]

The shah's rapport with the indigenous non-Muslim communities, too, suggests continuity, including a good deal of ambiguity. Until the end of his reign, ʿAbbas II resembled his two predecessors by curbing the effects of clerical bigotry, at least on a personal level. Chardin's claim that it was the secular authorities who protected non-Muslims, often against clerics who decried their presence and activities in the country, applies to Shah ʿAbbas I more than to any other Safavid ruler, but retains much of its validity for the reign of Shah ʿAbbas II. As the Frenchman put it, if it were not for the king and his men, Iran's hard-line clerics long ago would have forced all resident Jews and Christians to convert to Islam.[64] On several occasions, ʿAbbas II threatened high officials who mistreated Christian foreigners with dismissal and other sanctions.[65]

Shah ʿAbbas II's relaxed religious attitude is difficult to reconcile with the heightened persecution of Iran's Sufis as well as renewed pressure on the country's Armenians and Jews that took place under his watch. In a sign of the changing times, the prayer mat, a family heirloom and symbol of the Safavid connection to Sufism, was no longer used at his enthronement.[66] His reign also saw a new outburst of anti-populist and anti-Sufi writing by scholars such as Mir Lawhi and Muhammad Tahir Qummi, the shaykh al-islam of Qum, who criticized his teacher, Majlisi the Elder, for the latter's Sufi proclivities.[67] These were in part directed against the extremist, heretical forms of Shiʿism associated with the Abu Muslim tradition. They also targeted popular or "bazaari" Sufism of the Qalandar variety, with its antinomian practices involving song and dance, bizarre punk-like attire, and the use of various mind-altering stimulants.⁶⁸ The major clerics active in the time of Shah ʿAbbas such as Mir Damad and Shaykh Baha' al-Din had largely steered clear of literalist tendencies, leavening their thinking with philosophical and mystical notions. Their students, including the famous Mulla Sadra and Muhammad Taqi Majlisi (d. 1661), the father of the better known Muhammad Baqir and a formidable cleric in his own right, continued this tradition, so that until the reign of Shah Sulayman Isfahan remained a bastion of philosophically oriented thinking. Over time, however, a generation of clerics came to the fore to propagate, in Babayan's words, a "new synthesis in which notions of Iranian kingship merged with Shiʿi symbols to shape a new language of temporal authority."⁶⁹

Non-Muslims came under renewed attack as well in this period. At various times between 1645 and 1654 the Safavid authorities sought to force Iran's Jews to convert, forbade Christians from selling alcohol to Muslims, and took other measures targeting non-Shiʿis. In 1657 the Armenians were forced to leave Isfahan proper and to decamp to New Julfa, across the Zayandah Rud. The same period also saw increased pressure on Christians to convert to Islam, leading to mass conversion among Christians on account of the inheritance law.⁷⁰

In trying to explain this paradox, it is important to realize that, invariably, the measures were instigated by officials around the shah rather than by the monarch himself, with a succession of grand viziers beginning with Mirza Taqi taking the lead. Chardin claims that the latter constantly urged the shah to enact measures against Christians, recommending that, like the Jews, they be forced to wear a special insignia on their clothing. Shah Safi and his successor had always rebuffed the grand vizier on this, according to Chardin, who also attributed Mirza Taqi's demise in 1645 in part to ʿAbbas II's dislike of his vizier's aversion to Christianity.⁷¹ Part of this "antipathy" came in the form of fiscal pressure. During his tenure, Mirza Taqi is said to have levied ten times the annual tax on New Julfa in a period of five months—a measure that, if true, was of a piece with his overall zeal in increasing tax revenue for the royal coffers.⁷²

No ambiguity exists with regard to his successor, Khalifah Sultan. Khalifah Sultan no doubt was mainly chosen for his political experience and qualities, but by appointing him the shah may also have wanted to appease the clergy. Khalifah Sultan was known as a hardline ʿalim, and he proved to be much less accommodating to local Christians than any of his predecessors (although, like so many clerics, he did show an interest in Christian doctrine, querying visiting missionaries about their creed).⁷³ The Dutch report how, on 3 December

1645, one and a half months after his accession, Isfahan's Armenian fur manufacturers and vendors were forced to close their shops so as to make room for Muslim artisans. Khalifah Sultan also urged the shah to force the Julfan Armenians to wear distinctive clothing. The latter, not without resources, turned to the *qullar-aqasi*, Siyavush Beg, himself a former Christian. According to the *Tarikh-i jahan-ara-yi `Abbasi*, they also sent money to the *sarkar-i khassah* (crown domain), which probably refers to the queen-mother, the official patron of New Julfa. The same source insists that this did not have the desired effect. Yet the Dutch reveal that, after the occurrence of a public protest on the royal square, a compromise was reached whereby members of each group were allowed to have their shops in their own quarter.[74]

These measures, in conjunction with the ones enacted by the next grand vizier, Muhammad Beg, have been variously interpreted. The contemporary Persian-language chronicles describe the various decrees issued in this period as part of an overall morality campaign that also involved the outlawing of prostitution and an order for brothels to shut their doors, as well as measures designed to safeguard Shi`i society against pollution, such as a ban on Armenian fur merchants selling their wares to Muslims.[75] Foreign visitors and residents, by contrast, saw this policy as an example of growing intolerance vis-à-vis religious "minorities." Modern scholars have tended to interpret the episode in similar fashion.[76]

Khalifah Sultan's campaign, unleashed one month after the vizier assumed power, contained all the elements of a ritual cleansing, an attempt at purification by a high official keen to establish his credentials upon taking office. In typical fashion, the campaign was directed against symbols of depravity such as prostitution and the use of intoxicating substances. Also in keeping with tradition, it targeted members of ethnic and religious minorities, who were vulnerable because they paired (perceived) wealth to a relative lack of social and economic protection. Jews, Armenians, and Banyans—Hindu Indian—merchants were all conspicuous participants in economic life, active as traders, artisans, and money lenders.[77] Many, although by no means all, were well off and thus became the object of envy and rancor in a time of religious sensitivity sparked by economic distress. Unlike the Julfan Armenians, who could appeal to the queen-mother for support, Jews and Hindus did not have any obvious high-ranking defenders who might shelter them from oppression.

This context helps explain the targeting of Iran's religious minorities in this period, both in terms of the anxieties and the need for scapegoats lean times tend to generate, and in terms of the actual money the authorities clearly hoped to extract from them, either in the form of excessive taxation, or as a price for revoking bans on their activities. We know that in the campaign of late 1645 money played a role, if not as the motivating force, certainly in its dénouement. Less than a week after the institution of the ban, the Dutch reported how the headmen of the Armenian community of New Julfa had been incarcerated and falsely accused of having promised to raise 1,000 tumans for the shah for the right to work side by side with Muslims.[78]

Khalifah Sultan's successor, Muhammad Beg, became known as much for his eagerness to adopt and import Western technology as for his curiosity about Christianity. He befriended several Christian visitors, among them the prior of the Jesuit mission in Isfahan, the learned Father Chézaud, who impressed the chief minister with his debating skills during disputations with the ulama and who, with Muhammad Beg's assistance, was able to obtain the real estate property he needed to establish a convent in town.[79] Yet, like Khalifah Sultan, Muhammad Beg also has become notorious for the various anti-minority decrees that were issued during his administration, typically at his behest. His appointment as grand vizier in early 1654 was soon followed by measures targeting the country's *dhimmi* population (clients; i.e. Christians and Jews living under Islamic rule). Before the year was out, some Christian churches had been closed and bans had been issued on the construction of new ones in New Julfa as well as on the tolling of church bells.[80] Christians were also prohibited from selling wine to Muslims.[81] Also, with the exception of European East India Company merchants and resident missionaries, the Armenian residents of the capital in 1657 were no longer allowed to stay in Isfahan proper but had to move to New Julfa across the Zayandah Rud. Armenian sources suggest that this decision was motivated in part by a desire to prevent them from supplying wine to Muslims.[82]

More drastic new pressure was put on the Jews, not just in Isfahan, but in cities such as Kashan, Shiraz, and Lar as well. There was nothing new about this. Shah 'Abbas I had at various times countenanced or even ordered the conversion of Iran's Jews, either in the context of tensions caused by members of the Jewish community who, after converting to Islam, had conspired against their former coreligionists, or as a result of vengeful intrigues by Safavid officials who saw themselves thwarted in their attempts to overtax the community.[83] In 1654, the Jewish residents of the said cities were threatened with a loss of commercial employment and ultimately given a choice between conversion and expulsion. It is not known if their promise to offer the shah a large gift if he would repeal the measure had any effect. We do know that, to avoid being put to death, many complied by resorting to a variant of the Shi'i device of *taqiyah*, prudent dissimulation, by becoming *anusim*, Muslim against their will.[84] In Kashan, reportedly home to more than 1,000 Jewish families, some clerics, including the famous Fayz-i Kashani, stood up for the local Jews, acting as their spokesmen, yet some 150 were killed during Muhammad Beg's tenure.[85]

The Jewish part of the story has been variously interpreted as well. Habib Lavi (Levy), in an undocumented allegation that has meanwhile found its way into the modern Persian-language literature, attributes anti-Jewish sentiment to incitement by Christian missionaries. There are anti-Jewish passages in the writings of Gouvea, to be sure, yet no direct evidence exists that he and his men were in any way responsible for anti-Jewish sentiments in mid-seventeenth century Iran.[86] There is, on the other hand, the account of a French Jesuit, a resident of Isfahan at the time, who more plausibly put the campaign in a domestic context by referring to persistent Jewish boasting about the imminent return of the Messiah. This is a reference to the well-known Sabbatai Zevi movement and the messianic expectations it generated in various parts of the Middle East. The euphoria the movement created in Jewish circles, in Iran as well as in the Ottoman Empire, is well documented, and the Jesuit father is not the only one who connects this to the anti-Jewish agitation at the time. Such was the excitement of these expectations, Chardin reports, that, in response, the Jews of Astarabad (modern Gurgan) refused to pay the poll tax.[87] Annoyed, the Safavid authorities reacted by making the Jews promise that, if their savior would not appear within a period of thirty years, they would agree to convert to Islam.[88]

All fingers point to Muhammad Beg as the official who instigated the persecution that occurred during his time in office. Yet in this case, too, it is unlikely that he just acted on his own initiative. Clerical incitement played an unmistakable role in the agitation. The Dutch noted that the decision to target Christians had been taken at the behest of a cleric who had convinced the shah that having ritually unclean people—non-Shi'i Muslims—live amid Muslims would carry the risk of contamination. They are among several observers who refer to an unnamed zealous mullah who, preoccupied with ritual purity and contamination, apparently told the shah that Christians washed themselves, their clothes, and their wine jugs in the water of a canal that was connected to the royal palace.[89] This person is likely to have been none other than Muhammad Taqi Majlisi. In 1655 Majlisi the Elder finished a tract titled *Lavami' sahib-qirani*, which he subsequently presented to Shah 'Abbas II. In it he spelled out the reasons why the *ahl-i kitab* (People of the Book), could not be trusted and how they had violated their obligations. Suggesting that they should be put in their place, he recommended that they be forced to pay the *jiz'ya*, the poll tax, and even advocated waging jihad against them. The fatwa against the Jews proclaimed at this point may have been related to Majlisi's treatise, which was presented to the monarch in the same year. Similarly, it is telling that pressure on minorities, especially the Jews, abated with Majlisi's death and the dismissal of Muhammad Beg in 1661. The Jews ceased to be anusim in this period, and for the remainder of Shah 'Abbas II's reign no instances of outright persecution are on record.[90] Incidentally, the shah's critics included precisely this type of lackadaisical attitude that marked his later reign in their list of complaints about him.[91]

The Julfan-Armenian community of Isfahan meanwhile added its own dynamic to the complex circumstances. This included much internal division and feuding, fear, and resentment of European missionaries and their proselytizing activities, attempts to undermine the position of these interlopers, and enough financial power to give such attempts a goodly chance of success. Vasken Ghougassian has shown how the contested appointment of Dawit Julayec'i as head of the diocese of New Julfa in 1646 led to a serious rift in Iran's Armenian community. Some prominent members of the powerful Shahrimanian family, most notably its head, Khajah Sarhat, in that year declared themselves faithful to the Church of Rome. In the process they became the leaders of the (exiguous) Armenian Catholic community, creating strong animosity between them and the majority Gregorians (followers of the Gregorian rite who were called Schismatics by the missionaries), who remained the dominant force in New Julfa.

In the face of growing pressure, the Catholic New Julfans appear to have strengthened their existing ties to foreign lands. The fabulously rich Shahrimanian family had owned a house in Venice since 1613, and some of their members regularly spent long periods of time there as well as in Rome and Livorno. Their substantial loans to the Serenissima and the conversion to Catholicism of some of their members as well as other connections with the papacy on the basis of which they would eventually gain Roman citizenship, stretched out over more than half a century. The trade mission to Moscow organized by Sarhat Shahrimanian and executed by his son Zakharia in 1659 similarly represents a clear attempt to acquire an "insurance policy" against adversity in Iran. Zakharia, who served

Shah Sulayman as a royal merchant and who worked for Shaykh 'Ali Khan as well, took the so-called diamond throne with him as a gift. Arriving in the Russian capital, he presented this valuable object, made of silver and studded with diamonds and other precious stones valued at 80,000 gold ducats, to Czar Alexei Mikhailovich in hopes of obtaining trade privileges, notably an exclusive Armenian right to travel through his domain. But he clearly meant to strengthen political ties between the Julfan merchants and the Russian crown as well, so as to buy some protection against the Safavid regime.[92]

Catholicism also made inroads through a growing collaboration between the Catholic Armenians and southern European nations which made use of the former to gain access to and influence in the Safavid realm.[93] All this played itself out in mutual suspicion and recrimination between the majority of the Julfans and the missionaries. The entry into Iran of the Christian men of the cloth, beginning with the Augustinians under Shah 'Abbas I, from the outset had created tensions with the domestic Armenians. New complications arose with the arrival of the more activist French Jesuits in 1653, among the missionary orders themselves, in their relationship with the authorities, and in their interaction with Iran's Armenian community. Fierce rivalry developed between the Jesuits and especially the Capuchins, whose presence in Iran went back to 1628, when the French Father Pacifique de Provins had arrived in Isfahan. More importantly, the Jesuits became embroiled with Iran's Armenians, the main targets of their urge to guide Iranians to the true faith. More zealous in their beliefs and, still untried, more eager to convert than the Iberian orders, the French Jesuits tended to be less respectful of the Armenian religious authorities and thus encountered a great deal of opposition from the New Julfan community.[94]

With the conclusion of the Accord of Zuhab in 1639, the interests of the royal court and those of New Julfa's merchants—and those of missionaries and Christians in general—had ceased to converge. The Julfan Armenians continued to ply the trade routes between Iran and Europe, but as the shah lost interest in them as intermediaries, linguists, and diplomats, their clout in Isfahan diminished.[95] Yet this did not keep especially Dawit, the archbishop of the Gregorian community, from strongly resisting the establishment and activities of the newly arrived Jesuits in various ways. Anxious about the growing activities of the Christian preachers, he sent letters to the court arguing that the missionaries had come to convert Muslims. Pressure from the Armenian ecclesiastical authorities caused various missionary orders to recall their agents from New Julfa.[96] It also forced Chézaud's host, the *kalantar* of New Julfa, to evict his guest. Eventually Armenian complaints prompted Muhammad Beg to address the shah with a request to forbid the Jesuits from settling in the Armenian suburb until the promises conveyed by Chézaud and Rigordi had been fulfilled. This resulted in the issuance of a royal farman halting the construction of a Jesuit church in 1654, followed by the expulsion of all missionaries from the town.[97] A side effect of this move was bad blood between the orders, with the Capuchins holding the Jesuits responsible for their eviction, which in turn undermined the cause of the missionaries at large, contributing to suspicions that they were foreign agents intent on weakening Iran.[98]

Why Shah 'Abbas II himself gave such latitude to his scheming officials is not fully explained by these circumstances and remains a matter of speculation. The events of 1645 may be attributed in part to the weakness of a ruler who at the time was not yet thirteen years of age. But diffidence resulting from inexperience fails to explain the shah's muted reaction to the measures that were taken a decade later. As in the case of his great-grandfather, a gregarious personality combined with an interest in the philosophical aspects of Christianity had little bearing on the political question of how to approach Christians (or Jews) as a group, least of all if that group involved a domestic constituency in a politically contentious climate. Given mounting pressure from hard-line religious forces, it is easy to see political calculations at work. We know that, at some point in his reign, Shah 'Abbas II came under severe criticism from some Shi'i ulama, who argued that he should abdicate to make room for a more devout ruler on account of his unholy lifestyle. This was ostensibly based on his excessive drinking and his flirtation with Sufism but it also seems to have involved a perception among his critics that he was overly friendly with non-Muslims.[99] For the shah to give in to some of the demands of the ulama with regard to non-believers may have been a safety valve, an easy way of muting or deflecting criticism of his questionable lifestyle.[100]

THE PERIOD OF SHAH SULAYMAN (1666–94)

By the time Shah Safi II (Sulayman) came to power the Shi'i clergy were in the process of consolidating their power, and religion had become fully institutionalized, functioning as an arm of the state. Dissent was heard, to be sure, with some ulama complaining that the shah neglected his duties, but by and large a symbiotic relationship between the secular state and the religious elite had come into being, whereby the ulama benefited from the perquisites of high office and in return fully cooperated with the state, invoking the need for a "just and judicious king to administer and rule the world."[101] Shi'ism by this time had become state-sponsored performance, with the enactment of officially sanctioned popular rituals—an attempt to produce an alternative "carnival" of practices, in Sajjad Rizvi's words—in the form of Ghadir Khumm parades and `Ashura celebrations centering on the camel sacrifice ceremony. The process itself goes back to the days of Shah `Abbas I, yet in the late seventeenth century reached new heights of state-sponsored theatricality.[102]

In the three-way competition between advocates of popular Sufism, philosophically minded scholars, and shari`a-minded ulama, meanwhile, the last group definitively gained the upper hand.[103] The Shi`i clerics became ever more assertive following the accession of Shah Sulayman, taking advantage of a ruler who showed himself more interested in the pleasures his office entitled him to than the duties it entailed. This assertiveness manifested itself in growing insistence on orthopraxis and increased pressure on Iran's non-Shi`is.[104] In 1678 the ulama of the capital proclaimed Armenians and Jews responsible for the drought that afflicted much of the country in that year. Several rabbis had their bellies slit and the Jews of Isfahan only escaped a worse fate by paying 600 tumans.[105] Growing religious pressure manifested itself outside the capital as well. At an unspecified point during Shah Sulayman's administration, the ulama of Kirman forced the local Zoroastrian population to leave their quarter near the city center and move to the suburbs so as not to get mixed up with Muslims.[106]

Muhammad Baqir Majlisi in particular came to play a prominent role in official policies. Long before being appointed shaykh al-islam of Isfahan in 1687, he enjoyed the support of Shah Sulayman, who personally sent a representative to Yemen to help secure research material for the *Bihar al-anwar*, the monumental work of religious learning that Majlisi composed under his reign.[107] As soon as he took up his post as shaykh al-islam, Majlisi's zeal came out in various ways. He thus set out to make life difficult for the city's Armenians, with the apparent intent of forcing them to convert.[108] Within a year he managed to have the idols in the Hindu temple of Isfahan smashed, rejecting a suggestion by the local Banyans to have them transferred to India instead.[109] Over time Majlisi would target anyone who did not conform to his ideas about proper Islamic comportment. Sufis in particular suffered under his regime. Other major clerics of high official rank known for their strong anti-Sufi feelings include Mulla Muhammad Tahir Qummi, and Shaykh Hurr al-`Amili, who in this period served as shaykh al-islam of the shrine cities of Qum and Mashhad, respectively.[110]

Even if they typically had a legitimizing hand in the continued pressure exerted on non-Shi`is in this period, Iran's clerics were not necessarily the sole or even the principal driving force behind specific campaigns involving Christians or Jews. The death of Shah `Abbas II and the accession of Shah Safi II inaugurated a period of great uncertainty among Christians in Iran. They greeted the coming to power of the new shah with considerable apprehension, worrying that the young ruler might be overly impressionable. And they were right, for, following the shah's second enthronement as Sulayman in 1667, he quickly fell under the influence of *tufangchi–aqasi* (head of the musketeers) Budaq Sultan, an official who was known in Isfahan's foreign circles as a notorious enemy of Christianity, in part, it was said, out of conviction, in part because he was a sworn enemy of the *nazir* (steward of the royal household), who had the reputation of being well disposed to Christians.[111]

Conditions hardly improved when Shaykh `Ali Khan took over from Budaq Sultan as tufangchi–aqasi in 1668. Shaykh `Ali Khan became known for his dislike of Christians during his subsequent tenure as grand vizier. Indeed, Shaykh `Ali Khan is likely to have been instrumental in the mounting pressure on Iran's non-Muslim inhabitants. A catalyst for this is said to have been the conversion to Islam in 1671 of an Armenian bishop who next sought refuge with the shaykh al-islam and brought charges against the Armenian Church.[112] In the same year we hear of Christians being insulted on the street and publicly exhorted to convert, and of the churches of New Julfa being subjected to a tax increase involving the payment of an annual sum of 400 tumans.[113] In 1672 Armenians were banned from entering the Muslim part of Isfahan even for commercial purposes.[114] A year later the Armenian kalantar, Aqa Pir, one of the country's richest merchants, apostatized in a move that earned him great honors from the shah.[115] In 1674 it was reported that Sulayman had forced more than twenty of the most prominent Armenian residents of New Julfa to adopt Islam.[116]

This did not necessarily reflect personal animosity toward Christians on the part of the ruler. True, Shah Sulayman himself proved far less approachable than his father had been; under him the interaction that had been relaxed between Shah `Abbas II and the Franks gave way to a much more formal and distant relationship.[117]

And the visit he paid to New Julfa in 1690 was mostly designed to select young Armenian women for his harem. But he also used the occasion to go to the Vank church, where he showed a keen interest in the meaning of the icons displayed.[118] The events of 1674 notwithstanding, the shah is also said generally to have disapproved of forced conversions. On occasion, he allowed those who had thus been targeted to return to their original faith, and even annulled tax debts of certain poor Armenians to save them from conversion.[119] Here, too, the initiative is likely to have come from officials in his entourage, including religious functionaries, but above all the grand vizier. Inasmuch as Shaykh ʿAli Khan was a suspected crypto-Sunni, a perceived need to appear beyond reproach in devoutness almost certainly played a role in his religious zeal. But purely economic motives need to be considered as well. In his drive to increase revenue for the shah's coffers Shaykh ʿAli Khan after all was hardly discriminatory. Under his vizierate, taxes went up on church property in New Julfa. Zoroastrians were targeted as well. So were VOC and EIC, who felt the heat of his efforts to curb their illegal bullion exports.

Conditions were clearly affected as well by the intra-Armenian rivalry involving Catholics and Gregorians that flared up in this period—and which a weak shah allowed to go unchecked.[120] The prominent Catholic Armenian Shahrimanian family in this period drew ever closer to the Church of Rome and came to act as benefactors to the missionaries, building schools for catechism instruction and churches where the Latin rite was celebrated. This collusion raised suspicion among Safavid officials about the loyalty of the Catholic Armenians, contributing to their worsening conditions.[121] The Gregorians, led by Bishop Stepanos (in office 1683–96), did the bidding of the court; as did the kalantar of New Julfa, who is said to have incited the community against the Shahrimanians while assisting in the practice of recruiting pretty Armenian girls for the royal harem.[122] Under Alexander, who in 1696 succeeded Stepanos as archbishop of New Julfa, the Catholic Armenians would suffer even more pressure, prompting the Shahrimanians eventually to decamp to Italy.

Other rich New Julfa merchants, also members of the Gregorian branch, meanwhile schemed against the Catholic missionaries, exhorting the Safavid authorities to take measures against them by purchasing anti-missionary *raqams* from the crown. In the late spring of 1694, the consecration of Monsigneur Pidou de Saint Olon, Bishop of Babylonia, as Bishop of Isfahan in May, sparked a major controversy between the fathers and the Gregorian Armenians, who saw this event as yet another attempt by Rome to meddle in their affairs. Following a riot on the royal square Bishop Stepanos and his ecclesiastics took advantage of Shah Sulayman's terminal illness to obtain an anti-missionary decree from the queen-mother proclaiming the construction of a new Carmelite church and the procession of the Sacraments through the streets of the suburb to be unacceptable. Issued in July, the decree ordered the *divanbegi* (Chief Justice) to undertake the expulsion of the Carmelite fathers from New Julfa. A collective missionary protest, the intervention of Ignatius Zapolski, the Polish ambassador who happened to be in Isfahan at the time, and the warning that such ill-treatment of the Christian men of the cloth would have negative repercussions for Iran's relations with European countries were no match for the money the Armenians paid to various court officials, among them the queen-mother herself, to bolster their cause. The Carmelites—although not the other missionaries—were thus forced to leave, while their half-finished church was demolished. It would take two years and the intercession of a powerful court eunuch at the request of Father Elia de S. Alberto, the head of the resident Carmelites, before they were allowed to return.[123]

Chapter 8

From Stability to Turmoil: The Final Decades, 1700–1722

ولی با زن و خواجه ، طفل و حکیم   کریم و نعیم و حلیم و رحیم
چو آیینه و آب قلبش رقیق   لطیف و نظیف و رفیق و شفیق
به نامرد هم حرف تندی نزد   زبس بود راحم به هر نیک و بد
مبادا که بیچاره نفرین کند   عدو را نمی خواست غمگین کند
به رویش ز فرط غضب تف نمود   کسی گر ز امرش تخلف نمود
نمی کرد کاری به غیر از نماز   چو دشمن به ملکش زدی ترکتاز
همی کرد از غصه چشمی پر آب   نمودی اگر خصم ملکش خراب

Noble, gentle, soft, and compassionate with women, eunuchs, children, and doctors
Delicate, pure, friendly, affectionate, his heart like a mirror and limpid water
So accommodating with good and evil that he barely raised his voice with a scoundrel
Careful not to cause enemies grief lest he make hapless ones more miserable
If anyone contravened his orders all that his wrath would make him do was spit in his face,
If an enemy raided his territory he would do no more than pray
If a foe ruined his realm his eyes would fill up with sorrowful tears.

Mukafatnamah, in Ja`fariyan, *`Ilal-i bar uftadan-i Safaviyan*, 79

INTRODUCTION

On 29 July 1694 Shah Sulayman died, exhausted from excessive drinking and sexual debauchery. As the French cleric Gaudereau tells it, his last words were "Bring me some wine."[1] The shah had not left his palace since 24 March—when he had briefly come out of his private quarters to preside over a gathering of court elders. This lack of leadership, the Dutch commented, had created paralysis in government circles, giving court officials a free hand to act arbitrarily and allowing provincial magistrates to fleece the population with impunity.[2] Several incidents had preceded the shah's demise, including a major conflict between the *divanbegi* (Chief Justice) and the mullahs of Isfahan involving the violation of the right to seek *bast*, sanctuary, which led 3,500 clerics to stage a rally protesting royal negligence of the affairs of state.[3] Simultaneously, 500 Baluchis conducted raids deep into Safavid territory, coming as close as a day's march from Isfahan. People victimized by these marauders converged on the capital, where they staged noisy protests on the royal square. When their outrage failed to elicit a proper government reponse, they hurled rocks at the gates of the shah's palace and the *talar*, its reception hall. The grand vizier suffered injury in the commotion; the *sipahsalar*, caught by the mob, might well have been torn to pieces had a hastily assembled troop of mounted Georgian soldiers not managed to disperse the crowd.[4]

The previous chapters have shown how, by late Safavid times, the balance of power between the center and the periphery was in the process of tipping toward centrifugal forces. This is something of a paradox since, over time, the center had both grown tremendously in size and complexity, and become stationary. In early Safavid times the court had been small and ambulant, reflecting the shah's status as the approachable head of a mobile military band engaged in perpetual campaigning, a leader who, if he was not exactly a *primus inter pares*, operated as a warlord who had to be responsive to the expectations of his men. By the late seventeenth century, a very different ruler presided over the Safavid state. Turned sedentary, the shah now seemed adrift amid an immobile, multi-layered and faction-ridden court run by eunuchs and women.[5]

With the physical transformation, the nature of the court and the constellation of power emanating from it changed as well. With Shah Sulayman's retreat from public life, the monarch and his direct entourage all but disappeared from sight. Unlike the Arab ideal, which mandated a ruler who was close and accessible, the shah in the Iranian tradition of kingship had an exalted, god-like status. But in a curious paradox, his actual popularity was also bound up with the degree to which he was open to popular access.[6] In the late sixteenth century the people of Qazvin—at that time the capital—had shown their unhappiness with Shah Tahmasb's withdrawal from state affairs.[7] Shah `Abbas I's popularity was due in part to his famous approachability. Even Safi I and 'Abbas II presided over grievance councils and hosted foreign visitors during nightly drinking sessions. Under their successors this type of accessibility diminished. Sulayman still liked to leave the palace for riding parties, but his outings typically took the form of the insular *quruq*. Sultan Husayn went even further. He rarely left the confines of the harem, and the one major journey he undertook was a pilgrimage to the shrine of Imam Riza in Mashhad. He was also notorious for his gullibility, to the point where people openly mocked him, declaring that he had none of the characteristics of a king. According to legend the shah's simple-mindedness was such that whenever he lost at a game played for money he would be so embarrassed that he asked his opponent not to inform the *nazir*, steward of the royal household, who was to pay out the money.[8]

As a result, the shah, while still holding direct absolute power, no longer operated as the forceful ruler of previous times, feared and respected for his "punishing power." Iranian rulers had always relied on a circle of counselors, but strong ones had never allowed the officials in their orbit to amass enough power to challenge theirs.[9] Making and keeping subordinates dependent was a matter of a divide-and-rule policy. And for that policy to be successful, the shah had to take the lead, to diversify his sources of information, have a presence beyond the walls of the palace, not just physically but also in terms of inspiring fear through punishment or at least a credible threat of retribution. Drawing on the age-old maxims of Iranian kingship, the Persian sources recognize the link between a lack of respect for the ruler on the part of underlings, and their growing insubordination and abuse of power.[10] Shah Sulayman still met expectations when in 1680 he recalled Khusraw Khan, Kurdistan's tyrannical governor, and ordered him executed on the maydan.[11] Punishment under Shah Sultan Husayn never went beyond exile to the fortress of Alamut in the Alburz Mountains or, more often, to faraway Marv in Khurasan, where the condemned would languish until, as the Dutch cynically put it, their crimes were forgotten and they managed to get released with the help of their friends.[12] Forfeiture of property and monetary fines became the most common form of retribution.[13]

Naturally, the shah's reclusiveness and ignorance had a negative effect on the efficiency and cohesion of the court. Foreigners lamented the growing venality of Safavid officialdom in a stream of increasingly despondent reports. In the 1660s Tavernier noted how, over time, gift-giving had become more pervasive and lavish as provincial governors had lost autonomy vis-à-vis the central state.

He explained that, if they wished to remain in favor and power, local rulers were obliged to send ever richer gifts to Isfahan. They also paid off anyone who might complain about them. The money for all these costly obligations they extracted from the local population.[14] The venality only seems to have worsened over time, to the point of paralyzing the administration.[15] Shah Sultan Husayn himself is said to have taken the lead, requiring state officials to offer gifts once a month rather than once a year.[16] The Dutch in 1716 observed that the *qazi* (judge) of Shiraz had spent enough money to be appointed *shaykh al-islam* of Isfahan.[17] Krusinski had this to say about the effects:

> [...] every governor ... hasten'd to fill his Purse, that he might have wherewithal to purchase a new Palace, or to defend himself against any Prosecution he had to apprehend for his Oppressions, the whole at the expense of the poor People, who were fleeced in all Respects by those too frequent Alterations ... the People had a great deal to suffer under governors who regarded their Post no more than Palace to bait at, made it more their Study to pillage the Cities and Provinces, than to keep up good order; and this they did with the less Caution and Reserve, because they were very sensible that they might do it with Impunity.[18]

Nor were foreign observers the only ones to sound gloomy. Mirza Muhammad Khalil Mar`ashi ascribes the deteriorating state of affairs at Sultan Husayn's court to a surfeit of jealousy and an abundance of lust and lack of discipline, *band u bast*, among courtiers. He specifically laments the bribery it took to be appointed to high office, observing that the highest bidder would be given the job in a revolving-door process, so that the person installed as governor of Kashan would be called back before taking up his post to make room for someone else.[19] Officials, no longer kept in check by the ruler's oversight, would go all out in their mutual slander. Competent ones, unable to get the shah's attention, wound up shunning any responsibility. A loss of fear inevitably diminished respect for royal authority. Musa Beg, appointed governor of Tabriz in 1702–3 and ordered to move to Khurasan to combat raiding Turkmen, responded by saying that the court was in such disarray that he would surely be stripped of his position if he left Isfahan, and that he would rather be present in the capital if that were to happen. He was dismissed, arrested, briefly imprisoned, and eventually put under house arrest. Musa Beg's successor, Rustam Khan, who also served as sipahsalar, went even further. Dismayed at the shah's ignorance, he resigned in protest, with the argument that he could no longer serve such an incompetent ruler. Under earlier shahs this would surely have cost him his head, but Shah Sultan Husayn merely had him dismissed. Rustam Khan's friends next managed to to get him rehabilitated. Informed of the decision, he sneeringly repeated his refusal to work for an inept monarch and asked to be left alone, after which he was dismissed for good.[20] In 1715, finally, Safi Quli Khan, appointed *muhtasib*, supervisor of the city's victuals, and *amir-akhur-bashi* (master of the royal stables), as well as *zarrabi-bashi* (mintmaster), declined the latter two functions. He also requested to be relieved of the position of muhtasib. Asked by the shah why there was no improvement in the supply and the price of food, he openly blamed the crown. The people, he explained, did not fear the shah anymore, for miscreants were no longer punished, and without punishment there was no fear. His request for full authority to mete out justice was rejected by the shah who declared that he had lost his mind. The exchange was picked up by the *qurchibashi*, an enemy of Safi Quli Khan, who convinced Sultan Husayn that his rival was indeed insane. He thus was banished from Isfahan and went on hajj.[21]

CLERICS, EUNUCHS, AND WOMEN IN CHARGE

A retreating shah allowed the infighting among numerous contenders for power to go unchecked. Sulayman and, even more so, Sultan Husayn no longer practiced the time-honored policy of maintaining a balance among big egos and multiple factions. Among the main beneficiaries were the hard-line clerics. Shah Sultan Husayn's accession exemplified their prominence; the shah refused to let the Sufis gird him with the sword of state, and instead offered that privilege to the sepulchral shaykh al-islam of Isfahan, Muhammad Baqir Majlisi. Asked what he desired in compensation, Majlisi requested restrictions on various kinds of un-Islamic behavior, including a prohibition for women to go out in improper attire and unattended by their husbands. Following the enthronement, the shah issued a decree that banned prostitution, enforced proper veiling, and forbade women from strolling through public gardens. Alcohol consumption was banned, too, and the 6,000 bottles found in the royal cellar were demonstratively poured out on the royal square.[22] Sultan Husayn, who would soon take to the bottle himself, throughout his reign consorted with high-ranking clerics, frequently seeking their advice and especially that of Majlisi until the latter's death in 1699. In subsequent years the shah drew very close to Mir Muhammad Baqir Khatunabadi, his personal chaplain, or *mulla-bashi*. Given the nick-name of Mullah Husayn, he became known as a ruler all of whose acts were "in accordance with the shari'a."[23]

Majlisi and his students, such as the shaykh al-islam of Shushtar, Shaykh Ni'mat Allah al-Jaza'iri, continued the tradition of targeting non-Shi'is in their writings. Sunnis bore the brunt of Majlisi's vilifications.[24] Sufis, too, provoked his wrath, for their ecstatic practices involving song and dance and the use of hallucinants. Theory turned into action when the shah announced the closing of the *Tawhid-khanah*, a hang-out adjacent to the royal palace where Sufi shaykhs engaged in ecstatic rituals. He also committed himself to expelling all Sufis from his realm, unleashing a wave of persecution that is otherwise poorly documented.[25] Majlisi reciprocated by publicly praising the shah.[26] All this was part of a growing emphasis on the Shi'i nature of the Safavid polity entailing the marginalization of non-believers.

Eunuchs and women inhabiting the very center of the court, the royal harem, gained the most in executive power. Jean Chardin estimated the number of eunuchs in Shah Sulayman's entourage to be 3,000.[27] A generation later, Father Sanson spoke of approximately 14,000 courtiers without specifying the number of eunuchs among them.[28] Eunuchs were reviled for their perceived abuse of power. In 1643 Shah 'Abbas II had several of them, including the *rish sifid* (the official in charge of the black eunuchs), of the harem, apprehended and punished for the misuse of public funds.[29] Father Krusinski, suggesting how Safavid rulers used that same negative image to their advantage, claimed that Safavid rulers liked the disdain in which the eunuchs were held by the people for making these courtiers more dependent on them.[30] By the time Shah Sultan Husayn came to power their influence had become a crucial factor in the decision-making process. The Dutch report that the last six months before Shah Sulayman's death, the grand vizier was summoned to submit anything of importance in a sealed envelope to the harem, after which he had to wait until a decision was made public.[31] By 1714, according to the same source, the eunuchs not only had the shah's ear but determined who was appointed, who was dismissed, and who was promoted at the court.[32] When Sultan Husayn left on a trip to the north in 1706, he tellingly left Isfahan in charge, not of his grand vizier, but of Safi Quli Agha, a prominent eunuch who served as *amir-shika-bashi mirshikar-bashi*, master of the hunt.[33] Their conspicuous visibility during official ceremonies in this period is equally as telling. When the Ottoman envoy Dürri Efendi visited Isfahan in 1720, Qislar Agha, the first black eunuch, and Qapu Agha, the principal white eunuch, were seated on the right and left of the shah respectively.[34]

Women, too, played an important role in statecraft in these last decades of Safavid rule. As such, there was nothing new about female participation in statecraft. In the Turko-Mongol tradition, sovereignty was vested in the male and female members of the ruling clan, and women had always had a presence in the public sphere. Heirs to this tradition, the Safavids had long had their share of forceful females. The legendary Pari Khan Khanum, daughter of Shah Tahmasb, and Mahd-i `Ulya, the wife of Shah Muhammad Khudabandah, come to mind. Shah `Abbas, too, dealt with strong women, among them his aunt, Zaynab Bigum, the daughter of Shah Tahmasb, whose advice he is said to have valued above anyone else's.[35] The shah's mother especially was a formidable presence, traditionally accompanying the shah on campaigns and serving on the royal council.[36] `Abbas II's grandmother held the reins of power until the shah himself turned eighteen.[37] The formidable power of females in Safavid Iran is exemplified by the fact that, typically, prominent women were included in purges that marked a royal reach for real power.[38] Pari Khan Khanum thus ended up being killed. Zaynab Bigum fell out of favor in 1614 and was expelled from the royal harem.[39] With Sulayman, and even more under Sultan Husayn, the numbers and their influence seem to have grown. Raphaël du Mans and Engelbert Kaempfer estimated a number of 300 and 400 harem women, mostly concubines, respectively. In the 1690s Sanson claimed that more than 800 women inhabited the royal harem.[40] The Russian consul Semen Avramov, describing the entourage that accompanied Sultan Husayn while entering Kashan in late 1717, counted 525 camels, 200 eunuchs and some 1,000 women.[41] Such huge numbers make Krusinski's claim that the shah's harem "swallowed up the greatest part of his expenses" and that the cost of maintaining this entourage had trebled from his predecessors lose much of its apparent hyperbole.[42]

Under the last two shahs women wielded extraordinary power. It was apparently Sulayman's mother who proposed his recoronation with the argument that a bad constellation of the stars had led to her son's illness. She also instilled parsimony into him. It is not clear what happened to her in later years, but in the last phase of Sulayman's reign, when the shah was often ill, another woman came to the fore. Maryam Bigum, a daughter of Shah Safi and thus Sulayman's aunt, even secured the succession of Sultan Husayn.[43] The latter reigned under her spell until her death at an advanced age in September

1720. She persuaded her son to take up drinking in late 1694, a few short months after he had solemnly outlawed alcohol. It was she who quelled a court revolt against the shah in 1717, and it was at her behest that, after much dithering, the shah eventually mounted a campaign against Baluchi and Afghan invaders.[44] Upon her death she left 200,000 tumans in cash, aside from vast amounts of jewelry, gold, silver, and landed property.[45]

COURT POLITICS, 1700–15

In the first five year of Shah Sultan Husayn's reign, no single official seems to have dominated the court. The Dutch in 1698 called Mirza Muhammad Tahir wise and astute, but added that he had many enemies and kept a low profile. A few courtiers wielded disproportionate influence, most notably Safi Quli Beg, the *nazir*, and Mirza Rabi`ah, son of Mirza Rafi` al-Din, the *mustawfi al-mamalik*, and the author of the *Dastur al-muluk*, who was a great friend of the grand vizier and had been a rising star at the court for some time.[46] In May 1699 Shah Sultan Husayn dismissed Mirza Muhammad Tahir as grand vizier, ostensibly on account of old age, and replaced him with the *ishik-aqasi-bashi*, Muhammad Mu'min Khan Shamlu.[47] Quite advanced in age, too, the new grand vizier encountered his most formidable rival in Mirza Rabi`ah. The latter had accompanied Muhammad Husayn Beg as secretary on a diplomatic voyage to Siam in 1685. After his return he had become secretary of the grand vizier and later *mustawfi khassah* of the silk domains. In 1697 he had fallen out of royal favor.[48] Yet in January 1699, back in the shah's graces, he was appointed mustawfi khassah.[49] Whereas the Dutch characterized Muhammad Mu'min Khan as "not malevolent but greatly fond of gifts," they called Mirza Rabi`ah extraordinarily smart, full of self-confidence and eager to expose the flaws of other officials to the monarch. This naturally made him hated, yet he cleverly managed to survive amid slander and intrigue.[50] The English thought Mirza Rabi`ah a "most intolerable fellow," claiming that "under the pretence of being a true and faithful servant of the king," he called all manner of people to account and plundered them under pretences of gathering in the king's rents. He also opposed Muhammad Mu'min Khan in everything and, since he had free access to the shah—who at this point seems to have borne his grand vizier a grudge—he was in a position to summon "all the cans, viziers, beglerbegs to come themselves and make up their accompt with him."[51]

Not surprisingly, Mirza Rabi`ah made many enemies besides the grand vizier. One was the nazir. A dispute between the two men in 1702 escalated to the point where Safi Quli Beg beat Mirza Rabi`ah with a stick, resulting in the disgrace of the former when the grand vizier brought the incident to the shah's attention.[52] Another was the powerful eunuch and amir-shikar-bashi Ja`far Quli Agha. When Mirza Rabi`ah decided to go on pilgrimage in late 1704, he clearly sought to escape from a cloud of allegations about malfeasance brought up by this latter official, who sent a runner to Kung to apprehend him—by which time Mirza Rabi`ah had already set sail.[53] He was still in office as supervisor of the shah's finances when he died in 1712 while visiting the `atabat.[54]

The influence wielded by Muhammad Mu'min Khan, the scion of a tribal family, and Mirza Rabi`ah, a Tajik, suggests that there was more to the late Safavid court than ghulams and eunuchs. Both groups played an important role and the latter clearly rose to preeminence in this period, but their ascendance was neither uncontested nor linear. The Dutch in 1707–8 claimed that the eunuchs reigned supreme at the Safavid court, singling out Safi Quli Agha in particular for having the shah's ear.[55] Yet the tables seemed to turn with the appointment of a new grand vizier in the summer of 1708, following a serious bread riot caused by a poor harvest and exacerbated by the manipulation of the price of flour by Safi Quli Agha, leaving a number of casualties and property damage to the royal palace.[56] Clearly keen to assume real power, Shah Quli Khan, shortly after taking office became involved in a quarrel with the amir-shikar-bashi, Ja`far Quli Agha. The conflict escalated and Ja`far Quli Agha was beaten up for his alleged arrogance. He complained with the shah, only to be told that this incident should teach the eunuchs to be less engaged in politics. Later that year, implicated in the killing of Kalb `Ali Khan of Astarabad, he was demoted and his goods were confiscated. The Dutch, speculating that the Safi Quli Khan was as determined as his father had been to wield real power, insisted that his rival's fall had diminished the influence of the eunuchs.[57]

Yet less than two years later it became clear that the new grand vizier, whom the Dutch called "not as smart as his predecessor," had failed to build enough of a power base to break the grip of the eunuchs.[58] In early 1709 Ja`far Quli Agha was reinstated as amir-shikar-bashi; he would be an inveterate enemy of the grand vizier until his death in 1713. The nazir, too, remained a formidable rival.[59] And, as always, the religious forces were involved in the complex struggle for power and influence. Shah Quli Khan collaborated with the shaykh al-islam by endorsing a decree instigated by the latter that forbade non-Mulims to leave their homes during rainy or snowy weather lest they pollute Muslims. Their joint effort reportedly had its roots in the grand vizier's need for allies in his long-standing feud with the white eunuchs. By 1712 his power had become severely curtailed and he was clearly no longer in charge of state affairs. Much of his authority had been given to Safi Quli Khan, the divanbegi, who was now said to be a favorite of the shah. In 1713 Ja`far Quli Agha's died and Ahmad Agha (briefly) took on the position of amir-shikar-bashi. A "proud and arrogant person," this head of the white eunuchs would later serve as troop commander to end up as *qullar-aqasi* at the time of the Afghan invasion.[60] The eunuchs were back in power; yet, as always, it remained a contested authority.

FATH `ALI KHAN DAGHISTANI: RISE TO POWER

Fath `Ali Khan belonged to the Lezghi people, mountaineers from Daghistan who were kept in check by the Safavids by way of a tributary relationship.[61] Born in 1673 or 1674, he was the son of Safi Quli Khan, also known as Alqas Mirza b. Ildirim Khan Shamkhal, who under Shah Safi I had been sent to Isfahan by his own father, Aldas (Ildas) Mirza Shamkhal, to serve as a hostage at the Safavid court.[62] Taken to Iran with his brother under Shah Sulayman, Fath `Ali Khan, like his father, was probably reared in the royal harem.[63]

Fath `Ali Khan and his clan had long enjoyed a favorite status at the court. He served as governor of Kuh-i Giluyah when he was appointed amir-shikar-bashi mishikar-bashi in 1713.[64] He also held the post of qullar-aqasi, which entailed the management of the Caspian silk trade. Such prominence reflected his good standing with the shah as well as the good will of some important court eunuchs, if not that of his father-in-law and main rival, grand vizier Shah Quli Khan. In early 1714 Fath `Ali Khan briefly fell out of favor at the court, presumably for showing unusual frankness in informing the shah about the state of the country—this at a time when Sultan Husayn often resided in his newly built pleasure resort, Farahabad, outside Isfahan, for extended periods of time, blissfully unaware of the surging problems outside, from Lur tribesmen preying in the vicinity of the capital to insurrections in regions as far apart as Kirman, Luristan, Mashhad, Herat, Georgia, and Huwayza. Yet thanks to eunuch support Fath `Ali Khan soon managed to regain control over the silk-growing areas. His conflict with the grand vizier did not abate, though. In late 1714 Fath ʿAli Khan and his friend Safi Quli Khan, the divanbegi, openly quarreled with Shah Quli Khan in front of the shah.[65]

The grain hoarding scandal that broke the following year underscores the dire state of the country and the role played by the insouciance of its ruling elite, including Fath ʿAli Khan. Various sources report how in March, following a dramatic increase in bread prices, a riot erupted in front of the entrance to the royal palace. Shouting a thousand insults at the address of the shah, the mob threw rocks, damaging the masonry of the palace exterior. In response the shah convened the royal council. Fath ʿAli Khan, present at the meeting, made it known that the current *darughah*, mayor, of Isfahan, Qurchishah Beg, who also served as muhtasib, had been unable to force the owners of grain storage facilities to sell their cereals. The reason was that the hoarders included, aside from a number of palace eunuchs, high-ranking clerics, among them the aforementioned Mir Muhammad Baqir Khatunabadi, who reportedly had told the shah that if people were able to buy tobacco at 8 ʿ*abbasis* per *man-i shah* (*c.* 5.8 kg.) they could surely afford to buy bread at 8 *bistis*. It would thus be necessary to put someone of greater heft in charge as muhtasib. The shah thereupon appointed Imam Quli Khan Zanganah, the amir-akhur-bashi and a son of grand vizier Shah Quli Khan. The monarch also had officials dispatched to Khatunabadi's residence with the order to offer a large volume of grain on the royal square the next morning. In the meantime a mob congregated around the cleric's residence, ready to assail it. The demonstrators managed to set the door on fire, but before they could enter the house the shah, having heard the news, sent Fath ʿAli Khan to inform the rioters that there would soon be a surfeit of bread available. This calmed tempers and averted further unrest. The grand vizier next arranged for a large quantity of flour to be brought to the market; when the eunuchs and the mollahs followed suit, the price of bread fell to acceptable levels.[66]

The aftermath of this scandal further clarifies Fath ʿAli Khan's role in it, showing how he took advantage of the incident to weaken his rivals. Imam Quli Khan's success in bringing the price of cereals down was short-lived. Within two months after the events, bread prices had shot up again, a development that the Dutch attributed to grain vendors and bakers holding back supplies, in addition to machinations of Fath ʿAli Khan aimed at discrediting Imam Quli Khan and his father, Shah Quli Khan. By late spring, Imam Quli Khan had lost his position as muhtasib and the function had reverted to the (new) divanbegi, Isma'il Khan. Meanwhile, one of the grand vizier's brothers, Allah Virdi Beg, lost his post as darughah to Ibrahim Khan, a nephew of the influential eunuch Ibrahim Agha.[67]

Three days after Shah Quli Khan's death on July 22, Fath 'Ali Khan was appointed grand vizier. He immediately embarked on a campaign to garner revenue for the royal coffers and, as it later transpired, for his own pockets as well. Within two months the new grand vizier had dismissed various officials in the direct entourage of his predecessor while reducing the salaries of the ghulams and other high officials. Those who lost their jobs were asked to submit an account of the tax payments they had been supposed to make and to pay any arrears. Several officials, among them the former *mustawfi al-mamalik*, 'Ali Riza Khan, and the governor of Bandar 'Abbas and Lar, were forced to sell their homes and furniture. In late September, VOC director Oets reported how Fath 'Ali Khan collected money wherever he could, and how merchants increasingly feared being audited. Not a day passed, Oets claimed, without someone being taken into custody. The Armenians of New Julfa were among the first to experience the new minister's zeal. Not only did he demand that they pay the poll tax, but he made the obligation retroactive to the accession of Sultan Husayn in 1694, tearing up a *raqam* according to which the prominent Shahrimanian merchant family had been exempted from paying the *jiz'ya* since the days of Shah 'Abbas II. The lure of personal gain quickly caused him to bend, though. Armenian pleas and substantial bribery sufficed to have the order commuted so that the Shahrimanians were only charged for the preceding three years.[68]

Another example involves Fath 'Ali Khan's dealings with one of his enemies, Musa Khan, the former *tufangchi–aqasi*, and his family. When the shah relieved Musa Khan's brother, Husayn Khan, former governor of Shamakhi, of his 7,000-tuman debt and admitted him back into his graces, Fath 'Ali Khan informed him that Husayn Khan's fraudulent behavior was far worse than the king was aware of, and that he would launch an investigation into this affair if he were given permission to do so. The shah consented, Fath 'Ali Khan went to work, and Husayn Khan, condemned to paying 14,000 tumans, was imprisoned when he proved unable to come up with this enormous sum. He was eventually given a bastinado, losing a few toes in the process.[69]

Foreign merchants suffered as well. Within months of taking office, Fath 'Ali Khan instituted a new tax of ³/₅ *mahmudi* on each gold ducat leaving the country. He also questioned the agents of the maritime companies on the legitimacy of their commercial privileges, and only relented after the Dutch paid 6,900 ducats, 6,000 of which to him personally. In 1716 a ban was proclaimed on the production of gold and silver wire, the weaving and wearing of clothes made with gold and silver thread, as well as the use of brocaded horse covers. The ban was rescinded after the artisans handling gold brocade offered gifts to Fath ʿAli Khan and the shah's personal physician, *hakimbashi*, the influential Rahim Khan, to be replaced with a ban on the preparation of goatskins.[70] Fath ʿAli Khan's efforts to garner money for the shah's—and his own—treasury, continued right up to his last days in office. In early 1720 the Dutch report how the price of the Venetian ducat had risen considerably, pointing fingers at Fath ʿAli Khan for having ordered merchants to purchase as much gold as they possibly could regardless of the price.[71]

In the process the grand vizier amassed enormous executive power. The French consul Ange Gardane called Fath ʿAli Khan the "absolute ruler of the realm, who takes care of everything while the king has not the slightest knowledge of what goes on in the country."[72] Sultan Husayn built pleasure gardens while Fath ʿAli Khan extracted money from every possible source to finance these projects, treating those who refused to pay to the bastinado.[73] A few lines from a mocking verse written by a contemporary critic aptly reflect the perception of a chief minister encouraging his master to keep busy with a pet project—the restoration of the Bagh-i Farahabad—so that he would have a free hand with the business of state:[74]

بده اختیاری که کل جهان   مرا بنده باشند از مال و جان
به تعمیر "باغ فرح" روز و شب   به اقبال مشغول شو بی تعب

Give me a free hand so that the entire world
becomes beholden to me in money and life
Keep yourself busy with the auspicious
restoration of the Bagh-e Farah
day and night and indefatigably.

In keeping with custom, Fath ʿAli Khan's power was built on a vast network of family ties, confirming Maeda's claim that the imported ghulam cadres depended for their political survival on family connections as much as did the indigenous tribal elite.[75] Fath ʿAli Khan's brother Aslan Khan, who had been governor of Astarabad since 1708–9, is likely to have remained in function while Fath ʿAli Khan was chief minister. The same may have been true for Aslan Khan's son, Muhammad Khan, who had become vizier of Herat in 1708–9.[76] A nephew of Fath ʿAli Khan, Muhammad ʿAli Khan, was sipahsalar as well as khan of Yerevan. When Muhammad ʿAli Khan was killed in 1716, his (unnamed) twelve-year-old son succeeded him, besides being appointed *vali* of Georgia and governor of Tabriz.[77] In January 1717, another of Fath ʿAli Khan's nephews, Gida ʿAli Beg, became governor of Kuh-i Giluyah, the province that had formerly been in the hands of Fath ʿAli Khan himself.[78] This appointment seems to have been part of a campaign to sideline a competitor, Safi Quli Beg. The latter, who reportedly rivaled the grand vizier in wealth, had succeeded Fath ʿAli Khan as qullar-aqasi and had been appointed governor of Kuh-i Giluyah as well as Dashtistan and the entire region between Fars and Bandar ʿAbbas, shortly after Fath ʿAli Khan acceded as grand vizier.[79] In January 1717, Safi Quli Beg lost his position as qullar-aqasi (to be succeeded by Rustam Khan, also known as Husayn Quli Khan, a half-brother of Fath ʿAli Khan), and with that his governorship of Kuh-i Giluyah, which went to a nephew of Fath ʿAli Khan.[80] Yet another nephew, Mihr ʿAli Khan, the son of Fath ʿAli Khan's brother Kalb ʿAli Khan, in April 1717 succeeded his father as governor of Shushtar.[81] One of the grand vizier's brothers, Muhammad Khan, who had been deputy of the governor of Mashhad in 1714, served as *sardar*, army commander, while Fath ʿAli Khan was chief minister.[82] When the khan of Shamakhi died in early 1720, Fath Ali Khan managed to have his own godfather appointed in his stead.[83] Lutf ʿAli Khan, who would play an important role as sardar, was one of his many nephews as well as his brother-in-law. A daughter of Fath ʿAli Khan, finally, was married to Rustam Khan, who served as qullar-aqasi between 1717 and 1722 and in the former year was appointed governor of Kirman.[84]

Building up a network by way of nepotism was a necessary yet not sufficient precondition for an official's ascent to high office and his subsequent political survival. Even more crucial was a good relationship with the ruler, for even a withdrawn shah retained the power to dismiss any official at a moment's notice. By all accounts Fath ʿAli Khan's enjoyed an excellent rapport with the shah.[85] The total trust Shah Sultan Husayn put in his grand vizier lasted right up to the moment that the latter fell from grace in late 1720. Trying to explain the shah's passivity in the face of Fath ʿAli Khan's glaring abuse of power, Gardane insisted that Sultan Husayn was so sure of his minister's probity that all insinuations to the contrary fell on deaf ears, giving rise to a popular belief that the shah was bewitched by him.[86] Such insouciance fully two decades after taking power reflects the shah's persisting immaturity as much as his vizier's considerable abilities. After all, by raising substantial revenue for the royal coffers, Fath ʿAli Khan delivered what was most needed at the profligate court. He also proved to be an astute negotiator with the Dutch over matters of silk, and with the Russians concerning military matters and proposals for an anti-Ottoman coalition.[87] Yet none of this rendered Fath ʿAli Khan immune to innuendo by rivals, the more so given his outsider status. Like Shaykh ʿAli Khan Zanganah, he hailed from Iran's periphery, inhabited by people with a negative reputation among persophone, Shiʿi Iranians. Fath ʿAli Khan also shared the Sunni beliefs of his countrymen, the Lezghis. Since, unlike Shaykh ʿAli Khan, he never disguised his true beliefs, he offered his detractors ample opportunity to defame him, as a line in the aforementioned poem demonstrates:

سیرت همه قبح و کافر دلی   عمر را شده نام فتحعلی

With his ugly face and the heart of an unbeliever
Fath ʿAli Khan's name has become ʿUmar.

None of this might have been decisive and Fath ʿAli Khan might not have become as unpopular as he did if, following his appointment, he had not immediately set out to curtail many privileges accumulated by courtiers. Further, his ways of collecting revenue clearly crossed the fine line that separated expected peculation and excessive greed, creating enormous resentment. Gardane claimed that, during his five years in office, Fath ʿAli Khan had amassed a fortune that was seven times as large as the holdings of the royal treasury.[88] Be that as it may, there is ample evidence to suggest that Fath ʿAli Khan made himself hugely unpopular with his revenue gathering methods. One of these concerns the manipulation of cereal prices in time of scarcity. The Russian envoy Artemii Volynskii plausibly implicates Fath ʿAli Khan in yet another grain hoarding scandal in 1717, calling him the greatest speculator of them all:

> Anyone who has a manufactury or a shop is permitted [legally] to produce and sell food as well as the best brocaded silk fabric that is manufactured. But [in fact] these goods are sold and traded only by the i'timad al-dawlah, and any others must buy through him to sell. In the same way, no one is allowed to bring in grain to sell, only the grand vizier, and anyone who brings in grain must sell to his buyers, who then will sell it in the city.[89]

The grand vizier also profited from bribes paid by applicants for new positions. Since any post would go to the highest bidder, it was tempting for the official responsible for assigning positions to rotate these rather quickly. In 1716, for instance, the governor of Bandar ʿAbbas, Safi Quli Khan, lost his position to Safi Quli Beg, the *qapuchi-bashi*, head of the royal doorkeepers, who had paid 1,000 tumans to the grand vizier whereas his competitor, the son of former governor (and shahbandar) of the port city Zakhariya Khan, had only paid 500.[90] Fath 'Ali Khan was not above extortion either. This took various forms beyond his repeated demands for money from the agents of the maritime companies, which continued until the last days of his tenure. In 1720 VOC servant François Sahid went up to Qazvin, where the shah was encamped, to discuss the restitution of the various debts the court had with the VOC. He brought a *pishkash* (gift) worth 1,308 (Moorish) ducats for the grand vizier and other court officials with him. But Mirza Rafi'ah, acting as Fath 'Ali Khan's secretary, told him that the debt could only be settled if the grand vizier were given 2,000 to 2,500 ducats.[91] In its biting sarcasm, the full verse from which two fragments were quoted earlier again best illustrates the reputation that Fath 'Ali Khan enjoyed among his contemporaries:[92]

به صورت چو طاووش سیرت چو مار	به غیر از وزیر فریبنده کار
که ابلیس را داد بازی به فن	فریبنده طناز ساحر سخن
برآورد با دم ز سوراخ مار	زرگنج را از آن فسونگر شعار
عمر را شده نام فتحعلی	به سیرت همه قبح و کافر دلی
به همدستی کوسه و شیخ و میر	مشعبد وزیر فسونگر دبیر
حریفان بیچاره را کرد مات	ببرد آن همه از جماد و نبات
زخیل و بغال و بعیر و حمار	ز املاک و اسباب و نقد و عقار
که بودش گمان کرد اخذ از جفا	به هر صیغه از هر که در هر کجا
در اول چنین کرد با شه قرار	چو شد مسند آرای تدبیر کار
نه از محرمان و نه ناکس نه کس	که جز من کسی را مکن همنفس
مرا بنده باشند از مال و جان	بده اختیاری که کل جهان
به غیر از دو سه شغل بی اعتبار	تو خود هم مکن دخل در هیچ کار
به صحبت قرین باش و اکل و همان	برو فارغ از غصه ما خادمان
به اقبال مشغول شو بی تعب	به تعمیر "باغ فرح" روز و شب
	بگفت آفرین شاه و آسوده شد
	در فتنه با قیر اندوده شد

Who else but the deceitful minister with a face like a peacock and the character of a snake
playful impostor, magician with word—could fool the Devil himself?
That swindler got gold treasure out of a snake hole with his tail
with his ugly face and the heart of an unbeliever
Fath 'Ali Khan's name has become 'Umar
A juggler for a minister, a swindler for a scribe
In partnership with the inexperienced, clerics and princelings,[93]
he extracted all this from matter as well as from plants, confounding his poor competitors, property and goods, cash and real estate, elephants, mules, camels, and donkeys

Using any craft, he unjustly took from anyone and anyplace he thought of
When he became the ornament of the throne and master of the show, he first made arrangements with the shah:
Don't make anyone but me your intimate, not a relative, no one and nobody
Give me freedom so that all the world becomes enslaved to me in property and life
You yourself should not interfere in anything other than in a few inconsequential matters
Give me a free hand so that the entire world becomes beholden to me in money and life
Keep yourself free from the sorrow of us servants
Stay with conversation, and food and the like
Keep yourself busy with the auspicious restoration of the Bagh-i Farah day and night and indefatigably
The shah said, bravo and relaxed
The door of chaos became sealed with tar.

FATH 'ALI KHAN'S FALL

Opposition to the grand vizier was not long in coming. A few months after his appointment, qurchibashi Muhammad Quli Khan Shamlu accused Fath 'Ali Khan in the royal council of driving the country to ruin and of giving orders as if he were the shah. Muhammad Quli Khan threatened to resign, arguing that he did not wish to serve under the authority of a sodomite who was out to destroy the careers of old and faithful servants like Musa Khan while fleecing everyone for the sake of filling the royal coffers. Asked by the shah whether he had taken note of the accusations, the grand vizier replied that he had heard every single word but that, since Muhammad Quli Khan was crazy, he had chosen not to respond. This was followed by more verbal exchanges and even threats, according to the Dutch, who wondered how such a showdown could have taken place in the presence of the shah.[94]

More serious—and reflective of the hatred building up against Fath 'Ali Khan—was an attempt on his life in late February 1718 in Kashan, where the shah resided at the time. The bullets missed their target but killed one of the chief minister's servants. While the perpetrator could not be found suspicion fell on the son of Zakhariya Khan—the official who had been outspent in his bid for the position of governor of Bandar 'Abbas by Safi Quli Beg.[95] Fath 'Ali Khan retained the shah's full confidence for two more years. His downfall followed a classic pattern of court intrigue. On 21 September 1720 Ahmad Agha, the head of the white eunuchs, was exiled to Shiraz, allegedly for having pointed out the shah's ignorance, accusing the ruler of ruining the country by transferring all his authority to the grand vizier.[96] Fath 'Ali Khan's detractors, led by the mullabashi, Muhammad Husayn Tabrizi, and the royal physician, Rahim Khan, next found a way to accuse him of rebellion with the aim of overthrowing the shah. They charged that Fath 'Ali Khan had maintained a secret correspondence with Sunni collaborators, a Kurdish commander and agents of his kinsmen, the Lezghis, enjoining the former to move to Tehran with his troops, while giving the Lezghis carte blanche to continue their depredations provided they would not go beyond Yerevan, which was administered by the grand vizier's nephew. As proof, the two officials produced a fake letter supposedly written by Fath 'Ali Khan to the (unnamed) Kurdish leader.[97]

Upon hearing this, Sultan Husayn ordered the arrest of his chief minister. Before he was apprehended on 12 November, Fath 'Ali Khan is rumored to have dispatched a large caravan packed with his belongings to India. He may have been tortured to make him reveal the magnitude and whereabouts of his vast wealth. Eventually he had his eyes gouged with a dagger. Part of his assets was confiscated for the royal treasury and the remainder was distributed among the people.[98] Lutf 'Ali Khan who, like his uncle had apparently amassed great riches, was taken into custody as well. An inventory of the goods, cash, gold, silver, and jewels belonging to all the supects revealed an estimated sum of 2 million tumans.[99] Fath 'Ali Khan, blinded and found guilty of the charges brought against him, was deposed and replaced by Muhammad Quli Khan Shamlu, the son of former grand vizier Muhammad Mu'min Khan. Shaykh 'Ali Khan, a son of Shah Quli Khan and grandson of Shaykh 'Ali Khan Zanganah, who served as amir-shikar mishikar-bashi, was appointed qurchibashi. The post of amir-shikar mishikar-bashi was given to the eunuch Ahmad Agha, and Mirza Muhammad became inspector of the royal accounting office.[100]

The aftermath of this drama as told by Krusinski is revealing of Shah Sultan Husayn's management style. When the day following his grand vizier's blinding no trace of 3,000 Kurdish troops marching on Isfahan was found, the shah began to suspect a vast imposture and ordered a trial to uncover the truth. Fath 'Ali Khan mounted a spirited defense in which he refuted the charges brought against him involving treason, nepotism, and massive peculation one by one for being illogical and, ultimately, untrue. Overcome with remorse, the shah arranged for his former grand vizier to be taken to the citadel of Shiraz, ordering the governor to treat him with respect. Yet rather than punishing those who had betrayed Fath ʿAli Khan, Sultan Husayn decided to hush up the entire affair and to accept their apology. All were restored to their former estates, although those who had lost their positions were not reappointed.[101]

CONDITIONS IN THE COUNTRY AT LARGE: THE MILITARY, MONEY, AND MINORITIES

By 1700 Safavid Iran suffered from a series of interlocking problems that involved growing insecurity fed by weakening defenses and rampant corruption, in addition to a fractious political system overseen by a weak shah. All this was exacerbated by an unusual series of epidemics and droughts followed by famine that in the preceding two decades had gripped the country, affecting almost all regions at one time or another. Outbreaks of the plague are recorded as early as 1684–5 with parts of Gilan, always prone to epidemics, affected. In 1685, more than 80,000 people may have died in and around Ardabil.[102] In the latter year the disease raged around Hamadan as well.[103] In 1686–7 there were outbreaks in Azerbaijan, Mazandaran, Astarabad, and Isfahan.[104] In 1689 the epidemic surfaced in Shiraz, where it was said to have killed thousands.[105] At about the same time the plague extended over the entire arc that connects Baku with Basra via Mosul and Baghdad. A French missionary in 1690 visiting several villages in the vicinity of Baku commented on the great ravages the plague had caused in that area. When the epidemic struck Tiflis in 1691 it caused many Armenians to leave the city.[106] Mesopotamia, possibly the origin of the disease, suffered in particular. From Diarbakr to Mosul the epidemic had raged for three years by 1690, causing many thousands of deaths.[107] Said to have started in Basra—where as many as 80,000 people may have perished—the disease at its height in 1691 killed between 1,000 and 1,100 people a day in Baghdad alone. Qazvin, Kirmanshah, Erzurum, and Yerevan were also afflicted.[108] As will be seen shortly, southeastern Iran was affected as well. In 1696, finally, Fars again suffered a severe period of drought and famine.[109]

Iran's road scurity, under strain since the 1680s, further declined around this time. In 1697, travel routes around Isfahan were impassable, with highway robbers operating practically at the city gates. Few merchants dared send their caravans because of the risk of attack, and in November of the same year alone robbers managed to despoil three caravans.[110] Krusinski, commenting on the deteriorating safety in the early eighteenth century, insisted that "caravans did not dare to stop any longer in the villages, but chose rather to encamp under tents, because of the difficulty of avoiding peasant ambushes."[111]

Iran's external borders came under pressure as well. In the years following Sultan Husayn's accession, the western frontier area was threatened by Sulayman Baba, a Kurdish chieftain who, having pushed back the Ottomans, had been expanding his territory across a wide swath of northern Iraq and was now moving against Ardalan.[112] Turkmen tribesmen meanwhile raided the northern borderlands, entering Safavid territory as far as Astara and Farahabad in the Caspian region. In 1694 a 20,000-strong Uzbek force staged a major incursion into Khurasan, taking 15,000 captives.[113] In the same period Baluchi tribesmen became active in the southeast, penetrating Safavid territory as far as Yazd, while the Omani Arabs threatened Iran's Persian Gulf littoral with increasingly brazen naval raids.[114]

Isfahan took some steps to meet these challenges. The position of sipahsalar, suspended under Shah 'Abbas II, had already been revived in 1692, no doubt in response to the various tribal incursions. Neither this measure, nor the revival of the artillery corps in this same period did much to turn the tide for an army weakened by decades of neglect.[115] Murtaza Quli Beg Zanganah, the son of qurchibashi Shah Quli Khan and the assistant of the governor of Kirmanshah, was ordered to move against the rebel forces of Sulayman Baba with troops from the Kirmanshah region. But the response was half-hearted at best. The shah, opting not to antagonize the Ottomans, refrained from sending an all-out punitive expedition against a tribal leader whom he considered to be under the jurisdiction of the Porte. Instead, he dispatched an envoy named Abu'l Qasim Khan to Istanbul, first to congratulate Sultan Mustafa II (r. 1695–1703) with his recent accession and, second, to urge the new ruler to rein in Sulayman Baba. In 1698 the latter's troops, numbering 30,000, took Ardalan and Urmiyah. Shah Sultan Husayn responded by ordering 'Abbas Quli Khan Qajar, *sardar* (army commander) and former governor of Ganja, to confront the rebel with a force of 60,000 men.[116] The two parties initially seem to have reached a truce, but in July of the same year Sulayman Baba attacked again and defeated the Iranians, now led by 'Abbas Quli Khan Ziyad Ughlu, near Marivan.

He next retreated to Ottoman territory, after which Istanbul, keen to coopt him, offered him control over the province of Shahrizur. He would continue to stalk the Kurdish boderlands with his troops, until in 1700–1 the Ottomans sent an expeditionary force against him and ended his rule by having him executed.[117]

Isfahan responded to the Uzbek incursions by ordering Rustam Khan to assemble an army. In 1697 hapless peasants in Khurasan implored its soldiers to stay, offering money if they would defend them. Nevertheless, the Uzbeks the following year managed to lay siege to Astarabad.[118] In response to the Omani challenge, the court tried to mobilize resources in the south, a process that, the Dutch speculated, would take at least two months.[119] `Ali Mardan Khan, given control over Kuh-i Giluyah, was ordered to collect *suyursat*, provisions, from all over Fars and to send these to Bandar `Abbas and Kung. He also went to the port of Bandar Daylam, where he requested assistance from various shaykhs in preparation for war against Oman. None of this really addressed the problem, though. Lacking a navy the Safavids were poorly equipped to project power on the sea. For a naval deployment in the Persian Gulf they had to turn to foreign nations, the Portuguese, the Dutch, and the English, all of whom were reluctant to oblige. At any rate, a drought in the Garmsirat in 1695 scuttled the operation, so that an expedition had to be postponed.[120]

Shah Sulayman's reign had seen a creeping weakening of the military. The pace only quickened under Shah Sultan Husayn, even if the true extent of the problem only became apparent as relative stability turned to chaos at the turn of the eighteenth century. This was in part a matter of relative strength vis-à-vis the tribal peoples living on the edges, involving a shift in the balance of power. In their encounters with those living in the east, the early Safavids had generally held the upper hand owing to earlier and easier access to firearms. Shah Tahmasb, for instance, may have owed his crushing victory over the Uzbeks at the battle of Jam in 1528 to his imitation of the Ottoman *tabur cengi*, Wagenburg tactic, chaining wagons together and putting cannon within.[121] In the course of the seventeenth century the Iranians appear to have lost this advantage. In 1617 Pietro della Valle could still declare that the people from Balkh and Bukhara, lacking access to firearms, were weak against the Safavid army. Even a century later the tribes on the edges of of Khurasan did not necessarily use firearms.[122] But by the 1690s Sanson called the Baluchis "good shots."[123] Twenty years later, a resident missionary reported from Shamakhi that whereas earlier the

Lezghis had only carried bows, arrow and lances, they were now all equipped with pistols and sabers, which they had learned to manufacture and knew how to handle adroitly.[124] At that time the Afghans used *zamburaks*, swivel guns mounted on the backs of camels.[125]

The real problem of the Safavids, however, was their growing inability to organize and especially fund a credible military operation. At the turn of the eighteenth century, Israel Ori estimated that Iran's armed forces consisted of 100,000 men, all cavalry, and 10,000 royal guards, but lacked an infantry. He also reckoned that it would take Isfahan seven to eight months to mobilize a considerable force.[126] He was not far off the mark: Nasiri reports that in 1696 it took six months to field an army.[127] Artemii Volynskii, visiting Iran in 1717–18, described the country as extremely weak and an easy target for an outside power. Drawing attention to what he saw as the inability of the military to defend Iran against domestic rebels and outside aggressors, he presciently forsaw the coming destruction of the Safavid state.[128]

As always, the structural impediment to efficient recruitment was a lack of finances. To combat the woeful shortfall of available funds, the state continued the practices outlined in Chapter 4, proclaiming bans on the export of bullion from the Persian Gulf ports, and issuing silver coins of lower weight.[129] In 1710, grand vizier Shah Quli Khan Zanganah convened a meeing with the wealthiest Muslim merchants, Mirza Mahdi and Mirza Isma`il, to discuss possible ways of preventing this drain.[130] Yet large amounts of money continued to leave for India, in a movement now compounded by a growing outflow of gold ducats via the western border. Pilgrims to the `atabat and the Arabian shrine cities had always been forced to take large amounts of gold with them to cover their travel expenses. To prevent this type of bullion export was exactly one of the reasons why Shah `Abbas I had promoted the visitation of the domestic shrines of Qum and Mashhad. The late Safavid state, by contrast, keen to flaunt its religious zeal, encouraged pilgrims to visit Iraq and Arabia, appointing officials to accompany the travelers. Enormous amounts of gold left the country as a result, causing gold prices in Isfahan to rise in advance of the pilgrimage season and to drop again after the departure of the hajj caravan.[131] This became a growing problem at the turn of the century, judging by the increasing frequency of Dutch reporting on it. In 1703–4 a gigantic sum of 100,000 tumans is said to have left the country in this manner.[132] Court eunuchs were conspicuous participants in this traffic, and, according to the scathing remarks from contemporary observers, they used dubious means to collect the gold in question:

گرفتند زرها ز شاه و گدا   ز انعام و رشوه و از ربا
نموده حرام از پی مستحب   به دادند زرها به روم و عرب
که حاجی و هم کربلایی شوند   به هم چشمی ، هم مرائی شوند

> They took gold from the shah and the beggar
> From gifts and from bribes and from interests
> They gave the gold to the Christians and the Arabs
> So as to become hajjis and people who have visited Kerbala.
> While competing with each other being hypocrits.[133]

Particularly detrimental to the country's cohesion and defensive capabilities was Sultan Husayn's religious policy. Fath 'Ali Khan Daghistani's tenure as grand vizier shows that even in late Safavid times, when a literalist interpretation of Shi'ism had come to influence official policy, an official with questionable credentials hailing from a peripheral part of the realm could still operate at the very center of power. Like his predecessors, Sultan Husayn was also cordial with European men of the cloth, inviting the Polish Father Krusinski to his palace to explain the meaning of Christian iconography to him.[134] Following his accession the shah renewed the decrees that allowed European missionaries to operate in his realm, and in 1703 he gave Polish Jesuits permission to establish Jesuit mission in Ganja in the Caucasus.[135] The tradition of encouraging debate on religious issues with representatives of Christianity continued under him as well.[136]

None of this could obscure the growing religious tensions, however, in Isfahan as much as in the country at large. Kaempfer, residing in Iran in 1684–5, had noted how the vilification of 'Umar had become an integral part of the call to prayer, that cursing now included members of other minorities, and that this type of agitation had become so widespread that foreigners were frequently confronted with youngsters hurling insults at them as they walked around town.[137] Muslims in the capital in this period complained about impure infidels riding camels and donkeys in the city.[138] Matters only worsened under Shah Sultan Husayn. The measures taken on the occasion of the shah's enthronement in 1694 included a ban for non-Muslims to leave their homes at time of rain and snow lest they contaminate believers. Thanks to the mitigating influence of palace eunuch Agha Kamal the enforcement of such discriminatory measures remained lax. Yet the pressure did not let up. At the advice of orthodox clerics, Sultan Husayn in 1699 reaffirmed the Shi'i purity laws.[139] As we have seen, in 1708 the ban on non-Muslim outings during periods of rain or snow was reissued at the behest of Shah Quli Khan Zanganah and Isfahan's shaykh al-islam, Mir Muhammad Baqir Khatunabadi.[140] In

1714 the shah's religious advisors, arguing that the Islamic law did not allow Christians to employ Muslim servants, helped promulgate a ban on the practice. Not much seems to have come of it, even though rumors persisted that the shah was about to forbid Europeans from having Muslims work for them. In 1715 news spread about an imminent expulsion of all Westerners from Iran.[141]

This policy had serious economic as well as military consequences. The New Julfan Armenians exemplify the former. They had been targeted in the 1640s and 1650s and, though hardly suffering from outright and sustained persecution, they had a growing tax burden imposed on them. A missionary, writing in 1700, expressed the connection between weakening royal power and increased fiscal pressure on vulnerable groups by calling Shah Sultan Husayn a weak ruler with good intentions, as a result of which "officials and governors do not fear him and so they take money from the Armenians...."[142] Barely appointed mustawfi khassah in 1699, Mirza Rabi`ah advised the shah to tighten the accounting rules for provincial governors and to force Isfahan's Hindu merchants to convert to Islam, pay the jiz'ya, or leave the country. Following an outcry in their ranks and a slump in trade, he offered a way out, allowing them to pay 100 to 200 tumans to have the measure repealed. Mirza Rabi`ah also persuaded the shah to issue four raqams curtailing the rights of the New Julfa community. According to the first, no corn or wheat could be brought to New Julfa directly but all had to be taken to Isfahan proper first, there to be bought by the Julfans. The second stipulated that the Armenians could no longer sell fruit, vegetables and other foodstuffs to Muslims; the third raised rents paid by the New Julfans, and the fourth confiscated all gardens alongside the Zayandah Rud for the shah, forbidding Armenians from building on the land any longer.[143] In another act of deliberate humiliation, the Armenians were forced to wear distinctive clothing.[144] In 1699, finally, the imposition on New Julfa reached 5,000 tumans. This sum was substantially lowered after a number of Armenians fled the borough.[145] Once again, the right amount of money proved sufficient to have discriminatory measures repealed or softened. Groups with the wherewithal to buy off adversity also had the means to decamp. New Julfa's Catholic Armenians thus emigrated to Venice, Russia, and India in growing numbers in this period. The Sharimanians, under fire from their Gregorian colleagues as well as the fisc, are the best example of this type of flight. Two older members of the community, Markerat and Mankel, converted in the same period.[146] But most chose to leave. Having invested a great deal of capital and good will in Venice and Rome, they were offered trading privileges and granted citizenship in these Italian cities. In 1698 the family moved to Venice.[147]

We have little direct information about the fate of non-Shi`is beyond Isfahan. Jean Pitton de Tournefort, traveling in the Caucasus at the turn of the eighteenth century, reports that a poll tax amounting to 6 `abbasis per person was levied on Georgians and Armenians.[148] Growing religious intolerance coupled with new taxes led to a decrease in revenue accruing from monasteries in Armenia, antagonizing their clerics and drawing them into the orbit of the Ottomans.[149] Most dramatically, the Dutch in 1716 report how exorbitant food prices had driven thousands of starving Christians to convert to Islam,—presumably to find relief from those high taxes.[150] We also know that the sericulture of the Caspian provinces went into decline in this period, causing many caravanserais in Rasht to shut their gates. Fear of Russian aggression did the rest. Rasht, the Russian officer Soimonov insisted in about 1720, had changed from a thriving commercial center into an army camp. As a result, Armenians from all over the north in this period increasingly moved to Russia, so that by 1723 few were left in Gilan and Mazandaran.[151]

The subsequent Russian invasion brought more turmoil to the region. `Ali Muhammad Hazin, who hailed from the town of Lahijan in Gilan, desribes how his family lost all their property as a result of the chaos introduced by the occupation, and how their estate fell to ruin.[152]

Zoroastrians, Jews, and Banyans too, suffered growing pressure. Their overall numbers were small, although in the towns of Kirman and Yazd the former constituted a sizeable minority, and the recorded examples are telling. Shortly after coming to power, Shah Sultan Husayn signed a decree that stipulated the forced conversion of Iran's Zoroastrians. A few years later this decree was implemented in Isfahan, causing a temple in the city's Zoroastrian quarter to be destroyed to make room for a mosque and a school.[153] As will be seen below, the pressure extended to Yazd and Kirman as well, antagonizing the local Zoroastrians to the point of turning them into collaborators with the invaders. Local Jews may also have welcomed the Afghan invasion.[154] In Bandar `Abbas as in Kirman, the main victims of the increasingly desperate conditions in the last years of Safavid rule were the resident Banyans, who were forced to pay the jiz'ya. In September 1721, on the eve of the Safavid collapse, this impost was quadrupled. [155]

Because of their small numbers, Armenian, Jewish, Zoroastrian, and Banyan disaffection was ultimately of little consequence. Far more serious was the growing oppression of the Sunnis who inhabited the sensitive tributary *limes* in large numbers. The mostly Sunni Kurds in the western borderlands offer the best example. Notoriously fickle, they easily switched sides, and repressing their religious identity was the surest way of antagonizing them. The revolt of Sulayman Baba in 1694, with its clear sectarian roots, is a case in point. Members of the delegation sent to Isfahan by the Kurdish leader a year earlier had been killed by dervishes out of hatred for Sunnis.[156] And the Sulayman Baba uprising was not the only manifestation of sectarian tensions provoked by Isfahan. In the first years of the eighteenth century, the harsh, anti-Sunni rule of Hasan `Ali Khan of Ardalan in Kurdistan provoked an anti-Safavid revolt in the region.[157] The growing restiveness of the Baluchis in the southeast had a religious dimension as well. Targeted by the governor of Mashhad, Najaf Quli Khan, who waged a proselytizing campaign against these alleged pagans, they turned against the Safavids shortly after Sultan Husayn's accession.[158] Subsequent years would show many more examples of such stress and strain caused by religious zealotry.

THE LAST TWO DECADES

Developments in the north

When the Dutch traveler De Bruyn visited Shirvan in 1702 he called the province one of the most important for the Safavid government, and sang its praises as a land of fertility, high agricultural yield and low prices living under the firm but just rule of Allah Virdi Khan. Ganja, which rivaled the provincial capital, Shamakhi, in size, was one of Iran's most attractive cities, De Bruyn claimed, endowed as it was with wide streets, neat bazaars, and pretty caravanserais. Five years later De Bruyn returned to find conditions changed. Ganja's government was now in the hands of Allah Virdi Khan's son, a ruler who was mostly concerned with women and wine. Justice and security had lapsed. Local troops were not paid and lived from plunder. De Bruyn met local people who told him that they preferred to live under the tsar and would not mind a Russian invasion.[159]

Like the observations about the Caspian provinces mentioned earlier, this might appear as a snapshot of one region taken by one passing traveler. Yet the conditions observed by De Bruyn are emblematic of many parts of Iran in the early 1700s. The details are sparse but it appears that Azerbaijan, perhaps the most important region in terms of revenue and military recruitment, was in turmoil by 1711. In the early months of that year Tabriz suffered from unspecified internecine strife which reportedly cost 3,000 lives.[160] In subsequent years, astronomical prices and oppressive rule caused great hardship in the same city. In early 1719, its inahbitants revolted against their tyrannical governor, Muhammad `Ali Khan, forcing him to flee. Isfahan is said to have reacted by imposing a hefty fine on Tabriz and by ordering the populace to obey the authorities.[161] In 1721 a devastating earthquake leveled three-quarters of the city and reportedly killed more than 40,000 people.[162]

We have far more detailed information about Shirvan and adjacent regions in the years after De Bruyn passed through. In 1709 the province became a target of raiding Lezghi mountaineers, who took advantage of the vacuum created by the retreat of Safavid authority. Led by a spiritual leader, a Sunni cleric named Hajji Da'ud, they marched into Shirvan under a Sunni banner proclaiming an ardent desire to have the Safavid yoke lifted.[163] The people of neighboring Armenia revolted in 1716, killing their governor, Muhammad `Ali Khan. This nephew of grand vizier Fath `Ali Khan, who also happened to be the country's sipahsalar, was succeeded by his twelve-year-old son. Later that same year banditry in Georgia prevented caravans from passing through.[164] All this prompted one traveler to remark that the shah was forced to spend more treasure on Georgia than he derived from the region in profits simply to keep the Georgians from turning against Iran by uniting with the Turks, the Tatars, or the Kurds.[165] The Lezghi incursions into Shirvan intensified as of 1718; incited, it was rumored, by Fath `Ali Khan Daghistani. In April of that year they took the village of Ak Tashi near Nizovoi, after abducting a number of its inhabitants and plundering a caravan of forty people on the road to Shamakhi. More reports about Lezghi depredations followed. By early May some 17,000 Lezghi tribesmen had come to within twenty kilometers from Shamakhi, ready to attack the city after looting settlements in the surrounding area.[166]

The shah, residing in Qazvin, at this point tried to mobilize troops, but the effort was stymied by a pressing lack of money. Volynskii reports how in early March 1718 a courier arrived in Shirvan with a royal order for Khusraw Khan to direct a military force to Qazvin, where an insurrection had broken out. Rumor had it that the rebels had it in for the shah himself, intending to replace him with his brother, presumably `Abbas Mirza.[167] Reluctant to disobey the ruler this time, Khusraw Khan began to assemble troops, and by 26 March, having gathered 500 men, set out for Qazvin. The Georgians, who

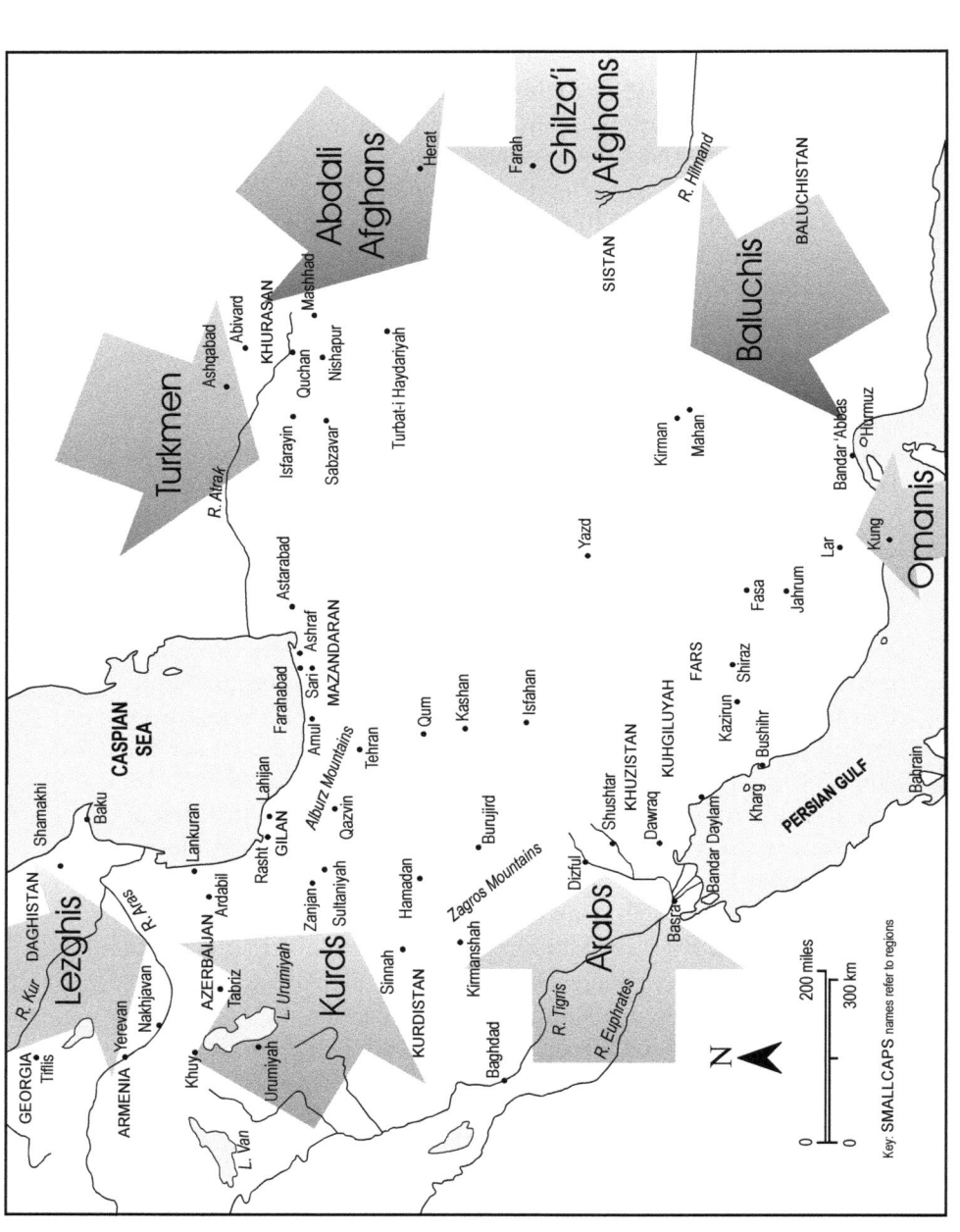

Map 5. Late Safavid Iran: tribal pressure on the periphery

were supposed to provide the shah's army with 40,000 soldiers in times of need, were barely more forthcoming.[168] Farsadan Beg, the governor of Tabriz, told Volynskii that the shah had repeatedly asked the vali of Georgia, Vakhtang VI, to come to Qazvin with his troops, reportedly consisting of 10,000 Georgians and 3,000 to 4,000 ethnic Iranians, but that the vali had refused to do so, with the argument that the Safavids did not pay their soldiers. Similar problems complicated the defense of the northern border against Russian aggression. For years, Isfahan had not paid the *shamkhal* of Tarku his customary subsidy, and when he requested military assistance against the Russians from the Safavids, the shah promised him (a token sum of) 1,000 tumans. He thus submitted to Russian authority in 1717, facilitating Peter I's march into Iran.[169]

Volynskii, returning to Shamakhi in 1718, found that the local authorities saw the grand vizier as an infidel, hence considered his orders invalid, and even questioned the authority of the shah himself.[170] The Italian Beneveni meanwhile insisted that the town's population was ready to revolt against their Safavid overlords for extorting large sums of money from them.[171] In 1719 Georgian troops were enlisted to confront the Lezghi threat to the region. Their commander was Khusraw Khan's half-brother Vakhtang VI, the vali of Georgia's central district of Kartli, who, after a long period of resisting, in 1716 had finally agreed to convert to Islam, after which he became known as Husayn Quli Khan. Appointed sipahsalar, he was sent back to Georgia with the task of taking on the Lezghis. Moving to Daghistan and assisted by the beglerbeg of Shirvan and the king of Kakhet'i, Georgia's eastern half, he managed to inflict heavy losses on the Daghistani rebels. Yet at the height of the campaign, in the winter of 1721, the shah recalled him. The order came after Fath 'Ali Khan's fall and was issued at the instigation of the eunuch court faction that included the mullabashi and the hakimbashi, who apparently had persuaded the shah that a victory for Vakhtang over the Lezghis would harm the country since it would enable the vali to form an alliance with the Russians with the aim of conquering Iran.[172]

In 1721, as Kurds staged raids into Iran from the Erzurum area and roamed close to Isfahan, the chaos in the north peaked with the Lezghi occupation of Shamakhi.[173] Suggesting how inflamed ethnoreligious sentiments had become at this point, between 4,000 and 5,000 of the town's Shi'i inhabitants were put to the sword.[174] Equally suggestive is a remark made by Dürri Efendi, the Ottoman envoy who came to Iran in early 1721, to the effect that the Lezghi aggression could have been avoided. In a private conversation, Muhammad Quli Khan, Fath ʿAli Khan's successor, had implied that the Lezghis—as well as the Afghans—might have been bought off. Their raiding activities, he claimed, were really meant to force the shah to acknowledge their vassal status with a robe of honor and the payment of their agreed-upon annuity. Only the ruler's obstinate refusal to do so had stood in the way of a solution.[175]

The Lezghi assault had other consequences as well; it resulted in the death of a large number of Russian merchants and the loss of a huge sum of money in merchandise. The numbers vary—Russian sources speak of more than 300 killed and 400,000 tumans in lost merchandise; but this is likely an exaggeration designed to bolster justifications for the subsequent Russians attack; more realistic reports speak of the killing of a few caravanserai wardens and the loss of 60,000 tumans. Regardless of the numbers, the events gave the Russians the excuse they needed to invade northern Iran through Daghistan as part of a larger project to forge a direct commercial link with India that Czar Peter had been preparing for years. In late 1714 his countrymen had equipped 300 to 400 large vessels at Astrakhan to attack the silk-growing parts of the Caspian littoral, prompting many people in Gilan to flee the region. Three years later, 30,000 Russian troops had arrived on the southern shores of the Caspian near Astarabad.[176] Isfahan failed to react to these events in any meaningful way and, with Gilan in the throes of a serious tax revolt, the north now seemed ripe for the picking.[177] Volynskii's reports about the lamentable state of the Safavid military must have convinced the czar that occupying northern Iran would be easy.[178] Before doing so, the Russians sent a manifesto justifying their intervention and promising protection for rulers, the populace, and all merchants. Fielding some 100,000 troops, including Cossack, Tatar, and Kalmyk auxiliaries, and supported by the shamkhal of Tarki, ʿAdil Giray, who provided provisions, the Russians in August 1722 took Darband.[179] After seizing Shamakhi, Hajji Da'ud sought Russian protection, declaring his loyalty to the czar. When the Russians rebuffed him, he turned to the Ottomans for protection.

In 1723 the latter moved into the Caucasus and took Yerevan and Tiflis, acquired protective status over Shamakhi, and eventually seized Ganja. They also took control of a large section of western Iran, including Kirmanshah, Hamadan, and Marand, crowning their conquest with the occupation of Tabriz in July 1725. The need to establish new spheres of influence in the Caucasus brought Moscow and Istanbul to the brink of a new conflict. Yet thanks to French mediation, they signed the Treaty of Constantinople in 1723, making Daghistan, parts of Shirvan, Gilan, and Mazandaran fall to the Russians while allowing the Ottomans to annex Georgia, Armenia, the western parts of Daghistan and Shirvan, Hamadan, Kirmanshah, and the surrounding tracts of Iraq-i ʿAjam.[180]

THE SOUTH AND THE PERSIAN GULF COAST

The southern part of Iran, too, erupted in chaos and anarchy in this period, as rebellions broke out among the tribesmen in ʿArabistan, Omanis engaged in piracy and naval aggression with increasing frequency, attacking and partly destroying Kung in 1695, while Baluchi tribesmen threatened the southeastern borderlands. Drought and its consquences, famine and epidemics, were a causal factor in all of this. ʿArabistan was hit hard by the devastating plague that raged in Basra in the early 1690s.[181] According to Shushtari, a local chronicler, the decline of Shushtar began in 1106/1694–5, a year marked by destructive flooding and harvest-destroying locust swarms.[182] The epidemic created great unrest among the region's Arab tribes, most notably the Muntafiq whose leader, the formidable Shaykh Maniʿ b. Mughamis, rose to prominence in this period.[183] Forced to pay full taxes in the face of famine, they revolted against their Ottoman overlords. In 1695, with the Ottomans tied up in Europe, Shaykh Maniʿ managed to take Basra without a struggle, expelling the Ottoman *basha* and his troops.

Shaykh Maniʿ's expansionist ambitions extended to neighboring ʿArabistan. The Safavids, whose hold over this region, located beyond the Zagros Mountains and inhabited by Arabs of the Mushaʿshaʿ tribe, had always been precarious, had long sent governors belonging to the tribe as valis to Huwayza.[184] Some 5,000 disgruntled Mushaʿshaʿ followers of Sayyid Mahmud, a nephew of Faraj Allah, the region's Safavid-appointed vali, had joined forces with Shaykh Maniʿ, assisting him in the seizure of Basra. The ensuing conflict between Shaykh Maniʿ and his Mushaʿshaʿ sympathizers and the forces loyal to Faraj Allah resulted in the latter taking Basra, forcing Shaykh Maniʿ to flee.[185] Yet Faraj Allah's occupation of Basra did not end the turmoil in the region. Shaykh Maniʿ managed to regroup, with the support of Arab tribes, the Banu Khalid, the Fudul, and the Rabiʿah, and turned around to attack Basra and even Huwayza itself. This prompted Isfahan to dispatch an army from Luristan, led by ʿAli Mardan Khan, the governor of Kuh-i Giluyah. On 26 March 1697 the Iranian troops seized Basra. ʿAli Mardan Khan initially was appointed governor, but later that same year was replaced by Ibrahim Khan, the governor of Dawraq.[186] For the next four years the Iranians ruled the port. Yet, ever cautious not to antagonize the Ottomans, Shah Sultan Husayn early on had keys of pure gold made and dispatched Rustam Khan Zanganah as ambassador to Istanbul to hand these over to the sultan in a symbolic gesture. Before the year was out Shaykh Mani`, seemingly recovered, made common cause with his erstwhile enemy, Faraj Allah, who had meanwhile been dismissed from his post as vali of Huwayza. Together they defeated a large Iranian force near the fortress of Khurma, killing most of the troops and capturing their general.[187]

What little we know about developments in `Arabistan in the last years of Safavid rule suggests continued turmoil. In 1713, a tyrannical vali was deposed by a rival, prompting Isfahan to send `Avaz Khan, a former governor of Bandar `Abbas, to Huwayza to apprehend the rebel and to install the latter's nephew, as well as to find out about the reasons why the inhabitants had revolted against the previous vali.[188] `Avaz Khan managed to reestablish order by having the old vali reinstated, prompting the deposed one to seek refuge with the Mughamis in Basra.[189] The next year saw a new Arab revolt against Huwayza.[190] In the summer of 1716 Safi Quli Khan, the qullar-aqasi and governor of Fars, moved against the Arabs but was defeated with great loss of life. In typical fashion, the disaster was kept secret from the shah.[191]

Elsewhere in the south it was much the same story. In 1707, with a drought afflicting large parts of the Garmsir, the inhabitants of Lar murdered their governor, `Abd al-Qasim Khan, who had already been dismissed by Isfahan. The people of Kuh-i Giluyah, too, killed their governor, in a clear reflection of disintegrating central control.[192] The greatest challenge to security in the region came from the sea in the form of growing naval aggression by the Ya`riba Arabs of Masqat in Oman. In 1714 the Omanis attacked Kung, drove out the Iranians, and ransacked the town, destroying the Portuguese residence and church in the process.[193] There may have been a religious angle to this; rumor had it that the Kurds used religious propaganda to incite the (Sunni) Omanis against Iran.[194] These events sparked serious recrimination among courtiers in Isfahan, with Fath `Ali Khan Daghistani and Safi Quli Khan accusing grand vizier Shah Quli Khan of mismanagement and blaming him for the Arab attack.[195]

Isfahan's initial response to the worsening situation in the south was to reshuffle positions. At the behest of Ahmad Agha, a major eunuch, the shah in 1713 dismissed `Ali Riza Khan as governor of

Bandar 'Abbas and appointed Zakhariya Khan, former darughah of Isfahan, in his stead. As said, Zakhariya Khan had apparently promised the shah 2,500 per year in toll revenue for the favor. The shahbandar, Nur Allah, was deposed as well. His successor, Ya'qub Khan, was ordered to appoint a deputy and to move to Qandahar with Mansur Khan. A year later Nur Allah was reappointed and Mirza Sayyid 'Ali received the post of mustawfi in Lar.[196] More appointments followed the next year. In the summer of 1715, Safi Quli Khan became beglerbeg of Kuh-i Giluyah and governor of Fars, including the vizierate of Jahrum, putting him in control of most of southern Iran. He was also to prepare for an expedition against the Omanis. His deputy in Shiraz, Mirza Maqsud, was ordered to go to Huwayza to try to solve the problems there.[197]

None of these measures did anything to stem the turmoil. Highway robbers infested the road between Isfahan and Bandar 'Abbas in the fall of 1715.[198] The Omanis, taking advantage of Iran's weakness, in the same year sailed toward Bahrain with a number of ships, causing fears among the Dutch that Fath 'Ali Khan might force them to render naval assistance. Yet the Iranian forces on the island managed to repel the invaders.[199] News also arrived that the Omanis were approaching Bandar 'Abbas. The Baluchis, meanwhile, split up into two groups, with a few thousand joining the Omanis and others moving toward Kashan. The few hundred soldiers sent by Isfahan to confront the latter contingent were defeated.[200]

In reaction to these developments the shah reshuffled yet more posts. In 1716 Safi Quli Khan, the qullar-aqasi, was replaced by the sipahsalar-cum-vali of Georgia, Husayn Quli Khan, also known as Vakhtang VI. A cousin of the grand vizier, Gida 'Ali Beg, became governor of Kuh-i Giluyah, while Murtaza Quli Khan received Shiraz. Safi Quli Khan initially retained Bandar 'Abbas and Lar but lost control over the region to Safi Quli Beg, the official who had outbid Zakharya Khan by 500 tumans for the position.[201] Armenian, Muslim and Banyan merchants, meanwhile, faced increasing demands for money. The hardest hit in Bandar 'Abbas, according to the Dutch, was one Mirza Sayyid, who was approached by the authorities to come up with 10,000 tumans, ostensibly to pay for the return of an envoy named Mirza Mustafa from India.[202]

The increasing Omani aggression finally compelled the Safavids to take more drastic measures. In the fall of 1717 the Omanis took Bahrain as well as the islands of Qishm and Larak. They also appeared in the harbor of Bandar 'Abbas, where they seized an English ship, presumably in the belief that it belonged to the Portuguese.[203]

In October Fath ʿAli Khan's nephew, the formidable Lutf ʿAli Khan, was appointed governor of Lar and Bandar ʿAbbas as well as Kuh-i Giluyah.[204] In February 1718 Yaʿqub Sultan arrived in town as deputy of the governor of Fars, accompanied by 2,000 soldiers. He immediately instituted a harsh regime, executing anyone who disobeyed his orders. In mid March the Omanis attacked the fortress of Hurmuz, but were repulsed and left, leaving more than 700 dead and 250 wounded.[205] The following month Lutf ʿAli Khan sent 4,000 soldiers to Bahrain to help recapture it for the shah. The operation nearly failed. Soldiers who had never seen salt water boarded ships and promptly fell seasick. Landing on the north side of the island, they failed to take appropriate precautions to safeguard the ships as well as the victuals, the horses, the weaponry and the ammunition they had brought with them. All of these fell into the hands of the Omanis, who quickly took on the exposed Iranians, massacring them all.[206] Yet in the summer of 1718 Lutf ʿAli Khan managed to retake Bahrain after all. Relieved, the shah ordered the lighting of bonfires and three days of celebratory drum-beating, despite the persistently grim news arriving from the northeast.[207] The jubilation was short-lived, though, for in November the Omanis once again took Bahrain, slaughtering some 6,000 Iranian soldiers in the operation.[208] In response, the Safavids sent increasingly urgent requests to the Dutch and the English to assist them in confronting the Omanis, yet these fell on deaf ears.[209]

By this time danger loomed from the land side as well. In early 1719 Baluchi tribesmen were roaming the countryside, plundering villages within four days from Bandar ʿAbbas and north of Minab. A small army of some 500 soldiers was dispatched to confront them, but, poorly paid, these took to plundering too. The Baluchis, 7,000 to 8,000 strong, killed some 200, causing great panic in Bandar ʿAbbas. Fresh soldiers were mobilized and the authorities brought in some new artillery, only to discover that the marauders had retreated to their own territory.[210] At this point, Fath ʿAli Khan himself offered to confront the Omanis and the Baluchis. As the Dutch tell it, he was prevented from doing so by a jealous monarch loath to concentrate even more power in the hands of an already very powerful chief minister. Lutf ʿAli Khan was chosen to lead the campaign instead. In July 1,500 soldiers were sent to Qishm, but by year's end they had yet to move against its fortress.[211] Lutf ʿAli Khan himself later that year led a force of 20,000 to the south.[212]

The expedition was a disaster from the outset. The sipahsalar made many enemies during his stay in the Garmsir, antagonizing some of the court eunuchs who had landed estates in the area by ravaging their property. The Dutch report how he billeted troops among an unwilling population, allowed his soldiers to harass and despoil the hapless population, requisitioned pack animals, and forced Bandar `Abbas's Banyan inhabitants to pay the poll tax. Many people living between Shiraz and Bandar `Abbas fled their homes, leaving behind their possession.[213] In Lar, Lutf `Ali Khan's demand of an extra tax of 12,000 tumans from the town and the surrounding villages—a sum that subsequently was reduced to 2,000—caused a popular uprising. He suppressed the revolt mercilessly, killing its leader, Mirza Rafi`ah, in a barbaric fashion.[214] In early 1720 Lutf `Ali Khan made a deal with the Omanis whereby the latter agreed to give up the territory they had gained, to pay annual tribute in the amount of 3,000 tumans to Isfahan, to allow free shipping in the Persian Gulf, and to assist the Iranians in driving the Portuguese from Kung. In exchange they would enjoy exemption from tolls in Kung and acquire a base on Qishm where they could repair their ships.[215] Naturally, this deal remained a dead letter.

Khurasan and Baluchistan

Perenially exposed to Uzbek and Turkmen raiding, Iran's northern frontier saw its share of unrest in the last decades of Safavid rule. In early 1708 the Dutch reported that the Safavid offensive against the Turkmen around Astarabad was going badly, and that Kalb `Ali Khan had been with 1,200 of his men. Later that year, the Turkmen, assisted by rebels from the town of Sayfja, moved and laid siege to Astarabad. This created great consternation at the court, which sent Aslan Khan with 2,000 soldiers to confront the enemy.[216] The Safavid army achieved some success in 1714–15, when an Afshar force led by Baba `Ali, the governor of Abivard in northern Khurasan, defeated an 8,000-strong band of marauding Yomut Turkmen and captured some 1,400.[217] But the following year the Turkmen, led by warlord Shir Ghazi, threatened Astarabad again. This prompted the court to ask Kalb `Ali Khan to lend support to the expedition of sipahsalar `Ali Quli Khan who was sent with 30,000 troops to counter the aggression.[218]

Iran's most vulnerable frontier ultimately proved to be the vast arid lands to the east, populated by tribal forces that neither the Safavids nor the Mughals had ever managed to pacify and that were driven to depair by drought and famine at the turn of the eighteenth century.

In the early 1670s the Iranians had organized various campaigns to punish rebellious Baluchis from Kitch and Makran.[219] In 1689 the Kirman region suffered its first major Baluchi attack, which targeted the town of Khabis, east of the town of Kirman. The vizier of Kirman barely responded to this challenge and subsequently tried to hush up his feeble reaction by blaming his colleague from Sistan for the aftermath. He falsely claimed that the chief of the Baluchis, Pur Dil Khan, and his son had written a letter stating that if Isfahan were to confirm their position as paid frontier guards, they would take on the security of the area. He was replaced with Muhammad 'Ali Khan. A year later the Afghans of the Ghilza'i tribe staged their first raids into the area, robbing a caravan coming from Isfahan. In October 1691 the Baluchis struck again, attacking Kubnan and Zarand. More than 200 people were killed in various skirmishes. The following year Pur Dil Khan assaulted Rudbar and threatened to lay siege to Kirman itself. Only negotiations initiated by the *kalantar* of Rayin, some 90 kilometers southeast of Kirman, prevented this from happening.[220]

If anything, the change of power in Isfahan in 1694 only increased the frequency of the raids. Riding swift camels and adept at the use of firearms, the Baluchi tribesmen at this point penetrated Safavid territory and plundered caravans as far as Yazd. In 1695 they even came within a day's march from the gates of Isfahan.[221] In subsequent years, as Pur Dil Khan joined forces with two other Baluchi leaders, Amir Shah Salim and Amir Khusraw Shah, their raids came to be an ever growing threat. Like the Afghans, the Baluchis likely were driven into Iran's settled territory by an unusually long period of drought and famine that struck the region in these years.[222] The weakening of regional alliances did not help either. The oppressive behavior of Kirman's darughah, Mansur Beg, alienated the rulers of Bam, vital for the defense of the eastern hinterland, making it hard to maintain stability in Baluchistan.[223]

Isfahan, paralyzed by the death of Shaykh Ali Khan in 1689, initially gave little serious attention to these challenges. Just as it took almost two years for Mirza Tahir Qazvini to replace Shaykh 'Ali Khan as grand vizier, so the appointment of a new governor in Kirman was delayed for years by administrative inertia and misplaced frugality. The resulting lack of authority led to growing unrest in Kirman, where matters turned so dire that officials no longer dared to go the bazaar or the city's back alleys. Only in May 1693, after years of pleading and bribery, was Shah Virdi Khan's appointment approved.[224] Like his predecessors, Shah Virdi Khan was charged with the task of ending Baluchi marauding. To that effect, he organized various armed expeditions to the centers of Baluchi activity, Khabis, Ravar and Kubnan.[225] It would be another five years before Isfahan itself mounted a more forceful military response. In 1699 the shah conferred the post of sipahsalar on Shahnavaz Khan, better known as Gurgin Khan (Giorgi XI), the former vali of Kartli in Georgia who had lost his thone for having revolted against the Safavids.[226]

Reappointed vali of Kartli and given control over Kirman and a huge area stretching east all the way to Kabul, Gurgin Khan set out to take on the Baluchis, whose raids now ravaged the country as far as Yazd.[227] He first dispatched his brother Levan, renamed Shah Quli Khan, with a contingent of troops to Kirman before moving to the region himself. Meanwhile, the city's defensive facilities were upgraded; in 1700-1 a new square was constructed to accommodate fresh troops numbering 30,000. Gurgin Khan soon thereafter faced off against Mir Samandar, a Baluchi chieftain whose incursions threatened Qandahar. Appointed beglerbeg of Qandahar in 1704 and aided by the Afshar, who had reemerged as a formidable force in Kirman, Gurgin Khan routed the numerically stronger Baluchis in several confrontations, forcing Mir Samandar to submit to him.[228]

Gurgin Khan would meet his match in Mir Ways b. Shah 'Alam, a chief of the Hotaki clan of the Afghan Ghilza'i tribe who held the post of kalantar of Qandahar. Mir Ways, who had long served the Safavids by patrolling the caravan traffic between Iran and India, at first cooperated with the Georgians, but soon became alienated from Isfahan. He must have been greatly disturbed when in 1706 his lucrative post was taken away from him, to be offered to 'Alam Shah Afghan.[229] Gurgin Khan's oppressive rule in Qandahar meanwhile quickly strained relations with the Afghans. The Georgians sequestered goods, commandeered Afghan girls and women, and raised taxes. Gurgin Khan even demanded Mir Ways's own daughter and partied on the anniversary of the murder of the Caliph 'Umar (by a Persian slave).[230] His (nominally Shi'i) Georgian soldiers also misbehaved toward the local population, violating a guarantee of religious freedom that the Sunni Aghans had obtained as a condition for submitting to the Safavids.[231] They reportedly desecrated Sunni mosques by bringing pigs and drinking wine inside, and are said to have abused underage girls and nine- to ten-year-old boys to the point of killing them, after which they dumped their bodies at their parents' homes. The resentful Afghans sent complaints to Isfahan but, intercepted by Gurgin Kan's men at court, these never reached the shah. Eventually, the outrages prompted Mir Ways to rebel against his Georgian masters. But before he could engage in a full-scale rebellion, Gurgin Khan, suspicious of Mir Ways's ambitions, had him arrested and escorted to Isfahan, urging the shah to get rid of him, or at least never to allow him to return to Qandahar.[232]

While in Isfahan, Mir Ways through skillful flattery and bribery managed to rehabilitate himself. He convinced the shah that Gurgin Khan could not be trusted, that he meant to turn Qandahar into an autonomous region, and that he threatened the Safavid realm by planning a Russo-Georgian coalition directed against Iran.[233] He was allowed to go on pilgrimage to Mecca, where he persuaded the religious authorities to grant him a fatwa giving the Afghans the right to break free from Iranian rule. In 1708 he was sent back to Qandahar to serve as a shadow administrator. Upon his return, Mir Ways instigated a full-scale rebellion against the Georgians. In April 1709 Gurgin Khan and his entourage met their death at the hands of the Afghans, taken by surprise during a punitive expedition and hacked down in their tents, after which the Afghans took Qandahar and massacred the city's Georgian garrison.[234] Upon the news of Gurgin Khan's death, the shah first dispatched an envoy and, when the latter was imprisoned by Mir Ways, followed up by sending Gurgin Khan's nephew, Khusraw Khan (Kay Khusraw), former darughah of Isfahan, against the Afghans. The new sipahsalar had great difficulty outfitting a campaign, for initially he had a risible 7,000 tumans to pay for 3,000 soldiers at his disposal, the work of an obstructionist rival, the grand vizier, who prevented the release of money from the royal treasury for his efforts. Members of the the anti-Georgian court faction, too, were keen to see him fail. They thus made sure that funds earmarked for his expedition were misappropriated and that the payment of the remainder was delayed. Relief only came in the form of military assistance from the Afghan Abdali tribe, the archenemies of the Ghilzai's who had their base in the Herat area. After two years of fighting interrupted by a truce, Khusraw Khan with their help managed to lay siege to Qandahar. After two months the Ghilzai's sued for peace. Yet the Iranians demanded unconditional surrender, so that their opponents resolved to keep fighting. The Georgians in October 1711 were forced to retreat, exhausted from the summer heat, disease and a lack of provisions, and harassed by Baluchi forces who had thrown in their lot with the Afghans. In the ensuing pursuit by the defenders, Khusraw Khan and many of his soldiers were killed and their military equipment fell to the Afghans.[235]

Mir Ways would continue to expand his territory relatively unopposed until his death in early 1715. In late 1712 he took Kabul after a siege. He next turned his 12,000 troops westward, toward Herat.[236] The Safavid response fell far short of the task at hand. Following Khusraw Khan's death, in late 1712 qurchibashi Muhammad Zaman Khan was appointed sardar and khan of Kirman, and ordered to move against the Afghans while collecting soldiers on the way. As always, money was the stumbling block. Instead of opening up his treasury, the shah had 14,000 tumans forcibly taken from merchants in Isfahan and New Julfa.[237] Zaman Khan's campaign, hampered by a lack of resources and illness, was a slow affair and fizzled when he died near Herat in the spring of 1712.[238] Mansur Khan Shahsivan, his successor, did not fare much better. While the shah forced his courtiers to pay for the construction of a new maydan in Farahabad, Mansur Khan in September of 1713 left Isfahan with fifty soldiers and virtually no money. A year later he was said to be camping out near Mashhad, still devoid of troops and funds.[239] Other news was just as depressing. In the summer of 1713 a mere five hundred soldiers headed for Khurasan. When, upon departing, they complained that they had received neither money nor horses, they were dispersed with sticks. Mahd 'Ali Khan, the Safavid governor of Farah, reported that a lack of funds prevented him and his 1,500 troops from advancing against Mir Ways. His soldiers refused to obey orders and many had deserted and were making the roads unsafe, causing the local population more grief than the Afghans did.[240] The local militia of Marv, meanwhile, rose in revolt for lack of pay, while 8,000 Turkmen were reportedly advancing toward Mashhad.[241] The latter city, too, seemed helpless at the approach of Abdali troops, devoid of money, people, and defenses. Many of its soldiers defected, and those who stayed refused to fight.[242] The Uzbeks managed to capture thousands of people near the city, carrying them off them into slavery.[243]

THE END

Kirman was to bear the brunt of the final assault. The drought of 1716, which killed many goats and caused food prices to skyrocket, was a turning point. The ensuing famine sparked unrest in the city. Governor Ibrahim Khan proved unable to pay his troops, prompting many soldiers to sell their arms.[244] The Baluchis, driven to depair by the same drought, next invaded the area and laid siege to the city. Ibrahim Khan led his troops, numbering 2,000, outside the walls, but suffered defeat. Wounded, he fled the battlefield and took refuge within the walls, leaving the spoils to the Baluchis. These next laid siege to the citadel after destroying a number of surrounding villages. Ibrahim Khan capitulated and only managed to spare the city by promising to pay the victors 2,000 tumans. A portion of the 1,700 tumans he eventually handed over was extracted from local Banyans and the VOC and EIC agents.[245]

In response Isfahan sent a contingent of some 1,000 soldiers under the command of a newly appointed sardar, Muhammad 'Ali Khan, but by the time they arrived in Kirman the Baluchis had already disappeared with a large amount of cattle.[246] The city was left in a state of famine; corpses littered the streets, and chaos caused by rampaging soldiers was now rife. Murder became common, and houses were routinely broken into. The prolonged drought forced people to leave the city in search of victuals. Food prices had soared to the point where a short trip to a mill to grind flour required an escort of five to six soldiers.[247]

Kirman next witnessed the outbreak of a popular uprising. The three-day rebellion was led by a local textile merchant, the head of the guilds, who had distributed arms among the populace. It only ended through the intervention of the local clergy and with the arrival of a message from Isfahan that qullar-aqasi Rustam Mirza had been appointed as the city's new governor. Rustam Mirza sent a deputy, his brother Muhammad Quli Mirza, a boy of only thirteen or fourteen. Because of his young age, Muhammad Quli Mirza in turn was represented by a ghulam named Muhammad Ja'far Beg. Muhammad Ja'far Beg proved to be an effective ruler. He immediately set out to mete out justice irrespective of rank and reputation, and made himself popular by announcing a year-long tax break for the populace. Transportation costs fell and abundant rains caused food prices to plummet as well.[248] The court meanwhile extended a hand to the Baluchis by sending another Georgian, Gurgin Beg, with six robes of honor for various Baluchis chiefs, promising to restore their former tribute if they would resubmit to the shah's authority.[249]

Conditions in Isfahan reflect the seriousness of the situation at this point. While the shah constructed pleasure gardens, Bakhtiyari and Lur depredations around the capital made it impossible for all but caravans accompanied by large contingents of soldiers to pass through. A military force was sent to take care of the problem but, overwhelmed, its soldiers returned mauled and deprived of arms.[250] Inside the city, the incidence of theft and murder was on the rise. Vagrants and beggars roamed the streets in great numbers, and poverty had reached such levels that people would quickly strip the flesh of any dead camel, mule or horse left out on the street. Europeans dared to go out only on horseback accompanied by a servant on foot whose task it was to disperse the throngs of beggars.[251] In July 1717 Volynskii referred to the panic among the Safavid elite caused by a slew of alarming news: A combined force of Afghans and Baluchis had taken Herat; much of Khurasan had been overrun by Uzbeks; Astarabad and Yerevan were threatened; and the governor of Marv was said to be moving against Iran with 40,000 men.[252] The loss of Bahrain finally caused the court to wake up from its slumber, as Dutch envoy Ketelaar put it. In reality the shah seems to have been prodded into action by his great-aunt, the octogenarian Maryam Bigum, who provided him with cash from her own vast treasury.[253] In preparation for a campaign, tents and ordnance in the form of zamburaks and cannon were gathered outside Isfahan. On 23 November 1717 the shah himself moved toward Kashan, leaving divanbegi Muhammad Quli Khan in charge of the capital.[254]

As always, money was the most pressing issue, forcing the government to take drastic, even desperate, measures. In 1123/1711–12 a pentagonal and oval coinage made its appearance. Its apparent aim was to mask the significant lowering in weight that the currency was undergoing at that time. Six years later the government devalued the coinage by lowering the `abbasi from 7.62 to 7.50 gr. or even less.[255] In 1714 the state resolved to strike gold ducats as pure as the Venetian ducat, with the intent of selling these to merchants for export, but a lack of available gold scuttled the plan.[256] The intent nevertheless persisted. In 1716 a (short-lived) ban was proclaimed on the use of gold and silver thread in textile manufacturing. Later that same year Shah Sultan Husayn, unable to pay his troops, again announced plans to issue a gold coin. Drastic measures were taken to secure the metal. On 27 July 1717, the royal council sent an order to have all the gold from the shrine of Imam Riza in Mashhad removed and transported to Isfahan, where it was used to strike new coins. A reported 100,000 tumans worth of gold was brought to the royal treasury in this manner. The shah even went so far as to remove the precious metals from his ancestors' graves in Qum. The result was the issue of the first Safavid gold coins since the reign of Shah `Abbas I.[257] Yet the initiative was more than offset by the increased outflow of gold via the pilgrimage. Grand vizier Shah Quli Khan, scheduled to go to Mecca in 1714, forbade Isfahan's money changers from selling the coins to anyone but him. Agha Kamal, the royal treasurer, is said to have carried 200,000 ducats with him to Arabia that year.[258] The hajj season of 1715 raised the precious metal drain to new heights. The Dutch, estimating the number of pilgrims at 30,000, calculated that, since each person took on average 10 tumans with him, this meant a loss of 300,000 tumans.²⁵⁹ The following year reports again spoke of court eunuchs buying up all the available gold in the market. Agha Kamal ordered his subordinates to collect all ducats in sight, after issuing a ban on vendors to sell to anyone else.²⁶⁰

In the fall of 1719 panic broke out in Kirman as news arrived from Sistan that Mahmud, Mir Ways's son and successor, had left Qandahar and was approaching with some 2,000 warriors.²⁶¹ Kirman's governor, Muhammad Quli Mirza, hastily set out to strengthen the city's defenses, fortifying the existing walls and pressing the inhabitants into corvée labor to build new ones. At the news that the invaders had already entered Kirman province, the resistance quickly dissipated. Instead of putting up a fight, Muhammad Quli Mirza and his Georgian soldiers in October fled the city, followed by many merchants and the majority of the inhabitants. Of the original population of 28,000 to 30,000, only 3,000—most of them old and disabled—are said to have stayed behind. Taking advantage of the confusion, the 200 troops sent by Isfahan took to plundering. The EIC representatives at this point decided to leave the city as well. In early November, with the Afghans already before the city walls, the VOC people abandoned Kirman as well, leaving a few local caretakers behind. As they found the passage to Bandar `Abbas blocked and the road to Shiraz via Yazd infested by Lurs and Arabs, they decided to head for Baft, until they heard that 3,000 Afghans were heading in that direction, so that they reached Yazd via a desert route.²⁶²

In response, Isfahan ordered the authorities in Bandar `Abbas to collect a force and move to Kirman. Muhammad Quli Khan, the divanbegi, was appointed sardar and told to head in the same direction with his 4,000 men. Lutf `Ali Khan, too, was summoned to head for Kirman with his troops. In January 1720, 6,000 soldiers left Kung and moved to within six days' marching from Kirman, where they waited to be joined by forces from Isfahan, Shiraz, and Lar. They appear to have plundered all the villages on their way.²⁶³ Yet they never arrived in Kirman. There is reason to believe Fath `Ali Khan's argument, made as part of his defense, that insufficient funding had fatally undermined his nephew's fighting capacity—against both the Omanis and the Afghans. Krusinski plausibly asserts that the eunuchs obstructed him for fear that a successful campaign against the Afghans would enhance his prestige with the shah to the point where, joining forces with his redoubtable uncle, he would be able to destroy them. They thus resolved to destroy the vizier and his nephew first.²⁶⁴

The Afghans next captured Kirman. General Darur Shah entered the city on 4 November with some 8,000 soldiers, and a day later Mahmud Ghilza'i followed with Asad Allah Khan, accompanied by three elephants and a quantity of artillery and ammunition.[265] At first, the invaders treated the populace quite well, even as they extorted large sums from the wealthy, incarcerated and in some cases killed those who resisted, and sought to convert all others to Sunnism. The remaining Banyans in particular suffered maltreatment. The Afghans chased them out of the city and forced the wealthy ones to disclose the whereabouts of their fortune, killing six or seven under torture.[266] Many local Zoroastrians, meanwhile, collaborated with the invaders, viewing them as liberators." Quite a few converted to Islam, and those who went to work for the Afghans appear to have engaged in revenge killings of local Muslims.[267]

The Afghan troops stayed in Kirman for less than six months, during which time they carried a fair amount of property to Qandahar and conducted punitive expeditions to the surrounding countryside and as far as Yazd. Many Kirmanis were driven out of the city, settled in the surrounding gardens, *bagh*, and were forced to defray the expenses of the occupying force. When the Afghans left in the spring of 1720—presumably to quell a revolt in Qandahar—the city lay in ruins; its caravanserais, bazaars, and the bagh as well as the Zoroastrian quarter having been destroyed.[268] Yet, in a remarkable demonstration of resilience, life resumed after the Afghan retreat. The Dutch and the English agents returned in June, and most of the inhabitants gradually came back as well. The new governor sent from Isfahan, Subhan Virdi Khan, soon made himself popular by energetically taking on the rebuilding of the city's defenses. The shah dispatched the royal architect (*mi`marbashi*), to help design a stronger fortress, while the inhabitants of Yazd had a 4,000-tuman contribution imposed on them to finance the project.[269]

The optimism was short-lived. In the spring of 1721 civil strife erupted between the governor and the kalantar, soon to be overshadowed by a new Afghan threat from Bam. In the fall Mahmud, advancing with 9,000 men, captured the suburbs, including the Zoroastrian quarter.[270] On 29 October the Afghans attacked the city proper. They took a mosque, killing many of the refugees inside, and destroyed the building. They next laid siege to the citadel, with thousands of people huddled insisde. This stronghold endured daily fire at a cost of large numbers of casualties and terrible starvation, yet proved resistant. Unable to breach the inner fortifications, the Afghans after three months offered to leave in exchange for a large sum of money.

Having collected what they could from the impoverished populace, they left in February 1722. Only some 3,000 people had survived the siege, the city again lay in ruins, and the surrounding countryside was devastated.[271]

While Kirman lay under siege, Bandar ʿAbbas, Kung and Lar came under Baluchi attack. Thousands of Baluchi and Lur tribesmen infested the roads connecting these towns, killing, looting, and burning at will.[272] Some relief troops were finally dispatched to end this scourge, but by the time these arrived in Lar, attention had shifted back to the Afghan threat to Isfahan itself. In early March 1722 Mahmud arrived at the town of Gulnabad, about twenty kilometers from the capital, with some 12,000 troops, 4,000 of them "well armed."[273] On March 8 the Afghans defeated a hastily assembled Iranian army of about 40,000 men supplemented by 30,000 infantry troops. The Georgian contingent, the only one said to have put up a decent fight, lost 4,000 to 5,000 men—ten times the Afghan casualties. The remainder of the Safavid army sought refuge in the city, with the exception of ʿAli Mardan Khan, the leader of the Bakhtiyaris, who with his troops returned to his home region.[274]

Lack of unity and coordination rather than military weakness per se accounted for the Iranian defeat at Gulnabad. ʿAli Mardan Khan, who had defected, was thought to have maintained a secret correspondence with Mahmud. Other commanders, engaged in mutual rivalry, worked at cross purposes. Sayyid ʿAbd Allah, the vali of ʿArabistan, is said to have advised the shah to attack the Afghans, whereas grand vizier Muhammad Quli Khan, who resented Sayyid ʿAbd Allahs's special position with Sultan Husayn, reportedly restrained his troops and turned his back on the enemy for fear that his rival would get credit for a victory. Other sources suggest that ʿAbd Allah had only attacked the Afghans to make the Iranians "believe that he had no secret correspondence with the Afghans."[275]

Mahmud next moved to Farahabad and took the suburb without meeting any resistance. He also seized New Julfa, whose inhabitants welcomed him with food and drank wine to his health. This collaboration kept the Armenians from suffering physical harm yet did not protect them from Mahmud's exactions in the form of a demand for 60,000 tumans and the selection of a number of women for himself and his commanders.[276] After a few days of panic during which the Afghans could have taken Isfahan proper, its inhabitants quickly reinforced the defenses, and a long siege ensued. Mahmud initially reached out to the shah, proposing to withdraw in return for being granted control over Khurasan and Kirman, but by the time the Iranians agreed to this felt secure enough to reject the offer. Safavid reinforcements from Hamadan, Luristan, and Kurdistan, meanwhile, were intercepted and defeated by the Afghans.[277] As the siege wore on, popular anger at the shah's inertia turned to unrest and rioting, and the call to have him replaced by his brother, 'Abbas Mirza, grew ever louder. In the course of the summer, as the shah frantically rotated muhtasibs, the city ran out of food. In July bread prices soared to 60 mahmudis per man, soon to reach the astronomical height of 120 mahmudis, causing many soldiers to desert for lack of food. Toward the end of the summer conditions became so dire that people took to eating tree bark, leaves, and dried excrement. Eventually they resorted to cannibalism.[278] On 23 October, the city finally fell to the Afghans, forcing Sultan Husayn to cede power to Mahmud.

Isfahan suffered greatly during the siege and the ensuing occupation. The city may have lost 100,000 of its inhabitants, many of its buildings lay in ruins, and its economy was in tatters. When the shah's treasury was opened it revealed a mere 4,000 tumans in cash and jewelry, a far cry from the 200,000 tumans that his great-aunt had presumably left behind and vastly reduced from its previous holdings on account of the payments in gold the monarch had eventually been forced to make to his soldiers.[279] Much wealth had remained in private hands. Muhammad Mustawfi recounts how he was sent from door to door to search for food and found fourteen bags each weighing 100 *man-i Tabriz* filled with freshly minted 'abbasis.[280] The Afghans did all they could to lay their hands on this wealth, extorting vast sums from anyone they suspected of owning anything, Armenians, Muslims, and the European maritime companies.[281]

Shortly after taking Isfahan, Mahmud sent a large force to Qazvin, intent on capturing Prince Tahmasb, a son of Sultan Husayn who had managed to escape from Isfahan. He also dispatched troops to Hamadan and Shiraz. A group of Kirmani Zoroastrians led by Nasr Allah Khan took part in the assault on the latter city, assisted by Sunni musketeers from Kazirun, Khunj, and Lar who had thrown in their lot with them.[282] Afghan troops also moved to Bihbahan in Kuh-i Giluyah, taking Dahdasht on the way. Armenian assistance in the undermining of the fortifications, notwithstanding, they failed to take the city and returned empty-handed.[283]

Conclusion

> Thus fell the Mighty Persian Monarchy by the hands of Seven or Eight Thousand Rebels, who were at first looked upon so very insignificant that this Haughty Lazy Court did not think fit to make any preparations against it till the Danger came to their very Doors.
> Owen Philips, English EIC agent, 20 June 1723

The trajectory of the Safavid state in some ways exemplifies Ibn Khaldun's famous paradigm about the flux and reflux of premodern Middle Eastern states. It does so better than the Ottoman Empire in the shortness of its life span and the abruptness of its collapse, and more closely than the Mughal state in the religious inspiration that fueled its rise and the sloth that hastened its fall—from the charismatic warrior Shah Isma`il I to the feeble, palace-bound Shah Sultan Husayn, from the Qizilbash fighters who helped the former conquer a land and turn it into a state in the name of a millenarian faith, to a sedentary court elite which, preferring the cushions of the palace to the rigors of the saddle, gave up on war and exposed the country to attack by a new cohort of vigorous tribesmen. The decline and fall of the Safavids may be seen as the natural fate of a regime precariously ruling over hardscrabble lands, one case in a long sequence stretching from the Achaemenids to the Qajars. A feeble entity that, like all premodern states, hardly inspired any inherent loyalty and that faced greater obstacles to control than most, the Safavid state was held together as much by inertia as by design. Its longevity thus is more remarkable than its sudden demise is puzzling, and only the association of the Safavid polity with Twelver Shi`ism, the overlapping religious and territorial boundaries it produced, and its (questionable) status as the first Iranian nation-state, sets it apart from all other Iran's dynastic regimes until the twentieth century.

In an attempt to analyze both the forces that animated it and those that contributed to its weakening, this book has explored early modern Iran from a holistic perspective, integrating economic performance, monetary policy, and military capabilities with issues of ideology, strategies of power, and political divisiveness. While keeping an eye on Safavid history in its entirety, the discussion focused on the second century of the dynasty's life span, the period between the death of Shah `Abbas I in 1629 and the dramatic fall of Isfahan in 1722. In an attempt to view this period not just as a prelude to the apocalypse but in its own right, I imposed an (imaginary) equilibrium on it, presenting state-society interaction as the outcome of a series of tensions between centrifugal and centripetal tendencies. In all this, the state appeared less as a Leviathan than as a forum for never-ending negotiation. Safavid shahs wielded tremendous power, to be sure, including the power over their subjects' life and death. Their rise and initial expansion involved violent conquest, and their ultimate weapon remained ruthless retribution. Yet their infrastructural reach was rather circumscribed. Governing a land of scarce resources populated by mostly tribal folks led by seditious chieftains, even the strongest ruler needed to forge and maintain alliances. What really held an "empire" such as Safavid Iran together was the ability of its governing elite to negotiate arrangements of mutual benefit with various constituencies—ensuring collaboration through cooptation by way of intra-elite marriage and tributary agreements.[1]

A series of substantive chapters put this functionalist model to the test of historical events and processes. The main conclusion of the investigation was that in the course of the seventeenth century Iran entered a deep crisis marked by failing political, administrative, and military leadership, and severe monetary problems.[2] The Safavid state failed, after all, in the single most crucial objective of all premodern and early modern military fiscal states, generating sufficient revenue for the dual purpose of besting adversaries and maintaining military and bureaucratic control over a refractory population.[3] The state's main task was, in Iskandar Beg Munshi's words, to preserve stability and road security; in other words, to levy taxes and put them to productive use, maintain an army strong enough to defend the borders, keep local government from abusing its power, and guaranteeing a modicum of safety for merchants and travelers.[4] That was the Safavid "project," as it was the project of all early modern states, and the late Safavid state fell short on most counts. It levied taxes, to be sure, but these became increasingly onerous and arbitrary; and it failed to put them to good use; the army visibly decreased in battle-readiness; and Iran's vaunted road security deteriorated to the point where by century's end marauders roamed close to Isfahan. As a blissfully oblivious shah built pleasure gardens while his court dissolved into feuding factions, peripheral tribal forces, no longer held in check by the threat of violence and the lure of money, pounced on the borders. Not only did the Safavids fall, quickly and dramatically; they did so at the hand of a rag-tag bunch of tribesmen whose numbers were far too small to bring down any state other than a severely weakened one. The assailants succeeded because they met with little resistance, and they met with little resistance because the Safavid state had lost its unity of purpose and its resolve at the highest command level. The Safavid political system, in sum, had become weakened to the point of atrophying prior to the fall of Isfahan.

It has been the book's aim to identity the causes, the nature, and the sequence of this crisis. I have used the term "crisis" consciously. While mindful of Randolph Starn's admonition about our tendency to see crises everywhere, one could argue that, in some ways, the Safavid state—sparsely populated, endowed with few (exportable) resources, undercapitalized—had always been in "crisis."[5] From its inception in the early sixteenth century it had been plagued by fiscal problems; revenue had always lagged behind expenditure and, although feared and formidable, its army had never been a match for the much more powerful Ottomans. If one focuses on military matters, the Safavids, like the Mongols before them, in some ways peaked early, and "decline" arguably set in with Shah Isma`il's defeat against the Ottomans at Chaldiran.[6] Chaldiran also set the stage for ideological indeterminacy, weakening the inspirational force of Shi`ism as a messianic creed. Given the difficulty of running a vast empire as a centrally directed enterprise, in sum, "some kind of devolution" was probably "inevitable."[7] One could argue about the first clear manifestations of Safavid retrenchment, either agree with Chardin, who famously insisted that Iran had ceased to prosper from the moment that Shah `Abbas I passed away, or with later commentators who have seen the accession of Shah Sulayman in 1666 or the enthronement of Shah Sultan Husayn in 1694 as the "beginning of the end."[8] Yet, as Minorsky argued, most of the ills plaguing the late Safavid state and society are *rooted* in long-term processes.[9] Some of their underlying causes have nothing to do with the Safavids, others go back to the very origins of the Safavid state, and yet others relate to the reign of Shah `Abbas I.

An assessment of the structural reasons for the weakening of Safavid Iran has to begin with the realm's physical features and its resource base rather than the dynasty. Most of Iran was arid to semi-arid, poorly endowed with arable land, and low in population density. Distances were great, communication was hazardous, and most people lived scattered in remote villages or led a nomadic or semi-nomadic existence. The state found it difficult to control these groups, let alone harness their economic activities for revenue purposes. Iran's narrow income base is one reason why Iranians had been migrating to India in search of employment and patronage—not since the reign of Shah `Abbas I, as Chardin claimed, but long before the rise of the Safavids. It is difficult to imagine any Safavid ruler abolishing the *jiz'ya* for non-Muslims, as Sultan Akbar did in 1564 with the argument that the impost was economically unnecessary.[10] Geography, moreover, prevented the Safavids from breaking out of the "arid zone dilemma" by way of military conquest. To the east of Iran's heartland lay the vast barrenness of Sistan and Baluchistan; beyond that loomed the formidable mountain range of the Hindu Kush, which prevented access to the immensely fertile plains of the Punjab. Central Asia's large oases, separated from Iran by the Kara Kum desert and hostile Uzbek territory, were too far to be incorporated as well. The only economically viable regions within military reach were the Caspian littoral, the southern Caucasus and Azerbaijan, and Iraq. The Safavids conquered and held on to the first two regions, both of incalculable economic significance to the state. Their control over Iraq, contested by the Ottomans, culturally unassimilable and climatologically alien to the Qizilbash, was intermittent and proved to be untenable in the long term.[11]

Only a "fully engaged, dynamic and ruthless ruler" could build a solid power structure on such shaky foundations, harnessing resources and bringing disparate groups together or at least keeping them from destroying each other.[12] To understand why the Safavid state failed as a military and fiscal apparatus we have to acknowledge the central position of the shah as the "collector and distributor of livelihood, wealth, honour, and reputation as well as the final arbiter of both reward and punishment over all his territories and their populations." This is not to ascribe to the "great men" theory of history, or to imply that the character and competence of the ruler were the only factors determining the fate of the land.[13] The Safavids were despots as well as tyrants according to the Aristotelian meaning of the first term as a ruler whose reign is based on the approval of his subjects, and of the second as a ruler whose power depends on fear and violence. The king's authority was based on his exalted position as God's vicegerent. But it was also engendered by a blend of hope and fear, hope of royal favor and clemency, and fear of royal wrath and retribution. Iranians, Chardin insisted, expected their rulers to be violent.[14] The Persianate Mirror for Princes literature had long stressed reward and revenge as two essential features of successful kingship.[15] Living large was another ingredient of power.[16] To be engaged in heavy drinking and unbridled carnal pleasure was both the ruler's natural right and a way to impress his subordinates and rivals.[17] In Rustam al-Hukama's words, rulers have the right to indulge in pleasure and entertainment provided they also take care of their subjects' well-being.[18] The latter task involved royal visibility, direct interaction with their subjects for the sake of rendering public justice.

Shah `Abbas I met these various expectations. He projected great military power, regained most of the lands lost by his predecessors, and adopted a set of forward-looking policies designed to optimize military strength, centralize state control, and expand Iran's internal and international commercial ambit. He paired ruthlessness with justice; he dealt harshly with threats to his power while remaining in touch with his people, to whom he was visible and whose concerns he appeared to share. A towering personality and a shrewd politician, he kept his officials in positions of subordination, relying on a good information system without becoming dependent on any one counselor. Most importantly, he managed to stay on top of the fray by fostering mutual rivalry among contending forces, outsiders—Arab clerics and Caucasian ghulams, whom he allowed to gain high administrative and military rank—as much as the Qizilbash, who were weakened yet not eliminated in the process.[19]

`Abbas successors sought to apply the same methods but did so as lesser personalities. Shah Safi I, young, weak and faced with the daunting task of replacing a legend, took more than three years to establish his authority. The bloody purge he enacted to do so was less an overall turning point in Safavid history than a pivotal moment in his own survival and subsequent reign. `Abbas II established his personal power with the execution of Mirza Muhammad "Saru" Taqi and Jani Khan Shamlu. These rulers also met the next challenge, not to become the plaything of the forces around them—the Qizilbash, the religious forces, the eunuchs—but to remain above the swirl of private interests, and to stay in touch with their subjects. Under `Abbas II ordinary people might still grab the reins of the ruler's horse and hand him their petitions before he set out on his morning ride. They also chose their grand viziers wisely, recruiting them from diverse backgrounds representing tribal, clerical, or ghulam interests, but primarily on the basis of their fiscal and administrative competence, and they gave them ample room to fashion their own policies. Still, replicating the example set by Shah Isma`il I a century earlier, both rulers ended their days in immoderate drinking to the point of losing effective control.

Shah Sulayman and Shah Sultan Husayn were different in that they never entered "political adulthood." Instead of taking control, they left the affairs of state to their grand viziers while they themselves retreated into "lust and play."[20] So long as he had a capable vizier on his side, and provided he himself intervened decisively at crucial moments, the fainéant shah was not necessarily fatal to good governance. With Shaykh `Ali Khan, Sulayman selected a competent vizier, to be sure. Yet instead of giving him a mandate and full support, he threw him to the welter of rival innuendo and intrigue, thus forcing him into inactivity.[21] Shaykh `Ali Khan represents the paradox of a vizier without whom nothing could be done yet who was not part of the inner circle of power. Shah Sulayman's reign saw the emergence of a functional duality of power between a chancery that continued to oversee the implementation of fiscal policy, and a privy council that often worked at cross purposes with it to the point of nullifying its decisions. The effect was a rudderless state

Shah Sulayman and Shah Sultan Husayn also gave up being warrior kings. Rarely appearing in public other than in the form of the insular *quruq* (the outings with his female entourage), they no longer projected the image of the ambulant ruler patrolling his realm to dispense justice through a blend of severity and generosity.[22] Although his stinginess sullied his reputation, Sulayman at least kept up the (often gratuitous) violence that made subordinates cower. Sultan Husayn, pusillanimous, gullible and uxorious, deeply influenced by Muhammad Baqir Majlisi, Fath `Ali Khan Daghistani, and especially his great-aunt, Maryam Bigum, just invited contempt and insubordination. The perception of a disengaged and spendthrift weakling surrounded by profiteering sycophants in time had a harmful effect on the reputation of the Safavids. Nadir Shah's rejection of several Safavid practices, most notably the abduction and rape of women, and the popular approval this policy met may be read as a significant comment on the last years of the Safavid dynasty.[23] But ultimately (perceived) royal weakness was less a moral issue than a cause for political alarm: it unleashed the centrifugal forces that allowed court eunuchs to engage in destructive factional strife, top clerics to run grain monopoly rackets, and provincial governors to fleece the people. A lack of fortitude ate away at the shah's legitimacy as well. The staying power of the *shah-seven* (love for the shah phenomenon) suggests that even in late Safavid times the mystique of the shah had not died altogether.[24] Yet especially Shah Sultan Husayn, ignoring Shah `Abbas's dictum that a successful ruler is one who leads his troops in person and is ready to die on the battlefield seems to have forgotten that there was a connection between the love people felt for the shah and the latter's actual performance.[25] Yet under Sultan Husayn doubts were heard not just about the ruler's competence but about the very link between kingship and the divine order—doubts that may well have expressed a creeping sentiment that the expectation of the shah as defender of the faith and the realm was not being met.[26]

The other issues, growing money problems, attempts by the state to generate more revenue, a weakening army, and the harassment of minorities, are all interlinked as well as intertwined with these political conditions, even if the roots and circumstances vary. In some we see the unintended consequences of Shah 'Abbas I's policies. This includes his decision to keep the heir-to-be immured in the palace, a policy that lessened the quality of leadership and allowed the crown domain and especially the women and eunuchs at its center to assume control. There are also the ghulams, whose power became firmly entrenched under his watch. The ghulams were not necessarily more useful or loyal than the Qizilbash they were supposed to supplant. They may have been more efficient, but with greater efficiency came an approach to control and revenue-collection that tended to alienate rather than engage and mollify the tax-paying populace. Maintaining kinship ties with their ancestral lands, they also added to the complexity of the ruling elite, fueling fierce competition between the "old" tribal Qizilbash forces, the "new" bureaucratic ghulams and eunuchs, and the ranks of the increasingly prominent religious estate. Far from just being a contest between "interest groups," the struggle occurred *within* the groups as well and typically took the form of personal rivalries between individual officials.

The impecuniousness of Safavid Iran was endemic, the result of a lack of precious metal deposits and a poor resource base. The unusual scarcity of ready money leading to the closing of a large number of mints and a worsening currency, in turn, was contingent, a function of a general bullion famine that afflicted all of Eurasia in the seventeenth century. Iran, wedged in between the Ottoman Empire and Russia, both prone to issue silver export bans, and silver-hungry India, was particularly vulnerable to the vagaries of the international money flows. The monetary policies adopted by the state did little to reverse the growing shortages and to shore up the soundness of the country's currency, and in some ways aggravated the problems. Unofficial policies in the form of hoarding may have been the greatest obstacle. If anything, low velocity rather than the available stock of wealth accounts for the monetary woes of the state and the society at large. The stunning wealth hoarded in the royal treasury—with glaring examples from Shah Tahmasb to Shah Sultan Husayn—in addition to the equally dazzling riches found in the cellars of Maryam Bigum, Mirza Taqi, and Fath `Ali Khan after their death or ouster, suggest the enormity of the sums that were hoarded by the elite.

With money in short supply, the demand for taxes escalated. Desperate for revenue and confident about internal stability, Shah `Abbas's successors continued his policy of converting large swaths of the country from state land to crown land. While the immediate fiscal advantages of this policy were obvious, they came at the high price of slackening military vigilance and growing abuse by officials with little incentive to look out for the long-term well-being of the land they supervised. Over time, such abuse appears to have increased in intensity and scope. As the case of Fars and Kirman suggests, the conversion to crown land also entailed the intrusion of alien elements little familiar with local conditions, resulting in mismanagement and religious and ethnic conflict.

Increased taxation also took the form of experimentation with the currency. Reducing the weight of the coinage was one time-honored device of producing revenue. Another was debasement, producing more coins from a given amount of metal. Both were short-term solutions in that they procured immediate revenue for the state while generating long-term inflation (which in the case of Iran appear to have been limited because of the unusually high scarcity and low velocity of money). Most importantly, tampering with the coinage undermined confidence in the currency. It created confusion among merchants and, by impeding both cash transactions and credit facilities by way of bills of exchange, was harmful to trade, making the elite even more eager to hoard "good" coins, and causing merchants to step up their precious metal exports. Trying to stanch this drain by issuing currency export bans without economic reform, finally, was no more than a palliative, for it drove out sound money without improving the quality of circulating coins. The religiously inspired policy adopted under Shah Sultan Husan, which encouraged the pilgrimage to Iraq and Arabia, only made matters worse, causing a gratuitous drain of enormous sums of gold from the country.

Rhoads Murphey cautions that it is simplistic automatically to associate a loss of military vigor with decline, arguing that the connection between the two must be demonstrated rather than assumed[27]. Early modern England exemplifies this proposition. The English ceased to be a military power after 1453 and remained "weak" until 1689, yet England in that period laid the foundation for its subsequent economic and governmental strength.[28] In the case of the

Safavids, whose sheer survival was predicated on a strong military, the link is inexorable. Modern scholars beginning with Walther Hinz have seen in early Safavid expansionism a spiritual urge involving the millenarian zeal of the shah and his warrior band. Yet their primary urge arguably was a matter of *mulk-giri*, of grabbing territory.[29] Like the early Mughals and Ottomans, the Safavids took territory for a living; they continued to do so for more than a century after their rise as a political dynasty. In the course of the seventeenth century mulk-giri lost its force as a rationale for power, the closure symbolized by the Accord of Zuhab and its result, the definitive loss of Iraq. The Safavid decision to appease their main adversaries followed a pragmatic realization that it would be impossible ever to defeat them. Cut-backs in military expenditure—a function of financial concerns and factional fighting pitting the old Qizilbash warrior elite against the new, insular forces that represented the concerns and interests of the inner palace—preceded the peace, made it inevitable, and then provided a compelling argument for further cost-cutting.

On purely strategic grounds, the Safavid decision to embrace peace made sense. But it was also a move borne of weakness, and one with far-reaching consequences. The Accord of Zuhab marked a dramatic rupture in more than one way. It symbolized the end of war as the natural condition of the state, and with that spelled an end to its many functions, practical as well as symbolic ones—keeping tribal forces engaged, bringing in booty and slaves, enhancing the shah's warrior aura and forcing him to patrol his realm. Most ominously, Zuhab reinforced a false sense of security. The same arid zone that limited expansion also shielded the Iranian heartland from outside threats. Inhospitable terrain surrounded the inner core on all sides but the northwest. The Zagros range protected the central plateau from tribal assault from the west. Iran's heartland was separated from the Indian subcontinent by a 500-mile barrier consisting of the arid and thinly populated vastness of Sistan and Baluchistan. A seasonally determined 1,000-mile military radius, moreover, made it difficult for the Ottomans and the Mughals to reach beyond Tabriz in the west and Qandahar in the east, respectively.

Zuhab, finally, allowed Iran to evolve beyond an agrarian-based military-fiscal polity into what Mann calls a "territorial empire," one in which ideology and culture rather than raw military power provide cohesion. This followed the diminishing status of the quasi-aristocratic Qizilbash, a force desirous to subjugate, willing to fight for a sacred cause, and die in bloody battle, and the ascendance of a series of alternative status groups of a different disposition. Most important among these were the bureaucrats, the "men of the pen," mainly ethnic Persians, the "new" clerical class composed of Arab immigrants from Lebanon and Bahrain and, eventually, the eunuchs who came to dominate court politics in the later seventeenth century. None of these was rooted in the old steppe politics and its central concerns, perpetual war and territorial expansion. The first group was given to administrative concerns; the second represented the institutionalized form of religion that came to buttress the new state; the third embodied the insular, claustrophobic type of court politics that was to mark the later Safavid state. The prominent role that these groups came to play in governance arguably prevented Iran from becoming a type of praetorian state in which military leaders exercise independent political power and function as kingmakers.

Isfahan's architecture reflects all this: it exudes Shah `Abbas's imperial vision, but it is a non-belligerent, non-expansionist vision. The mosques, the royal pace and the entire layout of the royal square bespeak enduring Persianate notions of urbane refinement and sophistication rather than raw military power, and in so far as the architecture is religious, it is tempered by civic-mindedness. The center as conceived by Shah `Abbas lacks in permanent triumphal arches celebrating victory in war; it finds expression in buildings that are slender, pious and decorative rather than bellicose and forbidding. The columns of the `Ali Qapu palace are open and inviting, neither projecting the raw power of the fortresses of Agra and Delhi, nor the secluded inwardness of the Topkapı Palace in Istanbul.[30]

The half century between 1650 and 1700 truly was a lull before the storm—an apparent equilibrium of stability and relative prosperity masking an underlying process of economic weakening, military neglect and religious oppression that invited barbarian invasion. As late as 1721 the Ottoman envoy Dürri Efendi observed that the Safavid realm looked prosperous and peaceful yet was ready to collapse for lack of a functioning government.[31] Decades earlier, Iran's army had already become a shadow of its former self, demoralized by poor leadership and insufficient pay, to the point where, arguably, only the Ottoman decision to refrain from war saved Iran from territorial loss for the remainder of century. The political elite, torn asunder by factionalism, now lacked the wherewithal to resist the growing nomadic pressure on Iran's borders. The few campaigns launched from Isfahan were little effective, stymied by court intrigue resulting in deliberate misinformation, the withholding of funds and other forms of obstructionism. Still, the relative ease with which a small band of marginal marauders managed to penetrate the heart of the country and bring down the regime remains remarkable. What turned these tribesmen into an existential threat to the Safavid state was less their fighting power than Iran's internal weakness after decades of elite infighting, mismanagement and neglect.

More corrosive than military neglect per se was the decrease in readiness to accommodate and to coopt, to create alliances by way of paying tribesmen to police borderlands—the recruitment formula that the British later would call the battle for "hearts and minds." Despite appearances, the demise of the Safavid state was less a thundering crash than the final tearing of the fabric after its myriad threads had slowly unraveled. And the most vital—as well as fragile—threads connected the center to the periphery, home to Arabs, Kurds, Lezghis, Turkmen, Uzbeks, Baluchis, and Afghans. It seems that, in most cases, these tribesmen might have been mollified with money, that their continued loyalty could have been bought at a time when frequent drought and famine drove them to a desperate search for resources in Iran's settled areas. The growing parsimony of the late Safavids jeopardized security above all because it alienated the peripheral elements whose cooperation was vital for the defense of the external borders. Lambton attributes the disintegration of the Safavids in part to a "tribal resurgence."[32] Allowing for a measure of dialectics, we might see this resurgence, if that is what took place, as perhaps less the cause than the *result* of weakening Safavid rule.

The growing oppression of religious "minorities" contributed to the fraying fabric as well. `Abbas I's savage suppression of heretical groups, his ill-treatment of Iran's Armenians other than the New Julfans, and the various anti-minority campaigns under `Abbas II belie the idea that religious intolerance had its origins in Shah Sultan Husayn's reign, and more particularly goes back to Muhammad Baqir Majlisi's nefarious influence at his court. Yet it is still true that minorities tended to fare best with a strong state in place. The last two, retreating shahs not only allowed the high Shi`i clergy to become full players in the political arena, but also facilitated the ascendance within their ranks of doctrinaire elements keen to foster unity through intolerance.[33] These were not the only ones responsible for pressure and persecution, to be sure; they found willing collaborators in various secular officials keen to firm up their religious credentials, to bring down rivals or, most often, to garner revenue from vulnerable groups in society. In the case of the Armenians this vulnerability was greatly enhanced by internal rifts between Catholics, who were wooed by resident missionaries, and Gregorians, who incited friendly elements in the state to bring down their rivals and to have the missionaries expelled. It is important to remember, finally, that as the state's search for revenue turned more desperate, Safavid officials squeezed money indiscriminately, singling out Armenians, Jews, Zoroastrians, and Hindus above all because they were easy targets. The effect was resentment and the weakening of the fragile bonds of loyalty. The Catholic Shahrimanians, buffeted by a growing tax burden and harassed by fellow Armenians, eventually chose to take their considerable wealth to Italy. Quite a few Armenians living in the north also decamped to Russia. The ones who stayed, most of the New Julfans, as well as the Zoroastrians of Kirman and Yazd, often collaborated with the invaders, even welcoming them as "liberators."

The doctrinaire clerics reserved their strongest invective for Iran's non-Twelver Shi`i Muslims, members of heretical sects, Sufis and Sunnis. Safavid staying power had always been predicated on pragmatic tolerance coexisting in relative harmony with the emphatically religious underpinnings of the state, and inclusion and exclusion traditionally followed self-proclaimed civilizational and political rather than strictly religious categories. Rulers dealt with heretical forces with great brutality, but in practice accommodated those on the margins just enough to enable them not just to survive but occasionally to operate near the center of power, to the point where, even toward the end, when doctrinaire Shi`ism had become a dominant force at the court, the shah was served by a Sunni grand vizier. This reflected the tradition of religious toleration, but insofar as various top officials of Sunni conviction hailed from frontier zones, it was arguably a matter of pragmatism as well, of giving peripheral regions a stake in the Safavid enterprise. This model unraveled as Isfahan began to espouse an exclusionary form of Shi`ism. The consequences were most dramatic for Iran's "Sunni fringe," which, though never an impenetrable "barrier of heterodoxy," was sensitive nonetheless.[34] It was the great mistake of the Safavids to alienate this frontier zone through financial shortsightedness and religious exclusion precisely at a time when its loyalty was most needed.[35]

Did the fall of the center spawn regional centers? In reaction to "Mughalist" assumptions about a backward, passive, and exploitable countryside, the "new" Indian historiography has tended to look for signs of invigoration in the countryside and the periphery in the face of a faltering center.[36] The staggering corruption and mismanagement notwithstanding, the Safavid state did not fully disintegrate until the very end. By 1715, only one of the criteria of local autonomy as listed by Richard Barnett (for India)—revenue formerly submitted to the center now remaining in the provinces—was in place in the Safavid realm. Local governors ruled in arbitrary fashion, brazenly fleecing their subjects, but they were not in a position to appoint their own successors or to conduct their own diplomatic and military activity.[37] Neither prior nor subsequent to the fall of Isfahan did any alternative centers of political power and economic activity emerge. The Safavid dynasty's mystique and mobilizing power continued to reverberate long after the demise of the actual state in 1722, with almost all successor dynasties claiming legitimacy in their name.[38] Yet Afghan rule was brief, and Mahmud's death in 1725 was followed by large-scale, long-term chaos that was exacerbated by the rapacious policies of Nadir Shah in the 1730s. It would take a full century before Iran regained a measure of stability. The Ottomans experienced serious problems in the seventeenth century, yet their state survived and went on to exist for another three hundred years. The Mughal state collapsed, but India, so much richer and with a far greater variety of local centers of real economic viability, took a different course as well. Hyderabad, Awadh, and Bengal picked up where the crumbling center left off. The collapse of Isfahan, by contrast, was accompanied by the disintegration and outside conquest of the country's most productive provinces, Azerbaijan, Shirvan, Armenia, Georgia, Gilan, and Mazandaran. Life went on, to be sure; the export of Kirman wool quickly revived, and Bandar `Abbas resumed its role as a maritime entrepôt, but such continuity did not provide a sufficiently strong foundation for a peripheral surge in the face of central decline.

Glossary

**`abbasi:** currency unit; one tuman equaled 50 `abbasis
amir al-umara: commander of tribal forces
amir-akhur-bashi: head of the royal stables
amir-shikar-bashi: master of the hunt
**`atabat:** Shi`i shrine cities in Iraq
barat: bill of exchange, assignment on revenue
beglerbeg: governor-general
dargah: palace
darughah: police prefect, mayor
divan: chancery, state administration
divanbegi: Chief Justice
garmsir: "warm region," name for Iran's Persian Gulf coast
ghulams: "royal slaves"
haram: inner palace, harem
ishik-aqasi-bashi: royal chamberlain
ishik-aqasi-bashi-yi haram: chamberlain of the inner palace
i`timad al-dawlah: grand vizier
jiz'ya: poll tax, to be paid by non-Muslims
kalantar: headman of a town, representative of an urban community
khassah: sector of the administration belonging and responding to the crown
majlis: gathering, session, audience
mahmudi: currency unit; one tuman equaled 100 mahmudis
mamalik: state sector of the administration
mihmandari: free upkeep and *per diem* granted to foreign envoys
mihtar: royal chamberlain
muhrdar: keeper of the seals
muhtasib: market inspector, supervisor of victuals
mullabashi: royal chaplain
mustawfi: comptroller
mustawfi baqaya: comptroller of arrears
mu`ayyir al-mamalik: assayer of the mint

na'ib: substitute
nazir-i buyutat: steward of the royal household
pishkash: gift
qahvahchi-bashi: royal coffee master
qaychachi-bashi: head tailor in the royal workshops
qazbegi (qazbaki): copper coin
qazi: judge
qullar-aqasi: head of the slave soldiers
qurchis: members of the tribal cavalry
qurchibashi: head of the tribal Qurchi forces
quruq: embargo, ban for males to be present during shah's outings
rahdar: road toll token
raqam: royal decree
ri`ayat: common people, peasants
rish-sifid-i haram: official in charge of the black eunuchs
sadr-i mamalik: head of the state religious administration
sadr-i khassah: head of the crown religious administration
sahib-i jam`: department head
sardar: army commander
sarkar-i khassah: royal domain
sarraf-bashi: head of the money changers
shahbandar: harbor master
shahi: currency unit; one tuman equaled 200 shahis
shah-seven: "love of the shah"
shaykh al-islam: highest religious functionary of a town
shirahchi-bashi: royal sommelier
sipahsalar: commander of the armed forces
suyurghal: land grant, fief
suyursat: purveyance, providing food and services, billeting of troops during war
tufangchi-aqasi: head of the musketeers
tuman: unit of account in the Safavid monetary system, ghost money
tupchibashi: cannon master, artillery commander
tushmal-bashi: royal food taster
tuyul: revenue assignment, land grant
vajibi: seigniorage
vali: viceroy, governor of a *vilayat*
vakil: regent, middleman
vaqa'i`-nivis: registrar
vaqf: religious endowment
vazifah: pension
vazir-i khassah: keeper of the accounts of the king's household
vilayat: semi-autonomous province
yasavul-bashi: head of the aides-de-camp
yuzbashi: commander of a hundred, centurion
zarrabi-bashi: mintmaster

Notes

PREFACE

1 For the hemispheric reach of the Julfan Armenians in this period, see Aslanian, *From the Indian Ocean to the Mediterranean*.
2 For a compelling recent study that situates the lag in Middle Eastern development vis-à-vis Europe in early modern times in legal and institutional differences, see Kuran, *The Long Divergence*.
3 Mokyr, *The Enlightened Economy*, 7.
4 Indeed, even in modern Iran rent-seeking, now lubricated by huge oil income, arguably is prevalent.
5 For a particularly egregious example of this type of conspirational historiography, which blames the English and British for every mishap in Iran from the early Safavid period onward, see Zavish, *Nakhustin karguzaran-i isti`mar*.

INTRODUCTION

1 Lockhart, *The Fall of the Safavi Dynasty*.
2 This does not mean that nothing has been written concerning the "decline and fall" of the Safavids. See, for instance, the various writings of premier Iranian scholars such as Ja`fariyan and Sifatgul and, in English and French, Foran, "The Long Fall"; Touzard, *Le Drogman Padery*; and Axworthy, *The Sword of Persia*, 37–56. For an English translation of part of the Dutch documentation on the last years of the period, see Floor, ed., *The Afghan Occupation*.
3 Dickson, review of Lockhart, *The Fall of the Safavi Dynasty*. Axworthy, *The Sword of Persia*, 302, 331–2, points out the reasons why Dickson's review is uncharitable.
4 Minorsky, ed., *Tadhkirat al-Mulūk*, introduction.

5 See, for instance, Arjomand, *The Shadow of God*; Babayan, *Monarchs, Mystics and Messiahs*; and Abisaab, *Converting Persia*. Of the three synthetic works, Savory, *Iran under the Safavids*, Roemer, *Persien auf dem Weg*, and Newman, *Safavid Iran*, Roemer comes closest to applying Minorsky's ideas. In his synthesis, Savory pays lip service to Minorsky in an attempt to go beyond dissolute kings and venal courtiers but basically reiterates the notion that after Shah `Abbas "the Great, Iran went into steep, unmitigated decline." The most recent attempt at synthesis is Newman, *Safavid Iran*, who resolutely avoids the entire issue of decline. Rejecting the very concept of the state, Newman does not refer to the Safavid state's weakening, and offers no explanation whatsoever for its collapse.
6 See Foran, "The Long Fall." Axworthy, *The Sword of Persia*, ch. 1, is an exception as well. For a good discussion embedded in a larger overview of the entire Safavid period, see Roemer, *Persien auf dem Weg*, and its English distillation, "The Safavid Period."
7 Kafadar, "The Question of Ottoman Decline," 32.
8 Lockhart, *The Fall of the Safavi Dynasty*, 29.
9 During the decade that Muhammad Beg served Shah `Abbas II as grand vizier, Istanbul saw the appointment and dismissal of seven grand viziers and a succession of six shaykh al-islams. See Goffman, *The Ottoman Empire and Europe*, 217.
10 Indeed, with the possible exception of Shah Isma`il II (r. 1576–8), who may have been assassinated but who probably died from a drug overdose, no Safavid ruler was ever killed in the 221-year lifespan of the dynasty.
11 Vatin and Veinstein, *Le sérail ébranlé*, ch. 1.
12 Richard, ed., *Raphaël du Mans*, 2:262.
13 Hodgson, *The Venture of Islam*, 3:49–50.
14 For this, see Aslanian, *From the Indian Ocean to the Mediterranean*.
15 Rahmani, *Azerbaidzhan*, 177.
16 See Emerson and Floor, "Rahdars and their Tolls." In the 1660s, Armenian merchants visiting Moscow for trade talks contrasted Iran's road security to the system of high tolls and dangerous conditions for travelers in Russia. See Parsamian, *Armiano-russkie otnosheniia*, 73, cited in Herzig, "The Armenian Merchants," 203.
17 Chardin, *Voyages*, 5:391; 6:123, 127.
18 For this, see Ali, "The Passing of Empire."
19 Hinz, *Esma`il II*, 95, even made a distinction between the tribal squabbles of Safavid Iran and "world history," to which he connected Shah `Abbas I. Shah `Abbas's reputation as one of the "good" kings in Iranian history endures to this day. Even the current Islamic Republic, although allergic to the idea of monarchy, upholds this characterization in its official interpretation of history.
20 The first to do so may have been Jan Smidt, Dutch envoy to Shah Safi's court, who left a lengthy description of his encounter with that ruler shortly after Shah `Abbas's death in 1629. He portrays the late

shah as a wise ruler who had been respected by all the country's grandees. See Smidt's diary, in Dunlop, ed., *Bronnen*, 731. Fryer, visiting Iran a half century after the shah's death, reports that his name was "invoked when any commendable or famous action is performed; saying 'Shaw Abas,' or 'Shabas,' as we are wont to say, 'Well done.'" See Fryer, *A New Account*, 2:245.

21 See, for instance, Kaempfer, *Am Hofe des persischen Grosskönigs*, 36–8.
22 This reputation is reflected in Western as much as in Iranian historiography. The author of the *Tarikh-i Tahmasiyah*, writing from India in the late eighteenth century, only brings up his narrative to 1071–2/1661–3, the last year recorded in the *Khuld-i barin*, with the argument that he had found no information on the subsequent period in libraries accessible to him and that, especially for the reign of Shah Sulayman, he was short on knowledge. See Röhrborn, *Provinzen und Zentralgewalt*, 1–2.
23 See Krusinski, *The History of the Late Revolutions*.
24 The phrase is from Edward Gibbon's *Decline and Fall of the Roman Empire*, as cited in Porter, *Gibbon*, 104. The chapter titled "Power" in this study analyzes the stereotypes of Asian despotism as depicted by Gibbon's work and other Georgian-era historiographers. For the Greek antecedents of the stubborn notion that royal women played a destructive role backstage, see Brosius, *Women in Ancient Persia*, 3–9.
25 Malcolm, *A History of Persia*, 1:552, 570–82, 588.
26 Browne, *A Literary History*, vol. 4: *Modern Times, 1500–1924*, 24. Browne seems to have been influenced by Iran's Poet-Laureate Malik al-Shu`ara Bahar. The assessment of Safavid literature as uninteresting survives until today. See, for example, Safa, "Persian Literature," 960. Of late, however, scholars have begun to take a fresh and more appreciative look at Safavid poetry in particular. See, for example, Losensky, *Welcoming Fighani*.
27 Bausani, "Notes on the Safavid Period."
28 Welch, "Worldly and Otherworldly Love," 301. Only recently have art historians begun to reassess the period and view it in more positive light. See, for example, Landau, "Farangī Sāzī at Isfahan."
29 Savory, "The Safavid Administrative System," 367.
30 Al-Azmeh, *Muslim Kingship*, 77.
31 Ibid., 113.
32 Sabzavari, *Rawzat al-anwar*, 70–100.
33 Quinn, "Rewriting Ni`matullāhī History"; Wood, "*Tarikh-i Jahanara*."
34 Gemelli Careri, *Giro del mondo*, 2:202.
35 Mar`ashi, *Majma` al-tavarikh*, 48, writing a few decades after the demise of Safavid rule, ascribed the rot to the hedonism, the cowardliness, the greed, and the jealousies of the elite. Findiriski *Tuhfat al-`alam*, 84, speaks of the desire for luxury which toward the end of Safavid rule had reached the point where merchants, artisans, and peasants wore brocade cloaks and expensive calico shawls and donned colorful

turbans of various provenance. Contemporary commentators differed on the role religion played in this process. Some blamed the decline they perceived on a lack of religious guidance after the death in 1699 of Iran's chief cleric, Muhammad Baqir Majlisi. According to al-Bahrani, *Lu'lu'at al-Bahrayn*, 55, "The moment Majlisi departed from this world, the reins of government affairs fell from the hands of the shah and disorder became apparent in the country; in the same year the city of Qandahar was lost to his government and decay overwhelmed the realm to the point where government was totally taken away from him." A similar tone is struck by Tunakabuni, *Qisas al-'ulama*, 205. But the generally secular genre of Iranian historiography more typically focused on a surfeit of religion, blaming the stranglehold that religious sentiments had on the shah for the downward spiral. Rustam al-Hukama, *Rustam al-tavarikh*, 98, for instance, called Shah Sultan Husayn just and friendly but led astray by bigoted mullahs, pious and ascetic types, so that the principle of good governance, *husn-i siyasat*, suffered.

36 Shushtari, *Tadhkira-i Shushtar*, 116.
37 Hazin Lahiji, "Vaqi`at-i Iran va Hind," 190.
38 Tihrani, *Mir'at-i varidat*, 98.
39 Rustam al-Hukama, *Rustam al-tavarikh*, 91–2, 98–9, 108–9, 328.
40 See, for example, Simnani, *Shah Sultan Husayn*, 335. For a discussion of the nationalist uses of the Safavids in Iran's modern popular historiography, see Amin, "Mujassama-i būd."
41 NA, VOC 1349, Gamron to Batavia, 25 Nov. 1679, fols. 1717v–19r. Most European observers, and especially the ones who just passed through the country and had an inadequate knowledge of its languages and customs, clearly offer a limited perspective on Iran's reality. The decay the classically educated ones observed was also inflected by invidious comparisons with a mythical Iranian past. Yet none of this precludes using their observations as source material. For a more detailed argument along these lines, see Matthee, "The Safavids under Western Eyes."
42 For this, see Carnot, *Représentations de l'Islam*, 237ff.
43 Van den Trille, aboard ship "Bueren", to Batavia, June 1634, in Dunlop, ed., "Bronnen", 474.
44 NA, VOC 1349, Gamron to Batavia, 25 Nov. 1679, fols. 1712v–13v; VOC 1379, Gamron to Heren XVII, 25 Nov. 1682, fol. 2723; VOC 1416, Casembroot off Qishm, to Heren XVII, 9 Sept. 1684, fol. 1626r.
45 Elliot, *Spain and Its World*, 242.
46 Widmer, "Niedergangskonzeptionen."
47 Thomson, *Decline in History*, 91.
48 Busse, "Persische Staatsgedanken," 63.
49 Hasan, *State and Locality*, 5.
50 For this and other tendencies inherent in documentation emanating from the center, see Berktay, "Three Empires," 250–1.

51 The situation in Kirman is not only known through the documentation of the Dutch and English East India companies, which were interested in the goat's wool produced in the surrounding area, but also happens to be the subject of two late-Safavid local chronicles that sequentially narrate the entire period from the 1660s until the fall of Isfahan. See Mashizi, *Tarikh-i Safaviyah-i Kirman*; and Kirmani, *Sahifat al-irshad*. The second text starts where the first leaves off, causing Bastani-Parizi, the editor of both texts, to conclude that the author of the second work was aware of the earlier one. See Kirmani, *Sahifat al-irshad*, introduction, 71.
52 For this term and its meaning, see Bayly, *Imperial Meridian*, 18.

CHAPTER 1

1 The "state" is used here in the institutional Weberian sense, containing the following elements, summarized by Mann, "The Autonomous Power of the State," as:
   a. A differentiated set of institutions and personnel embodying -
   b. Centrality in the sense that political relations radiate outwards from a center to cover -
   c. A territorially demarcated area, over which it exercises -
   d. A monopoly of authoritative binding rule-making, backed up by a monopoly of the legitimate means of physical violence.
2 Gorski, *The Disciplinary Revolution*, 29.
3 For the features of the patrimonial state, see Weber, *Economy and Society*, 1:1006–10. For its manifestation in the Mughal case, see Blake, "The Patrimonial-Bureaucratic Empire."
4 See Mann, "The Autonomous Power of the State," 4.
5 Mann, *The Sources of Social Power*, 1:80.
6 Wolf, *Europe and the People without History*, 79–82. Wolf's tributary mode aims to dissolve the traditional Marxian distinction between the Asiatic mode of production and the feudal mode of production, and subsume all precapitalist systems under one model. Though part of a larger, Marxist, theoretical construct, the tributary mode of production seems flexible enough and sufficiently attuned to the production and reproduction of political and social power in Safavid Iran to fit into the Weberian formation applied here.
7 See Hinz, *Irans Aufstieg zum Nationalstaat*.
8 For the Mongol manifestation of this, see Schurmann, "Mongolian Tributary Practices," 320–2.
9 Hasan, *State and Locality*, Introduction.
10 For the contrast between these two notions and the Central Asian antecedents of the former (in the case of the Ottoman state), see Togan, "Ottoman History by Inner Asian Norms."

11 For a definition of the state along these lines, see Tapper, *Frontier Nomads of Iran*, introduction, 10.
12 Das Gupta, *The World of the Indian Ocean Merchant*, 194.
13 See Adle, "Contributions à la géographie."
14 For the term "inner frontier" as applied to Mughal India, see Gommans, *Mughal Warfare*.
15 Maeda, "Exploitation of the Frontier," 481–2 calls the Caucasus the "nearest frontier" for the Safavids.
16 NA, VOC 1304, Report Willemson, Masqat, 1674, fol. 483v.; also in Floor, "A Description of Masqat." For the Arab and Iranian elements in the south, see Aubin, "Le royaume d'Ormuz," 138–40. As in India, Banyans in Iran were typically employed as small-scale merchants and shopkeepers. See Habib, "Merchant Communities"; and Dale, *Indian Merchants*.
17 The larin was an elongated silver coin, first mentioned in the Persian Gulf in the early 1500s and used throughout the western Indian Ocean until the eighteenth century. For early references to the larin and its spread, see Barbosa, *The Book of Duarte Barbosa*, 1:100–1; Pyrard, *The Voyage of François Pyrard*, 1:232–4; and Codrington, "Coins of the Kings of Hormuz," 160.
18 See Melville, "Qars to Qandahar."
19 See Mufid Mustawfi, *Mohtaṣar-e Mofīd*, 376–87. Iran only became a maritime nation in the twentieth century.
20 Chardin, *Voyages*, 4:268, 288.
21 Floor, *The Economy of Safavid Persia*, 2.
22 See the discussion in Minorsky, ed., *Tadhkirat al-Mulūk*, 173–82.
23 Floor, *The Economy of Safavid Persia*, 252.
24 For this, see Matthee, *The Politics of Trade*, 99–105.
25 For information on the traveling time between these places, see Heeringa, ed., *Bronnen*, 2:163; and Dunlop, ed., *Bronnen*, 625.
26 The records of the Dutch East India Company (VOC) in 1636 provide a telling example. The Dutch that year bought 107,040 pounds of wheat in Jahrum in Fars for 10,264 *mahmudis*, and transported this to Bandar 'Abbas. Although the distance involved was only half of that between Isfahan and the coast, the freight price they paid was 8,554 mahmudis, or almost 90 percent of the cost of the wheat. See NA, VOC, Factuur retourgoederen, 25 Mar. 1636, in Dunlop, ed., *Bronnen*, 572. Klein, "Trade in the Safavid Port City," 186, has criticized the validity of this point by arguing that the example is not representative since the period in question was one of drought. Yet, even if this explains the high price of the transportation, the same drought may have been responsible for the fact that the wheat was transported in the first place.
27 See Matthee, "The East India Company Trade."
28 This phenomenon was neither new nor unique to Iran. Parts of early modern Europe suffered from severe shortages of cash. War and

instability tended to aggravate this problem. Not infrequently, times of acute scarcity saw a re-emergence of barter trade. See Braudel, *The Mediterranean*, 1:452–3.
29 Quoted in Ferrier, "An English View of Persian Trade," 192–3.
30 Dunlop, ed., *Bronnen*, 199.
31 The Dutch observation in 1640 that copper coin did not have a significant role in commerce is a case in point, for they most likely only referred to the large-scale and long-distance trade they themselves engaged in. In addition, the Dutch noted that copper *qazbaki*s were mostly used by "poor people." NA, Coll. Gel. de Jongh, 142, "Reductie van de Parsiaensche munte," 1640, unfol. This is confirmed by an English report from 1701 which stated that the qazbaki was more common in Isfahan's bazaar than silver. See IOR, E/3/60/7115, Isfahan to Company, 24 Mar. 1701, fol. 15.
32 Della Valle, *Viaggi*, 1:586; Krusinski as quoted in Rabino di Borgomale, *Coins, Medals, and Seals*, 20. In some places this phenomenon seems to have applied to silver as well. See Gemelli Careri, *Giro del mondo*, 2:235.
33 For the limes, see Fryer, *A New Account*, 2:216; for the wax, see Tournefort, *Relation d'un voyage*, 2:318.
34 Chardin, *Voyages*, 5:414–15. The little direct evidence available on this issue is confined to the Caucasus and the borderlands with the Ottoman Empire, where a near-subsistence economy seems to have prevailed. For references to Georgia and Mingrelia, see Efendi, *Narrative of Travels*, 2:169; Chardin, *Voyages*, 1:186, 335–6; PF S.C., Giorgia 1, Notizie di Mengrelia, 17 Feb. 1687, fols. 368–81; and Tournefort, *Relation d'un voyage*, 2:301. For Khuzistan and the Ottoman borderlands, see Rebelo, *Un voyageur portugais*, 148–9; and [Vachet], "Journal d'un voyage," fols. 144–5. Remote parts of Iran operated on barter until the twentieth century. G. P. Tate, referring to the inhabitants of Sistan on the border with Afghanistan, noted that "previous to our mission of 1903 a large proportion of the people had never even handled silver money." See Tate, *Frontiers of Baluchistan*, 227.
35 For this process and the role of the concept of a capital, see Gronke, "The Persian Court."
36 For this, see Axworthy, *A History of Iran*, 161.
37 For this argument, see Fragner, "Historische Wurzeln."
38 For a good overview of these arrangements, see Murphey, "The Ottoman-Safavid Border Conflict;" and idem, "The Resumption of Ottoman-Safavid Border Conflict." Also see Matthee, "Between Arabs, Turks and Iranians."
39 See Sanandaji, *Tuhfah-i Nasiri*, 99–100. This equaled some 30,000 tumans.
40 Anon., *'Alam-ara-yi Safavi*, 137. Written in the 1670s as a popular history of the Safavids, this is not a primary source for the events.

41 The Ottoman ambassador Ahmad Dourry (Dürri) Efendy in 1720 estimated that no less than one-third of Iran's population consisted of Sunnis. See Dourry Efendy, *Relation*, 54.
42 For the position of Turkish versus Persian in Safavid Iran, see Gandjei, "Turkish in the Safavid Court"; and Perry, "Persian during the Safavid Period."
43 It is tempting to project the strong ties between the ulama and the merchants under the Qajars backward, yet there is precious little evidence for cooperation between the two in the Safavid period, probably because no compelling outside threat drove them yet together.
44 Several contemporary authors draw attention to this and compare it favorably to the situation in the Ottoman Empire and even Europe. See Matthee, "The Safavids under Western Eyes," 167–8.
45 `Shah Abbas I was the exception to this, at least according to Della Valle, *Delle conditioni*, 35–6, who insists that the shah's soldiers behaved well toward villagers and peasants, did not loot but paid for everything they needed.
46 Chardin, *Voyages*, 9:339, relating how the governor of Mazandaran pleaded with Shah Sulayman not to visit his province. This was a persisting phenomenon. As late as 1900, the news that Muzaffar al-Din Shah would travel from Tehran to Tabriz on his way to Europe sent many villagers en route into the mountains with their possessions for fear of being robbed. See AAE, CP, nouv. sér, Perse 1, Tehran to Paris, 6 Apr. 1900, fol. 119.
47 See Chardin, *Voyages*, 2:138; 4:428; 8:496–7; [Vachet], "Journal d'un voyage," fols. 383–4; and De la Maze, "Journal du voyage," 406. It should be noted that Iran was by no means unique in this respect. In Europe, too, villages were often situated at some distance from main routes. See Braudel, *The Mediterranean*, 1:277.
48 For the tension between the two traditions, see Fletcher, "The Turco-Mongolian Monarchic Tradition."
49 For this shift, see Babayan, *Mystics, Monarchs, and Messiahs*, 349ff.
50 The *Dastur al-muluk* is similar to the *Tadhkirat al-muluk* in being an eighteenth-century administrative manual written to instruct the new Afghan rulers in bureaucratic organization.
51 Barthold, *Turkestan*, 227; cited in Minorsky, ed. *Tadhkirat al-mulūk*, 24–5.
52 Chardin, *Voyages*, 10:49.
53 Kaempfer, *Am Hofe des persischen Grosskönigs*, 163. A good example of an appointee automatically sending a substitute is the case of Kirman. Its governor in the seventeenth century was often the *qurchibashi*, an official who had to have a presence at the court. See Vaziri, *Tarikh-i Kirman*, 642.
54 See Bill, "The Plasticity of Informal Politics," 143, for the enduring importance of the vakil in the Iranian political system. For the importance of having an intermediary in early Stuart England, see Peck, *Court Patronage*.

55 Kaempfer, *Am Hofe des persischen Grosskönigs*, 231–2.
56 For royal travel as an inherent part of the Mughal imperial structure, see Blake, "The Patrimonial-Bureaucratic Empire," 92–3. Shah Tahmasb is an exception among the early shahs, for he became a recluse after 1555.
57 See Della Valle, *Delle conditioni*, 30; and Chardin, *Voyages*, 5:287. In general, see Weber, *State and Society*, 1042–3. Institutionalized rivalry was not, of course, a phenomenon exclusive to Safavid Iran. Louis XIV said in his memoirs that rivalry between ministers helped to unite the full authority of the ruler in the king's person. See Lossky, "The Intellectual Development of Louis XIV."
58 See Mufid Mustawfi, *Mohtaṣar-e Mofid*, 1:12. This work was written in the 1680s, during the reign of Shah Sulayman. Mufid Mustawfi's self-consciousness in delineating Iran as a political and religious unit is unmistakable in that he conceives of a "greater Iran," which includes the entire Mesopotamian region that had been lost to the Ottomans in 1638–9. For the reintroduction of the term Iran, see Krawulsky, "Zur Wiederbelebung"; and Fragner, "Historische Wurzeln," 88–9.
59 Valah Qazvini Isfahani, *Khuld-i barin*, 589.
60 Axworthy, *A History of Iran*.
61 For more on this, see Matthee, "Was Safavid Iran an Empire?"
62 See Calmard, "Les rituels shiites"; idem, "Shi'i Rituals and Power"; and Rahimi, "The Rebound Theater State."
63 See Rizvi, *The Safavid Dynastic Shrine*.
64 For a good discussion of the history and background of the confluence of traditional Iranian, Islamic, and the Turko-Mongol concepts of power and legitimacy, see Arjomand, "Salience of Political Ethic."
65 Vicenzo Alessandri, report to Venetian Senate, 24 Sept. 1572, in Berchet, *La repubblica di Venezia*, 178.
66 Munajjim *Tarikh-i 'Abbasi*, 188.
67 Aram, *Andishah-i tarikh-nigari*, 260–3.
68 The Shahsivan phenomenon is generally mentioned in connection with Shah 'Abbas I, but instances are recorded until the very end of the dynasty. See, for example, Valah Qazvini Isfahani, *Khuld-i barin*, 204–5; letter Gaudereau, 5 Dec. 1695, in Kroell, ed., *Nouvelles d'Isfahan*, 73; and Kirmani, *Sahifat al-irshad*, 389. See Tapper, *Frontier Nomads of Iran*, 47–57, for the argument that the notion that the shah-seven were created as a new tribe goes back to a misreading of the sources by John Malcolm.
69 See Sifatgul, *Sakhtar-i nihad*, 310–13; and Floor, *A Fiscal History*, 59–62. For the *sadr*, see Floor, "The Sadr or Head."
70 For this, see Matthee, "The Politics of Protection."
71 See Sabzavari, as discussed in Sifatgul, *Sakhtar-i nihad*, 497; and Naji, *Risalah*.
72 Shah Isma'il II (r. 1576–7) may have been poisoned because of his Sunni tendencies.

73 Sifatgul, introduction to Tihrani, *Mir'at-i varidat*, 14–15.
74 For this process, see Matthee "The Career of Mohammad Beg," and idem, "Administrative Stability." See also Aubin, "L'avènement des Safavides," 115.
75 See Lambton, "Justice in the Medieval Theory"; and Perry, "Justice for the Underprivileged."
76 See, for example, Sabzavari, *Rawzat al-anwar*, 801–10.
77 Thus in 1645, a sum of 1,000 tumans was distributed among the poor of Isfahan to pray for the health of Shah 'Abbas II who had been injured falling from his horse. At the same time all those imprisoned for misdemeanors were released. See NA, Coll. Gel. de Jongh 283, Daghregister Winninx, Isfahan, 18 Sept. 1645, fol. 211. Gemelli Careri, *Giro del mondo*, 2:121, similarly noted that when Shah Sulayman fell ill in the early 1690s a sum of 37,000 tumans was distributed to the indigent, and all provincial governors received orders to release prisoners.
78 D'Alessandri, "Narrative," 216.
79 Hinz, "Schah Esma'il II," 91.
80 Diego di Santa Ana, Isfahan to Clement VIII, 7 Dec. 1607, in Alonso, "Due lettere," 161.
81 Minorsky, ed., *Tadhkirat al-Mulūk*, 82; Mirza Rafi'ah, "Dastur al-muluk," 73; Thevenot, *Travels*, 103; Fryer, *A New Account*, 3: 24.
82 Pacifique de Provins, *Relation d'un voyage*, 256.
83 [Anon., ed.] *A Chronicle of the Carmelites*, 159; and Ross, *Sir Anthony Sherley*, 230.
84 NA, VOC 1208, Sarcerius, Gamron to Batavia, 12 Apr. 1655, fol. 512; Vahid Qazvini, *Tarikh-i jahan-ara-yi 'Abbasi*, 556; Fasa'i, *Farsnamah-i Nasiri*, 1:480, 484–85. According to Qazvini, *Fava'id al-Safaviyah*, 69, a third day each week was set aside for the receipt of gifts from rulers.
85 See Perry, "Justice of the Underprivileged." For the judicial system in Safavid Iran, see Floor, "The Secular Judicial System."
86 This idea is discussed in general terms by Van Klaveren, "Die historische Erscheinung der Korruption."
87 See Vahid Qazvini, *Tarikh-i Jahan-ara-yi 'Abbasi*, 731 for the first example; Mardukh, *Tarikh-i Mardukh*, 111, for Khusraw Khan; and Röhrborn, "Regierung und Verwaltung," 44, for Gilan.
88 See Papazyan, *Agrarnie otnosheniia*, 189–91.
89 Maeda, "Forced Migrations," 246–8.
90 Maeda, "The Household of Allahverdi Khan," 63; Gellner, "Tribalism and the State," 114, too, argues that the term "slaves" is also not really appropriate, since the state owned them as much as they owned the state.
91 Rota, "Caucasians in Safavid Service," 109–10.
92 Della Valle, *Viaggi*, 1:468.
93 Poullet (d'Armainville), *Nouvelles relations*, 2:289–90.

94 For this, see Szuppe, "Kinship Ties"; and eadem, "La participation des femmes."
95 Maeda, "Hamza Mīrzā," 160–3.
96 Maeda, "Exploitation of the Frontier," 493–4.
97 For the important role of women in Safavid court politics, see Szuppe, "La participation des femmes." See also Chardin, *Voyages*, 8:47–8, for the marriage between Shah 'Abbas II's daughter Hava Bigum and the sadr.
98 See Chardin, *Voyages*, 2:31–2.
99 The Achaemenid roots of gift-giving in Iran are discussed in Sancisi-Weerdenburg, "Gifts in the Persian Empire." For the institution of pishkash in Islamic times, see Lambton, "Pishkash: Present or Tribute?"; and Matthee, "Gifts and Gift-Giving."
100 This practice may go back to Mongol times as well. See Allsen, "Mongol Princes," 120–1.
101 Chardin, *Voyages*, 3:197–8.
102 NA, VOC 1430, Isfahan to Batavia, 5 July 1686, fol. 1548v. Five percent went to "one of the shah's eunuchs." See Speelman, *Journaal*, 269. Chardin, *Voyages*, 5:359, and Kaempfer, *Am Hofe des persischen Grosskönigs*, 106, claim that the *ishik-aqasi-bashi* received 10 percent.
103 Chardin, *Voyages*, 5:286–7. As examples Chardin cites several Uzbek princes and the Mughal Prince Muhammad Akbar who in 1686 fled to Iran after rebelling against his father, Aurangzeb, to be given refuge in comfortable circumstances. For Muhammad Akbar, see Islam, *Indo-Persian Relations*, 131–2.
104 One understands Chardin's amazement at the appointment of Muhammad Quli Khan, who had been exiled by Shah 'Abbas II for thirteen years, to the sensitive position of khan of the frontier region of Qandahar. See Chardin, *Voyages*, 10:110–11.
105 Afushtah-i Natanzi, *Naqavat al-asar*, 541ff.
106 Valah Qazvini Isfahani, *Khuld-i barin*, 593.
107 De Bruyn, *Reizen over Moskovie*, 176.
108 Foreign observers noted the absence of a "nobility" along Western lines among the Iranian elite, and the attendant lack of feudal titles and attributes, and ascribed the remarkable rise of commoners to the absence of a fixed hierarchy among social groups. See, for example, Raphaël du Mans, "Estat de la Perse," in Richard, ed., *Raphaël du Mans*, 2:95–6. This is, of course, a main feature in Weber's patrimonial rule as well.
109 Findiriski, *Tuhfat al-'alam*, 123. Mirza Habib Allah was appointed sadr by the shah.
110 Monshi, *History of Shah 'Abbas*, 525, lists despotic behavior and an inclination to deal swiftly and severely with wrongdoers explicitly, not just as one of Shah 'Abbas's attributes but as one of his virtues.
111 Findiriski, *Tuhfat al-'alam*, 128.
112 Sabzavari, *Rawzat al-anwar*, 94.

113 See Junabadi, *Rawzat al-Safawiyah*, 675–7; Falsafi, *Zindigani-yi Shah ʿAbbas*, 3:165; and Reid, *Tribalism and Society*, 29–30. Reid erroneously presents this as an enduring and unchangeable feature of the Safavid polity.
114 In 1682 he was deposed from the latter post, only to be reinstated in 1691.
115 See Luft, "Iran unter Schāh ʿAbbās II," 109.
116 The exceptions to this unity are the southern larin and, to some extent, the coinage of Khuzistan, which fell within the Safavid standard but exhibited autonomous features. See Matthee, "The Safavid Mint of Huwayza."
117 This is argued by Michel Mazzaoui, "From Tabriz to Qazvin to Isfahan," 521–2, who questions the notion that Isfahan became the Safavid capital simply because the city was beyond the reach of the Ottomans.
118 See Gaube and Wirth, *Der Bazar von Isfahan*, 54. For population figures, see Floor, *The Economy of Safavid Persia*, 2–5. For a detailed analysis of the construction of the maydan and the surrounding premises, see McChesney, "Four Sources."
119 Writing in 1665, Raphael du Mans claimed that, during the previous twenty years, Isfahan had grown by one-fourth or one-fifth. See Raphaël du Mans, "Estat de la Perse 1665," in Richard, ed., *Raphaël du Mans*, 2:262, 277.
120 The significance of the *urdu bazaar* in Iran goes back to ancient times. Speaking about its significance in the Mongol period, Lambton says, "When the Il-Khan was in residence in Tabriz or Sultaniya, prices would be high because of the great concourse there. If he was absent, prices would decline sharply." See Lambton, *Continuity and Change*, 170.
121 Richard, ed., *Raphaël du Mans*, 2:119.
122 Chardin, *Voyages*, 10:2.
123 NA, VOC 1747, Isfahan to Gamron, 6 Oct. 1706, fol. 279.
124 NA, VOC 1307, Gamron to Heren XVII, 1 Aug. 1676, fol. 669r.
125 NA, VOC 1246, Gamron to Batavia, 8 Feb. 1664, fol. 774; VOC 1241, Gamron to Heren XVII, 15 Feb. 1664, fol. 573v.; VOC 1307, Gamron to Heren XVII, 28 Mar. 1676, fol. 634r. For a discussion of the urdu bazaar, see Hanway, *An Historical Account*, 4:247–8.
126 Floor, *The Persian Textile Industry*, 83–4, takes issue with the notion that the karkhanhas were supervised by the state, arguing that "most of the royal workshops were in fact privately owned...."
127 Stressing the Central Asian background of the Mughals, Stephen Dale draws attention to the Mongol habit of protecting trade and to engage in trading partnerships, and argues that this practice was similar to the business alliances that Mughal and Safavid rulers and nobles made with indigenous merchants of their societies. See Dale, *Indian Merchants*, 33. For an excellent discussion of the ways in which the Mongols approached trade, see Allsen, "Mongolian Princes," 121.

128 Thevenot, *Relation d'un voyage*, 130; Tavernier, *Les six voyages*, 1:119. Gemelli Careri, *Giro del mondo*, 2:76, in the 1690s called Iranian caravanserais so "uniform and well proportioned that they are not inferior to the best structures in Europe."
129 See Kleiss and Kiani, *Iranian Caravansarais*.
130 For this notion, see Perry, "Justice for the Underprivileged."
131 Florencio del Niño Jesús, *En Persia (1608–1624)*, 3:57; Bushev, *Posol'stvo Artemiia Volynskogo*, 61–2.
132 See, among others, Tavernier, *Les six voyages*, 1:2, and Bourges, *Relation du voyage*, 68, 122.
133 Tavernier, *Les six voyages*, 1:688; Chardin, *Voyages*, 6:129; Kaempfer, *Am Hofe des persischen Grosskönigs*, 168; Gemelli Careri, *Giro del mondo*, 2:188.
134 Allsen, "Mongolian Princes," 98–9.
135 Visnich, Isfahan to Amsterdam, 26 Sept. 1629, Dunlop, ed., *Bronnen*, 306.
136 Gemelli Careri, *Giro del mondo*, 2:188.
137 Tavernier, *Les six voyages*, 1:685–6, 92 ; Chardin, *Voyages*, 4:124–7. For details and context, see Floor, "The Secular Judicial System."
138 Banani, "Reflections," 89–90.
139 Floor, *The Economy of Safavid Persia*, 28.

CHAPTER 2

1 For a discussion of the formation and evolution of the ghulams, see Floor, *Safavid Government Institutions*, 166–76. For an example of a non-Caucasian ghulam, see Muzaffar Beg, in Maeda, "The Household of Allahverdi Khan," 62–3.
2 See Minorsky, ed., *Tadhkirat al-Mulūk*, 19, 23; Lockhart, *The Fall of the Safavi Dynasty*, 16–34; and Savory, *Iran under the Safavids*, 226–41.
3 Junabadi, *Rawzat al-Safaviyah*, fol. 292. See also Aubin, "Šah Ismāʿīl et les notables," 65–6.
4 Röhrborn, *Provinzen und Zentralgewalt*, 33.
5 Babayan, *Mystics, Monarchs, and Messiahs*, 382.
6 Babaie et al., *Slaves of the Shah*, 37.
7 For details, see ibid., especially ch. 5; Farhad, "Military Slaves"; and, for the house of Allah Virdi Khan, Maeda, "The Household of Allahverdi Khan."
8 Babaie et al., *Slaves of the Shah*, especially Babaie, "Launching from Isfahan"; Maeda, "Parsadan Gorgijanidze's Exile"; and Tokatlian, *Kalantars*, 24–5.
9 See, for example, Roemer, *Persien auf dem Weg*.
10 Gobineau, *Trois ans en Asie*, 328.
11 Khuzani Isfahani, "Afzal al-tavarikh," vol. 3, fol. 171a. On the complex identity of Tahmasb Quli Khan and his Mirimanidze clan, see Maeda, "On the Ethno-Social Background," 253–7.

12 This is the tenor of the depiction of ghulams in Babaie et al., *Slaves of the Shah*.
13 Afushtah'i Natanzi, *Naqavat al-asar*, 19, offers an isolated reference to a "qurchi-yi Gurji." Several high-ranking ghulams commanding Qurchi regiments appear in the sources. See Röhrborn, "Regierung und Verwaltung," 39; and Floor, *Safavid Government Institutions*, 139, 151.
14 See Turkaman, *Tarikh-i `alam-ara-yi `Abbasi*, 1106: talking about the composition of the tufangchi corps, he calls them collectively ghulams. Floor, *Government Institutions*, 167, misreads Turkaman and turns his meaning around by stating that ghulams, "at first, consisted also of Chagatay, Arab, and Persian tribes from Khorasan, Azerbaijan, and Tabaristan as well as riff-raff from the main urban centers."
15 Maeda, "The Household of Allahverdi Khan," 159.
16 Floor, "A Note on the Grand Vizierate," 478.
17 Sanson, "Nouvelles de Perse," 13 Aug. 1691, in Kroell, ed., *Nouvelles d'Ispahan*, 42.
18 As analyzed for Buyid society by Mottahedeh, *Loyalty and Leadership*.
19 Abisaab, *Converting Persia, passim*.
20 Gouvea, *Relaçam*, fol. 62.
21 Anon., ed., *A Chronicle of the Carmelites*, 314–16.
22 Krusinski, *The History of the Late Revolutions*, 1:100–1, 190–2, 194. For more details, see Chapter 8.
23 F. Franciscus Maria di S. Syro, n.d., in CA, O.C.D. 243, 1 bis.
24 Avril, *Voyage*, 60.
25 See, for example, Anon., ed., *A Chronicle of the Carmelites*, 253.
26 Chardin, *Voyages*, 2:42–3, 150. For other references to the reputation of Georgians in late Safavid Iran, see Lang, "Georgia and the Fall."
27 See Fryer, *A New Account*, 2:291.
28 Faroqhi, *The Ottoman Empire*, 44.
29 In Kirman, for instance, the position of shaykh al-islam was a hereditary function, *mansab-i mawrusi*. See Mashizi, *Tarikh-i Safaviyah-i Kirman*, 349.
30 Even in England, the personality of the king had a large impact on the trends of political life until the late eighteenth century and, some historians argue, until 1832. See Marshall, *The Age of Faction*, 14.
31 Gomes, "The Court Galaxy," 196.
32 As Kaempfer, *Am Hofe des persischen Grosskönigs*, 103, put it, the Safavid court knew a basic bureaucratic hierarchy but it was not rigid, since real ranking was often dependent on the favor of the shah.
33 Chardin, *Voyages*, 5:237.
34 Ibid., 347–8.
35 Della Valle, *Delle conditioni*, 12.
36 For this, see Matthee, "The Politics of Protection."
37 The problem may have been particularly acute in (Safavid) Iran, but there is nothing uniquely Safavid or Iranian about either endemic

court factionalism or the tendency of rulers to foster a competitive atmosphere among the members of their entourage; the same was true of contemporary European kings. The contemporary English and French courts were riven by similar forms of endemic factionalism. Louis XIV of France in his memoirs explicitly stated that rivalry between ministers helped to concentrate full authority in the king's person. See Lossky, *The Intellectual Development*, 119, and, in general, Mettam, *Power and Faction*. For England, see Marshall, *The Age of Faction*; for France, see Peck, *Court Patronage*.

38 Lambton, *Continuity and Change*, 28. The terms mamalik and khassah will be further explained in Chapter 6.
39 Kaempfer, *Am Hofe des persischen Grosskönigs*, 81; and Minorsky, ed., *Tadhkirat al-Mulūk*, 86, 114–15.
40 Sabzavari, *Rawzat al-anwar*, 614. In the story the shah himself is enjoined to be careful not to waste money on undue causes and not to engage in frivolous activities: see ibid., 808. For more on this dichotomy, see Barfield, "Tribe and State Relations," 172–3.
41 See Speelman, *Journaal*, 149ff; Chardin, *Voyages*, 9:480; Bushev, *Posol'stvo Artemiia Volynskogo*, 181–2.
42 Kaempfer, *Am Hofe des persischen Grosskönigs*, 81.
43 Sabzavari, *Rawzat al-anwar*, 614.
44 Rustam al-Hukama, *Rustam al-tavarikh*, 71ff.
45 De Bruyn, *Reizen over Moskovie*, 157.
46 Du Mans in Richard, ed., *Raphaël du Mans*, 2:10.
47 Della Valle, *Viaggi*, 1:662. Shah ʿAbbas told Della Valle that a successful king was a warrior king who did not depend on the self-serving advice of his ministers and clerics.
48 This is what Saru Shah Husayn, grand vizier to Shah Ismaʿil, successfully did with his master. See Qummi, *Khulasat al-tavarikh*, 109.
49 Brugsch, *Reise der K. Preusische Gesandtschaft*, 1:225.
50 Valah Qazvini Isfahani, *Khuld-i barin*, 187.
51 Murshid Quli Khan was the last effective vakil. See Turkaman, *Tarikh ʿalam-ara-yi ʿAbbasi*, 350–72, 399–405; Minorsky, ed., *Tadhkirat al-Mulūk*, 14–15; Röhrborn, "Regierung und Verwaltung," 19.
52 For the creation of the post of majlis-nivis as a shadow office to the vizierate, see Nasiri, *Titles and Emoluments*, 42.
53 Lockhart, *The Fall of the Safavi Dynasty*, 29.
54 Savory, *Iran under the Safavids*, 239–41.
55 For this argument, see Aubin, "L'avènement des Safavides," 115.
56 Anon., ed., *A Chronicle of the Carmelites*, 284–5, 308; Kutsia, "Ispahanis qartveli tarugebi."
57 According to Isfahani, *Khulasat al-siyar*, 40, the young king had no knowledge of the state of his realm.
58 Diary of Jan Smidt, 26 July–16 June 1628, in Dunlop, ed., *Bronnen*, 747; and IOR, E/3/13/1379, Isfahan to Company, 26 Sept. 1631, fol. 73b.

59 Olearius, *Vermehrte newe Beschreibung*, 341.
60 Anon., ed., *A Chronicle of the Carmelites*, 308.
61 Dunlop, ed., *Bronnen*, 359, Qazvin to Batavia, 30 June 1633; IOR, E/3/12/1314, Isfahan to Company, 30 Sept. 1630, fol. 148; Rota, *La vita e i tempi di Rostam Khan*, 82ff.
62 IOR, E/3/13/1317, Gombroon to Company, 6 Oct. 1630, fol. 151.
63 Dunlop, ed., *Bronnen*, 422, Isfahan to Heren XVII, 8 May 1633.
64 Exceptions were made, most notably in the case of the sons of one daughter of ʿAbbas, the wife of the shaykh al-islam of Isfahan, who had a very good relationship with her nephew. See Chardin, *Voyages*, 5:248.
65 Olearius, *Vermehrte newe Beschreibung*, 656–7.
66 Babaie et al., *Slaves of the Shah*, 31.
67 Isfahani, *Khulasat al-siyar*, 126; Turkaman and Muʾarrikh, *Zayl-i tarikh*, 90; Valah Qazvini Isfahani, *Khuld-i barin*, 104–8; Afandi Isfahani, *Riyaz al-ʿulama*, 2:52; Fasaʾi, *Farsnamah-i Nasiri*, 472.
68 Valah Qazvini Isfahani, *Khuld-i barin*, 6, 13–14, 201–3; Turkaman and Muʾarrikh, *Zayl-i tarikh*, 144–5; NA, VOC 1115, Isfahan to Heren XVII, 27 Oct. 1634, fols. 99–100; IOR, E/3/13/1317, Gombroon to Company, 6 Oct. 1630, fols. 151ff; Dunlop, ed., *Bronnen*, 372, Gamron to Heren XVII, 27 Mar. 1631; and ibid., 525, Gamron to Batavia, 15 Mar. 1635; Olearius, *Vermehrte newe Beschreibung*, 655–6.
69 Valah Qazvini Isfahani, *Khuld-i barin*, 53; Turkaman and Muʾarrikh, *Zayl-i tarikh*, 99–100; Dunlop, ed., *Bronnnen*, 422, Isfahan to Heren XVII, 8 May 1633.
70 Dunlop, ed., *Bronnnen*, 422, Isfahan to Heren XVII, 8 May 1633.
71 Tavernier, *Les six voyages*, 1:572–73.
72 Gabashvili, "The Undiladze Feudal House." The terror the massacres instilled in the ranks of the palace courtiers is vividly illustrated by the words of the Dutch, who told the story of how the shah, walking through the royal garden with some of his courtiers, pointed to tall trees and remarked that it was probably time to cut them down and replace them with new saplings. All those accompanying him at that point are said to have wished that they were 1,000 miles away from the court. See NA, VOC 1106, "Account of the circumstances, direction and management of commerce in Gujarat, Hindustan and Persia," 1633, unfol.
73 Tafrishi, *Tarikh-i Shah Safi*, 161.
74 For this purge, see Maeda, "Forced Migrations," 251–2; and Matthee, "Farhad Khan."
75 AN, VOC 1106, Isfahan to Heren XVII, 8 May 1633, unfol.; Valah Qazvini Isfahani, *Khuld-i barin*, 148–9.
76 Kutsia, "Ispahanis qartveli tarugebi."
77 Haneda, *Le Châh et les Qizilbâš*, 200–1.
78 Kirmani, *Sahifat al-irshad*, 66.

79 Babaie et al., *Slaves of the Shah*, 7–8.
80 Mar`ashi, *Tarikh-i Gilan*, 227; Turkaman, *Tarikh-i `alam-ara-yi `Abbasi*, 1093; Turkaman and Mu'arrikh, *Zayl-i tarikh*, 263–4.
81 Mar`ashi, *Tarikh-i Gilan*, 227; Isfahani, *Khulasat al-siyar*, 70.
82 Floor, "The Rise and Fall," 246.
83 Turkaman and Mu'arrikh, *Zayl-i tarikh*, 94–5.
84 Isfahani, *Khulasat al-siyar*, 189.
85 Tavernier, *Les six voyages*, 1:574.
86 Valah Qazvini Isfahani, *Khuld-i barin*, 171. Floor's dismissal of this point in Babayan's dissertation does not make sense. See Floor, "The Rise and Fall," 249.
87 Olearius, *Vermehrte newe Beschreibung*, 532.
88 Munajjim, *Tarikh-i `Abbasi*, 382.
89 NA, VOC 1158, Daghregister Winnincx, 11 Oct. 1645, fol. 204.
90 The sixteenth century had seen a series of strong chief counselors; Aqa Jahan and Ma`sum Beg Safavi, Najm-i Sani and Saru Shah Husayn Isfahani under Shah Isma`il come to mind. These had typically been able to display their strength at times when the shah was weak, as were Shah Isma`il after his terrible defeat at Chaldiran in 1514 and Shah Tahmasb in his early reign.
91 Valah Qazvini Isfahani, *Khuld-i barin*, 205; Turkaman and Mu'arrikh, *Zayl-i tarikh*, 296–7.
92 Turkaman and Mu'arrikh, *Zayl-i tarikh*, 207, 233–4, 281.
93 For this, see Matthee, *The Politics of Trade*, 132, 136–7, 148–55, 158–9.
94 NA, VOC 1146, Isfahan to Heren XVII, 6 Jan. 1644, fol. 977v.; ibid., Isfahan to Heren XVII, 13 July 1644, fol. 976v.; Tavernier, *Les six voyages*, 1:572–3.
95 NA, VOC 1144, Daghregister Walckaert, fol. 561; VOC 1141, Instruction for Van Tuynen and Walckaert, 20 Aug. 1642, fol. 547.
96 Mulla Kamal, *Tarikh-i Safaviyan*, 100.
97 NA, VOC 1144, Gamron to Batavia, 14 May 1643, fols. 488–94.
98 NA, Coll. Gel. de Jongh 157a, Gel. de Jongh to Gardenys, 17 Apr. 1643, unfol.; VOC 1144, Gamron to Batavia, 14 May 1643, 488–94. The Persian sources merely refer to "unbecoming behavior" as the reason why the shah had his sipahsalar executed. See Shamlu, *Qisas al-khaqani*, 1:282; and Vahid Qazvini, *Tarikh-i jahan-ara-yi `Abbasi*, 48.
99 NA, Coll. Gel. de Jongh 283, Daghregister Winnincx, 11 Oct. 1645, fol. 204.
100 Ibid.; Chardin, *Voyages*, 7: 308–9.
101 Different interpretations of the circumstances and motives of the murder are found in Babayan, *Mystics, Monarchs, and Messiahs*, 123–8, and Floor, "The Rise and Fall."
102 NA, VOC 1152, Daghregister Bastyncq, 30 Oct. 1645, fols. 246–9.
103 Mashizi, *Tarikh-i Safaviyah-i Kirman*, 211; Vaziri, *Tarikh-i Kirman*, 638; NA, VOC 1152, Daghregister Bastyncq, fol. 248. Da'ud Khan's

position was given to Safi Quli Beg. Jani Khan's two brothers, Ulugh Khan, who had continued to represent Jani Khan in Kirman, and Qara Khan, who was *sardar* (army commander) in Khurasan, were apprehended and lost their lives as well. The career of Jani Khan's son, `Abd al-Qasim Khan, on the other hand, did not suffer in the wake of his father's demise. He would be *mirab* (supervisor of irrigation) before becoming *divanbegi* (mayor) of Qazvin and later khan of Hamadan. See Mashizi, *Tarikh-i Safaviyah-i Kirman*, 373, 391; Chardin, *Voyages*, 9:361, 571–2; Sanson, "Nouvelles de Perse," 13 Aug. 1691, in Kroell, ed., *Nouvelles d'Ispahan*, 40; Sanson, *Estat présent*, 110–12.

104 AN, Coll. Gel. de Jongh 283, Isfahan to Gamron, 14 Oct. 1645, fol. 194.

105 Turkaman, *Tarikh-i `alam-ara-yi `Abbasi*, 2:1040–1, 1013; Shamlu, *Qisas al-khaqani*, 1:204. For another chronogram (*zaybandah-i afsar-i vizarat*) see Ma`sum, *Tarikh-i salatin-i Safaviyah*, 58.

106 AN, Coll. Gel. de Jongh 283, Isfahan to Gamron, 14 Oct. 1645, fol. 194.

107 The term is Abisaab's, in *Converting Persia*, 101. The argument is Babayan's, *Monarchs, Mystics, and Messiahs*, 409.

108 Valah Qazvini Isfahani, *Khuld-i barin*, 421.

109 Anon., ed., *A Chronicle of the Carmelites*, 1:353; Richard, ed., *Raphaël du Mans*, 2:208; Chardin, *Voyages*, 4:69; 9:516–17; Foster, ed., *The English Factories in India, 1646–50*, 43.

110 NA, VOC 1224, Gamron to Batavia, 3 Sept. 1657, fol. 316.

111 Matthee, *The Politics of Trade*, 157–8, 161–2.

112 Valah Qazvini Isfahani, *Khuld-i barin*, 141, 151; Vahid Qazvini, *Tarikh-i jahan-ara-yi `Abbasi*, 514, 745; AN, VOC 1379, Report Casembroot to Heren XVII, 25 Nov. 1682, fol. 2735r.

113 Foster, ed., *The English Factories in India, 1651–1654*, 63, 66; Speelman, *Journaal*, 70. Qazvini, *Fava'id-i Safaviyah*, 66, states that in 1650 `Abbas II regaled Allah Virdi Khan with gold-embroidered silk wovens inlaid with six rubies, and a gem-studded dagger.

114 Afandi, *Riyaz al-`ulama*, 2:52; Foster, *The English Factories in India, 1651–1654*, 271–2; Shamlu, *Qisas al-khaqani*, 1:XX–XXI; Khatunabadi, *Vaqa'i` al-sinnin*, 519.

115 Richard, ed., *Raphaël du Mans*, 2:268; Floor, "A Note on the Grand Vizier," 466–7; NA, VOC 1203, Gamron to Batavia, 21 Mar. 1653, fol. 798v; VOC 1201, Gamron to Batavia, 5 Apr. 1653, fol. 777v.

116 Turkaman and Mu'arrikh, *Zayl-i tarikh*, 281. See also Tavernier, *Les six voyages*, 1:616. On the qaychachi-bashi, see Minorsky, ed., *Tadhkirat al-Mulūk*, 65–6.

117 Tavernier, *Les six voyages*, 1:616.

118 AN, Coll. Gel. de Jongh, 283, Isfahan to Gamron, 4 Oct. 1646, fol. 437.

119 Tavernier, *Les six voyages*, 1:617. Muhammad ʿAli Beg died on 8 Dhu'l hijjah 1061/22 Nov. 1651. See Shamlu, "Qisas al-khaqani," fol. 91; and Speelman, *Journaal*, 54.
120 Speelman, *Journaal*, 181.
121 Ibid., 269–70.
122 NA, VOC 1203, Gamron to Batavia, 16 May 1654, fols. 807v–8r.
123 For the harsh winter and the inflation, see Nasrabadi, *Tazkirah-i Nasrabadi*, 603; and Afshar, "'Inqilab-i diram.'".
124 For this, see Matthee, *The Politics of Trade*, 160–3.
125 See Ansari, *Dastur al-moluk*, 80–1; and Savory, "The Office of Sipahsalar."
126 Chardin, *Voyages*, 5:312–13.
127 Chardin, *Voyages*, 7:137. Not surprisingly, no one came forward to buy these mansions, so that the stratagem came to nothing.
128 NA, VOC 1224, Gamron to Batavia, 1 Mar. 1658, fol. 800.
129 NA, VOC 1232, Gamron to Heren XVII, 25 Dec. 1660, fol. 368v.
130 See Röhrborn, *Provinzen und Zentralgewalt*, 122. Raphaël du Mans, whose description of Iran reflects the latter part of Shah ʿAbbas II's reign, claimed that crown lands (*mulk-i shahi*) comprised more land than that held in private hands (*arbabi*). See Richard, ed., *Raphaël du Mans*, 2:177.
131 Tavernier, *Les six voyages*, 1:617–20. See also Wilson, "History of the Mission," 699–700.
132 Ibid. The search for lead is also mentioned in Mashizi, *Tazkirah-i Safaviyah-i Kirman*, 273–4.
133 Chardin, *Voyages*, 7:283.
134 Tavernier, *Les six voyages*, 1:621–2.
135 Speelman, *Journaal*, 33, 70, 231.
136 Ibid., 54.
137 Coolhaas, ed., *Generale Missiven, 1639–1655*, 803.
138 This can be deduced from combining the information in Foster, ed., *The English Factories in India, 1655–1660*, 88, 127, with that in NA, VOC 1226, 1 Mar. 1658, fol. 806, that in the Generale Missiven, in Coolhaas, ed., *Generale Missiven, 1655–1674*, 276, and that in IOR, E/3/26/2868, Isfahan to Company, 25 Jan. 1660.
139 NA, VOC 1226, Gamron to Batavia, 1 Mar. 1658, fol. 806.
140 Vahid Qazvini, *Tarikh-i jahan-ara-yi ʿAbbasi*, 149.
141 Turkaman and Muʾarrikh, *Zayl-i tarikh*, 281; Coolhaas, ed., *Generale Missiven, 1639–55*, 803.
142 NA, VOC 1224, Gamron to Batavia, 1 Mar. 1658, fol. 800.
143 Wilson, "History of the Mission," 700. The embassy in question is the one sent in 1658 to congratulate the new Mughal ruler Aurangzeb on his accession to the throne. Muhammad Beg's nephew is unlikely to have been the head of this embassy, which was Budaq Beg, the son of commander of the musketeers (*tufangchi-aqasi*),

Qalandar Sultan, who upon his return was appointed tufangchi-aqasi himself.
144 NA, VOC 1224, Gamron to Batavia, 3 Sept. 1657, fol. 316.
145 The post of darughah of Isfahan was in hands of the son of the governor of Georgia following an agreement between Shah ʿAbbas I and the governor, who submitted to Isfahan in return for having his son fill the post in perpetuity. Rustam Khan had thus held the post for thirty years, but ordinarily a substitute held the actual position. Mir Qasim Beg was one such substitute, as is reflected in his official title, *naʾib-i darughah*. See Chardin, *Voyages*, 10:29.
146 Shamlu, "Qisas al-khaqani," fol. 132v.; Tavernier, *Les six voyages*, 1:626–30; Chardin, *Voyages*, 9:570.
147 For Farsadan, see Brosset, ed., *Histoire de la Géorgie*, 2:509–14, 541, 561–3; and Maeda, "Parsadan Gorgijanidze's Exile."
148 The story is told, in slightly different versions, by Vahid Qazvini, *Tarikh-i jahan-ara-ʿAbbasi*, 616–19; by Shamlu, "Qisas al-khaqani," fol. 133v; in NA, VOC 1224, Gamron to Batavia, 3 Sept. 1657, fol. 316v; also in VOC 1229, 30 Nov. 1657; by Thevenot, *The Travels*, 2:101–2; and in Chardin, *Voyages*, 9:567–70.
149 Tavernier, *Les six voyages*, 1:632.
150 The story of Mirza Hadi's dismissal and his replacement by the ghulam Babunah Beg is told by Tavernier, *Les six voyages*, 1:624–5; and in Shamlu, "Qisas al-khaqani," fol. 133. See also NA, VOC 1224, Gamron to Batavia, 9 Dec. 1656, fol. 272v; and ibid., Gamron to Batavia, 3 Sept. 1657, fol. 316v. The fall of the governor of Yerevan is narrated by Tavernier, *Les six voyages*, 1:622–3. For the names of the various governors, see Luft, "Iran unter Schāh ʿAbbās," 236–7, fn. 399.
151 NA, VOC 1236, Gamron to Heren XVII, 2 Sept. 1660, fols. 9ff; ibid., VOC 1232, Gamron to Heren XVII, 25 Dec. 1660, fols. 368v–9r.
152 IOR, E/3/26/2868, Isfahan to Company, 25 Jan. 1660.
153 Tavernier, *Les six voyages*, 1:632.
154 See Moreen, "The Downfall," 76.
155 Vahid Qazvini, *Tarikh-i jahan-ara-yi ʿAbbasi*, 719, 773; Shamlu, "Qisas al-khaqani," fol. 143.
156 NA, VOC 1234, Gamron to Heren XVII, 5 May 1662, fol. 207r.
157 NA, VOC 1239, Gamron to Heren XVII, 31 Dec. 1662, fol. 1209r, and VOC 1241, Gamron to Heren XVII, 15 Feb. 1664, fol. 576r.
158 Chardin, *Voyages*: 9:345–6, and NA, VOC 1307, Gamron to Batavia, 12 Dec. 1675, fol. 639v.
159 This date confirms Rasul Jaʿfariyan's conclusion that Mirza Mahdi was appointed grand vizier in 1071, not 1072, which he based on clues found in a poem. See Jaʿfariyan, *Naqsh-i khandan-i Karaki*, 398.
160 Vahid Qazvini, *Tarikh-i jahan-ara-yi ʿAbbasi*, 307, 517; Valah Qazvini Isfahani, *Khuld-i barin*, 654–55; Nasrabadi, *Tazkirah-i Nasrabadi*, 25.
161 Chardin, *Voyages*, 9:481; Abisaab, *Converting Persia*, 105.

162 Findiriski, *Tuhfat al-'alam*, 124–5.
163 NA, VOC 1240, Gamron to Batavia, 12 Apr. 1662, fol. 415.
164 NA, VOC 1264, Gamron to Batavia, 9 Apr. 1667, fol. 665.
165 Shamlu, "Qisas al-khaqani," fol. 146v; AN, VOC 1248, Gamron to Batavia, 31 May 1664, fols. 346–7.
166 NA, VOC, 1242, Gamron to Batavia, 30 Aug. 1662, fols. 1417v–18r.
167 Khatunabadi, *Vaqa'i' al-sinnin*, 525.

CHAPTER 3

1 Chardin, *Voyages*, 9:401ff. See also Kaempfer, *Am Hofe des persischen Grosskönigs*, 49–50.
2 Hanway, *An Historical Account*, 1:21.
3 Lockhart, *The Fall of the Safavi Dynasty*, 31.
4 Busse, *Untersuchungen*, 75–6.
5 Chardin, *Voyages*, 5:340.
6 Tavernier, *Les six voyages*, 1:538, 554; Kaempfer, *Am Hofe des persischen Grosskönigs*, 234.
7 Chardin, *Voyages*, 9:552–3. For more on quruq, see Matthee, "A Sugar Banquet," 206–8. Local officials also engaged in quruq: see Thevenot, *Suite de voyage*, 4:418–19. The practice would only begin to die out under the Qajar dynasty in the 1870s. See Curzon, *Persia and the Persian Question*, 1:404; and Wills, *In the Land of the Lion and the Sun*, 370.
8 D'Alessandri, "Narrative," 216.
9 Pacifique de Provins, *Relation d'un voyage*, 393.
10 Vahid Qavini, *Tarikh-i jahan-ara*, 557; Fasa'i, *Farsnamah-i Nasiri*, 480, 484–5.
11 Tavernier, *Les six voyages*, 1:526.
12 NA, VOC 1373, Gamron to Heren XVII, 29 May 1683, fol. 862v.
13 IOR, E/3/26/2868, Isfahan to Company, 25 Jan. 1660, unfol.
14 NA, VOC 1379, Report Casembroot to Heren XVII, 25 Nov. 1682, fols. 2731v–2r.
15 Richard, ed., *Raphaël du Mans*, 2:297.
16 Chardin, *Voyages*, 9:515. Chardin, *Voyages*, 6:46, calls the sadr the "grand pontife," similar to the mufti of the Turks.
17 Kaempfer, *Am Hofe des persischen Grosskönigs*, 98, 104; Sanson, Isfahan, 12 Sept. 1691, in Kroell, ed., *Nouvelles d'Ispahan*, 46.
18 Kaempfer, *Am Hofe des persischen Grosskönigs*, 66, 106–7; NA, VOC 1373, Gameron to Batavia, 19 Apr. 1683, fol. 883v.
19 For the Indian case, see Chandra, *Parties and Politics*, 199–220.
20 Chardin, *Voyages*, 9:424.
21 Krusinski, *The History of the Late Revolutions*, 1:79–80.
22 Brosset, ed., *Histoire de Géorgie*, 2/i, 561.

23 Retrospective information, without details, by Krusinki, *The History of the Late Revolutions*, 1:77–8.
24 Minorsky, ed., *Tadhkirat al-mulūk*, 56; Ansari, *Dastur al-Moluk*, 176; and Nasiri, *Titles and Emoluments*, 17. The Augustinian missionary P. Diego di Sant'Anna gives the fantastic number of 1,400 royal concubines for the period of Shah `Abbas I. See Alonso, "Due lettere," 160.
25 Chardin, *Voyages*, 8:82.
26 Della Valle, *Viaggi*, 2:86.
27 Turkaman and Mu'arrikh, *Zayl-i tarikh*, 207; and Minorsky, ed., *Tadhkirat al-mulūk*, 56.
28 Chardin, *Voyages*, 5:237–50, 9:405.
29 Chardin, *Voyages*, 6:24, 40–2; Kaempfer, *Am Hofe des persischen Grosskönigs*, 230; Tavernier, *Les six voyages*, 1:705.
30 Sanson, *Estat présent*, 146.
31 Ibid., 144–7. See also Chardin, *Voyages*, 5:430.
32 Olearius, *Vermehrte newe Beschreibung*, 671; Chardin, *Voyages*, 5:378; Kaempfer, *Am Hofe des persischen Grosskönigs*, 107.
33 Richard, ed., *Raphaël du Mans*, 2:14.
34 Chardin, *Voyages*, 5:377–9; Tavernier, *Les six voyages*, 1:648; Richard, ed., *Raphaël du Mans*, 2:14; Thevenot, *Relation d'un voyage*, 2:102; Kaempfer, *Am Hofe des persischen Grosskönigs*, 107.
35 Ansari, *Dastur al-Moluk*, 179–80; Chardin, *Voyages*, 5:349–50, 378–9; Thevenot, *Relation d'un voyage*, 2:102; Kaempfer, *Am Hofe des persischen Grosskönigs*, 107.
36 Minorsky, ed., *Tadhkirat al-Mulūk*, 96.
37 Chardin, *Voyages*, 7:421.
38 Kaempfer, *Am Hofe des persischen Grosskönigs*, 234–5.
39 Sanson, Isfahan 8 Apr. 1691, in Kroell, ed., *Nouvelles d'Ispahan*, 30.
40 Aubin, *L'ambassade de Gregório Pereira Fidalgo*, 65; NA, VOC 1897, Gamron to Batavia, 30 Nov. 1716, fol. 41.
41 Tavernier, *Les six voyages*, 1:647.
42 Kaempfer, *Am Hofe des persischen Grosskönigs*, 81 ff.
43 Sanson, *Estat présent*, 27–9.
44 Chardin, *Voyages*, 5:240; Kaempfer, *Am Hofe des persischen Grosskönigs*, 234–5; Sanson, *Estat présent*, 144–6.
45 Kaempfer, *Am Hofe des persischen Grosskönigs*, 82.
46 Shaykh `Ali Khan remained in office until his death in 1689. The period of his tenure is erroneously given as 1668–86 by Busse, *Untersuchungen*; as ca. 1673–90 by Braun, "Das Erbe Schah Abbas I," 189; as 1669–88, by Röhrborn, "Regierung und Verwaltung," 27; and as 1673–90 by Roemer, "The Safavid Period," 306.
47 Khatunabadi, *Vaqa'i` al-sinnin*, 530–1. The Zanganah were known for their bravery. See Nasrabadi, *Tazkirah-i Nasrabadi*, 36, where it is said that the manliness, courage, and loyalty of the Zanganah need no mentioning.

48 See Isfahani, *Khulasat al-siyar,* 264, 286; Turkaman and Mu'arrikh, *Zayl-i tarikh,* 227–8, 246; and Mardukh Kurdistani, *Tarikh-i Mardukh,* 101. He must have been amir-akhur-bashi until at least 1637, for Von Mandelso, *Beschrijvingh,* 2–3, mentioned being the guest of the shah's "stable master" ʿAli Bali Beg in that year. For more information, see Matthee, "Administrative Stability." For the difference between the amir-akhur-bashi "jilaw" and the amir-akhur-bashi "sahra," see Minorsky, ed., *Tadhkirat al-Mulūk,* 52, 87, 120.
49 Shamlu, "Qisas al-khaqani," fol. 154; Vahid Qazvini, *Tarikh-i jahanara,* 331, 569; Luft, "Iran unter Schah ʿAbbas II," 110; K. Röhrborn, *Provinzen und Zentralgewalt,* 9; Chardin, *Voyages,* 10:126; and Fasa'i, *Farsnamah-i Nasiri,* 480. For the Zanganah, see Kunke, *Nomadenstämme,* 74, 76, 85, 143, 154.
50 Chardin, *Voyages,* 10:126; Shamlu, "Qisas al-khaqani," fol. 153; Luft, "Iran unter Schah ʿAbbas II," 103, 110.
51 Chardin, *Voyages,* 10:126; NA, VOC 1266, Gamron to Heren XVII, 20 July 1669, fol. 952v.
52 Chardin, *Voyages,* 9:571, 10:2–4; IOR, G/36/105, Isfahan to Surat, 14 Aug. 1668, fol. 36; Kaempfer, *Am Hofe des persischen Grosskönigs,* 59; AME, vol. 349, Du Mans, Isfahan to Baron, Aleppo, 23 Apr. 1668, fols. 161–4. Information about the occurrence of a famine in the Kirman area may be found in Mashizi, *Tadhkirah-i Safaviyah-i Kirman,* 317, 352–3.
53 Chardin, *Voyages,* 10:65ff. The most complete discussion of the Uzbek wars during this period is found in Braun, "Das Erbe Schah ʿAbbas I," 56–65.
54 NA, VOC 1266, Gamron to Heren XVII, 28 Feb. 1669, fols. 916–17v, 929v. This tells the story of how Cossacks raided the town of Farahabad in Mazandaran disguised as merchants. Chardin, *Voyages,* 10:135–8, recounts the same event.
55 NA, VOC 1270, Gamron to Heren XVII, 24 Apr. 1670, fol. 892v; Chardin, *Voyages,* 9:331, 10:86; and Kaempfer, *Am Hofe des persischen Grosskönigs,* 65–6.
56 NA, VOC 1288, Gamron to Batavia, 31 Jan. 1672, fol. 887r; VOC 1360, Memorandum Casembroot to Van den Heuvel, 4 Mar. 1679, fol. 1906v. In the latter source, it is said that the vizier of Isfahan charged with the payment of duties did not receive a penny for his service.
57 NA, VOC 1266, Gamron to Heren XVII, 20 July 1669, fol. 952v.
58 NA, VOC 1270, Gamron to Heren XVII, 24 Apr. 1670, fol. 892v; VOC 1284, Gamron to Batavia, 7 Mar. 1671, fols. 2329v–30r; Chardin, *Voyages,* 8:194; and Ghougassian, *The Emergence of the Armenian Diocese,* 41, 108–9.
59 NA, VOC 1304, Gamron to Heren XVII, 24 May 1674, fol. 451v.
60 Kaempfer, *Am Hofe des persischen Grosskönigs,* 88–9.
61 NA, VOC 1284, Gamron to Batavia, 26 Aug. 1670, fol. 2278r.

62 The nazir returned to Iran in late 1672. He was granted permission to resume his old post but died while waiting to make his appearance before the shah. His nephew Najaf Quli Beg was thereupon installed as permanent nazir. See NA, VOC 1285, Gamron to Batavia, 5 Dec. 1672, fol. 5r.

63 NA, VOC 1288, Gamron to Heren XVII, 16 May 1672, fols. 924r, 927r, 928r; VOC 1295, Gamron to Batavia, 19 Sept. 1672, fol. 393v; Chardin, *Voyages*, 3:29. No source gives a precise date for the demotion, but since Chardin and the Dutch note that Shaykh 'Ali Khan's reinstatement took place on 26 June 1673 and that the vizier's discomfiture had lasted fourteen months, the event must have taken place in April 1672.

64 Chardin, *Voyages*, 3:29; Mashizi, *Tadhkirah-i Safaviyah-i Kirman*, 387; and Ange de Saint Joseph, *Souvenirs de la Perse safavide*, 182–3, who claimed that the grand vizier had been out of office for eight months and preferred to remain unemployed rather than follow the shah's command to shave his beard and drink wine. Mashizi claimed that courtiers had had to implore the shah to spare Shaykh 'Ali Khan's life and that Sulayman had eventually put his vizier under house arrest. A more colorful English account insisted that the shah had in one of his intoxicated moods ordered the blinding of one of his own brothers. The queen-mother had intervened on behalf of the victim, but this only provoked a greater fury in the shah, who drew his sword and wounded her. Denied medical treatment at her son's orders, she reportedly committed suicide by jumping from the top of the palace. Shaykh 'Ali Khan's disapproval of this royal cruelty apparently provoked the shah's displeasure and thus caused his dismissal. See IOR, G/36/106, Gombroon to Surat, 29 Apr. 1672, fol. 96; ibid., Gombroon to Surat, 27 Nov. 1672, fol. 38. In reality Sulayman's mother survived her son, for upon his death in 1694 she made an endowment of a copy of the Koran on his tomb. See Mudarrisi Tabataba'i, *Turbat-i pakan*, 1:170.

65 Carré, *Le courrier du Roi*, 461–2.

66 NA, VOC 1285, Isfahan to Shiraz, 11, 16, and 30 Aug. 1673, fols. 416r–17v; ibid., Shiraz to Batavia, 13 Sept. 1673, fol. 412v; VOC 1307, Gamron to Batavia, 12 Dec. 1675, fol. 639v.

67 See Chardin, *Voyages*, 3:116, 121–7; and NA, VOC 1285, Shiraz to Batavia, 13 Sept. 1673, fol. 411v, for various examples of humiliation, such as the shah forcing his vizier to become drunk, throwing wine in his face, and, most denigrating, making him shave his beard.

68 Kaempfer, *Am Hofe des persischen Grosskönigs*, 88–90.

69 NA, VOC 1373, Gamron to Batavia, 28 Aug. 1683, fol. 1003v; and Kaempfer, *Am Hofe des persischen Grosskönigs*, 73.

70 The persistence of an urban bias against people from rural backgrounds is reflected in the words of Fasa'i, *Farsnamah-i Nasiri*, 488, when he notes of Shaykh 'Ali Khan's son Husayn 'Ali Khan that,

although he was a country dweller and of tribal descent (*mard-i sahra-gard-i ilati*), he was well versed in the official sciences and especially in *fiqh* (the study of Islamic law).

71 Kaempfer, *Am Hofe des persischen Grosskönigs*, 88.
72 See Bastani-Parizi, *Siyasat va iqtisad*, 146.
73 Baladouni and Makepeace, eds., *Armenians*, 67. For a similar opinion, see Chardin, *Voyages*, 3:119; and NA, VOC 1183, Daghregister Bastyncq, 23 Oct.–13 Dec. 1645, fols. 246–9. The ban was revoked after Shaykh ʿAli Khan's temporary dismissal. See NA, VOC 1288, Gamron to Batavia, 19 Sept. 1672, fol. 393v.
74 ARSI, Gall. 97ⁱⁱ, letter Claude Ignace Mercier, S.J., Isfahan, 28 Feb. 1672, fol. 350.
75 Kaempfer, *Am Hofe des persischen Grosskönigs*, 90; Gemelli Careri, *Giro del Mondo*, 2:128.
76 Sanson, Isfahan, 12 Sept. 1691, in Kroell, ed., *Nouvelles d'Ispahan*, 49.
77 Kaempfer, *Am Hofe des persischen Grosskönigs*, 204.
78 Ibid., 165; and Chardin, *Voyages*, 9:206.
79 Chardin, *Voyages*, 9:370–1; Brosset, ed., *Histoire de la Géorgie*, 2/ii, 9; Lang, *The Last Years*, 89–90. For the wider context, see Matthee, "Gorgin Khan."
80 Gemelli Careri, *Giro del Mondo*, 2:29ff.
81 Chardin, *Voyages*, 3:30.
82 Minorsky, ed., *Tadhkirat al-Mulūk*, 25, 45, 123–4.
83 NA, VOC 1364, Gamron to Batavia, 7 Sept. 1682, fol. 390v.
84 NA, VOC 1355, Gamron to Batavia, 21 Aug. 1681, fol. 426v; and VOC 1379, Gamron to Batavia, 6 Mar. 1682, fols. 2664v–5r. According to the latter document, the vizier accused the mustawfi of having accepted 6,000 tumans in protection money from the Portuguese.
85 NA, VOC 1416, Gamron (ship "Blauwe Hulck") to Batavia, 20 Oct. 1684, fols. 1609v–10r.
86 IOR, G/36/108, Gombroon to Surat, 23 Feb. 1680, fols. 57–8; NA, VOC 1343, Gamron to Heren XVII, 25 Mar. 1680, fol. 599r; ibid., Gamron to Batavia, 13 Apr. 1680, fol. 509v.
87 NA, VOC 1355, Gamron to Batavia, 5 Mar. 1681, fol. 400r.
88 Kaempfer, *Am Hofe des persischen Grosskönigs*, 81ff.
89 NA, VOC 1373, Gamron to Batavia, 19 Apr. 1683, fol. 883v.
90 NA, VOC 1364, Gamron to Batavia, 14 June 1682, fol. 365v; Brosset, ed., *Histoire de Géorgie*, 2/i, 560. Saru Khan's father, Murtaza Quli Khan, had been qurchibashi as well as sipahsalar under Shah ʿAbbas II from 1645–6 until 1663, when he had been killed on the shah's orders. A member of the Qajar tribe, he had held a variety of other posts, including the governorship of Hamadan, which he held in tuyul until the area became khassah land.
91 Kaempfer, *Am Hofe des persischen Grosskönigs*, 85, 89.
92 NA, VOC 1360, Memorandum Casembroot to Van den Heuvel, 4 Mar. 1679, fol. 1908v.

93 Chardin, *Voyages*, 9:331; NA, VOC 1307, Gamron to Heren XVII, 12 Dec. 1675, fol. 639v.
94 Chardin, *Voyages*, 3:119.
95 Mashizi, *Tadhkirah-i Safaviyah-i Kirman*, 23, 420–3, 487, 500, 512–13, 521.
96 NA, VOC 1379, Report Casembroot to Heren XVII, 25 Nov. 1682, fol. 2734r–v.
97 Sanson, *Estat présent*, 109.
98 Sefatgol, "Awqaf under the Afsharids," 213.
99 Shah Sulayman had apparently decided on this project, for which the French engineer M. Genet was engaged. Genet had, according to Sanson, already taken all the necessary measures to drill through the mountains when he was obstructed by Shaykh `Ali Khan, who convinced the shah that the water of the Karun River was bad and would spoil that of the Zayandah Rud. See Sanson, *Estat présent*, 78–9.
100 Chardin, *Voyages*, 10:126; Sanson, letter from Isfahan, 13 Aug. 1691, in Kroell, ed., *Nouvelles d'Ispahan*, 36; idem, "Relation de la mort de Schah Abbas," in ibid., 70; Hedges, *The Diary*, 1:216; NA, VOC 1360, Memorandum Casembroot to Van den Heuvel, 4 Mar. 1679, fol. 1908v; Khatunabadi, *Vaqa'i` al-sinnin*, 548. Shah Quli Khan ruled in Kirmanshah from at least 1675 to 1691.
101 Chardin, *Voyages*, 2:202. This unspecified son must have lost his position, however, for Chardin, *Voyages*, 8:452, tells the story of the execution in 1673 of Khusraw Khan, governor of Gilan and Mazandaran and tufangchi-aqasi.
102 NA, VOC 1360, Memorandum Casembroot to Van den Heuvel, 4 Mar. 1679, fol. 1908v.
103 Kaempfer, *Am Hofe des persischen Grosskönigs*, 89.
104 Turkaman and Mu'arrikh, *Zayl-i tarikh*, 246; Kaempfer, *Am Hofe des persischen Grosskönigs*, 89; Nasrabadi, *Tazkirah-i Nasrabadi*, 36–7.
105 Shamlu, "Qisas al-khaqani," fols. 52 and 73. Vahid Qazvini, *Tarikh-i jahan-ara*, 495, mentions Dust `Ali Khan's appointment as khan of Bust in 1061/1651. Also see NA, VOC 1360, Memorandum Casembroot to Van den Heuvel, 4 Mar. 1679, fol. 1908v.
106 NA, VOC 1360, Memorandum Casembroot to Van den Heuvel, 4 Mar. 1679, fol. 1908v.
107 Kaempfer, *Am Hofe des persischen Grosskönigs*, 89.
108 Sanson, Isfahan, 8 Apr. 1691, in Kroell, ed., *Nouvelles d'Ispahan*, 29, mentioned how this nephew came to kiss Shah Sulayman's feet at the New Year ceremony of 1691, "for the post of army commander, for the government of Tabriz which is attached to the former post, and for that of head of the infantry, which ranks fourth in the empire."
109 The amir-shikar-bashi generally also supervised the Armenians of Isfahan and relayed their requests to the court. `Abbas `Ali Beg, whose name we learn from Mashizi, *Tazkirah-i Safaviyah-i Kirman*, 485, was said

to be sympathetic to the Christians, unlike his father. He died in 1682. See NA, VOC 1379, Gamron to Heren XVII, 25 Nov. 1682, fol. 2735r.
110 Fasa'i, *Farsnamah-i Nasiri*, 488, mentions 1086/1675–6 as the year in which Husayn `Ali Khan became governor of Bihbahan and Kuh-i Giluyah. See also Khatunabadi, *Vaqa'i` al-sinnin*, 547. Kaempfer, *Am Hofe des persischen Grosskönigs*, 89, mentions two deceased sons of Shaykh `Ali Khan, one as governor (*hakim*) of Qazvin, the other as ruler of Kirmanshah.
111 Mashizi, *Tazkirah-i Safaviyah-i Kirman*, 442, 433; Muhammad Mardukh, *Tarikh-i Mardukh*, 110.
112 NA, VOC 1360, Memorandum Casembroot to Van den Heuvel, 4 Mar. 1679, fol. 1988r.
113 AME, vol. 353, Sanson to Raimond Marcye, 4 Oct. 1689, fols. 115–18.
114 Khatunabadi, *Vaqa'i` al-sinnin*, 547, claims that he died on 11 Muharram 1101 (Wednesday, 25 Oct. 1689) at 4 o'clock in the afternoon. Sanson reported in a letter he wrote on 4 October that the grand vizier was dying. See AME, vol. 353, Sanson to Raimond Marcye, 4 Oct. 1689, fols. 115–18.
115 Brosset, ed., *Histoire de la Géorgie*, 2/ii, 561.
116 This was not unique to Iran. Upon Mazarin's death in 1661 Louis XIV declared his intention of ruling without a minister of state. See Burke, *The Fabrication of Louis XIV*, 49.
117 Tahir Vahid was a son of Mirza Muhammad, who had been *vaqa'i`-nivis* under Shah `Abbas I. See Nasrabadi, *Tazkirah-i Nasrabadi*, 115.
118 Sanson, Isfahan, 8 Apr. 1691, in Kroell, ed., *Nouvelles d'Ispahan*, 30.
119 NA, VOC 1501, Daghregister Van Leene, 8 and 13 Aug. 1690, fols. 632b, 648; see also Aubin, ed., *L'ambassade de Gregório Pereira Fidalgo*, 30–1, 88–9; and Gemelli Careri, *Giro del mondo*, 2:127. Also see Brosset, ed., *Histoire de la Géorgie*, 2/i:566.
120 Gaudereau, "Relation de la mort de Schah Soliman," in Kroell, ed., *Nouvelles d'Ispahan*, 59; NA, VOC 1501, Daghregister Van Leene, fols. 716v–17.
121 Mashizi, *Tadhkirah-i Safaviyah-i Kirman*, 395.
122 See NA, VOC 1364, Gamron to Batavia, 14 June 1682, fol. 365v; Brosset, ed., *Histoire de la Géorgie*, 2/i, 560.
123 Sanson, *Estat présent*, 30.
124 Minorsky, ed. *Tadhkirat al-Mulūk*, 46.
125 Aubin, ed., *L'ambassade de Gregório Pereira Fidalgo*, 59.
126 Haneda, *Le Chāh et les Qizilbaš*, 197.
127 Sanson, "Nouvelles d'Ispahan," 13 Aug. 1691, in Kroell, ed., *Nouvelles d'Ispahan*, 36.
128 The story of Saru Khan's downfall in 1691 is told in Sanson, *Estat présent*, 112–35; and in idem, "Nouvelles d'Ispahan," 13 Aug. 1691, in Kroell, ed., *Nouvelles d'Ispahan*, 35ff; other versions of the same letter are found in AME, vol. 351, fols. 317–30, 335–8; and vol. 353, fols. 176–80.

129 Sanson, *Voyage*, 30.
130 NA, VOC 1501, Daghregister Van Leene, fol. 531; Aubin, ed., *L'ambassade de Gregório Pereira Fidalgo*, 30–1.

CHAPTER 4

1 See Matthee, "Merchants in Safavid Iran."
2 Membré, *Mission to the Lord Sophy*, 14.
3 Efendy, *Narrative of Travels*, 2:169. Barter continued to be common in Iran into the twentieth century. G. Tate, visiting Iran in the early twentieth century, writes: "Previous to our mission of 1903 a large proportion of the people [of Sistan] had never even handled silver money. In 1899 I was compelled to send to the village of Chilling in order to change a few rupees of Indian currency into Persian coin." See Tate, *The Frontiers of Baluchistan*, 227.
4 PF, SC, Georgia I, Notizie di Mengrelia, 17 Feb. 1687, fols. 368–81.
5 Tournefort, *Relation d'un voyage*, 2:301.
6 Chardin, *Voyages*, 5:414–15.
7 For the tas'ir system, see Lambton, *Continuity and Change*, 191; and Floor, *A Fiscal History*, 53, 189.
8 Martinez, "Regional Mint Output," 137, estimates that about 35 percent of the total mint output in the Il-Khanid state was in gold.
9 Smith and Plunkett, "Gold Money in Mongol Iran."
10 See Matthee, "Between Venice and Surat"; and Chelebi, *Travels*, 44.
11 The term qazbaki (qazbegi) seems to go back to Ghazi Beg, who ruled Shirvan in 1501–2. See Shirazi "Navidi," *Takmilat al-akhbar*, 135.
12 Olearius, *Vermehrte newe Beschreibung*, 561–2.
13 Krusinski, *The History of the Late Revolutions*, 1:89. For a more extensive discussion of the Safavid copper coinage, see Floor, *The Economy of Safavid Persia*, 66–70.
14 Seigniorage around 1675 amounted to roughly 2 percent. See Chardin, *Voyages*, 5:398.
15 Simmons, "The Evolution of Persia's Monetary System," 91.
16 See the discussion in Schultz, "Mamluk Money," 38–41. For the differences between the Mughals, the Safavids, and the Ottomans, see Subrahmanyam, "Precious Metal Flows," 215.
17 See Matthee, "Between Venice and Surat."
18 Iran did have copper mines but the quality of the copper was low and it had to be mixed with foreign copper to be useable. There were some silver mines too, but, given their location in remote areas, their exploitation was not cost-effective. The country therefore imported almost all its copper and silver. See Floor and Clawson, "Safavid Iran's Search," 253.

19 The robbery in 1673 of a rich caravan near Qandahar, involving the theft of the enormous (and no doubt exaggerated) sum of at least 150,000 tumans, suggests that the volume carried overland was considerable indeed. See NA, VOC 1291, Gamron to Heren XVII, 21 Mar. 1673, fol. 558r; VOC 1304, Gamron to Heren XVII, 24 May 1674, fol. 437r; Chardin, *Voyages*, 2:232–3; Pelsaert, *De geschriften*, 279.
20 Richard, ed., *Raphaël du Mans*, 2:149.
21 Floor, *The Economy of Safavid Persia*, 197.
22 This does not mean that merchandise just flowed through Iran without leaving a trace or that the country did not consume any of the imports: many of the spices and virtually all of the enormous amount of imported sugar remained in the country. It is clear, however, that Iran's role in all this was proportionally much larger than its consumption levels warranted. For more on this, see Matthee, "The Safavid Economy."
23 The following statement by H. J. Whigham from the turn of the twentieth century illustrates the existence of regional variations long after the Safavids: "it is impossible to prove that prices have risen as a whole in Persia. Silver prices have, of course, been doubled in the last twenty years owing to the depreciation of silver. Land, and food, and labour has become intrinsically dearer in Teheran, where there is a steady increase in the foreign element, and it is here, perhaps, that observations are most frequently made. Yet throughout Western Persia the price of grain is lower to-day than it has ever been in the memory of living man as far as I can discover...." See Whigham, *The Persian Problem*, 359.
24 Government debasement would ordinarily generate inflation because it increased the nominal value of the bullion and the nominal money supply. For a historical example, see Sussman, "Debasements," 52. See Pamuk, *A Monetary History*, 124–5, for the argument that, in spite of severe monetary problems, long-term inflation remained low in the Ottoman Empire as well.
25 Aubin, "L'avènement des Safavides," 62–3. Budaq Munshi Qazvini, *Javahir al-akhbar*, 140, describes the shah as a ruler in whose treasury no one ever saw more than 100 tumans in gold.
26 See Rumlu, *Ahsan al-tavarikh*, 635. This may of course have been as much a matter of lack of willingness as of inability.
27 Aubin, "L'avènement des Safavides," 21.
28 Relazione della Persia fatta al Senato Veneto Anno MDLXXX, in BA, cod. 46-IX-23, fol. 330v; and Teodoro Balbi, in Berchet, ed., *La repubblica di Venezia*, 279.
29 Monshi, *History of Shah 'Abbas*, 1: 406–7.
30 Ferrier, "An English View," 192–3.
31 Dunlop, ed., *Bronnen*, 199, Isfahan to Heren XVII, 17 Aug. 1626.

32 Don Juan, *Don Juan of Persia*, 221–2; the amount is surely wildly exaggerated, as is often the case with Don Juan's figures.
33 Della Valle, *Delle conditioni*, 40; Ferrier, "Anglo-Persian Relations," 330.
34 Brosset, ed., *Collection*, 2:26–7.
35 See Matthee, *The Politics of Trade*.
36 Pamuk, *A Monetary History*, 135–9; Şahillioğlu, "The Role of International Monetary and Metal Movements," 285.
37 Pamuk, *A Monetary History*, 135–9.
38 See, for example, IOR, E/3/6/700, enclosure letter Pettus to Company, 27 Sept. 1618, unfol.
39 Compare thirteenth-century Europe, where political expansion partly explains the contraction of mints. See Spufford, *Money and Its Use*, 193.
40 Coolhaas, ed., *Generale Missiven, 1639–1655*, 34. According to Turkaman and Mu'arrikh, *Zayl-i tarikh*, 210, Qandahar brought in 50,000 tumans in annual revenue.
41 NA, VOC 1162, Gamron to Batavia, 16 Apr. 1647, fols. 317–20.
42 This is contrary to the suggestion of Simmons, who assumes that, generally, Safavid Iran allowed the free import and export of bullion and that only the export of foreign coins was subject to a fee. He attributes this freedom in part to the absence of a need to curtail exports in a situation where Gresham's Law did not operate, because in Iran the monetary value of coins generally exceeded their bullion value. See Simmons, "The Evolution of Persia's Monetary System," 167–9.
43 NA, VOC 908, Uitgaande Brieven, 21 Oct. 1682.
44 Minorsky, ed., *Tadhkirat al-Mulūk*, 128.
45 Supple, *Commercial Crisis*, 194.
46 The idea that Tahmasb issued an export ban in or before 1572, voiced by Floor, *The Economy of Safavid Persia*, 77, rests on a misunderstanding which derives from an incomplete translation of a statement by D'Alessandri. This observer, claiming that the importation of precious metals was forbidden "into the aforementioned country," referred to Iran. This means that the Ottomans banned money exports to Iran. The English translation obscures this and makes it sound as if Iran banned money exports by saying that "the exportation of metals is forbidden." See Berchet, ed., *La repubblica di Venezia*, 180; and D'Alessandri, "Narrative," 226.
47 Quoted in Ferrier, "An English View," 193.
48 Letter Pettus to the EIC, in Sainsbury, ed., *A Calendar of State Papers, 1617–1621*, 199.
49 Meilink-Roelofsz, "The Earliest Relations," 35–6.
50 NA, VOC 1150, Gamron to Batavia, 10 Mar. 1644, fol. 136.
51 Speelman, *Journaal*, 235.
52 NA, VOC 1178, Gamron to Batavia, 15 May 1650, fol. 809v.
53 Gaastra, "The Export of Precious Metals," appendix 4. See also NA, VOC 317, Copie Brieven Heren XVII, 4 Oct. 1647, fol. 83, where

a different figure for the export for 1646–7 is given, i.e. fl. 980,000, as opposed to fl. 1,246,605 in Gaastra's list; and VOC 1167, 18 Jan. 1649, where the fl. 715,606 listed by Gaastra for 1647 is presented as the sum sent in 1648.

54 NA, VOC 882, Uitgaande Brieven, 21 Sept. 1658, fol. 482.
55 NA, VOC 886, Uitgaande Brieven, 18 Sept. 1662, fol. 474. Gaastra, "The Export of Precious Metals," 474, has a list with estimated bullion export figures from Iran.
56 NA, VOC 1226, Gamron to Heren XVII, 16 Sept. 1658. fol. 800. See also ibid., Surat to Batavia, 16 Feb. 1658, fol. 864v.
57 NA, VOC 1233, fol. 95.
58 NA, VOC 1239, Gamron to Heren XVII, 31 Dec. 1662, fol. 1208v. In 1663, the export duty was raised to 4.5 stuivers or two-fifths of a mahmudi. See NA, VOC 1239, fol. 1670.
59 Floor, *The Economy of Safavid Persia*, 80.
60 Foster, ed., *The English Factories in India, 1646–1650*, 123.
61 NA, VOC 1170, Gamron to Batavia, 15 May 1648, fol. 738. This latter figure closely matches Stephen Album's estimate of this development. See Album, "Iranian Silver Denominational Names," 1:20.
62 Foster, ed., *The English Factories in India, 1646–1650*, 123.
63 NA, VOC 1170, Gamron to Batavia, 15 May 1648, fol. 738.
64 NA, VOC 1185, Gamron to Batavia, 18 May 1651, fol. 546.
65 In 1638–9 the interest rate was 20 percent in Bandar `Abbas. This rate remained virtually unchanged in the next thirty years. The lowest recorded rate in this period was 12 percent, in 1660. This compares with interest rates at Surat that dropped from 12 to 6 percent in the same period, and a 6 percent rate in Holland in 1660. See Dunlop, ed., *Bronnen*, 642; Coolhaas, ed., *Generale Missiven, 1639–1655*, 32, 143; and NA, Coll. Gel. de Jongh, 141, 1641, unfol. Tavernier, *Les six voyages*, 1:471, claims that Banyan money lenders in Isfahan charged up to 18 percent.
66 Zak`aria of Agulis, *The Journal*, 66. These panj shahi coins may have already been struck before 1662. See Hinz, "The Value of the Toman," 94. For the "small" and "large" `abbasis, see also Avery, Fragner, and Simmons, "`Abbasi."
67 Kuteliia, *Gruziia i sefevidskii Iran*, 36.
68 Zak`aria of Agulis, *The Journal*, 78.
69 Simmons, "The Evolution of Persia's Monetary System," 38–46, 164.
70 See Pamuk, *A Monetary History*, 131ff.
71 For the English recoinage of the late seventeenth century, see Li, *The Great Recoinage of 1696 to 1699*. The difference between Iran and early modern European governments is that the latter tended not to resort to semi-secret schemes. Monetary manipulation often occurred in an atmosphere of open discussion over alternative options. The public

debate over the advisability of devaluing the currency that preceded the English recoinage is a good example of this.
72 Relazione della Persia fatta al Senato Veneto Anno MDLXXX, in BA, cod. 46-IX-23, fol. 330v; Balbi, in Berchet, ed., *La repubblica di Venezia*, 279; and Nasrabadi, *Tazkirah-i Nasrabadi*, 421.
73 Nasrabadi, *Tazkirah-i Nasrabadi*, 421.
74 The meaning of this line is ambiguous. It can mean that people became heavy with money that was adulterated with heavy copper, in the way a fish is heavy with scales. The fish can also be a reference to the fish that, according to a prevalent cosmological belief, carried the earth on its back. The first meaning, a pun on the double meaning of the word *fals*, "money" or "fish scale," is indicated in the article by Iraj Afshar on this poem, "'Inqilab-i diram'." The reference to the function of the fish in the second meaning recurs later in the poem.
75 This poem is included in Afshar, "'Inqilab-i diram'," 273.
76 Mustawfi Bafqi, *Jami`-i mufidi*, 3:205.
77 Deyell, "The Development of Akbar's Currency System," 33–8.
78 See Matthee, "Mint Consolidation."
79 Pamuk, "In the Absence of Domestic Currency," 347.
80 Attman, *Russian and Polish Markets*, 192.
81 IOR, EIC, E/3/37/4258, Swally to Company, 22 Jan. 1677; Von Glahn, *Fountain of Fortune*, 228.
82 Arasaratnam, *Merchants, Companies, and Commerce*, 195.
83 IOR, EIC, E/3/37/4258, Swally to Company, 22 Jan. 1677, unfol.
84 Ferrier, "British-Persian Relations," 204.
85 Cipolla, *Money, Prices, and Civilization*, 9.
86 For the mint of Huwayza in the Safavid period, see Matthee, "The Safavid Mint of Huwayza."
87 See, for example, NA, VOC 1285, Gamron to Heren XVII, 6 May 1673, fol. 385r.
88 NA, VOC 1304, Gamron to Batavia, 4 Sept. 1674, fol. 519v; VOC 1294, Gamron to Heren XVII, 5 Oct. 1674, fol. 32v.
89 See Album, "Iranian Silver Denominational Names," 20.
90 Şahillioğlu, "The Role of International Monetary and Metal Movements," 287.
91 Haidar, "Precious Metal Flows," 340, 353. The mint of Bombay was reportedly out of money in 1676. See Fawcett, ed., *The English Factories in India*, 160–1.
92 Chardin, *Voyages*, 9:571, 10:2–4; NA, VOC 1266, Surat to Heren XVII, 8 Nov. 1668, fols. 155, 941.
93 Chardin, *Voyages*, 10:6. The severe winter and the price increases of 1672 are mentioned in the margin of a drawing by Mu`in Musavvir in the collection of the Boston Museum of Fine Arts. The drawing and the translation of the marginal text are reproduced in Ettinghausen, "Stylistic Tendencies." According to this source, snow fell eighteen

times in Isfahan between mid-Sha`ban and 20 Shavval 1082, January to February 1672. The harsh weather in this period is confirmed in an EIC report from Isfahan, which mentioned great quantities of snow and many deaths between Isfahan and Shiraz. See IOR, G/36/106, Isfahan to Gombroon, 27 Jan. 1672, fol. 90. These prices acquire some meaning against the salaries of ordinary people. In 1682 the Dutch paid their local personnel, gardeners, doormen, and messengers, monthly salaries of between 60 and 70 shahis. See NA, VOC 1364, Memorandum Van den Heuvel to Burghgraaff, 28 Mar. 1682, fol. 393r.

94 Chardin, *Voyages*, 291–2.
95 NA, VOC 1364, Memorandum Casembroot to Van den Heuvel, 14 June 1682, fol. 368r.
96 Thevenot, *Relation d'un voyage*, vol. 2, *Suite du voyage*, 169; Tavernier, *Les six voyages*, 1:133–4; NA, VOC 1355, Gamron to Heren XVII, 21 Aug. 1681, fol. 426v; VOC 1373, Gamron to Heren XVII, 29 May 1683, fol. 862v.
97 Kaempfer, *Am Hofe des persischen Grosskönigs*, 71–2.
98 For the role of money in the fall of the Ming dynasty, see Von Glahn, *Fountain of Fortune*, 207ff.
99 Kaempfer, *Am Hofe des persischen Grosskönigs*, 71–2.
100 NA, VOC 1291, Gamron to Heren XVII, 21 Mar. 1674, fol. 558r; and VOC 1304, Gamron to Batavia, 24 May 1674, fol. 437; ibid., Gamron to Batavia, 4 Sept. 1674, fol. 519v; VOC 1343, "Overview of trade conditions in Persia," 13 Feb. 1680, fol. 600.
101 Stephen Album, personal communication to the author, 19 Dec. 1990.
102 Chardin, *Voyages*, 5:414. See also Kaempfer, *Am Hofe des persischen Grosskönigs*, 124. If this is true, royal income must have been substantial, for the growing panoply at the court, the shah's energetic building program, and the frequent hunting parties all required staggering amounts of revenue. One battue, held in 1683, is reported to have cost 200,000 tumans (and anywhere between 500 and 800 human lives). See Kaempfer, *Am Hofe des persischen Grosskönigs*, 73; NA, VOC 1373, Gamron to Batavia, 28 Aug. 1683, fol. 1003v.
103 Chardin, *Voyages*, 8:194–5.
104 NA, VOC 1285, Gamron to Heren XVII, 17 Jan. 1673, fol. 1r.
105 NA, VOC 1332, Gamron to Batavia, 1 June 1679, fol. 917v; ibid., Gamron to Isfahan, 1 June 1679, fol. 921v; VOC 1349, Gamron to Batavia, 25 Nov. 1679, fol. 1712r; VOC 1343, Basra to Heren XVII, 8 Aug. 1680, fol. 619r. For details about the weight issue, see Matthee, "Mint Consolidation."
106 For further details, including tables, see Matthee, "Mint Consolidation," and idem, "The Safavid Mint of Huwayza."
107 NA, VOC 1323, Gamron to Batavia, 12 Aug. 1677, fol. 675r.
108 NA, VOC 1315, Gamron to Batavia, 5 June 1677, fol. 733r.

109 NA, VOC 1355, Gamron to Batavia, 5 Mar. 1681, fol. 401r; ibid., Gamron to Batavia, 26 July 1681, fol. 431v; ibid., Gamron to Heren XVII, 21 Aug. 1681, fol. 426v.
110 NA, VOC 1364, Memorandum Casembroot to Van den Heuvel, 14 June 1682, fol. 368r.
111 NA, VOC 908, Uitgaande Brieven, 21 Oct. 1682.
112 NA, VOC Generale Missiven, 30 Jan. 1666, fol. 205; Anon., ed., *A Chronicle of the Carmelites*, 442.
113 There is no good explanation for the court's demand for a 9½ dang 'abbasi. Presumably, the request was for 'abbasis that were equivalent to the "small" ones struck under Shah 'Abbas II, which equaled 120 troy grains or ca. 7.39 grams. A weight of 9½ dang, however, only yields 114 grains or ca. 7.29 grams. (The dang is a Persian weight equaling 0.768 grams. Thanks to Stephen Album for pointing out the discrepancy to me.)
114 NA, VOC 1315, Gamron to Batavia, 5 June 1677, fol. 733r.
115 NA, VOC 1270, Gamron to Heren XVII, 24 Apr. 1670, fol. 892v.
116 NA, VOC 1274, Gamron to Heren XVII, 22 Apr. 1671, fol. 735r; ibid., Gamron to Heren XVII, 10 Sept. 1671, fol. 746r; VOC 1284, Gamron to Batavia, 15 May 1671, fols. 2353v–4r.
117 NA, VOC 1284, Gamron to Batavia, 15 May 1671, fols. 2353v–4r.
118 IOR, EIC, G/36/106, Gombroon to Surat, 13 Nov. 1671, fol. 51.
119 NA, VOC 1285, Gamron to Heren XVII, 17 Jan. 1673, fol. 1r.
120 NA, VOC 1373, Missive Van den Heuvel, 31 July, fol. 901v; also in VOC 1388, fol. 2337r–v.
121 NA, VOC 1373, Missive Van den Heuvel, 31 July 1683, fol. 901v; also in VOC 1388, fols. 2337r–8r.
122 NA, VOC 1406, Gamron to Batavia, 28 Feb. 1684, fol. 1182v.
123 IOR, G/36/109, 2d fasc., Isfahan to Surat, 13 Nov. 1684, fols. 74–5.
124 NA, VOC 1383, Gamron to Batavia, 28 Aug. 1684, fol. 720; the same report is found in VOC 1406, fols. 1245r–7r.
125 IOR, G/36/109, 2nd fasc., Isfahan to Surat, 13 Nov. 1684, fols. 75–6.
126 Kaempfer, *Briefe, 1683–1715*, 205–7.
127 NA, VOC 1416, Gamron (ship "Blauwe Hulck") to Batavia, 20 Oct. 1684, fol. 1619v. Due to the occupation of Qishm and the warlike state with Iran, the Dutch factor at this time did not reside in Bandar 'Abbas but was aboard this ship, which was anchored off the Persian Gulf coast.
128 NA, VOC 1398, Gamron (ship "Blauwe Hulck") to Surat, 4 Dec. 1684, fol. 493v. According to the French cleric Sanson, the new coins were minted at various mints around the country: Isfahan, Iravan (Yerevan), Dadiyan, Tabriz, Ardabil, Hamadan, and Huwayza. Dadiyan and Hamadan, however, are not known as mints in this period. See Sanson, *Estat présent Voyage*, 159–60.
129 NA, VOC 1416, Gamron to Batavia, 9 Apr. 1685, fols. 1676v–7r.

130 NA, VOC 1416, Gamron to Batavia, 20 Oct.1684, fols. 1619v–20r.
131 NA, VOC 1398, Isfahan to Batavia, 30 Sept. 1685, fol. 693v.
132 NA, VOC 1416, Gamron to Batavia, 9 Apr. 1685, fol. 1677r.
133 The text mentions 13½ and 14 mahmudis, but in light of the well-attested fluctuation of the riyal between 6 and 8 mahmudis, shahis, each worth half a mahmudi, must have been meant here. Instead of substituting shahis, I have chosen to halve the amounts.
134 NA, VOC 1398, Isfahan to Batavia, 30 Sept. 1685, fol. 640r.
135 Ibid., fols. 639v–40v. The date of this report, September 1685, contradicts the timing given by Kaempfer, *Am Hofe des persischen Grosskönigs*, 71, who asserted that all money, with the exception of mahmudis from Huwayza, was declared invalid in November of that year.
136 This is, after all, what happened in England too, after the recoinage of the 1690s: money continued to be carried out and newly minted coin would disappear as soon as it came out of the mint. See Li, *The Great Recoinage*, 143–50.
137 Kasravi, *Tarikh-i pansad salah-i Khuzistan*, 87; Shubbar, *Tarikh al-Musha`sha`yin*, 155; Ranjbar, *Musha`sha`iyan*, 328.
138 IOR, G/36/109, 2nd fasc., Gombroon to Surat, 9 Dec. 1684, fols. 72–3.
139 Hedges, *The Diary*, 1:216.
140 Khatunabadi, *Vaqa`ih al-sinnin*, 537, mentioning the master of the mint, Saru Khan Sahandlu, as the one who had ordered the currency "reform."
141 Anon., ed., *A Chronicle of the Carmelites*, 1:434, letter Fr. Elias, 16 Jan. 1688; based on CA, S.N.R., vol. 1, fol. 493.
142 For gold and its role in Safavid monetary matters, see Matthee, "Between Venice and Surat."
143 NA, VOC 1430, Isfahan to Batavia, 5 July 1686, fols. 1537v–40r.
144 Bushev, "Puteshestvic Mokhammada Khossein-Khan," 143–4.
145 NA, VOC 1434, Gamron to Batavia, 2 June 1688, fol. 555r.
146 NA, VOC 1425, Gamron to Batavia, 21 Aug. 1687, fol. 441r; and Coolhaas, ed., *Generale Missiven, 1686–1697*, 371.
147 NA, VOC 1644, "Twee placcaten wegens het stempelen der persiaensche abasis en het billioen verklaren der valsche ditos," Colombo, 7 Dec. 1688 and 27 Jan. 1691. See also Codrington, *Ceylon Coins and Currency*, 113, 164.
148 NA, VOC 1476, Gamron to Isfahan, 12 Aug. 1690, fols. 473r–4r.
149 See Matthee, "The East India Company Trade."
150 See NA, VOC 1416, Gamron to Batavia, 16 July 1685, fol. 1726r; and Coolhaas, ed., *Generale Missiven, 1686–1697*, 2–3.
151 NA, VOC 1559, Gamron to Batavia, 31 Oct. 1693, fols. 804–7.
152 NA, VOC 1476, 20 Sept. 1690, fols. 479–83; Sanson, *Estat présent*, 13–14.
153 Sanson, Isfahan, 8 Apr. 1691, in Kroell, ed., *Nouvelles d'Ispahan*, 30.
154 AME, vol. 351, Sanson, letter 29 Sept. 1691, fol. 319.

155 NA, VOC 1501, Notulen van Leene, 31 Mar. 1691, fol. 520.
156 NA, VOC 1493, Gamron to Batavia, 15 Mar. 1692, fol. 320v; VOC 1501, Generale Missiven, 11 Dec. 1692, fol. 245.
157 NA, VOC 1493, Gamron to Batavia, 13 Oct. 1691, fols. 281v–2v.
158 IOR, E//3/48/5760, Gombroon to Company, 10 Mar. 1691; VOC 1501, Generale Missiven, 11 Dec. 1692, fol. 245r.
159 NA, VOC 1507, Gamron to Heren XVII, 2 Aug. 1693, fol. 469r.
160 Coolhaas, ed., *Generale Missiven, 1686–1697*, 705.
161 Lockyer, *An Account of the Trade in India*, 241.
162 Ferrier, "British-Persian Relations," 317; NA, VOC 1843, 6 Sept. 1712, fols. 92–3, with text of farman; VOC 1947, 1 Nov. 1719, fol. 280; VOC 1875, 19 Aug. 1721, fols. 169–74.

CHAPTER 5

1 Haneda, *Le Chāh et les Qizilbaš*, 129–33, 136–7, 141; Floor, *Safavid Government Institutions*, 128ff.
2 Poullet, *Nouvelles relations*, 2:145; Richard, ed., *Raphaël du Mans*, 2:118, 286–7.
3 Trausch, *Anpassung und Abbilding*, 90–8.
4 Bacqué-Grammont, "Les Ottomans et les Safavides," 13.
5 "Della guerra tra Persiani e Turchi," in BA, Cod. 46-X-X, fol. 374r–v.
6 NA, VOC 1178, Gamron to Batavia, 16 Oct. 1649, fol. 628v.
7 Murphey, *Ottoman Warfare*, 36–7. The latter numbers are given in Giovanni Maria Malvezzi to King Ferdinand, 22 July 1548, in Džaja and Weiss, eds., *Austro-Turcica*, 267–71.
8 Bacqué-Grammont, *Les Ottomans, les Safavides*, 146, 157, 165.
9 Tucci, "Una relazione," 154, 156.
10 Vaziri, *Tarikh-i Kirman*, 2:598; Dickson, "Shah Tahmasb and the Uzbeks," 129.
11 Bacqué-Grammont, *Les Ottomans, les Safavids*, 172.
12 Ágoston, *Guns for the Sultan*, 194. The Safavids did benefit from the defection of Prince Bayazid and his army to Iran in 1559, which entailed the inclusion of Ottoman gunners in Shah Tahmasb's army.
13 Poullet, *Nouvelles relations*, 2:146–7.
14 McNeill, *The Pursuit of Power*, 95. For Russia's dependence on waterways, see Smith, "Muscovite Logistics."
15 Tucci, "Relazione," 154, 156.
16 Bacqué-Grammont, *Les Ottomans, les Safavides*, 168.
17 Parker, *The Military Revolution*, 125–6.
18 Kaempfer, *Am Hofe des persischen Grosskönigs*, 94. See also De Bruyn, *Reizen over Moskovie*, 157. The persistence of prejudice against the army formations fitted for the use of firearms is reflected in an observation by the French officer and military adviser Trezel in 1808, who noted

that the infantry in Iran had been "despised until today." See Archives Militaires, Vincennes, Paris, #1673, Report Alphonse Camille Trézel à Gardanne, 27 April 1808, fol. 310.
19 Savory, "The Office of Sipahsalar," 612. For a different view, see Floor, *Safavid Government Institutions*, 18.
20 Savory, "The Office of Sipahsalar," 603.
21 This number is given by Fryer, *A New Account*, 2:290. Lang, "Georgians and the Fall," 525, thinks this number is too high.
22 Floor, *Safavid Government Institutions*, 162.
23 Speelman, *Journaal*, 149ff; Sanson, *Estat present*, 26, 30, who does not list the sipahsalar among the top court officials, probably because the position had not yet been reinstated at the time he wrote; Bushev, *Posol'stvo Artemiia Volynskogo*, 181–2; and Floor, *Safavid Government Institutions*, 164.
24 Vahid Qazvini, *Tarikh-i jahan-ara-yi ʿAbbasi*, 121.
25 Ra'is al-Sadat, "Tasarruf-i Qandahar," 452.
26 Luft, "Iran unter Schah ʿAbbās II," 33.
27 Nasiri, *Dastur-i shahriyaran*, 246.
28 Haneda, *Le Chāh et les Qizilbaš*, 206ff. Herbert, *The Travels*, 123, refers to their loyalty, arguing that this is why they were placed in positions of authority, especially in the confrontation with the Turks.
29 Kirmani, *Sahifat al-irshad*, 14–15.
30 Babinger, *Hans Derschwamm's Tagebuch*, 31.
31 Don Juan, *Don Juan of Persia*, 221.
32 Aubin, "L'avènement des Safavides," 39, 62, 63.
33 Shamlu, "Qisas al-khaqani," 94; D'Alessandri, "Narrative," 218.
34 "Relazione della Persia fatta al Senato Veneto Anno MDLXXX," in BA, Cod. 46-IX-23, fol. 330v; and Balbi, in Berchet, ed., *La repubblica di Venezia*, 279.
35 De Chinon, *Relations nouvelles*, 72.
36 Turkaman, *Tarikh-i ʿAlam-ara-yi ʿAbbasi*, 228.
37 Shamlu, "Qisas al-khaqani," 107. Floor, *Safavid Government Institutions*, 204, erroneously situates this payment in the reign of Ismaʿil II.
38 Turkaman, *Tarikh-i ʿalam-ara-yi ʿAbbasi*, 1:468.
39 Chardin, *Voyages*, 3:315.
40 Della Valle, *Viaggi*, 2:301.
41 Della Valle, *Delle conditioni*, 40.
42 Arakel, trans. in Brosset, ed., *Collection*, 2:26–7.
43 Tucci, "Le emissioni," 310.
44 IOR, E3/13/1379, Isfahan to London, 26 Sept. 1631, fol. 73; and Dunlop, ed., *Bronnen*, 391–2, Isfahan to Batavia, 3 Nov. 1632.
45 Turkaman and Muʿarrikh, *Zayl-i tarikh*, 233–4, 281.
46 For this, see Matthee, *The Politics of Trade*, 132, 136–7, 148–55, 158–9.
47 Riazul Islam, *Indo-Persian Relations*, 103–4; Floor, "The Rise and Fall," 253.
48 Tavernier, *Les six voyages*, 1:592.

49 Feynes, *Voyage*, 63. This number is probably exaggerated, especially given the much smaller number of troops his son Imam Quli Khan is said to have commanded.
50 Tavernier, *Les six voyages*, 1:594; Chardin, *Voyages*, 5:253. Silva y Figueroa, *Comentarios*, 1:358–9, claims 10,000 as the number of troops that Imam Quli Khan was obliged to field for the shah.
51 NA, VOC 1242, Gamron to Heren XVII, 20 June 1664, fol. 1091.
52 See, in particular, Babaie et al., *Slaves of the Shah*.
53 Turkaman and Mu'arrikh, *Zayl-i tarikh*, 263–4.
54 NA, Coll. Gel. de Jongh 283, Daghregister Winnincx, 11 Oct. 1645, fol. 204.
55 Dunlop, ed., *Bronnen*, 527.
56 Colenbrander, ed., *Daghregister Batavia...anno 1636*, 116.
57 Falsafi, "Sar-guzasht," 297; Floor, "The Rise and Fall," 257.
58 For a Persian translation of the accord, see Mazandarani, ed., *Majmu'ah-i 'ahdnamah'ha*, 3:81–2. An English translation of the accord's preamble appears in Edmonds, *Kurds, Turks and Arabs*, 125–7. For a good discussion of the terms of the treaty, see Braun, "Das Erbe Schah 'Abbas I," 22, 37–41.
59 Holloway, *Relation of the Late Seidge*, 11–12, 23.
60 Della Valle, *Viaggi*, 2:98. For the Ottoman proposal, see the letter Sultan Murad wrote to Shah 'Abbas, in Nava'i, ed., *Shah 'Abbas*, 3:53–61. The religious forces, by contrast, are said to have played a role in the decision to reopen hostilities with the Ottomans: see Gouvea, *Relaçam*, fol. 62.
61 Diary of Jan Smidt, 26 July 1628–14 July 1630, in Dunlop, ed., *Bronnen*, 748.
62 Chardin, *Voyages*, 5:250–1.
63 For the continuation of Ottoman-Safavid diplomatic relations in the eighteenth century, see Tucker, "The Peace Negotiations of 1736."
64 NA, VOC 1152, Daghregister Basra, fol. 281.
65 For details, see Matthee, "Between Arabs, Turks and Persians."
66 Braun, "Das Erbe Schah 'Abbas I," 42. The information in this study is mostly based on the *'Abbasnamah*, more recently edited in a critical edition as *Tarikh-i jahan-ara-yi 'Abbasi*. See also Sabitiyan, ed., *Asnad va namah'ha-yi tarikhi*. 342–4; and 'Abidini, "Munasibat-i siyasi."
67 When he fell ill, he was cured by the shah's own physician. See Valah Qazvini Isfahani, *Khuld-i barin*, 585–7; Vahid Qazvini, *Tarikh-i jahan-ara-yi 'Abbasi*, 621.
68 See Riyahi, *Sifaratnamah'ha-yi Iran*, 43–4. Diminished Iranian diplomatic activity following the cessation of Safavid-Ottoman hostilities is also reflected in the leveling off of contact with Russia in this period. See Matthee, "Anti-Ottoman Alliances."
69 Kütükoğlu, *Osmanlı-Iran siyasi münasebetleri (1578–1590)*; and idem, *Osmanlı-Iran siyasi münasebetleri (1578–1612)*, only go up to 1612. In

addition, a few letters written to Safavid rulers by Sultans Murad IV, Mehmet IV, and Ahmad II, appear in Nava'i, ed., *Asnad va mukatibat, 1038–1105*, 39–42, 203–5, 250–7, and 271–7.
70 Nasiri, *Dastur-i shahriyaran*. A few letters sent to the Porte by Shah Sulayman and his grand vizier, Muhammad Tahir Qazvini, in the early 1690s appear in Nava'i, ed., *Asnad va mukatibat, 1038–1105*, 278, 280–1.
71 Mantran, "L'état ottoman au XVIIe siècle," 237.
72 Luft, "Iran unter Schah `Abbās II," 120–2.
73 As reported by the Ottoman historian Na`im, in Braun, "Das Erbe Schah `Abbas I," 34; and `Abidini, "Munasibat-i siyasi," 66.
74 Della Valle, *Viaggi*, 2:195–6. For more details on the Safavids and Iraq, see Matthee, "Iraq-i `Arab."
75 Valah Qazvini Isfahani, *Khuld-i barin*, 509–10; Tahir Vahid, *Tarikh-i jahan-ara-yi `Abbasi*, 536–7; and Qazvini, *Fava'id-i Safaviyah*, 67.
76 Gommans, *Mughal Warfare*, 108–9, with a map indicating the Mughal radius of action.
77 Tahir Vahid, *Tarikh-i jahan-ara-yi `Abbasi*, 286 ff.; and Islam, *Indo-Persian Relations*, 102–4.
78 Saksena, *The History of Shahjahan*, 219.
79 NA, VOC 1137, Gamron to Heren XVII, 20 Feb. 1642, fol. 237v; and Coll. Gel. de Jongh 157a, Isfahan to Aleppo, 13 Sept. 1642, unfol.
80 Mirot, "Le séjour du Père Bernard," 230–1, fn.
81 Krusinski, *The History of the Late Revolutions*, 1:144. For references and descriptions, see Razaviyan, "Naqsh-i Qandahar," 5–6.
82 NA, Coll. Gel. de Jongh 283, Daghregister Winnincx, 12 Oct. 1645, fol. 204.
83 NA, Coll. Gel. de Jongh 283, Isfahan to Gamron, 13 July 1646, fol. 403; Chardin, *Voyages*, 10:44, who claims that Jamshid Khan collected 4,000 soldiers in Isfahan.
84 Mashizi, *Tazkirah-i Safaviyah*, 230–1; Inayat Khan, *The Shah Jahan Nama*, 412.
85 Shamlu, "Qisas al-khaqani," 327–8; Valah Qazvini Isfahani, *Khuld-i barin*, 455; Tahir Vahid, *Tarikh-i jahan-ara-yi `Abbasi*, 457; Mulla Kamal, *Tarikh-i Mulla Kamal*, 106–7.
86 Riazul Islam, ed., *A Calendar of Documents*, 1:297–8; and idem, *Indo-Persian Relations*, 107–10.
87 Andersen and Iversen, *Orientalische Reise-Beschreibungen*, 154. The number of 50,000 appears in NA, VOC 1178, Gamron to Batavia, 16 Oct. 1649, fol. 628v. The Mughal Inayat Khan, *The Shah Jahan Nama*, 232, at this time insisted, on the basis of reports by people "well acquainted with the statistics of Iran," that the Safavid state supported "a regular standing army of 30,000 cavalry, comprised of 7,000 cuirass horsemen, 3,000 pages, and 10,000 matchlockmen the special service of the Shah, with the remainder being maintained by the nobles."

88 Andersen and Iversen, *Orientalische Reise-Beschreibungen*, 155–6; Saksena, *The History of Shahjahan*, 225. Other sources give different dates in February for the Safavid capture of the city: see Burton, *The Bukharans*, 258.
89 Foster, ed., *The English Factories in India, 1646–50*, 266–7, Isfahan to Company, 26 July 1649; and 270, Isfahan to Company, 21 Nov. 1649.
90 De Chinon, *Relations nouvelles*, 73; Speelman, *Journaal*, 211–12.
91 Sanson, *Estat présent*, 162.
92 NA, VOC 1178, Gamron to Batavia, 16 Oct. 1649, fol. 627v.
93 Nicoll, *Shah Jahan*, 225.
94 Mashizi, *Tazkirah-i Safaviyah-i Kirman*, 230–1; Manucci, *Storia di Mogor*, 1:38; Speelman, *Journaal*, 249.
95 NA, VOC 1215, Gamron to Isfahan, 11 Dec. 1655, fol. 810.
96 Alam Khan, "The Indian Response to Firearms," 27, fn. 98.
97 Raverty, *Notes on Afghánistan*, 22–8.
98 Sanson, *Estat présent*, 162.
99 Anon., ed., *A Chronicle of the Carmelites*, 354.
100 Krusinski, *The History of the Late Revolutions*, 1:143–4.
101 Valah Qazvini Isfahani, *Khuld-i barin*, 531, 585. Manucci, *Storia do Mogor*, 1:40, in the 1640s called Iran "very well governed, having no rebellions or treasons, neither robbers nor highwaymen on the roads...."
102 Chinon, *Relations nouvelles*, 69; AME, 350, De la Maze, Isfahan to Baron, Aleppo, 7 Nov. 1667, fols. 259–62; and Sanson, *Estat présent*, 162.
103 Chardin, *Voyages*, 10:30–2.
104 Mashizi, *Tazkirah-i Safaviyah-i Kirman*, 308, 322; IOR, E/3/29/3185, Surat to Company, 25 Sept. 1666, unfol.
105 Sarkar, "The Asian Balance of Power," 203. See also IOR, E/3/29/3213, Surat to Company, 26 Mar. 1667, unfol.; and Bernier, *Travels in the Mogul Empire*, 185.
106 Chardin, *Voyages*, 10:46–7, claims on the basis of reports by "very intelligent" persons that Aurangzeb called a halt to these preparations at the behest of a sister who persuaded him that there was little glory in trying to recover Qandahar, a difficult enterprise that had twice been attempted in vain by his father.
107 NA, VOC 1264, Gamron to Batavia, 9 Apr. 1667, fol. 665. `Ali Quli Khan was to die in the summer of the same year.
108 Chardin, *Voyages*, 10:58–66; AME, 350, Mercier, Isfahan to Baron, Aleppo, 20 July 1668, fol. 295; Burton, *The Bukharans*, 285–6.
109 NA, VOC 1265, 8 July 1667, fol. 955v; VOC 1255, 6 Aug. 1667, fols. 904–5; VOC 1266, Gamron to Heren XVII, 28 Feb. 1669, fol. 930; Chardin, *Voyages*, 10:67–8; Zak`aria of Agulis, *The Journal*, 84.
110 Chardin, *Voyages*, 10:80; Caskel, *Beduinenstämme*, 418.
111 Longrigg, *Four Centuries*, 116.
112 Ibid., fn. 4.

113 Richard, ed., *Raphaël du Mans*, 2:266.
114 IOR, G/36/105, Gombroon to Surat, 26 Nov. 1668, fol. 41.
115 Chardin, *Voyages*, 5:498.
116 Chardin, *Voyages*, 3:315.
117 Kaempfer, *Am Hofe des persischen Grosskönigs*, 96.
118 Chardin, *Voyages*, 5:317, 325–6, 427.
119 AME, 350, letter De la Maze, 7 Nov. 1667, 259–62.
120 NA, VOC 1355, Gamron to Batavia, 5 Mar. 1681, fol. 399v.
121 Ezov, ed., *Snosheniia Petro Velikogo*, 39; Richard, ed., *Raphaël du Mans*, 2:287.
122 Zak`aria of Agulis, *The Journal*, 115–16, 144.
123 Della Valle, *Delle conditioni*, 35–6.
124 Della Valle, *Viaggi*, 1:827.
125 Chardin, *Voyages*, 2:138; 4:428; 8:496–7; [Vachet], "Journal d'un voyage," fols. 383–4; and De la Maze, "Journal du voyage," fol. 406.
126 Quoted in Rota, *Under Two Lions*, 45.
127 Zevakin, "Persidskii vopros," 143.
128 Poumarède, *Pour en finir*, 289.
129 Gaudereau, "Relation d'un mission…pour la réunion des Arméniens à l'Eglise catholique" (Paris, 1692), 2, quoted in Bonnerot, *La Perse*, 18.
130 NA, VOC 1291, Gamron to Heren XVII, 27 Apr. 1674, fol. 596v.
131 Richard, ed., *Raphaël du Mans*, 1:97.
132 Carré, *Le courrier du Roi*, 1063.
133 Chardin, *Voyages*, 9:232–3, 243; and Kaempfer, *Am Hofe des persischen Grosskönigs*, 75–6.
134 BN, Collection Clairambault 297, Lettre de Nointel à Colbert sur ce qui se passe du costé de Perse; Aleppo, 10 Aug. 1674, fols. 141–8.
135 Chardin, *Voyages*, 9:337; Baibourtian, *International Trade*, 166.
136 Gemelli Careri, *Giro del mondo*, 2:128.
137 The story was repeated by Father Krusinski and in modern times taken up by Lockhart and others as an illustration of Shah Sulayman's spinelessness. See Krusinski, *The History of the Late Revolutions*, 1:40; and Lockhart, *The Fall of the Safavi Dynasty*, 30.
138 NA, VOC 1279, Gamron to Heren XVII, 4 Mar. 1672, fol. 904v. Provisions for this campaign in the form of cereals and lead were sent from, among other places, Kirman, Sistan, and Bandar `Abbas. See Mashizi, *Tarikh-i Safaviyah-i Kirman*, 374–5, 383–7, 393.
139 Carré, *Le courrier du Roi*, 280–1.
140 Chardin, letter to Cosimo III, Grand Duke of Tuscany, Tabriz, 15 May 1673, in Kroell, ed., "Douze lettres," 318–19.
141 Zak`aria of Agulis, *The Journal*, 117–18.
142 See Eszer, "Zu einigen bisher ungeloesten Problemen," 272. That Shaykh `Ali Khan's pacifism was not unconditional either is suggested by the report that he was the leader of the court faction that favored a confrontational policy vis-à-vis the Russians, following an incident

of Iranian merchants being harassed and plundered by the forces of the rebel Sten'ka Razin in Russian territory in 1673. See Baibourtian, *International Trade*, 166.
143 For this, see Matthee, "Administrative Stability."
144 Kaempfer, *Am Hofe des persischen Grosskönigs*, 106.
145 IOR, G/36/105, Isfahan to Surat, 14 Aug. 1668, fol. 68; NA, VOC 1268, Gamron to Batavia, 26 May 1668, fol. 1369v; VOC 1270, Gamron to Batavia, 18 June 1669, fol. 967; more details in Matthee, "Between Arabs, Turks and Iranians."
146 Disappointed, Husayn Basha moved to Bandar Rig, where he embarked for India, never to return to either Iran or Basra. NA, VOC 1270, Gamron to Batavia, 18 June 1669, fol. 968; Anon., ed., *A Chronicle of the Carmelites*, 1153, letter 31 Aug. 1669; Richard, ed., *Raphaël du Mans*, 1:218, letter Du Mans, Isfahan 3 Apr. 1668; ibid., 224, letter 23 Apr. 1668.
147 Gemelli Careri, *Giro del mondo*, 2:128.
148 See Matthee, "Administrative Stability," and the sources quoted therein.
149 Meserve, *Empires of Islam*, 235–6.
150 Chardin, *Voyages*, 9:337.
151 Chardin, *Voyages*, 3:203.
152 Zedginidze, "Iz istorii pol'sko-russkikh diplomaticheskikh otnoshenii," 20–1; and Kaempfer, letter to Johan Bergenhielm, Shamakhi, 12 and 22 Apr. 1684, in *Briefe, 1683–1715*, 168–9.
153 Letters of 5 Aug. 1683 to Sebastian Knab and of 26 Sept. 1683 to Sulayman, in HHSt, Persien 1.
154 Casanatense Library, Rome, Miscella 608/43. For further information on this issue, see Matthee, "Iran's Ottoman Diplomacy."
155 Letter Knab to Leopold I, 29 April 1685, in Eszer, "Zu einigen bisher ungeloesten Problemen," 270.
156 Richard, ed., *Raphaël du Mans*, 1:296. See also Levi-Weiss, "Le relazioni fra Venezia e la Turchia," 72.
157 Chowaniec, "Z dziejów polityki Jana III," 156.
158 Richard, ed., *Raphaël du Mans*, 1:121–2, quoting Nicolà Beregani, *Historia delle guerre d'Europa dalla comparsa dell'armi ottomane nell'Hungheria l'anno 1683* (Venice, 1698), 1:421–2.
159 Eszer, "Zu einigen bisher ungeloesten Problemen," 267. For the issue of the pilgrim traffic, see Tucker, "The Peace Negotiations of 1736."
160 This occurs in Gravier d'Ortières, *Estat des places que les princes Mahometans possèdent sur les côtes de la Mer Méditerranée...*, as quoted in Bilici, *Louis XIV et son projet*, 283.
161 Quoted in Setton, *Venice, Austria, and the Turks*, 281, without a reference.
162 Fabritius, "Kurtze Relation von meine drei gethane Reisen," in Konovalov, "Ludvig Fabritius's Account," 99–100.
163 Sanson, *Estat présent*, 140–4.
164 NA, VOC 1343, Gamron to Heren XVII, 23 July 1680, fol. 608.

165 Sanson, Isfahan, 13 Sept. 1691, in Kroell, ed., *Nouvelles d'Ispahan*, 48–9.
166 Kaempfer, *Am Hofe des persischen Grosskönigs*, 75. According to the same observer, this also explained the shah's lackadaisical attitude vis-à-vis the Uzbek raids in Khurasan.
167 In Fasa'i, *Farsnamah-i Nasiri*, 152–3.
168 Sanson, Isfahan, 13 Sept. 1691, in Kroell, ed., *Nouvelles d'Ispahan*, 50.
169 Farooqi, *Mughal-Ottoman Relations*, 10–56.
170 Schillinger, *Persianische und Ostindianische Reise*, 218.

CHAPTER 6

1 Lambton, "Islamic Society in Persia."
2 Malcolm, *A History of Persia*, 2:324–5.
3 Mustawfi Bafqi, *Jami`-i mufidi*, 3:810; and Hazin, *The Life of Hazin*, 42–3.
4 Arjomand, "Oriental Despotism," 38; Ashraf, "Iranian Identity."
5 Floor, *A Fiscal History*, 107ff.
6 Sumer, *Naqsh-i Turkan-i Anatuli*, 102, 111–12.
7 Ibid., 119; and Turkaman and Mu'arrikh, *Zayl-i tarikh*, 147.
8 Junabadi, *Rawzat al-Safaviyah*, 700–13; Sumer, *Naqsh-i Turkan-i Anatuli*, 121–2. The first recorded Afshar governor of Kirman is Bayram Beg, whose name appears in ca. 916/1510. See Bastani-Parizi, *Ganj `Ali Khan*, 17.
9 Nasiri, *Alqab*, 14; Röhrborn, *Provinzen und Zentralgewalt*, 29.
10 Vahid Qazvini, *Tarikh-i jahan-ara-yi `Abbasi*, 316; and Chardin, *Voyages*, 2:383–4.
11 Junabadi, *Rawzat al-Safaviyah*, 746; Khuzani Isfahani, "Afzal al-tavarikh," fol. 113; Valah Qazvini Isfahani, *Khuld-i barin*, 204; Turkaman and Mu'arrikh, *Zayl-i tarikh-i*, 147; Tumanovich, *Gerat*, 197; and Matthee, "Hajeb, Safavid and Qajar Period."
12 Khuzani Isfahani, "Afzal al-tavarikh," fol. 81b.
13 Vaziri, *Tarikh-i Kirman*, 642.
14 Quiring-Zoche, "Isfahan," 183–6.
15 Khuzani-Isfahani, "Afzal al-tavarikh," fols. 38–9.
16 Ansari, *Dastur al-Moluk*, 11–15.
17 Kaempfer, *Am Hofe des persischen Grosskönigs*; and Valah Qazvini Isfahani, *Khuld-i barin*, 205.
18 Kuteliia, *Gruziia i sefevidskii Iran*, 30.
19 Mustawfi, "Amar," 406.
20 Vachet, "Journal d'un voyage," 337.
21 Bembo, *The Travels*, 108.
22 Perry, "Deportations," 310.
23 Isfahani, *Khulasat al-siyar*, 64, 71.

24 The shah subsequently decided to settle many of them near Isfahan. See Herzig, "The Deportation of the Armenians."
25 Perry, "Forced Migrations," 205–6.
26 In 1691 the court ordered an investigation after a Qajar tax collector had forced the é to pay 1,500 tumans and after they had been raided by the Yomut. See Zabihi-Situdah, *Az Astara ta Astarabad*, 7:52–3, doc. 30; Schimkoreit, *Regesten*, 323–4, doc. 347.
27 Vahid Qazvini, *Tarikh-i jahan-ara-yi `Abbasi*, 706–7; Mawliyani, *Gurjiha*, 161.
28 Fraser, *A Narrative of Khorasan*, 42–4.
29 Turkaman and Mu'arrikh, *Zayl-i tarikh*, 132; Bastani-Parizi, *Ganj `Ali Khan*, 17.
30 Chardin, *Voyages*, 5:323–4.
31 Crone, *Pre-Industrial Societies*, 38ff.
32 As was true for the Ottoman Empire and the Mughal state; see Barkey, *Empire of Difference*, passim; and Hasan, *State and Locality*, passim, respectively.
33 Röhrborn, *Pronvinzen und Zentralgewalt*, 29.
34 Chardin, *Voyages*, 5:275, 346–7.
35 Chardin, *Voyages*, 9:549, and 5:260.
36 Gouvea, *Relaçam*, fol. 53v.
37 Zak`aria of Agulis, *The Journal*, 75.
38 Kirmani, *Sahifat al-irshad*, 80.
39 Giovanni Michele, "Relazione delle successi della guerra," BA, Cod. 46-X-10, fol. 312v.
40 As was true for the frontiers of premodern India, it is foreign rather than indigenous sources that described these linear borders. For India, see Embree, "Frontiers into Boundaries," 262.
41 For the Roman strategy of using friendly tribes to patrol their eastern frontiers, see Whittaker, *The Frontiers of the Roman Empire*, 136. According to Sanson, *Estat présent*, 176, the shah maintained a correspondence with the ruler of Masqat for the same purposes, in this case as a policy against the Portuguese.
42 Valah Qazvini Isfahani, *Khuld-i barin*, 175–6; Turkaman and Mu'arrikh, *Zayl-i tarikh*, 147.
43 Père Bachoud, in Fleuriau, ed., *Lettres édifiantes et curieuses*, 4:118. For a study of the elusive term and office of shamkhal, see Floor, "Who Were the Shamkhal and the Usmi?"
44 Bushev, *Istoriia posol'stv i diplomaticheskikh otnoshenii*, 253.
45 Anon. ed., *A Chronicle of the Carmelites*, 1149.
46 For examples, see Sanandaji, *Tuhfah-i Nasiri*, 96ff; and Özoğlu, "State-Tribe Relations," 15.
47 NA Coll., Gel. de Jongh 283, Daghregister Winnincx, 7 Oct. 1645, fol. 217.
48 Luft, "Iran unter Schāh `Abbās II," 108–9. He was next sent into exile in Khurasan, though.

49 Sanson, *Estat présent*, 176.
50 Monshi, *History of Shah 'Abbas*, 1299.
51 Kirmani, *Sihafat al-irshad*, 361.
52 Chardin, *Voyages*, 9:205–6.
53 "Mémoire de la province de Sirvan," in Fleuriau, ed., *Letters édifiantes et curieuses*, 4:28; Krusinski, *The History of the Late Revolutions*, 1:243; Dourry Efendy, *Relation*, 33; Mustawfi, "Amar," 405; and Khodarkovsky, *Russia's Steppe Frontier*, 68–9. The payment of an annuity to subordinates was common practice for the Russians as well; see ibid., 55, 63.
54 Chardin, *Voyages*, 10:58, 64.
55 Krusinski, *The History of the Late Revolutions*, 1:243; Efendy, *Narrative of Travels*, 33; Chardin, *Voyages*, 10:58, 64ff.
56 Chardin, *Voyages*, 5:396.
57 Turkaman, *Tarikh-i 'alam-ara-yi 'Abbasi*, 614, 1098–9.
58 Vahid Qazvini, *Tarikh-i jahan-ara-yi 'Abbasi*, 393ff; and Luft, "Iran unter Schāh 'Abbās II," 108–9.
59 Chardin, *Voyages*, 5:251–3, and Kaempfer, *Am Hofe des persischen Grosskönigs*, 167, wrongly attributed the beginnings of the conversion to khassah land to the reign of Shah Safi.
60 Valah Qazvini Isfahani, *Khuld-i barin*, 576–7; Tahir Vahid, *Tarikh-i jahan-ara-yi 'Abbasi*, 566, 612; Röhrborn, *Provinzen und Zentralgewalt*, 37, 122.
61 Chardin, *Voyages*, 5:252.
62 See Berktay, "Three Empires," 253–4, for this argument.
63 Subrahmanyam, "Aspects of State Formation," 371.
64 Vahid Qazvini, *Tarikh-i jahan-ara-yi 'Abbasi*, 748.
65 Chardin, *Voyages*, 5:387ff, 428, 551–3.
66 Floor, *The Economy of Safavid Persia*, 28.
67 Brosset, *Collection*, 2:204; and Mar'ashi Safavi, *Majma' al-tavarikh*, 48–9.
68 Chardin, *Voyages*, 5:276–7; Brosset, *Collection*, 2:204; Mar'ashi Safavi, *Majma' al-tavarikh*, fol. 52a. When Safi Quli Beg became the new governor of Kirman in 1658–9, he arrived with an entirely new administration numbering 150 officials. See Mashizi, *Tarikh-i Safaviyah-i Kirman*, 289–90.
69 Farman by Shah Sulayman, in Puturidze, ed., *Persidskie istoricheskie dokumenty*, 1:2, no. 5; Chardin, *Voyages*, 2:345–7, 10:35–6, 50; Petis de la Croix, *Extrait du journal*, 145; Gemelli Careri, *Giro del mondo*, 2:42–3.
70 For the kalantar, see Herzig, "The Armenians," 97; and Floor, "Kalantar."
71 Kaempfer, *Am Hofe des persischen Grosskönigs*, 169.
72 Richard, ed., *Raphaël du Mans*, 2:262.
73 Vahid Qazvini, *Tarikh-i jahan-ara-yi 'Abbasi*, 342.
74 Chardin, *Voyages* 3:154.
75 For this, see Matthee, "The Safavids under Western Eyes."

76 Manucci, *Storia di Mogor*, 1:40.
77 Boullaye-le-Gouze, *Voyages*, 91.
78 Carré, *Le courrier du Roi*, 268.
79 Deslandes, *The Beauties of Persia*, 8.
80 Bembo, *The Travels*, 296, 391.
81 Chardin, *Voyages*, 5:391.
82 Vachet, "Journal d'un voyage," fol. 336.
83 Donazzolo, "Viaggi in Oriente," 424.
84 Rakhmani, *Azerbaidzhan*, 156.
85 Tavernier, *Les six voyages*, 1:415–16.
86 Geidarov, *Remeslennoe proizvodstvo*, 174.
87 Deslandes, *The Beauties of Persia*, 11; Struys, *Drie aanmerkelijke en seer rampspoedige reysen*, 317.
88 Kaempfer, *Reisetagebücher*, 74, 77.
89 Richard, ed., *Raphaël du Mans*, 2:321–3.
90 Bushev, *Posol'stvo Artemiia Volynskogo*, 166.
91 Struys, *Drie aanmerkelijke en seer rampspoedige reysen*, 253–4.
92 NA, VOC 1266, Gamron to Heren XVII, 28 Feb. 1669, fols. 916–17b, 929b; Chardin, *Voyages*, 10:135–8; Struys, *Drie aanmerkelijke en seer rampspoedige reysen*, 195–6, 199; and Borob'eva, "K voprosy prebyvanii."
93 Matthee, "Jesuits."
94 Mashizi, *Tarikh-i Safaviyah-i Kirman*, 290.
95 De la Maze, description of travel through northern Iran, ARSI, Gal. 97^{II}, fol. 371v.
96 Ibid, fols. 371v–2.
97 NA, VOC 1360, Gamron to Batavia, 4 Mar. 1680, fols. 1886v–87r.
98 Bembo, *The Travels*, 300.
99 See Mitchell, "Provincial Chancelleries," and the sources quoted therein.
100 See Smith, ed., *The First Age*, 27. The figure of 200,000 for 1514, given in Berchet, ed., *La repubblica di Venezia*, 275, is no doubt exaggerated. Chardin, *Voyages*, 8:435, gave Shiraz 12,000 households or perhaps 60,000 inhabitants in the mid-seventeenth century, claiming that the number of households had fallen to 4,000 after a terrible flood in 1668.
101 Thevenot, *Voyage*, 3:434ff.
102 Carré, *Le courier du Roi*, 227–8.
103 Petis de la Croix, *Extrait du journal*, 114.
104 Fryer, *A New Account*, 2:211–18.
105 Bembo, *The Travels*, 296.
106 Hedges, *The Diary*, 1:207.
107 Tavernier, *Les six voyages*, 1:596.
108 Chardin, *Voyages*, 5:251, 253–4; 8:446.
109 Diary of Jan Smidt, in Dunlop, ed., *Bronnen*, 734.
110 NA, VOC 1158, Daghregister Winnincx, 18 July 1645.

111 NA, VOC 1217, Gamron to Isfahan, 22 June 1656, fol. 399; Chardin, *Voyages*, 3:270–2; Speelman, *Journaal*, 101–2.
112 Vahid Qazvini, *Tarikh-i jahan-ara-yi `Abbasi*, 332.
113 NA, VOC 1224, Gamron to Batavia, 9 Dec. 1656, fol. 272v; VOC 1217, Gamron to Isfahan, 22 June 1656, fol. 399.
114 Tavernier, *Les six voyages*, 1:624–5; Shamlu, "Qisas al-khaqani," fol. 133; Nasrabadi, *Tazkirah-i Nasrabadi*, 1:101.
115 Vahid Qazvini, *Tarikh-i jahan-ara-yi `Abbasi*, 610. In 1656, when Sulayman Khan was ousted, Kurdistan similarly was divided into six regions. See Mardukh Kurdistani, *Tarikh-i Mardukh*, 110, and Röhrborn, *Provinzen und Zentralgewalt*, 80.
116 Vahid Qazvini, *Tarikh-i jahan-ara-yi `Abbasi*, 741.
117 IOR, G/36/105, Gombroon to Surat, 11 Jan. 1669, fols. 55–6.
118 NA, VOC 1340, Gamron to Batavia, 12 Feb. 1678, fol. 1549; and Fryer, *A New Account*, 2:227–8, 339.
119 CA, OCD 238k, letter Fr. John Baptist, 11 Sept. 1678. See also Anon., ed., *A Chronicle of the Carmelites*, 1:445; NA, VOC 1351, Gamron to Heren XVII, 1 Sept. 1679, fols. 2584v–5r.
120 NA, VOC 1434, Gamron to Batavia, 2 June 1688, fol. 555v.
121 CA, OCD, letter Elia de S. Alberto, Isfahan, 19 June 1689, fol. 237v.
122 NA, VOC 1291, Gamron to Heren XVII, 21 Mar. 1674, fol. 559v.
123 Fryer, *A New Account*, 2:215–16.
124 Bastani-Parizi, *Ganj `Ali Khan*, 17.
125 Mu'min Kirman, *Sahifat al-irshad*, introd., 63.
126 Ibid.
127 Mashizi, *Tazkirah-i Safaviyah-i Kirman*, 248.
128 Golombek, "The Safavid Ceramic Industry at Kirman."
129 NA, VOC 1217, Gamron to Isfahan, 27 Aug. 1656, fol. 416.
130 For more details, see Matthee, "The East India Company Trade."
131 Mashizi, *Tazkirah-i Safaviyah-i Kirman*, 207–9, 234, 276–7, 332–3; Vaziri, *Tarikh-i Kirman*, 635–7.
132 Mashizi, *Tazkirah-i Safaviyah-i Kirman*, 211; Vaziri, *Tarikh-i Kirman*, 638; NA, VOC 1152, Daghregister Bastincq, fol. 248.
133 Mashizi, *Tazkirah-i Safaviyah-i Kirman*, 68.
134 Tavernier, *Les six voyages*, 1:771.
135 Mashizi, *Tazkirah-i Safaviyah-i Kirman*, 433.
136 Ibid., 98, 545.
137 Ibid., 251.
138 Ibid., 28–9, 40–1, 51–4, 515, 570.
139 Ibid., 538, 563, 636.
140 Ibid., 94–5, 460–1.
141 Chardin, *Voyages*, 10:32ff, 41ff, 100ff.
142 Chardin, *Voyages*, 2:347–50; 3:155.
143 Mashizi, *Tazkirah-i Safaviyah-i Kirman*, 86–7, 98, 102, 546, 583.
144 Ibid, 102, 617.

145 Pearson, "Merchants and States," 71.
146 Sanson, *Estat présent*, 98.
147 Masters, *The Origins of Western Economic Dominance*, 57.
148 NA, VOC 1201, Gamron to Batavia, 16 Aug. 1653, fols. 821–38.
149 Coolhaas, ed., *Generale Missiven, 1639–1655*, 803.
150 Foster, ed., *The English Factories in India, 1655–1660*, 88, 127.
151 NA, VOC 1520, Report van Leene to Batavia, 20 June 1692, fol. 213; VOC 1507, Gamron to Heren XVII, 2 Aug. 1693, fol. 466v. For Mirza Sharif Jahan, see also Aubin, *L'ambassade de Gregório Pereira Fidalgo*, 6 and 84, where he is called Miriza Serrafujão.
152 NA, VOC 1559, Gamron to Batavia, 8 July 1694, fols. 858–9v.
153 Pearson, *The Indian Ocean*, 118.
154 In Coolhaas, ed., *Generale Missiven, 1639–1655*, 803.
155 NA, VOC 1226, Gamron to Batavia, 19 Apr. 1658, fols. 809v–12; IOR, G/36/84, sect. 3, Swally to Gombroon, 16 Oct. 1658, fol. 242. See also Foster, *The English Factories in India, 1655–1660*, 171.
156 IOR, E/3/26/2729, Gombroon to Madras, 2 Apr. 1659; idem in IOR, G/40/30, fol. 182.
157 IOR, E/3/26/2868, Isfahan to Company, 25 Jan. 1660, unfol.
158 NA, VOC 1241, Gamron to Heren XVII, 17 Mar. 1664, fol. 638v. Coolhaas, ed., *Generale Missiven, 1655–1674*, 107, cites 20,000 tumans for 1656.
159 The Iranians constantly used "coloring" as an excuse not to give the EIC a sum in toll money that even remotely approached half of the total receipts, their legitimate share. Thus in 1659 the English received 500 tumans; they had to be content with 450 tumans in 1660, 600 in 1661, and 660 in 1662. Every time much haggling preceded the payments. IOR, E/3/27/2890, Isfahan to Company, 15 June 1661, fol. 44v; NA, VOC 1232, Gamron to Heren XVII, 4 July 1661; VOC 1234, Gamron to Heren XVII, 14 June 1661, fols. 303v–4r.
160 Murtaza Quli Khan, the Dutch admitted, was a decent man who had no choice but to do his job. Nasrabadi, *Tazkirah-i Nasrabadi*, 2:41 and 303, emphasizes his gentle nature and care for the poor.
161 NA, VOC 1241, Gamron to Heren XVII, 17 Mar. 1664, fols. 637v–8v; VOC 1248, Gamron to Batavia, 31 May 1664, fol. 3039.
162 IOR, E/3/27/2894, Isfahan to Company, 11 Aug. 1661, unfol.
163 IOR, G/36/108, Gombroon to Surat, 24 Apr. 1682, fol. 80.
164 Chardin, *Voyages*, 5:402–3.
165 Carré, *The Travels*, 802–3.
166 NA, VOC 1245, Gamron to Heren XVII, 29 Apr. 1665, fol. 515r–v; IOR, G/36/104, Gombroon to Surat, 24 and 29 Apr. 1665, fols. 225, 227; Shamlu, "Qisas al-khaqani," fol. 153v.
167 NA, VOC 1255, Gamron to Heren XVII, 8 Aug. 1667, fols. 901–2.
168 IOR, G/36/105, Gombroon to Surat, 26 Nov. 1668, fol. 40v; NA, VOC 1266, Gamron to Heren XVII, 28 Feb.1669, fols. 925v–6r.

169 NA, VOC 1270, Gamron to Batavia, 18 Jan. 1669, fols. 962v–3r; VOC 1266, Gamron to Heren XVII, 20 July 1669, fol. 952v; IOR, G/36/105, Gombroon to Surat, 27 March 1669, fols. 60–1. The list of khans and shahbandars in Floor, *The Persian Gulf*, 301, is unreliable here.

170 IOR, G/36/106, Gombroon to Surat, 13 Nov. 1671, fol. 51, where it is said that four days earlier the khan had left Bandar `Abbas with an army of 14,000 men to fight in Makran. NA, VOC 1285, Gamron to Heren XVII, 6 May 1673, fol. 386, reports that, according to news in January of 1673, Murtaza Quli Khan had been defeated by the Baluchis from Kitch. See also IOR, G/36/106, 2nd fasc., Gombroon to Surat, 19 Apr. 1673, fol. 103.

171 NA, VOC 1251, Gamron to Heren XVII, 6 Apr. 1666, fol. 1338; IOR, E/3/29/3173, Gombroon to Company, 18 May 1666; and E/3/29/3198, 26 Oct. 1666, unfol.

172 NA, VOC 1268, Gamron to Heren XVII, 26 May 1668, fol. 1361v.

173 Chardin, *Voyages*, 5:403.

174 NA, VOC 1274, 1671, fol. 735v; VOC 1274, Gamron to Heren XVII, 22 Apr. 1671, fol. 735v. See also IOR, G/36/105, Gombroon to Surat, 23 Feb. 1671, fol. 168, which mentions that the young shahbandar's assistant was one "Delour Agga" (Dilavar Agha?), born a Christian, who had been taken by the "deceased shawbunders father that time the Persians tooke Bagdat," and who had himself been shahbandar of Kung for some time; and ibid., Gombroon to Surat, 22 Apr. 1671, which mentions one Mahmud Baqir Beg, a ghulam, as having come down to take up the shahbandar's duties.

175 De Bruyn, *Reizen over Moskovie*, 159. Kaempfer, who visited Iran in 1684, was clearly misinformed and referred to the old situation when he wrote that the shahbandar rotated every year. See Kaempfer, *Am Hofe des persischen Grosskönigs*, 112, 120.

176 See IOR, G/36/106, Gombroon to Surat, 29 Apr. 1672, fol. 96; NA, VOC 1297, Gamron to Heren XVII, 1 Apr. 1675, fol. 1011r; VOC 1323, Gamron to Batavia, 12 Feb. 1678. The figure for 1699 may be found in IOR, G/40/5, Abstracts of letters, Isfahan to Surat, 24 May 1699, fol. 76v.

177 NA, VOC 1323, Gamron to Batavia, 12 Aug. 1677, fol. 675r.

178 IOR, G/36/106, Gombroon to Surat, 29 Apr. 1672, fol. 96.

179 NA, VOC 1862, Gamron to Batavia, 15 Feb. 1716, fol. 2552.

180 NA, VOC 1315, Gamron to Batavia, 5 June 1677, fol. 732r–v.

181 NA, VOC 1355, Gamron to Heren XVII, 17 Apr. 1681, fol. 394v; VOC 1370, Gamron to Paliacatta (Pulicat), 16 July 1681, fol. 2527v.

182 NA, VOC 1549, Gamron to Batavia, 31 May 1695, fol. 589.

183 NA, VOC 1364, Memorandum Casembroot to Van den Heuvel, 14 June 1682, fol. 367v; VOC 1582, Gamron to Batavia, 1 Nov. 1695, fol. 24.

184 NA, VOC 1297, Gamron to Heren XVII, 1 Apr. 1675, fol. 1011r; VOC 1340, Gamron to Batavia, 12 Feb. 1678, fol. 1549v; NA, VOC 1332, Report Bent to Casembroot, 1 June 1679, fol. 920v.
185 NA, VOC 1323, Gamron to Isfahan, 27 Dec. 1677, fol. 683r; ibid., Gamron to Batavia, 12 Feb. 1678, fol. 678r; VOC 1323, Gamron to Batavia, 12 Feb. 1678, fol. 678v.
186 NA, VOC 1323, Isfahan to Gamron, 23 Jan. 1678, fol. 685r.
187 Fryer, *A New Account*, 2:225.
188 NA, VOC 1329, Gamron to Batavia, 20 Jan. 1677, fol. 1511r–v.
189 Fryer, *A New Account*, 2:302; NA, VOC 1323, Gamron to Isfahan, 11 and 13 Dec. 1677, fol. 682r.
190 IOR, G/36/107, Gombroon to Surat, 19 Apr. 1678, fol. 82.
191 NA, VOC 1340, 12 Feb. 1678, fol. xxx; IOR, E/3/39/4563, Surat to Company, 24 Jan. 1679, unfol.; Tavernier, *Les six voyages*, 1:174; Fryer, *A New Account*, 2:227–8, 339, 361; and Anon., ed., *A Chronicle of the Carmelites*, 400.
192 IOR, G/36/87, Gombroon to Surat, 15 Nov. 1677, fol. 11; G/36/107, Gombroon to Surat, 24 Apr. 1678; Fryer, *A New Account*, 2:339.
193 NA, VOC 1323, Isfahan to Gamron, 2 Mar. 1678, fol. 688r; ibid., Isfahan to Gamron, 26 May 1678, fol. 662r.
194 See the translation of a letter from Nasir ʿAli Khan to Bent, written from Shiraz on 3 Feb. 1679, in VOC 1333, fol. 692v, in which it is reported how the khan sent a gift to the VOC director in the form of a horse and requested friendship in the future.
195 NA, VOC 1333, Gamron to Batavia, 25 Feb. 1679, fol. 693r–v; VOC 1360, Gamron to Batavia, 4 Mar. 1680, fols. 1871r–2r.
196 It is typical of the accommodating nature of Shah Sulayman's reign that Nasir ʿAli Khan's possessions were later returned to him. See NA, VOC 1373, Gamron to Batavia, 19 Apr. 1683, fol. 883r.
197 NA, VOC 1355, Gamron to Batavia, 5 Mar. 1681, fol. 399r.
198 Fryer, *A New Account*, 2:302.
199 Coolhaas, ed., *Generale Missiven, 1655–1674*, 41; IOR, G/36/107, 25 Jan. 1675, fol. 66.
200 See, for example, IOR, G/40/2, 2 Nov. 1668, fol. 36, where it is said that Basra was outstripping Bandar ʿAbbas in commercial activity.
201 NA, VOC 1245, Gamron to Heren XVII, 9 Jan. 1665, fol. 365v; VOC 1406, Van den Heuvel to Batavia, 28 Feb. 1684, fol. 1161; Thevenot, *Livre troisième de la suite du voyage*, 609.
202 NA, VOC 1270, Surat to Batavia, 30 Nov. 1669, fol. 857; and IOR, G/36/105, Isfahan to Surat, 5 Sept. 1669, fol. 86v.
203 NA, VOC 1307, Gamron to Batavia, 12 Dec. 1675, fol. 636v. For the story of the Portuguese, see also Chardin, *Voyages*, 9:243ff; VOC 1304, Gamron to Batavia, 4 Sept. 1674, fol. 521; VOC 1297, Gamron to Heren XVII, 12 July 1675, fol. 1017v; and IOR, E/3/35/4077, Surat to Company, 13 Feb. 1675, unfol.

CHAPTER 7

1. Van Bruinessen, *Agha, Shaykh and State*, 167–8.
2. Tenreiro, *Itinerários*, 20–1.
3. In Aubin, "Šah Ismā'īl et les notables," 58.
4. Turkaman, *Tarikh-i 'alam-ara-yi 'Abbasi*, 628; Monshi, *History of Shah 'Abbas*, 819.
5. For Isfahan's traditionally Shi'i orientation, see Ja'fariyan, "Pishinah-i tashayyu' dar Isfahan."
6. Ja'fariyan, "Tashayyu' dar Qazvin," 57–9.
7. Aubin, "Les Sunnites de Lārestan," 151.
8. Olearius, *Vermehrte newe Beschreibung*, 700.
9. Posch, "Der Fall Alkas Mirza," 158.
10. Ja'fariyan "Tashayyu'-i Astarabad," 271–2.
11. Turkaman, *Tarikh-i 'alam-ara-yi 'Abbasi*, 579ff; Monshi, *History of Shah 'Abbas*, 766ff.
12. Aubin, "Les Sunnites de Lārestan," 155–6.
13. Danishpazhuh, ed., "Amar,"
14. Dourry Efendy, *Relation*, 54. The claim, made by an envoy with an agenda and a superficial perspective on Iranian society, cannot be taken at face value. Yet we have no other numbers.
15. Ja'fariyan, *'Ilal-i bar uftadan-i Safaviyan*, 368. Vahid Qazvini, *Tarikh-i jahan-ara-yi 'Abbasi*, 503, speaks of the "fanaticism of the empty school of Sunnism" in the context of the war of 1648.
16. This is a controversial issue. Newman has argued that this migration is largely fictional. Stewart, "Notes on the Migration," and Abisaab, *Converting Persia*, 51, by contrast, demonstrate that it was real and important.
17. Abisaab, *Converting Persia*, 50.
18. Ja'fariyan, *Naqsh-i khandan-i Karaki*, 173ff.
19. Dickson, "Shah Tahmasb and the Uzbeks," 190.
20. Della Valle, *Viaggi*, 2:330; Arjomand, *The Shadow of God*, 198–9; Babayan, *Mystics, Monarchs, and Messiahs*, 349ff.
21. Falsafi, *Zindigani*, 896–9.
22. Sherley, *Sir Anthony Sherley*, 74.
23. For a discussion, see Rota, "Caucasians in Safavid Service," 111–12.
24. See Rebelo, *Un voyageur portugais en Perse*, 125.
25. For this, see Matthee, "The Politics of Protection."
26. Anon., ed., *A Chronicle of the Carmelites*, 157; Sanson, *Estat présent*, 254–5.
27. Herzig, "The Armenian Merchants," 82.
28. Monshi, *History of Shah 'Abbas*, 1181–2.
29. Della Valle, *Delle conditioni*, 53, 65–8.
30. Anon., ed., *A Chronicle of the Carmelites*, 271. Little more is known about this than that the persecution had stopped by the fall of 1624, possibly after payments had been made by the community in question.
31. Abisaab, *Converting Persia*, 79; Della Valle, *Delle conditioni*, 54.

32 Anon., ed., *A Chronicle of the Carmelites*, 288.
33 For this, see Herzig, "The Deportation of the Armenians." At the request of Allah Virdi Khan, the governor of Fars, 500 Armenian families were also settled in Shiraz, "en raison du bon caractère et de la loyauté de ces gens," as chronicler Arakel of Tabriz put it. Some were also sent to Farahabad in Mazandaran. See Brosset, ed. and trans., *Collection*, 1:291, 488.
34 Florencio del Niño Jesús, *Biblioteca Carmelitano-Teresiana*, 2:109.
35 Alonso, "El primer viage desde Persia," 525.
36 Gouvea, *Relaçam*, fol. 11.
37 Gulbenkian, "Deux lettres surprenantes."
38 Anon., ed., *A Chronicle of the Carmelites*, 169.
39 Ibid., 281–2. They were not allowed to return until a year later, when it had become clear that they were innocent of "the troubles."
40 Falsafi, *Zindigani*, 883–7.
41 Gouvea, *Relaçam*, fols. 69–70v., tells an interesting story about Shah `Abbas's octogenarian *mihmandar*, `Ali Beg, who was said to be quite zealous in his faith. On one occasion this official told the Portuguese diplomat-cum-missionary: "If only a few years ago one would have told us about the existence of a Christian church in this city, we would have burned both you and the church itself. Now, however, not only do you have a church, but the shah enters it and even allows you to remove slaves from his own house to take them to Christian lands."
42 Alonso, "Una embajada de Clemente," 51.
43 Abisaab, *Converting Persia*, 79–80; Anon., ed., *A Chronicle of the Carmelites*, 255; Della Valle, *Viaggi*, 2:143–4. For Baha' al-Din's advice to the shah with regard to Zoroastrians and Jews, see Moreen, *Iranian Jewry's Hour*, 90. For a fuller discussion of the shah's treatment of the missionaries, see Matthee, "The Politics of Protection."
44 Alonso, "Una embajada de Clemente," 54.
45 Abisaab, *Converting Persia*, 67.
46 Gouvea, *Relaçam*, fol. 230.
47 Anon., ed., *A Chronicle of the Carmelites*, 1:206–7; for the larger context, see Matthee, "The Politics of Protection."
48 Anon., ed., *A Chronicle of the Carmelites*, 245; Chardin, *Voyages*, 6:48; "Lettre du Révérend Père H. B***, Missionnaire en Perse, à Monsieur le Comte de M***," in Fleuriau, ed., *Lettres édifiantes et curieuses*, 4:108.
49 Ghougassian, *The Emergence of the Armenian Diocese*, 73, 75.
50 Malcolm, *A History of Persia*, 1:574. Simeon of Yerevan, an eighteenth-century Armenian chronicler, while confusing him with his successor, Shah `Abbas II, called Safi "peace-loving and benevolent." See Siméon of Erevan, *Jambr*, 168–9. For Safi's treatment of the Jews, see Moreen, *Iranian Jewry's Hour*, 93–94.
51 Anon., ed., *A Chronicle of the Carmelites*, 1:352.

52 Babayan, *Monarchs, Mystics, and Messiahs*, 375.
53 Ibid., 403–4.
54 Mirot, "Le séjour du Père Bernard," 227.
55 Anon., ed., *A Chronicle of the Carmelites*, 350–1.
56 Quinn, "Coronation Narratives," 327–8.
57 Aram, *Andishah-i tarikh*, 318–19.
58 Chardin, *Voyages*, 9:514.
59 Moreen, *Iranian Jewry's Hour*, 73–4.
60 For this, see Matthee, *The Pursuit of Pleasure*, 56.
61 Richard, ed., *Raphaël du Mans*, 1:67.
62 Krusinski, *The History of the Late Revolutions*, 1:129–30.
63 Zimmel, "Vorgeschichte," 5–7. For the larger context, see Matthee, "Jesuits."
64 Chardin, *Voyages*, 6:73–4.
65 Kaempfer, *Am Hofe des persischen Grosskönigs*, 46. Kaempfer even claimed that Shah 'Abbas II threatened to impale the shaykh al-islam of Isfahan who had criticized him for his friendliness to Christians.
66 Quinn, "Coronation Narratives," 327–8.
67 Babayan, *Mystics, Monarchs, and Messiahs*, 462.
68 Ja'faryan, *Safaviyah dar arsah-i din*, 525–6. For these polemics, see Babayan, *Mystics, Monarchs, and Messiahs*, 403ff.
69 Ibid., 376.
70 Baghdiantz-McCabe, "The Socio-Economic Conditions," 379.
71 Chardin, *Voyages*, 9:517; Krusinski, *The History of the Late Revolutions*, 1:129.
72 Chardin, *Voyages*, 7:315.
73 Richard, ed., *Raphaël du Mans*, 2:208, fn. 20.
74 Vahid Qazvini *Tarikh-i jahan-ara-yi 'Abbasi*, 415–16; NA, VOC 1152, Daghregister Bastynck, fols. 246–9; Anon., ed., *A Chronicle of the Carmelites*, 353; Richard, ed., *Raphaël du Mans*, 2:208; Chardin, *Voyages*, 4:69; 9:516–17; Foster, ed., *The English Factories in India, 1646–50*, 43.
75 Mulla Kamal, *Tarikh*, 98, 102; Vahid Qazvini, *Tarikh-i jahan-ara-yi 'Abbasi*, 414–15; and Keyvani, *Artisans and Guild Life*, 129, quoting Muhammad Tahir Vahid, "Divan-i Rizvan," University of Tehran Library, Ms. 4344.
76 See, for example, Lockhart, *The Fall of the Safavi Dynasty*; and Moreen, *Iranian Jewry's Hour*.
77 For the important role of Indians in Safavid economic life, see Dale, *Indian Merchants*.
78 NA, VOC 1152, Extract daghregister Bastyncq, fols. 246–9.
79 Wilson, trans. and ed., "History of the Mission," 697–9; [Villotte], *Voyage*, 134–5; and Zimmel, "Vorgeschichte," 22–4.
80 Richard, ed., *Raphaël du Mans*, 2:217–18, 143; Manucci, *Storia di Mogor*, 4:192.
81 Chardin, *Voyages*, 7:411.

82 Brosset, trans. and ed., *Des historiens arméniens*, 57; and Darhuhaniyan, *Tarikh-i Julfa-yi Isfahan*, 60–1.
83 Moreen, *Iranian Jewry's Hour*, 80–93.
84 Moreen, "The Problem of Conversion," 220.
85 Naraqi, *Tarikh-i ijtima`i-yi Kashan*, cited in Sharifi, *Dard-i dil-i Zimmah*, 38–9. For a discussion of these events, see Moreen, *Iranian Jewry's Hour*, 94ff.
86 Levy, *Tarikh-i jami`-i Yahudiyan*, 174–84.
87 Chardin, *Voyages*, 6:135.
88 Wilson, "History of the Mission," 695.
89 NA, VOC 1215, Gamron to Batavia, 30 Mar. 1657, fol. 864; idem in VOC 1224, fol. 285v; Richard, ed., *Raphaël du Mans*, 1:143.
90 Moreen, *Iranian Jewry's Hour*, 95.
91 Sharifi, *Dard-i dil-i Zimmah*, 71–8.
92 Baibourtian, *International Trade*, 152-3; Bellingeri, "Sugli Sceriman rimasti a Giulfa," 109; Aslanian, "The Circulation of Men and Credit," 152–3; Aslanian and Berberian, "The Sceriman Family."
93 Ghougassian, *The Emergence of the Armenian Diocese*, 248. Also see Aslanian, "The Circulation of Men and Credit," 153; and Baibourtian, *International Trade*, 153.
94 Richard, ed., *Raphaël du Mans*, 1:44.
95 Baghdiantz-McCabe, "The Socio-Economic Conditions," 375–6.
96 Anon., ed., *A Chronicle of the Carmelites*, 2:1075.
97 Richard, ed., *Raphaël du Mans*, 2: 215–18; Tokatlian, *Kalantars*, 53.
98 Richard, ed., *Raphaël du Mans*, 1:45.
99 See Kaempfer, *Am Hofe des persischen Grosskönigs*, 46.
100 There are striking similarities with the contemporary Ottoman Empire here. Sultan Murad IV (r. 1623–40) maintained friendly relations with Sufis to the point of patronizing them. Yet he also endorsed some of the measures propagated by the Kazızadeli movement, though only those, such as closing unruly coffeehouses, that "benefited his authoritarian rule." See Baer, *Honored by the Glory*, 68.
101 Calder, "Legitimacy and Accommodation," 102.
102 Rizvi, "Sayyid Ni`mat Allah al-Jaza'iri," 238; Chardin, *Voyages*, 10:14. For examples, see Calmard, "Shi`i Rituals of Power," 147ff.; and Rahimi, "The Safavid Camel Sacrifice Ritual." Specific examples from the reign of Shah Sulayman may be found in Sanson, letters from Isfahan, 12 and 13 Sept. 1691, in Kroell, ed., *Nouvelles d'Ispahan*, 43 and 47–8.
103 For this three-way struggle, see Babayan *Mystics, Monarchs, and Messiahs*, 412ff.
104 Richard, ed., *Raphaël du Mans*, 1:77, 82.
105 Anon., ed., *A Chronicle of the Carmelites*, 408. The Julfan Armenians, who enjoyed the protection of the queen-mother, paid less.
106 Vaziri Kirmani, *Jughrafiya-yi Kirman*, 28.
107 Tarimi, `*Allamah Majlisi*, 145.
108 NA, VOC 1439, Gamron to Batavia, 25 Nov. 1687, fol. 1413r.

109 In Sifatgul, *Sakhtar-i nihad*, 221.
110 Ibid., 452, 542.
111 Chardin, *Voyages*, 9:518–19.
112 Ibid., 406–7; Chardin, *Voyages*, 3:119; Darhahuniyan, *Tarikh-i Julfa-yi Isfahan*, 573–4; Ghougassian, *The Emergence of the Armenian Diocese*, 41, 108–9.
113 CA, OCD 236i, Ange de St Joseph, 2 Oct. 1672; and Anon., ed., *A Chronicle of the Carmelites*, 407.
114 Richard, ed., *Raphaël du Mans*, 1:82; anon., ed., *A Chronicle of the Carmelites*, 406-07.
115 Chardin, *Voyages*, 3:142–6.
116 In Metzler, "Nicht erfüllte Hoffnungen," 693.
117 In Richard, ed., *Raphaël du Mans*, 1:64–5, fn. 150.
118 See [Villotte], *Voyages*, 148–51; and Ja`fariyan, introduction to *Tarjumah-i anajil-i arba`ah*, 30.
119 Sanson, *Estat présent*, 10–12.
120 Anon., ed., *A Chronicle of the Carmelites*, 416.
121 The connection between European powers and indigenous Christian communities in Iran goes back to the early days of the Safavids. Iran's Nestorians in 1502 expressed a desire to be put under Portuguese protection. See Neck, "Diplomatische Beziehungen," 74.
122 Anon., ed., *A Chronicle of the Carmelites*, 457.
123 Gaudereau, Isfahan, 16 Feb. 1695, in Kroell, ed., *Nouvelles d'Ispahan*, 78; idem, "Relation de ce qui est passé à la consecration de Monsieur Pidou de Saint Olon," 9 May 1694, in ibid., 79–86; Anon., ed., *A Chronicle of the Carmelites*, 461–9, 862; Donazzolo, "Viaggi in Oriente," 423; and Zedginidze, "Iz istorii pol'sko-russkikh diplomaticheskikh otnoshenii," 21–2.

CHAPTER 8

1 Gaudereau, "Relation de la mort de Schah Abbas," in Kroell, ed., *Nouvelles d'Ispahan*, 64. Gaudereau erroneously gives July 28 as the date of the shah's death.
2 NA, VOC 1559, Gamron to Batavia, 8 July 1694, fol. 854v–855; VOC 1571, Gamron to Heren XVII, 23 July 1694, fol. 57.
3 NA, VOC 1559, Gamron to Batavia, 20 Mar. 1694, fol. 840.
4 Gaudereau, "Relation de la mort de Schah Abbas," in Kroell, ed., *Nouvelles d'Ispahan*, 65–66.
5 Aubin, ed., *L'ambassade de Gregório Pereira Fidalgo*, 65.
6 Busse, "Persische Staatsgedanke," 62–63.
7 D'Allesandri, "Narrative," 216.
8 De Bruyn, *Reizen over Moskovie*, 165.
9 Axworthy, *The Sword of Persia*, 27, 34, 50.

10 See, for instance, Afushtah'i Natanzi, *Naqavat al-asar*, 74–75, who posits a link between Shah Isma'il's lack of concern for his people and the arrogance of subordinate officials.
11 Mardukh Kurdistani, *Tarikh-i Mardukh*, 111.
12 NA, VOC 1779, Memorandum Backer to Macare, 12 Mar. 1709, fols. 471–72.
13 Krusinski, *The History of the Late Revolutions*, 1:107–8.
14 Tavernier, *Les six voyages*, 1:597.
15 See Ja'faryan,'*Ilal-i bar uftadan-i Safaviyan*, 46–48, for contemporary Persian observations and criticism of the phenomenon.
16 Krusinski, *The History of the Late Revolutions*, 1:86–87. The Dutch, by contrast, during the reign of Shah Safi had complained that bribery had grown worse for the opposite reason—as a result of a *loss* of central control following the reign of Shah 'Abbas I. They claimed that the need to give presents to Safavid officials had been much less under Shah 'Abbas than under Shah Safi. See Van den Trille, aboard Ship "Bueren," to Batavia, June 1634, in Dunlop, ed., *Bronnen*, 475.
17 NA, VOC 1897, 4th fasc., Gamron to Batavia, 30 Nov. 1716, fol. 4.
18 Krusinksi, *The History of the Late Revolutions*, 1:100.
19 Mar'ashi, *Majma' al-tavarikh*, 48–49.
20 De Bruyn, *Reizen over Moskovie*, 164. A slightly different version of the story can be found in Harrach, "Voyage," fol. 24.
21 NA, VOC 1886, Isfahan to Gamron, 23 Oct. 1715, fols. 270–1.
22 Nasiri, *Dastur-i shahriyaran*, 31; Findiriski, *Tuhfat al-'alam*, 35–6.
23 Khatunabadi, *Vaqa'i' al-sinnin*, 557.
24 Muhammad Baqir Majlisi's *Haqq al-yaqin*, written in Persian in 1697, is emblematic of this for including vehement denunciations of the first three caliphs, calling them hypocrites and unbelievers. See Turner, *Islam without Allah*, 169; and Rizvi, "Sayyid Ni'mat Allāh al-Jazā'irī."
25 Sanson, *Estat présent*, 41–42; Röhrborn, *Provinzen und Zentralgewalt*, 37; and Nayrizi Shirazi, *Risalah-i siyasi*, 34–35. See also Lockhart, *The Fall of the Safavi Dynasty*, 38.
26 Nasiri, *Dastur-i shahriyaran*, 22.
27 Chardin, *Voyages*, 6:24, 40–2.
28 Sanson, *Estat présent*, 102.
29 Shuja', *Zan, siyasat va haramsara*, 158.
30 Krusinski, *The History of the Late Revolutions*, 1:79–80.
31 NA, VOC 1571, Gamron to Heren XVII, 23 July 1694, fol. 57.
32 NA, VOC 1856, Gamron to Isfahan, 24 May 1714, fol. 1117.
33 NA, VOC 1747, Isfahan to Gamron, 26 Aug. 1706, fol. 245. When he fell into disgrace a year later, he was succeeded by Khusraw Mirza, the former vali of Georgia. See ibid., 12 July 1707, fols. 238–9.
34 Dourry Efendy, *Relation*, 48.
35 Gouvea, *Relaçam*, fol. 288.

36 Olearius, *Vermehrte newe Beschreibung*, 657.
37 Berchet, ed., *La repubblica di Venezia*, 222; Tavernier, *Les six voyages*, 1:572.
38 Babayan, *Monarchs, Mystics, and Messiahs*, 366ff.
39 As was seen in chapter 3, she made a brief comeback under Shah Safi, to be definitively banned from the palace by the same ruler.
40 Richard, ed., *Raphaël du Mans*, 2:19; Kaempfer, *Am Hofe des persischen Grosskönigs*, 231.
41 Bushev, *Posol'stvo Artemiia Volynskogo*, 204.
42 Krusinski, *The History of the Late Revolutions*, 119, 124, 127.
43 Anon., ed., *A Chronicle of the Carmelites*, 1:470.
44 MAE, MD, Perse 1, Gardane to Dubois, Shamakhi, 5 Jan. 1720, fol 41.
45 NA, VOC 1964, Garmon to Batavia, 15 Feb. 1721, fol. 54.
46 NA, VOC 1611, Memorandum Hoogcamer to Casteleyn, 31 May 1698, fols. 66–8.
47 NA, VOC 1603, Gamron to Batavia, 1 July 1699, fol. 1853v; VOC 1639, Gamron to Batavia, 25 Aug. 1699, fol. 7. The position of ishik-aqasi-bashi had been with the Shamlu for the duration of the Safavid dynasty.
48 NA, VOC 1611, Isfahan to Gamron, 10 Sept. 1697, fol. 38.
49 IOR, E/3/54, 6614, Isfahan to Company, 7 Feb. 1699, unfol.
50 NA, VOC 1732, Memorandum Casteleyn to Backer, fols. 39–40.
51 In Ferrier, "British-Persian Relations," 303–4.
52 He was paraded on a mule through the streets of Isfahan. See NA, VOC 1679, Isfahan to Gamron, 12 Aug. 1702, fols. 102–3.
53 He would return to Isfahan in late 1704. See NA, VOC 1694, Isfahan to Gamron, 26 Jan. 1704, fol. 206; VOC 1714, Isfahan to Gamron, 10 Oct. 1704, fols. 94–5.
54 Khatunabadi, *Vaqa'i` al-sinnin*, 564. According to the Dutch, he died in 1712. See Coolhaas, ed., *Generale Missiven, 1675–1685*, 905.
55 NA, VOC 1763, Isfahan to Gamron, 25 Mar. 1708, fol. 542.
56 Agha Hushyar, the head eunuch, used this opportunity to make Safi Quli Agha fall from royal grace. For the details, see NA, VOC 1747, Isfahan to Gamron, 1 July 1707, fols. 233-4; VOC 1763, Isfahan to Gamron, 25 Oct. 1707, fol. 252; VOC 1763, Gamron to Batavia, 21 Dec. 1707, fol. 106. Muhammad Zaman Khan, a nephew of the old grand vizier and ishik-aqasi-bashi, became the new qurchibashi.
57 NA, VOC 1763, Isfahan to Gamron, 25 Oct. 1707, fol. 253; VOC 1779, 12 Mar. 1709.
58 NA, VOC 1779, Memorandum Backer to Macare, 12 Mar. 1709, fol. 474.
59 NA, VOC 1763, Isfahan to Gamron, 25 Mar. 1708, fol. 542; VOC 1779, Isfahan to Gamron, 20 Jan. 1709, fol. 545; VOC 1779, Casteleyn, Isfahan to Batavia, 12 Jan 1709, reported that the influence

of treasurer Agha Kamal made that the decree was already observed more in the breach than in the observation.

60 NA, VOC 1779, 10 Dec. 1708, fol. 313; VOC 1802, 31 Oct. 1712, fol. 2208; VOC 1856, Isfahan to Gamron, 11 Aug. 1713, fol. 408; Isfahan to Gamron, 19 Oct. 1713, fol. 496.

61 In the early eighteenth century, the Daghistanis each year sent an envoy with two cowhides and as many sheep skins to the Safavid court as a token gift. In return they received an annual stipend in the amount of 1700 tumans, which was designed to buy their peace and allegiance. See Krusinski, *The History of the Late Revolutions*, 1:243; and Dourry Efendy, *Relation*, 33.

62 Valah Qazvini Isfahani, *Khuld-i barin*, 641; Al-Husaini, *Tadhkira-i Shushtar*, 65; I'timad al-Saltanah, *Tarikh-i muntazam-i Nasiri*, 2:1014; Rota "Le favayedo's-safaviyeh," 439. Upon entering the court, he had been renamed Safi Quli Khan.

63 AAE, CP, Perse 5, Gardane, Shamakhi to Paris, 5 Jan. 1720, fol. 259v.; Bell of Antermony, *Travels from St. Petersburg*, 76.

64 NA, VOC 1856, Gamron to Isfahan, 30 Sept. 1713, fols. 953–4. Hirotake Maeda tells me that there may have been two different officials with the same name, and that the Fath 'Ali Khan holding the governor ship of Kuh-i Giluyah was a Georgian of the Baratishvili family. This issue requires more research.

65 NA, VOC 1856, Isfahan to Gamron, 30 Sept. 1713, fol. 471; ibid., Isfahan to Gamron, 15 Apr. 1714, fol. 740; VOC 1834, Gamron to Heren XVII, 23 Apr. 1714, fol. 2645v; VOC 1856, Gamron to Heren XVII, 13 June 1714, fol. 221; VOC 1870, Gamron to Batavia, 27 Dec. 1714, fol. 21.

66 For more details, see NA, VOC 1870, Isfahan to Gamron, 9 Mar. 1715, fols. 609–12; and Khatunabadi, *Vaqa'i` al-sinnin*, 567–8. Although Mir Muhammad Baqir Khatunabadi appears as the shaykh al-islam in the sources, he was in fact the first Safavid mullabashi. See Arjomand, "The Office of Mullabashi." One 'abbasi equaled 10 bistis. Eight bistis for a *man*, 2.9 kg, of bread was higher than usual, though less than during the famine of 1667, when the government had fixed the price at one 'abbasi or 10 bistis per man.

67 NA, VOC 1848, Isfahan to Heren XVII, 24 May 1715, fol. 2299.

68 NA, VOC 1886, Isfahan to Gamron, 9 Sept. 1715, fol. 209; ibid., Isfahan to Jacobsz., Gamron, 29 Sept. and 23 Oct. 1715, fols. 230, 278.

69 NA, VOC 1886, Isfahan to Gamron, 17 Nov. 1715, fols. 352–3.

70 NA, VOC 1886, Isfahan to Gamron, 9 Sept. 1715, fols. 202–4.

71 NA, VOC 1947, 2nd fasc., Isfahan Gamron, 5 Jan. 1720, fol. 293.

72 MAE, CP, Perse 5, Gardane, Shamakhi to Paris, 5 Jan. 1720, fol. 259v. For other opinions, see Bushev, *Posol'stvo Artemiia Volynskogo*, 104; and NA, VOC 1901, Daghregister Johan van Dinter, fol. 1079; and Matthee, "Blinded by Power," 192–3.

73 NA, VOC 1897, Isfahan to Gamron, 3 Dec. 1716, fol. 247.
74 In Ja'fariyan, `Ilal-i bar uftadan-i Safaviyan, 53. For the Bagh-i Farahabad, see Krusinski, *The History of the Late Revolutions*, 1:125. For its dedication as vaqf property, see Ja'fariyan, *Safaviyah dar `arsah-i din*, 903ff.
75 Maeda, "On the Ethno-Social Background."
76 Al-Husaini, *Tadhkira-i Shustar*, 66; Khatunabadi, *Vaqa'i` al-sinnin*, 558.
77 NA, VOC 1879, Isfahan to Gamron, 22 Aug. 1716, fol. 281; AAE, CP, Perse 5, Gardane, Yerevan to Paris, 5 Oct. 1717, fol. 145v. There is some difference about the age of this boy-ruler. According to the Dutch he was eight when he was appointed. Gardane, who was in Yerevan in 1717, at that point called him thirteen years old.
78 NA, VOC 1897, Isfahan to Gamron, 22 Jan. 1717, fol. 271.
79 NA, VOC 1886, Gamron to Batavia, 24 Mar. 1716, fol. 21.
80 NA, VOC 1897, Isfahan to Gamron, 22 Jan. 1717, fol. 271.
81 Al-Husaini, *Tadhkira-i Shushtar*, 69.
82 Mustawfi, *Zubdat al-tavarikh*, 120; Ja'fariyan, `Ilal-i bar uftadan-i Safaviyan, 149.
83 Beneveni, Shamakhi to St. Petersburg, 1 July 1720, in Beneveni, *Poslannik Petra I na Vostoke*, 48.
84 NA, VOC 1897, Isfahan to Gamron, 22 Jan 1717, fol. 271; Lang "Georgia and the Fall," 536; Bushev, *Posol'stvo Artemiia Volynskogo*, 182.
85 Ibid., 155.
86 AAE, MD, Perse 1, Gardane, Shamakhi to Paris, 5 Jan. 1720, fol. 41.
87 For more details, see Matthee, *The Politics of Trade*, 216–7. Also see Lockhart, *The Fall of the Safavi Dynasty*, 105; Bushev, *Posol'stvo Artemiia Volynskogo*, 58, 165–6.
88 AAE, MD, Perse 1, Gardane, Shamakhi to Paris, 5 Jan. 1720, fol. 41.
89 Bushev, *Posol'stvo Artemiia Volynskogo*, 106–7.
90 NA, VOC 1897, Isfahan to Gamron, 22 Jan. 1717, fol. 271.
91 NA, VOC 1964, 2nd fasc., Gamron to Heren XVII, 18 Sept. 1720, fols. 103–5.
92 Ja'fariyan, `Ilal-i bar uftadan-i Safaviyan, 125–6.
93 The Persian word *kusah* (shark), here translated as "inexperienced," is used for someone without a beard. According to Ja'fariyan, `Ilal-i bar uftadan-i Safaviyan, 125, it refers to Mirza Rafi`.
94 NA, VOC 1886, Isfahan to Gamron, 23 Oct. 1715, fols. 279ff.
95 NA, VOC 1913, 2nd fasc., Isfahan to Gamron, 7 Mar. 1718, fol. 276; Bushev, *Posol'stvo Artemiia Volynskogo*, 212. According to Volynskii, who heard the news while in Shamakhi, the incident had taken place on the evening of the day that the shah had arrived from Savah in Qum. Someone had fired a gun at Fath `Ali Khan while he was on his way to the shah's quarters rather than returning from a gathering with the monarch.
96 NA, VOC 1964, 2nd fasc., Gamron to Isfahan, 23 Oct. 1720, fols. 158–9.

97 Mar'ashi, *Majma' al-tavarikh*, 49–50. Fath 'Ali Khan's reputation as a Sunni may have prompted the mullabashi and his son to take a personal role in his blinding. See Ja'fariyan, *'Ilal-i bar uftadan-i Safaviyan*, 301. Lockhart, *The Fall of the Safavid Dynasty*, 117, notes that Muhammad Husayn disliked Fath 'Ali Khan for his presumed Sunni beliefs.

98 Beneveni, Tehran to St. Petersburg, 25 May 1721, in Beneveni, *Poslannik Petra I na Vostoke*, 52–54; AAE, MD, Perse 1, Gardane, Shamakhi to Paris, 5 Jan. 1720, fol. 41; Krusinski, *The History of the Late Revolutions*, 1:125–9, 234; Dourry Efendy, *Relation*, 69; Anon., ed., *A Chronicle of the Carmelites*, 556–7. The name of the Kurdish chief remains obscure. It may have been Khanah Pasha who, having grabbed power in 1720, ruled Kurdistan from Kirkuk to Hamadan until 1723–24. See Sanandaji, *Tuhfah-i Nasiri*, 135. For more details on the conspiracy, see Matthee, "Blinded by Power."

99 Krusinski, *The History of the Late Revolutions*, 1:125–9, 234; Dourry Efendy, *Relation*, 69; Anon., ed., *A Chronicle of the Carmelites*, 556–7.

100 NA, VOC 1964, 2nd fasc., Gamron to Batavia, 15 Feb. 1721, fol. 58; ibid., Isfahan to Heren XVII, 7 Jan. 1721, fols. 133–4. The farman appointing Muhammad Quli Khan Shamlu as the new grand vizier contains a passage about the blinding of his predecessor that referrs to the punishment as a "warning to the seeing," *'ibrat li'l-nazirin*. See Nava'i, ed., *Asnad va mukatibat*, 155.

101 Krusinski, *The History of the Late Revolutions*, 1:219ff.

102 Khatunabadi, *Vaqa'i' al-sinnin*, 537.

103 AME, vol. 351, Roch, Hamadan to Paris, 31 Oct. 1686, fol. 223. This missionary, referring to an outbreak the year before, foresaw a possible recurrence as a result of the extraordinary amount of rain that had fallen. The abundant rainfall in the winter of 1685–6 and the resulting spread of the plague are confirmed in a letter by Sanson written from Hamadan on 19 Apr. 1686, in ibid., fols. 186–8.

104 Khatunabadi, *Vaqa'i' al-sinnin*, 538–40, 543–4, claims 20,000 deaths in Tabriz; See also Witsen, *Noord en oost Tartaryen*, 694.

105 CA, O.C.D. 237h, Elia de S. Alberto, Isfahan to Rome, 18 June, 1689.

106 PF, SC. Giorgia 1, Giulio da Cremona Capp., 22 Oct. 1691, fol. 429; ibid., 26 Nov. 1691, fol. 438.

107 AME, vol. 348, "Relation du voyage de M. Gaudereau, " fols. 451–2; and 516 ; and [Vachet], "Journal du voyage," fols. 185–6.

108 This figure is given by Hamilton, *A New Account*, 1:82–3. Al-'Azzawi, *Tarikh al-'Iraq*, 5:129, 131, speaks of 100,000 deaths in Baghdad in 1689 and of up to 1,000 casualties a day for 1690. Other references to the plague in Basra and Khuzistan in 1691 are found in CA, O.C.D. 184a, "Annales de la mission de Bassorah," 1691, fols. 54–5; NA, VOC 1476, Kung to Heren XVII, 19 May 1691, fol. 633a; VOC 1493, Isfahan to Batavia, 13 Oct. 1691, fol. 283b; and in Ja'fariyan, *'Ilal-i*

bar uftadan-i Safaviyan, 331. For other cities, see [Vachet], "Journal du voyage," fols. 561–2, 574, 578.
109 Nasiri, *Dastur-i shahriyaran*, 153.
110 NA, VOC 1611, Isfahan to Gamron, 10 Sept. 1697, fol. 38; ibid. to ibid., 26 Nov. 1697, fol. 46.
111 Krusinski, *The History of the Late Revolutions*, 1:116.
112 Ardalan, *Les Kurdes Ardalân*, 50–1.
113 Gaudereau, "Relation de la mort de Schah Abbas," in Kroell, ed., *Nouvelles d'Ispahan*, 72.
114 NA, VOC 1611, Isfahan to Gamron, 26 Nov. 1697, fol. 46.
115 Floor, *Safavid Government Institutions*, 19.
116 Nasiri, *Dastur-i shahriyaran*, 129, 132–3, 177; NA, VOC 1611, Gamron to Heren XVII, 6 May 1698, fol. 37.
117 Nasiri, *Dastur-i shahriyaran*, 222ff. `Abbas Quli Khan was exiled to Alamut for his poor performance. See NA, VOC 1626, Isfahan to Gamron, 22 Feb. 1699, fol. 99; Ardalan, *Les Kurdes Ardalân*, 52–53, according to whom Sulayman Baba was defeated by the Safavids in 1698.
118 Nasiri, *Dastur-i -shahriyaran*, 244–7.
119 NA, VOC 1562, Gamron to Batavia, 25 Oct. 1696, fol. 664v.
120 Nasiri, *Dastur-i shahriyaran*, 153.
121 Inalcik, "The Socio-political Effects," 207.
122 Della Valle, *Viaggi*, 1:625.
123 Gaudereau, "Relation de la mort de Schah Abbas," in Kroell, ed., *Nouvelles d'Ispahan*, 65.
124 Bachoud, "lettre de Chamakié," in Fleuriau, ed., *Lettres édifiantes et curieuses*, 4:118.
125 Gilanentz, *The Chronicle*, 7.
126 Letter Israel Ori, in Ezov, ed. *Snosheniia Petra Velikogo*, 28–44.
127 Nasiri, *Dastur-i shahriyaran*, 104.
128 Bushev, *Posol'stvo Artemiia Volynskogo*, 155–6.
129 This included a plan to issue a new `abbasi weighing 16 1/6 percent less than the current ones, in order to prevent the outflow of money. NA, VOC 1798, Isfahan to Gamron, 15 May 1710, fol. 46.
130 NA, VOC 1798, Isfahan to Gamron, 15 May 1710, fol. 46.
131 NA, VOC 1732, Isfahan to Gamron, 23 July 1705, fol. 126; VOC 1737, Isfahan to Heren XVII, 20 Sept. 1708, fol. 120; VOC 1779, Isfahan to Gamron, 1 Nov. 1708, fol. 283; VOC 1798, Isfahan to Gamron, 4 Sept. 1709, fol. 222; NA, VOC 1856, Isfahan to Gamron, 23 Nov. 1713, fol. 558; NA, VOC 1856, Isfahan to Gamron, 23 Nov. 1713, fol. 558; AAE, Perse 5, "Mémoire sur les monnoyes de Perse et autres qui y ont cours," fols. 209–11. For more detailed information on these fluctuations, see Matthee, "Between Venice and Surat."
132 Khatunabadi, *Vaqa`i`c al-sinnin*, 553.
133 *Mukafatnamah*, in Ja`fariyan, *`Ilal-i bar uftadan-i Safaviyan*, 47.

134 Ja'fariyan, introduction to *Tarjumah-i anajil-i arba'ah*, 35; and Pucko, "The Activity of Polish Jesuits," 313.
135 Krzyszkowskie, "Entre Varsovie et Ispahan," 114–15.
136 Ja'faryan, *Safaviyah dar 'arsah-i din*, 986.
137 Kaempfer, *Am Hofe des persischen Grosskönigs*, 35–6.
138 Ja'fariyan, *Safaviyah dar 'arsah-i din*, 791–92.
139 NA, VOC 1626, Isfahan to Gamron, 22 Feb. 1699, fol. 99.
140 NA, VOC 1779, Isfahan to Gamron, 10 Dec. 1708, fol. 313.
141 NA, VOC 1856, Isfahan to Gamron, 15 Apr. 1714, fol. 742; ibid. to Batavia, 15 June 1714, fols. 86–7; VOC 1886, Isfahan to Gamron, 9 Sept. 1715, fol. 189. NA, VOC 1886, Isfahan to Gamron, 9 Sept. 1715, fol. 189.
142 Anon, ed., *A Chronicle of the Carmelites*, 484.
143 IOR, E/3/54, 6614, Isfahan to Company, 7 Feb. 1699, unfol.; and 6614, Isfahan to Gombroon, 7 Feb. 1699, unfol.
144 Ja'faryan, *Safaviyah dar 'arsah-i din*, 985.
145 Darhuhaniyan, *Tarikh-i Julfa-yi Isfahan*, 144, 150.
146 Harrach, "Voyage," fol. 22.
147 Anon., ed., *A Chronicle of the Carmelites*, 485; White, *Zaccaria Seriman*, introduction; Darhuhaniyan, *Tarikh-i Julfa-yi Iran*, 220–21; Aslanian, "The Circulation of Men and Credit," 152–3.
148 Tournefort, *Relation du voyage*, 2:312.
149 Arunova and Ashrafiyan, *Gosudarstvo Nadir-Shakha*, 51–2.
150 NA, VOC, 4th fasc., Gamron to Batavia, 30 Nov. 1716, fol. 16.
151 Soimonov, "Auszug aus dem Tage-Buch," 354–55; Ghougassian, *The Emergence of the Armenian Diocese*, 46.
152 Hazin. *The Life of Sheikh Muhammad Ali Hazin*, 112–13.
153 Lockhart, *The Fall of the Safavi Dynasty*, 73.
154 Moreen, *Iranian Jewry's Hour*, 15.
155 NA, VOC 1928, 3rd fasc., Gamron to Isfahan, 14 Jan. 1719, fols. 330–31; VOC 1964, Gamron to Isfahan, 13 Sept. 1721, fol. 343.
156 Gaudereau, "Relation de la mort de Schah Soliman," in Kroell, ed., *Nouvelles d'Ispahan*, 72.
157 Lockhart, *The Fall of the Safavi Dynasty*, 47, 72.
158 Gaudereau, "Relation de la mort de Schah Abbas," in Kroell, ed., *Nouvelles d'Ispahan*, 72.
159 De Bruyn, *Reizen over Moskovie*, 103–4, 434. De Bruyn presciently concluded that, given the region's economic importance, it would indeed be worth the Russians' while to invade, and that it would be a relatively simple operation, only requiring a small force.
160 Anon., ed., *A Chronicle of the Carmelites*, 519.
161 AAE, CP, Perse 5, Issoudroun to Michel, Tabriz, 12 June 1717, fol. 139a; NA, VOC 1904, Gamron to Heren XVII, 5 May 1719, fol. 2281v.; VOC 1947, 3rd fasc., Gamron to Heren XVII, 25 May 1719, fol. 75.

162 AAE, CP, Perse 6, Gardane, Shamakhi, 10 June 1721, fol. 13.
163 Kemper, *Herrrschaft, Recht und Islam*, 139.
164 NA, VOC 1879, Isfahan to Gamron, 22 Aug. 1716, fol. 281; VOC 1897, Isfahan to Gamron, 14 Nov. 1716, fol. 237.
165 Tournefort, *Relation d'un voyage*, 2:318.
166 Bushev, *Posol'stvo Artemiia Volynskogo*, 215–19.
167 His status as the eldest of the two sons and the support of his influential great-aunt Maryam Bigum had been responsible for the choice of Sultan Husayn as Shah Sulayman's successor in 1694. Many had favored the younger brother, `Abbas Mirza, however, for being much stronger of character and will than his sibling. See Lockhart, *The Fall of the Safavid Dynasty*, 35–6. Beneveni fails to give the name of the nazir, but from the Dutch sources we learn that Rajab `Ali Beg was the incumbent between 1714 and 1720. His name also occurs as nazir in Ansari, *Dastur al-Moluk*, 29, 219.
168 Letter Israel Ori, in Ezov, ed., *Snosheniia Petra Velikogo*, 39.
169 Bushev, *Posol'stvo Artemiia Volynskogo*, 212–13, 222; Kemper, *Herrschaft, Recht und Islam*, 142.
170 Bushev, *Posol'stvo Artemiia Volynskogo*, 224.
171 Beneveni, Shamakhi to St. Petersburg, 5 Jan. 1720, in Beneveni, *Poslannik Petra I na Vostoke*, 39–40.
172 Tardy, "Georgische Teilnahme," 325–6. It seems that Husayn Quli Khan resented the Iranians on account of his forcible conversion. We also know that he secretly expressed pro-Russian feelings to Volynskii. See Lang, "Georgia and the Fall," 534, 536; idem, *The Last Years*, 109–10; Lockhart, *The Fall of the Safavi Dynasty*, 118.
173 Dourry Efendy, *Relation*, 69.
174 Bushev, *Posol'stvo Artemiia Volynskogo*, 215–16, 219–20, AAE, Perse 5, Padery, Shamakhi, to Paris, 5 Jan. 1720, fols. 258–60; Lystsov, *Persidskii pokhod*, 103; Bachoud, "lettre de Chamakié," in Fleuriau, ed., *Lettres édifiantes et curieuses*, 4 :98–9.
175 Dourry Efendy, *Relation*, 41–42.
176 NA, VOC 1913, Gamron to Batavia, 31 Dec. 1717, fol. 49.
177 NA, VOC 1870, Isfahan to Gamron, 7 Jan. 1715, fol. 572; Bushev, *Posol'stvo Artemiia Volysnkogo*, 107, 161–2.
178 Ibid., 265–6.
179 Kemper, *Herrschaft, Recht und Islam*, 139–42.
180 Sotavov, *Severnii Kavkaz*, 63–9; Zarinebaf-Shahr, "Tabriz under Ottoman Rule," 105.
181 Ja`fariyan, *Safaviyah dar `arsah-i din*, 776.
182 Shushtari, *Tadhkira-i Shushtar*, 66.
183 NA, VOC 1571, Gamron to Batavia, 26 June 1695, fols.167–8.
184 Gaudereau, "Relation de la mort de Schah Abbas," in Kroell, ed., *Nouvelles d'Ispahan*, 62.
185 Ibid.; Ranjbar, *Musha`sha`iyan*, 330–1.

186 Nasiri, *Dastur-i shahriyaran*, 249; NA, VOC 1598, Gamron to Batavia, 8 June 1697, fol. 80; Gollancz, *Chronicle of Events*, 415; Ranjbar, *Musha`sha`iyan*, 331.
187 Afandi, *Gulshan-i khulafa*, 307; NA, VOC 1611, 2nd fasc., Gamron to Batavia, 11 Jan. 1698, fol. 19; idem to Heren XVII, 6 May 1698, fol. 37; idem to Batavia, 20 Aug. 1698, fol. 6.
188 NA 1843, Gamron to Isfahan, 11 May 1713, fols. 154–5. `Avaz Khan had served as governor of Bandar `Abbas in 1698–99. See Nasiri, *Dastur-i Shahriyaran*, 273.
189 NA, VOC 1856, Isfahan to Gamron, 29 June 1713, fols. 311–12.
190 NA, VOC 1856, Isfahan to Gamron, 20 Mar. 1714, fol. 682; VOC 1870, Gamron to Isfahan, 26 July 1714, fol. 91.
191 NA, VOC 1879, Gamron to Batavia, 30 Nov. 1716, fol. 16.
192 NA, VOC 1763, Isfahan to Gamron, 20 Sept. 1707, fol. 237; ibid., Gamron to Batavia, 21 Dec. 1707, fol. 106.
193 NA, VOC 1856, Gamron to Batavia, 15 June 1714, fols. 109–10.
194 Gaudereau, "Relation de la mort de Schah Soliman," in Kroell, ed., *Nouvelles d'Ispahan*, 72.
195 NA, VOC 1870, Isfahan to Gamron, 21 June 1714, fols. 173, 178–9.
196 NA, VOC 1856, Isfahan to Gamron, 11 Aug., 1713, fols. 382–3; ibid., Gamron to Heren XVII, 13 June 1714, fol. 257; VOC 1870, Isfahan to Gamron, 21 June 1714, fols. 178–9.
197 NA, VOC 1886, Isfahan to Gamron, 9 Sept. 1715, fol. 211; and ibid., Gamron, to Isfahan, 14 Sept. 715, fols.113–4.
198 NA, VOC 1886, Isfahan to Gamron, 23 Oct. 1715, fol. 302.
199 NA, VOC 1886, Isfahan to Gamron, 17 Nov. 1715, fol. 326–9; ibid., Gamron to Batavia, 15 Feb. 1716, fol. 95.
200 NA, VOC 1886, Isfahan to Gamron, 9 Sept. 1715, fol. 213.
201 NA, VOC 1897, Isfahan to Gamron, 22 Jan. 1717, fol. 271.
202 NA, VOC 1886, Gamron to Isfahan, 27 Feb. 1716, fols. 450–1.
203 NA, VOC 1913, Gamron to Batavia, 31 Dec. 1717, fol. 28.
204 NA, VOC 1913, 2nd fasc., Report Ketelaar to Van Swols, 31 Mar. 1718, fol. 499; and Floor, ed., *The Afghan Occupation*, 31.
205 NA, VOC 1913, 3d fasc., Daghregister Gamron, 24 Feb. 1718, fol. 307; 16 Mar., fol. 312; 19 Mar., fol. 314; 3 Apr., fols. 328–9. The Dutch thought that these numbers might be exaggerated.
206 Ibid., 17 April 1718, fol. 347; Mar`ashi Safavi, *Majma` al-tavarikh*, 39–40.
207 NA, VOC 1928, Isfahan to Gamron, 3 Sept. 1718, fol. 77; 12 Sept. 1718, fol. 81.
208 NA 1928, Gamron to Isfahan, 1 Dec. 1718, fol. 186; ibid., 3rd fasc., Gamron to Batavia, 30 Jan. 1719, fol. 139.
209 NA, VOC 1913, 2nd fasc., Gamron to Batavia, 31 Dec. 1717, fol. 49; VOC 1913, Isfahan to Gamron, 3 Feb. 1718, fol. 270; VOC 1913, Gamron to Isfahan, 6 Mar. 1718, fol. 291; VOC 1913, 2nd fasc.,

Report Ketelaar to Van Swols, 31 Mar. 1718, fols. 489–90, 498–9; ibid., Gamron to Isfahan, 12 Apr. 1718, fol. 295; NA, VOC 1913, 3rd fasc., Daghregister Gamron, 2 Mar. 1718, fol. 309 and 9 Mar. , fol. 311; VOC 1928, Letter I'timad al-dawlah to Oets, 24 Sept. 1718, fols. 225–8; VOC 1928, 3rd fasc., Gamron to Batavia, 30 Jan. 1719, fols. 135–6.

210 NA, VOC 1928, 3rd fasc., Gamron to Batvia, 20 Mar. 1719, fol. 258; VOC 1904, Gamron to Heren XVII, 5 May 1719, fol. 2280v; VOC 1947, 3rd fasc., Gamron to Heren XVII, 25 May 1719, fol. 74.

211 NA, VOC 1947, 3rd fasc., Isfahan to Gamron, 1 Sept. 1719, fol. 97; ibid., Gamron to Batavia, 25 Nov. 1719, fol. 51.

212 NA, VOC 1947, 3rd fasc., Lutf 'Ali Khan to Van Biesum, rec'd 28 Sept. 1719, fols. 118–20.

213 NA, VOC 1928, 3rd fasc., Gamron to Batavia, 20 Mar. 1719, fols. 257–8; 261–2; VOC 1947, 3rd fasc., Isfahan to Gamron, 1 Sept. 1719, fol. 97; ibid., Gamron to Batavia, 25 Nov. 1719, fol. 51.

214 NA, VOC 1964, Gamron to Oets, Isfahan, 10 Dec. 1720, fol. 211.

215 NA, VOC 1947, 3rd fasc., Gamron to Batavia, 29 Feb. 17120, fol. 235.

216 NA, VOC 1763, Isfahan to Gamron, 23 Feb. 1708, fol. 508; VOC 1779, Isfahan to Gamron, 29 July 1708, fol. 245.

217 Marvi Yazdi, 'Alam-ara-yi Nadiri, 1:11. The future Nadir Shah was sent to Isfahan to convey the news of the victory to the shah. See Axworthy, *The Sword of Persia*, 22.

218 Kirmani, *Sahifat al-irshad*, 445, 448.

219 See Floor, *The Persian Gulf*, 275–6.

220 Mashizi, *Tarikh-i Safaviyah-i Kirman*, 98–103, 546, 557–8, 583, 617.

221 Kirmani, *Sahifat al-irshad*, 229, 233–7, 240, 245, 267, 283ff.; Gaudereau, "Relation de la mort de Schah Abbas," in Kroell, ed., *Nouvelles d'Ispahan*, 65.

222 Kirmani, *Sahifat al-irshad*, introd., 77.

223 Mashizi, *Tarikh-i Safaviyah-i Kirman*, 94–5, 460–1.

224 Ibid., 537–38, 563, 636.

225 Nasiri, *Dastur-i shahriyaran*, 68, 72–4; Matthee, "The East India Company Trade," 358.

226 For details, see Gaudereau, "Relation de la mort de Schah Abbas," in Kroell, ed., *Nouvelles d'Ispahan*, 75–6; *Nouveaux mémoires*, 3:262; Zakaria in Brosset, *Collection*, 122–3; Brosset, ed., *Histoire de la Géorgie*, 2/ii, 15; Aubin, *L'ambassade de Gregório Pereira Fidalgo*, 73–5.; and Lang, *The Last Years*, 96–7.

227 Nasiri, *Dastur-i shahriyaran*, 277; Brosset, ed., *Histoire de la Géorgie*, I2/ii, 16; Krusinski, *The History of the Late Revolutions*, 1:150–1; Tardy, "Georgische Teilnahme," 321.

228 Kirmani, *Sahifat al-irshad*, 14, 298–301; 337, 346–7; Brosset, ed., *Histoire de la Géorgie* I2/ii:16–20; Lockhart, *The Fall of the Safavid Dynasty*, 46–7, 84–5.

229 Kirmani, *Sahifat al-irshad*, 351–4, 363–9.
230 Ibid., 368–9. The date given in this text, Rabi` al-thani 1121/17 June 1709 must be incorrect, both because it does not correspond to the anniversary of Umar's assassination and because Gurgin Khan was killed in April 1709.
231 Krusinski, *The History of the Late Revolutions*, 1:162.
232 Ibid., 154; Tihrani, *Mir'at-i varidat*, 108–9; Brosset, ed., *Histoire de la Géorgie*, 2/ii, 26; Lockhart, *The Fall of the Safavid Dynasty*, 85. Lockhart suggests that Mir Ways rebelled before being sent to Isfahan, but as Axworthy, *The Sword of Persia*, 295, fn. 49, observes, this is not the way Krusinski tells the story and anyhow not plausible.
233 Krusinski, *The History of the Late Revolutions*, 1:179–81; Tardy, "Georgische Teilnahme," 323-3, Lockhart, *The Fall of the Safavi Dynasty*, 86–7.
234 Ibid., 112–13; Kirmani, *Sahifat al-irshad*, 378–9; NA, VOC 1753, Isfahan to Gamron, 23 June 1709, fol. 292v.; "Traduction d'un mémoire," fols. 254–7; Soimonov, "Auszug aus dem Tage-Buch", 299; Tardy, "Georgische Teilnahme," 325; Lang, *The Last Years*, 1957, 99-101; the different versions are summed up in Lockhart, *The Fall of the Safavi Dynasty*, 87-8.
235 Mustawfi, *Zubdat al-tavarikh*, 116-17, 168; NA, VOC 1768, Gamron, to Heren XVII, 1 Oct. 1710, fol. 2059v; Krusinski, *The History of the Late Revolutions*, 1:100-01, 190-2, 194; and Lockhart, *The Fall of the Safavi Dynasty*, 89-91. The figure of 3,000 soldiers is given in NA, VOC 1798, Isfahan to Gamron, 4 Sept. 1709, fols. 218-9; VOC 1753, 23 June 1709, fol. 293v; Mustawfi gives the number of 12,000 soldiers.
236 NA, VOC 1843, Gamron to Isfahan, 11 May 1713, fols. 153-4; ibid., Isfahan to Gamron, 25 May 1713, fol. 165; VOC 1856, Isfahan to Gamron, 13 June 1714, fol. 798.
237 NA, VOC 1843, Isfahan to Heren XVII, 14 Nov. 1712, fol. 193; AAE, CP, Perse, 3, Pidou de St Olon, Isfahan, 3 Dec. 1712, fol. 25v.
238 NA, VOC 1843, Gamron to Isfahan, 30 May 1713, fol. 61; VOC 1865, Isfahan to Gamron, 13 June 1713, fol. 273.
239 NA, VOC 1856, Isfahan to Gamron, 11 Aug. 1713, fols. 382-3; 30 Sept., fol. 473; VOC 1870, Gamron to Isfahan, 6 June 1714, fol. 130.
240 NA, VOC 1856, Isfahan to Gamron, 1 Sept. 1713, fol. 452; ibid., Gamron to Isfahan, 3 Oct. 1713, fol. 939.
241 NA, VOC 1856, Gamron to Isfahan, 1 Sept. 1713, fol. 452; ibid., Gamron to Isfahan, 3 Oct. 1713, fol. 939.
242 NA VOC 1856, Isfahan to Gamron, 23 Nov. 1713, fol. 541; VOC 1856, Isfahan to Gamron 27 Feb. 1714, fol. 672; ibid., Isfahan to Gamron, 10 Mar. 1714, fol. 683; ibid., Gamron to Heren XVII, 23 Apr. 1714, fol. 202.
243 NA, VOC 1886, Isfahan to Gamron, 2 Feb. 1716, fols. 429-30; Gamron to Batavia, 15 Feb. 1716, fol. 92.
244 Kirmani, *Sahifat al-irshad*, 86-8.

245 NA, VOC 1886, Gamron to Isfahan, 27 Feb. 1716, fol. 451-2; and VOC 1897, Isfahan to Gamron, 4 Oct. 1716, fol. 293; ibid., Gamron to Batavia, 30 Nov. 1716, fols. 26-8; ibid., trans. Armenian wool buyers Auwanees and Gatjatoer, 2 Jan. 1717, fols. 359-65.
246 NA, VOC 1897, Isfahan to Gamron, 4 Oct. 1716, fol. 293.
247 NA, VOC 1897, report Armenian wool collectors, 2 Jan. 1717, fols. 361-3.
248 NA, VOC 1913, Kirman to Gamron, 8 Apr. 1717, fol. 183; ibid., Kirman to Gamron, 11 May, fol. 186; Kirman to Gamron, 14 Aug. 1717, fol. 197; VOC 1913, Kirman to Gamron, 2 Nov. 1717, fols. 219–21; VOC 1928, Kirman to Gamron, 25 July 1718, fol. 110.
249 Kirmani, *Sahifat al-irshad*, introd., 90–91; NA, VOC 1913, Kirman to Gamron, 8 Apr. 1717, fols. 180–3. For more information, see Matthee, "The East India Company Trade," 373–5.
250 NA, VOC 1856, Isfahan to Gamron, 9 Oct. 1713, fols. 494–5.
251 NA, VOC 1897, Isfahan to Gamron, 14 Nov. 1716, fol. 237; ibid., Isfahan to Gamron, 3 Dec. 1716, fol. 268; ibid., Gamron to Batavia, 30 Nov. 1716, fol. 16; Worm, *Ost-Indian- und persianische Reisen*, 293.
252 Bushev, *Posol'stvo Artemiia Volynskogo*, 162.
253 The extent of Maryam Bigum's private assets was revealed when, upon her death on 17 September 1720, she is said to have left behind the enormous sum of 200,000 tumans in cash in addition to large amounts of jewelry, gold, silver and landed property. See NA, VOC 1964, Gamron to Batavia, 15 Feb. 1721, fol. 54.
254 NA, VOC 1913, 2nd fasc., Gamron to Batavia, 31 Dec. 1717, fol. 49; VOC 1913, Isfahan to Gamron, 3 Feb. 1718, fol. 270; ibid., Gamron to Isfahan, 6 Mar. 1718, fol. 291; ibid., 2nd fasc., Report Ketelaar to van Swols, 31 Mar. 1718, fols. 489–90; ibid., Gamron to Isfahan, 12 Apr. 1718, fol. 295; ibid., 3rd fasc., Daghregister Gamron, 2 Mar. 1718, fol. 309; and 9 Mar., fol. 311.
255 Rabino, *Coins, Medals, and Seals* 34; Radzhabli, "Iz istorii monetnogo dela," 55; Kuteliia, *Gruziia i sefevidskii Iran* 28.
256 NA, VOC 1856, Isfahan to Gamron, 10 Mar. 1714, fol. 690.
257 Bushev, *Posol'stvo Artemiia Volynskogo*, 163, 257; Mustawfi, *Zubdat al-tavarikh*, 118–9; NA, VOC 1897, Isfahan to Gamron, 14 Nov. 1716, fols. 230–1; VOC 1879, 4th fasc., Gamron to Batavia, 30 Nov. 1716, fol. 17; VOC 1913, Gamron to Batavia, 31 Dec. 1717, fol. 49.
258 NA, VOC 1856, Isfahan to Gamron, 14 Jan. 1714, fol. 625; VOC 1870, Isfahan to Gamron, 25 Aug. 1714, fol. 222.
259 NA, VOC 1886, Isfahan to Gamron, 23 Oct. 1715, fol. 272.
260 NA, VOC 1879, Gamron to Batavia, 30 Jan. 1716, fol. 41; ibid., Gamron to Batavia, 30 Nov. 1716, fol. 41.
261 Mir Ways was initially succeeded by a nephew named Aqa Pir Muhammad, who, killing a number of Mir Ways's sons and all Iranian prisoners, kept up the pressure on Herat, plundering many villages around and luring many poorly paid Safavid soldiers to his ranks. See NA, VOC 1886,

Isfahan to Gamron, 2 Feb. 1716, fol. 429–30; ibid., Gamron to Batavia, 15 Feb. 1716, fol. 92. Floor, ed., *The Afghan Occupation*, 39–40, mistakes him for a son of Mir Ways and conflates him with Mahmud.

262 NA, VOC 1947, Kirman to Gamron, 3 Nov. 1719, fols. 130–1; ibid., Kirman to Gamron, 19 and 24 Oct. 1719, fols. 130–35; VOC 1937, Gamron to Batavia, 25 Nov. 1719, fols. 2153v–54; VOC 1947, Armenian wool buyers, Kirman, sent from Isfahan to Gamron, 3 Dec. 1719, fols. 301–6.

263 NA, VOC 1947, 3rd fasc., Isfahan to Gamron, 5 Jan. 1720, fol. 293; ibid., Armenian wool buyers, Kirman to Isfahan, 5 Jan. 1720, fol. 308; VOC 1947, 3rd fasc., Gamron to Batavia, 29 Feb. 1720, fol. 223.

264 Krusinki, *The History of the Late Revolutions*, 1:223–5.

265 NA, VOC 1947, Report Armenian wool buyers, Kirman, 3 Dec. 1719, fol. 304.

266 NA, VOC 1964, missives Qalb 'Ali Fazlullah, Muhammad Ibrahim "Della" (Allah?) and Shir 'Ali Munajjim, Kirman to wool buyers in Isfahan, early 1720, fols. 305–12; NA 1947, Armenian wool buyers, Isfahan to Gamron, 5 Jan. 1720, fols. 307–08.

267 Krusinski, *The History of the Late Revolutions*, 1:220; Lockhart, *The Fall of the Safavi Dynasty*, 73.

268 NA, VOC 1947, Armenian wool buyers, Isfahan, 5 Jan. 1720, fol. 308; VOC 1947, 2nd fasc., Gamron to Batavia, 29 Feb. 1720, fol. 223; VOC 1964, Kirman to Isfahan, 18 Apr. 1720, fol. 306; Lockhart, *The Fall of the Safavi Dynasty*, 112; and Matthee, "The East India Company Trade," 376. The Dutch sources seem to confirm Lockhart's suspicion that the Afghan retreat from Kirman was caused by a revolt in Qandahar rather than by Lutf 'Ali Khan—who never arrived at Kirman.

269 NA, VOC 1964, Kirman to Gamron, 18 July 1720, fol. 299.

270 NA, VOC 1983, Kirman to Gamron, 2 Feb. 1722, fols. 530–2.

271 NA, VOC 1983, 9 Nov. 1721, fols. 247–9; ibid., 21 and 28 Feb. 1722, fols. 288–9, 532–42; VOC 1999, Report Lispensier, fols. 352–6; Mar'ashi, *Majma' al-tavarikh*, 55–6; Floor, ed., *The Afghan Occupation*, 55–62.

272 Narrative in Floor, ed., *The Afghan Occupation*, 63ff.

273 Spahans Daghregister, in Floor, ed., *The Afghan Occupation*, 85.

274 Ibid., 87; Lockhart, *The Fall of the Safavi Dynasty*, 130–43; Alexander of Malabar, "The Story of the Sack of Isfahan," 646.

275 Krusinski, *The History of the Late Revolutions*, 2:22; Floor, ed., *The Afghan Occupation*, 88; Alexander of Malabar, "The Story of the Sack of Isfahan," 647.

276 Ibid., 648–49; Spahans Daghregister, in Floor, ed. *The Afghan Occupation*, 96–7, 100, 105–06; Krusinski, *The History of the Late Revolutions*, 2:120; Gilanentz, *The Chronicle*, 11–12. Iran's Zoroastrians, too, seem to have lent a hand to the Afghans. It was a Zoroastrian qanat-digger who delivered the village of Gaz, nine miles from Isfahan, to the Afghans by tunneling under its walls.

277 Gilanentz, *The Chronicle*, 13–8.
278 Spahans Daghregister, 2 Apr., 27 Apr., 24 July, 31 Aug. 1722, in Floor, ed., *The Afghan Occupation*, 110–1, 119–21, 150, 171.
279 Gilanentz, *The Chronicle*, 21. For Maryam Bigum's assets, see fn. 254.
280 Mustawfi, *Zubdat al-tavarikh*, 134.
281 Gilanentz, *The Chronicle*, 21.
282 Fasa'i, *Farsnamah-i Nasiri*, 1:502.
283 Bihbahani, *Bada`i-al-akhbar*, 41.

CONCLUSION

1 For the question of whether Safavid Iran was an empire, see Matthee, "Was Safavid Iran an Empire?"
2 Morony, "'In a City without Watchdogs."
3 For these objectives, see Tilly, "Reflections on the History," 23–4.
4 Monshi, *History of Shah 'Abbas*, 523. For the second listing, see Floor, "A Note on the Grand Vizier," 443.
5 Starn, "Historians and 'Crisis.'"
6 Consider the similarities with the Mongol Empire which, in Morgan's words, "dissolved" around the year 1260, a little over thirty years after the death of its founder, Chinggis Khan. See Morgan, "The Decline and Fall," 3.
7 Ibid., 4.
8 Chardin, *Voyages*, 3:291–2. Al-Shushtari, like many after him, insisted that matters deteriorated with the feeble and incompetent Shah Sultan Husayn. Shushtari, *Tadhkira-i Shushtar*, 116. Mirza Naqi Nasiri, writing during the Afghan interregnum, contends that the Safavid state began to decline with Shah Sulayman. See Nasiri, *Titles and Emoluments*, 53. Isfahani, the author of the nineteenth-century *Nisf-i jahan*, 181, insisted that the decline began with the death of Shaykh 'Ali Khan in 1689. Another Qajar historian, the I'timad al-Saltanah, saw decline start with the accession of Shah Sultan Husayn, five years later. See I'timad al-Saltanah, *Tarikh-i muntazam-i Nasiri*, 2:996.
9 Minorsky, ed., *Tadhkirat al-Mulūk*, 23.
10 Abu'l Fazl, *Akbarnama*, 2:317.
11 For this, see Matthee, "Iraq-i 'Arab."
12 Dale, *Muslim Empires*, 248.
13 Paraphrasing Murphey, *Exploring Ottoman Sovereignty*, 15.
14 Chardin, *Voyages*, 5:219.
15 Amanat, *The Pivot of the Universe*, 257.
16 Dubbed a "nursery of lust and intemperance," the court of England's James I, a contemporary of Shah 'Abbas I, was filled with drinking, gambling and sexual antics. See Houston, *James I*, 111.
17 For this, see Matthee, *The Pursuit of Pleasure*, especially chs. 2 and 3.

18 Rustam al-Hukama, *Rustam al-tavarikh*, 91–2, 98–9, 108–9, 328.
19 Chardin, *Voyages*, 5:237. For ʿAbbas's policy of diversifying his sources of advice, see Della Valle, *Delle conditioni*, 28. Morgan, "The Decline and Fall," 4–5. In Morton's words, "ʿAbbas's system required not their destruction but their continued existence to balance the new forces he had favored at their expense." Morton, "The Chūb-i Tarīq," 243.
20 See Amanat, *The Pivot of the Universe*, 160, for the relationship between shahs and grand viziers in Iranian history. In contemporary Europe, France and Spain in particular, one witnesses a similar dilemma. Several newly confident monarchs did away with their minister-favorites to take on the reins of government themselves—Louis XIII who did not replace Mazarin after the latter's death in 1661, and Leopold I of Austria who acted similarly when Ferdinand Portia died in 1665.
21 In the Ottoman Empire, badly shaken by waves of turbulence in the 1640s, the weak Sultan Mehmet IV at least allowed Köprülü Mehmet Pasha to "restore" the empire with a free and ruthless hand. See Baer, *Honored by the Glory*, 79, 105–6.
22 Sultan Aurangzeb (r. 1658–1708) resembled Sultan Husayn in being heavily influenced by doctrinal religion, but as the most peripatetic of all Mughal rulers he still continued to project authority. See Blake, "The Patrimonial-Bureaucratic Empire," 93.
23 See Axworthy, *The Sword of Persia*, 166–8.
24 Letter Gaudereau, 5 Dec. 1695, in Kroell, ed., *Nouvelles d'Ispahan*, 73.
25 Della Valle, *Viaggi*, 1:662.
26 Tihrani, *Miras-i varidat*, 14–15.
27 Murphey, "Mustafa Ali," 246.
28 Brewer, *The Sinews of Power*, 7–8.
29 For this, in reference to Sultan Babur, the founder of the Mughal dynasty (r. 1526–30), see Dale, *The Garden of the Eight Paradises*, 94, 153.
30 For some comparative observations on the differences in palace architecture between the three empires, see Necipoğlu, "Framing the Gaze."
31 ʿAbidini, "Munasibat-i siyasi," 80; and Faroqhi, "Der osmanische Blick nach Osten," 379.
32 Lambton, "The Tribal Resurgence."
33 Marx, *Faith in Nation*, 93–4, 120–1, 127.
34 For this term, see McChesney, "'Barrier of Heterodoxy.'"
35 The contrast with India is instructive. Following the reign of the zealous Aurangzeb, Zu'l Fiqar Khan sought to revive the liberal tradition of Sultan Akbar by trying to coopt peripheral groups, by abolishing the *jizʾya* in 1712, and by making concessions to the Rajputs and the Marathas. See Chandra, *Parties and Politics*, 125.
36 The most forceful representatives of the "Mughalist" school are Habib, *The Agrarian System*, and Chandra, *Parties and Politics*.
37 Barnett, *North India*, 21–2.
38 Perry, "The Last Safavids."

Bibliography

I. ARCHIVAL SOURCES

The Netherlands

Nationaal Archief (NA), The Hague. Eerste afdeling (first section).
Records of the Verenigde Oostindische Compagnie (VOC) (Dutch East India Company).
Overgekomen brieven en papieren (Letters and papers received). Vols. 1130–1999 (1639–1722). Papers relating to the VOC factories in Isfahan, Shiraz, Kirman, Gamron (Bandar ʿAbbas), and Surat, written from these factories to the VOC Asian headquarters in Batavia and its general headquarters in Amsterdam, respectively.
Bataviasch uitgaand brievenboek (Batavia's outgoing Letterbook). Vols. 850–974 (1623–1721). Letters relating to Iran, written from the VOC headquarters in Batavia to the factory in Gamron.
Resoluties van de Heren XVII (Resolutions of the Heren XVII). Vols. 106–11 (1660–95). Resolutions taken by the VOC directors in Holland.
Copieboek van brieven (Copy book of letters). Vols. 315–22 (1627–96). Copies of letters, instructions, and other papers sent by the Heren XVII and the Amsterdam Chamber to the Indies and the Cape).
Collectie Geleynssen de Jongh. Vols. 28, 142, 148, 157, 157a, 283.

Great Britain

British Library, London.
    Shamlu, Vali Quli b. Davud Quli. "Qisas al-khaqani." Ms. Or. 7656.
India Office Records (IOR), London.
    Records of the English East India Company (EIC).
    Letters from Persia, Original Correspondence. Vols. E/3/6-E/3/60 (1618–1701).
    Despatch Books (Letters from the London Council to Asia). Vols. E/3/84-E/3/92 (1653–95).
    Factory Records Persia and Persian Gulf G/29/1.

Factory Records Surat G/36/84-G/36/110 (1653–94).
Factory Records Miscellaneous G/40/2–5; G/40/30.
University of Cambridge.
Khuzani Isfahani, Fazli. "Afzal al-tavarikh," vol. 3, Christ's College, ms. Dd.5.6

France

Archives des Affaires Etrangères (AE), Paris.
Memoires et documents (MD), Coll. Perse. Vols. 5–6.
Archives de la Société des Missions Etrangères (AME), Paris.
Vol. 347. Vachet, Bénigne, "Journal d'un voyage en Perse."
Vol. 348. Gaudereau, M., "Relation du voyage de M. Gaudereau à Ispahan adressée aux supérieurs et directeurs du séminaire de Tours, le 22 janvier 1691."
Vols. 349–53.
Bibliothèque Nationale, Paris. Collection Clairambault 297.
[Vachet], "Journal d'un voyage en Perse commencé au mois de Décembre de l'année 1689." Mss. Fr. 24516.

Italy

Carmelite Archives, Rome.
O.C.D. series. Vols. 236, 237, 238, 241, 242, 243.
Casanatense Library, Rome.
Miscella 608/43.
Propaganda Fide Archives, Rome.
Scritture referite nei Congressi (S.C).
Mesopotamia, Persia, Caldei. Vol. 1 (1614–1690). Vol. 2 (1691–1707).
Giorgia. Vol. 1 (1626–1707).
Archivum Romanum Societatis Iesu, Rome (ARSI).
Gall. 97[ii], letter Claude Ignace Mercier, S.J., Isfahan, 28 Feb. 1672
Gall. 97[ii,] De la Maze, description of travel through northern Iran.

Portugal

Biblioteca da Ajuda, Lisbon.
Codex 46-X-10 G. Michele, "Relazione delli successi della Guerra fra il Turco e Persiano dall' anno 1577 al 1587."
Codex, 46-IX-23. "Relazione della Persia fatta al Senato Veneto Anno MDLXXX."

Austria

Haus-, Hof- und Staatsarchiv (HHSt), Vienna.
Harrach, Ferdinand Amadeus von. "Voyage en Perse." Handschriften, Hs. Weiss 706/30.

II. COLLECTIONS OF DOCUMENTS AND REFERENCE WORKS

Anon, ed. *A Chronicle of the Carmelites in Persia and the Papal Mission of the XVIIth and XVIIIth Centuries*. 2 vols. edited as one. London, 1939.
Brosset, M. -F., trans. and ed. *Chronique Géorgienne*. Paris, 1830.
——, trans. and ed. *Collection d'historiens arméniens*. 2 vols. St. Petersburg, 1874–76.
——, trans. and ed. *Histoire de la Géorgie depuis l'antiquité jusqu'au XIXe siècle*. 2 vols. St. Petersburg, 1856–57.
——, trans. and ed. *Des historiens arméniens des XVIIe et XVIIIe siècles: Arakel de Tauriz, régistre chronologique*. St. Petersburg, 1873.
Coolhaas, W. Ph., ed. *Generale missiven van Gouverneurs-Generaal en Raden aan Heren XVII der Verenigde Oost-Indische Compagnie*. 9 vols. The Hague, 1960–88.
Dunlop, H., ed. *Bronnen tot de geschiedenis der Oostindische Compagnie in Perzië, 1611–1638*. The Hague, 1930.
Džaja, Srećko M., and Günter Weiss, eds. *Austro-Turcica 1541–1552. Diplomatische Akten des habsburgischen Gesandtschaftsverkehrs mit der Hohen Pforte im Zeitalters Süleymans des Prächtigen*. Munich, 1995.
Fawcett, Charles, ed. *The English Factories in India*. 4 vols. Oxford, 1936–55.
Fleuriau, Père, ed. *Lettres édifiantes et curieuses, écrites des missions étrangères*. 8 vols. Toulouse, new ed., 1810.
Floor, Willem, trans. and ed. *The Afghan Occupation of Safavid Persia 1721–1729*. Paris, 1998.
Foster, Sir William, ed. *The English Factories in India, 1618–1669*. 13 vols. Oxford, 1906–27.
Gollancz, Sir Hermann. *Chronicle of Events between the Years 1629 and 1733 relating to the Settlement of the Order of Carmelites in Mesopotamia (Bassora)*. Oxford, 1927.
——, ed. *Chronicle of Events between the Years 1623 and 1733 relating to the Settlements of the Order of the Carmelites in Mesopotamia (Basra)*. Oxford, 1927.
Heeres, J. E., and F. W. Stapel, eds. *Corpus diplomaticum Neerlando-Indicum*. 5 vols. of *Bijdragen tot de Taal-, Land- en Volkenkunde van Nederlandsch-Indië*. The Hague, 1907–55.
Heeringa, K., ed. *Bronnen tot de geschiedenis van de Levantsche handel*. 2 vols. The Hague, 1910–17.
Islam, Riazul, ed. *A Calendar of Documents on Indo-Persian Relations (1500–1750)*. 2 vols. Tehran/Karachi, 1979.
Kaempfer, Engelbert. *Briefe, 1683–1715*. Edited by Dieter Haberland. Munich, 2001.
Mazandarani, Ghulam `Ali Vahid, ed. *Majmu`ah-i `ahdnamah'ha-yi tarikhi-yi Iran*. Tehran, 1350/1971.

Nava'i, 'Abd al-Husayn, ed. *Asnad va mukatibat-i siyasi-yi Iran az sal-i 1038 ta 1105 h.q.* Tehran, 1360/1981.

——. *Shah 'Abbas. Asnad va mukatibat-i tarikhi hamrah ba yaddashtha-yi tafsili.* 3 vols. Tehran, 2nd ed., 1366/1987.

Parsamian, V. A., et al., eds. *Armiano-russkie otnosheniia v VXII veke.* Erevan, 1953.

Puturidze, V. S., ed. *Persidskie istoricheskie dokumenty v knigokhraniloshchakh Gruzii.* 4 vols. Tiflis, 1961–77.

Sabitiyan, Z., ed. *Asnad va namah'ha-yi tarikhi va ijtima`i-yi, dawrah-i Safaviyah.* Tehran, 1343/1964.

Sainsbury, W. Noel, ed. *Calendar of State Papers, Colonial Series, East Indies, China and Japan, 1617–1621.* London, 1870; repr. Vaduz, 1964.

Schimkoreit, Renate, ed. *Regesten publizierter safawidsicher Herrscherurkunden: Erlasse und Staatsschreiben der frühen Neuzeit Irans.* Berlin, 1982.

Tajbakhsh, Ahmad. *Tarikh-i Safaviyah. Asnad va tarikh.* Shiraz, 1372/1994.

Zabihi, Masih, and Manuchihr Situdah, eds. *Az Astara ta Astarabad.* Vols. 6. and 7. Tehran, 1054/1975.

III. PRINTED PRIMARY SOURCES

Abu'l Faiz. *Akbarnama.* Trans. by H. Beveridge, 2 vols. Calcutta, 1907–39.

Afandi, 'Abd Allah b. 'Isa. *Riyaz al-`ulama va hiyaz al-fuzala.* Mashhad, 1366/1987.

Afushta'i Natanzi, Mahmud b. Hidayat Allah. *Naqavat al-asar fi zhikr al-akhyar.* Edited by Ihsan Ishraqi. Tehran, 2nd ed., 1373/1994.

Alexander of Malabar. "The Story of the Sack of Isfahan by the Afghans in 1722." *Journal of the Royal Central Asian Society* 33 (1936): 643–53.

Alonso, Carlos, O.S.A. "Due lettere riguardanti i primi tempi delle missioni agostiniane in Persia," *Analecta Augustiniana* 24 (1961): 152–201.

Andersen, Jürgen, and Volquard Iversen. *Orientalische Reise-Beschreibungen.* Schleswig, 1669; repr. edited by Dieter Lohmeier, Tübingen, 1980.

Ange de St. Joseph. *Souvenirs de la Perse safavide et autres lieux de l'Orient (1664–1678).* Translated and annotated by Michel Bastiaensen. Brussels, 1985.

Anon. *`Alam-ara-yi Safavi.* Edited by Yad Allah Shukri. Tehran.1363/1984.

Ansari, Mohammd Rafi` al-Din. *Dastur al-Moluk. A Safavid State Manual.* Edited by Willem Floor and Mohammad H. Faghfoory. Costa Mesa, 2007.

Astarabadi, Sayyid Hasan Murtaza Husayni. *Tarikh-i sultani. Az Shaykh Safi ta Shah Safi.* Edited by Ihsan Ishraqi. Tehran, 1364/1985–86.

Aubin, Jean, ed. *L'ambassade de Gregório Pereira Fidalgo à la cour de Châh Soltân Hosseyn 1696–1697.* Lisbon, 1971.

Avril, Philippe, S. J. *Voyage en divers états d'Europe et d'Asie entrepris pour découvrir un nouveau chemin à la Chine.* Paris, 1692.

Bachoud, Père. "Lettre de Chamakié, le 25 septembre 1712, au Père Fleuriau." In Fleuriau, ed., *Lettres édifiantes et curieuses*, 4:91–100.
Bahrani, Shaykh Yusuf. *Lu'lu'at al-Bahrayn*. N.p., n.d.
Barbosa, Duarte. *The Books of Duarte Barbosa*. Trans. and edited by M. Longworth Dames, 2 vols. London, 1918.
Bedik, Bedros. *Cehil Sutun, seu explicatio utriusque celeberrimi, ac prettiosissimi theatri quadraginta columnarum in Perside orientis, cum adjecta fusiori narratione de religione, moribus*. Vienna, 1678.
Bell of Antermony, John. *Travels from St Petersburg to Various Parts of Asia*. Edinburgh, new ed. in one vol., 1805.
Bembo, Ambrosio. *The Travels and Journal of Ambrosio Bembo*. Trans. by Clara Bargellini; edited and annotated by Anthony Welch. Berkeley, 2007.
Beneveni, Florio. *Poslannik Petra I na Vostoke. Posol'stvo Florio Beneveni v Persiiu i Bukhari v 1718–1725 godakh*. Edited by M. L. Vais et al., Moscow, 1986.
Berchet, Gugliemo, ed. *La repubblica di Venezia e la Persia*. Turin, 1865; repr. Tehran, 1976.
Bihbahani, Mirza ʿAbd al-Nabi Shaykh al-Islam. *Badaʿi al-akhbar (Vaqaʾi'-i Bihbahan dar zaman-i hamlah-i Mahmud Afghan)*. Edited by Sayyid Saʿid Mir Muhammad Sadiq. Tehran, 1389/2010.
Boullaye-le-Gouz, Sieur de la. *Les voyages et observations du Sieur Boullaye-le Gouz*. Paris, 1657; repr. 1994.
Brugsch, H. *Reise der K. Preussische Gesandtschaft nach Persien 1860 und 1861*. 2 vols. Leipzig, 1862–63.
Busse, Heribert. *Untersuchungen zum islamischen Kanzleiwesen an Hand turkmenischer und safawidischer Urkunden*. Cairo, 1959.
Carré, Barthélemy. *Le courrier du roi en Orient. Relations de deux voyages en Perse et en Inde 1668–1674*. Edited and annotated by Dirk van der Cruysse. Paris, 2005.
———. *The Travels of Abbé Carré in India and the Near East 1672 to 1674*. Translated by Lady Fawcett; edited by Sir Charles Fawcett and Sir Richard Burn, 3 vols. paginated as one. London, 1947–48.
Chardin, Jean. *Voyages du chevalier Chardin, en Perse, et autres lieux de l'Orient*. Edited by L. Langlès. 10 vols. and map. Paris, 1810–11.
Chelebi, Evliya. *Travels in Iran and the Caucasus, 1647–1654*. Trans. and edited by Hasan Javadi and Willem Floor. Washington D.C., 2010.
Chinon, Gabriel de. *Relations nouvelles du Levant ou traités de la religion, du gouvernement et des coûtumes des Perses, des Arméniens, et des Gaures*. Lyon, 1671.
Curzon, George N. *Persia and the Persian Question*, 2 vols. London, 1892.
D'Alessandri, Vincenzio. "Narrative of the Most Noble Vincentio d'Alessandri." In Grey, ed., *A Narrative of Italian Travels*, 211–29.
De Bourges, Jacques. *Relation du voyage de monseigneur l'évêque de Beryte vicaire apostolique du royaume de la Cochinchine par la Turquie, la Perse, les Indes etc... jusqu'au royaume de Siam*. Paris, 1666.
De Bruyn, Cornelis. *Reizen over Moskovie, door Persie en Indië: Verrykt met Driehondert konstplaten, Vertoonende de beroemdste lantschappen en steden, ook de byzondere dragten, beesten, gewassen en planten die daer gevonden worden: Voor al derzelver oudheden En wel*

voornamentlyk heel uitvoerig die van heerlyke en van oudts de geheele werrelt door befaemde Hof van Persepolis, by de Persianen Tchilminar genaemt. Amsterdam, 1714.

De la Maze, Jean-Baptiste, S. J. "Journal du Père de la Maze, de Chamakie à Ispahan, par la province du Guilan." In Fleuriau, ed., *Lettres édifiantes et curieuses*, 4:43–90.

———. "Mémoire de la province de Sirvan, en forme de lettre adressée au Fleuriau." In Fleuriau, ed., *Lettres édifiantes et curieuses*, 4:11–42.

Della Valle, Pietro. *Delle conditioni di Abbàs Rè di Persia*. Venice, 1628; repr. Tehran, 1976.

———. *Viaggi di Pietro della Valle. Il pellegrino descritti da lui medesimo in lettere familiari all-erudito suo amico Mario Schipano divisi in tre parti cioè: la Turchia, la Persia e l'India*. 2 vols. Edited by G. Gancia. Brighton, 1843.

Dernschwamm, Hans. *Hans Dernschwamm's Tagebuch einer Reise nach Konstantinopel und Kleinasien (1553/55)*. Edited by Franz Babinger. Berlin, 1986.

Deslandes, André Daulier. *The Beauties of Persia or an Account of the Most Interesting Features in that Kingdom*. Paris, 1673; repr. London, 1926.

Don Juan. *Don Juan of Persia. A Shi`ah Catholic 1560–1604*. Translated and edited by G. Le Strange. London, 1926.

Dourry Efendy, Ahmad. *Relation de Dourry Efendy, ambassadeur de la Porthe Otomane auprès du roy de Perse*. Translated by M. de Fiennes; edited by L. Langlès. Paris, 1810.

Efendi, Evliya. *Narrative of Travels in Europe, Asia, and Africa in the Seventeenth Century*. Translated by Joseph von Hammer. 2 vols. London, 1834; repr., New York and London, 1968.

Ezov, G. A., ed. *Snosheniia Petra Velikogo s armianskim narodom*. St. Petersburg, 1898.

Fasa'i, Hajj Mirza Hasan Husayn. *Farsnamah-i Nasiri*, 2 vols. paginated as one. Tehran, 1894–95; new ed. edited by Mansur Rastegar Fasa'i, 1367/1988.

Ferrier, R.W. "An English View of Persian Trade in 1618." *JESHO* 19 (1976): 182–214.

Feynes, Henri de. *Voyage faict par terre depuis Paris jusques à la Chine par le Sieur de Feynes avec son retour par mer*. Paris, 1630.

Findiriski, Sayyid Abu Talib Musavi. *Tuhfat al-`alam. Dar awsaf va akhbar-i Shah Sultan Husayn Safavi*. Edited by Rasul Ja`fariyan. Tehran, 1388/2009.

Florencio del Niño Jesús, P. Fr. *Biblioteca Carmelitano-Teresiana de Misiones*. 3 vols. Vol. 2, *A Persia (1604–1609)*; Vol. 3, *En Persia (1608–1624). Su fundaciòn-Sus embajadas-Su apostolado*. Pamplona, 1928–30.

Floyer, E. A. "Journal of a Route from Jask to Bampur." *Journal of the Royal Geographic Society* 47 (1877): 188–201.

Fraser, James B. *Narrative of a Journey to Khorasan in the Years 1821 and 1822, including Some Account of the Countries North of Persia*. London, 1825.

Fryer, John A. *A New Account of East India and Persia, Being 9 Years' Travels, 1672–1681*. Edited by W. Crooke. 3 vols. London, 1909–15.

Gemelli Careri, Giovanni Francesco. *Giro del Mondo del dottor D. Gio. Francesco Gemelli Careri*. 6 vols. Naples, 1699.

Gilanentz, Petros di Sarkis. *The Chronicle of Petros di Sarkis Gilanentz Concerning the Afghan Invasion of Persia in 1722, the Siege of Isfahan and the Repercussions in Northern Persia, Russia and Turkey.* Trans. and edited by Caro Owen Minasian. Lisbon, 1959.

Gobineau, Joseph-Arthur Comte de. *Trois ans en Asie.* In idem, *Oeuvres,* 29–401. Paris, 1983.

Gouvea, Antonio de. *Relaçam em quem se tratao as guerras e grandes victories que alcancou o grande Rey da Peresia Xa Abas do Grao Turco Mahometo e seu filho Amette as quaes resultarao das embaxaidas que pr mandado da Catholica Real magestade de Rey D. Filippe II de Poretugal fizereao alguns religiosos da Ordem dos Eremeitaas de Santo Agostinho a Persia.* Lisbon, 1611.

Grey, Charles, ed. and trans. *A Narrative of Italian Travels in Persia in the Fifteenth and Sixteenth Century.* London, 1873.

Hanway, Jonas. *An Historical Account of the British Trade over the Caspian Sea: With a Journal of Travels through Russia into Persia...to which are added, The Revolutions of Persia during the Present Century, with the Particular History of the Great Usurper Nadir Kouli.* 4 vols. London, 1753.

Hazin Lahiji, Muhammad Ali. *The Life of Sheikh Muhammad Ali Hazin.* Translated and edited by F. C. Belfour. London, 1830.

———. "Vaqi`at-i Iran va Hind." In idem, *Rasa'il-i Hazin-i Lahiji,* 189–246. Edited by `Ali Awjabi et al. Tehran, 1377/1998.

Hedges, William. *The Diary of William Hedges, Esq., during his Agency in Bengal; as well as on his Voyage Put and Return Overland (1681–1687).* Edited by R. Barlow and H. Yule. 3 vols. London, 1887–89.

Herbert, Thomas. *Travels in Persia, 1627–1629.* Abridged an edited by William Foster. London, 1928.

Hidayat, Riza Quli Khan. *Rawzat al-safa-yi Nasiri.* 10 vols. Tehran, 1853–56.

Holloway, William. *A Relation of the late Seidge and Taking of the City of Babylon by the Turke. As it Was Written from Thence by Zarain Aga.* London, 1639.

Inayat Khan. *The Shah Jahan Nama of Inayat Khan: An Abridged Histdory of the Mogul Emperor Shah Jahan, Compiled by his Royal Librarian.* Trans. by A. R. Fuller; edited by W. E. Begley and Z. A. Desai. Delhi, 1990.

Isfahani, Muhammad Ma`sum b. Kh\`ajigi. *Khulasat al-siyar. Tarikh-i ruzgar-i Shah Safi.* Tehran, 1368/1389.

I`timad al-Saltanah, *Tarikh-i muntazam-i Nasiri.* Edited by Muhammad Isma`il Rizvani, 3 vols., Tehran, 1364/1985.

Ja`fariyan, Rasul, ed. *`Ilal-i bar uftadan-i Safaviyan. Mukafat namah.* Tehran, 1372/1993.

Kaempfer, Engelbert. *Am Hofe des persischen Grosskönigs 1684–1685.* Trans. by Walther Hinz. Leipzig, 1940; new ed., Tübingen, 1977.

Katib, Ahmad b. Husayn b. `Ali. *Tarikh-i jadid-i Yazd.* Edited by Iraj Afshar. Tehran, 1345/1966.

Khatunabadi, Sayyid `Abd al-Husayn. *Vaqa'i` al-sinnin va al-a`vam.* Tehran, 1352/1973.

Kirmani, Mulla Muhammad Mu'min. *Sahifat al-irshad (Tarikh-i Afshar-i Kirman—payan-i kar-i Safaviyah)*. Edited by Muhammad Ibrahim Bastani-Parizi. Tehran, 1384/2005.

Konovalov, S. "Ludvig Fabritius's Account of the Razin Rebellion." *Oxford Slavonic Papers* 6 (1955): 72–101.

Kroell, Anne. "Douze lettres de Jean Chardin." *Journal Asiatique* 170 (1982): 295–338.

Krusinski, Judasz Tadeusz. *The History of the Revolutions of Persia*. 2 vols. London, 1733.

Lockyer, Charles. *An Account of the Trade in India. Containing Rules for Government in Good Trade, Price Courants and Tables*. London, 1711.

Malcolm, John. *The History of Persia. From the Most Early Period to the Present Time*. 2 vols. London, 1815.

Manucci, Nicolao. *Storia do Mogor or Mugul India 1653–1708*. Translated by William Irvine. 4 vols. London, 1907.

Mar`ashi, Mir Taymur. *Tarikh-i khandan-i Mar`ashi-yi Mazandaran*. Edited by Manuchihr Situdah. Tehran, 1364/1985.

Mar`ashi, Sayyid Zahir al-Din b. Sayyid Nasir al-Din. *Tarikh-i Gilan va Daylamistan*. Edited by Manuchihr Situdah. Tehran, 2nd ed., 1364/1985.

Mar`ashi Safavi, Mirza Muhammad Khalil. *Majma` al-tavarikh dar tarikh-i inqiraz-i Safaviyah va vaqa'i`-i ba`d ta sal-i 1207 h.q.* Edited by `Abbas Iqbal Ashtiyani. Tehran, 1362/1983.

Mardukh Kurdistani, Ayatullah Shaykh Muhammad. *Tarikh-i Mardukh*. Tehran, 3rd ed. Tehran, 1359/1980.

Marvi, Muhammad Kazim. *`Alam-ara-yi Nadiri*. 3 vols. Edited by Muhammad Amin Riyahi. Tehran, 2nd ed., 1369/1990.

Ma`sum, Mirza Muhammad. *Tarikh-i salatin-e Safaviyah*. Edited by Amir Hasan `Abidi. Tehran, 1351/1972.

Mashizi Bardsiri, Mir Muhammad Sa`id. *Tazkirah-i Safaviyah-i Kirman*. Edited by Muhammad Ibrahim Bastani-Parizi. Tehran, 1369/1990.

Membré, Michele. *Mission to the Lord Sophy of Persia (1539–1542)*. Translated and edited by A. H. Morton. London, 1993.

Minorsky, Vladimir, trans. and ed. *Tadhkirat al-Mulūk. A Manual of Safavid Administration*. London, 1943; repr. 1980.

Monshi, Eskandar Beg. See Turkaman, Iskandar Bayg.

Mudarrisi Tabataba'i, *Turbat-i pakan. Asar va banaha-yi qadim-i mahdudah-i kanuni-yi dar al-mu`minin-i Qum*. 2 vols. Qum, 1335/1956.

Mulla Kamal. *Tarikh-i Safaviyan: Khulasat al-tavarikh. Tarikh-i Mulla Kamal ta'lif-i du nafar az darbariyan-i Shah `Abbas-i divvum*. Edited by Ibrahim Dihqan. Tehran, 1334/1955.

Munajjim, Mulla Jalal al-Din. *Tarikh-i `Abbasi ya ruznamah-i Mulla Jalal al-Din Munajjim*. Edited by Sayf Allah Vahid Niya. Tehran, 1366/1987.

Mustawfi, Mirza Muhammad Husayn. "Amar-i mali va nizami-yi Iran dar 1128 ya tafsil-i `asakir-i fayruzi-yi mu`asir-i Sultan Husayn Safavi." Edited by M. T. Danishpazhuh. *Farhang-i Iran Zamin* 20 (1353/1975): 396–421.

Mustawfi, Muhammad Muhsin. *Zubdat al-tavarikh*. Edited by Behruz Gudarzi. Tehran, 1375/1996.
Mustawfi Bafqi, Muhammad Mufid. *Jami`-i mufidi ya tarikh-i Yazd*. 3 vols. Edited by Iraj Afshar. Tehran, 1342/1963.
——. *Mohtasar-e Mofid des Mohammad Mofid Mostoufi*. 2 vols. Edited by Seyfeddin Najmabadi. Wiesbaden, 1989–91.
Naji, Muhammad Yusuf. *Risalah dar padishahi-yi Safaviyan*. Edited by Rasul Ja'fariyan and Firishtah Kushki. Tehran, 1387/2009.
Nasiri, Mirza Naqi. *Titles and Emoluments in Safavid Iran: A Third Manual of Safavid Administration*. Trans. and edited by Willem Floor. Washington D.C., 2008.
Nasiri, Muhammad Ibrahim b. Zayn al-`Abidin. *Dastur-i shahriyaran*. Edited by Muhammad Nadir Nasiri Muqaddam. Tehran, 1373/1994.
Nasrabadi, Muhammad Tahir. *Tazkirah-i Nasrabadi. Tazkirah-i shu`ara*. 2 vols. paginated as one. Edited by Muhsin Naji Nasrabadi. Tehran, 1378/1999.
Nayrizi Shirazi, Qutb al-Din Muhammad. *Risalah-i siyasi dar tahlil-i `ilal-i suqut-i dawlat-i Safaviyah va rah-i hal-i bazgasht-i an bih qudrat*. Edited by Rasul Ja`fariyan. Qum, 1371/1992.
Nikitine, B. "Les valis d'Ardalan." *Revue du Monde Musulman* 49 (1922):70–104.
Olearius, Adam. *Vermehrte newe Beschreibung der muscowitischen und persischen Reyse sodurch gelegenheit einer holsteinischen Gesandschaft an den Russischen Zaar und König in Persien geschehen*. Schleswig, 1656; facs. repr. edited by D. Lohmeier, Tübingen, 1971.
Pacifique de Provins, Père. *Relation d'un voyage de Perse faict par le R.P. Pacifique de Provins prédicateur capucin*. Paris, 1631; repr. 1939.
Pelsaert, Francisco. *De geschriften van Francisco Pelsaert, 1627. Kroniek and remonstrantie*. Edited by O. H. A. Kolff and H. W. van Santen. The Hague, 1979.
Petis de la Croix, François. *Extrait du journal du sieur Petis, Fils, Professeur en Arabe, et secrétaire interprète entretenu en la marine renfermant tout ce qu'il a vu en fait en Orient*. In Doury Efendy, *Relation de Dourry Efendy*, 73–174.
Poullet (d'Armainville). *Nouvelles relations du Levant. Avec une exacte description... du Royaume de Perse*. 2 vols. Paris, 1668.
Pyrard, François. *The Voyages of François Pyrard of Laval to the East Indies, the Moluccas and Brazil*. 2 vols. Edited by Pierre de Bergeron and Jérôme Bignon. London, 1887.
Qazvini, Abu'l Hasan. *Fava'id al-Safaviyah. Tarikh-i salatin va umara-yi Safavi pas az suqut-i dawlat-i Safaviyah*. Edited by Maryam Mir-Ahmadi. Tehran, 1367/1988.
Qazvini, Budaq Munshi. *Javahir al-akhbar*. Edited by Muhsin Bahramnizhad. Tehran, 1379/2000.
Qummi, Qazi Ahmad b. Sharaf al-Din al-Husayn al-Husayni. *Khulasat al-tavarikh*. Edited by Ihsan Ishraqi, 2 vols. paginated as one. Tehran, 1362/1983; repr. 1383/2004.

Rebelo, Nicolao Orta. *Un voyageur portugais en Perse au début du XVIIe siècle. Nicolau Orta Rebelo.* Edited by Joaquim Veríssimo Serrão. Lisbon, 1972.

Richard, Francis, ed. *Raphaël du Mans missionnaire en Perse au XVIIe s.* 2 vols. Paris, 1995.

Riyahi, Muhammad Amin. *Sifaratnamah'ha-yi Iran: Guzarishha-yi musafirat va ma'muriyat-i safiran-i `Usmani dar Iran.* Tehran, 1368/1989.

Rota, Giorgio, ed. and trans. *La vita e i tempi di Rostam Khan (Edizione e traduzione italiana del Ms. British Library Add 7,655).* Vienna, 2009.

Rumlu, Hasan Big. *Ahsan al-tavarikh.* Edited by `Abbas Husayn Nava'i. Tehran, 1357/1978.

Rustam al-Hukama (Muhammad Hashin Asif). *Rustam al-tavarikh.* Edited by Muhammad Mushiri. Tehran, 1348/1969; 2nd ed., 1352/1973.

Sabzavari, Muhammad Baqir. *Rawzat al-anvar-i `Abbasi (Dar akhlaq va shivah-yi kishvardari).* Edited by Isma`il Changizi Ardahani. Tehran, 1377/1998.

Sanandaji, Mirza Shukr Allah. *Tuhfah-i Nasiri dar tarikh va jughrafiya-yi Kurdistan.* Edited by Hishmat Allah Tabibi. Tehran, 1366/1987.

Sanson, François. *Estat présent du royaume de Perse.* Paris, 1694.

Schillinger, Père Franz Caspar. *Persianische und Ost-Indianische Reise.* Nuremberg, 1707.

Shamlu, Vali Quli b. Davud Quli. *Qisas al-khaqani.* 2 vols. Edited by Sayyid Hasan Sadat Nasiri. Tehran, 1371–74/1992–95.

Sherley, Antony. *Sir Anthony Sherley His Relation of His Travels into Persia.* London, 1613; facs. repr. 1972.

Shirazi, `Abdi Bayg "Navidi." *Takmilat al-akhbar.* Edited by `Abd al-Husayn Nava'i. Tehran, 1369/1990.

Ash-Shushtari, Sayyid `Abdallah bin Nur ad-Din bin Ni`matallah al-Husaini. *Tadhkira-i Shushtar.* Calcutta, 1924.

Silva y Figueroa, Don Garcia de. *Comentarios de D. Garcia de Silva y Figueroa de la embajada que de parte del Rey de España don Felipe III hize al Rey Xa Abas de Persia.* 2 vols. Madrid, 1903–05.

Simēon of Erevan, Kat`oghikos. *Jambr.* Trans. and edited by George A. Bournoutian. Costa Mesa, Cal. 2009.

Smith, Ronald Bishop, ed. *The First Age of the Portuguese Embassies, Navigations and Peregrinations in Persia (1507–1524).* Bethesda, MD, 1970.

Soimonov, Fedor I. "Auszug aus dem Tage-Buch des ehemahligen Schiff-Hauptmanns und jetzigen geheimen Raths und Gouverneurs von Siberien, Herrn Fedor Iwanowitsch Soimonov, von seiner Schiffahrt der Caspische See." In G. F. Müller, ed., *Sammlung russischer Geschichte.* 10 vols. Vol. 7, 155–530. St. Petersburg, 1762.

Speelman, Cornelis. *Journaal der reis van den gezant der O. I. Compagnie Joan Cunaeus naar Perzië in 1651–1652.* Edited by A. Hotz. Amsterdam, 1908.

Stanley of Alderley, ed. *Travels to Tana and Persia by Josafa Barbaro and Ambrogio Contarini.* Transl. by Thomas and S. A. Roy. London, 1873.

Struys, J. J. *Drie aanmerkelijke en seer rampspoedige reysen door Italie, Griekenlandt, Lijflandt, Moscovien, Tartarijen, Meden, Persien, Oost-Indien, Japan, en verscheyden andere gewesten.* Amsterdam, 1676.

Tate, G. *The Frontiers of Baluchistan: Travels on the Borders of Persia and Afghanistan.* London, 1909.

Tavernier, Jean Baptiste. *Les six voyages de Jean Bapt. Tavernier en Turquie, en Perse, et aux Indes.* 2 vols. Utrecht, 1712.

Tenreiro, António. "Itinerário de de António Tenreiro." In Antonio Baião, ed., *Itinerários da Índia a Portugal por terra.* Coimbra, 1923.

Thevenot, Jean de. *Relation d'un voyage fait au Levant.* Vol. 2, *Suite du voyage de Levant.* Paris, 1674.

———. *Livre troisième de la suite du voyage de Mr. de Thévenot au Levant.* Paris, 1689.

Tihrani, Muhammad Mirza. *Mir'at-i varidat. Tarikh-i suqut-i Safaviyan. Payamadha-yi an va farmanrava'i-yi Malik Mahmud Sistani.* Edited by Mansur Sifatgul. Tehran, 1373/2004.

Tournefort, Jean Pitton de. *Relation d'un voyage du Levant,* 2 vols. Paris, 1717.

Tunakabuni, Muhammad b. Sulayman. *Tazkirat al-`ulama.* Edited by Riza Azhari and Ghulamriza Parandah. Mashhad, 1372/1993.

Turkaman, Iskandar Bayg. *Tarikh-i `alam-ara-yi `Abbasi.* 2 vols. paginated as one. Edited by Iraj Afshar. Tehran, 1350/1971.

———. (Eskandar Beg Monshi). *History of Shah `Abbas the Great.* Translated and edited by Roger M. Savory. 3 vols. paginated as one. Boulder, Co, 1978.

Turkaman, Iskandar Bayg, and Muhammad Yusuf Mu'arrikh. *Zayl-i tarikh-i `alam-ara-yi `Abbasi.* Edited by Suhayli Khvansari. Tehran, 1317/1938.

Vahid Qazvini, Mirza Muhammad Tahir. *Tarikh-i jahan-ara-yi `Abbasi.* Edited by Sayyid Sa`id Mir Muhammad Sadiq, Tehran, 1383/2004.

Valah Qazvini Isfahani, Muhammad Yusuf. *Khuld-i barin. Iran dar zaman-i Shah Safi va Shah `Abbas divvum.* Edited by Muhammad Riza Nasiri. Tehran, 1380/2001.

Valentyn, François. *Oud en Nieuw Oost-Indiën.* 5 vols. Vol. 5, *Keurlyke beschryving van Choromandel, Pegu, Arrakan, Bengale, Mocha, van 't Nederlandsch comptoir in Persien en zaken overblyvzlen; een net beschryving van Malacca...Sumatra...Malabar... Japan...Kaap der goede hoope...Mauritius.* Dordrecht-Amsterdam, 1726.

Vaziri Kirmani, Ahmad `Ali Khan. *Jughrafiya-yi Kirman.* Edited by Muhammad Ibrahim Bastani-Parizi. Tehran, 1353/1974.

———. *Tarikh-i Kirman.* Edited by Muhammad Ibrahim Bastani-Parizi, 2 vols. paginated as one. Tehran, 3rd ed.,1364/1985.

Villotte, Père Jacques (attributed to). *Voyages d'un missionnaire de la Compagnie du Jésus en Iran, aux Indes, en Arabie et en Barbarie.* Paris, 1730.

Von Mandelso, Johann. *Beschrijvingh van de gedenkwaerdige zee- en landreyze deur Persie naar Oost-Indien.* Amsterdam, 1658.

Whigham, H. J. *The Persian Problem. An Examination of the Rival Positions of Russia and Great Britian in Persia with Some Accounts of the Persian Gulf and the Bagdad Railway.* New York, 1903.

Wills, C.J. *In the Land of the Lion and the Sun or Modern Persia. Being Experiences of Life in Persia from 1866 and 1881.* London, 1883; repr. 1891.

Witsen, Nicolaas. *Noord en oost Tartaryen; behelzende eene beschryving van verscheidene Tartersche en nabuurige gewesten in de noorder en oostelijkste deelen van Aziën en Europa.* Amsterdam, 1705.

Worm, Johan Gottlieb. *Ost-Indian- und persianische Reisen, oder: zehenjärige auf Gross-Java, Bengala, und im Gefolge Herrn Joann Josua Kötelär, holländischen Abgesandtens an den Sophi in Persien geleistete Kriegsdienste.* Dresden and Leipzig, 1737.

Zak`aria of Agulis, *The Journals of Zak`aria of Agulis.* Translated and edited by George A. Bournoutian. Costa Mesa, 2003.

IV. MODERN STUDIES

Abisaab, Rula Jurdi. *Converting Persia: Religion and Power in the Safavid Empire.* London, 2004.

`Abidini, Abu'l Fazl. "Munasibat-i siyasi-yi dawlat-i Safavi ba Impiraturi-yi `Usmani az mu`ahidah-i Zuhab ta suqut-i Isfahan (1049–1135/1639–1722)." *Tarikh-i ravabit-i khariji* 8:30 (1386/2007): 63–85.

Adle, Chahriyar. "Contributions à la géographie historique du Damghan." *Le Monde Iranien et l'Islam* 1 (1971): 69–104

Afshar, Iraj. "'Inqilab-i diram' dar zaman-i Shah `Abbas-i divvum." *Tarikh: Zamimah-i Majallah-i Danishkadah-i Adabiyat va `Ulum-i Insani* 1 (2535/1976): 267–74.

Ágoston, Gábor. *Guns for the Sultan: Military Power and the Weapons Industry in the Ottoman Empire.* Cambridge, 2005.

Alam, Muzaffar and Sanjay Subrahmanyam. *Indo-Persian Travels in the Age of Discoveries 1400–1800.* Cambridge, 2007.

Album, Stephen. "Iranian Silver Denominational Names, 907–1295/1501–1878," part one. *Pricelist* 52 (1987), 20.

Allsen, Thomas. "Mongolian Princes and Their Merchant Partners." *Asia Minor,* 3rd ser., pt. 2 (1989): 83–125.

Alonso, Carlos. *Antonio de Gouvea, O.S.A. Diplomático y visitador apostólico en Persia (†1628).* Valladolid, 2000.

———. "Una embajada de Clemente VIII a Persia (1600–1609)." *Archivum Historiae Pontificiae* 34 (1996): 7–125.

Ali, M. Athar. "The Passing of Empire: The Mughal Case." *Modern Asian Studies* 9 (1975): 385–96.

Amanat, Abbas. *The Pivot of the Universe: Nasir al-Din Qajar and the Iranian Monarchy, 1851–1896.* Berkeley and Los Angeles, 1997.

Amin, Camron Michael. "Mujassama-i būd mujassama-i nabūd: The Image of the Safavids in 20th-Century Iranian Popular History." In *History and Historiography of Post-Mongol Central Asia and the Middle East. Studies in Honor of John E. Woods,* edited by Judith Pfeiffer and Shohleh A. Quinn, 343–59. Wiesbaden, 2006.

Aram, Muhammad Baqir. *Andishah-i tarikh-nigari-yi `asr-i Safavi.* Tehran, 1386/2007.
Ardalan, Shireen. *Les Kurdes Ardalân entre la Perse et l'Empire ottoman.* Paris, 2004
Arjomand, Said Amir. "Coffeehouses, Guilds and Oriental Despotism. Government and Civil Society in Late 17th to Early 18th-Century Istanbul and Isfahan, and as Seen from Paris and London." *Archives Européennes de Sociologie* 65 (2004): 23–42.
———. "The Mujtahid of the Age and the Mullābāshi: An Intermediate Stage in the Institutionalization of Religious Authority in Shi`ite Iran." In *Authority and Political Culture in Shi`ism*, edited by idem, 80–89. Albany, 1988.
———. "The Office of Mullabashi in Shi`ite Iran." *Studia Islamica* 57 (1983): 135–46.
———. "The Salience of Political Ethic in the Spread of Persianate Islam." *Journal of PersianateStudies* 1 (2008): 5–29.
———. *The Shadow of God and the Hidden Imam.* Chicago, 1984.
Arunova, M. R. and K. Z. Ashrafiyan, *Gosudarstvo Nadir-Shakha Afshara. Ocherki obshchestvennikh otnoshenii v Irane 30–40-x godov XVIII veka.* Moscow, 1958.
Ashraf, Ahmad. "Iranian Identity. Medieval Islamic Period." *EIr.* 13 (2006), 507–22.
Aslanian, Sebouh. "The Circulation of Men and Credit: The Role of the Commenda and the Family Firm in Julfan Society." *JESHO* 50 (2007): 124–171.
———. *From the Indian Ocean to the Mediterrranean: The Global Trade Networks of Armenian Merchants from New Julfa.* Berkeley and Los Angeles, 2011.
Aslanian, Sebouh, and Houri Berberian. "Sceriman Family," *EIr*, online version.
Attman, Artur. *Russia and Polish Markets in International Trade 1500–1650.* Gotenburg, 1973.
Aubin, Jean. "L'avènement des Safavides reconsidéré." *Moyen Orient et Océan Indien* 5 (1988): 1–130.
———. "Le royaume d'Ormuz au début du XVIe siècle." *Mare Luso Indicum* 2 (1972): 77–179.
———. "Šah Ismā'īl et les notables de l'Iraq persan," *JESHO* 2 (1959): 37–79.
———. "Les Sunnites de Lāristān et la chute des Safavides." *Revue des Etudes Islamiques* (1965): 151–71.
Avery, P. B. G. Fragner, and J. B. Simmons. "`Abbasi." *EIr.* 1 (1985), 86.
Axworthy, Michael. "The Army of Nader Shah." *IS* 40 (2007): 635–46.
———. *A History of Iran. Empire of the Mind.* New York, 2008.
———. *The Sword of Persia. Nadir Shah, from Tribal Warrior to Conquering Tyrant.* London and New York, 2006.
al-Azmeh, Aziz. *Muslim Kingship: Power and the Sacred in Muslim, Christian and Pagan Polities.* London, 1997.
al-`Azzawi, `Abbas. *Tarikh al-`Iraq bayn al-ihtilalayn.* 7 vols. Baghdad, 1372/1953.

Babaie, Sussan. *Isfahan and its Palaces: Statecraft, Shi`ism and the Architecture of Conviviality in Early Modern Iran.* Edinburgh, 2008.

Babaie, Sussan et al. *Slaves of the Shah: New Elites of Safavid Iran.* London and New York, 2004.

Babayan, Kathryn. *Mystics, Monarchs, and Messiahs: Cultural Landscapes of Early Modern Iran.* Cambridge, Mass., 2003.

——. "The Waning of the Qizilbash: The Temporal and the Spiritual in Seventeenth-Century Iran." Ph.D. dissertation. Princeton University, 1993.

Bacqué-Grammont, Jean-Louis. "Les Ottomans et les Safavides dans la première moitié du XVIe siècle." In *Convegno sul tema La Shī`a nell'impero Ottomano,* edited by Francesco Gabrieili, 7–21. Rome, 1993.

——. *Les Ottomans, les Safavides et leurs voisins, Contributions à l'histoire des relations internationales dans l'Orient islamique de 1514 à 1524.* Leiden, 1987.

Baer, Marc David. *Honored by the Glory of Islam: Conversion and Conquest in Ottoman Europe.* Oxford, 2008.

Baghdiantz, Ina. "The Socio-Economic Conditions in New Julfa Post-1650: The Impact of Conversions to Islam on International Trade." *Revue des Etudes Arméniennes* 26 (1996–97): 367–96.

Baibourtian, Vahan. *International Trade and the Armenian Merchants in the Seventeenth Century.* New Delhi, 2004.

Banani, A. "Reflections on the Social and Economic Structure of Safavid Persia at Its Zenith." *IS* 11 (1978): 83–116.

Barfield, Thomas. "Tribe and State Relations: The Inner Asian Perspective." In *Tribes and State Formation in the Middle East,* edited by Philip S. Khoury and Joseph Kostiner, 153–182. Berkeley and Los Angeles, 1990.

Barnett, Richard B. *North India between Empires: Awadh, the Mughals and the British, 1720–1801.* Berkeley and Los Angeles, 1980.

Barthold, W. *Turkestan Down to the Mongol Invasion.* London, 1928; 4th ed., 1977.

Bastani-Parizi, Muhammad Ibrahim. *Ganj `Ali Khan.* Tehran, 3rd edn., 1368/1989.

——. "Sha`r-i gulnar." In idem, *Farmanfarma-yi `alam,* 163–303. Tehran, 2nd ed., 1367/1988.

——. *Siyasat va iqtisad dar `asr-i safavi.* Tehran, 3rd ed., 1362/1983.

Bausani, Alessandro. "Notes on the Safavid Period: Decadence or Progress." In *Proceedings of the Ninth Congress of the Union Européenne des Arabistants et Islamisants,* edited by Rudolph Peters, 15–30. Leiden, 1981.

Bayly, C. A. *Imperial Meridian: The British Empire and the World 1780–1830.* London and New York, 1989.

Bellingeri, Giampiero. "Sugli Sceriman rimasti a Giulfa: devozione agli ultimi Safavidi?" In *Gli Armeni e Venezia. Dagli Sceraman a Mechitar: il momento culminante di una consuetudine millenaria,* edited by G. L. Zekiyan and A. Ferrari, 93–124. Venice, 2004.

Berktay, Halil. "Three Empires and the Societies They Governed: Iran, India and the Ottoman Empire." In *New Approaches to State and Peasant in*

Ottoman History, edited by Halil Berktay and Suraiya Faroqhi, 242-66. London, 1992.
Bilici, Faruk. *Louis XIV et son projet de conquête d'Istanbul*. Ankara, 2004.
Bill, James A. "The Plasticity of Informal Politics: The Case of Iran." *The Middle East Journal* 27 (1973): 131-51.
Blake, Stephen P. "The Patrimonial-Bureaucratic Empire of the Mughals." *Journal of Asian Studies* 39 (1979): 77-94.
Bonnerot, H. *La Perse dans la littérature française du XVIIIe siècle*. Paris, 1988.
Borob'eva, A.G. "K voprosu o prebyvanii Stepana Razina v Azerbaidzhane i Persii." *Izvestiia Akademii Nauk Azerbaidzhanskoi SSR, seriia istorii, filosofii i prava* (1983), 3:32-37.
Braudel, Fernand. *The Mediterranean and the Mediterranean World in the Age of Philip II*, 2 vols. Trans. by Siân Reynolds. Berkeley, 1973.
Braun, Hellmut. "Das Erbe Schah `Abbas I. Iran und seine Könige, 1629-1694." Diss. Phil. University of Hamburg, 1969.
———. "Ein iranischer Grosswesir des 17. Jahrhunderts: Mirza Muhammad-Taqi." In *Festgabe deutscher Iranisten zur 2500 Jahresfeier Irans*, edited by W. Eilers, 1-7. Stuttgart, 1971.
Brewer, John. *The Sinews of Power: War, Money and the English State, 1688-1783*. Cambridge, Mass., 1990.
Brosius, Maria, Brosius, *Women in Ancient Persia 559-331 BC*. Oxford, 1996.
Browne, E. G. *A Literary History of Persia*, vol. 4, *Modern Times, 1500-1924*. London, repr. 1969.
Bruinessen, Martin van. *Agha, Shaykh and State: On the Social and Political Organization of Kurdistan*. Utrecht, 1978.
Burton, Audrey. *The Bukharans: A Dynastic, Diplomatic and Commercial History 1550-1702*. New York, 1997.
Bushev, P. P. *Istoriia posol'stv i diplomaticheskikh otnoshenii russkogo i iranskogo gosudarstv v 1586-1612*. Moscow, 1976.
———. *Posol'stvo Artemiia Volynskogo v Iran v 1715-1718 gg*. Moscow, 1978.
———. "Puteshestvie Mokhammada Khosein-Khan Beka v Moskvu v 1690-1692 gg." *Strany i Narody Vostoka* 18 (1976), 135-72.
Busse, Heribert. "Der Persische Staatsgedanke im Wandel der Geschichte." *Saeculum* 28 (1977): 53-74.
Calder, Norman. "Legitimacy and Accommodation in Safavid Iran: The Juristic Theory of Muhammad Bāqir al-Sabzavārī (d. 1090/1679)." *Iran* 25 (1987): 91-105.
Calmard, Jean. "Les rituels shiites et le pouvoir. L'imposition du shiisme safavide: eulogies et malédictions canoniques." In idem, ed., *Etudes Safavides*, 109-50.
———. "Shi`i Rituals and Power. II. The Consolidation of Safavid Shi`ism: Folklore and Popular Relgion." In Melville, ed., *Safavid Persia*, 139-90.
Calmard, Jean, ed. *Etudes Safavides*. Paris-Tehran, 1993.
Carnot, Dominique. *Représentations de l'Islam dans la France du XVIIe siècle. La ville des tentations*. Paris, 1998.

Chandra, Satish. *Parties and Politics at the Mughal Court, 1707–1740.* New Delhi, 1959, 4th ed., 2002.

Chowaniec, "Z dziejów polityki Jana III na Bliskim Wschodzie 1683–1686." *Kwartalnik Historyczny* 40 (1926): 150–60.

Cipolla, Carlo M. *Money, Prices, and Civilisation in the Mediterranean World, Fifth to Seventeetnh Centuries.* Princeton, 1956.

Codrington, H. W. "Coins of the Kings of Hormuz." *Numismatic Chronicle* 4th ser., 14 (1914): 156–67.

———. *Ceylon Coins and Currency*, Series A, no. 3 of *Memoirs of the Colombo Museum.* Colombo, 1924.

Crone, Patricia. *Pre-Industrial Societies: Anatomy of the Pre-Modern World.* Oxford, 2nd ed., 2003.

Dale, Stephen Frederic. *The Garden of the Eight Paradises: Babur and the Culture of Empire in Central Asia, Afghanistan and India (1483–1530).* Leiden, 2004.

———. *Indian Merchants and Eurasian Trade, 1600–1750.* Cambridge, 1994.

———. *The Muslim Empires of the Ottomans, Safavids, and Mughals.* Cambridge, 2010.

Darhahuniyan, Harutun. *Tarikh-i Julfa–yi Isfahan.* Trans. Leon Minassian and Musavi Faridani. Tehran, 1379/2000.

Das Gupta, Ashin. *The World of the Indian Ocean Merchant 1500–1800.* Delhi, 2001.

Deyell, John S. "Akbar's Currency System and Monetary Integration of the Conqured Kingdoms." In *The Imperial Monetary System of Mughal India*, edited by D. S. Richards, 13–16. Delhi, 1987; repr. 2000.

Dickson, Martin. "The Fall of the Safavi Dynasty." Review article. *Journal of the American Oriental Society* 82 (1962): 503–17.

———. "Shah Tahmasp and the Uzbeks (The Duel for Khurasan with ʿUbayd Khan)." Ph.D. dissertation. Princeton University, 1958.

Donazzolo, Pietro. "Viaggi in Oriente ed in Occidente (Sec. XVII-XVIII) del Fratello Francisco Maria di S. Siro (Carmelitano Scalzo) al secolo Antonio Gorla di Portabella." *Rivista Geografica Italiana* 19 (1912): 337–54; 423–36; 530–37; 584–605.

Eisenstein, Elizabeth. *The Printing Revolution in Early Modern Europe.* Cambridge, 1983.

Elliot, J. H. *Spain, Europe, and the Wider World 1500–1800.* New Haven and London, 2009.

Embree, Ainslie T. "Frontiers into Boundaries: From the Traditional to the Modern State." In *Realm and Region in Traditional India*, edited by Richard G. Fox, 255–80. Durham, NC, 1977.

Emerson, John. "Ex Oriente Lux: Some European Sources on the Economic Structure of Persia between about 1630 and 1690." Ph.D. dissertation. Cambridge University, 1969.

Emerson, John and Willem Floor. "Rahdars and their Tolls in Safavid and Afsharid Iran." *JESHO* 30 (1987): 318–27.

Eszer, Ambrosius. "Zu einigen bisher ungeloesten Problemen im Sebastianus Knab O.P." *Archivum Fratrum Praedicatorum* 44 (1974): 263–70.
Ettinghausen, Richard. "Stylistic Tendencies at the Time of Shah 'Abbas." *IS* 7 (1974): 593–628.
Falsafi, Nasrullah. Sarguzasht-i 'Saru Taqi'" In idem, *Chand maqalah-i tarikhi va adabi*, 285–310. Tehran, 1342/1963.
———. *Zindigani-yi Shah 'Abbas-i avval*. 5 vols. paginated as one. Tehran, 4th ed., 1369/1990.
Farooqi, Naimur Rehman. *Mughal-Ottoman Relations*. Delhi, 1989.
Faroqhi, Suraiya. "An Ottoman Ambassador in Iran: Dürri Ahmad Efendi and the Collapse of the Safavid Empire in 1720–21." In eadem, *Another Mirror for Princes: The Public Image of the Ottoman Sultans and Its Reception*, 165–87. Istanbul, 2008.
———. *The Ottoman Empire and the World around It*. London, 2005.
Ferrier, R. W. "British-Persian Relations in the 17th century." Ph.D. dissertation. University of Cambridge, 1970.
Floor, Willem M. *Commercial Conflict between Persia and the Netherlands 1712–1718*. Durham, 1988.
———. "A Description of Masqat and Oman anno 1673 A.D./1084Q." *Moyen Orient et Océan Indien* 2:1 (1985): 1–69.
———. *The Economy of Safavid Persia*. Wiesbaden, 2001.
———. *A Fiscal History of Iran in the Safavid and Qajar Periods 1500–1925*. New York, 1998.
———. "Kalantar." *EIr.* 15 (2010), 366–67.
———. "A Note of the Grand Vizierate in Seventeenth-Century Persia." *ZDMG* 155 (2005): 435–81.
———. *The Persian Gulf. A History, 1500–1730*. Washington D.C, 2006.
———. *The Persian Textile Industry in Historical Perspective, 1500–1925*. Paris, 1999.
———. "The Rise and Fall of Mirza Taqi, the Eunuch Grand Vizier (1043–55/1633–45) Makhdum al-Omara va Khadem al-Foqara." *St.Ir.* 26 (1997): 237–66.
———. "The Sadr or Head of the Safavid Religious Adminsitration, Judiciary and Endowments, and Other Members of the Religious Institution." *ZDMG* 150 (2000): 461–500.
———. "The Secular Judicial System in Safavid Persia." *St.Ir.* 29 (2000): 9–60.
———. "Who were the Shamkhal and the Usmi?" *ZDMG* 160 (2010): 341–81.
Floor, Willem and Patric Clawson. "Safavid Iran's Search for Silver and Gold." *IJMES* 32 (2000): 345–68.
Floor, Willem, and Edmund Herzig, eds. *Safavid Iran and the World*. London, 2011.
Foran, John. "The Long Fall of the Safavid Dynasty: Moving beyond the Standard Views."*IJMES* 24 (1992): 281–304.
Fragner, Bert G. "Historische Wurzeln neuzeitlicher iranischer Identität. Zur Geschichte des politischen Begriffs 'Iran' im späten Mittelalter und in der Neuzeit." In *Studia Semitica Necnou Iranica Rudolpho Macuch Septuagenario*

ab amicis et discipulis dedicata, edited by Maria Macuch et al., 79–100. Wiesbaden, 1989.

Gaastra, F. "The Export of Precious Metals from Europe to Asia by the Dutch East India Company, 1602–1795." In Richards, ed., *Precious Metals*, 447–75.

Ganjei, Tourkhan. "Turkish in the Safavid Court of Isfahan." *Turcica* 21–23 (1991–2): 311–18.

Geidarov, M. Kh. *Remeslennoe proizvodstvo v gorodakh Azerbaidzhana v XVII v.* Baku, 1967.

Gellner, Ernest. "Tribalism and the State in the Middle East." In *Tribes and State Formation in the Middle East*, edited by Philip S. Khoury and Joseph Kostiner, 109–26. Berkeley and Los Angeles, 1990.

Ghabashvili, Valerian N. "The Uniladze Feudal House in the Sixteenth to Seventeenth-Century Iran According to the Georgian Sources." *IS* 40 (2007): 37–58.

Ghougassian, Vazken Sarki. *The Emergence of the Armenian Diocese of New Julfa in the Seventeenth Century*. Atlanta, 1998.

Golombek, Lisa. "The Safavid Ceramic Industry at Kirman." *Iran* 41 (2003): 253–67.

Gomes, Rita Costa. "The Court Galaxy." In *Finding Europe. Discourses on Margins, Communiteisd, Images ca. 13th-ca. 18th Centuries*, edited by Anthony Moho, Diogo Ramada Curto and Niki Koniordos, 185–204. New York and Oxford, 2007.

Gommans, Jos. *Mughal Warfare. Indian Frontiers and High Roads to Empire, 1500–1700*. London and New York, 2002.

Gorski, Philip S. *The Disciplinary Revolution: Calvinism and the Rise of the State in Early Modern Europe*. Chicago and London, 2003.

Gronke, Monika. "The Persian Court between Palace and Tent: From Timur to `Abbas I," in *Timurid Art and Culture: Iran and Central Asia in the Fifteenth Century, Muqarnas*, suppl., edited by Lisa Golombek and Maria Subtelny (Leiden, 1992): 18–22.

Gulbenkian, Roberto. "Deux lettres surprenantes du Catholicos arménien David IV à Phippe III d'Espagne, II de Portugal 1612–1614." In Idem, *Estudios Históricos*, vol. 1, *Relações entre Portugal, Arménia e Médio Oriente*, 301–56. Lisbon, 1995.

Habib, Irfan. *The Agrarian Revolution of Mughal India, 1556–1707*. Delhi, 2nd ed., 2005.

Haidar, Najaf. "Precious Metal Flows and Currency Circulation in the Mughal Empire." *JESHO* 39 (1996): 298–364.

Halft, Dennis OP. "Schiitische Polemik gegen das Christentum im safawidischen Iran des 11./17. Jhdts. Sayyid Ahmad `Alawīs Lawāmi`-i rabbānī dar radd-i subha-yi nasrānī." In *Contacts and Controversies between Muslims, Jews and Christians in the Ottoman Empire and Pre-Modern Iran*, edited by Camilla Adang and Sabine Schmidtke, 273–334. Würzburg, 2010.

Haneda, Masashi. *Le Chāh et les Qizilbaš. Le systeme militaire safavide*. Berlin, 1987.

Hasan, Farhat. *State and Locality in Mughal India: Power Relations in Western India, c. 1572–1730.* Cambridge, 2004.

Herzig, Edmund. "The Armenian Merchants of New Julfa, Isfahan: A Study in Pre-Modern Asian Trade." Ph.D. dissertation. University of Oxford, 1991.

———. "The Deportation of the Armenians in 1604–1605 and Europe's Myth of Shah 'Abbas I." In Melville, ed., *Persian and Islamic Studies*, 59–71.

Hinz, Walther. *Irans Aufstieg zum Nationalstaat im fünfzehnten Jahrhundert.* Berlin, 1936.

———. "Schah Esma'il II. Ein Beitrag zur Geschichte der Safaviden." *Mitteilungen des Seminars für Orientalische Sprachen an der Friedrich-Wilhelms-Universität zu Berlin*, 2. Abt., Westasiatische Studien 36 (1933): 19–99.

———. "The Value of the Toman in the Middle Ages." In M. Minovi and I. Afshar, eds., *Yadnamah-i irani-yi Minorsky*, 90–95. Tehran, 1969.

Hodgson, Marshall. *The Venture of Islam: Conscience and History in a World Civilization.* 3 vols. Chicago, 1974.

Houston, S. J. *James I.* London. 1995.

Isfahani, Muhammad Mihdi b. Muhammad Riza. *Nisf-i jahan fi ta'rif al-Isfahan.* Edited by Manuchihr Situdah. Tehran, 1340; 2nd ed., 1368/1989.

Islam, Riazul. *Indo-Persian Relations: A Study of the Political and Diplomatic Relations between the Mughul Empire and Iran.* Tehran, 1970.

Ismailov, E. E. "Grecheskie i gruzinskie predki Shakha Ismaila Khatai (Voskhodyashie rodoslovnye rospisi)." *Azerbaycan Tarixi Şecara Cemiyyetinin Xeberleri* (Baku) 5 (2004): 40–47.

Ja'fariyan, Rasul. "Adabiyat zidd-i masihi dar dawrah-i Safavi," introduction to *Tarjumah-i anajil-Safavi.* Translated by Mir Muhammad Baqir Isma'il Husayni Khatunabadi. Tehran, 1375/1996.

———. *Naqsh-i Khandan-i Karaki dar ta'sis va tadavum-i dawlat-i Safavi.* Tehran, 1387/2008.

———. "Pishinah-i tashayyu' dar Isfahan," in idem, *Maqalat-i tarikhi*, 305–339. Qum, 2nd ed., 1376/1997.

———. *Safaviyah dar 'arsah-i din, farhang va siyasat*, 3 vols. paginated as one. Qum, 1379/2000.

———. "Tashayyu'-i Astarabad va naqsh-i an dar ustuvari-yi dawlat-i Shi'i-yi Safavi," in idem, *Kavishha-yi tazah dar bab-i ruzgar-i Safavi*, 263–316. Tehran, 1384/2005.

———. "Tashayyu' dar Qazvin az aghaz ta dawrah-i Safaviyah," in idem, *Maqalat-i tarikhi* 6, 13–62. Qum 1379/2000.

Kafadar, Cemal. "The Question of Ottoman Decline." *Harvard Middle Eastern and Islamic Review* 4 (1997–98): 30–75.

Kamen, Henry. *Philip of Spain.* New Haven, 1997.

Kasravi, Ahmad. *Tarikh-i pansad salah-i Khuzistan.* Tehran, 1312/1934; 2nd ed. 1373/1994.

Kemper, Michael. *Herrrschaft, Recht und Islam und Daghestan. Von den Khanaten und Geheimbünden zum ğihād-Staat.* Wiesbaden, 2005.
Keyvani, Mehdi. *Artisans and Guild Life in the Later Safavid Period: Contributions to the Social-Economic History of Persia.* Berlin, 1982.
Khan, Iqtidar Alam. "Indian Response to Firearms [1300–1750]." *Proceedings Indian History Congress* 58 (1998): 1–29.
Khodarkosvky, Michael. *Russia's Steppe Frontier: The Making of a Colonial Empire 1500–1800.* Bloomington, 2002.
Klein, Rüdiger. "Trade in the Safavid Port City Bandar Abbas and the Persian Gulf Area (ca. 1600–1680): A Study of Selected Aspects." Ph.D. dissertation. University of London, 1993/94.
Kleiss, W. and M. Y. Kiani, *Iranian Caravansarais.* Tehran, 1373/1995.
Krawulsky, Dorothea. "Zur Wiederbelebung des Begriffes 'Iran' zur Ilhanzeit." In eadem, *Das Reich der Ilhane. Eine Topographisch-historische Studie,* 11–17. Wiesbaden, 1978.
Krzyszkowski, P. Joseph, S. I. "Entre Varsovie et Ispahan. Le P. Ignace-François Zapolski S.I." *Archivum Historicum Societas Jesu* 18, 35 (1949): 85–117.
Kunke, Marina. *Nomadenstämme in Persien im 18. und 19. Jahrhundert.* Berlin, 1991.
Kuran, Timur. *The Long Divergence: How Islamic Law Held Back the Middle East.* Princeton and Oxford, 2011.
Kuteliia, T. S. *Gruziia i sefevidskii Iran (po dannym numizmatiki.* Tiflis, 1979.
Kutsia, Karlo. "Ispahanis qartveli tarugebi." (Georgian Darughahs of Isfahan). In *Maxlobeli, Agmosavletis istoriis sakitxebi* (Some Issues in Near Easten History), vol. 1, 93–103. Tbilisi, 1963.
Kütükoglu, Bekir S. "Les relations entre l'empire ottoman et l'Iran dans la seconde moitié du XVIe siècle." *Turcica* 6 (1975): 128–45.
———. *Osmanlı-Iran siyasi münasebetleri, 1578–1590.* Istanbul, 1962.
———. *Osmanlı-Iran siyasi münasebetleri, 1578–1612.* Istanbul, 1993.
Lambton, Ann K. S. *Continuity and Change in Medieval Persia: Aspects of Administrative, Economic and Social History, 11th-14th Century.* London, 1988.
———. "Islamic Society in Persia." In A. K. S. Lambton, *Theory and Practice in Medieval Persian Government.* Part VII, 3–32. London, 1980.
———. "Justice in the Medieval Persian Theory of Kingship." *Studia Islamica* 17 (1962): 91–119.
———. "Pishkash: Present or Tribute?" *BSOAS* 57 (1994): 145–58.
——— "The Tribal Resurgence and the Decline of the Bureaucracy in the Eighteenth Century." In *Studies in Eighteenth-Century Islamic History,* edited by Thomas Naff and Roger Owen, 108–29, 377–82. Carbondale, Ill., 1977.
Landau, Amy. "Farangī Sāzī at Isfahan: The Court Painter Muhammad Zamān, the Armenians of New Julfa and Shāh Sulaymān (1666–1694)." Ph.D. dissertation. University of Oxford, 1995.
Lang, D. M. "Georgia and the Fall of the Safavi Dynasty." *BSOAS* 14 (1952): 523–39.
———. *The Last Years of the Georgian Monarchy 1658–1832.* New York, 1957.

Lavi, Habib. *Tarikh-i jami`-i Yahudiyan-i Iran: Guzidah-i tarikh-i Yahud-i Iran.* Beverly Hills, 1377/1998.
Levi-Weiss, D. "Le relazioni fra Venezia e la Turchia dal 1670 al 1684 e la formazione della sacra lega." *Archivio Veneto-Tridentino* 8 (1925): 1–46.
Li, Ming-Hsun. *The Great Recoinage of 1696 to 1699.* London, 1963.
Lockhart, Laurence. *The Fall of the Safavi Dynasty and the Afghan Occupation of Persia.* Cambridge, 1958.
Longrigg, Stephen Helmsley. *Four Centuries of Modern Iraq.* Oxford, 1925.
Losensky, Paul E. *Welcoming Fighānī: Imitation and Poetic Individuality in the Safavid-Mughal Ghazal.* Costa Mesa, 1998.
Lossky, A. "The Intellectual Development of Louis XIV from 1661 to 1715." In Ragnhild R. Hatton, ed., *Louis XIV and Absolutism,* 101–29. Columbus, OH, 1976.
Luft, Paul. "Iran unter Schāh `Abbās II (1642–1666)." Phil. Dissertation. University of Göttingen, 1968.
Lystov, V. P. *Persidskii pokhod Petra I 1722–1723.* Moscow, 1951.
McChesney, Robert D. "'Barrier of Heterodoxy'?: Rethinking the Ties Between Iran and Central Asia in the 17th Century." In Melville, ed., *Safavid Persia,* 231–67.
———. "Four Sources on Shah `Abbas's Building of Isfahan." *Muqarnas* 5 (1988): 103–34.
McNeill, William H. *The Pursuit of Power: Technology, Armed Force, and Society since A.D. 1000.* Chicago, 1982.
Maeda, Hirotake. "Exploitation of the Frontier: Shah Abbas I's Policy towards the Caucasus." In Floor and Herzig, eds., *Safavid Iran and the World,* 487–505.
———. "The Forced Migrations and Reorganisation of the Regional Order in the Caucaus by Safavid Iran: Preconditions and Developments Described by Fazli Khuzani." In *Reconstruction and Interaction of Slavic Eurasia and Its Neighbouring Worlds,* edited by Osamu Ieda and Tomohiko Uyano, 237–73. Sapporo, 2006.
———. "Hamza Mīrzā and the 'Caucasian Elements' at the Safavid Court: A Path toward the Reforms of Shah `Abbas I." *Orientalist* (Tbilisi) 1 (2001): 155–71.
———. "The Household of Allahverdi Khan: An Example of Patronage Network in Safavid Iran." In *Géorgie et sa capitale Tbilissi entre Perse et Europe,* edited by Florence Hellot-Belier and Irène Natchkebia, 43–55. Paris, 2009.
———. "On the Ethno-Social Background of Four *Gholām* Families from Georgia in Safavid Iran." *St. Ir.* 32 (2003): 243–78.
———. "Parsadan Gorgijanidze's Exile in Shustar: A Biographical Episode of a Georgian Official in the Service of the Safavids." *Journal of Persianate Studies* 1 (2008): 218–29.
Mahdavi, Sayyid Muslih al-Din. *Zindiginamah-i `Allamah Majlisi,* 2 vols. Tehran, 1378/2000.

Mann, Michael. "The Autonomous Power of the State: Its Origins, Mechanisms and Results." *Archives Européennes de Sociologie* 25 (1984), 185–213.

———. *The Sources of Social Power.* Vol. 1: *A History of Power from the Beginning to A.D. 1760.* Cambridge, 1986.

Mantran, Robert. "L'état ottoman au XVIIe siècle: stabilisation ou déclin?" In idem, ed., *Histoire de l'Empire Ottoman,* 227–64. Paris, 1989.

Manz, Beatrice Forbes. *Power, Politics and Religion in Timurid Iran.* Cambridge, 2007.

Markaryan, S. A. "Georgii XI I Kandagarskoe vosstanie 1709 gg. *Vostok Oriens* (2009): 5:41–45.

Marshall, Alan. *The Age of Faction. Court Politics, 1660–1702.* Manchester and New York, 1999.

Martinez, A. P. "Regional Mint Output and the Dynamics of Bullion Flows through the Il-Xanate." *Journal of Turkish Studies* 7 (1983): 121–73.

Marx, Anthony W. *Faith in Nation: Exclusionary Origins of Nationalism.* New York, 2003.

Masters, Bruce. *The Origins of Western Economic Dominance in the Middle East: Mercantilism and the Islamic Economy in Aleppo, 1600–1750.* New York, 1988.

Matthee, Rudi (Rudolph). "Administrative Stability and Change in Late-17th-Century Iran: The Case of Shaykh `Ali Khan Zanganah (1669–1689)." *IJMES* 26 (1994): 77–98.

———. "Between Arabs, Turks and Iranians: The Town of Basra, 1600–1700." *BSOAS* 69 (2006): 53–78.

———. "Between Venice and Surat: The Trade in Gold in Late Safavid Iran." *Modern Asian Studies* 33 (1999): 231–65.

———. "Blinded by Power: The Rise and Fall of Fath `Ali Khān Dāghistāni, Grand Vizier under Shāh Sultān Safavi (1127/1715–1133/1720)." *St.Ir.* 33 (2004): 179–220.

———. "The Career of Mohammad Beg, Grand Vizier of Shah `Abbas II (r. 1642–1666)." *IS* 24 (1991): 17–36.

———. "The East India Company Trade in Kerman Wool, 1658–1730." In Calmard, ed., *Etudes Safavides,* 343–83.

———. "Farhad Khan." *EIr.* 9 (1999), 258–60.

———. "Hajeb. In the Safavid and Qajar Periods." *EIr.* 11 (2002), 545–48.

———. "Iran's Ottoman Policy under Shah Sulayman, 1666/1076–1695/1105)." In *Iran and Iranian Studies: Papers in Honor of Iraj Afshar,* edited by Kambiz Eslami, 148–77. Princeton, 1998.

———. "Jesuits." *EIr.* 14 (2009), 634–38.

———. "Merchants in Safavid Iran: Participants and Perceptions." *Journal of Early Modern History* 4 (2000): 233–68.

———. "Mint Consolidation and the Worsening of the Late Safavid Coinage: The Mint of Huwayza." *JESHO* 44 (2001): 505–39.

———. "Negotiating Across Cultures: The Dutch Van Leene Mission to the Iranian Court of Shah Sulayman, 1689–92." *Eurasian Studies* 3:2 (2004): 35–63.

———. "Politics and Trade in late Safavid Iran: Commercial Crisis and Government Reaction under Shah Solayman (1666–1694)." Ph.D. dissertation. University of California, Los Angeles, 1991.
———. "The Politics of Protection: European Missionaries in Iran during the Reign of Shah Abbas I (1587–1629)." In *Contacts and Controversies between Muslims, Jews and Christians in the Ottoman Empire and Pre-Modern Iran*, edited by Sabine Schmidtke and Camille Adang, 245–71. Würzburg, 2010.
———. *The Politics of Trade in Safavid Iran: Silk for Silver, 1600–1730*. Cambridge, 1999.
———. *The Pursuit of Pleasure: Drugs and Stimulants in Iranian History, 1500–1900*. Princeton, 2005.
———. "The Safavid Economy as Part of the World Economy." In Floor and Herzig, eds., *Iran and the World in the Safavid Age*.
———. "The Safavid Mint of Huwayzah: The Numismatic Evidence." In *Society and Culture in the Early Modern Middle East: Studies on Iran in the Safavid Period*, edited by Andrew J. Newman, 265–91. Leiden, 2003.
———. "The Safavid-Ottoman Frontier: Iraq-i Arab as Seen by the Safavids." *International Journal of Turkish Studies* 9 (2003): 157–73.
———. "A Sugar Banquet for the Shah: Anglo-Dutch Rivalry at the Iranian Court of Šāh Sulaymān (r. 1666–1694)." *Eurasian Studies* (2006): 195–217.
Mawliyani, Sa`id. *Jaygah-i Gurjiha dar tarikh va farhang va tamaddun-i Iran*. Isfahan, 1379/2000.
Mazzaoui, Michel. "From Tabriz to Qazvin to Isfahan: Three Phases of Safavid History." *ZDMG*, suppl. 3, pt. 1 (1977): 521–22.
Meilinck-Roelofsz, M.A.P. "The Earliest Relations between Persia and the Netherlands. *Persica* 6 (1977): 1–50.
Melville, Charles. "Qars to Qandahar: The Itineraries of Shah `Abbas I (995–1038/1587–1629)." In Calmard, ed., *Etudes Safavides*, 195–224.
———, ed. *Persian and Islamic Studies in Honour of P. W. Avery*. Cambridge, 1990.
———, ed. *Safavid Persia: The History and Politics of an Islamic Society*. London, 1996.
Meserve, Margaret. *Empires of Islam in Renaissance Historical Thought*. Cambridge, Mass., 2008.
Mettam, Roger. *Power and Faction in Louis XIV's France*. Oxford and New York, 1988.
Metzler, Josef. "Nicht erfüllte Hoffnungen in Persien." In *Sacrae congregationis de Propaganda Fide memoria rerum, 350 anni a servizio delle missioni*, edited by idem, vol. I/1, 680–706. Rome, 1971.
Mirot, Léon. "Le séjour du Père Bernard de Sainte-Thérèse en Perse (1640–1642)." *Études Carmélitaines. Mystiques et missionnaires* 18 (1933): 213–36.
Mitchell, Colin P. "Provincial Chancelleries and Local Lines of Authority in Sixteenth-Century Safavid Iran." *Oriente Moderno*, n.s. 27 (2008): 483–507.
Mokyr, Joel. *The Enlightened Economy: An Economic History of Britain 1700–1850*. New Haven and London, 2009.

Moreen, Vera Basch. "The Downfall of Muhammad [Ali] Beg, Grand Vizier of Shah ʿAbbās II (reigned 1642–1666)." *Jewish Quarterly Review* 72 (1981): 81–99.

——. *Iranian Jewry's Hour of Peril and Heroism: A Study of Bābāī Ibn Lutf's Chronicle (1617–1662)*. Jerusalem, 1987.

——. "The Problem of Conversion among Iranian Jews in the Seventeenth and Eighteenth Centuries." *IS* 19 (1986): 216–28.

——. Risāla-yi Sawāʿiq al-Yahūd [The Treatise Lightning Bolts against the Jews] by Muhammad Bāqir b. Muhammad Taqī al-Majlisī (d. 1699)." *Die Welt des Islams* 32 (1992): 177–95.

Morgan, David. "The Decline and Fall of the Mongol Empire." *Journal of the Royal Asiatic Society*, 3rd ser., 19 (2009): 1–11.

Morony, M. "'In a City without Watchdogs the Fox is Overseer': Issues and Problems in the Study of Bureaucracy." In *The Organization of Power*, edited by McGuirre Gibson and Robert D. Biggs, 7–18. Chicago, 1987.

Morton, Alexandre. "Morton, "The Chūb-i Tarīq," and Qizilbāsh Ritual in Safavid Persia." In Calmard, ed., *Etudes Safavides*, 225–45.

Mottahedeh, Roy. *Loyalty and Leadership in an Early Islamic Society*. Princeton, 1980.

Murphey, Rhoads. "Continuity and Discontinuity in Ottoman Administrative Theory and Practice during the Late 17th Century." *Poetics Today* 14 (1993): 419–43.

——. *Exploring Ottoman Sovereignty: Tradition, Image and Practice in the Ottoman Imperial Household, 1400–1800*. London and New York, 2008.

——. "Mustafa Ali and the Politics of Cultural Despair." *IJMES* 21 (1989): 243–55.

——. *Ottoman Warfare 1500–1700*. New Brunswick, NJ, 1999.

——. "Ottoman-Safavid Border Conflict, 1603–1638." *Orientwissenschaftliche Hefte* 12 (2003): 151–70.

——. "The Resumption of Ottoman-Safavid Border Conflict, 1603–1638: Effects of Border Destabilization on the Evolution of State –Tribe Relations. In *Shifts and Drifts on Nomad-Sedentary Relations*, edited by Stefan Leder and Bernard Streck, 307–32. Wiesbaden, 2005.

Necipoğlu, Gülru. "Framing the Gaze in Ottoman, Safavid and Mughal Palaces." *Ars Orientalis* 23 (1993): 303–42.

Neck, Rudolf. "Diplomatische Beziehungen zum Vorderen Orient unter Karl V." *Mitteilungen des Österreichischen Staatsarchivs* 5 (1952): 63–86.

Newman, Andrew. *Safavid Iran. Birth of a Persian Empire*. London, New York, 2006.

——. "Towards a Reconsideration of the 'Isfahan School of Philosophy': Shaykh Baha'i and the Role of the Safawid Ulama'." *St.Ir.* 15 (1986): 165–99.

Nicoll, Fergus. *Shah Jahan: The Rise and Fall of the Mughal Emperor*. London, 2009.

Özoğlu, Hakan. "State-Tribe Relations: Kurdish Tribalism in the 16th and 17th-Century Ottoman Empire." *British Journal of Middle Eastern Studies* 23:1 (1996): 5–27.

Pamuk, Şevket. "The Disintegration of the Ottoman Monetary System during the Seventeenth Century." *Princeton Papers in Near Eastern Studies* 2 (1993), 67–81.

———. "In the Absence of Domestic Currency: Debased European Coinage in the Seventeenth-Century Ottoman Empire." *The Journal of Economic History* 57 (1997): 345–66.

———. *A Monetary History of the Ottoman Empire*. Cambridge, 2000.

Parker, Geoffrey. *The Military Revolution: Military Innovation and the Rise of the West, 1500–1800*. Cambridge, 1988.

Pearson, M.N. *The Indian Ocean*. London and New York, 2003.

———. "Merchants and States." In *The Political Economy of Merchant Empires: State Power and World Trade 1350–1750*, edited by James D. Tracy, 41–116. Cambridge, 1991.

Peck, Linda Levy. *Court Patronage and Corruption in Early Stuart England*. Boston and London, 1990.

Perry, John R. "Deportations." *EIr.* 7 (1996), 309–10.

———. "Forced Migration in Iran during the Seventeenth and Eighteenth Centuries." *IS* 8 (1975): 199–215.

———. "Justice for the Underprivileged: The Ombudsman Tradition of Iran." *Journal of Near East Studies* 37 (1978): 203–15.

———. "Persian during the Safavid Period: Sketch for an *Etat de Langue*." In Melville, ed., *Safavid Persia*, 269–85.

———. "The last Safavids." *Iran: Journal of the British Institute of Persian Studies* 9 (1971): 59–71.

Porter, Roy. *Gibbon: Making History*. London, 1995.

Posch, Walter. *Der Fall Alkâs Mîrzâ und der Persienfeldzug von 1548–1549*. Würzburg, 2000.

Poumarède, Géraud. *Pour en finir avec la Croisade. Mythes et réalites de la lutte contre les Turcs aux XVIe et XVIIe siècles*. Paris, 2004.

Pucko, Zygmunt. "The Activity of Polish Jesuits in Persia and Neighbouring Countries in the 17th and 18th Centuries." In *Proceedings of the Third European Conference of Iranian Studies*, pt. 2, *Mediaeval and Modern Persian Studies*, edited by Charles Melville, 309–15. Wiesbaden, 1999).

Quinn, Sholeh. "Coronation Narratives in Safavid Chronicles." In *History and Historiography of Post-Mongol Central Asia and the Middle East. Studies in Honor of John E. Woods*, edited by J. Pfeiffer and S. A. Quinn, 311–31. Wiesbaden, 2006.

———. "Rewriting Ni`matullāhī History in Safavid Chronicles." In *The Heritage of Sufism: Late Clasical Persianate Sufism (1501–1750)*, edited by Leonard Lewisohn and David Morgan, 201–24. London, 1999.

Quiring-Zoche, Rosemarie. *Isfahan im 15. und 16. Jahrhundert. Ein Beitrag zur persischen Stadtgeschichte*. Berlin, 1980.

Rabino di Borgomale, H. L. *Coins, Medals, and Seals of the Shahs of Iran. 1500–1941.* Hertford, 1945.

Radzhabli, A. M. "Iz istorii monetnogo dela v sefevidskom gosudarstve." *Trudy Muzeia istorii Azerbaidzhana* 4 (1961): 44–67.

Rahimi, Babak. "The Rebound Theater State: The Politicis of the Safavid Camel Sacrifice Rituals, 1598–1695." *IS* 37 (2004): 451–79.

Rahmani, A. A. *Azerbaidzhan v kontse XVI i XVII vekov.* Baku, 1981.

Ra'is al-Sadat, Sayyid Hasan. "Tasarruf-i Qandahar dar dawrah-i Shah `Abbas-i divvum." In *Iran-zamin dat gustarah-i tarikh-i Safaviyah*, edited by Maqsud `Ali Sadiqi, 445–62. Tabriz, 1384/2005.

Ranjbar, Muhammad `Ali. *Musha`sha`iyan. Mahiyat-i fikri-ijtima`i va farayand-i tahavullat-i tarikhi.* Tehran, 1382/2003.

Raverty, Major H. G. *Notes on Afghánistan and Part of Baluchistan.* London, 1888.

Razaviyan, Raziyah. "Naqsh-i Qandahar dar ravabit-i Iran va Hind (Safaviyan va Gurkaniyan)." *Tarikh-i ravabit-i khariji* 5/18 (1383/2004): 5–24.

Reid, James J. *Tribalism and Society in Islamic Iran 1500–1629.* Malibu, 1983.

Richards, D. S., ed. *Precious Metals in the Late Medieval and Early Modern Worlds.* Durham, NC, 1980.

Rizvi, Kishwar. *The Safavid Dynastic Shrine: Architecture, Religion and Power in Early Modern Iran.* London and New York, 2010.

Rizvi, Sajjad H. "Sayyid Ni`mat Allāh al-Jazā'irī and his Anthologies: Anti-Sufism, Shi`ism and Jokes in the Safavid World." *Die Welt des Islams* 50 (2010): 224–42.

Roemer, Hans Robert. *Persien auf dem Weg in die Neuzeit: Iranische Geschichte von 1350–1750.* Beirut, 1989.

———. "The Safavid Period." In *CHI*, vol. 6, 189–350. Cambridge, 1986.

Röhrborn, Klaus Michael. *Provinzen und Zentralgewalt Persiens im 16. und 17. Jahrhundert.* Berlin, 1966.

———. "Regierung und Verwaltung Irans unter den Safawiden." *Handbuch der Orientalistik: Regierung und Verwaltung des vorderen Orients in islamischer Zeit.*"

———. "Staatskanzlei und Absolutismus im safawidischen Persien." *ZDMG* 127 (1977): 313–43.

Rota, Giorgio. "Caucasians in Safavid Service in the 17th Century." In *Caucasia between the Ottoman Empire and Iran, 1555–1914*, edited by R. Motika and M. Ursinus, 107–20. Wiesbaden, 2000.

———. "Le favayedo's-safaviyeh e la storia della Georgia." *Annali de Ca' Foscari* 33 (1994): 427–44.

———. *Under Two Lions: On the Knowledge of Persia in the Republic of Venice (ca 1450–1797).* Vienna, 2009.

Safa, Z. "Persian Literature in the Safavid Period." In *CHI*, vol. 6, 948–64. Cambridge, 1990.

Şahillioğlu, Halil. "The Role of International Monetary and Metal Movements in Ottoman Monetary History 1300–1750." In Richards, ed., *Precious Metals*, 269–292.

Saksena, Banarsi Prasad. *History of Shahjahan of Dihli*. Allahabad, 1958.

Saray, Mehmet. *Türk-Iran münasebetlerinde ülin rolü*. Ankara, 1990.

Sarkar, "Asian Balance of Power in the Light of Mughal-Persian Rivalry in the 16th and 17th Centuries." In *Studies in the Foreign Relations of India*, edited by P. M. Joshi and M. A. Nayeem, 195–222. Hyderabad, 1975.

Savory, Roger. *Iran under the Safavids*. Cambridge, 1980.

——. "The Safavid Administrative System." In *CHI*, vol. 6, 351–72. Cambridge, 1990.

——. "The Office of Sepahsalar (Commander of State in the Safavid State)." *Proceedings of the Second European Conference of Iranian Studies*, edited by Bert Fragner et al., 597–615. Rome, 1995.

Schultz, "Mamluk Money from Baybars to Barquq: A Study Based on the Literary Sources and the Numismatic Evidence." Ph.D. dissertation. University of Chicago, 1995.

Schurmann, H. F. "Mongolian Tributary Practices of the Thirteenth Century." *Harvard Study of Asiatic Studies* 19 (1956): 304–89.

Sefatgol (Sifatgul), Mansour. "The Question of Awqaf under the Afsharids." In *Matériaux pour l'histoire économique du monde iranien*, edited by Rika Gyselen and Maria Szuppe, 209–32. Paris, 1999.

——. "Persian Historical Writing during the Last Safavids: The Historiography of Decline." *Eurasian Studies* 5 (2006): 319–33.

——. *Sakhtar-i nihad va andishah-i dini dar Iran-i `asr-i Safavi. (Tarikh-i tahavul-lat-i dini-yi Iran dar sadah'ha-yi dihum ta davazdihum hijri qamari)*. Tehran, 1381/2002.

Setton, Kennet M. *Venice, Austria, and the Turks in the Seventeenth Century*. Philadelphia, 1991.

Sharifi, Yusuf. *Dard-i dil-i Zimmah. Nigarishi bar zindigi-yi ijtima`i-yi aqaliyatha-yi mazhabi dar avakhir-i `asr-i Safavi*. Los Angeles, 2009.

Shubbar, Jasim Hasan. *Tarikh al-Musha`sha`yin wa tarajim `alayhim*. Najaf, 1385/1965.

Shujja`, `Abd al-Majid. *Zan, siyasat va haramsara dar `asr-i Safaviyah*. Tehran, 1384/2005.

Sidorko, Clemens P. "'Kampf den ketzerischen Qizilbaš!.' Die Revolte des Haǧǧī Dā'ūd (1718–1728)." In *Caucasia between the Ottoman Empire and Iran, 1555–1914*, edited by R. Motika and M. Ursinus, 133–46. Wiesbaden, 2000.

Simmons, Jeremiah Benn. "The Evolution of Persia's Monetary System between Safavid Power's Consolidation in 1502 and the Employing of Belgian Mint Management Experts in 1901." Ph.D. dissertation. Cambridge University, King's College, 1977.

Simnani, Panahi. *Shah Sultan Husayn Safavi. Trazhidi-yi natavani-yi hukumat*. Tehran, 1373/1994.

Siroux, M. *Caravanserails d'Iran.* Mémoires de l'Institut Français d'Archéologie du Caire 81, Cairo, 1949.
Smith, Dianne L. "Muscovite Logistics, 1462–1598." *Studies on Eastern Europe and Russia* 71 (1993): 35–65.
Smith, John Masson Jr., and Frances Plunkett. "Gold Money in Mongol Iran." *JESHO* 11 (1968): 275–98.
Sotavov, N. A. *Severnii Kavkaz v russko-iraniskikh i russko-turechkikh otnosheniiakh v XVIII v.* Moscow, 1991.
Spufford, Peter. *Money and Its Use in Medieval Europe.* Cambridge, 1988.
Starn, Randolph. "Historians and 'Crisis.'" *Past and Present* 52 (1971): 3–52.
Stewart, Devin J., "Notes on the Migration of `AmilīScholars to Safavid Iran." Journal of Near Eastern Studies 55 (1996): 81–103.
Subrahmanyam, Sanjay. "Aspects of State Formation in South India and South-East Asia, 1500–1650." *Indian Economic and Social History Review* 23 (1986): 357–77.
———. "Precious Metal Flows and Prices in Western and Southern Asia, 1500–1750: Some Comparative and Conjunctorial Aspects." *Studies in History,* n. s. 7 (1991): 79–105.
Sumer, Faruq. *Naqsh-i Turkan-i Anatuli dar tashkil va tawsi`ah-i dawlat-i Safavi.* Translated by Ihsan Ishraqi and Muhammad Taqi Imami. Tehran, 1371/1992.
Supple, B. E. *Commercial Crisis and Change in England 1600–1642: A Study in the Instability of a Mercantile Economy.* Cambridge, 1959.
Sussman, Nathan. "Debasements, Royal Revenues, and Inflation in France during the Hundred Years' War, 1415–1422." *Journal of Economic History* 53 (1993): 44–70.
Szuppe, Maria. "Kinship Ties between the Safavids and the Qizilbash Amirs in Late Sixteenth-Century Iran: A Case Study of the Polticial Careeer of Members of the Sharaf al-Din Oghli Tekelu Family." In Melville, ed., *Safavid Persia,* 79–104.
———. "La participation des femmes de la famille royale à l'exercice du pouvoir en Iran safavide au XVIe siècle." *St.Ir.* 23 (1994): 211–58; and 24 (1995): 61–122.
Tapper, Richard. *Frontier Nomads of Iran: A Political and Social History of the Shahsevan.* Cambridge, 1997.
Tardy, Lajos. "Georgische Teilnahme an den persisch-afghanischen Kriegen 1711–1725 im Spiegel eines Missionsberichtes." *Bedi Kartlisa/Revue de Kartvélogie* 40 (1982): 316–29.
Tarimi, Hasan. `Allamah Majlisi.* Tehran, 1375/1996.
Thomson, J. K. J. *Decline in Hstory: The European Experience.* Cambridge, 1998.
Tilly, Charles. "Reflections on the History of European State-Making." In *The Formation of National States in Western Europe,* edited by idem, 3–83. Princeton, 1975.
Togan, Isenbeke. "Ottoman History by Inner Asian Norms." In *New Approaches to State and Peasant in Ottoman History,* edited by Halil Berktay and Suraiya Faroqhi, 185–210. London, 1992.

Tokatlian, Armen. *Kalantars. Les seigneurs arméniens dans la Perse safavide.* Paris, 2009.
Touzard, Anne-Marie. *Le Drogman Padery, émissaire de France en Perse (1719–1725).* Paris, 2005.
Trausch, Tilmann. *Anpassung und Abbilding. Das Türkenbild in safawidischen Chroniken des 16. Jahrhunderts.* Berlin, 2008.
Tucci, Ugo. "Le emissioni monetarie di Venezia e i movimenti internazionali dell'oro." In idem, *Mercanti, navi, monete nel Cinquecento Veneziano,* 275–316. Bologna, 1981.
———. "Una relazione di Giovan Battista Vechietti sulla Persia e sul Regno di Hormuz 1587." *Oriente Moderno* 35:4 (1955): 149–60.
Tucker, Ernest. "The Peace Negotiations of 1736: A Conceptual Turning Point in Ottoman-Safavid Relations." *Turkish Studies Association Bulletin* 20:1 (Spring 1996): 16–37.
Tumanovich, N. N. *Gerat v XVI-XVIII vekakh.* Moscow, 1989.
Turner, Colin. *Islam without Allah? The Rise of Religious Externalism in Safavid Iran.* Richmond, Surrey, 2000.
Van Klaveren, Jacob. "Die historische Erscheinung der Korruption." *Vierteljahrschrift für Sozial-und Wirtschaftsgeschichte* 44 (1957): 289–324; and 45 (1958): 433–504.
Van Santen, H. W. "De Verenigde Oost-Indische Compagnie in Gujarat en Hindustan, 1620–1660." Ph.D. Dissertation. Leiden University, 1982.
Vatin, Nicolas, and Gilles Veinstein, *Le Sérail ébranlé. Essai sur les morts, dépositions et avènements des sultan ottomans XVIe-XIXe siècle.* Paris, 2003.
Volovnikova, V.G. et al., eds. *Poslannik Petra I na vostoke. Posol'stvo Florio Beneveni v Persiiu i Bukharu v 1718–1725 godakh.* Moscow, 1986.
Von Glahn, Richard. *Fountain of Fortune. Money and Monetary Policy in China, 1000–1700.* Berkeley and Los Angeles, 1996.
Vusuqi, Muhammad Baqir. *Tarikh-i muhajirat-i aqvam dar khalij-i Fars. Muluk-i Hurmuz.* Shiraz, 1380/2001.
Weber, Max. *Economy and Societ.* 2 vols. Edited by Guenther Roth and Claus Wittich. Berkeley and Los Angeles, 1978.
White, D. Maxwell. *Zaccaria Seriman 1709–1784 and the Viaggi di Enrico Wanton.* New York, 1961.
Whittaker, C. R. *Frontiers of the Roman Empire: A Social and Economic Study.* Baltimore and London, 1994.
Widmer, Paul. "Niedergangskonzeptionen, zwischen Erfahrung und Erwartung." In *Niedergang. Studien zu einem geschichtlichen Thema,* edited by Reinhart Koselleck and Paul Widmer, 12–30. Munich, 1980.
Wilson, Sir Arnold T. "History of the Mission of the Fathers of the Society of Jesus, Established in Persia by the Reverend Father Alexander of Rhodes." *BSOAS* 3 (1923–25): 675–716.
Wolf, Eric. *Europe and the People without History.* Berkeley and Los Angeles, 1984.
Wood, Barry D. "The *Tarikh-i Jahanara* in the Chester Beatty Library: An Illustrated Manuscript of the – 'Anonymous Histories of Shah Isma'il.'" *IS* 37 (2004): 89–108.

Zarinebaf-Shahr, Fariba. "Tabriz under Ottoman Rule (1725–1731)." Ph.D. dissertation. University of Chicago, 1991.

Zavish, H. M. *Nakhustin karguzaran-i isti`mar.* Tehran, 1366/1988.

Zedginidze, G.E. "Iz istorii pol'sko-russkikh diplomaticheskikh otnoshenii s Iranom. Deiatel'nost Bogdana Gurdzhinskogo." Avtoreferat dissertatsii. Tiflis, 1971.

Zevakin, E. S. "Konflikt Rossii s Persiei v serednie XVII stoletiia." *Azerbaidzhan v nachale XVIII veka* 8:4 (Baku, 1929): 24–31.

———. "Persidskii vopros v russko-evropeiskikh otnosheniiakh XVII v." *Istoricheskie Zapiski* 8 (1940): 129–62.

Zimmel, Bruno. "Vorgeschichte und Gründung der Jesuitenmission in Isfahan (1642–1657)." *Zeitschrift für Missionswissenschaft und Religionswissenschaft* 53 (1969): 1–26.

Index

Abarquh 143
'Abbas I, Shah xxii, xxiii, xxvi, 3, 5, 15,
    16, 17, 18, 19, 20, 21, 22–23, 24,
    27, 33, 34, 35, 37, 38, 39, 57, 60,
    62, 75, 78, 81, 85, 88, 98, 110, 113,
    115, 116, 118, 122, 125, 128, 129,
    140, 142, 143, 144, 145, 146, 147,
    148, 151, 153, 154, 155, 157, 159,
    163, 174, 177–82, 190, 198–9, 218,
    244, 245, 246, 247, 249, 253, 314n
'Abbas II, Shah xxii, xxiii, 12, 16, 17,
    23, 30, 42, 43, 45, 49, 50, 51, 52,
    53, 55–6, 57, 58, 60, 61, 63, 64,
    92, 93, 94, 98, 99, 100, 102, 106,
    113, 119, 121, 122, 123, 124, 126,
    127, 128, 129, 145, 147, 148, 149,
    150, 151, 157, 164, 166, 167, 168,
    183–5, 189, 191, 202, 247, 253,
    268n, 311n
'Abbas 'Ali Beg 284n
'Abbas Beg Zanganah 72
'Abbas Mirza 223, 241, 321n
'Abbas Quli Beg Zanganah 72
'Abbas Quli Khan 160
'Abbas Quli Khan Qajar 216, 319n
'Abbas Quli Khan Ziyad Ughlu 216
'Abd Allah, Sayyid 240
'Abd Allah b. Nur ad-Din b.
    Ni'matallah al-Husayni al-
    Shushtari 227, 327n
'Abd al-Qasim Beg 164
'Abd al-Qasim Khan (son of Jani Khan)
    23, 276n
'Abd al-Qasim Khan (governor of Lar)
    230

Abdali Afghans 234, 235
Abhar 143
Abisaab, Rula 30, 309n
Abivard 231
Abu Ishaq Kaziruni 174
Abu'l Ghazi Khan 127, 148
Abu'l Qasim Beg Iv Ughli 37
Abu'l Qasim Khan 216
Abu Muslim 176, 184
Abu Talib Musavi Findiriski 22, 52,
    261n
'Adil Giray (Tartar chief) 147
'Adil Giray (Shamkhal) 226
Adle, Chahriyar 4
Afghanistan and Afghans 9, 10, 114,
    126, 136, 147, 162, 174, 204, 218,
    226, 232–5, 237–41, 253, 265n
Afshar 40, 114, 142, 143, 159, 174,
    231
Agha Kafur 55, 61, 62
Agha Hajji 60
Agha Kamal 61, 219, 237–8
Agha Mubarak 55, 56, 61, 62
Agha Vali 89
Agra 252
Aguletsi, Zakariya 89
Ahmad Agha 214
Ahmad b. Zayn al-'Abidin 'Alavi 180
Ahmad Agha 206, 228
Aix-la-Chapelle 130
Akbar, Prince 136
Akbar, Sultan 83, 92, 178, 246, 328n
Ak Tashi 223
'Alam Shah Afghan 233
Alamut 199, 319n

Alburz Mountains 4, 141, 199
Aldas (Ildas) Mirza Shamkhal 206
Aleppo 85, 127
Alexander, Bishop 194
Alexander, King 146
Alexandretta (Iskenderun) 131
Alexei Mikhailovich, Czar 190
'Ali, Imam 15
'Ali al-Karaki 52, 176, 183
'Ali Bali Beg 281n
'Ali Beg 310n
'Ali Beg Zanganah 62
'Ali Khan 21
'Ali Kirmani 41
'Ali Mardan Khan 117, 118, 122, 159, 217, 227, 240
'Ali Muhammad Hazin Lahiji xxvii, 141
'Ali Quli Beg 42
'Ali Quli Khan 38, 39, 128, 232
'Ali Riza Khan 208, 228
Allah Virdi Beg 168
Allah Virdi Khan (governor of Fars) 27, 28, 30, 38, 113, 117, 143, 155, 178
Allah Virdi Khan (ruler of Shirvan) 222
Allah Virdi Khan Musahib (amir-shikar-bashi) 45, 46, 50, 51, 122, 276n, 309n
Alqas Mirza 146
Alqas Mirza b. Ildirim Khan Shamkhal 206
Amasya, Peace of 119
Amin Beg 87
Amir-akhur-bashi 113, 281n
Amir al-umara 35, 143
Amir-shikar-bashi 37, 45, 46, 143, 284n
Amir Khusraw Shah 232
Amir Shah Salim 232
Anatolia 5, 97, 105, 173
Andkhud 174
Andrusovo, Peace of 130
Anna Khanum 42, 43, 44
Anusa 68
Anusha Khan 127
Aq-Quyunlu 77, 112, 173
Aqa Jahan 275n
Aqa Pir 193
Aqa Pir Muhammad 325n
'Arab Khan Shamlu 44

Arabia 78, 156, 218, 237, 250
'Arabistan 4, 10, 93, 98, 132, 143, 146, 227–8
Arabs 9, 10, 121, 147
Aras River 24, 145, 178
Ardabil 40, 47, 50, 122, 149
Ardalan 148, 216, 222
Armenia and Armenians xxxiii, 5, 8, 10, 16, 18, 24, 27, 29, 30, 31, 45, 46, 67, 70, 85, 98, 105, 106, 107, 114, 129, 130, 132, 144, 145, 152, 155, 158, 159, 177, 179, 181, 182, 184–6, 189–91, 192–5, 208, 220, 221, 223, 227, 240, 241, 253, 254, 255, 259n, 283n, 284n, 312n
'Asab Khan 37
Asad Allah Khan 239
Ashraf 5
Aslan Khan 209, 231
Astara 122, 216
Astrakhan 226
Astarabad (Gurgan) 15, 52, 127, 142, 153, 188, 205, 209, 215, 227, 231, 237
'atabat 15, 205, 218
Augustinians 180, 181, 190
Aurangzeb, Sultan 124, 125, 126, 136, 277, 298n, 328n
Austrians 180
'Avaz Khan 228
Avramov, Semen 203
Avril, Philippe S. J. 31
Awad 255
Axworthy, Michael 14, 259n
Azerbaijan 5, 6, 39, 40, 43, 68, 72, 85, 94, 112, 114, 122, 142, 149, 150, 152, 154, 157, 173, 215, 222, 246, 255

Babayan, Kathryn 39, 40, 185
Banu Khalid tribe 227
Babunah Beg 278n
Badakhshan 124
Baft 238
Baghdad 37, 41, 81, 85, 104, 112, 116, 117, 118, 120, 123, 127, 130, 131, 133, 134, 179, 215
Bagh-i Farahabad 209
Baha' al-Din al-'Amili, Shaykh 180, 181, 185, 310n

Bahar, Malik al-Shu`ara 261n
Bahrain 5, 38, 106, 176, 229, 230, 237, 252
Bakharz 71
Bakhtiyari 23, 136, 143, 147, 149, 153, 179, 236
Baku 154, 215
Balkh 127, 217
Baluchistan and Baluchis 9, 10, 114, 131, 136, 142, 145, 147, 161–2, 167, 198, 204, 216, 217, 222, 227, 229, 230, 231–41, 246
Bam 161, 232, 239
Bandar `Abbas 7, 46, 48, 87, 98, 100, 102, 104, 105, 129, 140, 150, 152, 163–72, 184, 208, 210, 211–2, 217, 221, 229–31, 238, 240, 255, 308n
Bandar Daylam 217
Bandar Rig 172, 300n
Banu Khalid 227
Banyans 86, 107, 165, 170, 172, 186, 192, 221, 229, 231, 236, 239, 264n
Barnett, Richard 254
Barthold, V. V. 12
Basra 5, 88, 93, 103, 107, 119, 127, 132, 148, 158, 172, 215, 227–8, 318n
Bastani-Parizi, Muhammad Ibrahim 159, 263n
Bausani, Alessandro xxvi
Bayazid, Prince 294n
Bayram Beg 301n
Bengal 255
Bembo, Ambrosio 144, 152, 155, 156
Beneveni, Florio 225, 321n
Bih Pas 21
Bihbahan 72, 241
Biktash Khan 159
Bill, James 12
Birjand 159
Bizhan Beg 68
Boullay-le-Gouze, Sieur de la 151
Browne, E. G. xxv–xxvi, 261n
Brugsch, Heinrich 34
Budaq Beg 277n
Budaq Sultan 53, 193
Bukhara 127, 217
Busse, Heribert 56

Bust 124, 125
Buyids 272n
Cairo 83
Candia, War of 85, 120, 130
Capuchins 190
Carmelites 195
Carré, Barthélemy 131, 152, 156, 166
Casembroot, Reynier 71, 102
Caspian Sea 64, 143, 149, 155, 226
Caucasus 5, 9, 18, 30, 67, 115, 122, 147, 179, 219, 246
Ceylon 5, 106
Chaldiran, Battle of 15, 111, 118, 175, 245
Chapelle de Han 47–48
Chardin, Jean xxiv, xxviii, 6, 8, 21, 24, 31, 52, 55, 56, 60, 68, 76, 96, 97, 115, 127, 128, 145, 146, 149, 152, 156, 161, 162, 166, 167, 181, 183, 184, 188, 202, 246
Chelebi, Evliya 76
Chézaud, Aimé 184, 191
China 96, 156
Chiragh Khan Zahidi (Pirzadah) 36, 37
Christianity 177–88
Chugur–i Sa`d 122, 142
Cipolla, Carlo 93
Circassians 18, 27, 37, 67
Clement IX, Pope 130
Colbert, Jean-Baptiste 89
Constantin Mirza 146
Constantinople, Treaty of 227
Coromandel 87
Cossacks 64, 127, 129, 149, 155, 226, 281n
Crone, Patricia 145
Cunaeus, Joan 47

Daghistan 67, 76, 122, 145, 146, 206, 226–8, 315n
Dahdasht 241
Dale, Stephen 270n
Dara Shikuh 124, 125
Darband 122, 136, 148, 153, 226
Darughah 19, 62
Darughah-i daftar 62
Darur Shah 239
Dasht-i Kavir 141
Dasht-i Lut 141
Dashtistan 210

Da'ud Khan 38, 39
Da'ud Khan Shamlu 44, 276n
David of Kakheti, Prince 20
Dawit Julayec'i 189, 190
Dawraq 94, 228
Daylaman 18
De Bruyn, Cornelis 34, 222
De la Maze, Jean-Baptiste S. J. 129, 154–5
Delhi 252
Della Valle, Pietro 115, 121, 129, 179, 217
Deslandes, André Daulier 152–3
Diarbakr 127, 215
Dickson, Martin xxi
Diego di Sant'Anna 280n
Divanbegi 36
Dizful 94
Don Juan of Persia *see* Uruch Beg
Drought 63, 158, 160, 162, 169, 192, 215, 217, 231–2, 235–6
Du Mans, Raphaël 24, 59, 61, 80, 102, 115, 132, 134, 151, 153, 183, 184, 203, 277n
Dürri Efendi (Dourry Efendy), Ahmad 174, 202, 225, 252
Dust 'Ali Khan Zanganah 71
Dutch *see* VOC

Echmiadzin 179
EIC (English East India Company) 42, 108, 159, 166, 170, 173, 194, 306n
Elia di S. Alberto, Father 195
Elliot, John xxix
England and English 89, 217, 250, 266n, 272n, 289n, 293n
Erekle, Prince 68
Erzurum 215, 225
Eunuchs 28, 30, 55, 60, 61–2, 202, 205–6, 214, 218, 251–2

Fabritius, Ludvig 135–6
Famine 63, 96, 101, 158, 215, 231–2, 235–6, 249
Farah 124, 235
Farahabad (Mazandaran) 5, 57, 64, 127, 153, 216, 281n
Farahabad (Isfahan) 235
Faraj Allah b. 'Ali Khan 99, 227–8
Farhad Khan Qaramanlu 39, 142

Faroqhi, Suraiya 31
Fars 5, 25, 27, 38, 50, 140, 143, 144, 150, 152, 155–8, 159, 164, 174, 210, 215, 229, 230
Farsadan Beg 224–5
Farsadan Gorgijanidze 50
Fath 'Ali Khan Daghistani 22, 59, 73, 206–15, 219, 223, 225, 228, 248, 250, 315n
Findiriski *see* Abu Talib Musavi Findiriski
Firaydun Khan 167
Firdawsi, Abu'l Qasim 22
Firearms 111–2, 144, 217–8
Floor, Willem 30, 41, 52, 270n, 275n
France 89, 328n
Fryer, John 156, 158, 170, 261n
Fudul tribe 227

Ganj 'Ali Khan 40, 122, 142
Ganja 38, 40, 142, 145, 216, 219, 226
Gardane, Ange de 209, 210, 211, 317n
Garmsir(at) 5, 6, 71, 217, 228, 230–1
Garusi 174
Gaskar 18
Gaudereau, Abbé Martin 197, 313n
Gaz 326n
Gemelli Careri, Giovanni 68, 132–3, 150
Georgia and Georgians 5, 8, 16, 18, 19, 20, 27, 28, 30, 31, 36, 38–9, 56, 61, 67–8, 72, 76, 113–4, 122, 143, 145, 146, 167, 178, 206, 210, 223, 227, 229, 233–4, 238, 240, 255, 265n
Germans 137
Ghadir Khumm 192
Gharib Shah 36
Ghazan Khan 77
Ghilza'i Afghans 232–41
Ghougassian, Vasken 189
Ghulams 18–19, 21, 27, 28–30, 36–40, 109, 112–3, 143, 164, 178, 249, 272n
Ghuzz Turks 1
Gibbon, Edward 261n
Gida 'Ali Beg 210
Giyas al-Din Mansur 162
Gifts 20–21, 268n, 269n
Gilan 4, 6, 18, 19, 21, 25, 36, 40, 44, 76, 83, 143, 149, 153, 155, 174, 215, 221, 226–7, 255

Giorgi X, King 20
Giorgi XI *see* Gurgin Khan
Gobineau, Joseph Arthur Comte de 29
Göklen 145
Golconda 93
Gouvea, António de 179–80, 188
Grand Vizier 33–5, 62
Gritti, Francesco 130
Gujarat 5
Gul-Mihr Beg 122
Gulnabad 240
Gulpaygan 38
Gurdziecki, Bogdan 130
Gurgan *see* Astarabad
Gurgin Beg 236
Gurgin Khan 146, 233–4, 323n

Hajj 69, 78, 201, 218–9, 237–8
Hajji ʿAli Khan 72
Hajji Daʾud 223, 226
Hajji Manuchihr Khan 122, 124
Hajji Muhammad ʿAli Beg 89
Hajji Muhammad Baqir Beg 92
Hajji Muʾmin 170
Hajji Piri 107
Hakkari 147
Hamadan 23, 40, 44, 71, 73, 121, 136, 149, 152, 160, 174, 215, 226, 227, 241
Hamzah Mirza (son of Shah Muhammad Khudabandah) 19, 115, 146
Hamzah Mirza (son of ʿAbbas II) 56
Haneda, Masashi 40
Hanway, Jonas 56
Hasan ʿAli Khan 222
Hasan Basha 158
Hasan Beg 37, 49
Hasan Khan Ustajlu 37, 40
Hatim Beg 161
Hatim Beg Urdubadi 41
Haydar Beg 53
Hazar Jarib 57
Hazin Lahiji *see* ʿAli Muhammad Hazin Lahiji
Hedges, William 104, 156
Herat 40, 177, 206, 209, 234, 235, 237, 325n
Herzig, Edmund 178
Hindu Kush 246

Hindus 186, 220, 254
Hinz, Walther 2, 251, 260n
Hizar-pishah 61, 73
Hodgson, Marshall xxiii
Holland xxii
Hotaki 233
Hurmuz 38, 163, 179, 230
Hurr al-ʿAmili, Shaykh 193
Hurufiya 177
Husayn ʿAli Khan Zanganah 71, 72, 283n, 285n
Husayn Basha Afrasiyab 119, 127–8, 132, 300n
Husayn Beg 48, 49, 164
Husayn Beg Tabrizi 46
Husayn Khan 208
Husayn Khan Beg (nazir) 42
Husayn Khan Beg (envoy to Russia) 105
Husayn Khan Shamlu 40
Husayn Quli Khan 210, 321n
Husayn Quli Khan (Vakhtang VI) 225, 229
Huwayza 92, 94, 98–99, 103–4, 147, 167, 227–9
Hyderabad 141, 255

Ibn Khaldun 243
Ibrahim I, Sultan 120
Ibrahim Agha 208
Ibrahim Beg 72
Ibrahim Khan (darughah) 208
Ibrahim Khan (governor of Dawraq) 229, 126–7
Il-Khans 14, 22, 77
Imam Quli Khan 23, 28, 38, 39, 117, 143, 148, 156, 157, 164
Imam Quli Khan Zanganah 207
Imam Riza 199, 237
Inayat Khan 297n
India 80, 81, 83, 86, 87, 88, 93–4, 96, 105, 107, 115, 141, 156, 220, 255
Iqtaʿ 141
Iraq 4, 46, 78, 114, 115, 119, 121, 127, 152, 174, 216, 218, 227, 246, 250
ʿIsa Khan Beg 49, 164–5
ʿIsa Khan Shaykhavand 36, 37, 74
Isfahan 4, 8, 12, 16, 19, 23, 29, 45, 50, 63, 71, 85, 88, 90, 98, 103, 105,

107, 126–7, 136, 139, 143, 151, 152, 165, 167, 173–4, 178, 181, 182, 184–7, 192, 200, 215, 218, 237–8, 241–2, 244, 252, 270n
Ishik-aqasi-bashi 21, 36, 37, 60, 113, 315n
Iskandar Beg Munshi 81, 147, 179, 244
Isma'il I, Shah 9, 10, 15, 39, 40, 78, 81, 83, 111–13, 115, 118, 142, 148, 155, 173–6, 243, 245, 247, 260n, 267n, 275n
Isma'il II, Shah 16, 17, 176–7
Isma'il Aqa Mutafarriqeh 120
Isma'il Beg Zanganah 72
Isma'il Khan 208
Istanbul 83, 184, 252
Italy 194, 220, 254
I'timad al-dawlah see grand vizier
'Ivaz Beg 61
Izmir 155

Jabal 'Amil 176
Ja'far Quli Agha 205, 206
Ja'far Quli Khan 146
Jahan, Shah 122, 124, 125
Jahrum 25, 156, 157, 229
Jala'ir 40
Jam, Battle of 111, 217
Jamshid Khan 53, 123, 126, 162
Jani Khan Shamlu 23, 43–4, 118, 123, 160, 247, 276n
Janissaries 120
Japan 93, 156
Jerusalem 179
Jesuits 184, 187, 190–1, 219
Jews 10, 152, 181, 182, 183, 184, 185, 186, 187–9, 191, 192, 193, 221, 254, 310n
Jirun 38
Jiz'ya 160, 189, 208, 220, 221, 246, 328n
Julfa 24, 29, 178

Kabul 233–4
Kaempfer, Engelbert 34, 61, 65, 67, 71–2, 89, 96, 97, 102, 128, 132, 136, 151, 153, 203, 219, 311n
Kafadar, Cemal xxii
Kakhet'i 68, 225
Kalantar 17, 62
Kalhuri 174

Kalb 'Ali Khan (qurchibashi) 70, 72, 119–20, 148
Kalb 'Ali Khan (of Astarabad) 205, 210, 231
Kalhur 63
Kalmyks 64, 226
Kara Kum 246
Kara Qaytaq 122
Kartli 36, 39, 68, 225, 233
Karun River 48, 71, 284n
Kashan 4, 18, 143, 187, 203, 213, 229, 237
Kay Khusraw *see* Khusraw Khan
Kazirun 73, 241
Kazızadeh Movement 312n
Kemanskesh Kara Mustafa Pasha 120
Ketelaar, Joshua 237
Khabis 162, 232–3
Khʿaf 71
Khajah Mahabbat 42, 60
Khajah Mushfiq 42
Khajah Sarhat 189
Khalifah Sultan (Sultan al-'Ulama) 36, 41, 44–5, 49, 52, 58, 149, 185–6
Khalil Khan 23, 147
Khan Ahmad Beg 72
Khanah Pasha 318n
Khʿar 149
Khassah land 143, 148–9
Khazanah-dar 60
Khristoforov, K. 131
Khunj 241
Khurasan 5, 63, 70, 71, 73, 83, 115, 123, 127, 136, 142, 145, 149, 174, 199, 200, 216, 217, 235, 240
Khurma 228
Khusraw Khan (governor of Kurdistan) 18, 199
Khusraw Khan (amir-shikar-bashi) 45, 56
Khusraw Khan (tufangchi-aqasi) 65
Khusraw Khan (governor of Shirvan) 122
Khusraw Khan (governor of Gilan and Mazandaran) 284n
Khusraw Khan (Gurgin Khan's nephew) 223, 225, 234–5
Khusraw Mirza *see* Rustam Khan

Khuzistan 4, 142, 174, 265n, 270n, 318n
Kirman 4, 8, 9, 40, 43, 44, 47, 70, 106, 111, 114, 123, 124, 126, 127, 131–2, 140, 142, 143, 149, 158–62, 174, 192, 206, 210, 221, 233–41, 254, 255, 263n, 272n, 301n, 326n
Kirmanshah 63, 71, 74, 103–4, 127, 132, 145, 215, 216, 226–7
Kishik-khanah 62
Kitch 131, 145, 161, 232
Klein, Rüdiger 264n
Knab, Sebastianus 134
Koy Su River 122
Krusinski, Judasz Thadeusz S.J. xxv, 60, 125, 184, 200, 202, 203, 219, 238, 299n, 324n
Kubnan 162, 232, 233
Kuchab 131
Kuh-i Giluyah 38, 46, 72, 142, 174, 206, 210, 217, 228, 229, 230
Kung 167, 168, 172, 205, 217, 228, 231, 238, 240, 319n
Kurdistan and Kurds 4, 8, 9, 18, 21, 62, 67, 72, 114, 121, 131, 132, 142, 143, 145, 147, 160, 174, 177, 199, 214, 222, 223, 225, 241, 304n, 318n

Lahore 125
Lambton, Ann K. S. 253
Lar 38, 61, 131, 144, 152, 164, 167, 174, 187, 208, 229, 230, 231, 240, 241
Larak 229
Lashkargah 124
Lavi, Habib 188
Lebanon 176, 252
Leopold I, Emperor 133, 328n
Levan *see* Shah Quli Khan
Lezghis 5, 9, 145, 147, 148, 174, 206, 211, 214, 217–8, 223, 225–6, 253
Livorno 189
Lockhart, Laurence xxi–xii, 56, 299n
Louis XIII, King 184, 328n
Louis XIV, King 267n, 273n, 285n
Luristan and Lurs 4, 63, 67, 136, 143, 179, 206, 227, 236, 238, 240–1
Lutf `Ali Khan 210, 214, 230–1, 238, 326n

Maeda, Hirotake 209, 316n
Mahd `Ali Khan 235
Mahd-i `Ulya 203
Mahmud Baqir Beg 307n
Mahmud b. Mir Ways 238–41, 255
Mahmud, Sayyid 227
Mahmud Mu'min 167
Majlis-nivis 35, 273n
Majlisi *see* Muhammad Baqir Majlisi and Muhammad Taqi Majlisi
Makran 9, 131, 145, 161, 232, 306n
Maldive Islands 5
Malcolm, John xxv, 141
Mamalik land 142–3, 149–50
Mani` b. Mughamis, Shaykh 227
Mann, Michael 2
Mansur Beg 232
Mansur Khan 147, 161
Mansur Khan Shahsivan 235
Manucci, Nicolao 151
Manuchihr Khan (son of Qarchaqay Khan) 28
Manuchihr Khan (Lur leader) 63
Maqsud Beg 53, 65
Marand 226
Marathas 328n
Mardin 127
Maria di S. Siro, Francesco 152
Marivan 216
Marivan, Battle of 37, 116
Mar `ashi Sayyids 41, 44
Marv 50, 71, 177, 199, 235
Maryam Bigum 74, 203–4, 238, 248, 250, 321n, 325n
Mashhad 4, 7, 15, 21, 24, 28, 37, 81, 124, 127, 177, 199, 206, 210, 218, 235, 237
Masqat 136, 229, 302n
Ma`sum Beg 110, 275n
Mazandaran 4, 5, 19, 40, 41, 44, 45, 127, 143, 146, 149, 153, 157, 182, 221, 226–8, 255
Mazarin, Cardinal Jules 285n, 328n
Mecca 65, 69, 78, 134, 175, 234, 237
Mehmet III, Sultan 83
Mehmet IV, Sultan 132, 134
Membré, Michele 76
Mihmandari 59, 151

Mihr 'Ali Khan 210
Mihrab Khan 167
Mihtar 60–61
Mihtar Da'ud 61
Minab 159, 170, 230
Mingrelia 265n
Minorsky, Vladimir xxi–xxii, 86, 178, 245, 260n
Mir Damad 183, 185
Mir Lawhi 184
Mir Muhammad Baqir Khatunabadi 201–2, 207, 219, 316n
Mir Muhammad Tahir Simnani 37
Mir Qasim Beg 49–50
Mir Rafi' al-Din Muhammad Shahristani 37
Mir Samandar 233
Mir Ways b. Shah 'Alam 148, 233–5, 325n
Mirza Abu Talib Khan Urdubadi 37, 38, 41
Mirza Habib Allah 22
Mirza Hadi 50, 157, 278n
Mirza Ibrahim 150, 152
Mirza Isma'il 218
Mirza Mahdi 218
Mirza Makhdum Khan 177
Mirza Maqsud 229
Mirza Masih 164, 169
Mirza Ma'sum 42, 116
Mirza Muhammad (*vaqa'i'-nivis*) 285n
Mirza Muhammad 214
Mirza Muhammad Mahdi 51, 52–3, 55, 87
Mirza Muhammad Khalil Mar'ashi 200
Mirza Muhammad "Saru" Taqi xxiii, 21, 22, 38, 40–2, 43–4, 47, 60, 116–118, 122, 123, 149, 185, 247, 250
Mirza Muhammad Tahir Vahid Qazvini 72, 73, 74, 107, 113, 154, 161, 232
Mirza Mu'in al-Din Muhammad 157
Mirza Murtaza 164
Mirza Mustafa 229
Mirza Qasim 43
Mirza Qavam al-Din Muhammad 45
Mirza Rabi'ah 204–5, 220

Mirza Rafi'ah 212
Mirza Rafi'ah (rebel) 231
Mirza Rafi' al-Din 204
Mirza Razi 69, 70
Mirza Sadiq 65, 150, 157–8
Mira Sadiq (shahbandar) 164
Mirza Sayyid 229
Mirza Sayyid 'Ali 164, 229
Mirza Sharif Jahan 164, 305n
Mirza Sharif Khan 164, 169
Mirza Tahir 150, 154, 163
Mirza Yahya 73
Mirza Yusuf 167
Mongols 9, 77
Mosul 215
Mu'ayyir al-mamalik 46, 49
Mufid Mustawfi Yazdi 141, 267n
Mughals 9, 10, 14, 21, 59, 83, 85, 92, 93, 96, 111, 122–7, 128, 130, 135, 136, 149, 161–2, 175, 243, 245, 255
Mughamis 227–8
Muhammad Akbar 269n
Muhammad 'Ali Beg 43, 46, 164, 168–9
Muhammad 'Ali Khan 209–10, 232
Muhammad Amin Beg 47, 48, 49, 163
Muhammad b. Sulayman Tunakabuni 262n
Muhammad Baqir Majlisi 185, 192, 201–2, 248, 253, 262n, 314n
Muhammad Baqir Mirza 149
Muhammad Baqir Sabzavari xxvi, 34
Muhammad Beg (grand vizier) 42–3, 45, 46–52, 58, 87, 88, 149, 157, 164, 186, 187–9
Muhammad Beg (envoy to Poland) 130
Muhammad Husayn Beg 204
Muhammad Husayn Tabrizi 214
Muhammad Ibrahim b. Zayn al-'Abidin Nasiri 218
Muhammad Isma'il 157
Muhammad Ja'far Beg 236
Muhammad Khan 37
Muhammad Khan (vizier of Herat) 209–210
Muhammad Khan, Sayyid 37
Muhammad Khudabandah, Shah 83, 115, 203

Muhammad Mirza Tahir 30
Muhammad Muhsin Mustawfi 241
Muhammad Mu'min Khan Shamlu 204, 214
Muhammad Quli Beg 48, 163–4
Muhammad Quli Khan 50, 269n
Muhammad Quli Khan Shamlu 213, 214, 226, 237, 238, 240, 318n
Muhammad Quli Mirza 236
Muhammad Salih Khan 41
Muhammad Tahir 37
Muhammad Tahir Qummi 184, 193
Muhammad Taqi Majlisi 184, 185, 188–9
Muhammad Zaman Khan 235
Muhsin Fayz-i Kashani, Mulla 183
Muhtasib 207–8
Mu'in Musavvir 290n
Mukri 177
Mulla Qudrati 90–2, 100
Mullabashi 202, 316n
Muntafiq 127, 227
Muqaddam 18
Murad IV, Sultan 83, 296n, 312n
Murtaza Quli Beg Zanganah 216
Murtaza Quli Khan (shahbandar) 158, 165, 166, 167, 168, 172, 306n
Murshid Quli Khan Ustajlu 23, 39, 81
Murtaza Quli Khan Bigdili Shamlu 74, 283n
Murtaza Quli Khan Qajar 44, 53
Murtaza Quli Khan Sa'dlu 73
Musa Khan 200, 208, 213
Musha`sha` 10, 227–8
Mustafa II, Sultan 216
Mustawfi al-mamalik 62
Mustawfi khassah 62, 69
Muzaffar al-Din Shah 266n
Muzaffar Beg 30
Muzaffar Husayn 161

Nadir Shah 9, 248, 255, 323n
Najaf Quli Beg Zanganah 65, 69–70, 71, 281n
Najaf Quli Khan 222
Najm-i Sani 275n
Nakhjavan 153
Naqdi Khan 44
Nasir al-Din Tusi 22

Nasr Allah Khan 241
Nasir `Ali Khan 168, 169–71, 308n
Nayriz 159
Nazir-i buyutat 32, 43, 45, 46, 53, 146
Nazir `Ali Khan Süglün 50
Nazir Najaf Quli Khan 151
Nestorians 313n
New Julfa xxiii, 24, 46, 67, 70, 150, 178, 181, 184, 185, 186, 187, 189–91, 193–5, 208, 220, 240
Newman, Andrew 260n, 309n
Nikahat Khanum 56
Ni`mat Allah al-Jaza'iri 202
Nisa 177
Nizovoi 154
Nuqtavis 177
Nur Allah 229

Oets, Jan 208
Olearius, Adam 41
Oman and Omanis 5, 6, 172, 216, 227–31
Ori, Israel 218
Ottoman Empire and Ottomans 9, 10, 14, 21, 31, 65, 77–8, 80, 81, 83, 88, 94, 97, 98, 110, 111, 112, 114, 116, 117, 118, 120, 121, 122, 123, 127, 128–37, 142, 144, 145, 147, 152, 175, 179–80, 181, 216, 217, 227–9, 243, 245, 252

Pacifique de Provins, R. P. 190
Pahlavis 12
Pari Khan Khanum 203
Parker, Geoffrey 112
Parthians 119
Pearson, Michael 164
Persian Gulf 36, 64, 97, 131, 163, 216, 217, 227
Peter I, Czar 225–6
Petis de la Croix, François 156
Philip II, King xxii
Pidou de Saint Olon, Bishop 194–5
Pishkash-nivis 21
Plague 215
Poland and Poles 130, 133–6, 137, 195, 219
Pontchartrain, Jérôme Phélypeaux 89
Portia, Ferdinand 328n

Portuguese 36, 115, 163, 170, 172, 179–80, 217, 228, 231, 302n
Priklonski, A. 131
Punjab 246
Pur Dil Khan 162, 232

Qajars (tribe) 40, 142
Qajars (dynasty) 9, 141, 279n
Qalandar Sultan 278n
Qalandars 184–5
Qandahar 7, 45, 57, 71, 85, 112, 117, 118, 119, 121, 122, 123–6, 130, 136, 145, 149, 160, 161–2, 229, 233, 234, 238, 239, 251, 288n, 298n, 326n
Qapu Agha 203
Qara Khan 276n
Qarabagh 38, 40, 142, 144
Qarchaqay Khan 28, 113
Qasim Beg 41
Qasr-i Shirin *see* Zuhab, Accord of
Qaychachi-bashi 46, 276n
Qazaqlu 144
Qazi Jahan Qazvini 177
Qazvin 5, 6, 17, 23, 72, 94, 131, 129, 174, 198, 212, 215, 223, 241
Qishm 36, 105, 229, 230
Qislar Agha 202–3
Qizilbash xxix, 1, 3, 5, 11, 18, 27, 28–30, 36, 39, 40, 44, 111, 112–3, 115, 118, 121, 124, 142, 145, 164, 173, 175, 176, 180, 243, 246, 247, 249, 251
Qullar-aqasi 36, 45, 53, 143, 206
Qum 6, 15, 51, 52, 146, 153, 184, 218, 237
Qurchibashi 23, 73–4, 113, 266n
Qurchishah Beg 207
Qurchis 60, 73, 74, 113, 117, 272n
Qurkhmas Khan 50
Quruq 57–58, 199, 279n
Quruqchis 57

Rabi`ah tribe 227
Rahdars 31, 64, 150, 153
Rahim Khan 209
Rajab `Ali Beg 183, 321n
Rajputs 125, 328n
Ramhurmuz 94
Rasht 18, 61, 221

Ravar 233
Rayin 159, 162, 232
Red Sea 156
Rigordi, François S.J. 184, 191
Rizvi, Sajjad 192
Roemer, Hans Robert 260n
Röhrborn, K. M. xxi–xxii
Romans 119
Rome 220–21
Rudbar 162, 232
Russia and Russians 25, 64, 80, 83, 85, 93, 97, 119, 122–4, 130, 131, 133, 135, 138, 145, 153, 190, 211, 220, 221, 222, 225, 254
Rustam al-Hukama xxvii, 247, 262n
Rustam Beg 36, 37
Rustam Khan (qullar-aqasi) 36, 39, 45, 68, 113
Rustam Khan (son) 68
Rustam Khan (grandson) 200–1, 210
Rustam Khan Zanganah 228
Rustam Mirza 236

Sabbatai Zevi Movement 188
Sabzavar 123
Sabzavari *see* Muhamamd Baqir Sabzavari
Sadr-i khassah 16, 59
Sadr-i mamalik 16, 45, 52
Safi I, Shah 12, 21, 22, 23, 30, 35–6, 39, 41, 44, 62–3, 83, 93–4, 98, 116, 122, 143, 156, 182–3, 185, 201, 206, 274n, 310n, 314n, 315n
Safi II (Sulayman) Shah 53, 55, 56, 94, 126, 167, 191
Safi, Shaykh 15
Safi Mirza 35–6
Safi Quli Agha 205
Safi Quli Beg (governor of Kirman) 303n
Safi Quli Beg (shahbandar) 212, 213–14, 229
Safi Quli Beg (shirahchi-bashi) 43, 276n
Safi Quli Beg (nazir) 204, 205
Safi Quli Khan (Alqas Mirza) 146
Safi Quli Khan (divanbegi, muhtasib) 201, 207
Safi Quli Khan (shahbandar) 212
Safi Quli Khan (qullar-aqasi) 228, 229

Sahid, François 212
Sa`ib-i Tabrizi 92
Sam Mirza (Shah Safi II; Shah Sulayman) 53
Sanson, François 60, 61, 67, 70, 72, 74, 136, 163, 202, 217
Saru Khan Husayn 273n, 275n
Saru Khan Sahandlu 70, 73, 74, 90, 106, 283n, 285n
Sarvistan 169, 171
Sasanians 119
Savah 153
Savory, Roger xxvi, 260n
Sayfja 231
Schillinger, Caspar 137
Sebastian, Pedro Cubero 131
Shahbandar 146, 163, 307n
Shah Navaz Khan 136
Shahnavaz I (Vakhtang V) 68
Shahnavaz II (Giorgi XI) *see* Gurgin Khan
Shah Quli Khan (Levan) 233
Shah Quli Khan Zanganah 71, 74, 104, 205–6, 207–8, 214, 216, 218, 237
Shahrimanian, Mankel 220
Shahrimanian, Markerat 220
Shahrimanian, Sarhat 189
Shahrimanian, Zakharia 189–90
Shahrimanians 189–90, 194, 220, 254
Shahrizur 216
Shahrukh Sultan Zanganah 63
Shahsivan tribe 40, 267n
Shah-seven 16, 147, 248, 267n
Shah Virdi Khan 67, 72, 161, 232–3
Shamakhi 153, 208, 210, 217, 222, 223, 225–6
Shamil 170
Shamkhal 147
Shamlu 40, 142, 315n
Shamshir Beg 48, 164
Shaykh `Ali Khan Zanganah 22, 48, 52, 59, 62–72, 74, 97, 101, 103–4, 106, 127, 132–3, 151, 160, 161, 168, 170, 172, 190, 193, 194, 211, 248, 280n, 282n, 284n, 300n, 327n
Shaykh `Ali Khan (grandson) 214
Shaykhavand 18, 110
Sherley, Anthony 177

Shi`ism 14–5, 173–92, 202, 219–22, 254
Shirahchi-bashi 43
Shiraz xxiii, 4, 7, 8, 88, 131, 132, 155–8, 167, 171, 172, 178, 184, 187, 214, 215, 229, 238, 304n
Shir Ghazi Khan 231
Shirvan 6, 18, 19, 40, 122, 140, 153–5, 173, 222–23, 225–7, 255
Shushtar 94, 210
Shushtari, *see* `Abd Allah b. Nur ad-Din b. Ni`matallah al-Husayni al-Shushtari
Silk 7, 25, 47, 86, 106, 171, 206
Simeon of Yerevan 310n
Simmons, J. 90, 92
Simnan 47, 73, 149, 177
Sind 5
Sipahsalar 37, 47, 113, 124–6, 143, 216
Sistan 9, 114, 124, 126, 238, 246, 251, 265n
Smidt, Jan 260n
Sobieski, King Jan III 131, 134
Soimonov, Fedor I. 221
Sorkhay Khan Shamkhal 122
Spain xxii, 114, 328n
Speelman, Cornelis 157
Starn, Randolph 245
Sten'ka Razin 64, 153, 299n
Stepanos, Bishop 194–5
Stewart, Devin 309n
Struys, Jan 153
Subhan Virdi Khan 239
Sufis and Sufism 176, 183, 184, 191, 192, 202, 254
Sulayman, Shah 16, 19, 52, 53, 55–9, 61, 62–8, 72, 81, 89, 94, 96, 97, 98, 125, 126, 127, 130–6, 144, 149, 167, 191, 192, 195, 197–9, 201, 206, 245, 248, 266n, 268n, 284n, 312n
Sulayman Baba 216–7, 222, 319
Sulayman Khan Zanganah 21, 71, 304n
Süleyman, Sultan xxiv
Sultan Husayn, Shah xxvii, 21, 24, 57, 61, 74, 81, 137, 168, 199–210, 219–20, 221, 228, 237, 240, 243, 245, 248, 250, 253, 262n, 327n
Sultaniyah 143, 153

Sunnism and Sunnis 10, 67, 134–5, 137, 138, 159, 160, 173–7, 194, 202, 211, 222–3, 226, 229, 234, 240, 254
Sunqur 63
Surat 107, 184
Suyurghal 16, 19, 155
Sweden and Swedes 135

Tabriz xxiii, 4, 5, 97, 102, 111, 112, 179, 184, 200, 223–4, 225, 226, 251
Tahir Mirza 48
Tahmasb I, Shah 11, 15, 17, 18, 23, 27, 37, 38, 58, 81, 90, 115, 118, 142, 146, 147, 175, 176, 177, 198, 250, 275n, 288n
Tahmasb, Prince 241
Tahmasb Quli Khan 29
Takallu 142
Takhtah Khan Ustajlu 37
Talib Khan 167
Talish 153
Tarku 225
Tatars 135, 147, 223
Tate, G. 286n
Tavernier, Jean-Baptiste xxviii, 25, 38, 41, 61, 96, 152, 156, 157, 199–200
Taxation 63–7, 70, 76–7, 100, 140, 151, 153, 154, 157, 159, 160, 161, 170, 182, 183, 194, 208, 220, 221, 227, 231, 250
Taymur Khan 9
Taymuraz Khan I, King 39
Tehran 4, 214
Tenreiro, António 174
Thevenot, Jean de 96
Tiflis 89, 94, 142, 215
Tournefort, Jean Pitton de 76
Trézel, Alphonse Camille 294n
Tufangchi-aqasi 53, 126, 143
Tumurids 77
Tunakabuni *see* Muhammad b. Sulayman Tunakabuni
Tupchibashi 47, 113, 125
Turkmen 9, 145, 174, 200, 216, 231, 235, 253
Turks 152
Tushmal-bashi 61
Tuyuls 64

Ughan Beg 48
Ughurlu Beg Shamlu 37, 50
Ulama 176–7, 180–2, 183, 187, 191–3, 198
Ulugh Khan 160, 276n
'Umar, Caliph 212, 219, 233, 323n
Uniladze clan 38, 39
Urdu bazaar 24, 129, 270n
Urganj 127
Urmiyah 216
Uruch Beg (Don Juan of Persia) 114
Uzbeks 5, 9, 10, 14, 36, 63, 64, 70, 81, 96, 111, 124, 126–8, 135, 136, 142, 145, 148, 175, 177, 216, 217, 231, 235, 253, 300n

Vachet, Bénigne 144
Vahid Qazvini *see* Mirza Muhammad Tahir Vahid Qazvini
Vakhtang V *see* Shahnavaz I
Vakhtang VI (Husayn Quli Khan) 225, 229
Vakil 145–6
Vakil-i divan 36–7
Vali 143–4
Van 147
Van Leene, Johan 74, 107
Vaqa'i`-nivis 146
Vazir al-muli 62
Vechietti, Giovanni Battista 111
Venice xxii, 189, 220
Vienna 133, 134
Vilayat 141, 143–4
VOC (Dutch East India Company) xxvii–xxviii, 8, 24, 42, 47, 51, 64, 87, 100–4, 106–8, 157, 166, 169, 170, 194, 212, 236, 264n
Volynskii, Artemii Petrovich 211, 218, 225, 317n, 321n

Weber, Max 2, 31–32
Whigham, H. J. 287n
Winnincx, Leonard 157
Wolf, Eric 263n
Women 201–4
Wool 8, 106, 159

Ya`qub Khan Zu'l Qadr 155
Ya`qub Khan 229

Ya`qub Sultan 230
Ya`riba Arabs 228
Yasavul-bashi 37–8
Yazd 4, 9, 141, 159, 216, 221, 238, 239, 254
Yemen 192
Yerevan 8, 50, 51, 89, 103, 112, 116, 132, 135, 146, 155, 179, 210, 214, 215
Yomut 145, 174, 231, 302n
Yusuf Agha 36, 37, 60
Yusuf Khan 38

Zagros Mountains 4, 141, 227, 251
Zakhariya Khan 212, 213–4, 229
Zaman Beg 52–3
Zanganah 62–3, 280n
Zanjan 153
Zapolski, Ignatius 195
Zarand 162, 232
Zayandah Rud 48, 57, 71, 185, 220, 284n
Zaynab Bigum 37, 203
Zaynal Khan 36–7, 69
Zaynal Khan (khan of Bandar `Abbas) 167
Zoroastrians 10, 67, 70, 160, 192, 194, 221, 239, 254, 310n, 326n
Zubaydah Bigum 37
Zuhab, Accord of xxx, 118–21, 125, 130, 182, 190, 251
Zu'l Fiqar Khan 59, 328n
Zu'l Fiqar Qaramanlu 40

1. View of Isfahan, 1703, from Cornelis de Bruyn, *Reizen over Moskovie, door Persie en Indie*, 2nd ed., 1714.

2. Royal Square of Isfahan, 1703, from Cornelis de Bruyn, *Reizen over Moskovie, door Persie en Indie*, 2nd ed., 1714.

3. Mint of Isfahan, from Ambrosio Bembo, "Viaggio e giornale per parte dell'Asia di quattro anni incirc fatto da me Ambrosio Bembo Nob. Veneto".

4. View of Sa'adabad, 1703, from Cornelis de Bruyn, *Reizen over Moskovie, door Persie en Indie*, 2nd ed., 1714.

5. View of Shamakhi, 1702, from Cornelis de Bruyn, *Reizen over Moskovie, door Persie en Indie*, 2nd ed., 1714.

6. View of Lar, 1704, from Cornelis de Bruyn, *Reizen over Moskovie, door Persie en Indie*, 2nd ed., 1714.

7. Grand Vizier Khalifah Sultan, by Mu'in Musavvir, *c.*1650, opaque watercolor, ink and gold on paper.

8. Safavid surrender at Qandahar, *c.*1640.

9. Shah Sulayman, *c.*1680, opaque watercolor on paper.

10. Grand Vizier Shah Quli Khan, by Hajii Muhammad, 1696, opaque watercolor, ink and gold on paper.

11. Shah Sultan Husayn, 1703, from Cornelis de Bruyn, *Reizen over Moskovie, door Persie en Indie*, 2nd ed., 1714.

Lightning Source UK Ltd.
Milton Keynes UK
UKHW021008061119
352993UK00004B/88/P